AMERICA

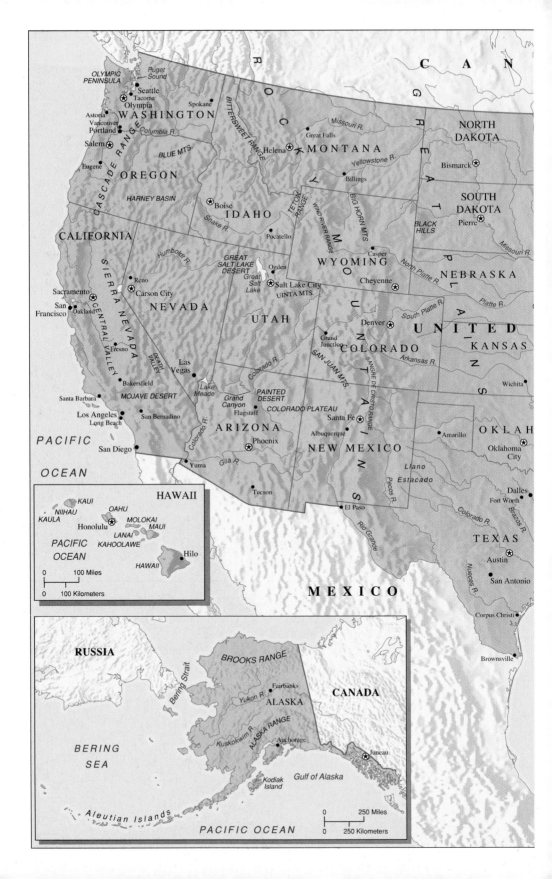

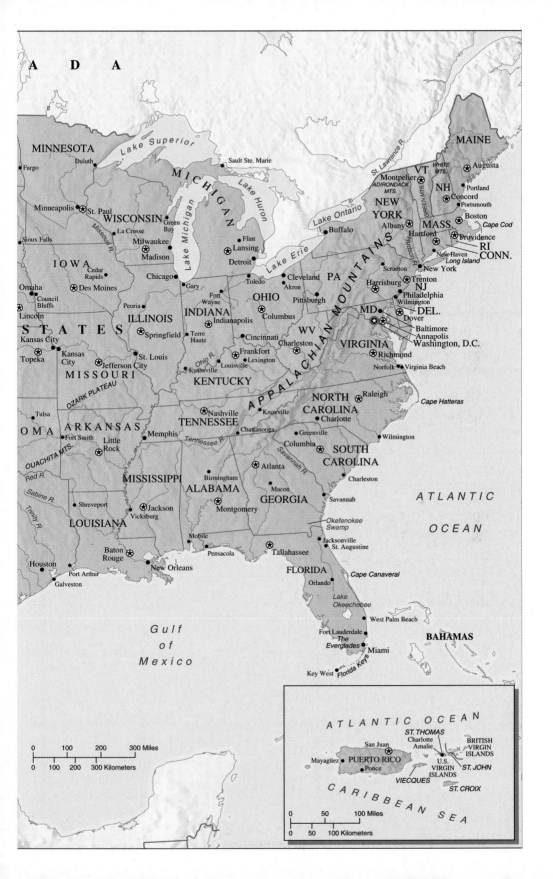

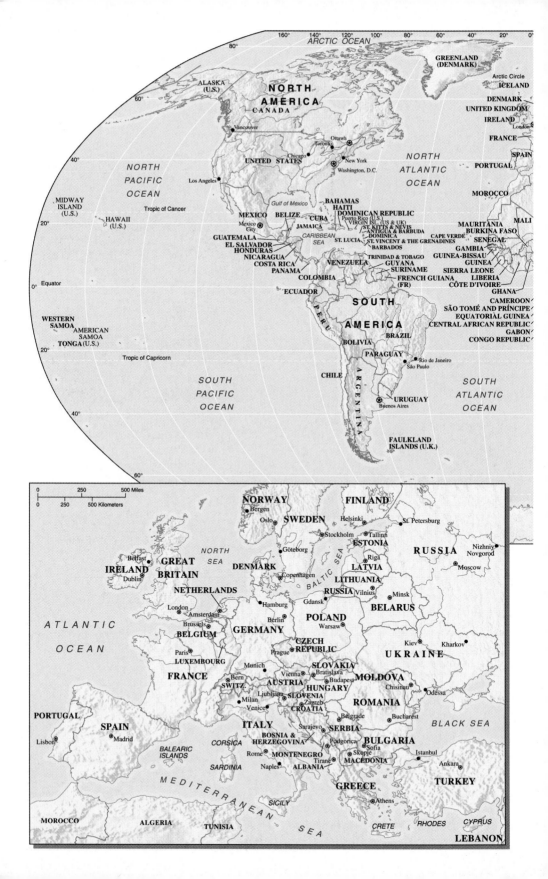

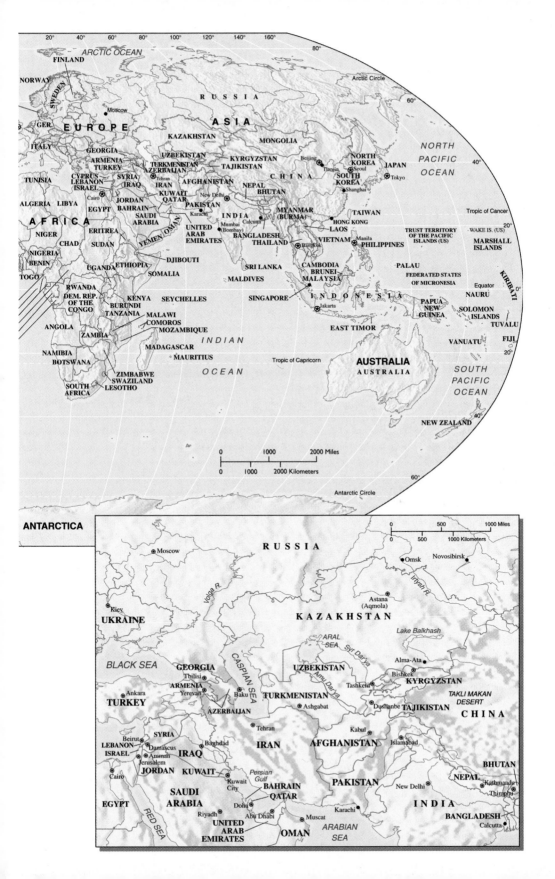

AMERICA

A NARRATIVE HISTORY

Brief Seventh Edition

Volume One

GEORGE BROWN TINDALL

DAVID EMORY SHI

W · W · NORTON & COMPANY · NEW YORK · LONDON

Composition: TechBooks
Manufacturing: Quebecor, Taunton
Book design: Jo Anne Metsch
Editor: Karl Bakeman
Editorial assistant: Rebecca Arata
Manuscript editor: Abigail Winograd
Project editor: Carla L. Talmadge
Associate managing editor, College: Lory A. Frenkel
Director of Manufacturing, College: Roy Tedoff
Cartographer: CARTO-GRAPHICS/Alice Thiede and William Thiede

Acknowledgments and copyrights continue on page A104,
which serves as a continuation of the copyright page.

The Library of Congress has cataloged the one-volume edition as follows:

Tindall, George Brown.
    America : a narrative history / George Brown Tindall,
David E. Shi.—Brief 7th ed.
        p.   cm.
    Includes bibliographical references and index.
    ISBN 13: 978-0-393-92734-4 (pbk.)
    ISBN 10: 0-393-92734-2 (pbk.)
    I. Shi, David E.   II. Title.

    E178.1.T55 2007   2006046845
    973—dc22
    ISBN 13: 978-0-393-92735-1 (pbk.)
    ISBN 10: 0-393-92735-0 (pbk.)

W. W. Norton & Company, Inc., 500 Fifth Avenue, New York, NY 10110
www.wwnorton.com

W. W. Norton & Company Ltd., Castle House, 75/76 Wells Street, London W1T 3QT

1 2 3 4 5 6 7 8 9 0

*W. W. Norton & Company has been independent since its founding in 1923,
when William Warder Norton and Mary D. Herter Norton first published
lectures delivered at the People's Institute, the adult education division of
New York City's Cooper Union. The Nortons soon expanded their program
beyond the Institute, publishing books by celebrated academics from America
and abroad. By mid-century, the two major pillars of Norton's publishing
program—trade books and college texts—were firmly established. In the 1950s,
the Norton family transferred control of the company to its employees, and
today—with a staff of four hundred and a comparable number of trade, college, and professional titles published each year—W. W. Norton & Company
stands as the largest and oldest publishing house owned wholly by its employees.*

For Bruce and Susan
and for Blair

For
Jason and Jessica

CONTENTS

Part Two / BUILDING A NATION

Part Three | AN EXPANSIVE NATION

Part Four | A HOUSE DIVIDED AND REBUILT

MAPS

PREFACE

Just as history is never complete, neither is a historical textbook. We have learned much from the responses of readers and instructors to the first six editions of *America: A Narrative History.* Perhaps the most important and reassuring lesson is that our original intention has proved valid: to provide a compelling narrative history of the American experience, a narrative animated by human characters, informed by analysis and social texture, and guided by the unfolding of events. Readers have also endorsed the book's distinctive size and format. *America* is designed to be read and to carry a moderate price. While the book retains its classic look, *America* sports a new color design for the Seventh Edition. We have added new eye-catching maps and included new art in full color. Despite these changes, we have not raised the price between the Sixth and the Seventh Editions.

As in previous revisions of *America,* we have adopted an overarching theme that informs many of the new sections we introduce throughout the Seventh Edition. In previous editions we have traced such broad-ranging themes as immigration, the frontier and the West, popular culture, and work. In each case we blend our discussions of the selected theme into the narrative, where they reside through succeeding editions.

The Seventh Edition of *America* highlights environmental history, a relatively new field that examines how people have shaped—and been shaped by—the natural world. Geographic features, weather, plants, animals, and diseases are important elements of environmental history. Environmental historians study how environments have changed as a result of natural processes such as volcanic eruptions, earthquakes, hurricanes, wildfires, droughts, floods, and climatic changes. They also study how societies have used and abused their natural environment through economic activities such as hunting, farming, logging and mining, manufacturing, building dams, and irrigation. Equally interesting is how different societies over time have perceived nature, as reflected in their religion, art, literature, and popular culture, and how they have reshaped nature according to those perceptions through the creation of parks, preserves, and designed landscapes. Finally, another major area of inquiry among environmental historians centers on the development of laws and regulations to govern the use of nature and maintain the quality of the natural environment.

Some of the new additions to the Seventh Edition related to environmental history are listed below.

- Chapter 1 includes discussions of the transmission of deadly infectious diseases from Europe to the New World and the ecological and social impact of the arrival of horses on the Great Plains.
- Chapter 3 examines the ways in which European livestock reshaped the New World environment and complicated relations with Native Americans.
- Chapters 5 and 6 describe the effects of smallpox on the American armies during the Revolution.
- Chapter 12 details the impact of early industrialization on the environment.
- Chapter 19 includes new material related to the environmental impact of the sharecrop-tenant farm system in the South after the Civil War, industrial mining in the Far West, and the demise of the buffalo on the Great Plains.
- Chapter 21 describes the dramatic rise of large cities after the Civil War and the distinctive aspects of the urban environment.
- Chapter 24 surveys the key role played by sportsmen in the emergence of the conservation movement during the late nineteenth century and details Theodore Roosevelt's efforts to preserve the nation's natural resources.
- Chapter 37 discusses President George W. Bush's controversial environmental policies and describes the devastation in Mississippi and Louisiana wrought by Hurricane Katrina.

Beyond these explorations of environmental history we have introduced other new material throughout the Seventh Edition. Fresh insights from important new scholarly works have been incorporated, and we feel confident that the book provides students with an excellent introduction to the American experience.

To enhance the pedagogical features of the text, we have added Focus Questions at the beginning of each chapter. Students can use these review tools to remind themselves of the key themes and central issues in the chapters. These questions are also available online as quizzes, the results of which students can e-mail to their instructors. In addition, the maps feature new enhanced captions designed to encourage students to think analytically about the relationship between geography and American history.

We have also revised the outstanding ancillary package that supplements the text. *For the Record: A Documentary History of America,* Third Edition, by David E. Shi and Holly A. Mayer (Duquesne University), is a rich resource with over 300 primary source readings from diaries, journals, newspaper articles, speeches, government documents, and novels. The *Study Guide,* by Charles Eagles (University of Mississippi), is another valuable resource. This edition contains chapter outlines, learning objectives, timelines, expanded vocabulary exercises, and many new short-answer and essay questions. *America: A Narrative History* Study Space is an online collection of tools for review and research. It includes chapter summaries, review questions and quizzes, interactive map exercises, timelines, and research modules, many new to this edition. *Norton Media Library* is a CD-ROM slide and text resource that includes images from the text, four-color maps, additional images from the Library of Congress archives, and audio files of significant historical speeches. Finally, the *Instructor's Manual and Test Bank,* by Mark Goldman (Tallahassee Community College) and Stephen Davis (Kingwood College) includes a test bank of short-answer and essay questions, as well as detailed chapter outlines, lecture suggestions, and bibliographies.

In preparing the Seventh Edition, we have benefited from the insights and suggestions of many people. Some of these insights have come from student readers of the text and we encourage such feedback. Among the scholars and survey instructors who offered us their comments and suggestions are: James Lindgren (SUNY Plattsburgh), Joe Kudless (Raritan Valley Community College), Anthony Quiroz (Texas A&M University – Corpus Christi), Steve Davis (Kingwood College), Mark Fiege (Colorado State University), David Head (John Tyler Community College), Hutch Johnson (Gordon College), Charles Eagles (University of Mississippi), Christina White and Eddie Weller at the South campus of San Jacinto College, Blanche Brick, Cathy Lively, Stephen Kirkpatrick, Patrick Johnson, Thomas Stephens, and others at the Bryan Campus of Blinn College, Evelyn Mangie (University of South Florida), Michael McConnell (University of Alabama – Birmingham), Alan Lessoff (Illinois State University), Joseph Cullon (Dartmouth University), Keith Bohannon (University of West Georgia), Tim Heinrichs (Bellevue Community

College), Mary Ann Heiss (Kent State University), Edmund Wehrle (Eastern Illinois University), Adam Howard (University of Florida), David Parker (Kennesaw State University), Barrett Esworthy (Jamestown Community College), Samantha Barbas (Chapman University), Jason Newman (Cosumnes River College), Paul Cimbala (Fordham University), Dean Fafoutis (Salisbury University), Thomas Schilz (Miramar Community College), Richard Frucht (Northwest Missouri State University), James Vlasich (Southern Utah University), Michael Egan (Washington State University), Robert Goldberg (University of Utah), Jason Lantzer (Indiana University), and Beth Kreydatus (College of William & Mary). Our special thanks go Tom Pearcy (Slippery Rock University) for all of his work on the timelines. Once again, we thank our friends at W. W. Norton, especially Steve Forman, Steve Hoge, Karl Bakeman, Neil Hoos, Lory Frenkel, Roy Tedoff, Dan Jost, Rebecca Arata, and Matt Arnold, for their care and attention along the way.

—George B. Tindall
—David E. Shi

Part One

A

NEW

WORLD

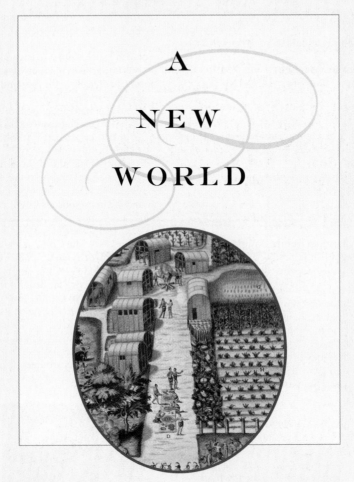

900

Classical Mayan civilization collapses
(A.D. 900)

Aztecs found capital city of Tenochtitlán
(1325)

1400

Aztec Empire flourishes (1400–1519)
Inca Empire flourishes (1438–1538)

1500

Juan Ponce de León explores Florida (1513)
Hernando Cortés conquers Aztecs for Spain
(1519)
Francisco Pizarro conquers Incas for Spain
(1531)

Spanish establish St. Augustine (1565)

1600

James I charters Virginia Company (1606)
English establish Jamestown (1607)
French establish Quebec (1608)

House of Burgesses meets in Virginia, becoming the first representative assembly
in the English colonies (1619)
Pilgrims land at Plymouth, draft and sign
the Mayflower Compact (1620)
Virginia becomes a royal colony (1624)
Dutch found New Amsterdam (1625)
Massachusetts Bay Company is founded
(1629)

Charles I grants Maryland to Lord
Baltimore as a proprietary colony
(1634)

Roger Williams establishes the town of
Providence, Rhode Island (1636)
Settlers from Massachusetts Bay Colony organize the self-governing colony of Connecticut (1637)

Massachusetts Bay Company charter
evolves into two-house legislature
(1644)

Colonies are left to themselves and practice
home rule during the Commonwealth
(1653–1658)

Viking Leif Eriksson sails along the coast of
North America (1001)
Italian city-states begin to trade with Asia
(1050–1300)
Crusades further open up West to knowl-
edge and trade with the East (1095–1270)
Marco Polo travels to China (1275)
Europeans seek westward sea route to Far
East (1290s–1520s)

Spanish expel Moors; Christopher Colum-
bus undertakes his first voyage (1492)
John Cabot, sailing for England, reaches
North America (1497)
Vasco da Gama reaches port of Calicut,
India, in search of spices (1498)
Martin Luther protests Catholic practice of
selling indulgences (1517)
Ferdinand Magellan's crew circumnavi-
gates the earth in pursuit of Asian riches
(1519–1522)
John Calvin establishes Calvinism (1536)
Nicolaus Copernicus describes helio-
centric universe (1543)

English East India Company is chartered
(1600); Dutch East India Company is
chartered (1602)
Dutch send Henry Hudson to find northwest passage to China (1609)
Galileo Galilei describes planets revolving
around sun (1610)
Thirty Years' War is fought in Europe
(1618–1648)
Dutch West India Company is chartered
(1623)

English Civil War (1642–1649) culminates
in the execution of King Charles I (1649)

Oliver Cromwell governs the Commonwealth of England as lord protector
(1653–1659)

900

SOCIAL

European exploitation of Native Americans begins centuries of unrest between colonists and natives (1490s–1500s)

Native Americans die by the thousands, devastated by smallpox and other diseases brought from Europe (1500s–1600s)

Population of English settlers in America increases from 105 to more than 2 million (1607–1770)
Iroquois Confederacy serves as buffer between French and English (1609–1770s)

First Africans are brought to English America as slaves (1619)
First Thanksgiving is celebrated (1621)

John Winthrop calls the Massachusetts Bay Colony the "city upon a hill" (1630)
Great Migration to America results from enclosure movement and religious persecution in England (1630s)
Maryland becomes refuge for English Catholics (1634)
Rhode Island legislates freedom of religion (1636)
Harvard College is founded (1636)
Colonists kill hundreds of natives in the Pequot War (1637)
Anne Hutchinson is tried (1637) and banished (1638)

Massachusetts Bay Colony mandates public education (1647)

ECONOMIC

1400

Export of American agricultural goods (such as maize, potatoes, and cocoa) to Europe fundamentally alters Europeans' diet (1490s–1600s)
Spanish *encomienda* extracts tribute from natives (1500s)   1500
Proprietors and chartered companies seek wealth by establishing colonies in America (1580s–1600)

1600

Colonists continue the English practice of coverture, which requires married women to surrender their right to own property (1600s–1700s)
Mercantilism, based on state-supported manufacturing and trade, is dominant economic system (1600s–1750)
French begin trading fur pelts with various Indian nations (1607)
"Starving time" takes place as Jamestown falls into ruin (1609–1610)
John Rolfe begins experimenting with tobacco in Virginia (1612)

Iroquois League completely depletes its hunting grounds and expands into neighboring areas (1630s–1640s)

Triangular trade begins between Europe, Africa, and the Americas (1643)

Navigation Act excludes foreign shipping from English and colonial trade (1651)

1660

Carolina is established as a proprietary colony (1663)

Dutch surrender New York to British (1664)

Duke of York establishes New Jersey as a proprietary colony (1664)

Bacon's Rebellion is suppressed by royal officials (1675–1676)

Charles II gives Pennsylvania and Delaware to William Penn as proprietary colonies (1681)

Dominion of New England reestablishes royal control by merging Connecticut, Rhode Island, Massachusetts Bay, and Plymouth colonies into a royal province (1686)

Dominion colonies revert to self-government (1688)

King William's War (1689–1697)

Vice-admiralty courts established by the crown (1696)

England's monarchy is restored under Charles II (1660)

French explore along the Mississippi River (1673–1682)

Germans migrate to America as a result of incessant wars (1680s–1690s)

Revocation of Edict of Nantes in France leads to Huguenot migration to Holland and America (1685)

Isaac Newton theorizes that natural law governs all things (1687)

England's Glorious Revolution establishes a constitutional monarchy (1688)

War of the League of Augsburg (1689–1697)

John Locke sets forth his contract theory of government (1690)

Bank of England is founded (1694)

1700

Queen Anne's War (1702–1713)

French establish New Orleans (1718)

Georgia is set up as philanthropic experiment and military buffer (1732)

Trial of John Peter Zenger confirms the right of the press to criticize the government (1735)

King George's War (1744–1748)

French begin to settle Louisiana (1699)

War of the Spanish Succession (1701–1714)

Treaty of Utrecht (1713)

Many Ulster Scots fleeing Anglican persecution come to America (1717–1775)

War of the Austrian Succession (1740–1748)

1750

Albany Congress enacts the Plan of Union (1754)

French and Indian War (Seven Years' War in Europe) (1754–1763)

Royal Proclamation limits expansion beyond the Appalachians (1763)

Boston Massacre (1770)

Population of Europe begins to increase (ca. 1750)

Many areas of Europe are devastated by resumed fighting in the Seven Years' War (1756–1763)

First Continental Congress meets (1774)

King George III of England declares colonists "open and avowed enemies" (1775)

Battles of Lexington and Concord (1775)

Second Continental Congress meets (1775)

Battle of Bunker Hill (1775)

1776

Congress adopts the Declaration of Independence (1776)

King Philip's War is fought between colonists and natives (1675–1676)	Navigation Act requires three quarters of the crews of ships trading with England and its colonies to be English subjects (1660)	**1660**
Pueblos under Popé revolt against the Spanish in New Mexico (1680)		
Pennsylvania becomes a haven for Quakers and other persecuted religious groups (1681)		

Navigation Act requires colonial governors to enforce Navigation Acts of 1651 and 1660 (1696)

Salem witch trials take place (1692)

The Wonders of the Invisible World:

Being an Account of the

TRYALS

OF

Several Witches.

Lately Executed in

NEW-ENGLAND:

And of several remarkable Curiosities therein Occurring.

Together with,

I. Observations upon the Nature, the Number, and the Operations of the Devils.
II. A short Narrative of a late outrage committed by a knot of Witches in Swede-Land, very much resembling, and so far explaining, that under which New-England laboured.
III. Some Councels directing a due Improvement of the Terrible things lately done by the unusual and amazing Range of Evil-Spirits in New-England.
IV. A brief Discourse upon those Temptations which are the more ordinary Devices of Satan.

By COTTON MATHER.

Published by the Special Command of his EXCELLENCY the Governour of the Province of the Massachusetts-Bay in New-England.

Printed first, at Boston in New-England; and Reprinted at London, for John Dunton, at the Raven in the Poultrey. 1693.

College of William and Mary is founded (1693)

Carolinas trade with Cherokees, Creeks, and Chickasaws and export an average of 54,000 deerskins annually (1699–1715)

South Carolina exports 100,000 pounds of rice annually (1700) **1700**

Enlightenment thinkers challenge monarchical abuses of power (1700s)

Non-native colonial population grows from 250,000 (1700) to 2.5 million (1775)

Iroquois tribes negotiate peace with French (1701)

Florida Indians are on the verge of extinction (1710)

Creek and Choctaw tribes revolt in the massive Yamasee War (1715)

Great Awakening leads to religious revival and widespread evangelism (1730s–1740s)

Benjamin Franklin establishes the American Philosophical Society (1743)

Iroquois, Cherokees, and Shawnees are pushed to give up land to white settlers (1760s–1770s)

American nationalism reaches its zenith as Revolution approaches (1760s–1770s)

English Molasses Act prevents colonies from trading with the French sugar islands (1733) **1750**

To raise tax revenues, Lord Grenville enacts the Sugar Act and Currency Act (1764), and the Stamp Act and Quartering Act (1765)

Townshend Acts provoke a boycott of British goods (1767)

South Carolina and Georgia export 65 million pounds of rice annually (1770s)

In response to Boston Tea Party (1773), British pass Coercive Acts (1774)

Thomas Paine publishes *Common Sense*, directly attacking allegiance to British monarchy (1776)

Adam Smith's *The Wealth of Nations* promotes free-market competition (1776) **1776**

Long before Christopher Columbus accidentally discovered the New World in his effort to find a passage to Asia, the tribal peoples he mislabeled Indians had occupied and shaped the lands of the Western Hemisphere. By the end of the fifteenth century, when Columbus began his voyage west from Europe, there were millions of natives living in the "New World." Over the centuries they had developed diverse and often highly sophisticated societies, some rooted in agriculture, others in trade or imperial conquest.

The indigenous cultures were, of course, profoundly affected by the arrival of people from Europe and Africa. The Indians were exploited, enslaved, displaced, and exterminated. Yet this conventional tale of conquest oversimplifies the complex process by which Indians, Europeans, and Africans interacted. The Indians were more than passive victims; they were also trading partners and rivals of the transatlantic newcomers. They became enemies and allies, neighbors and advisers, converts and spouses. As such they fully participated in the creation of the new society known as America.

The Europeans who risked their lives to settle in the New World were themselves quite varied. Young and old, men and women, they came from Spain, Portugal, France, Great Britain, the Netherlands, Italy, and the various German states. A variety of motives inspired them to undertake the harrowing transatlantic voyage. Some were adventurers and fortune seekers eager to find gold and spices. Others were fervent Christians determined to create kingdoms of God in the New World. Still others were convicts, debtors, indentured servants, or political or religious exiles. Many were simply seeking a plot of land, higher wages, and greater economic opportunity. A settler in Pennsylvania noted that "poor people (both men and women) of all kinds can here get three times the wages for their labour than they can in England or Wales."

Yet such enticements did not attract enough workers to keep up with the rapidly expanding colonial economies. So the Europeans began to force Indians to work for them, but there were never enough laborers to meet the unceasing demand. Moreover, the captive Indians often escaped or were so rebellious that their use was banned. The Massachusetts legislature instituted such a ban because Indians were of "a malicious, surly and revengeful spirit; rude and insolent in their behavior, and very ungovernable."

Beginning early in the seventeenth century, more and more colonists turned to the African slave trade for their labor needs. In 1619 white traders began transporting captured Africans to the English colonies. This development would transform American society in ways that no one at the time envisioned. Few Europeans during the colonial era saw the contradiction between the New World's promise of individual freedom and the expanding institution of race-based slavery. Nor did they imagine the problems associated with introducing into the new society a race of people they considered alien and unassimilable.

The intermingling of people, cultures, plants and animals from the continents of Africa, Europe, and North America gave colonial American society its distinctive vitality and variety. In turn, the diversity of the environment and the climate led to the creation of quite different economies and patterns of living in the various regions of North America. As the original settlements grew into prosperous and populous colonies, the transplanted Europeans had to fashion social institutions and political systems to manage growth and control tensions.

At the same time, imperial rivalries among the Spanish, French, English, and Dutch produced numerous clashes and costly wars. The monarchs of Europe struggled to manage and exploit this fluid and often volatile colonial society. Many of the colonists, they discovered, had brought with them to the New World a feisty independence that led them to resent government interference in their affairs. A British official in North Carolina reported that the residents of the Piedmont region were "without any Law or Order. Impudence is so very high, as to be past bearing." As long as the reins of imperial control were loosely applied, mother countries and their colonists parties maintained an uneasy partnership. But as the British authorities tightened their control during the mid–eighteenth century, they met resistance, which escalated into revolt and culminated in revolution.

1

THE COLLISION
OF CULTURES

FOCUS QUESTIONS

· What were the reasons for the founding of the colonies?

· How did Europeans and Native Americans adapt to each other's presence?

· What was the Spanish influence in North America?

To answer these questions and access additional review material, please visit www.wwnorton.com/studyspace.

The "New World" discovered by Christopher Columbus was in fact home to civilizations thousands of years old. Until recently archaeologists had long assumed that the first human residents were Siberians who some 12,000 to 15,000 years ago crossed the Bering Strait on a land bridge to Alaska made accessible by receding waters during the last Ice Age. Over the next 500 years the Asian migrants fanned out in small bands from the Arctic Circle to the tip of South America. Recent archaeological discoveries in Pennsylvania, Virginia, and Chile, however, suggest that humans may have arrived by sea much earlier (perhaps 18,000 to 40,000 years ago) from various parts of Asia—and some of them may even have crossed the Atlantic Ocean from southwestern Europe.

PRE-COLUMBIAN INDIAN CIVILIZATIONS

Whatever their place of origin and time of arrival, the first peoples in the Western Hemisphere spread across North and South America, establishing new communities and cultures. In the high altitudes of Mexico and Peru, Mayas, Aztecs, Incas, and others built great empires and a monumental architecture, supported by large-scale agriculture and far-flung commerce.

INDIAN CULTURES OF NORTH AMERICA Of the hundreds of Indian tribes inhabiting the present-day United States, the ancestors of only a few, such as the Pueblos, Creeks, and Iroquois, ever approached the level of social organization or cultural sophistication achieved by the Mayas and Aztecs in Central America and Mexico. North American tribes tended to be smaller, more scattered, and less settled. Most of them migrated with the seasons in search of food and temperate locales. They built few permanent structures and tended to own land communally, although individuals were allowed to own the food they produced or gathered.

In the Ohio and Mississippi River valleys many tribes developed a thriving village culture. While still primarily dependent upon hunting and gathering for subsistence, they also cultivated squash, beans, and maize. But even the most developed Indian societies of the sixteenth century were ill equipped to resist the dynamic European cultures invading their world. There were fatal gaps in Indian knowledge and technology. The Indians of Mexico, for example, had copper and bronze but no iron, except a few specimens of meteorites. They had domesticated dogs, turkeys, and llamas, but horses were unknown until the Spaniards arrived. When fighting erupted, arrows and tomahawks were seldom a match for guns. And the new diseases contracted from European invaders proved to be catastrophic for the Native Americans.

Yet against the odds the Indians resisted European invaders for centuries. They displayed an amazing capacity for adapting to changing circumstances, incorporating European technology and weaponry, forging new alliances, changing their community structures, and often converting whites to their way of life. Many Spanish, English, and French settlers voluntarily joined Indian society or chose to stay after being captured.

FIRST CONTACTS

The discovery of the New World coincided with the spread of European power and culture around the world. The expansion of Europe derived from, and in turn affected, the peculiar patterns and institutions that distinguished modern times from the medieval: the revival of learning and the rise of the inquiring spirit; the explosive growth of trade, towns, and modern corporations; the decline of feudalism and the rise of national states; the religious zeal generated by the Protestant Reformation and the Catholic Reformation; and on the darker side some old sins—greed, conquest, racism, and slavery.

By the fifteenth century these forces had combined to focus European eyes on new lands to conquer or settle and on new peoples to convert, civilize, or exploit. Europeans were especially attracted by the lure of Asia, a near-mythical land of silks, jewels, and millions of "heathens" to be Christianized. Equally valued were the spices—pepper, nutmeg, clove—so essential to the preservation of food, especially in southern Europe, where the warm and humid climate accelerated spoilage.

THE VOYAGES OF COLUMBUS Asia's wealth tantalized Christopher Columbus, a gold-loving adventurer. Born in 1451, the son of an Italian weaver, Columbus took to the sea at an early age. During the 1480s he hatched a scheme to reach Asia by sailing west. After years of disappointment and disgrace, he finally won the financial support of Ferdinand and Isabella, the Spanish monarchs.

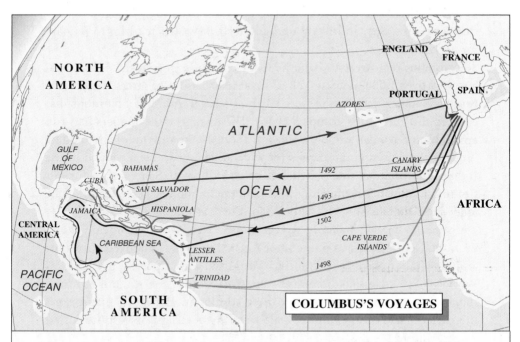

How many voyages did Columbus make to the Americas? What is the origin of the name for the Caribbean Sea? What happened to the colony that Columbus left on Hispaniola in 1493?

Columbus chartered one small ship, the *Santa María,* and the Spanish city of Palos supplied two smaller caravels, the *Pinta* and the *Niña.* From Palos this little squadron, with eighty-seven men, set sail on August 3, 1492. Early on October 12, 1492, a lookout called out, "*Tierra! Tierra!*" (Land! Land!) It was an island in the Bahamas that Columbus named San Salvador (Blessed Savior). Columbus assumed they were near the Pacific "East Indies," so he called the islanders *Indios,* Indians. Their docile temperament led him to write in his journal that "with fifty men they could all be subjugated and compelled to do anything one wishes."

At the moment, however, Columbus was not interested in enslaving "noble savages"; he was seeking the East Indies and their fabled gold. He therefore continued to search through the Bahamas down to Cuba, a place-name that suggested Cipangu (Japan), and then eastward to the island he named Española (or Hispaniola), where he first found significant amounts of gold jewelry. On the night before Christmas in 1492, the *Santa María* ran aground off Hispaniola. Columbus, still believing he had reached Asia, decided to return home. He left about forty men behind and seized a dozen natives to present as gifts to Spain's royal couple. After Columbus reached Palos, he received a hero's welcome. The news of his discovery spread rapidly throughout Europe, and Ferdinand and Isabella instructed him to prepare for a second voyage.

Columbus recrossed the Atlantic in 1493 with seventeen ships, livestock, and well over 1,000 men, as well as royal instructions to "treat the Indians very well." Once back in the New World, however, Admiral Columbus discovered the Europeans' camp in chaos. The unsupervised soldiers had run amok, raping women, robbing villages, and as Columbus's son later added, "committing a thousand excesses for which they were mortally hated by the Indians." The natives finally struck back and killed ten Spaniards. A furious Columbus launched a wholesale attack on the Indian villages, after which he loaded 550 Indians onto ships bound for the slave market in Spain.

Columbus made two more voyages to the New World. Ironically, however, the New World was named not for its European "discoverer" but for another Italian explorer, Amerigo Vespucci, who traveled to the New World in 1499. He sailed along the coast of South America and reported that it was so large it must be a new continent. European mapmakers thereafter began to label the new world using a variant of Vespucci's first name: America.

THE GREAT BIOLOGICAL EXCHANGE European contact with the New World produced a worldwide biological exchange that had profound consequences. If anything, the plants and animals of the two worlds were more different from each other than were the peoples and their ways of life. Europeans had never seen such creatures as the iguana, the flying squirrel, the catfish, and the rattlesnake, nor had they seen anything quite like several other species native to America: bison, cougars, armadillos, opossums, sloths, anacondas, toucans, condors, and hummingbirds. Among the Native Americans' few domesticated animals they could recognize the dog and the duck, but turkeys, guinea pigs, llamas, and alpacas were all new. Nor did the Native Americans know of horses, cattle, pigs, sheep, and goats, which soon arrived from Europe in abundance.

The transfer of plant life transformed the diets of both hemispheres. Before 1492 maize (corn), potatoes (sweet and white), and many kinds of beans (snap, kidney, lima, and others) were unknown in the Old World. Columbus returned to Spain with a handful of corn kernels, and within a few years corn had become a staple crop throughout Europe. The white potato, although commonly called Irish, actually migrated from South America to Europe and reached North America only with the Scotch-Irish immigrants of the 1700s. Other New World food plants include peanuts, squash, peppers, tomatoes, pumpkins, pineapples, papayas, avocados, cacao (the source of chocolate), and chicle (for chewing gum). Europeans in turn soon introduced into the New World rice, wheat, barley, oats, wine grapes, melons, coffee, olives, bananas, "Kentucky" bluegrass, daisies, dandelions, and clover.

The beauty of the ecological exchange between Old and New Worlds was that the food plants were more complementary than competitive. Indian corn spread quickly throughout the world. Before the end of the 1500s, American maize and sweet potatoes were staple crops in China. Plants initially domesticated by Native Americans now make up about one third of the world's food crops.

Europeans also adopted many Native American devices, such as canoes, snowshoes, moccasins, hammocks, kayaks, ponchos, dogsleds, toboggans, and parkas. The rubber ball and the game of lacrosse have Indian origins as well. Still other New World contributions include tobacco and several other drugs, among them coca (for cocaine), curare (a muscle relaxant), and cinchona bark (for quinine).

Unfamiliar Wildlife

A box tortoise drawn by John White, one of the earliest English settlers in America.

By far the most significant aspect of the biological exchange, however, was the transmission of infectious diseases from Europe and Africa to the New World. European colonists and enslaved Africans brought with them deadly pathogens that Native Americans had never experienced: smallpox, typhus, diphtheria, bubonic plague, malaria, yellow fever, and cholera. In dealing with such diseases over the centuries, people in the Old World had developed antibodies that enabled most of them to survive infection. Disease-toughened adventurers, colonists, and Africans invading the New World thus carried viruses and bacteria that consumed Indians, who lacked the immunity that forms from experience with the diseases.

The results were catastrophic. Epidemics are one of the most powerful forces shaping history, and disease played a profound role in decimating the indigenous peoples of the Western Hemisphere. Far more Indians died from contagions than from combat. Major diseases such as typhus and smallpox produced pandemics in the New World on a scale never witnessed in history. The social chaos caused by the arrival of European invaders contributed to the devastation of native communities. In the face of such terrible and mysterious diseases, panic-stricken and often malnourished Indians fled to neighboring villages, unwittingly spreading the diseases in the process. Unable to explain or cure the contagions, Indian chiefs and religious leaders often lost their stature. As a consequence, tribal cohesion and cultural life disintegrated, and efforts to resist European assaults collapsed. Over time, Native Americans adapted to the presence of the diseases and better managed their effects. They began to quarantine victims and infected villages to confine the spread of germs, and they developed elaborate rituals to sanctify such practices.

Smallpox was an especially ghastly and highly contagious disease in the New World. Santo Domingo boasted almost 4 million inhabitants in 1496; by 1570 the number of natives had plummeted to 125. In central Mexico alone, some 8 million people, perhaps one third of the entire Indian population, died of smallpox within a decade of the arrival of the Spanish. Smallpox brought horrific suffering. The virus passes through the air on moisture droplets or dust particles that enter the lungs of its victims. After incubating for twelve days, the virus causes headaches, backache, fever, and nausea. Victims then develop sores in the mouth, nose, and throat. Within a few days gruesome skin eruptions cover the body. Death usually results from massive internal bleeding.

In colonial America, as Indians died by the thousands, disease became the most powerful weapon of the European invaders. A Spanish explorer noted that "half the natives" died from smallpox and "blamed us." Many Europeans, however, interpreted such epidemics as diseases sent by God to punish Indians who resisted conversion to Christianity.

EXPLORATION AND CONQUEST OF THE NEW WORLD

Excited by Columbus's discoveries, professional explorers, mostly Italians, probed the shorelines of America during the early sixteenth century and greatly increased European knowledge of the New World. The first to sight the North American continent was John Cabot, a Venetian sponsored by King Henry VII of England. Cabot sailed across the North Atlantic in 1497. His landfall at what the king called "the newe founde lande" gave England the basis for a later claim to all of North America. During the early sixteenth century, however, the British became so preoccupied with internal divisions and conflicts with France that for several decades they failed to follow up Cabot's discoveries.

The New World thus was a Spanish preserve, except for Brazil, which was a Portuguese colony. The Caribbean Sea served as the funnel through which Spanish power entered the New World. After establishing colonies on Hispaniola and at Santo Domingo, which became the capital of the West Indies, the Spaniards proceeded eastward to Puerto Rico (1508) and westward to Cuba (1511–1514). Their motives were explicit. Said one soldier, "We came here to serve God and the king, and also to get rich."

A CLASH OF CULTURES The encounter between Spaniards and Indians in North America brought together quite different forms of technological development. Whereas Indians used dugout canoes for transportation, Europeans sailed oceangoing warships and brought steel swords, firearms, explosives, and armor, as well as greyhounds, which the Spaniards used to guard their camps. The advanced military tools and attack dogs help explain why the Europeans were able to defeat far superior numbers of Indians.

The Europeans also enjoyed other cultural advantages. For example, the only domesticated four-legged animals in North America were dogs and llamas. The Spaniards, on the other hand, brought horses, pigs, and cattle, all of which served as sources of food and leather. Horses provided greater speed in battle and introduced a decided psychological advantage.

The first European conquest of a major Indian civilization began in 1519, when the Spaniard Hernando Cortés and 600 men landed at the site of Vera

Cortés in Mexico

Page from the Tlaxcala Lienzo, a historical narrative from the sixteenth century. The scene, in which Cortés is shown seated on a throne, depicts the arrival of the Spaniards in Tlaxcala.

Cruz, in Mexico. Cortés then set about a daring conquest of the Aztec Empire. The 200-mile march from Vera Cruz through difficult mountain passes to the magnificent Aztec capital of Tenochtitlán (near present-day Mexico City) and the subjugation of the Aztecs, who thought themselves "masters of the world," were two of the most remarkable feats in human history. Tenochtitlán, with some 200,000 inhabitants, was by far the largest city in North America, much larger than Seville, the most populous city in Spain. Graced by wide canals and featuring beautiful stone pyramids and buildings, the fabled capital seemed impregnable to invasion.

Cortés, however, made the most of his assets. His invasion force had landed in a region where the natives were still resisting the spread of Aztec power and were ready to embrace new allies, especially those who possessed powerful weapons. By a combination of threats and deception, Cortés entered Tenochtitlán peacefully and made the emperor, Montezuma II, his puppet. This state of affairs lasted until the spring of 1520, when the Aztecs rebelled, took over the city, and stoned Montezuma to death. The Spaniards' Indian allies remained loyal, however, and Cortés gradually regrouped his forces; in 1521 he took the city again.

Within twenty years the Spanish soldiers had established a sprawling empire in the New World. Between 1522 and 1528 various lieutenants of Cortés's conquered the remnants of Indian culture in the Yucatán Peninsula and Guatemala. Then, in 1531, Francisco Pizarro led a band of soldiers down the Pacific coast from Panama toward Peru, where they brutally subdued the Inca Empire. From Peru, conquistadores extended Spanish authority south through Chile and north to present-day Colombia.

SPANISH AMERICA   The Spanish conquistadores transferred to America a system known as the *encomienda,* whereby favored officers became privileged landowners (*encomenderos*) who controlled Indian villages or groups of villages. They were called upon to protect and care for the villages and support missionary priests. In turn they could require tribute from the native villagers in the form of goods and labor. Spanish America therefore developed from the start a society of extremes: wealthy European conquistadores at one end of the spectrum and native peoples held in poverty at the other end.

Yet by the mid-1500s Indians were nearly extinct in the West Indies, killed more often by European diseases than by Spanish exploitation. To take their place, the colonizers as early as 1503 began to import Africans to work as slaves. In all of Spain's New World empire, the Indian population dropped from about 50 million at the outset to 4 million in the seventeenth century and slowly rose again to 7.5 million by the end of the eighteenth century. Whites, who totaled no more than 100,000 in the mid–sixteenth century, numbered over 3 million by the end of the colonial period.

The Indians, however, did not always lack advocates. Many Catholic missionaries offered a sharp contrast to the conquistadores. They ventured into remote areas, often without weapons or protection, to spread the gospel—sometimes risking their lives. Where conquistadores sought to wrest gold, land, and labor from the Indians, the Spanish missionaries wanted their souls, and they had a tremendous impact upon Native American culture. At their worst the missionaries were bigots determined to rid "heathen" people of their native religion and many of their cultural practices. At their best, however, missionaries were impassioned defenders of the Indians.

THE SPANISH HERITAGE   Throughout the sixteenth century much of what is now the United States belonged to Spain, and Spanish culture has left a lasting imprint upon American ways of life. Spain's colonial presence lasted more than three centuries, much longer than either England's or France's, and its possessions were much more far-reaching. The vice royalty of New Spain was centered in Mexico, but its frontiers extended from the Florida Keys to Alaska and included areas not currently thought of as formerly Spanish, such as the Deep South and the lower Midwest. Spanish place-names— San Francisco, Santa Barbara, Los Angeles, San Diego, Tucson, Santa Fe, San Antonio, Pensacola, and St. Augustine—survive to this day, as do Spanish influences in art, architecture, literature, music, law, and cuisine.

Although Spain's influence was strongest from Mexico southward, the "Spanish borderlands" of the southern United States, from Florida to California, preserve many reminders of the Spanish presence. The earliest known exploration of Florida was made in 1513 by Juan Ponce de León, then governor of Puerto Rico. He sought the mythic fountain of youth but instead found alligators, swamps, and abundant wildlife. Meanwhile, other Spanish explorers skirted the Gulf coast from Florida to Vera Cruz, scouted the Atlantic coast from Key West to Newfoundland, established a town at St. Augustine, Florida, and a mission at Santa Fe, New Mexico, and planted a short-lived colony on the Carolina coast.

Spain established provinces in North America not so much as commercial enterprises but as defensive buffers protecting its more lucrative trading empire in Mexico and South America. The Spaniards were concerned about French traders infiltrating from Louisiana, English settlers crossing into Florida, and Russian seal hunters wandering down the California coast. Yet the Spanish settlements in what is today the United States never flourished. England and France surpassed Spain in America because Spain failed to embrace what the other imperial powers decided early on: that developing a thriving Indian trade in goods was more important than the conversion of "heathens" and the often fruitless search for gold and silver.

THE SPANISH SOUTHWEST   Spain eventually founded other permanent settlements in present-day New Mexico, Texas, and California. Eager to pacify rather than fight the far more numerous Indians of the region, the Spanish used religion as an instrument of colonial control. Missionaries, particularly Franciscans and Jesuits, established isolated Catholic missions where they imposed Christianity upon the Indians. The soldiers who were sent to protect the missions were housed in presidios, or forts, while their families and the merchants accompanying the soldiers lived in adjacent villages.

The land that would later be called New Mexico was the first center of mission activity in the American Southwest. In 1598 Juan de Oñate, the

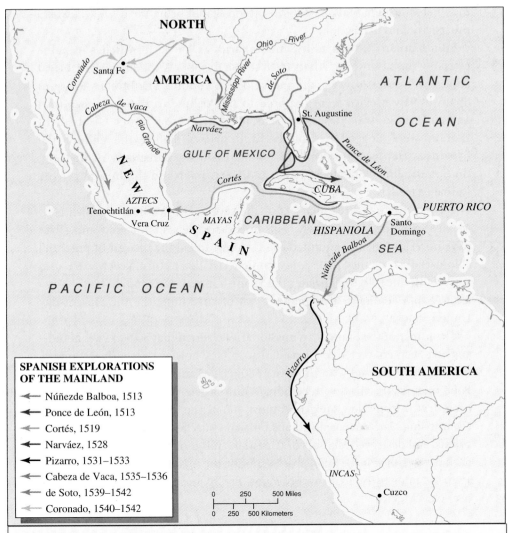

NORTH AMERICA

Ohio River

de Soto

ATLANTIC OCEAN

Coronado

Santa Fe

Cabeza de Vaca

Mississippi River

Rio Grande

Narváez

St. Augustine

GULF OF MEXICO

Ponce de León

N E W

Cortés

CUBA

PUERTO RICO

AZTECS
Tenochtitlán

Vera Cruz

MAYAS

CARIBBEAN

HISPANIOLA

Santo Domingo

S P A I N

Núñez de Balboa

SEA

PACIFIC OCEAN

Pizarro

SOUTH AMERICA

SPANISH EXPLORATIONS OF THE MAINLAND

- Núñez de Balboa, 1513
- Ponce de León, 1513
- Cortés, 1519
- Narváez, 1528
- Pizarro, 1531–1533
- Cabeza de Vaca, 1535–1536
- de Soto, 1539–1542
- Coronado, 1540–1542

INCAS

Cuzco

| 0 | 250 | 500 Miles |
| 0 | 250 | 500 Kilometers |

What were the Spanish conquistadores' goals for exploring the Americas? How did Cortés conquer the Aztecs? Why did the Spanish first explore North America, and why did they establish St. Augustine, the first European settlement in what would become the United States?

wealthy son of a Spanish family in Mexico, received a patent for the territory north of Mexico above the Rio Grande. With an expeditionary military force made up of Mexican Indians and mestizos (sons of Spanish fathers and native mothers), he took possession of New Mexico, established a capital at San Gabriel, and dispatched expeditions to look for gold and silver. He promised the Pueblo leaders that Spanish dominion would bring them peace, justice, prosperity, and protection.

Some Indians welcomed the missionaries as "powerful witches" capable of easing their burdens. Others tried to use the Spanish as allies against rival tribes. Still others saw no alternative but to submit. The Indians living in Spanish New Mexico were required to pay tribute to their *encomenderos* and perform personal tasks for them, including sexual favors. Disobedient Indians were flogged by soldiers and priests. Before the end of the province's first year, the Indians revolted. During three days of fighting, the Spanish killed 500 Pueblo men and 300 women and children. Survivors were enslaved.

During the first three quarters of the seventeenth century, Spanish New Mexico expanded very slowly. The hoped-for deposits of gold and silver were never found, and a limited food supply dulled the interest of potential colonists. In 1608 the Spanish government decided to turn New Mexico into a royal province. Two years later the Spanish moved the capital of New Mexico to Santa Fe, the first permanent seat of government in the present-day United States.

The leader of the Franciscan missionaries claimed that 86,000 Pueblo Indians had been converted to Christianity. In fact, however, resentment among the Indians increased with time. In 1680 a charismatic Indian leader named Popé organized a massive rebellion. Within a few weeks the Spaniards had been driven from New Mexico. Almost 400 of the Europeans were killed in the uprising. The outraged Indians burned churches, tortured and executed priests, and destroyed all relics of Christianity. It took fourteen years and four military assaults for the Spaniards to subdue the region. Thereafter, except for sporadic raids by Apaches and Navajos, the Spanish exercised stable control over New Mexico.

HORSES AND THE GREAT PLAINS Another major consequence of the Pueblo Revolt was the opportunity it afforded Indian rebels to acquire hundreds of coveted Spanish horses (Spanish authorities had made it illegal for Indians to own horses). The Pueblos in turn established a thriving horse trade with the Navajos, Apaches, and other tribes. By 1690 horses were evident in Texas, and they soon spread across the Great Plains, the vast rolling grasslands extending from the Missouri River valley in the east to the base of the Rocky Mountains in the west.

Horses were a disruptive ecological force in North America. Prior to the arrival of horses, Indians hunted on foot and used dogs as their beasts of burden, hauling their supplies on travois, devices made from two long poles connected by leather straps. But dogs are carnivores, and it was often difficult to find enough meat to feed them. Horses thus changed everything, providing the pedestrian Plains Indians with a transforming source of mobility and power. They are grazing animals, and the endless grasslands of the Great Plains offered plenty of forage. Horses could also haul up to seven times as much weight as dogs, and their speed and endurance made the Indians much more effective hunters and warriors. In addition, horses enabled Indians to travel farther to trade and fight.

The ready availability of large numbers of horses thus worked a revolution in the economy and ecology of the Great Plains. Such tribes as the Arapaho, Cheyenne, Comanche, Kiowa, and Sioux reinvented themselves as equestrian societies. They left their traditional woodland villages on the fringes of the plains and became nomadic bison (buffalo) hunters. Using horses, they could haul larger tepees and more meat and hides with them, building temporary camps as they migrated year-round with the immense bison herds, wintering in sheltered glades along rivers. The once-deserted plains soon were a crossroads of activity.

Plains Indians

The horse-stealing raid depicted in this hide painting demonstrates the essential role horses played in Plains life.

Indians used virtually every part of the bison they killed: meat for food; hides for clothing, shoes, bedding, and shelter; muscles and tendons for thread and bowstrings; intestines for containers; bones for tools; horns for eating utensils; hair for headdresses; and dung for fuel. One scholar has referred to the bison as the "tribal department store." The Plains Indians supplemented bison meat with roots and berries they gathered along the way. In the fall the nomadic tribes would travel south to exchange hides and robes for food or to raid Indian farming villages.

In the short run the horse brought prosperity and mobility to the Plains Indians. Horses became the center and symbol of Indian life on the plains. Yet the noble animal also brought insecurity, instability, and conflict. Indians began to kill more bison than the herds could replace. In addition, the herds of horses competed with the bison for food, depleting the grass and compacting the soil in the river valleys during the winter. As tribes traveled greater distances and encountered more people, infectious diseases spread more widely.

Horses became so valuable that they provoked thievery and intensified intertribal competition and warfare. Within tribes a family's status was determined by the number of horses it possessed. Horses eased some of the physical burdens on women but imposed new demands. Women and girls were assigned the responsibility of tending to the horses. They also had to butcher and dry the buffalo meat and tan the hides. As the value of the hides grew, male hunters began to indulge in polygamy: more wives could process more buffalo. The rising economic value of wives eventually led Plains Indians to raid farming tribes in search of captive brides as well as horses. The introduction of horses into the Great Plains, then, was a decidedly mixed blessing. By 1800 a plains trader could observe that "this is a delightful country, and were it not for perpetual wars, the natives might be the happiest people on earth."

CHALLENGES TO THE SPANISH EMPIRE   The Spanish monopoly on the New World colonies did not go unchallenged. The French were the first to pose a serious threat. In 1524 the French king sent the Italian Giovanni da Verrazano in search of a passage to Asia. Sighting land (probably at Cape Fear, North Carolina), he ranged along the coast as far north as Maine, but it would be another seventeen years before the French made their first effort at colonization. Jacques Cartier explored the Gulf of St. Lawrence and ventured up the St. Lawrence River as far as present-day Montreal. Near Quebec he established a short-lived colony in 1541.

Thereafter, however, French interest in Canada waned, as the French were preoccupied with the religious civil wars racking their country. Not

until the early seventeenth century, when Samuel de Champlain established settlements in Acadia (Nova Scotia) and at Quebec, did French colonization in America begin in earnest. Enterprising French traders negotiated with Indians for their fur pelts, and French Jesuit missionaries
cultivated their souls.

Acquiring furs and ministering to "heathens" took the French southward
as well. In 1673 Louis Jolliet and Père Jacques Marquette, a Jesuit priest, explored the Mississippi River, but fearing an encounter with the Spaniards,
they turned back before reaching the Gulf of Mexico. Nine years later René-
Robert Cavelier, sieur de La Salle, did the same, but he ventured all the way
to the Gulf of Mexico. There, near the river's delta, the French in the early
eighteenth century would establish a settlement called New Orleans. The
French thereby came to control not only Canada but also the major inland
waterway in North America, the Mississippi River. But because the French
monarchy never emphasized permanent settlement, French America remained only sparsely populated.

From the mid-1500s greater threats to Spanish power in the New World
arose from the growing strength of the Dutch and the English. The prosperous provinces of the Netherlands, which had passed by inheritance to the
Spanish king and had become largely Protestant, rebelled against Spanish
Catholic rule in 1567. A bloody struggle for independence was interrupted
by a twelve-year truce, but Spain did not accept the independence of the
Dutch republic until 1648.

Almost from the beginning of the Dutch revolt against Spain, Dutch privateers plundered Spanish ships. The Dutch raiders soon had their counterpart in England's sea dogges: John Hawkins, Francis Drake, and others.
While Queen Elizabeth of England steered a tortuous course to avoid open
war with Catholic Spain, she encouraged both Dutch and English sea captains to attack Spanish vessels. In 1577 Francis Drake set out on his famous
adventure around South America to raid Spanish towns along the Pacific
coast. Three years later he returned in triumph.

Sporadic British piracy against the Spanish continued until 1587, when
Queen Elizabeth had her Catholic cousin, Mary, Queen of Scots, beheaded
for her involvement in a plot to kill the English queen and elevate herself to
the throne. In revenge for Mary's execution, Spain's King Philip II decided to
crush Protestant England and began to gather his ill-fated invasion fleet,
called the Armada. The ambitious enterprise quickly became a case of incompetence and mismanagement accompanied by bad luck. The heavy
Spanish galleons could not cope with the smaller, faster English vessels. Defeat of the Spanish Armada convinced the English that the Spanish navy was

SETTLING THE CHESAPEAKE

With the death of Queen Elizabeth, the Tudor family line ended, and the throne fell to Elizabeth's cousin James VI of Scotland, the son of the ill-fated Mary, Queen of Scots. The first of the Stuarts, he ruled England as James I. The Stuart dynasty spanned most of the seventeenth century, a turbulent time of religious and political tensions, civil war, and foreign intrigues. During those eventful years in English history, all but one of the thirteen North American colonies had their start. They were quite diverse in geography, motives, and composition, a diversity that has since been a trademark and a strength of American society.

In 1606, having made peace with Spain, thereby freeing up resources and men for colonization, James I chartered what was called the Virginia Company, with two divisions, the First Colony of London and the Second Colony of Plymouth. The stockholders expected a potential return from gold and products such as wine, citrus fruits, olive oil, and forest products needed for naval use. Many also still hoped to discover a passage to India. Few if any investors foresaw what the first English colony would become: a fertile place to grow tobacco.

From the outset the pattern of English colonization diverged significantly from the Spanish activities in the New World. The autocratic Spaniards conquered people and regulated all aspects of colonial life. The English had a different model, based on their settlements, or "plantations," in Ireland, which the English had conquered by military force under Queen Elizabeth. Within their own pale (or limit) of settlement in Ireland, the English had set about transplanting their familiar way of life insofar as possible. Thus the English subjugated the Indians of North America much as they had the Irish in Ireland. In America the English settled along the Atlantic seaboard, where the native populations were relatively sparse. There was no Aztec or Inca Empire to conquer.

VIRGINIA   The London group of the Virginia Company planted the first permanent colony in Virginia, named after Elizabeth I, "the Virgin Queen." On May 6, 1607, three tiny ships loaded with 105 men reached Chesapeake Bay after four storm-tossed months at sea. They chose a river with a northwest bend—in the hope of finding a passage to Asia—and settled about forty miles inland to hide from marauding Spaniards.

The river they called the James and the colony, Jamestown. After building a fort, thatched huts, a storehouse, and a church, the colonists began planting, but most were either townsmen unfamiliar with farming or "gentlemen" adventurers who scorned manual labor. They had come to find gold, not to live as homesteaders. Ignorant of woodlore, they did not know how to exploit the area's abundant game and fish. Supplies from England were undependable, and only firm leadership and trade with the Indians, who taught the colonists to grow maize, enabled them to survive.

The Indians of the region were loosely organized. Powhatan was the charismatic chief of some thirty Algonquian-speaking tribes in eastern Virginia. The Indians making up the so-called Powhatan Confederacy were largely an agricultural people; corn was their primary crop. Despite occasional clashes with the colonists, the Indians initially adopted a stance of cautious assistance and watchful waiting. Powhatan hoped to develop a lucrative trade and military alliance with the newcomers; he realized too late that the newcomers intended to expropriate his lands and subjugate his people.

Ould Virginia

A 1624 map of Virginia by John Smith, showing Chief Powhatan in the upper left.

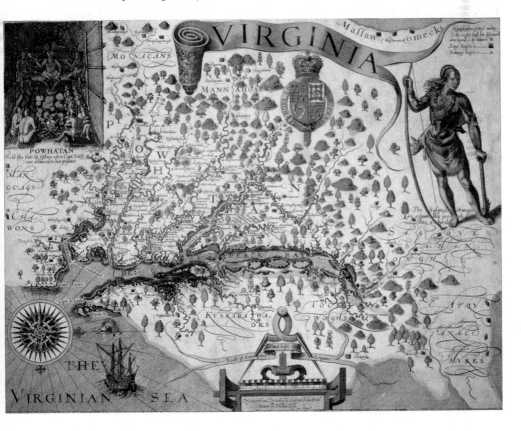

The colonists, as it happened, had more than a match for Powhatan in Captain John Smith, a soldier of fortune with rare powers of leadership and self-promotion. With the colonists on the verge of starvation, Smith imposed strict discipline and forced all to labor, declaring that "he that will not work shall not eat." Smith also bargained with the Indians and mapped the Chesapeake region. Despite his efforts, only 38 of the original 105 colonists survived the first nine months.

John Smith's efforts to save the struggling colony abruptly ended when he suffered a gunpowder burn and sailed back to England in 1609. More colonists were dispatched, including several women. The colony lapsed into anarchy and suffered the "starving time," the winter of 1609–1610, during which most of the colonists, weakened by hunger, fell prey to disease. A relief party found only about sixty settlers still alive in 1610.

For the next seven years the colony limped along until it gradually found a reason for being: tobacco. In 1612 John Rolfe had begun to experiment with the harsh-tasting Virginia tobacco, and by 1616 a smoother-tasting variety of the weed had become a valuable export. As Virginia's tobacco production soared, planters purchased indentured servants, thus increasing the flow of immigrants to the colony. Meanwhile John Rolfe had made another contribution to stability by marrying Pocahontas, the daughter of Powhatan. Their marriage helped ease deteriorating relations between the Indians and the English settlers.

In 1618 officials in London initiated a series of reforms intended to shore up their struggling American colony. They first inaugurated a new "headright" policy. Anyone who bought a share in the company or could transport himself to Virginia could have fifty acres and fifty more for any servants he might send or bring. The following year the company relaxed its tight legal code and promised that the settlers would have the "rights of Englishmen," including a representative assembly. On July 30, 1619, the first General Assembly of Virginia met in the Jamestown church and deliberated for five days, "sweating and stewing, and battling flies and mosquitoes." It was an eventful year in two other respects. During 1619 a ship arrived with ninety "young maidens" to be sold to husbands of their own choice for the cost of transportation (about 125 pounds of tobacco). And a Dutch warship dropped off "20 Negars," the first Africans known to have been brought to English America.

Yet the English foothold in Virginia remained tenuous. Some 14,000 people had migrated to the colony since 1607, but the population in 1624 stood at a precarious 1,132. The king appointed a commission to investigate the running of the struggling colony by the Virginia Company, and on the commission's recommendation a court dissolved the company. In 1624 Virginia became a royal colony.

Relations with the Indians continued in a state of what the governor's council called "perpetual enmity" until the Indians staged a major attack in 1644. The English suffered as many casualties as they had twenty-two years before, but they put down the uprising with such ferocity that nothing quite like it happened again. The combination of warfare and disease decimated the Indians of Virginia. The 24,000 Algonquians who inhabited the colony in 1607 were reduced to 2,000 by 1669.

MARYLAND   In 1634, ten years after Virginia became a royal colony, a neighboring settlement, named Maryland, appeared on the northern shores of Chesapeake Bay. It was the first so-called proprietary colony, granted not

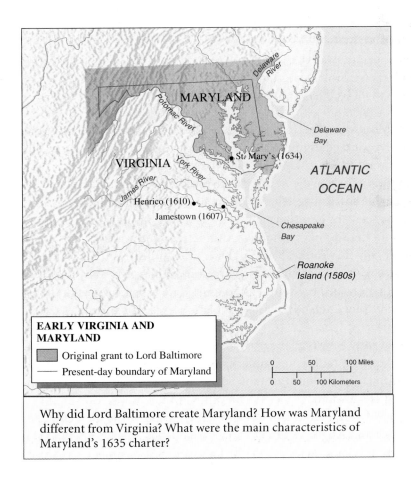

EARLY VIRGINIA AND MARYLAND

☐ Original grant to Lord Baltimore

— Present-day boundary of Maryland

Why did Lord Baltimore create Maryland? How was Maryland different from Virginia? What were the main characteristics of Maryland's 1635 charter?

to a joint-stock company but to an individual, Lord Baltimore. Sir George Calvert, the first Lord Baltimore, had announced in 1625 his conversion to Catholicism and sought the colony as a refuge for English Catholics, who were subjected to discrimination at home. The charter for such a colony was finally issued in 1632, after his death.

His son, Cecilius Calvert, the second Lord Baltimore, founded the colony in 1634 at St. Marys, on a small stream near the mouth of the Potomac River. Calvert brought along Catholic gentlemen as landholders, but a majority of the servants were Protestants. The charter gave Calvert power to make laws with the consent of the freemen (all property holders). The first legislative assembly met in 1635 and later divided into two houses, with governor and council sitting separately. The charter also empowered the proprietor to grant huge manorial estates, and Maryland had some sixty before 1676. But the Lords Baltimore soon found that to draw large numbers of settlers they had to offer small farms. The colony was meant to rely upon mixed farming, but its fortunes, like those of Virginia, soon came to depend upon tobacco.

Settling New England

Meanwhile, far to the north of the Chesapeake Bay, quite different colonies were emerging. The New England colonists were generally made up of middle-class families who could pay their own way across the Atlantic. In the Northeast there were relatively few indentured servants, and there was no planter elite. Most male settlers were small farmers, merchants, seamen, or fishermen. New England also attracted more women than did the southern colonies. Although its soil was not as fertile and its farmers not as wealthy, New England was a much healthier place to settle. Because of its colder climate, the region did not foster the infectious diseases that ravaged the southern colonies. Life expectancy was much longer. By 1700 New England's white population exceeded that of Maryland and Virginia.

Most early New Englanders were devout Puritans, who embraced a much more rigorous faith and simpler rituals than the Anglicans of Virginia and Maryland. The zealous Puritans believed themselves to be on a divine mission to create a model society committed to the proper worship of God. In the New World these self-described "saints" could purify their churches of all Catholic and Anglican rituals, supervise one another in practicing a communal faith, and enact a code of laws and a government structure based upon biblical principles. Such a holy settlement, they hoped, would provide a beacon of righteousness for a wicked England to emulate.

PLYMOUTH   The Pilgrims who established Plymouth Colony were bent not on finding gold or making a fortune but on building a Christian commonwealth. They belonged to the most uncompromising sect of Puritans, the Separatists, who had severed all ties with the Church of England. Persecuted by King James I and Anglican officials, they had fled to Holland in 1607.

The Separatists grew uneasy with Dutch folkways, however, and decided to move to America. These "Pilgrims" secured a land patent from the Virginia Company, and in 1620, 102 men, women, and children, led by William Bradford, crammed into the *Mayflower* for the transatlantic voyage. Only half the voyagers were Pilgrim "saints," Christians recognized as having been elected by God for salvation; the rest were non-Pilgrim "strangers": ordinary settlers, hired hands, and indentured servants.

A stormy voyage led them to Cape Cod, off the coast of Massachusetts, far north of Virginia. Exploring parties hit upon a place called Plymouth for their settlement. Since they were outside the jurisdiction of any organized government, forty-one of the Pilgrims entered into a formal agreement to abide by laws made by leaders of their own choosing—the Mayflower Compact of November 21, 1620. Used later as a model by other New England settlers, the compact helped establish the distinctive American tradition of consensual government.

Throughout its separate existence, until it was absorbed into Massachusetts in 1691, the Plymouth colony's government grew out of the Mayflower Compact, which was not a formal constitution but an agreement among members of a religious group who believed that God had made a covenant (or agreement) with them to provide a way to salvation. Thus the civil government evolved naturally out of the church government, and the members of each were initially identical.

Nearly half the Pilgrims died of exposure and disease, but friendly relations with the neighboring Wampanoag Indians proved their salvation. In the spring of 1621, the colonists met Squanto, who showed them how to grow maize. By autumn the Pilgrims had a bumper crop of corn, a flourishing fur trade, and a supply of lumber for shipment. To celebrate, they held a harvest feast with the Wampanoags, an annual ritual that would later be dubbed Thanksgiving.

MASSACHUSETTS BAY   The Plymouth colony's population never rose above 7,000, and after ten years it was overshadowed by its larger neighbor,

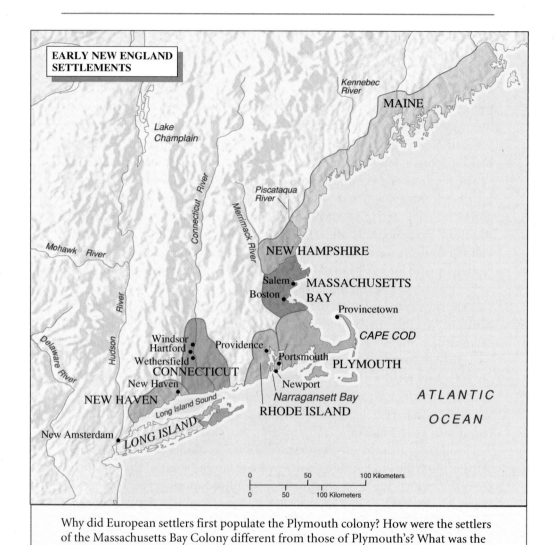

EARLY NEW ENGLAND SETTLEMENTS

Why did European settlers first populate the Plymouth colony? How were the settlers of the Massachusetts Bay Colony different from those of Plymouth's? What was the origin of the Rhode Island colony?

the Massachusetts Bay Colony. It, too, was intended to be a holy common-wealth made up of religious settlers bound together in the harmonious worship of God and the pursuit of their "callings." The colony got its start in 1629, when a group of Puritans and merchants convinced King Charles I (son of James I) to grant their newly formed Massachusetts Bay Company an area north of the Plymouth colony for settlement. Leaders of the company at first looked upon it mainly as a business venture, but a majority faction, led by

John Winthrop, a respected lawyer animated by intense religious convictions, resolved to use the colony as a refuge for persecuted Puritans and as an instrument for building a "wilderness Zion" in America.

Winthrop was a courageous leader who reflected the strengths and weaknesses of the Puritan movement. In 1629 he was forty years of age, had a large family, and found himself managing a floundering English estate that could not support his seven sons. Even more unsettling was the government's heightened persecution of Puritans and other dissenters. Hence he eagerly supported the idea of establishing a spiritual plantation in the New World, and he agreed to head up the enterprise. Winthrop shrewdly took advantage of a fateful omission in the royal charter for the Massachusetts Bay Company: the usual proviso that the company maintain its home office in England. Winthrop's group took its charter with them, thereby transferring government authority to Massachusetts Bay, where they hoped to ensure Puritan control.

In 1630 the *Arbella*, with John Winthrop and the charter aboard, embarked with six other ships for Massachusetts. In "A Modell of Christian Charity," a speech delivered on board, Winthrop told his fellow Puritans that "we must consider that we shall be a city upon a hill"—a shining example of what a truly godly community could be. By the end of 1630, seventeen ships bearing 1,000 more colonists had arrived in Massachusetts. As settlers—Puritan and non-Puritan—poured into the region, Boston became the chief city and capital.

The transfer of the Massachusetts charter, whereby an English trading company evolved into a provincial government, was a unique venture in colonization. Under this royal charter, power rested with the Massachusetts General Court, which elected the governor and his assistants and consisted of shareholders, called freemen (those who had the "freedom of the company"), but of those who came, few besides Winthrop and his assistants had such status. That suited Winthrop and his friends, but soon other settlers demanded a share of political power. Rather than risk trouble, the inner group invited applications and finally admitted 118 additional freemen in 1631. The

John Winthrop

The first governor of Massachusetts Bay Colony, in whose vision the colony would be as "a city upon a hill."

inner group also stipulated that only official church members, a limited category, could become freemen.

At first the freemen had no power except to choose "assistants," who in turn elected the governor and deputy governor. The procedure violated provisions of the charter, but Winthrop kept the document hidden, and few knew of its exact provisions. Controversy simmered until 1634, when each town sent two delegates to Boston to confer on matters coming before the Massachusetts General Court. There they demanded to see the charter, which Winthrop reluctantly produced, and they read that the power to pass laws and levy taxes rested in the General Court. Winthrop argued that the body of freemen had grown too large, but when it met, the General Court responded by turning itself into a representative body with two or three deputies to represent each town. A final stage in the evolution of the government, a two-house legislature, came in 1644, with the deputies and assistants sitting apart and all decisions requiring a majority in each house.

Thus over a period of fourteen years, the Massachusetts Bay Company, a trading corporation, evolved into the governing body of a commonwealth. Membership in a Puritan church replaced the purchase of stock as a means of becoming a freeman, which was to say a voter. The General Court, like Parliament, became a representative body of two houses, with the House of Assistants corresponding roughly to the House of Lords and the House of Deputies corresponding to the House of Commons. The charter remained unchanged, but practice under the charter differed considerably from the original expectation.

RHODE ISLAND More by accident than design, Massachusetts became the staging area for the rest of New England as new colonies grew out of religious quarrels. Puritanism created a volatile mixture: on the one hand, the search for God's will could lead to a rigid orthodoxy; on the other hand, it could lead troubled consciences to diverse, radical, or even bizarre convictions.

Young Roger Williams, who had arrived from England in 1631, was among the first to cause problems, precisely because he was the purest of Puritans, a Separatist troubled by the failure of the Massachusetts Nonconformists to repudiate the Church of England entirely. Williams held a brief pastorate in Salem, then moved to Plymouth. Governor Bradford found him gentle and kind in his personal relations and a charismatic speaker, but noted that he "began to fall into strange opinions." A quarrel with the authorities over their treatment of Indians led Williams to return to Salem. There he continued to challenge social and religious norms. Williams's belief that a true church must have no relations with the English government, the

Anglican establishment, or the unregenerate eventually led him to the conclusion that no true church was possible, unless perhaps one consisting of his wife and himself.

In Williams's view the purity of the church required complete separation of church and state and freedom from all coercion in matters of faith. "Forced worship," he declared, "stinks in God's nostrils." Such radical views were too advanced even for the progressive church of Salem, which finally removed him, whereupon Williams charged that the churches were "ulcered and gangrened." In 1635 the General Court banished him to England. Aided by Narragansett Indian friends, however, Williams and a few followers headed into the wilderness in the dead of winter and were eventually taken in by the Narragansetts. In the spring of 1636, he bought land from the Indians and established the town of Providence at the head of Narragansett Bay, the first permanent settlement in Rhode Island and the first in America to legislate freedom of religion.

Thus the colony of Rhode Island, the smallest in America, grew up in Narragansett Bay as a refuge for dissenters who believed that the state had no right to coerce religious belief. In 1640 they formed a confederation and in 1643 secured their first charter of incorporation as Providence Plantations. Roger Williams lived until 1683, an active and beloved citizen of the commonwealth he founded. During his lifetime at least, Rhode Island lived up to his principles of religious freedom and a government based on the consent of the people.

Anne Hutchinson quarreled with the Puritan leaders for different reasons. She was married to a prominent merchant and had given birth to thirteen children. Strong-willed and articulate, she also worked as a healer and midwife and hosted meetings in her Boston home to discuss sermons. Soon, however, those discussions turned into large forums for Hutchinson's commentaries on religious matters. She claimed to have had direct revelations from the Holy Spirit that convinced her that only two or three Puritan ministers actually preached the appropriate "covenant of grace." The others, she charged, were godless hypocrites, deluded and incompetent. They were promoting a "covenant of works" that led people to believe that good conduct would ensure their salvation.

Hutchinson's beliefs were provocative for several reasons. Puritan theology presumed that people could be saved only by God's grace rather than through their own willful actions. But Puritanism in practice also insisted that ministers were necessary to interpret God's will for the people so as to "prepare" them for the possibility of their being selected for salvation. In challenging the very legitimacy of the ministerial community as well as the hard-earned assurances of salvation enjoyed by current church members, Hutchinson was undermining the stability of an already fragile social system and theological order. What made the situation worse in such a male-dominated society, of course, was that a *woman* had the audacity to make such charges and assertions. Anne Hutchinson had both offended authority and sanctioned a disruptive self-righteousness.

A pregnant Hutchinson was hauled before the General Court in 1637, and for two days she verbally sparred with the presiding magistrates and testifying ministers. Her skillful deflections of the charges and her ability to cite biblical chapter-and-verse defenses of her actions led an exasperated Governor Winthrop to explode, "We do not mean to discourse with those of your sex." He found Hutchinson to be "a woman of haughty and fierce carriage, of a nimble wit and active spirit, and a very voluble tongue."

As the trial continued, an overwrought Hutchinson was eventually lured into convicting herself by claiming direct divine inspiration. Banished in 1638 as "a woman not fit for our society," she walked through the wilderness and settled with her family and a few followers on an island south of Providence, near what is now Portsmouth, Rhode Island. The arduous journey had taken a toll, however. Hutchinson grew sick, and her baby was stillborn, leading her critics in Massachusetts to assert that the "monstrous birth" was God's way of punishing her for her sins. Hutchinson's spirits never recovered. After her husband's death in 1642, she moved to what is now New York, then under Dutch jurisdiction, and the following year she and five of her children were massacred during an Indian attack.

CONNECTICUT, NEW HAMPSHIRE, AND MAINE   Connecticut had a more orthodox beginning than Rhode Island. It was founded by groups of Massachusetts Puritans seeking better land and access to the fur trade farther west. In 1636 three entire church congregations trekked westward by the "Great Road," driving their hogs and cattle before them, and settled the Connecticut River towns of Wethersfield, Windsor, and Hartford.

Led by Thomas Hooker, they organized the self-governing colony of Connecticut in 1637 as a response to the danger of attack from the Pequot Indians, who lived nearby. In 1639 the Connecticut General Court adopted the Fundamental Orders, a series of laws providing for a government like that of Massachusetts. In the Connecticut colony, however, voting was not limited to church members.

Although it would later become part of Connecticut, a separate colony was initially established in New Haven. A group of English Puritans led by their minister, John Davenport, had migrated first to Massachusetts and then, seeking a place to establish themselves in commerce, had settled in

New Haven, on Long Island Sound, in 1638. Like all the other offshoots of Massachusetts, the New Haven colony lacked a charter and maintained its independence. In 1662 it was absorbed into Connecticut.

To the north of Massachusetts, most of what are now the states of New Hampshire and Maine was granted in 1622 by the Council for New England to Sir Ferdinando Gorges and Captain John Mason. In 1629 Gorges and Mason divided their territory at the Piscataqua River, Mason taking the southern part, which he named New Hampshire, and Gorges taking the northern part, which became the province of Maine. In the 1630s Puritan immigrants began filtering in, and in 1638 the Reverend John Wheelwright, one of Anne Hutchinson's followers, founded Exeter, New Hampshire. Maine consisted of a few small, scattered settlements, mostly fishing stations, the chief of them being York.

INDIANS IN NEW ENGLAND

The English settlers who poured into New England found not a "virgin land" of uninhabited wilderness but a developed region populated by over 100,000 Indians. The white colonists viewed the Native Americans as an alien race and an impediment to their economic and spiritual goals. To the Indians the newcomers seemed like magical monsters, and they coped with their changing circumstances in different ways. Many resisted, others sought accommodation, and still others grew dependent upon European culture. The interactions of the two cultures involved misunderstandings, the mutual need for trade and adaptation, and sporadic outbreaks of epidemics and warfare.

In general, the English colonists adopted a strategy for dealing with the Native Americans quite different that was from that of the French and the Dutch. Merchants from France and the Netherlands were preoccupied with exploiting the fur trade. Thus they established permanent trading outposts, which led them to nurture amicable relations with the Indians, who were far more numerous than they. In contrast, the English colonists were more interested in pursuing their "God-given" right to fish and farm. They were quite willing, therefore, to manipulate and exploit the Indians they encountered rather than deal with them on an equal footing. Their goal was subordination rather than reciprocity.

Initially the coastal Indians helped the white settlers develop a subsistence economy. They taught the Europeans how to plant corn and use fish for fertilizer. They also developed a flourishing trade with the newcomers, exchanging furs for manufactured goods and "trinkets." The various Indian

The Broiling of Their Fish Over the Flame

In this drawing by John White, reproduced in an engraving by Theodor de Bry, Algonquian men in North Carolina broil fish, a dietary staple of coastal societies.

tribes of New England fought among themselves, usually over disputed land. Had they been able to forge a solid alliance, they would have been better able to resist the encroachments of white settlers. As it was, they were not only fragmented but also vulnerable to the infectious diseases carried on board the ships transporting European settlers to the New World. Epidemics of smallpox soon devastated the Indian population, leaving the coastal areas "a widowed land." Between 1610 and 1675 the Abenakis, a tribe in Maine, declined from 12,000 to 3,000 and the southern New England tribes from 65,000 to 10,000.

THE PEQUOT WAR   Indians who survived the epidemics and refused to yield their lands were dislodged by force. In 1636 settlers in Massachusetts accused a Pequot of murdering a colonist. Joined by Connecticut colonists, they exacted their revenge by setting fire to a Pequot village on the Mystic River. As the Indians fled their burning huts, the Puritans shot and killed them—men, women, and children. In less than an hour, all but seven of the Pequot villagers were dead.

Sassacus, the Pequot chief, organized the survivors among his followers and attacked the whites. During the Pequot War of 1637, the colonists and their Narragansett allies indiscriminately killed hundreds of Pequots. The colonists captured most of the surviving Pequots and sold them into slavery in Bermuda. Under the terms of the Treaty of Hartford (1638), the Pequot Nation was declared dissolved.

RENEWED SETTLEMENT

By 1640 English settlers in New England and around Chesapeake Bay had established two great beachheads on the Atlantic coast, with the Dutch colony of New Netherland in between. After 1640, however, the power struggle between king and Parliament, which erupted into civil war in 1642 between those who backed Parliament and those who supported the king, distracted attention from colonization. As a result, migration to America dwindled to a trickle for more than twenty years. During the time of the English Civil War and Oliver Cromwell's Puritan dictatorship, the struggling colonies were left pretty much alone. Virginia and Maryland remained almost as independent from British authority as New England did.

The Restoration of King Charles II in 1660 involved scarcely any changes in colonial governments. Immigration rapidly expanded the populations of Virginia and Maryland. Fears of reprisals against Puritan New England on account of the reestablishment of the Anglican Church as the official church of England proved unfounded, at least for the time being. The charter of Massachusetts was reconfirmed in 1662, and Connecticut and Rhode Island received their first royal charters in 1662 and 1663. All three colonies retained their status as self-governing corporations.

The Restoration also opened a new season of enthusiasm for colonial expansion. Within twelve years the English would conquer New Netherland, settle Carolina, and nearly fill out the shape of the American colonies. In the middle region, formerly claimed by the Dutch, four new colonies sprang into being: New York, New Jersey, Pennsylvania, and Delaware. Without exception, the new colonies were proprietary, awarded by the king to "proprietors," men who had remained loyal during the civil war.

THE CAROLINAS   Carolina from the start comprised two widely separated areas of settlement. The northernmost part, long called Albemarle, remained a remote scattering of settlers along the shores of Albemarle Sound, isolated from Virginia by the Dismal Swamp and lacking easy access to oceangoing vessels. The eight lords proprietors to whom the king had given Carolina neglected Albemarle from the outset and focused on more promising sites to the south. Eager to find settlers who had already been seasoned in the colonies, they looked first to Barbados. In 1669 three ships left London with

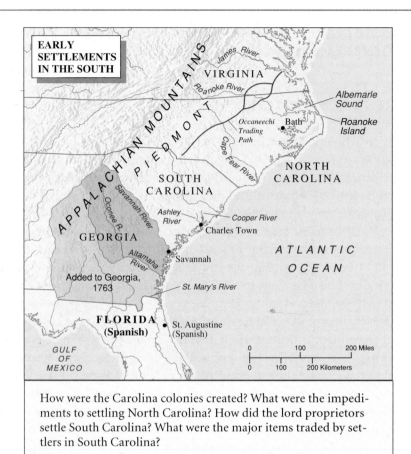

EARLY
SETTLEMENTS
IN THE SOUTH

VIRGINIA

James River

Roanoke River

APPALACHIAN MOUNTAINS

PIEDMONT

Occaneechi
Trading
Path

Cape Fear River

Bath

Albemarle
Sound

Roanoke
Island

NORTH
CAROLINA

SOUTH
CAROLINA

Savannah River

Oconee R.

GEORGIA

Ashley
River

Cooper River

Charles Town

Altamaha
River

Savannah

Added to Georgia,
1763

St. Mary's River

ATLANTIC

OCEAN

FLORIDA
(Spanish)

St. Augustine
(Spanish)

GULF
OF
MEXICO

0   100   200 Miles

0   100   200 Kilometers

How were the Carolina colonies created? What were the impedi-
ments to settling North Carolina? How did the lord proprietors
settle South Carolina? What were the major items traded by settlers in South Carolina?

about 100 settlers recruited in England; they sailed first to Barbados to pick
up more settlers and then north to Bermuda. The expedition landed in
America at a place several miles up the Ashley River, which they named
Charles Town (later known as Charleston).

The government of South Carolina rested upon one of the most curious
documents of colonial history, the Fundamental Constitutions of Carolina,
drawn up by one of the proprietors, Lord Anthony Ashley Cooper, with the
help of his secretary, the philosopher John Locke. Its cumbersome form of
government and its provisions for an almost feudal social system and an
elaborate nobility had little effect in the colony except to encourage a practice of large land grants. From the beginning, however, smaller headrights
were given to immigrants who could afford the cost of transit. The provision
that had greatest effect was a grant of religious toleration, designed to
encourage immigration, which gave South Carolina a distinctive degree of
indulgence (extending even to Jews and "heathens") and ethnic pluralism.

Ambitious English planters from Barbados dominated South Carolina and soon organized a major trade in Indian slaves. The first major export other than furs and slaves was cattle, and a true staple crop was not developed until the introduction of rice in the 1690s. South Carolina became a separate royal colony in 1719. North Carolina remained under the proprietors' rule for ten more years, when they surrendered their governing rights to the crown.

THE SOUTHERN INDIANS   The English proprietors of South Carolina wanted the colony to focus on producing commercial crops for profit (staples). Such production took time to develop, however. Land had to be cleared, and crops planted and harvested. These activities required laborers. Some of the South Carolina planters from Barbados brought enslaved Africans and British indentured servants with them. But many more workers were needed, and slaves and servants were expensive. The quickest way to raise capital in the early years of South Carolina's development was through trade with the Indians.

Beginning in the late seventeenth century the Creeks developed a flourishing trade with the British settlers, exchanging deerskins and slaves from rival tribes for manufactured goods. By 1690 traders from Charleston, South Carolina, made their way up the Savannah River to arrange deals with the Indians.

The trade with the English not only exposed the Indians to contagious diseases but also entwined them in a dependent relationship that would prove disastrous to their way of life. Eager to receive more finished goods, weapons, and ammunition, the Indians became pliable trading partners, easily manipulated by wily English entrepreneurs and government officials. The English traders began providing the Indians with firearms and rum as incentives to persuade them to capture members of rival tribes to be sold as slaves.

While colonists themselves captured and enslaved Indians, the Westos, Creeks, and most other tribes willingly captured other Indians and drove them to the coast to be exchanged for British trade goods, guns, and rum. Colonists, in turn, put some of the Indian

A War Dance

The Westo Indians of Georgia, pictured here doing a war dance, were among the first Native Americans to obtain firearms and used this advantage to enslave natives throughout Georgia, Florida, and the Carolinas.

captives to work on their plantations. But because Indian captives often ran away, the traders preferred to ship the enslaved Indians to New York, Boston, and the West Indies and import Africans to work in the Carolinas.

The complex profitability of Indian captives prompted a frenzy of slaving activity. Slave traders turned Indian tribes against one another in order to ensure a continuous supply of captives. As many as 50,000 Indians, most of them women and children, were sold as slaves in Charles Town between 1670 and 1715. More Indians were exported during that period than Africans were imported. Thousands more captured Indians circulated through such New England ports as Boston and Salem. Although the South Carolina proprietors in England expressly prohibited the enslavement of Indians, the traders paid no attention. The burgeoning trade in Indian slaves caused bitter struggles between tribes, gave rise to unprecedented colonial warfare, and spawned massive internal migrations across the southern colonies.

During the last quarter of the seventeenth century, the trade in Indian slaves spread across the entire Southeast. Slave raiding became the region's single most important economic activity and a powerful weapon in Britain's global conflict with France and Spain. During the early eighteenth century, Indians equipped with British weapons and led by English soldiers crossed into Spanish territory in south Georgia and north Florida. They destroyed thirteen Spanish missions, killed hundreds of Indians and Spaniards, and enslaved over 300 Indians. By 1710 the Florida tribes were on the verge of extinction. In 1708, when the total population of South Carolina was 9,580, including 2,900 Africans, there were 1,400 enslaved Indians in the colony.

SETTLING THE MIDDLE COLONIES AND GEORGIA

NEW NETHERLAND BECOMES NEW YORK   In London, King Charles II resolved to pluck out that old thorn in the side of the English colonies: New Netherland. The Dutch colony was older than New England, having been started when the two Protestant powers, England and the Netherlands, allied in opposition to Catholic Spain. The Dutch East India Company (organized in 1602) had hired an English captain, Henry Hudson, to seek the elusive passage to China. In 1609 Hudson had discovered Delaware Bay and had explored the river named for him to a point probably beyond Albany, where he helped initiate a lasting trade between the Dutch and the Iroquois Nations. In 1610 the Dutch established fur-trading posts on Manhattan Island and upriver at Fort Orange (later Albany). In the 1620s a newly organized Dutch

West India Company began to establish permanent settlements. In 1626 Governor Peter Minuit purchased Manhattan from the Indians, and the new village of New Amsterdam became the capital of New Netherland.

The colony's government was under the almost absolute control of a governor sent out by the West India Company. The governors depended upon a small army garrison for defense, and the inhabitants (including a number of English on Long Island) showed almost total indifference in 1664 when Governor Peter Stuyvesant called them to arms against a threatening British fleet. Almost defenseless, the old soldier Stuyvesant blustered and stomped about on his wooden leg, but he finally surrendered to the English without firing a shot.

The plan of conquest had been hatched by Charles II's brother, the duke of York, later King James II. When he and his advisers counseled that New Netherland could easily be conquered, Charles II simply granted the region to his brother. The English transformed New Amsterdam into New York and Fort Orange into Albany, and they held the country thereafter, except for a brief Dutch reoccupation in 1673–1674. Nonetheless, the Dutch left a permanent imprint on the land and the language. Whereas the Dutch vernacular faded away, place-names like Wall Street (named for the original wall that provided protection against the Indians) and Broadway (Breede Wegh) remained, along with family names like Rensselaer, Roosevelt, and Van Buren.

THE IROQUOIS LEAGUE   One of the most significant effects of European settlement in North America during the seventeenth century was the intensification of warfare among Indian peoples. The same combination of forces that weakened the Indian populations of New England and the Carolinas befell the tribes around New York City and the lower Hudson Valley. Dissension among the Indians and susceptibility to infectious disease left them vulnerable to exploitation by whites and other Indians.

In the interior of New York, however, a different situation arose. There the tribes of the Iroquois (an Algonquian term signifying "Snake" or "Terrifying Man") forged an alliance so strong that the outnumbered Dutch and, later, English traders were forced to work with the Indians in exploiting the lucrative fur trade. The Iroquois League represented a federation of five tribes that spoke related languages: the Mohawk, Oneida, Onondaga, Cayuga, and Seneca (a sixth tribe, the Tuscaroras who lived in the Carolinas, joined them in 1712). When the Iroquois began to deplete the local game during the 1640s, they used firearms supplied by their Dutch trading partners to seize the Canadian hunting grounds of the neighboring Hurons and Eries. During the so-called Beaver Wars the Iroquois defeated the western tribes and thereafter hunted the region to extinction.

During the second half of the seventeenth century, the relentless search for furs led Iroquois war parties to range across eastern North America. They gained control over a huge area from the St. Lawrence River to Tennessee and from Maine to Michigan. The Iroquois's wars helped reorient the political relationships in the whole eastern half of the continent. Besieged by the Iroquois League, the western tribes forged defensive alliances with the French.

In the 1690s the French and their Indian allies gained the advantage over the Iroquois. They destroyed crops and villages and infected the Iroquois with smallpox. Facing extermination, the Iroquois made peace with the French in 1701. During the first half of the eighteenth century, the Iroquois maintained a shrewd neutrality in the struggle between the two rival European powers, which enabled them to play the British off against the French while creating a thriving fur trade for themselves.

NEW JERSEY   Shortly after the English conquest of New Netherland, the duke of York granted his lands between the Hudson and Delaware rivers to Sir George Carteret and Lord John Berkeley and named the territory for Carteret's native island of Jersey. In East Jersey, peopled first by perhaps 200 Dutch, new settlements gradually arose: disaffected Puritans from New Haven founded Newark, and a group of Scots founded Perth Amboy. In the west, facing the Delaware River, a scattering of Swedes, Finns, and Dutch remained, soon to be overwhelmed by swarms of English Quakers. In 1702 East and West Jersey were united as a royal colony.

PENNSYLVANIA AND DELAWARE   The Quaker sect, as the Society of Friends was called in ridicule (because they were supposed to "tremble at the word of the Lord"), became the most influential of many radical groups that sprang from the turbulence of the English Civil War. Founded in Great Britain by George Fox in about 1647, the Quakers carried further than any other group the doctrine of individual spiritual inspiration and interpretation—the "inner light," they called it. They discarded all formal sacraments and formal ministry, refused deference to persons of rank, used the familiar *thee* and *thou* in addressing everyone, declined to take oaths, claiming they were contrary to Scripture, and embraced simple living and pacifism. Quakers experienced intense persecution—often in their zeal they seemed to invite it—but never inflicted it on others. Their tolerance extended to complete religious freedom for everyone and to the equality of the sexes, including the full participation of women in religious affairs.

The settling of Quakers in New Jersey encouraged others to migrate, especially to the Delaware River side of the colony. And soon across the river arose the Quaker commonwealth, the colony of Pennsylvania. William Penn, the

The Quakers Meeting

A Quaker meeting, at which the presence of women is evidence of Quaker views on the equality of the sexes.

colony's founder, was raised as a proper English gentleman but in 1667 became a Quaker. In 1681 King Charles II gave Penn proprietary rights to a huge tract of land in America and named it Pennsylvania (literally, "Penn's Woods"). William Penn vigorously recruited settlers to his new colony, and religious dissenters from England and the Continent—Quakers, Mennonites, Amish, Moravians, Baptists—flocked to the region. Indian relations were good from the beginning because of the Quakers' friendliness and Penn's careful policy of purchasing land titles from the Indians.

Pennsylvania's government resembled that of other proprietary colonies except that the councilors as well as the assembly were elected by the freemen (taxpayers and property owners) and the governor had no veto—although Penn, as proprietor, did. "Any government is free . . . where the laws rule and the people are a party to the laws," Penn wrote in the 1682 Frames of Government.

Mohawk River

Albany
(Fort Orange)

MASSACHUSETTS

NEW YORK
(NEW NETHERLAND)
(1624–1664)

42° parallel

Connecticut River

CONNECTICUT

PENNSYLVANIA

Delaware River

Susquehanna River

Newark

Elizabethtown

Perth Amboy

LONG ISLAND

NEW SWEDEN
(1638–1655)

Schuylkill River

EAST
JERSEY

New York
(New Amsterdam)

Philadelphia

Fort Christina
(Wilmington)

NEW JERSEY

MARYLAND

WEST
JERSEY

ATLANTIC
OCEAN

Delaware Bay

DELAWARE

Chesapeake Bay

VIRGINIA

THE MIDDLE
COLONIES

0   50   100 Miles

0   50   100 Kilometers

Why was New Jersey divided in half? Why did Quakers chose to settle in Pennsylvania? How did the relations between European settlers and Native Americans in Pennsylvania differ from those in the other colonies?

He hoped to show that a government could run in accordance with Quaker principles, that it could maintain peace and order without oaths or wars, that religion could flourish without an established church and with absolute freedom of belief.

In 1682 the duke of York also granted Penn the area of Delaware, another part of the former Dutch territory. At first, Delaware became part of Pennsylvania, but after 1704 the settlers were granted the right to choose their own assembly. From then until the American Revolution, Delaware had a separate assembly but shared Pennsylvania's governor.

GEORGIA   Georgia was the last of the British colonies to be established in North America—half a century after Pennsylvania. In 1732 King George II gave the land between the Savannah and Altamaha rivers to the twenty-one trustees of Georgia. In two respects, Georgia was unique among the colonies: it was set up both as a philanthropic experiment and as a military buffer against Spanish Florida. General James E. Oglethorpe, who accompanied the first colonists as resident trustee, represented both concerns: he served as a soldier who organized the colony's defenses and as a philanthropist who championed prison reform and sought a colonial refuge for the poor and the religiously persecuted.

In 1733 General Oglethorpe and about 120 colonists founded Savannah near the mouth of the Savannah River. Soon thereafter they were joined by Protestant refugees from central Europe, who made the colony for a time more German than English. The addition of Welsh, Highland Scots, Portuguese (Sephardic) Jews, and others gave the early colony a cosmopolitan character much like that of Charleston, South Carolina.

As a buffer against Spanish Florida, the colony succeeded, but as a philanthropic experiment it failed. Efforts to develop silk and wine production foundered. Landholdings were limited to 500 acres, rum was prohibited, and the importation of slaves forbidden, partly to leave room for servants brought on charity, partly to ensure security. But the utopian rules soon collapsed. The regulations against rum and slavery were widely disregarded and finally abandoned. By 1759 all restrictions on landholding had been removed.

In 1754 the trustees' charter expired, and the province reverted to the crown. As a royal colony, Georgia acquired an effective government for the first time. The province developed slowly over the next decade and grew rapidly in population and wealth after 1763. Instead of wine and silk, Georgians exported rice, indigo, lumber, naval stores, beef, and pork and carried on a lively trade with the West Indies. The colony had become a commercial success.

THRIVING COLONIES

After a late start and with little design, the English had outstripped both the French and the Spanish in the New World. British America had become the most populous, prosperous, and powerful region on the continent. By the mid–seventeenth century, American colonists on average were better fed, clothed, and housed than their counterparts in Europe, where a majority of the people lived in destitution. But the English colonization of North America included many failures as well as successes. Lots of settlers found only hard labor and an early death in the New World. Others flourished only at the expense of Indians, indentured servants, or African slaves.

The British succeeded in creating a lasting American empire because of crucial advantages they had over their European rivals. The lack of plan

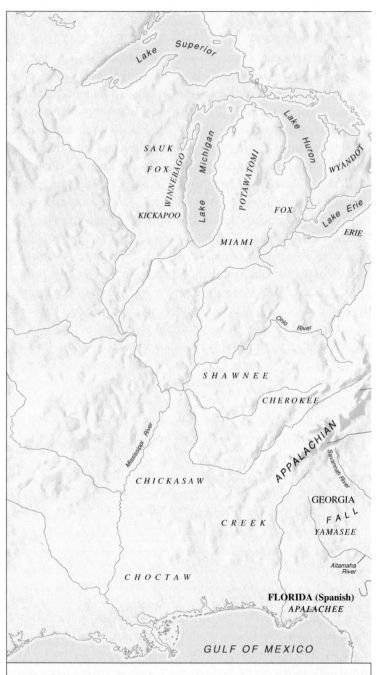

Why did European settlement lead to the expansion of hostilities among Indian peoples? What were the consequences of the trade and commerce between the English settlers and the southern Indian tribes? How were the relationships between the settlers and the members of the Iroquois League different from those between settlers and tribes in other regions?

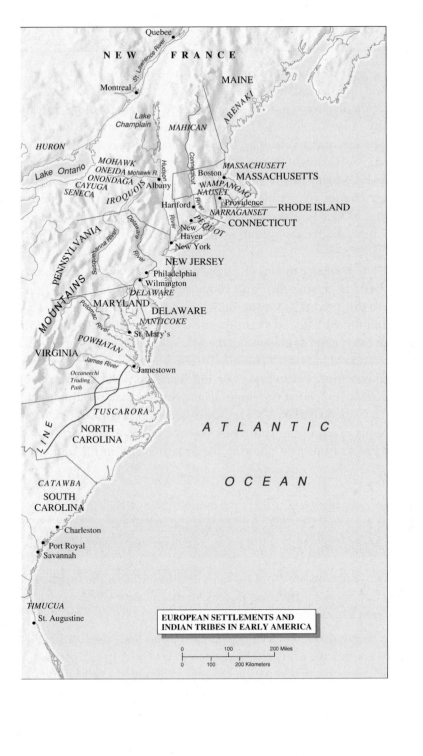

Quebee

NEW FRANCE

St. Lawrence River

MAINE

Montreal

ABENAKI

Lake Champlain

MAHICAN

HURON

Hudson

Connecticut

MASSACHUSETT

Lake Ontario

MOHAWK
ONEIDA *Mohawk R.*
ONONDAGA
CAYUGA
SENECA

IROQUOIS Albany

Boston

MASSACHUSETTS

WAMPANOAG
NAUSET

Hartford

Connecticut

River

Providence

RHODE ISLAND

NARRAGANSET

PENNSYLVANIA

Delaware

Susquehanna River

River

PEQUOT

CONNECTICUT

New Haven

New York

NEW JERSEY

Philadelphia
Wilmington

DELAWARE

MOUNTAINS

Potomac River

MARYLAND

DELAWARE

NANTICOKE

St. Mary's

POWHATAN

VIRGINIA

James River

Occaneechi Trading Path

Jamestown

ATLANTIC

TUSCARORA

NORTH
CAROLINA

LINE

OCEAN

CATAWBA

SOUTH
CAROLINA

Charleston

Port Royal
Savannah

TIMUCUA

St. Augustine

EUROPEAN SETTLEMENTS AND
INDIAN TRIBES IN EARLY AMERICA

0   100   200 Miles

0   100   200 Kilometers

marked the genius of English colonization, for it gave free rein to a variety of human impulses. The centralized control imposed by the monarchs of Spain and France got their colonies off the mark more quickly but eventually caused their downfall because it hobbled innovation in response to new circumstances. The British preferred private investment with minimal royal control. Not a single colony was begun at the direct initiative of the crown. In the English colonies poor immigrants had a much greater chance of getting at least a small parcel of land, and a greater degree of self-government made the English colonies more responsive to new challenges—though they were sometimes hobbled by controversy.

Moreover, the compact model of English settlement contrasted sharply with the pattern of Spain's far-flung conquests and France's far-reaching trade routes to the interior by way of the St. Lawrence and Mississippi rivers. Geography reinforced England's bent for the concentrated settlement of its colonies. The rivers and bays indenting the Atlantic seaboard served as veins of communication along which colonies first sprang up, but no great river offered a highway to the far interior. For 150 years the western outreach of British settlement stopped at the slopes of the Appalachian Mountains. To the east lay the wide expanse of ocean, which served not only as a highway for the transport of European culture to America but also as a barrier that separated old ideas from new, allowing the new to evolve in the new environment.

MAKING CONNECTIONS

- What we now know about the early settlements sets the stage for the regional differences in social patterns that will be discussed in the next chapter.

- This chapter concluded with the observation that "the lack of plan marked the genius of English colonization." In Chapter 4 we will see how that situation changes, as England begins to take control of the American colonies.

- Later relations between colonists and Native Americans, described in Chapter 4, had their roots in the history of these early settlements.

Further Reading

Bernard Bailyn's Voyagers to the West: *A Passage in the Peopling of America on the Eve of the Revolution* (1986) provides a comprehensive view of European migration. Carl Bridenbaugh's *Vexed and Troubled Englishmen, 1590–1642* (1968) helps explain why so many sought a new home in a strange land. English constitutional traditions and their effect on the colonists are examined in Edmund S. Morgan's *Inventing the People: The Rise of Popular Sovereignty in England and America* (1988). Jack P. Greene provides a brilliant synthesis of British colonization in *Pursuits of Happiness: The Social Development of Early Modern British Colonies and the Formation of American Culture* (1988). Alfred W. Crosby's *Ecological Imperialism: The Biological Expansion of Europe, 900–1900*, rev. ed. (2004) explores the ecological effects of European settlement. Alfred A. Cave's *The Pequot War* (1996) and Jill Lepore's *The Name of War: King Philip's War and the Origins of American Identity* (1998) describe the conditions leading to the wars between settlers and Indians.

A succinct overview of Puritanism can be found in Alan Simpson's *Puritanism in Old and New England* (1955). Andrew Delbanco's *The Puritan Ordeal* (1989) is a powerful study of the tensions inherent in the Puritan outlook. The best biography of John Winthrop is Francis Bremer's *John Winthrop: America's Forgotten Founding Father* (2004). Useful works on the problem of dissent in a theocracy include Edmund S. Morgan's *Roger Williams: The Church and the State* (1967) and Emery John Battis's *Saints and Sectaries: Anne Hutchinson and the Antinomian Controversy in Massachusetts Bay Colony* (1962).

The pattern of settlement in the middle Atlantic colonies is illuminated in Barry Levy's *Quakers and the American Family: British Settlement in the Delaware Valley* (1988). Randall Balmer's *A Perfect Babel of Confusion: Dutch Religion and English Culture in the Middle Colonies* (1989) describes how the English conquest of New Netherland intensified the cultural complexity of the middle colonies. On the early history of New York, see Russell Short's *The Island at the Center of the World: The Epic Story of Dutch Manhattan and the Forgotten Colony That Shaped America* (2004). The influence of Quakers can be studied in Gary B. Nash's *Quakers and Politics: Pennsylvania, 1681–1726* (1968).

Settlement of the areas along the southern Atlantic coast is traced in Wesley F. Craven's *The Southern Colonies in the Seventeenth Century, 1607–1689* (1949) and Clarence Lester Ver Steeg's *Origins of a Southern*

Mosaic (1975). Robert M. Weir's *Colonial South Carolina: A History* (1983) covers the activities of the lords proprietors. On the flourishing trade in captive Indians, see Allan Gallay's *The Indian Slave Trade: The Rise of the American South, 1670–1717* (2003). Those interested in the colonization of Georgia should consult *Oglethorpe in Perspective: Georgia's Founder after Two Hundred Years* (1989), edited by Phinizy Spalding and Harvey H. Jackson.

3

COLONIAL WAYS OF LIFE

FOCUS QUESTIONS

- What were the social and economic differences among the southern, middle, and New England colonies?
- How did various groups of people of different genders, races, and classes fit into colonial society?
- What was the impact of the Enlightenment and the Great Awakening on the American colonies?

To answer these questions and access additional review material, please visit www.wwnorton.com/studyspace.

Those who colonized America during the seventeenth and eighteenth centuries were part of a massive social migration occurring throughout Europe and Africa. They moved for different reasons. Most were responding to powerful social and economic forces: rapid population growth, the rise of commercial agriculture, and the early stages of the Industrial Revolution. Others sought political security or religious freedom. An exception was the Africans, who were captured and moved to new lands against their will.

THE SHAPE OF EARLY AMERICA

Most of the new Americans were young (over half were under twenty-five), and most were male. Almost half were indentured servants or slaves.

England also transported some 50,000 convicted felons to the North American colonies. Only one third of the newcomers journeyed with their families. Most immigrants were of the "middling sort," neither very rich nor very poor. Whatever their status or ambition, however, this extraordinary mosaic of ordinary yet adventurous people created America's enduring institutions and values.

SEABOARD ECOLOGY   America's ecosystem was shaped by both Native Americans and European settlers. For thousands of years, Indian hunting practices produced what one scholar has called the "greatest known loss of wild species" in American history. In addition, the Indians burned woods and undergrowth to provide cropland, ease travel through hardwood forests, and nourish the grasses, berries, and other forage for the animals they hunted. This "slash-and-burn" agriculture halted the normal forest succession and, especially in the Southeast, created large stands of longleaf pine, still the most common source of timber in the region.

Equally important in shaping the ecosystem of America was the European attitude toward the environment. Whereas the Native Americans tended to be migratory, considering land and animals communal resources to be shared and consumed only as necessary, many European colonizers viewed natural resources as privately owned commodities. Settlers thus looked with disdain upon the subsistence level of Indian agriculture and quickly set about evicting Indians; clearing, fencing, improving, and selling land; growing surpluses; and trapping game for furs to be sold or traded.

European ships brought to America domesticated animals—cattle, oxen, sheep, goats, horses, and pigs—that were unknown in the New World. By 1650 English farm animals outnumbered the colonists. Rapidly multiplying livestock reshaped the American environment and affected Indian life in unexpected ways. British settlers discovered that they did not have time to feed and care for livestock in pens, as they had in the Old World. Chesapeake farmers, for example, were too busy tending profitable tobacco plants to devote time to animal husbandry. So from late spring to harvest time in New England and year-round in Maryland and Virginia, hard-pressed farmers allowed their cows, horses, and pigs to roam freely through the woods, clipping their ears to identify them. Such free-range husbandry made sense in the short run, since the labor shortage made it too expensive to pen the animals in barnyards or fence them in pastures. In the longer term, however, the failure to constrain farm animals denied the planted fields dung for use as a valuable fertilizer. The fertility of the soil declined with each passing year. The Virginia planter Robert Beverley chastised his neighbors for engaging in such "exceeding illhusbandry" and for making their hogs "find their own support in the woods."

Hogs, in particular, thrived in the New World. The animals eat virtually anything and breed frequently. A sow can give birth three times a year to as many as sixteen piglets at a time. In a few years a dozen transplanted English pigs had spawned thousands of hogs throughout the colonies. In 1700 a visitor to Virginia observed that the pigs "swarm like vermin upon the earth. . . . The hogs run where they want and find their own support in the woods without any care of the owners."

Many of the farm animals turned wild (feral), ran amok in Indian cornfields, and devastated native flora and fauna. In New England, rooting pigs devoured the shellfish that local Indians depended upon for subsistence. Colonists often had trouble finding their wandering herds. One Marylander spent three days hunting for stray hogs. Others hired Indians to track them down. As livestock herds grew, settlers felt the need to acquire more land from the Indians. A single cow needed five acres of woodland to subsist. Trespassing livestock and expanding colonial settlements caused friction with the Indians, which occasionally helped ignite violent confrontations. One historian, in fact, has referred to roaming English livestock as four-legged "agents of empire" invading Indian land. As a frustrated Maryland Indian charged in 1666, "Your hogs & cattle injure us. You come too near us to live & drive us from place to place. We can fly no farther. Let us know where to live & how to be secured for the future from the hogs & cattle."

Roaming livestock exacerbated other environmental problems. European ships brought weeds as well as animals. Native weeds, such as ragweed, goldenrod, and milkweed, were not nearly as tenacious as the weeds that arrived from Europe: dandelion, thistle, plantain, and sedge. Their seeds were transported in the hay and grain brought from abroad. As pigs, cattle, and horses ate the hay, the weed seeds passed through their digestive tracts and were deposited in manure wherever the animals roamed. In 1672 a British naturalist reported that he had identified twenty-two English weeds that were flourishing in America. The

Colonial Farm

This plan of a newly cleared American farm shows how trees were cut down and the stumps left to rot.

Indians nicknamed plantain Englishman's foot because it seemed to sprout wherever the colonists walked. Today biologists estimate that half the weeds in the United States originated in Europe or Africa.

In time a denser population of humans and their domestic animals created a landscape of fields, meadows, fences, barns, and houses. Such innovations radically altered the ecology of the New World. Foraging cattle, sheep, horses, and pigs gradually changed the distribution of trees, shrubs, and grasses. Because cleared and grazed land is warmer and drier, it floods and erodes more easily. Indians, far from being passive observers, contributed to the process of environmental change by trading furs for metal or glass trinkets. The increased hunting decimated the populations of large mammals that had earlier been central to Indian culture—and to the ecological balance. By 1800 such unintended consequences had markedly changed the physical environment. New England, for example, had become a commercial success but was essentially an agricultural wasteland.

POPULATION GROWTH   England's first footholds in America were bought at a fearsome price. Many settlers died in the first years. But once the brutal seasoning was past and the colonies were on their feet, Virginia and its successors grew at a prodigious rate. After the last major Indian uprising in 1644, Virginia's population quadrupled, from about 8,000 to 32,000 over the next thirty years, then more than doubled, to 75,000, by 1704. In 1700 the English at home outnumbered the colonists by about twenty to one; by 1775, on the eve of the American Revolution, the ratio had fallen to three to one.

America's plentiful land beckoned immigrants and induced them to replenish the earth with large families. Where labor was scarce, children could lend a hand and, once grown, find new land for themselves if need be. Colonists tended, as a result, to marry and start families at an earlier age than their European counterparts.

BIRTHRATES AND DEATH RATES   The initial scarcity of women in the colonies had significant social effects. Whereas in England the average age of women at marriage was twenty-five or twenty-six, in America it dropped to twenty or twenty-one. Men also married younger in the colonies than in the Old World. The birthrate rose accordingly, because women who married earlier had time for about two additional pregnancies during the childbearing years. Given the better economic prospects in the colonies, a greater proportion of American women married, and the birthrate remained much higher than in Europe.

Equally important in explaining rapid population growth in the New World was its much lower death rate, at least in the New England colonies (in the South, death rates remained higher due to malaria, dysentery, and other warm-climate diseases). After the difficult first years of settlement, infants generally had a better chance of reaching maturity, and adults had a better chance of reaching old age than their counterparts in Europe. This greater longevity resulted less from a more temperate climate than from the character of the settlements themselves. Since the land was initially bountiful, famine seldom occurred after a settlement's first year. Although the winters were more severe than those in England, firewood was plentiful. Being younger on the whole—the average age in the colonies in 1790 was sixteen!—American adults were less susceptible to disease than were Europeans. More widely scattered, they were also less exposed to disease. That began to change, of course, as cities grew and trade and travel increased. By the mid–eighteenth century the colonies were beginning to experience levels of contagion much like those in Europe.

WOMEN IN THE COLONIES   Colonists brought to America deeply rooted convictions about the inferiority of women. God and nature, it was widely assumed, had stained women with original sin and made these "weaker vessels" smaller in stature, feebler in mind, and prone to both excited emotions and psychological dependency. Women were expected to be meek and model housewives. Their role in life was clear: to obey and serve their husbands, nurture their children, and maintain their households. John Winthrop insisted that a "true wife accounts her subjection [as] her honor and freedom" and would find true contentment only "in subjection to her husband's authority."

Such commonly held attitudes meant that most women were conditioned to accept their subordinate status in a male-dominated society. A Virginia woman explained that "one of my first resolutions I made after marriage was never to hold disputes with my husband." Both social custom and legal codes ensured that women remained deferential and powerless. They could not vote, preach, hold office, attend public schools or colleges, bring lawsuits, make contracts, or own property except under extraordinary conditions. In the eighteenth century, "women's work" typically involved activities in the house, garden, and yard. Despite the conventions that limited women, the scarcity of labor in the colonies opened social opportunities. Quite a few women, either by necessity or choice, worked in traditionally male vocations. In the towns, women commonly served as tavern hostesses and shopkeepers, and some worked as doctors, printers, upholsterers, painters, silversmiths, or shipwrights. They often, but not always, were widows who carried on their husbands' trades. Some women in the South managed plantations.

The First, Second, and Last Scene of Mortality

Prudence Punderson's needlework (ca. 1776) shows the domestic path, from cradle to coffin, followed by most colonial women.

The acute shortage of women in the early years of colonial settlement made them more highly valued than in Europe, and the Puritan emphasis on well-ordered family life led to laws protecting wives from physical abuse and allowing for divorce. In addition, colonial laws gave wives greater control over property that they contributed to a marriage or that was left after a husband's death. But the traditional notion of female subordination and domesticity remained firmly entrenched in the New World. As a Massachusetts boy maintained in 1662, the superior aspect of life was "masculine and eternal; the feminine inferior and mortal."

SOCIETY AND ECONOMY IN THE SOUTHERN COLONIES

CROPS   The southern climate enabled colonists to grow exotic staples (market crops) prized by the mother country. In Virginia by 1619, annual tobacco production had reached 20,000 pounds, and by 1688 it was up to 18 million

Virginia Plantation

Southern colonial plantations were constructed with easy access for oceangoing vessels, as shown on this 1730 tobacco label.

pounds. Tobacco, however, was only one of many cash crops being grown in the southern colonies. After 1690 rice became the staple crop in South Carolina. The southern woods also provided for the production of lumber and naval stores (tar, pitch, and turpentine). From their early leadership in the latter trade, North Carolinians would later derive the nickname of Tar Heels.

The economy of the southern colonies centered on a fundamental fact: land was plentiful, and laborers were scarce. The low cost of land lured most colonists. In 1614 each of the Virginia Company's colonists received three acres, and this policy marked the beginning of a "headright" system that provided every settler in the colony with a plot of land. In 1618 the company increased the land grants, giving 100 acres each to those already in the colonies and 50 acres each to new settlers or anyone paying the passage of immigrants (for example, indentured servants) to Virginia.

If one distinctive feature of the South's commercial agriculture was a ready market in England, another was a trend toward large-scale production. Those who planted tobacco discovered that it quickly exhausted the soil, thereby giving an advantage to the planter who had extra fields in which to plant beans and corn or to leave fallow. With the increase of the tobacco crop, moreover, a fall in prices meant that economies of scale might come into play—the large planter with the lower cost per unit might still make a profit. Gradually he would extend his holdings along the riverfronts and thereby secure the advantage of direct access to the oceangoing vessels that moved freely up and down the waterways of the Chesapeake. So easy was the access, in fact, that the Chesapeake colonies never required a city of any size as a center of commerce.

INDENTURED SERVANTS AND SLAVES The plantation economy depended upon manual labor, and voluntary indentured servitude accounted for probably half the white settlers in all the colonies outside New England. The name derived from the indenture, or contract, by which a person agreed to work for a fixed number of years in return for transportation to the New World.

Although many servants saw the opportunity to go to the New World as a chance to better themselves, not all went voluntarily. The London underworld developed a flourishing trade in "kids," who were "spirited" into servitude. On occasion, orphans were bound off to the New World, and from time to time the mother country sent convicts into colonial servitude. Once an indenture had run its course, usually after four to seven years, a servant claimed the freedom dues set by law—some money, tools, clothing, food—and often took up land-owning.

Slavery, long a dying institution in Europe, evolved in the Chesapeake after 1619, when a Dutch vessel dropped off twenty Africans in Jamestown. Some of the first slaves were treated as indentured servants. Those who worked out their term of indenture gained freedom and a fifty-acre parcel of land. They themselves sometimes acquired slaves and white indentured servants. But gradually the practice of perpetual black slavery became the custom and the law of the land.

AFRICAN ROOTS AND BLACK CULTURE Enslaved Africans came from lands as remote from one another as the Congo is from Senegal, and they spoke Mandingo, Ibo, Kongo, and countless other languages. For all their differences, however, the many peoples of Africa did share similar kinship and political systems. African societies were often matrilineal: property and political status descended through the mother rather than the father. Priests and the nobility lorded over the masses of farmers and craftspeople. Below the masses were the slaves, typically war captives, criminals, or debtors.

THE AFRICAN SLAVE TRADE, 1500–1800

How were Africans captured and enslaved? What were some of the experiences faced by most Africans on the Middle Passage? How did enslaved African Americans create a new culture?

Most of the Africans who arrived in British North America during the seventeenth century did not come directly from Africa, however. Instead, they had first been brought to the sugar-producing colonies in Brazil and the Caribbean. Once in North America, they often worked alongside white indentured servants, and personal relations between the two groups tended to be more open and casual than they would be a century later. A surprising number of the early slaves were able to earn money on the side and buy their freedom. Thus, the enslaved Africans of the seventeenth century had a more fluid and independent existence than their successors.

African Heritage

The survival of African culture among enslaved Americans is evident in this late-eighteenth-century painting of a South Carolina plantation. The musical instruments, pottery, and clothing are of African (probably Yoruban) origin.

During the eighteenth century, with the rapid development of a plantation economy in the Chesapeake Bay region and coastal South Carolina, the demand for slaves grew so quickly that a much higher proportion came directly from the African interior. Captured by ruthless traders, many of them Africans, the people destined for slavery were packed together in slave ships and subjected to a grueling transatlantic voyage that killed one in seven of them. Planters wanted field hands, so most of these newer slaves were young males who had had no exposure to European culture or languages, a factor that discouraged relations between the races.

Some of the enslaved blacks rebelled against their new masters, resisting work orders, sabotaging crops and tools, or running away to the frontier. In a few cases they organized rebellions, which were ruthlessly suppressed. "You would be surprised at their perseverance," noted one white planter. "They often die before they can be conquered." Those still alive when recaptured frequently faced ghastly retribution. After capturing slaves who participated in the Stono Uprising in South Carolina in 1739, enraged planters "cutt off their heads and set them up at every Mile Post."

In the process of being forced into bondage, blacks from diverse home-lands forged a new identity as African Americans while entwining in the fabric of American culture more strands of African heritage than historians and anthropologists can ever disentangle. Most important are African influences in music, folklore, and religious practices. On one level, slaves used songs, stories, and sermons to distract themselves from their toil; on another level these compositions conveyed coded messages of distaste for masters or overseers. Slave religion, a unique blend of African and Christian beliefs, centered on the theme of deliverance: God, slaves believed, would eventually free them and open up the gates to the promised land. The planters, however, sought to strip slave religion of its liberationist hopes. In 1667 the Virginia legislature declared that "the conferring of baptism does not alter the condition of the person as to his bondage or freedom."

Africans brought to America powerful kinship ties. Although most colonies outlawed slave marriages, many masters realized that slaves would work harder and more reliably if allowed to form families. Though many couples were broken up when one partner was sold, slave culture was remarkable for its powerful domestic ties. It was also remarkable for developing sex roles distinct from those of white society. Most enslaved women were by necessity field workers as well as wives and mothers responsible for household affairs. They worked in proximity to enslaved men and in the process were treated more equally than were most of their white counterparts.

SOCIETY AND ECONOMY IN NEW ENGLAND

TOWNSHIPS   In contrast to the seaboard planters, who transformed the English manor into the southern plantation, the Puritans transformed the English village into the New England town, although there were many varieties. Land policy in New England had a stronger social and religious purpose than elsewhere. The headright system of the Chesapeake never took root in New England. There were cases of large individual grants, but the standard practice was one of township grants to organized groups. A group of settlers, often already gathered into a congregation, would petition the general court for a town and then divide the parcel according to a rough principle of equity—those who invested more or had larger families or greater status might receive more land—retaining some pasture and wood-land in common and holding some for later arrivals. In some early cases the towns arranged each settler's land in separate strips after the medieval prac-tice, but with time land was commonly divided into separate farms away from the central village, to which landholders would move.

ENTERPRISE   New England farmers and their families led hard lives. The growing season was short, and the harsh climate precluded profitable cash crops. The crops and livestock were those familiar to the English coun-tryside: wheat, barley, oats, some cattle, swine, and sheep. With abundant fishing grounds that stretched northward to Newfoundland, it is little won-der that New Englanders turned to the sea for their livelihood. New Eng-land's proximity to waters rich in cod, mackerel, halibut, and other varieties of fish made it America's most important maritime center. Whales, too, abounded in New England waters and supplied oil for lighting and lubrica-tion, as well as ambergris, a secretion used in perfumes.

New England's fisheries, unlike its farms, supplied a product that could be profitably exported to Europe, with lesser grades of fish going to the West Indies as food for slaves. Fisheries encouraged the development of shipbuilding, and experience at seafaring spurred commerce. This in turn led to wider contacts in the Atlantic world and a degree of materialism and cosmopolitanism that clashed with the Puritan credo of plain living and high thinking. In 1714 a worried Puritan deplored the "great extravagance that people are fallen into, far beyond their circumstances, in their purchases, buildings, families, expenses, apparel, generally in the whole way of living." But such laments failed to stop the material growth of the New England colonies.

NEW ENGLAND SHIPBUILDING   The abundant forests of New Eng-land represented a source of enormous wealth. Old-growth trees were espe-cially prized by the British government for use as ships' masts and spars. At the same time, British officials encouraged the colonists to develop their own shipbuilding industry. The New England economy was utterly depen-dent upon fishing and maritime commerce, and this placed a premium on the availability of boats and ships—and shipbuilders. American seaports ag-gressively sought to entice shipwrights to emigrate, and American-built ships quickly became prized by European traders for their quality and price. It was much less expensive to purchase American-built ships than to trans-port American timber to Britain for ship construction, especially since a large ship might require the timber from as many as 2,000 trees.

Profitable Fisheries

Fishing for, curing, and drying codfish in Newfoundland in the early 1700s. For centuries the rich fishing grounds of the North Atlantic provided New Englanders with a prosperous industry.

Nearly one third of all British ships were made in the colonies. By the mid–seventeenth century bustling shipyards had appeared in many New England towns where rivers flowed into the ocean. By the eighteenth century, Massachusetts was second only to London in the number of ships produced. Shipbuilding was one of colonial America's first big industries, and it in turn nurtured many other businesses: timber, sawmills, iron foundries, sail lofts, fisheries, and taverns.

TRADE   By the end of the seventeenth century, America had become part of a great North Atlantic commercial network, trading not only with the British Isles and the British West Indies but also—and often illegally—with Spain, France, Portugal, Holland, and their colonies. Since the colonists lacked the means to produce goods themselves, they imported manufactured goods from Europe. Their central economic problem was finding the means to pay for those imports—the eternal problem of the balance of trade.

The mechanism of trade in New England and the middle Atlantic colonies differed from that in the South in two respects: the northern colonies were at a disadvantage in their lack of cash crops to exchange for English goods, but the abundance of their shipping and mercantile enterprise worked in their

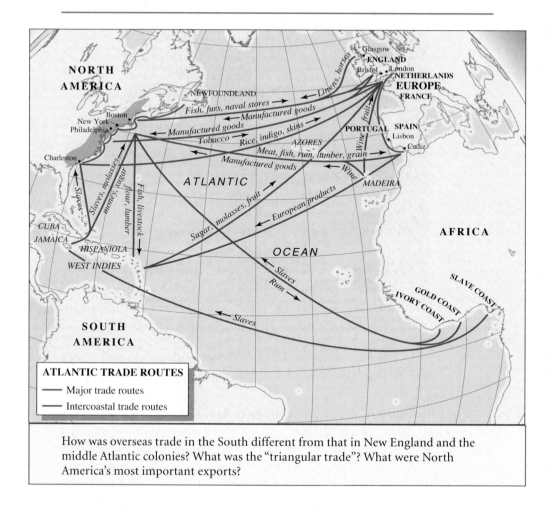

ATLANTIC TRADE ROUTES
— Major trade routes
— Intercoastal trade routes

How was overseas trade in the South different from that in New England and the middle Atlantic colonies? What was the "triangular trade"? What were North America's most important exports?

favor. After 1660, in order to protect England's agriculture and fisheries, the English government placed prohibitive duties (taxes) on certain major products exported by the northern colonies—fish, flour, wheat, and meat—while leaving the door open to timber, furs, and whale oil. As a consequence, in the early eighteenth century New York and New England bought more from England than they sold there, incurring an unfavorable trade balance.

The northern colonies solved the problem in two ways: they used their own ships and merchants, thus avoiding the "invisible" charges for trade and transport, and they found other markets for the staples excluded from England, thus acquiring goods or bullion to pay for imports from the mother country. These circumstances gave rise to the famous "triangular trade" (more a descriptive convenience than a rigid pattern), in which New Englanders shipped rum to the west coast of Africa, where they bartered for slaves; took the slaves on the "Middle Passage" to the West Indies; and returned home with various commodities, including molasses, from which they manufactured rum. In another version they shipped provisions to the West Indies, carried sugar and molasses to England, and returned with goods manufactured in Europe.

The generally unfavorable balance of trade left the colonies with a chronic shortage of hard currency, which drifted away to pay for imports and invisible charges. Various expedients met the money shortage. Most of the colonies at one time or another issued bills of credit, on promise of payment in hard currency later (hence the dollar "bill"), and most set up land banks that issued paper money for loans to farmers on the security of their land, which was mortgaged to the banks. Colonial farmers, recognizing that an inflation of paper money led to an inflation of crop prices, asked for more and more paper. Thus began in colonial politics what was to become a recurrent issue in later times: currency inflation. Wherever the issue arose, debtors commonly favored growth in the money supply, which would make it easier for them to settle accounts, whereas creditors favored a limited money supply, which would increase the value of their capital.

RELIGION   New England was settled by religious fundamentalists. The Puritans were God-fearing colonists who looked to the Bible for authority and inspiration.They read the Bible daily and memorized its passages and stories. They read it silently alone and aloud as families and in church services, which lasted from eight until noon on Sunday mornings. The Christian faith was a living source of daily inspiration and obligation for most New Englanders. The Puritans who settled Massachusetts, unlike the Separatists of Plymouth, proposed only to form a purified version of the Anglican Church. They believed that they could remain loyal to the Church of England. But their remoteness from England led them very quickly to a congregational form of church government identical with that of the Pilgrim Separatists.

In the Puritan version of Genevan John Calvin's theology, God had voluntarily entered into a covenant, or contract, with worshippers through which they could secure salvation. By analogy, therefore, an assembly of true Christians could enter into a church covenant, a voluntary union for the common worship of God. From this it was a fairly short step to the idea of a voluntary union for the purpose of government.

The covenant theory contained certain kernels of democracy in both church and state, but democracy was no part of Puritan political thought, which like so much else in Puritan belief began with original sin. Innate human depravity made governments necessary. The Puritan was dedicated to seeking not the will of the people but the will of God. The ultimate source of authority resided in the Bible, but the Bible had to be explained by "right reason." Hence, most Puritans deferred to an intellectual elite for a true knowledge of God's will. Church and state were but two aspects of the same unity, the purpose of which was to carry out God's will on earth. Although Puritan New England has often been called a theocracy, the church in theory was entirely separate from the state. By law, however, each town had to support a church through taxes levied on every household. And every resident was required to attend midweek and Sunday religious services. The average New Englander heard over 7,000 sermons in a lifetime.

DIVERSITY AND SOCIAL STRAINS   The harmony sought by Puritans settling New England was elusive. Increasing diversity and powerful disruptive forces combined to erode the consensual society envisioned by the founding settlers. Social strains and worldly pursuits increased as time passed, a consequence primarily of population pressure on the land and increasing disparities of wealth. Initially fathers exercised strong patriarchal authority over their sons through their control of the land. They kept the sons in town, not letting them set up their own households or get title to their farmland until they reached middle age. In New England as elsewhere, the tendency was to subdivide the land among all the children. But by the eighteenth century, with land scarcer, the younger sons were either getting control of the property early or moving on. Often the younger male children were forced, with family help and blessings, to seek land elsewhere, or find new kinds of work in the commercial cities along the coast or inland rivers. With the growing pressure on land in the settled regions, poverty and social tension increased in what had once seemed a country of unlimited opportunity.

Sectarian disputes and religious indifference also fractured many communities. The emphasis on a direct accountability to God, which forms the base of all Protestant theology, led believers to challenge authority in the name of private conscience. Massachusetts repressed such heresy in the 1630s, but it resurfaced during the 1650s among Quakers and Baptists, and in 1659–1660 the colony hanged four Quakers who persisted in returning after they had been expelled. These acts caused such revulsion—and an investigation by the crown—that they were not repeated, although heretics continued to face harassment and persecution.

More damaging to the Puritan utopia was the growing materialism of New England, which strained church discipline. More and more children of the "visible saints" found themselves unable to testify that they had received the gift of God's grace. In 1662 an assembly of ministers at Boston accepted the "Half-Way Covenant," whereby baptized children of church members could be admitted to a "halfway" membership. Their own children could be baptized, but such "halfway" members could neither vote nor take communion. A further blow to Puritan convention and control came with the Massachusetts royal charter of 1691, which required toleration of dissenters and based the right to vote on property rather than church membership.

NEW ENGLAND WITCHCRAFT   The strains accompanying Massachusetts's transition from Puritan utopia to royal colony reached an unhappy climax in the witchcraft hysteria at Salem Village (now the town of Danvers) in 1692. Belief in witchcraft pervaded European and New England society in the seventeenth century. Prior to the dramatic episode in Salem, almost 300 New Englanders (mostly lower-class, middle-aged spinsters or widows) had been accused of being witches, and more than 30 had been hanged.

Still, the Salem outbreak exceeded all precedents in its scope and intensity. The episode began when a few teenage girls became entranced by African tales told by Tituba, a West Indian slave, and began acting strangely—shouting, barking, groveling, and twitching for no apparent reason. The town doctor concluded that they had been bewitched, and the girls pointed to Tituba and two older white women as the culprits. Town dwellers were seized with panic as word spread that the devil was in their midst. At a hearing before the magistrates, the "afflicted" girls rolled on the floor in convulsive fits as the three women were questioned by the magistrates. In the midst of this hysterical carnival, Tituba shocked her listeners by not only confessing to the charge but also divulging that many others in the community were performing the devil's work.

With that the crazed girls began pointing accusing fingers at dozens of residents, including several of the most respected members of the community. Within a few months the Salem jail overflowed with townspeople— men, women, and children—accused of practicing witchcraft. Before the hysteria ran its course ten months later, nineteen people (including some men) had been hanged, one man—stubborn Giles Corey, who refused to plead either guilty or not guilty—was pressed to death by heavy stones, and more than 100 others were jailed.

But as the net of accusation spread wider, extending far beyond the confines of Salem, colonial leaders feared that the witch hunts were out of control. When the afflicted girls charged Samuel Willard, the distinguished pastor of Boston's First Church and president of Harvard College, the stunned magistrates had seen enough. Shortly thereafter the governor intervened when his own wife was accused of serving the devil. He disbanded the special court and ordered the remaining suspects released. Nearly everybody responsible for the

Salem executions later recanted, and nothing quite like it happened in the colonies again.

What explains the witchcraft hysteria at Salem? Some historians have argued that it represented nothing more than a contagious exercise in adolescent imagination intended to enliven the dreary routine of everyday life. Yet adults pressed the formal charges against the accused and provided most of the testimony. This fact has led some scholars to speculate that long-festering local feuds and property disputes may have triggered the prosecutions. One of the leaders of the young girls, for instance, was twelve-year-old Anne Putnam, whose older male kinfolk pressed many of the complaints. The Putnam clan were landowners whose power was declining, and their frenetic pursuit of witches might have served as a psychic weapon to restore their prestige.

More recently historians have focused on the most salient fact about the accused witches: almost all of them were women. Many of the accused women, it turns out, had in some way defied the traditional roles assigned to females. Some had engaged in business transactions outside the home; others did not attend church; some were curmudgeons; many were worried about Indian attacks. Most of them were middle-aged or older, beyond child-bearing age, and without sons or brothers. They thus stood to inherit property and live as independent women. The notion of autonomous spinsters flew in the face of prevailing social conventions. Whatever the precise cause, there is little doubt that the witchcraft hysteria reflected the peculiar social dynamics of the Salem community.

SOCIETY AND ECONOMY IN THE MIDDLE COLONIES

AN ECONOMIC MIX   Both geographically and culturally the middle Atlantic colonies stood between New England and the South, blending their own influences with elements derived from the older regions on either side. In so doing, they more completely reflected the diversity of colonial life and more fully foreshadowed the pluralism of the American nation than did the other regions. Their crops were those of New England but more bountiful, owing to better land and a longer growing season, and they developed surpluses of foodstuffs for export to the plantations of the South and the West Indies: wheat, barley, and livestock. The region's commerce rivaled that of New England, and indeed Philadelphia in time supplanted Boston as the largest city in the colonies.

Land policies in the middle colonies followed the headright system of the South. In New York the early royal governors carried forward, in practice

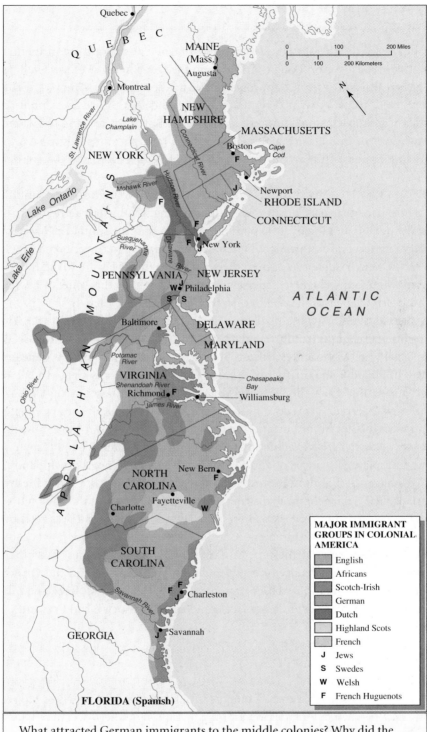

MAJOR IMMIGRANT GROUPS IN COLONIAL AMERICA

- English
- Africans
- Scotch-Irish
- German
- Dutch
- Highland Scots
- French
- **J** Jews
- **S** Swedes
- **W** Welsh
- **F** French Huguenots

What attracted German immigrants to the middle colonies? Why did the Scotch-Irish spread across the Appalachian backcountry? What major population changes were reflected in the 1790 census?

if not in name, the Dutch device of the patroonship, granting influential friends vast estates on Long Island and up the Hudson and Mohawk valleys. These realms most nearly approached the medieval manor. They were self-contained domains farmed by tenants who paid fees to use the landlords' mills, warehouses, smokehouses, and wharves. But with free land elsewhere, new waves of immigrants avoided these autocratic patroonships in favor of broader opportunities in the promised land of Pennsylvania.

AN ETHNIC MIX   In the makeup of their population, the middle colonies stood apart from both the mostly English Puritan settlements of New England and the biracial plantation colonies to the south. In New York and New Jersey, for instance, Dutch culture and language lingered, along with the Dutch Reformed Church. Up and down the Delaware River, the few Swedes and Finns, the first settlers, were overwhelmed by the influx of English and Welsh Quakers, followed in turn by Germans and Scotch-Irish.

The Germans came mainly from regions devastated by incessant war. The promise of religious freedom in the New World appealed to persecuted sects, especially the Mennonites, whose beliefs resembled those of the Quakers. West of Philadelphia thrifty immigrant farmers and artisans created a belt of settlement in which the "Pennsylvania Dutch" (a corruption of *Deutsch*, meaning "German") predominated. The Scotch-Irish began to arrive later and moved still farther out into the backcountry throughout the eighteenth century. (*Scotch-Irish* is an enduring misnomer for Ulster Scots, Presbyterians transplanted from Scotland to confiscated lands in northern Ireland to give that country a more Protestant tone.) The Scotch-Irish, mostly Presbyterians, fled from economic disaster and Anglican persecution. They settled first in Pennsylvania and then fanned out across the fertile valleys stretching southwestward into Virginia and Carolina. With the Germans they became the most numerous of the non-English groups in the colonies, but others also enriched the diversity of the population in New York and the Quaker colonies: Huguenots (French Protestants), Irish, Welsh, Swiss, Jews, and others. By 1790 barely half the populace could trace their origins to England.

COLONIAL CITIES

Since commerce was their chief reason for being, colonial cities hugged the coastline or, like Philadelphia, sprang up on rivers where oceangoing vessels could reach them. Never having more than 10 percent of the colonial population, they exerted an influence in commerce, politics, and culture out of proportion to their size. Five port cities outdistanced the rest. By the end of the colonial period, Philadelphia had some 30,000 people and was the largest city in the colonies, second only to London in the British Empire; New York, with about 25,000, ranked second; Boston numbered 16,000; Charleston, South Carolina, 12,000; and Newport, Rhode Island, 11,000.

THE SOCIAL AND POLITICAL ORDER   Merchants formed the upper crust of urban society, and below them came a middle class of craftspeople, retailers, innkeepers, and artisans. Almost two thirds of the adult male workers were artisans, people who made their living at handicrafts. They included carpenters, shoemakers, tailors, blacksmiths, weavers, and potters. At the bottom of the pecking order were sailors and unskilled workers. Such class stratification in the cities became more pronounced during the eighteenth century and thereafter.

Problems created by urban growth are nothing new. Colonial cities were busy, crowded, and dangerous. They required not only paved roads and street lights but regulations to protect children and animals from reckless riders. Other regulations restrained citizens from tossing their garbage into the street. Devastating fires led to building codes, restrictions on burning rubbish, and the organization of fire companies. Rising crime and violence required more police protection. And in cities the poor became more visible than they were in the countryside. Colonists responded according to the English principle of public responsibility for the needy. Most of the aid went to "outdoor" relief in the form of money, food, clothing, and fuel, but almshouses also appeared to house the destitute.

THE URBAN WEB   Transit within and between early-American cities was initially difficult. The first roads were Indian trails, which themselves often followed the tracks of bison through the forests. Those trails widened with travel, then were made into roads by order of provincial and local authorities. Land travel was initially by horse or by foot.The first stagecoach line for the public opened in 1732. From the main ports good roads might reach thirty or forty miles inland, but all were dirt roads subject to washouts and mud holes. Aside from city streets, there was not a single hard-surfaced road constructed during the entire colonial period.

Taverns were an important aspect of colonial travel, since movement by night was risky. By the end of the seventeenth century, there were more taverns in America than any other business, and they became the most important social institution in the colonies—and the most democratic. By 1690 there were fifty-four taverns in Boston alone, half of them operated by women.

Taverns

A tobacconist's business card from 1770 captures the atmosphere of late-eighteenth-century taverns. Here men in a Philadelphia tavern share conversation while they drink ale and smoke pipes.

Colonial taverns and inns were places to drink, relax, read the newspaper, play cards or billiards, gossip about people or politics, learn news from travelers, or conduct business. Local ordinances regulated them, setting prices and usually prohibiting them from serving liquor to African Americans, Indians, servants, or apprentices.

Taverns served as a collective form of social discourse; long-distance communication, however, was more complicated. Postal service in the seventeenth century was almost nonexistent—people entrusted letters to travelers or sea captains. Massachusetts set up a provincial postal system in 1677 and Pennsylvania in 1683. Under a parliamentary law of 1710, the postmaster of London named a deputy in charge of the colonies, and a postal system eventually extended the length of the Atlantic seaboard. Benjamin Franklin, who served as deputy postmaster for the colonies from 1753 to 1774, sped up the service with shorter routes and night-traveling post riders, and he increased the volume by inaugurating lower rates.

More reliable mail delivery gave rise to newspapers in the eighteenth century. Before 1745 twenty-two newspapers had been started: seven in New England, ten in the middle colonies, and five in the South. An important landmark in the progress of freedom of the press was John Peter Zenger's trial for seditious libel, for publishing criticisms of New York's governor in his newspaper, the *New York Weekly Journal.* Zenger was imprisoned for ten months and brought to trial in 1735. English common law held that one might be punished for criticism that fostered "an ill opinion of the government." The jury's function was only to determine whether the defendant had published the opinion. Zenger's lawyer startled the court with his claim that the editor had published the truth—which the judge ruled an unacceptable defense. The jury, however, agreed with the assertion and held the editor not guilty. The libel law remained standing as before, but editors thereafter were emboldened to criticize officials more freely.

THE ENLIGHTENMENT

Through their commercial contacts, newspapers, libraries, and other channels, cities became the centers for the discussion of new ideas. In the world of ideas a new development dazzled minds: the Enlightenment. During the seventeenth century, Europe experienced a scientific revolution in which the prevailing notion of an earth-centered universe was overthrown by the sun-centered system discovered by the sixteenth-century Polish astronomer Nicolaus Copernicus. The scientific revolution climaxed in 1687 when England's Sir Isaac Newton set forth his theory of gravitation. Newton had, in short, proposed a design of a mechanistic universe moving in accordance with natural laws that could be grasped by human reason and explained by mathematics.

By analogy to Newton's view of the world as a machine, one could reason that natural laws govern all things—the orbits of the planets and the orbits of human relations: politics, economics, and society. Reason could make people aware, for instance, that the natural law of supply and demand governs economics or that the natural rights to life, liberty, and property determine the limits and functions of government.

Much of enlightened thought could be reconciled with established beliefs: the idea of natural law existed in Christian theology, and religious people could reason that the worldview of Copernicus and Newton simply showed the glory of God. Yet Deists carried the idea to its ultimate conclusion, reducing God to a remote Creator, a master clockmaker who planned the universe and set it in motion. Evil in the world, one might reason further, resulted not from original sin so much as from an imperfect understanding of the laws of nature. People, the English philosopher John Locke argued in his *Essay Concerning Human Understanding* (1690), reflect the impact of their environment, the human mind being a blank tablet at birth that gains knowledge through experience. Corrupt society therefore might corrupt the mind. The way to improve both society and human nature was by the application and improvement of Reason—which was the highest Virtue (Enlightenment thinkers often capitalized both words).

THE AMERICAN ENLIGHTENMENT However interpreted, such "enlightened" ideas profoundly affected the climate of thought in the eighteenth century. The premises of Newtonian science and the Enlightenment, moreover, fitted the American experience, which placed a premium on observation, experiment, and the need to think anew. America was therefore especially receptive to the new science.

Benjamin Franklin epitomized the Enlightenment. He rose from the ranks of the common folk and never lost the common touch, a gift that accounted for his success as a publisher. Born in Boston in 1706, Franklin was the son of a maker of candles and soap. Apprenticed to his older brother, a printer, Franklin left home at the age of seventeen and relocated to Philadelphia. There, before he was twenty-four, he owned a print shop, where he edited and published the *Pennsylvania Gazette.* When he was twenty-six, he brought out *Poor Richard's Almanack,* a collection of homely teachings on success and happiness. Before he retired from business, at the age of forty-two, Franklin, among other achievements, had founded a library, set up a fire company, helped start the academy that became the University of Pennsylvania, and organized a debating club that grew into the American Philosophical Society. After his early retirement, he intended to devote himself to public affairs and the sciences.

Benjamin Franklin

Shown here as a young man in a portrait by Robert Feke.

The course of events allowed Franklin less and less time for science, but that remained his passion. His speculations extended widely to the fields of medicine, meteorology, geology, astronomy, and physics. He invented the Franklin stove, the lightning rod, and a glass harmonica for which Mozart and Beethoven wrote works. The triumph of this untutored genius further confirmed the Enlightenment trust in the powers of Nature and Reason.

EDUCATION IN THE COLONIES The heights of abstract reasoning, of course, were remote from the everyday concerns of most colonists. For the colonists at large, education in the traditional ideas and manners of society—even literacy itself—remained primarily the responsibility of family and church.

Conditions in New England, however, proved most favorable for the establishment of schools. The Puritan emphasis on Scripture reading, which all Protestants shared to some degree, implied an obligation to ensure literacy. In 1647 the Massachusetts Bay Colony required every town of fifty or more families to set up a grammar school (a "Latin school" that could prepare a student for college). Although the act was widely evaded, it set an example that the rest of New England emulated.

In Pennsylvania the Quakers never heeded William Penn's instructions to establish public schools, but they did respect the usefulness of education and financed a number of private schools, where practical as well as academic subjects were taught. In the southern colonies, efforts to establish schools were hampered by the more scattered population and in parts of the backcountry by indifference and neglect. Some of the wealthiest planters and merchants of the Tidewater sent their children to England or hired tutors, who in some cases would also serve the children of neighbors. In some places wealthy patrons or the people collectively managed to raise some kind of support for academies.

The Great Awakening

The new currents of learning and the questioning outlook spawned by the Enlightenment led many people to drift away from the moorings of orthodox religion during the eighteenth century. Many of those in the educated classes were attracted to Deism (which denied that God interfered with the laws and working of the universe) and skepticism (which questioned accepted assumptions and religious beliefs). The pious feared that the great Puritan and Quaker merchants of Boston and Philadelphia were prospering because the devil had lured them into the vain pursuit of worldly gain. Meanwhile, out along the fringes of settlement there grew up a great backwater of the unchurched, people who had no minister to preach or administer sacraments or perform marriages. By the 1730s the sense of spiritual decline had prepared the time for a revival of faith, the Great Awakening, a wave of evangelism that within a few years swept the colonies from one end to the other, America's first mass movement.

EDWARDS AND WHITEFIELD   In 1734–1735 a remarkable spiritual revival occurred in the congregation of Jonathan Edwards, a Congregationalist minister in Northampton, in western Massachusetts. One of America's most brilliant philosophers and theologians, Edwards had entered Yale in 1716, at age thirteen, and graduated as valedictorian four years later. In 1727 Edwards took charge of the Congregational church in Northampton and found the congregation's spirituality at a low ebb. He was convinced that Christians had become preoccupied with making and spending money and that religion had become too intellectual and in the process had lost its animating force. "Our people," he said, "do not so much need to have their heads stored [with education] as to have their hearts touched." He added that he considered it a "reasonable thing to endeavor to fright persons away from hell." His own vivid descriptions of the torments of hell and the delights of heaven helped rekindle spiritual fervor among his congregants. By 1735 Edwards could report that "the town seemed to be full of the presence of God; it never was so full of love, nor of joy."

The true catalyst of the Great Awakening, however, was a young English minister, George Whitefield, whose reputation as a spellbinding evangelist preceded him to the colonies. Congregations were lifeless, he claimed, "because dead men preach to them." Too many ministers were "slothful shepherds and dumb dogs." To restore the fires of religious fervor to American congregations, Whitefield reawakened the notion of individual salvation. In the autumn of 1739, Whitefield arrived in Philadelphia and late in that year preached to huge crowds. After visiting Georgia, he made a triumphal procession northward to New England, drawing great crowds and releasing "Gales of Heavenly Wind" that dispersed sparks throughout the colonies.

George Whitefield

The English minister's dramatic eloquence roused American congregants, inspiring many to experience a religious rebirth.

Whitefield enthralled audiences with his unparalleled eloquence. The English revivalist stressed the need for individuals to experience a "new birth," a sudden and emotional moment of conversion and salvation. By the end of his sermon, one listener reported, the entire congregation was "in utmost Confusion, some crying out, some laughing, and Bliss still roaring to them to come to Christ, as they answered, *I will, I will, I'm coming, I'm coming.*"

Jonathan Edwards heard Whitefield preach and wept through most of the sermon. Thereafter he spread his own revival gospel throughout New England. The Great Awakening in New England reached its peak in 1741 when Edwards delivered his most famous sermon. Titled "Sinners in the Hands of an Angry God," it represented a devout appeal to repentance. Edwards reminded the congregation of the reality of hell, the omnipotence of God's vision, and the certainty of his judgment. He warned that God "holds you over the pit of hell, much as one holds a spider, or some loathsome insect, over the fire, abhors you, and is dreadfully provoked . . . he looks upon you as worthy of nothing else, but to be cast into the fire."

The message and technique of Edwards and Whitefield were infectious, and imitators sprang up everywhere. Once unleashed, however, spiritual enthusiasm was hard to control, and in many ways the Great Awakening backfired on those who had intended it to bolster church discipline and social order. Some revivalists began to court those at the bottom of society—laborers, seamen, servants, and farmers. The Reverend James Davenport, for instance, a fiery New England Congregationalist, set about shouting, raging, and stomping on the devil and beseeching his listeners to renounce the established clergy, whom he branded unconverted, and become the agents of their own salvation. The radical revivalists, said one worried conservative, were breeding "anarchy, levelling, and dissolution."

PIETY AND REASON Whatever their motive or method, the revivalists succeeded in awakening the piety of many Americans. Between 1740 and 1742 some 25,000 to 50,000 New Englanders, out of a total population of 300,000, joined churches. The Great Awakening also helped fragment spiritual life. It spawned a proliferation of new religious groups and sects that helped undermine the notion of state-supported churches. Everywhere the revivals induced splits, especially in the more Calvinist churches. Traditional clergymen found their position undermined as church members chose sides and either dismissed their old ministers or deserted them.

By the middle of the eighteenth century, New England Puritanism had finally fragmented. The precarious balance in which the founders had held the elements of piety and reason was shattered, and more and more Baptists, Presbyterians, Anglicans, and members of other denominations began establishing footholds in formerly Congregationalist Puritan communities. Yet the revival frenzy scored its most lasting victories along the chaotic frontiers of the middle and southern colonies. In contrast, in the more sedate churches of Boston, rational religion ultimately got the upper hand in a reaction against the excesses of revival emotion. The rationality of Newton and Locke, the idea of natural law, crept more and more into the sermons of Boston ministers, and they embarked on the road to Unitarianism and Universalism.

In reaction to taunts that the "born-again" revivalist ministers lacked learning, the Great Awakening gave rise to the denominational colleges that became characteristic of American higher education. The three colleges already in existence had their origins in religious motives: Harvard College, founded in 1636 because the Puritans dreaded "to leave an illiterate ministry to the church when our present ministers shall lie in the dust"; the College of William and Mary, created in 1693 to strengthen the Anglican ministry; and Yale College, set up in 1701 to serve the Puritans of Connecticut, who believed that Harvard was drifting from the strictest orthodoxy. The College of New Jersey, later Princeton University, was founded by Presbyterians in 1746 as the successor to William Tennent's Log College. In close succession came King's College (1754) in New York, later Columbia University, an Anglican institution; the College of Rhode Island (1764), later Brown University, which was Baptist; Queens College (1766), later Rutgers, which was Dutch Reformed; and the Congregationalist Dartmouth College (1769), the outgrowth of an earlier school for Indians. Among the colonial colleges only the University of Pennsylvania, founded as the Academy of Philadelphia in 1751, arose from a secular impulse.

The Great Awakening, like the Enlightenment, set in motion powerful currents that still flow in American life. It implanted permanently in American culture evangelical energies and the appeal of revivalism. The movement weakened the status of the established clergy, encouraged believers to exercise their own judgment, and thereby weakened habits of deference generally. The proliferation of denominations heightened the need for toleration of dissent. In some respects the Great Awakening, characterized by piety and emotion, and the Enlightenment, dominated by reason and rationality, led by different roads to similar ends. Both movements emphasized the power and right of individual choice and popular resistance to established authority, and both aroused millennial hopes that America would become the promised land in which people might approach the perfection of piety or reason, if not both. Such hopes had both social and political, as well as religious, implications. As the eighteenth century advanced, fewer and fewer people were willing to defer to the ruling social and political elite, and many such rebellious if pious folk would be transformed into revolutionaries.

MAKING CONNECTIONS

- This chapter reveals social and racial tensions in colonial Virginia society; in the next chapter, these tensions will come to a head with Bacon's Rebellion.

- During the imperial crisis of the 1760s and 1770s, the ideas of the Great Awakening and especially the Enlightenment helped shape the American response to British actions and thereby contributed to a revolutionary mentality.

FURTHER READING

The diversity of colonial societies may be seen in David Hackett Fischer's *Albion's Seed: Four British Folkways in America* (1989). Other useful works include Richard Hofstadter's *America at 1750: A Social Portrait* (1971) and James A. Henretta's *The Evolution of American Society, 1700–1815* (1973). For a fascinating account of the impact of livestock on colonial history, see Virginia DeJohn Anderson's *Creatures of Empire: How Domestic Animals Transformed Early America* (2004).

Bernard Rosenthal challenges many myths concerning the Salem witch trials in *Salem Story: Reading the Witch Trials of 1692* (1993). Mary Beth Norton's *In the Devil's Snare: The Salem Witchcraft Crisis of 1692* (2002) emphasizes the role of Indian violence. Discussions of women in the New England colonies can be found in Laurel Thatcher Ulrich's *Good Wives: Image and Reality in the Lives of Women in Northern New England, 1650–1750* (1980), Joy Day Buel and Richard Buel Jr.'s *The Way of Duty: A woman and Her Family in Revolutionary America* (1984), and Carol F. Karlsen's *The Devil in the Shape of a Woman: Witchcraft in Colonial New England* (1987). John Demos describes family life in *A Little Commonwealth: Family Life in Plymouth Colony*, new ed. (2000).

For the social history of the southern colonies, see Allan Kulikoff's *Tobacco and Slaves: The Development of Southern Cultures in the Chesapeake, 1680–1800* (1986) and *Colonial Chesapeake Society* (1988), edited by Lois Green Carr, Philip D. Morgan, and Jean B. Russo. Edmund S. Morgan's *American Slavery, American Freedom: The Ordeal of Colonial Virginia* (1975) examines Virginia's social structure, environment, and labor patterns in a biracial context. On the interaction of the cultures of blacks and whites, see Mechal Sobel's *The World They Made Together: Black and White Values in Eighteenth-Century Virginia* (1987). African-American viewpoints are presented in Timothy H. Breen and Stephen Innes's *"Myne Owne Ground": Race and Freedom on Virginia's Eastern Shore, 1640–1676,* new ed. (2004). David W. Galenson's *White Servitude in Colonial America: An Economic Analysis* (1981) looks at the indentured labor force.

Henry F. May's *The Enlightenment in America* (1976) examines intellectual trends in eighteenth-century America. Lawrence A. Cremin's *American Education: The Colonial Experience, 1607–1783* (1970) surveys educational developments.

On the Great Awakening, see Edwin S. Gaustad's *The Great Awakening in New England* (1957), Patricia U. Bonomi's *Under the Cope of Heaven: Religion, Society, and Politics in Colonial America* (1986), and Timothy D. Hall's *Contested Americn Boundaries: Itinerancy and the Reshaping of the Colonial American Religious World* (1994). The political impact of the new religious enthusiasm is shown in Rhys Issac's *The Transformation of Virginia, 1740–1790* (1982). Patricia J. Tracy's *Jonathan Edwards, Pastor* (1980) stresses the Northampton minister's relations to his community.

4

THE IMPERIAL
PERSPECTIVE

FOCUS QUESTIONS

· How did England's political and economic administration of
the colonies change?

· How were the colonial governments structured?

· What were relations like between the English colonists and
their neighbors in North America: the French, the Spanish,
and the Indians?

To answer these questions and access additional review material, please visit
www.wwnorton.com/studyspace.

For the better part of the seventeenth century, England remained too distracted by the struggle between Parliament
and the Stuart kings to perfect either a systematic colonial
policy or effective agencies of imperial control. The English Civil War, which
lasted from 1642 to 1649, ushered in Oliver Cromwell's Puritan Commonwealth and Protectorate, during which the colonies were given a respite from
royal control. After the Restoration of King Charles II and the Stuart dynasty
in 1660, the British government slowly developed a new plan of colonial
administration. By the end of the seventeenth century, however, it still lacked
coherence and efficiency, leaving Americans accustomed to rather loose
colonial reins.

ENGLISH ADMINISTRATION
OF THE COLONIES

Throughout the colonial period the British king exercised legal authority in America, and land titles derived ultimately from royal grants to individuals and groups. All important colonial officials held office at the pleasure of the monarch. Before the English Civil War the king supervised colonial officials through the Privy Council, a body of thirty to forty advisers, eleven of whom in 1634 were made responsible for colonial administration. After the Restoration the king tried to reassert his control over the colonies, but administration by the mother country continued to be inconsistent and inefficient. The British government regarded English colonists as citizens, but it refused to grant them the privileges of citizenship. It insisted that the settlers contribute to the expense of maintaining the colonies, but it refused to allow them a voice in the shaping of administrative policies. Such inconsistencies bred tension that festered over time. By the mid–eighteenth century, when the British tried to impose on their colonies in America the kinds of controls that were reaping such profits in India, it was too late. British Americans had developed a far more powerful sense of their rights than had any other colonial people, and they were determined to assert and defend those rights.

THE MERCANTILE SYSTEM   In developing national economic policy, Restoration England under Charles II adopted the mercantile system, or mercantilism, which was based on the assumption that the world's supply of gold and silver remained essentially fixed, with only a nation's share in that wealth subject to change. Thus one nation could gain wealth only at the expense of another—by seizing its gold and silver and dominating its trade. To acquire gold and silver, a government had to control all economic activities, limiting foreign imports and preserving a favorable balance of trade. Thus a mercantilist government had to encourage manufacturing, through subsidies and monopolies if need be, to develop and protect its own shipping and to exploit colonies as sources of raw materials and markets for its finished goods.

During the English Civil War, Dutch shipping companies had taken over the trade with England's colonies. To win it back, Oliver Cromwell persuaded Parliament in 1651 to adopt the Navigation Act, which required that all goods imported by England or the colonies arrive on English ships and that the majority of the crew be English.

With the Restoration, Parliament passed the Navigation Act of 1660, which added a twist to Cromwell's act; ships' crews had to be three-quarters English, and "enumerated" products not produced by the mother country, such as tobacco, cotton, and sugar, were to be shipped from the colonies only to England or other English colonies. Not only did England (and its colonies) become the sole outlet for these colonial exports, but the Navigation Act of 1663 required that all ships carrying goods from Europe to America dock in England, be offloaded, and pay a duty before proceeding. A third major act rounded out the trade system. The Navigation Act of 1673 (sometimes called the Plantation Duty Act) required that every captain loading enumerated articles in the colonies pay a duty, or tax, on them.

ENFORCING THE NAVIGATION ACTS   The Navigation Acts supplied a convenient rationale for a colonial system: to serve the economic needs of the mother country. Their enforcement in far-flung colonies, however, was another matter. In 1675 Charles II designated certain members of his Privy Council the Lords of Trade. These officials were to make the colonies abide by the mercantile system and make them more profitable for the crown. To these ends the Lords of Trade served as the clearinghouse for all colonial affairs, building up a staff of colonial experts. They also named colonial governors,

Boston from the Southeast

This view of eighteenth-century Boston shows the importance of shipping and its regulation in the colonies, especially in Massachusetts Bay.

wrote or reviewed the governors' instructions, and handled all reports and correspondence dealing with colonial affairs.

Between 1673 and 1679 British collectors of customs duties arrived in all the colonies, and with them appeared the first seeds of colonial resentment. New England's Puritan leaders in particular harbored a persistent distrust of royal intentions. The Massachusetts Bay Colony not only ignored royal wishes; it also tolerated violations of the Navigation Acts. This led the Lords of Trade to begin legal proceedings against the colonial charter in 1678. The issue remained in legal snarls for another six years; in 1684 the Lords of Trade won a court decision annulling the Massachusetts charter.

THE DOMINION OF NEW ENGLAND   Temporarily the Massachusetts Bay government fell under the control of a special royal commission. Then, in 1685, King Charles II died and was succeeded by his brother the duke of York, as King James II, the first Catholic sovereign since Queen Mary (r. 1553–1558). Plans long maturing in the Lords of Trade for a general reorganization of colonial government coincided with the autocratic notions of James II, who asserted power more forcefully than his brother had. The new king therefore readily approved a proposal to create a Dominion of New England that included all the colonies south through New Jersey.

The Dominion was to have a government named by royal authority; a governor and council would rule without any colonial assembly. The royal governor, Sir Edmund Andros, appeared in Boston in 1686 to establish his rule, which he soon extended over Connecticut and Rhode Island and, in 1688, over New York and East and West Jersey. Not surprisingly, a rising resentment greeted Governor Andros's measures, especially in Massachusetts. Andros levied taxes without the consent of the General Court, suppressed town governments, enforced the trade laws, and clamped down on smuggling. Most ominous of all, he and his lieutenants took over one of Boston's Puritan churches for Anglican worship. Puritan leaders believed, with good reason, that he proposed to break their power and authority.

But the Dominion was scarcely established before word arrived that the Glorious Revolution of 1688 had erupted in England. King James II, like Andros, had aroused resentment by instituting arbitrary measures and openly parading his Catholic faith. The birth of a son who was sure to be reared a Catholic put the Anglican opposition on notice that James's pro-Catholic system would survive him. In 1688, therefore, parliamentary leaders, their patience exhausted, invited James's Protestant daughter Mary and her husband, the Dutch leader William III, to assume the throne as joint monarchs. James II, his support dwindling, fled to France.

THE GLORIOUS REVOLUTION IN AMERICA   When news reached Boston that William and Mary had landed in England, the city staged its own Glorious Revolution. Andros and his councilors were arrested, and Massachusetts reverted to its former government, as did the other colonies that had been absorbed into the Dominion. All were permitted to retain their former status except Massachusetts Bay and Plymouth, which after some delay were united under a new charter in 1691 as the royal colony of Massachusetts Bay.

The Glorious Revolution in England had significant long-term effects on American history. The Bill of Rights and the Toleration Act, passed in England in 1689, limited the powers of the country's monarchs and affirmed a degree of freedom of worship for all Christians, thereby influencing attitudes—and the course of events—in the colonies. And what was more significant for the future, the overthrow of James II set a precedent for revolution against the monarch. In defense of that action, the English philosopher John Locke published his *Two Treatises on Government* (1690), which had an enormous impact on political thought in the colonies. Whereas the first treatise refuted theories of the divine right of kings, the more important second treatise set forth Locke's contract theory of government, which argued that people were endowed with natural rights to life, liberty, and property. When a ruler violated these rights, the people had the right—in extreme cases—to overthrow the monarch and change their government.

In the American experience colonial governments had actually grown out of contractual arrangements such as John Locke had described; a good example is the Mayflower Compact. The royal charters themselves also constituted a sort of contract between the crown and the settlers. Such precedents made John Locke's writings especially appealing to colonial readers, and his philosophy probably had more influence in America than in England.

AN EMERGING COLONIAL SYSTEM   William and Mary oversaw a refinement of the Navigation Acts and the administrative system for regulating the American colonies. The Navigation Act of 1696, officially called the Act to Prevent Frauds and Abuses, required colonial governors to enforce the Navigation Acts, allowed customs officials to use "writs of assistance" (general search warrants that did not have to specify the place to be searched), and ordered that accused violators be tried in admiralty courts, because colonial juries habitually refused to convict their peers. Admiralty cases were decided by judges whom the royal governors appointed.

Also in 1696 King William III created a Lords Commissioners of Trade and Plantations to take the place of the Lords of Trade. Intended to ensure that the colonies served England's economy, the new Board of Trade oversaw the enforcement of the Navigation Acts and recommended ways to limit manufacturing in the colonies and encourage their production of raw materials.

From 1696 to 1725, the Board of Trade sought to bring more efficient royal control to the administration of the colonies. After 1725, however, its energies and activities waned. The Board of Trade became chiefly an agency of political patronage, studded with officials whose main interest was their salaries.

The Habit of Self-Government

Government within the American colonies, like colonial policy, evolved essentially without plan. In broad outline the governor, council, and assembly in each colony corresponded to the king, lords, and commons of the mother country. At the outset all the colonies except Georgia had begun as projects of trading companies or feudal proprietors holding charters from the crown, but eight colonies eventually relinquished or forfeited their charters and became royal provinces. In these the crown named the governor. Connecticut and Rhode Island were the last of the corporate colonies; they elected their own governors to the end of the colonial period. In the corporate and proprietary colonies and in Massachusetts, the charter served as a rough equivalent to a written constitution. Over the years certain anomalies appeared as colonial governments diverged from trends in England. On the one hand, the governors retained powers and prerogatives that the king had lost in the course of the seventeenth century. On the other hand, the assemblies acquired powers, particularly with respect to government appointments, that Parliament had yet to gain.

POWERS OF THE GOVERNORS   The crown never vetoed acts of Parliament after 1707, but the colonial governors, most of whom were mediocre or incompetent, still held an absolute veto over the assemblies, and the crown could disallow (in effect, veto) colonial legislation on advice of the Board of Trade. With respect to the assembly, the governor still had the power to determine when and where it would meet, prorogue (adjourn or recess) legislative sessions, and dissolve the assembly for new elections or postpone elections indefinitely. In contrast, in the mother country the crown had pledged to summon Parliament every three years and call elections at least every seven and could not prorogue sessions. The royal or proprietary governor, moreover, nominated for life appointment the members of his council (except in Massachusetts, where they were chosen by the lower house), and the council functioned as both the upper house of the legislature and the highest court of appeal within the colony.

With respect to the judiciary, in all but the charter colonies the governor still held the prerogative of creating courts and naming and dismissing judges, powers explicitly denied the king in England. Over time, however, the colonial assemblies generally made good their claim that courts should be created only by legislative authority, although the crown repeatedly disallowed acts to grant judges life tenure in order to make them more independent.

As chief executive, the governor could appoint and remove officials, command the militia and naval forces, grant pardons, and as his commission often put it, "execute everything which doth and of right ought to belong to the governor," which might cover a multitude of powers. In these respects, his authority resembled the crown's, for the king still exercised executive authority and had the power to name administrative officials.

POWERS OF THE ASSEMBLIES   Unlike the governor and members of the council, who were appointed by either king or proprietor, the colonial assembly was elected. Whether called the House of Burgesses (Virginia), or Delegates (Maryland), or Representatives (Massachusetts), or simply the assembly, the lower houses were chosen by popular vote in counties, towns, or, in South Carolina, parishes. Religious tests for voting were abandoned during the seventeenth century, and the chief restriction remaining was a property qualification, based upon the notion that only men who held a "stake in society" could vote responsibly. Yet the property qualifications generally set low hurdles in the way of potential voters. Property holding was widespread, and a greater proportion of the population could vote in the colonies than anywhere else in the world of the eighteenth century. Women, Indians, and African Americans were excluded—few then questioned this—and continued to be excluded for the most part into the twentieth century.

By the early eighteenth century the colonial assemblies, like Parliament, held two important strands of power. First, they controlled the budget by their right to vote on taxes and expenditures. Second, they held the power to initiate legislation. They used these powers to pull other strands of power into their hands when the chance presented itself. For example, they held governors on a tight leash by their control of political salaries. Throughout the eighteenth century the assemblies expanded their power and influence, sometimes in conflict with the governors and sometimes in harmony with them. Often in the course of routine business, the assemblies passed laws and set precedents the collective significance of which neither

The Boston Statehouse

Built in 1713.

they nor the imperial authorities fully recognized. Once established, however, these laws and practices became fixed principles, part of the "constitution" of the colonies. Self-government in the colonies became first a habit, then a "right."

TROUBLED NEIGHBORS

Self-government was not the only institution that began as a habit during the colonial period. The claims of white settlers on Indian lands had their roots in the first English settlements, where relations between the colonists and the Indians were at times cooperative and at times hostile. Indian-white relations transformed the human and ecological landscape of colonial North America, stirred up colonial politics, and disrupted or destroyed the fabric of Indian culture. Relations between European settlers and North American Indians were themselves agitated by the fluctuating balance of power in Europe. The French and the English each sought to use Indians to their advantage in fighting each other for control of New World territory.

DISPLACING THE INDIANS   The English invasion of North America would have been a different story had the English encountered greater resistance. Instead, in the coastal regions they found scattered and mutually hostile Indian tribes, whom they subjected to a policy of divide and conquer. Whether tempted by trade goods or the promise of alliances or intimidated by a show of force, most of the Native Americans let matters drift until the English were too entrenched to be pushed back into the sea.

During the first half of the seventeenth century, the most severe tests of the colonists' will to prevail came with the Virginia troubles in 1644 and Connecticut's Pequot War of 1637. In both colonies, Indian leaders engaged in last-chance efforts to save their lands; in both instances they failed. For the Pequots the result was virtual extermination—Puritans killed Pequots with such savagery that they offended their allies, the Narragansetts, who had never seen such total war. In Virginia, according to a census taken in 1669, only eleven of twenty-eight tribes described by John Smith in 1608, and only about 2,000 of some 30,000 Indians, remained in the colony. Indian resistance had been broken for the time.

Then, in the mid-1670s, both New England and Virginia went through another time of troubles: an Indian war in New England and a civil war masquerading as an Indian war in Virginia. The spark that set New England ablaze was the murder of John Sassamon, a "praying Indian" who had attended Harvard, strayed from the faith while serving King Philip (Metacom) of the Wampanoag tribe, and then returned to the Christian fold. When Plymouth tried and executed three Wampanoags for Sassamon's murder, King Philip's tribesmen attacked.

Thus began King Philip's War, which the land-hungry leaders of Connecticut and Massachusetts quickly enlarged by assaulting the peaceful Narragansetts at their chief refuge in Rhode Island, a massacre the Rhode Island authorities were helpless to prevent. From June to December 1675, Indian attacks ravaged the interior of Massachusetts Bay and Plymouth, and guerrilla war continued through 1676. Finally, depleted supplies and the casualty toll wore down Indian resistance. Philip's wife and son were captured and sold into slavery. In August 1676 Philip himself was tracked down and killed. Sporadic fighting continued until 1678 in New Hampshire and Maine. Indians who survived the slaughter had to submit to colonial authority and accept confinement to ever-dwindling plots of land.

BACON'S REBELLION   The news from New England heightened tensions among colonists in the sparsely settled Virginia interior and contributed to the tangled events thereafter known as Bacon's Rebellion. The roots of the revolt grew out of a festering hatred for the domineering colonial governor, William Berkeley. Appointed by the king in 1641, he served as Virginia's governor for most of the next thirty-five years. Berkeley was an unapologetic elitist who limited his circle of friends to the wealthiest and most ambitious planters. He granted them most of the frontier land and public offices, and he rarely allowed new elections to the assembly for fear that his cronies might be defeated. The large planters who dominated the assembly levied high taxes to finance Berkeley's regime, which in turn supported their interests at the expense of the small farmers and servants. With little nearby land available, newly freed indentured servants were forced to migrate westward in their quest for farms. Their lust for land led them to displace the Indians. When Governor Berkeley failed to support the aspiring farmers, they rebelled.

The discontent turned to violence in 1675 when a petty squabble between a frontier planter and the Doeg Indians on the Potomac River led to the murder of the planter's herdsman. Frontier militiamen retaliated by killing ten or more Doegs and, by mistake, fourteen Susquehannocks. Soon a force of Virginia and Maryland militiamen laid siege to the Susquehannocks and murdered five chieftains. The enraged Indian survivors took their revenge on frontier settlements. Scattered attacks continued down to the James River, where Nathaniel Bacon's overseer was killed.

In 1676 Bacon defied Governor Berkeley's authority by assuming command of a group of frontier vigilantes. The vain, ambitious, and hot-tempered Bacon had a talent for trouble and an enthusiasm for terrorizing peaceful Indians. After threatening to kill the governor and the assemblymen if they tried to intervene, Bacon began preparing for a total war against all Indians. Berkeley opposed Bacon's genocidal plan not because he liked Indians but because he wanted to protect his lucrative monopoly over the deerskin trade with them. To prevent any government interference, Bacon ordered the governor arrested, thus pitting his own followers (who were largely servants, small farmers, and even slaves) against Virginia's wealthy planters and political leaders. Berkeley's forces resisted—but only feebly—and Bacon's men burned Jamestown in 1676. But Bacon could not savor the victory long; he fell ill and died of dysentery a month later.

Governor Berkeley quickly regained control and subdued the leaderless rebels. In the process he hanged twenty-three men and confiscated several estates. For such severity the king recalled Berkeley to England. A royal commission then made treaties of pacification with the remaining Indians, some of whose descendants still live on tiny reservations guaranteed them in 1677. For the colonists the fighting had opened new lands and confirmed the power of an inner group of established landholders who sat on the Virginia council.

SPANISH AMERICA IN DECLINE   By the start of the eighteenth century, the Spanish were ruling over a huge colonial empire spanning North America. Yet their settlements in the borderlands north of Mexico were a colossal failure when compared with Spanish Mexico and the colonies of the other European powers. The Spanish failed to create thriving colonies in the American Southwest for several reasons. Perhaps the most obvious was that the region lacked the gold and silver, as well as the large native populations, that attracted Spain to Mexico and Peru. In addition, the Spanish were distracted by their need to control the perennial unrest in Mexico among the natives and the mestizos (people of mixed Indian and European ancestry). Moreover, those Spaniards who led the colonization effort in the borderlands were so preoccupied with military and religious control that they never produced viable settlements with self-sustaining economies. Only rarely, for example, did the Spanish send many women to their colonies in North America. Even more important, they never understood that the main

Champlain in New France

Samuel de Champlain firing at a group of Iroquois, killing two chiefs (1609).

factor in creating a successful community was a thriving market economy. Instead, they concentrated on building missions and forts and looking—in vain—for gold. Whereas the French and the English based their Indian policies on trade (that included providing Indians with firearms), Spain emphasized conversion to Catholicism and stubbornly adhered to an outdated mercantilism that forbade manufacturing within the colonies and strictly limited trade with the natives.

NEW FRANCE AND LOUISIANA   Permanent French settlements in the New World began in 1608, when the French explorer Samuel de Champlain founded a settlement at Quebec. From there he pushed his explorations into the Great Lakes as far as Lake Huron and southward to the lake that still bears his name. There, in 1609, he joined a band of Indian allies in a fateful encounter, fired his gun into the ranks of their Iroquois foes, and thereby kindled a hatred that pursued New France to the end. Thenceforth the Iroquois stood as a buffer against any French designs to move toward the English of the middle Atlantic colonies and as a constant menace on the flank of the French waterways to the interior.

From the Great Lakes, French explorers moved southward down the Mississippi River. The French thus enjoyed access to the great water routes that led to the heartland of the continent. Yet French involvement in North America never approached that of the British. In part this was because the French-held areas were less enticing than the English seaboard settlements. Few Frenchmen were willing to challenge the interior's rugged terrain, fierce winters, and hostile Indians. In addition, the French government impeded colonization by refusing to allow Huguenots to migrate. New France was to remain Roman Catholic. It was also to remain a howling wilderness, home to a mobile population of traders, trappers, missionaries—and, mainly, Indians. In 1750, when the English colonists in America numbered about 1.5 million, the French population was no more than 80,000.

In some ways, however, the French had the edge on the British. Their relatively small numbers forced them to develop cooperative relationships with the Indians. Unlike the English settlers, the French established trading outposts (to trade European goods for furs) rather than farms, mostly along the St. Lawrence River, on lands not claimed by Indians. Thus they did not have to confront initial hostility. The heavily outnumbered and disproportionately male French settlers sought to integrate themselves with Indian culture rather than displace it. Many French traders married Indians and raised families, in the process exchanging languages and customs. They also encouraged the Indians to embrace Catholicism and to hate the English. This more fraternal bond between the French and the Indians proved to be a source of strength in the wars with the English. French governors could mobilize for action without any worry about quarreling assemblies or ethnic and religious diversity. New France was thus able to survive until 1760, despite the lopsided disparity in numbers between the colonies of the two powers.

The Colonial Wars

For most of the seventeenth century, the French and the British Empires in America developed in relative isolation from each other; for most of that century, the homelands remained at peace. After the Restoration in 1660, Charles II and then James II pursued a policy of friendship with Louis XIV. The Glorious Revolution of 1688 abruptly reversed English diplomacy, however. William III, the new British king from the Dutch republic, had engaged in a running conflict with the ambitions of Louis XIV in Europe. His ascent to the throne brought England almost immediately into a Grand Alliance against the French in the War of the League of Augsburg, known in the colonies simply as King William's War (1689–1697). This was the first of four great European and intercolonial wars to be fought over the next seventy-four years.

Thereafter the major European wars of the period were the War of the Spanish Succession (known in the colonies as Queen Anne's War, 1702–1713); the War of the Austrian Succession (known in the colonies as King George's War, 1744–1748); and the Seven Years' War (known in the colonies as the French and Indian War, which lasted nine years in America, from 1754 to 1763). In all except the last, the battles in America were but a sideshow accompanying greater battles in Europe, where British policy aimed to keep a balance of power with the French. The multinational alliances shifted from one fight to the next, but Britain and France were pitted against each other every time.

So for much of the century after the great Indian conflicts of 1676, the colonies were embroiled in global wars and rumors of war. The effect on much of the population was devastating. The New England colonies, especially Massachusetts, suffered more than the rest, for they were closest to the centers of French population. It is estimated that 900 Boston men (about 2.5 percent of the men eligible for service) died in the fighting. One result of such carnage was that Boston's population stagnated through the eighteenth century while the population of Philadelphia and New York continued to grow, and Boston had to struggle to support a large population of widows and orphans. Eventually the economic impact of the four imperial wars left increasing numbers of poor people in New England, and many of them would participate in the popular unrest leading to the Revolutionary movement. Moreover, these prolonged conflicts led the English government to incur an enormous debt, establish a huge navy and standing army, and excite a militant sense of nationalism. These changes would ultimately lead to a reshaping of the relationship between the mother country and its American colonies.

THE FRENCH AND INDIAN WAR Of the four major wars involving the European powers and their New World colonies, the climactic conflict between Britain and France in North America was the French and Indian War. It began in 1754, after enterprising Virginians during the early 1750s had crossed the Allegheny Mountains into the upper Ohio River valley in order to trade with Indians and survey 200,000 acres granted them by King George. The incursion by the Virginians infuriated the French, and they set about building a string of forts in the disputed area.

The Virginia governor sent an emissary to warn off the French. An ambitious young officer in the Virginia militia, Major George Washington, having volunteered for the mission, received a polite but firm French refusal. In the spring of 1754 the Virginia governor sent Washington back to the disputed region with a small force to erect a fort at the strategic fork where the Allegheny and Monongahela rivers meet to form the Ohio River in southwestern Pennsylvania. The twenty-two-year-old Washington, hungry for combat and yearning for military glory, led his 150 volunteers and Iroquois allies across the Alleghenies, only to learn that French soldiers had beaten them to the strategic site and erected Fort Duquesne, named for the French governor of Canada. Washington decided to make camp about forty miles from the fort and await reinforcements. The next day the Virginians ambushed a French detachment. Ten French soliders were killed, one escaped, and twenty-one were captured. The Indians then scalped several of the wounded soldiers as a stunned Washington looked on. Washington was unaware that the French had been on a peaceful mission to discuss the disputed fort. The mutilated soliders were the first fatalities in what would become the French and Indian War.

Washington and his troops retreated and hastily constructed a crude stockade at Great Meadows, dubbed Fort Necessity, which a large force of vengeful French soliders attacked a month later, on July 3, 1754. After a daylong battle, George Wahington surrendered, having seen all his horses and cattle killed and one third of his 300 men killed or wounded. The French permitted

The First American Political Cartoon

Benjamin Franklin's exhortation to the colonies to unite against the French in 1754 would become popular again twenty years later, when the colonies faced a different threat.

the surviving Virginians to withdraw after stripping them of their weapons. After the regiment limped home, Washington decided to resign rather than accept a demotion. His blundering expedition triggered a series of events that would ignite a protracted world war. As a prominent British politician exclaimed, "The volley fired by a young Virginian in the backwoods of America set the world on fire."

Back in London the Board of Trade had already taken notice of the growing conflict in the American backwoods. The British government decided to force a showdown with the French in America, but things went badly at first. In 1755 the British fleet failed to halt the landing of French reinforcements in Canada. The British buttressed their hold on Nova Scotia by expelling most of its French population. Some 5,000 to 7,000 Acadians who refused to take an oath of allegiance were scattered through the colonies, from Maine to Georgia. Impoverished and homeless, many of them desperately found their way to French Louisiana, where they became the Cajuns (a corruption of the term *Acadians*) whose descendants still preserve elements of the French language along the remote bayous and in many urban centers.

A WORLD WAR For two years, war raged along the American-Canadian frontier without igniting war in Europe. In 1756, however, the colonial war merged with what became the Seven Years' War in Europe. In the final alignment of European powers, France, Austria, Russia, Saxony, Sweden, and Spain

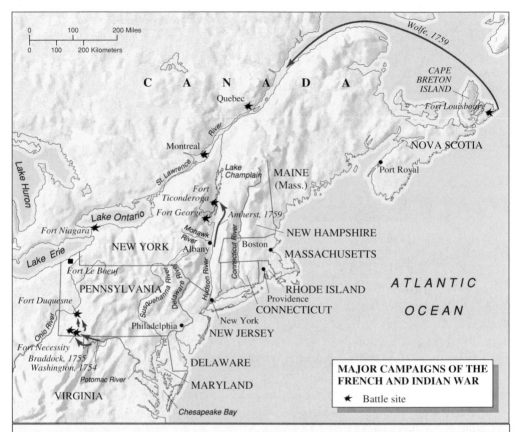

MAJOR CAMPAIGNS OF THE
FRENCH AND INDIAN WAR

✶   Battle site

What was the significance of the siege of Fort Necessity? What was the Plan of
Union? How did the three-pronged offensive of 1759 lead to a British victory in
North America?

fought against Britain, Prussia, and Hanover. The onset of world war brought
into office a new British government, with the popular, eloquent William Pitt
as head of the ministry. Pitt's ability and assurance ("I know that I can save
England and no one else can") instilled confidence at home and abroad.

British sea power cut off French reinforcements and supplies to the New
World—and the goods with which they bought Indian allies. In 1758 the
tide began to turn. Fort Louisbourg in Canada fell to the British. When a
new expedition marched against Fort Duquesne, the outnumbered French
burned the fort and fled the scene. On the site arose the British Fort Pitt and,
later, the city of Pittsburgh.

In 1759 the decisive battle occurred at Quebec, in Canada. Commanding
the British expedition up the St. Lawrence River was General James Wolfe, a

dedicated professional soldier who, at the age of thirty-two, had already spent more than half his life in military service. For two months, Wolfe probed the French defenses of Quebec, seemingly impregnable on its fortified heights and manned by alert forces under General Louis-Joseph de Montcalm. Finally Wolfe's troops found a path up the cliffs behind Quebec. During the night of September 12–13, they scrambled up the sheer walls and emerged on the Plains of Abraham, athwart the main roads to the city. There, in a battle more like conventional European warfare than a frontier skirmish, the British forces allowed the French to advance within close range and then fired two devastating volleys that ended French power in North America for all time. News of the victory was clouded by word of Wolfe's—and Montcalm's—deaths in the battle.

The war in North America dragged on until 1763, but the rest was a process of mopping up. In the South, where little significant action had occurred, the Cherokee Nation flared into belated hostility, but a force of British regulars and provincials broke their resistance in 1761.

Just six weeks after the capture of Montreal in 1760, King George II died, and his twenty-two-year-old grandson ascended the throne as George III. The new king took a more active role in colonial affairs than his Hanoverian predecessors had. The new king yearned for peace, which entailed forcing his chief minister, William Pitt, out of office. Pitt had wanted to declare war on Spain before the French could bring that other Bourbon monarchy into the conflict. He was forestalled, but Spain belatedly entered the war, in 1761. During the next year the Spanish met the same fate as the French: in 1762 British forces took Manila in the Philippines and Havana in Cuba. By 1763 the French and the Spanish were ready to negotiate a surrender. Britain ruled the world.

THE PEACE OF PARIS   The war culminated in the Treaty of Paris of 1763. It ended French power in North America, and Britain took all of France's North American possessions east of the Mississippi River (except New Orleans), several islands in the West Indies, and all of Spanish Florida. The English invited the Spanish settlers to remain and practice their Catholic religion, but few accepted the offer. The Spanish king ordered them to evacuate the colony and provided free transportation to Spanish possessions in the Caribbean Sea. Within a year most of the Spaniards sold their property at bargain prices to English speculators and began an exodus to Cuba and Mexico. When the Indian tribes that had been allied with the French learned of the 1763 peace settlement, they were despondent. Their lands were being given over to the British without any consultation. The Shawnees, for instance,

NORTH AMERICA, 1713

- England
- France
- Spain

0   500   1000 Miles

0   500   1000 Kilometers

What events led to the first clashes between the French and the British in the late seventeenth century? Why did New England suffer more than other regions of North America during the wars of the eighteenth century? What were the long-term financial, military, and political consequences of the wars between France and Britain?

demanded to know "by what right the French could pretend" to transfer Indian territory to the British. The Indians also worried that a victorious Britain had "grown too powerful & seemed as if they would be too strong for God itself." The Indians had hoped that the departure of the French from the Ohio Valley would mean that the area would revert to their control. Instead, the British cut off the trade and gift-giving practices that had bound the

NORTH AMERICA, 1763

- England
- Spain
- Proclamation line of 1763

How did the map of North America change between 1713 and 1763? How did Spain win Louisiana? What were the consequences of the British winning all the land east of the Mississippi?

Indians to the French. General Jeffrey Amherst, the British military governor for the western region, demanded that the Indians learn to live without "charity." British forces also moved into the French frontier forts. In a desperate effort to recover their autonomy, tribes struck back in the spring of 1763, capturing most of the British forts around the Great Lakes and in the Ohio Valley. They also raided colonial settlements in Pennsylvania, Maryland, and Virginia, destroying hundreds of homesteads and killing several thousand people. In the midst of the Indian attack on Fort Pitt (formerly Fort Duquesne), General Amherst approved the distribution of smallpox-infested blankets and handkerchiefs, from the fort's hospital, to the Indians besieging the garrison. His efforts at germ warfare were intended to "extir-pate this execrable race" of Indians.

Called Pontiac's Rebellion because of the prominent role played by the Ottawa chief, the far-flung attacks on the frontier forts convinced most colonists that all Indians must be removed. The British government, mean-while, negotiated an agreement with the Indians that allowed redcoats to reoccupy the frontier forts in exchange for a renewal of trade and gift giving. Still, as Pontiac stressed, the Indians asserted their independence and denied the legitimacy of the British claim to their territory under the terms of the Treaty of Paris. He told a British official that the "French never conquered us, neither did they purchase a foot of our Country, nor have they a right to give it to you." The British may have won a global empire as a result of the Seven Years' War, but their grip on the American colonies grew ever weaker.

In compensation for the loss of Florida, Spain received Louisiana (New Orleans and all French land west of the Mississippi River) from France. Un-like the Spanish in Florida, however, few of the French settlers left Louisiana after 1763. The French government encouraged them to stay and work with their new Spanish governors to create a bulwark against further English expansion. Spain would hold title to Louisiana for nearly four decades but would never succeed in erasing the region's French roots. The French-born settlers always outnumbered the Spanish.

The loss of Louisiana left France with no territory on the continent of North America. After 1763 British power reigned supreme over North America east of the Mississippi River. In gaining Canada, however, the British government put in motion a train of events that would end twenty years later with the loss of the rest of British North America. Britain's success against France threatened the Indian tribes of the interior because they had long depended upon playing the two European powers off against each other. Now, with the British dominant on the continent, American settlers were emboldened to encroach even more upon Indian land. In addition, vic-tory on the battlefields encouraged the British to tighten their imperial con-trol over the Americans and demand more financial contributions from the colonists to defray the cost of British army troops. Meanwhile, humiliated France thirsted for revenge. In London, Benjamin Franklin, agent for the colony of Pennsylvania from 1764 to 1775, found the French minister inor-dinately curious about America and suspected him of wanting to ignite the coals of controversy. Less than three years after Franklin left London and only fifteen years after the conquest of New France, he would be in Paris arranging an alliance on behalf of Britain's rebellious colonists.

MAKING CONNECTIONS

- Although the British victory in the French and Indian War brought the colonies and England closer together in some ways, it was also an important factor in the approach of the American Revolution, as will be demonstrated in Chapter 5.

- One of the great struggles of the Revolution would be transforming the dependent British colonies, as described in this chapter, into independent American states, as described in Chapter 6.

FURTHER READING

The economics motivating colonial policies are covered in John J. McCusker and Russell R. Menard's *The Economy of British America, 1607–1789*, rev. ed. (1991). The problems of colonial customs administration are explored in Micheal Kammen's *Empire and Interest: The American Colonies and the Politics of Mercantilism* (1970).

Jack P. Greene's *The Quest for Power: The Lower Houses of Assembly in the Southern Royal Colonies, 1689–1776* (1963) describes the politics of the southern colonies, and Richard P. Johnson's *Adjustment to Empire: The New England Colonies, 1675–1715* (1981) examines New England. The Andros crisis and related topics are treated in Jack M. Sosin's *English America and the Revolution of 1688: Royal Administration and the Structure of Provincial Government* (1982). Stephen Saunders Webb's *The Governors-General: The English Army and the Definition of the Empire, 1569–1681* (1979) argues that the crown was more concerned with military administration than with commercial regulation, and Webb's *1676: The End of American Independence* (1984) shows how the Indian wars undermined the autonomy of the colonial governments.

The early Indian wars are treated in Jill Lepore's *The Name of War: King Philip's War and the Origins of American Identity* (1998) and in Francis

Jennings's *The Invasion of America: Indians, Colonialism, and the Cant of Conquest* (1975). See also Jennings's *The Ambiguous Iroquois Empire: The Covenant Chain Confederation of Indian Tribes with English Colonies* (1984) and *Empire of Fortune: Crowns, Colonies, and Tribes in the Seven Years War in America* (1988) and Richard Aquila's *The Iroquois Restoration: Iroquois Diplomacy on the Colonial Frontier, 1701–1754* (1983).

A good introduction to the imperial phase of the colonial conflicts is Howard H. Peckham's *The Colonial Wars, 1689–1762* (1964). More analytical is Douglas Edward Leach's *Arms for Empire: A Military History of the British Colonies in North America, 1607–1763* (1973). Fred Anderson's *Crucible of War: The Seven Years' War and the Fate of Empire in British North America, 1754–1766* (2000) is the best history of the Seven Years' War.

5

FROM EMPIRE TO INDEPENDENCE

FOCUS QUESTIONS

· What were the changes in British colonial policy after 1763?

· How did Whig ideology shape the colonial response to changes in British policy?

· What was the role of Revolutionary leaders, including Samuel Adams, John Dickinson, Thomas Paine, and Thomas Jefferson?

To answer these questions and access additional review material, please visit www.wwnorton.com/studyspace.

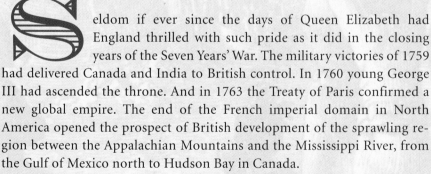

Seldom if ever since the days of Queen Elizabeth had England thrilled with such pride as it did in the closing years of the Seven Years' War. The military victories of 1759 had delivered Canada and India to British control. In 1760 young George III had ascended the throne. And in 1763 the Treaty of Paris confirmed a new global empire. The end of the French imperial domain in North America opened the prospect of British development of the sprawling region between the Appalachian Mountains and the Mississippi River, from the Gulf of Mexico north to Hudson Bay in Canada.

The American colonists shared in the euphoria of victory over the French, but the celebration masked festering resentments and new problems. Underneath the pride in the sprawling British Empire, a sense of an American nationalism was maturing. For over a generation the colonists had essentially been

George III

At age thirty-three, the young king of a victorious empire.

allowed to govern themselves and were beginning to think and speak of themselves more as American than as English or British. With vast new western lands to exploit, they could look to the future with confidence.

The Heritage of War

The colonists had a new sense of importance after fighting a major war with such success. Many in the early stages of the war had lost their awe of the British soldiers, who were vigorously inept at frontier fighting. American colonists were also dismayed by the sharp social distinctions between officers and men in the British army. The provincials, by contrast, presumed that by volunteering, they had formed a contract with a particular American officer from their community.

During the war many Americans became convinced of their moral superiority to their British allies. Although they admired the courage and discipline of British redcoats under fire, New Englanders abhorred the carefree cursing, whoring, and Sabbath breaking they observed among the British troops. Most upsetting were the brutal punishments imposed by British officers on their wayward men. Minor offenses might earn hundreds of lashes. The war thus heightened the New Englanders' sense of their separate identity and of their greater worthiness to be God's chosen people.

In the aftermath of victory, the British government faced massive new problems. How should it manage the defense and governance of the new territories acquired from France? How were they to pay an unprecedented debt built up during the war and bear the new financial and administrative burdens of greater colonial administration and more far-flung global defense? And—the thorniest problem of all, as it turned out—what role should the colonies play in all this? The problems were of a magnitude and complexity to challenge men of the greatest statesmanship and vision, but those qualities were rare among the ministers of George III. The king himself, while a conscientious and deeply religious man, was obstinate, unimaginative, and overly dependent upon his advisers and ministers.

In the English government of the eighteenth century, nearly every politician called himself a Whig, as did the king. *Whig* had been the name given to those who opposed James II, led the Glorious Revolution of 1688, and secured the Protestant Hanoverian succession in 1714. The Whigs were the champions of liberty and parliamentary supremacy, but with the passage of time Whiggism had drifted into complacency, and leadership settled upon an aristocratic elite of the Whig gentry. In the absence of party organization, parliamentary politics hinged upon factions bound together by personal loyalties, family connections, local interests, and the pursuit of royal patronage in the form of government appointments. Throughout the 1760s the king turned first to one and then to another mediocre prime minister, and the government grew more unstable just as the new problems of colonial administration required forceful solutions. Colonial policy remained marginal to the chief concerns of British politics. The result was inconsistency and vacillation followed by stubborn inflexibility.

WESTERN LANDS

No sooner was peace arranged in 1763 than the problem of America's western lands provoked a crisis in the British government. The Indians of the Ohio River valley, fearing the arrival of English settlers, joined Ottawa chief Pontiac's attempt to renew frontier warfare. Within a few months, Indians had wiped out every British post in the Ohio Valley region except Forts Detroit and Pitt.

To secure peace on the frontier, the ministers in London postponed further settlement of the western lands. The immediate need was to stop Pontiac's warriors and pacify the Indians. The king had signed the Royal Proclamation of 1763, which drew an imaginary line along the crest of the Appalachians, beyond which settlers were forbidden to go and colonial governors were forbidden to authorize surveys or issue land grants. It also established the new British colonies of Quebec and East and West Florida.

But Pontiac did not agree to peace until 1766, and Britain's proclamation line did not remain intact for long. Hardy pioneers ignored the line and pushed over the Appalachian ridges. By 1770 the town of Pittsburgh had twenty log houses, and four years later Daniel Boone and a party of settlers cut the Wilderness Road through the Cumberland Gap, in southwestern Virginia, to the Kentucky River.

GRENVILLE'S COLONIAL POLICY

As the Royal Proclamation of 1763 was being drafted, a new ministry in London began to grapple with the problems of imperial finances. The new chief minister, George Grenville, first lord of the Treasury, wanted to keep a large army (10,000 men) in America to avoid a rapid demobilization that would force many influential officers to retire and thereby spark political criticism at home. On top of an already staggering government debt, however, he faced sharply rising costs for defense of the American colonies.

CUSTOMS AND CURRENCY   Because there was a heavy tax burden at home and a much lighter one in the colonies, Grenville reasoned that the prosperous Americans should share the cost of their own defense. He also learned that the royal customs service in America was amazingly inefficient. Evasion and corruption were rampant. Grenville thus issued stern orders to colonial officials and dispatched the navy to patrol the coast in search of smugglers evading royal duties. Parliament agreed to set up a new maritime court in Halifax, Nova Scotia, granting it jurisdiction over all the colonies. Decisions would be made by judges appointed by the crown rather than by

The Great Financier, or British Economy for the Years 1763, 1764, 1765

This cartoon, critical of Grenville's tax policies, shows America, depicted as an Indian (at left), groaning under the burden of new taxes.

juries of colonists sympathetic to smugglers. The old habits of "salutary neglect" in the enforcement of the Navigation Acts were coming to an end, to the growing annoyance of American shippers.

The Molasses Act of 1733 had set a sixpence-per-gallon customs duty on molasses in order to prevent trade with the French sugar islands. New England merchants evaded this tax, smuggling in French molasses to make rum. Recognizing that the duty, if enforced, would ruin the rum distillers, Grenville put through the Sugar Act (1764), which cut the duty in half. This, he believed, would reduce the temptation to smuggle or to bribe customs officers. In addition, the Sugar Act levied new duties (taxes) on imports of foreign textiles, wine, coffee, indigo, and sugar. The act, Grenville estimated, would bring in enough revenue to help defray "the necessary expenses of defending, protecting, and securing" the colonies. For the first time, Parliament had adopted taxes on trade explicitly designed to raise revenues in the colonies rather than just regulate trade.

Another key element in Grenville's colonial program was the Currency Act of 1764. The colonies faced a chronic shortage of hard currency, which kept going out to pay debts in England. To meet the shortage, they issued their own paper money. British creditors feared receiving payment in such a depreciated paper currency, however. To alleviate their fears, Grenville prohibited the colonies from printing money. The value of existing paper money soon plummeted, since nobody was obligated to accept it in payment of debts, even in the colonies. The deflationary impact of the Currency Act, combined with new duties on commodities and stricter enforcement, jolted a colonial economy already suffering a postwar slump.

THE STAMP ACT   Grenville's strategy to raise revenue from the colonies entailed one more key provision. Because the Sugar Act would defray only part of the cost of maintaining British troops along the western frontier, he proposed another measure to raise money in America, a stamp tax. Enacted on February 13, 1765, the Stamp Act created revenue stamps that were to be purchased and attached to printed matter and legal documents of all kinds: newspapers, pamphlets, almanacs, bonds, leases, deeds, licenses, insurance policies, ship clearances, college diplomas, even playing cards. The requirement was to go into effect on November 1.

In March 1765 Grenville put through the final measure of his new program, the Quartering Act. It required the colonies to supply British troops with provisions and provide them barracks or submit to their use of inns and vacant buildings owned by colonists. The Quartering Act applied to all colonies but affected mainly New York, headquarters of the British forces.

THE IDEOLOGICAL RESPONSE   The cumulative effect of Grenville's measures outraged colonists. Unwittingly he stirred up a storm of protest and set in motion a profound exploration of English traditions and imperial relations. By this time the radical ideas of the so-called Real Whig minority in England had slowly begun to take hold in the colonies. The Real Whigs sought to safeguard citizens against government abuse of power.

Whig radicals charged that Grenville had loosed upon the colonies the very engines of tyranny from which Parliament had rescued England in the seventeenth century. A standing army, Whigs believed, encouraged despots, and now, with the French gone and Chief Pontiac subdued, several thousand British soldiers remained in the colonies. Among the fundamental English rights were trial by jury and the presumption of innocence, but the new vice-admiralty courts excluded juries and put the burden of proof on the defendant. Most important, the English had the right to be taxed only by their elected representatives. Parliament claimed that privilege in England, and the colonial assemblies had long exercised it in America. Now, with the Stamp Act, Parliament sought to usurp the assemblies' power of the purse strings. This could only lead to tyranny and enslavement.

PROTEST IN THE COLONIES   In a flood of colonial pamphlets, speeches, and resolutions, critics of the Stamp Act repeated a slogan familiar to all Americans: "No taxation without representation." The Stamp Act became the chief target of colonial protest because it burdened all colonists who did any kind of business. And it affected most of all the articulate elements in the community: merchants, planters, lawyers, printer-editors—all strategically placed to influence public opinion.

Through the spring and summer of 1765, popular resentment against Grenville boiled over in meetings, parades, bonfires, and other demonstrations. Calling themselves Sons of Liberty, colonial militants met underneath "liberty trees"—in Boston a great elm, in Charleston a live oak. One day in mid-August 1765, nearly three months before the effective date of the Stamp Act, an effigy of Boston's royal stamp agent swung from the city's liberty tree. In the evening a mob carried it through the streets, destroyed the stamp office, and used the wood to burn the effigy. Somewhat later another mob sacked the homes of the lieutenant governor and the local customs officer. The stamp agent in Boston, thoroughly shaken, resigned his commission, and stamp agents throughout the colonies felt impelled to follow his example.

The widespread protests encouraged colonial unity, as rebellious Americans discovered that they had more in common with each other than with

London. In May 1765 the Virginia House of Burgesses struck the first blow against the Stamp Act with the Virginia Resolves, a series of resolutions inspired by the young Patrick Henry. Virginians, the burgesses declared, were entitled to all English rights, and the English could be taxed only by their own representatives. Virginians, moreover, had always been governed by laws passed with their own consent. Newspapers spread the resolutions throughout the colonies, and other assemblies hastened to copy Virginia's example. In June 1765 the Massachusetts House of Representatives invited the various colonial assemblies to send delegates to confer in New York on appeals for relief from the king and Parliament.

Nine responded, and on October 7 the twenty-seven delegates of the Stamp Act Congress issued a Declaration of the Rights and Grievances of the Colonies, a petition to the king for relief, and a petition to Parliament for repeal of the Stamp Act. The delegates argued that Parliament might have powers to legislate for the regulation of colonial trade, but it had no right to levy taxes, which were a gift granted by the people through their elected representatives.

By November 1, its effective date, the Stamp Act was a dead letter. Business activities were conducted without the revenue stamps. Newspapers appeared with the skull and crossbones where the stamp belonged. Colonial rebels were beginning to sense their power. After passage of the Sugar Act, rebels began to boycott British goods rather than pay the new import duties. Now colonists adopted nonimportation agreements to exert pressure on British merchants. Americans knew they had become a major market for British products. By shutting off imports from the home country, they could exercise real leverage. Sage and sassafras took the place of British tea, and homespun garments became the fashion as symbols of colonial defiance.

REPEAL OF THE STAMP ACT   The storm had scarcely broken before Grenville's ministry was out of office, dismissed not because of the colonial turmoil but because of tensions with the king over the distribution of lucrative government appointments. In July 1765 the king installed a new minister, the marquis of Rockingham, leader of the "Rockingham Whigs," who sympathized with the colonists' views. Rockingham resolved to end the quarrel with America by repealing the Stamp Act, but he needed to move carefully in order to win a majority. Simple repeal was politically impossible without some affirmation of parliamentary authority over the colonies. When Parliament assembled early in 1766, the powerful parliamentary leader William Pitt demanded that the Stamp Act be repealed "absolutely, totally, and immediately,"

The Repeal, or the Funeral Procession of Miss America-Stamp

This 1766 cartoon shows Grenville carrying the dead Stamp Act in its coffin. In the background, trade with America starts up again.

but he urged that Britain's authority over the colonies "be asserted in as strong terms as possible," except on the point of taxation.

In March 1766 Parliament repealed the Stamp Tax but passed the Declaratory Act, which asserted the full power of Parliament to make laws binding the colonies "in all cases whatsoever." It was a cunning evasion that made no concession with regard to taxes but made no mention of them either. It reinforced a distinction between "external" taxes on trade and "internal" taxes within the colonies, a distinction that would have fateful consequences. To be sure, the Sugar Act remained on the books, but Rockingham reduced the molasses tax from threepence to onepence a gallon, less than the cost of a bribe.

FANNING THE FLAMES

Meanwhile, King George continued to play musical chairs with his ministers. After Rockingham lost the king's confidence, William Pitt formed a

ministry that included the major factions of Parliament. Soon thereafter, however, Pitt slipped over the fine line between genius and madness, and he resigned in 1768. For a time in 1767 the guiding force in the ministry was Charles Townshend, chancellor of the Exchequer (Treasury). The witty but erratic Townshend took advantage of Pitt's mental confusion to reopen the question of colonial taxation. He asserted that "external" taxes were tolerable to the colonies—not that he believed it for a moment.

THE TOWNSHEND ACTS   In 1767 Townshend put his plan through the House of Commons, and in September he died, leaving a bitter legacy: the Townshend Acts. With this legislation, Townshend had sought to bring the New York assembly to its senses. That body had defied the Quartering Act and refused to provide beds or supplies for the king's troops. Parliament, at Townshend's behest, had suspended all acts of the New York assembly until it would yield. New York finally caved in, inadvertently confirming the British suspicion that too much indulgence had encouraged colonial bad manners. Townshend had followed up with the Revenue Act of 1767, which levied duties ("external taxes") on colonial imports of glass, lead, paints, paper, and tea. Next, he had set up a Board of Customs Commissioners at Boston, the hotbed of colonial smuggling. Finally, he had reorganized the vice-admiralty courts, providing four in the continental colonies: at Halifax, Boston, Philadelphia, and Charleston.

The Townshend duties increased government revenues, but the intangible costs were greater. The duties taxed goods exported from England, indirectly hurting British manufacturers, and they had to be collected in colonial ports, increasing collection costs. More important, the new taxes accelerated colonial resentment and resistance. The Revenue Act of 1767 posed a more severe threat to colonial assemblies than Grenville's taxes had, for Townshend proposed to apply the revenues to pay the salaries of royal governors and other officers and thereby release them from financial dependence on the colonial assemblies.

DICKINSON'S "LETTERS"   The Townshend Acts inspired the colonists to boycott British goods and to develop their own manufactures. Once again the colonial press spewed out protests, most notably the essays of John Dickinson, a Philadelphia lawyer who hoped to resolve the dispute by persuasion. Late in 1767 his twelve "Letters from a Farmer in Pennsylvania" (as he chose to style himself) began to appear in the *Pennsylvania Chronicle,* from which they were copied in other newspapers. He argued that Parliament might regulate American commerce and collect duties incidental to that

purpose, but it had no right to levy taxes for revenue, whether they were internal or external.

SAMUEL ADAMS AND THE SONS OF LIBERTY But British officials could neither conciliate moderates like Dickinson nor cope with firebrands like Boston's Samuel Adams, who was now emerging as the supreme genius of revolutionary agitation. Born in 1722, Adams graduated from Harvard and soon thereafter inherited the family brewery, which he proceeded to run into bankruptcy. His distant cousin John Adams described Sam as a "universal good character," a "plain, simple, decent citizen, of middling stature, dress, and manners" who prided himself on his frugality and his distaste for ceremony and display. Politics, not profit, excited his passion, and he spent most of his time debating political issues with sailors, roustabouts, and stevedores at local taverns. Adams insisted that Parliament had no right to legislate for the colonies, that Massachusetts must return to the spirit of its Puritan founders and defend itself from a new royal conspiracy against its liberties.

Adams was a relentless rebel. He whipped up the Sons of Liberty, writing incendiary newspaper articles and letters and organizing protests at the Boston town meeting and in the provincial assembly. The royal governor called him "the most dangerous man in Massachusetts." Early in 1768 Adams and Boston lawyer James Otis formulated a letter that the Massachusetts assembly dispatched to the other colonies. It restated the illegality of parliamentary taxation, warned that the new duties would be used to pay colonial officials, and invited the other colonies to join in a boycott of British goods.

In mid-May 1769 the Virginia assembly reasserted its exclusive right to tax Virginians and called upon the colonies to unite in protest. Virginia's royal governor promptly dissolved the assembly, but the members met independently and adopted a new set of nonimportation agreements. Once again, as with the Virginia Resolves against the Stamp Act, most of the other colonial assemblies followed suit.

THE BOSTON MASSACRE In Boston roving gangs enforced the boycott of goods from England, intimidating Loyalist merchants and their customers. This led the governor to appeal for military support, and two British regiments arrived from Canada. The presence of British soldiers in Boston had always been a source of provocation, but now tensions heightened. On March 5, 1770, in the square before the custom house, a mob began heaving taunts, icicles, and oyster shells at the British sentry, whose call for help brought reinforcements. Then somebody rang the town fire bell,

drawing a larger crowd to the scene. Among the mob was Crispus Attucks, a runaway mulatto slave who had worked for some years on ships out of Boston. The riotous crowd began striking at the troops with sticks, and it knocked one soldier down. He rose to his feet and fired into the crowd. Others fired, too, and when the smoke cleared, five people lay dead or dying, and eight more were wounded.

The cause of colonial resistance now had its first martyrs, and the first to die was Crispus Attucks. News of the Boston Massacre sent shock waves through the colonies. The incident, remembered one Bostonian, "created a resentment which emboldened the timid" and "determined the wavering." But late in April 1770 news arrived that Parliament had repealed all the Townshend duties save one. The cabinet, by a vote of five to four, had advised keeping the tea tax as a token of parliamentary authority. Colonial diehards insisted that pressure should be kept on British merchants until

The Bloody Massacre

Paul Revere's partisan engraving of the Boston Massacre.

Parliament gave in altogether, but the nonimportation movement soon faded. Parliament, after all, had given up most of the taxes, and much of the colonists' tea was smuggled from Holland anyway.

For two years thereafter colonial discontent simmered down. The Stamp Act was gone, as were all the Townshend duties except that on tea. Yet most of the hated regulations remained in effect: the Sugar Act, the Currency Act, the Quartering Act, the vice-admiralty courts, the Board of Customs Commissioners. The redcoats had left Boston, but they remained nearby, and the British navy still patrolled the coast, looking for smugglers. Each remained a source of irritation and the cause of occasional incidents. As Sam Adams stressed, "Where there is a Spark of patriotick fire, we will enkindle it."

DISCONTENT ON THE FRONTIER

Many colonists showed no interest in the disputes over British regulatory policies raging along the seaboard. Parts of the backcountry had stirred with quarrels that had nothing to do with the Stamp and Townshend Acts. Rival land claims to the east of Lake Champlain pitted New York against New Hampshire and the Green Mountain Boys, led by Ethan Allen, against both. Eventually the residents of the area would simply create their own state, Vermont, in 1777, although it was not recognized as a member of the Union until 1791.

In Pennsylvania a group of frontier ruffians took the law into their own hands. Outraged at the lack of frontier protection provided by the Quaker-influenced assembly during Chief Pontiac's Rebellion, a group called the Paxton Boys took revenge by massacring peaceful Susquehannock Indians in Lancaster County, then threatened the so-called Moravian Indians, a group of Moravian converts near Bethlehem. When the Moravian Indians took refuge in Philadelphia, some 1,500 Paxton Boys marched on the capital, where Benjamin Franklin talked them into returning home by promising more protection along the frontier.

Farther south settlers along the South Carolina backcountry complained about the lack of protection from horse thieves, cattle rustlers, and Indians. They organized societies called Regulators to administer vigilante justice in the region and refused to pay taxes until they gained effective government. In 1769 the assembly finally set up six new circuit courts in the region and revised the taxes, but it still did not respond to the backcountry's demand for representation in the legislature.

In North Carolina the protest was less over the lack of government than over the abuses and extortion by government appointees from the eastern part of the colony. In 1766 farmers organized to resist, but their efforts were more pitiful than potent. In the spring of 1771, the royal governor and 1,200 militiamen defeated some 2,000 ill-organized Regulators in the Battle of Alamance. The pitched battle illustrated the growing tensions between back-country settlers and the wealthy planters in the eastern part of the colony, tensions that would erupt again during and after the Revolution.

These disputes and revolts within the colonies illustrate the fractious diversity of opinion and outlook evident among Americans on the eve of the Revolution. Colonists were of many minds about many things, including British rule. Frontier conflicts in colonial America also helped convince British authorities that the colonies were inherently unstable and that they required firmer oversight, including the use of military force to ensure civil stability.

A Worsening Crisis

Two events in June 1772 shattered the period of calm in the quarrels with the mother country. Near Providence, Rhode Island, a British schooner, the *Gaspee,* patrolling for smugglers, ran aground. Under cover of darkness, colonial rebels boarded the ship, removed the crew, and set fire to the vessel. Three days after the burning, Massachusetts's angry royal governor, Thomas Hutchinson, told the provincial assembly that his salary thenceforth would come out of the customs revenues. Massachusetts Superior Court judges would be paid from the same source and would no longer be dependent upon the assembly for their income. The assembly feared that this portended "a despotic administration of government."

To keep the pot simmering, in November 1772 Sam Adams convinced the Boston town meeting to form the Committee of Correspondence, which issued a statement of rights and grievances and invited other towns to do the same. Committees of Correspondence soon sprang up in other colonies. In March 1773 the Virginia assembly proposed the formation of such committees on an intercolonial basis, and a network of the committees spread across the colonies, maintaining contact, mobilizing public opinion, and keeping colonial resentments at a simmer.

THE BOSTON TEA PARTY Frederick, Lord North, who had replaced Townshend as chancellor of the Exchequer, soon brought colonial resentment to a boil. In May 1773 he contrived a scheme to bail out the foundering East

India Company. The company had in its British warehouses some 17 million pounds of unsold tea. Under the Tea Act of 1773, the government would refund the British duty of twelvepence per pound on all tea shipped to the colonies and collect only the existing threepence duty payable at the colonial port. By this arrangement, colonists could get tea more cheaply than the English could. North miscalculated, however, in assuming that price alone would govern colonial reaction.

The Committees of Correspondence, backed by colonial merchants, alerted colonists to the British conspiracy to purchase their loyalty and passivity with cheap tea. Before the end of the year, large shipments of tea had gone out to major colonial ports. In Charleston it was unloaded into warehouses—and later sold to finance the Revolution. In Boston, however, Governor Hutchinson and Sam Adams engaged in a test of will. The ships' captains, alarmed by the rebel opposition, proposed to turn back, but Hutchinson refused permission until the tea was unloaded and the duty paid. Then, on December 16, 1773, a group of colonial Patriots, disguised as Mohawk Indians, boarded the three ships and threw the 342 chests of tea overboard—cheered on by a crowd along the shore. One participant later testified that Sam Adams and John Hancock were there.

Given a more tactful response from London, the Boston Tea Party might easily have undermined the radicals' credibility. Many people, especially merchants, abhorred the wanton destruction of property. British authorities, however, had reached the end of their patience. They were now convinced that the very existence of the empire was at stake. The rebels in Boston were inspiring what could become a widespread effort to evade royal authority and imperial regulations. A firm response was required. "The colonists must either submit or triumph," George III wrote to Lord North, and North hastened to make the king's judgment a self-fulfilling prophecy.

THE COERCIVE ACTS In April 1774 Parliament enacted four harsh measures designed by Lord North to discipline Boston. The Boston Port Act closed the harbor from June 1, 1774, until the lost tea was paid for. An Act for the Impartial Administration of Justice let the governor transfer to England the trial of any official accused of committing an offense in the line of duty. A new Quartering Act directed local authorities to provide lodging for British soldiers, in private homes if necessary. Finally, the Massachusetts Government Act made the colony's governing council and law-enforcement officers all appointive, rather than elective, declared that sheriffs would select jurors, and stipulated that no town meeting could be held without the governor's consent, except for the annual election of town officers. In May,

The Able Doctor, or America Swallowing the Bitter Draught

This 1774 engraving shows Lord North, the Boston Port Act in his pocket, pouring tea down America's throat and America spitting it back.

General Thomas Gage replaced Hutchinson as governor of Massachusetts and assumed command of the British forces in the colonies.

Designed to isolate Boston and make an example of the colony, the Coercive Acts of 1774 instead cemented colonial unity and emboldened resistance. At last, it seemed to the colonists, their worst fears were being confirmed. If these "Intolerable Acts," as the colonists labeled the Coercive Acts, were not resisted, they would eventually be applied to the other colonies.

Further confirmation of British "tyranny" came with news of the Quebec Act, passed in June 1774. That act provided that the government in Canada would not have a representative assembly and would be led by an appointed governor and council. It also gave a privileged position to the Catholic Church. Americans viewed the measure as another indicator of British authoritarianism. In addition, colonists pointed out that they had lost many lives in an effort to liberate the trans-Appalachian West from the control of French Catholics. Now the British seemed to be protecting papists at the expense of their own Protestant colonists. What was more, the act placed within the boundaries of Quebec the western lands north of the Ohio River, lands that Pennsylvania, Virginia, and Connecticut had long claimed.

Meanwhile, colonists rallied to the cause of besieged Boston, taking up collections and sending provisions. When the Virginia assembly met in

May 1774, a young member of the Committee of Correspondence, Thomas Jefferson, proposed to set aside June 1, the effective date of the Boston Port Act, as a day of fasting and prayer in Virginia. The irate British governor thereupon dissolved the Virginia assembly, whose members then retired to a nearby tavern and resolved to create a "Continental Congress" to represent all the colonies. Similar calls were coming from Providence, New York, Philadelphia, and elsewhere, and in June the Massachusetts assembly suggested a September meeting in Philadelphia. Shortly before George Washington left to represent Virginia at the meeting, he wrote to a friend that "the crisis is arrived when we must assert our rights, or submit to every imposition that can be heaped upon us, till custom and use shall make us as tame and abject slaves, as the blacks we rule over with such arbitrary sway."

THE CONTINENTAL CONGRESS   On September 5, 1774, the First Continental Congress assembled in Philadelphia. The fifty-five delegates represented twelve continental colonies, all but Georgia, Quebec, Nova Scotia, and the Floridas. Peyton Randolph of Virginia was elected president, and Charles Thomson, "the Sam Adams of Philadelphia," became secretary. In effect, the delegates functioned as a congress of ambassadors, gathered to join forces on common policies, neither to govern nor to rebel but to adopt and issue a series of resolutions and protests.

The Congress endorsed the radical Suffolk Resolves, resolutions that declared null and void the recent acts of Parliament intended to coerce the colonies, urged Massachusetts to arm for defense, and called for economic sanctions against British commerce. The Congress also adopted a Declaration of American Rights, which conceded only Parliament's right to regulate commerce and those matters that were strictly imperial affairs. It denied Parliament's authority with respect to internal colonial affairs and proclaimed the right of each assembly to determine the need for troops within its own province.

Finally, the Congress adopted the Continental Association of 1774, which recommended that every county, town, and city form committees to enforce a boycott of all British goods. These committees would become the organizational and communications network for the Revolutionary movement, connecting every locality to the leadership. The Continental Association also included provisions for the nonimportation of British goods (implemented in December 1774) and the nonexportation of American goods to Britain (to be implemented in September 1775 unless colonial grievances were addressed).

In London the king fumed. In late 1774 he wrote his prime minister that the "New England colonies are in a state of rebellion," and "blows must decide whether they are to be subject to this country or independent." British critics of the American actions reminded the colonists that Parliament had absolute sovereignty. Power could not be shared.

Parliament declared Massachusetts in rebellion and prohibited the New England colonies from trading with any nation outside the empire. Lord North's Conciliatory Resolution, adopted on February 27, 1775, was as far as they would go to avert a crisis. Under its terms, Parliament would levy taxes only to regulate trade and would grant to each colony the duties collected within its boundaries, provided the colonies would contribute voluntarily to a quota for defense of the empire. It was a formula not for peace but for new quarrels.

SHIFTING AUTHORITY

Events were already moving beyond conciliation. All through late 1774 and early 1775 the defenders of American rights were seizing the initiative. The unorganized Loyalists (or Tories), if they did not submit to nonimportation agreements, found themselves confronted with tar and feathers. The Continental Congress urged each colony to mobilize its militia. The militia organized special units of "Minutemen" to be ready for quick mobilization. Royal and proprietary officials were losing control as provincial congresses assumed authority and colonial militias organized and gathered arms and gunpowder. Still, British military officials remained smugly confident. Major John Pitcairn wrote home from Boston in March, "I am satisfied that one active campaign, a smart action, and burning two or three of their towns, will set everything to rights."

LEXINGTON AND CONCORD   Pitcairn soon had his chance. On April 14, 1775, General Thomas Gage, the British commander, received orders to suppress the "open rebellion." Gage decided to seize Sam Adams and John Hancock in Lexington and destroy the militia's supply depot at Concord, about twenty miles northwest of Boston. But local Patriots got wind of the plan, and on April 18 Boston's Committee of Safety sent silversmith Paul Revere and tanner William Dawes by separate routes on their famous ride to spread the alarm. Revere reached Lexington about midnight and alerted John Hancock and Samuel Adams. Joined by Dawes and Samuel Prescott, who had been visiting in Lexington, Revere rode on toward Concord. A British patrol intercepted the trio, but Prescott slipped through and continued to deliver the warning.

The Battle of Lexington

Amos Doolittle's impression of the Battle of Lexington as combat begins.

At dawn on April 19, the British advance guard found Captain John Parker and about seventy "Minutemen" lined up on the Lexington village green. Parker apparently intended only a silent protest, but Major Pitcairn rode onto the green, swung his sword, and brusquely yelled, "Disperse, you damned rebels! You dogs, run!" The Americans had already begun backing away when someone fired a pistol shot, whereupon the British soldiers loosed a volley into the Minutemen and then charged them with bayonets, leaving eight dead and ten wounded.

The British officers hastily reformed their men and proceeded to Concord. There the Americans had already carried off most of their valuable supplies, but the British destroyed what they could. In the meantime, American Patriots were swarming over the countryside, eager to wreak vengeance on the hated British troops. At Concord's North Bridge the growing American militia inflicted fourteen casualties on a British platoon, and by about noon the exhausted redcoats had begun marching back to Boston.

By then, however, the road back had turned into a gauntlet of death as the rebels from "every Middlesex village and farm" sniped at the redcoats from behind stone walls, trees, barns, and farmhouses all the way back to the Charlestown peninsula. By nightfall the redcoat survivors were under the protection of the fleet and army at Boston, having suffered over 250 killed or wounded; the Americans had lost less than 100. A British general reported to

London that the rebels, though untrained, had earned his respect: "Whoever looks upon them as an irregular mob will find himself much mistaken."

THE SPREADING CONFLICT   The Revolutionary War had begun. When the Second Continental Congress convened at Philadelphia on May 10, 1775, British-held Boston was under siege by Massachusetts militia units. On the very day that Congress met, a force of Green Mountain Boys under Ethan Allen of Vermont and Massachusetts volunteers under Benedict Arnold of Connecticut captured the strategic Fort Ticonderoga in upstate New York. In a prodigious feat of daring energy, the Americans then transported sixty captured British cannons down rivers and over ridges to support the siege of Boston.

The Continental Congress, with no legal authority and no resources, met amid reports of spreading warfare; it had little choice but to assume the role of Revolutionary government. The Congress accepted a request that it "adopt" the motley army gathered around Boston and on June 15 named George Washington to be general and commander in chief of a Continental army. He accepted on the condition that he receive no pay. The Congress fastened on the charismatic Washington because his service in the French and Indian War had made him one of the most experienced officers in America. The fact that he was from influential Virginia, the most populous province, heightened his qualifications.

On June 17, the very day that George Washington was commissioned, the colonial rebels and British troops engaged in their first major fight, the Battle of Bunker Hill. While the Continental Congress deliberated, both American and British forces around Boston had increased. Militiamen from Rhode Island, Connecticut, and New Hampshire joined in the siege. British reinforcements included three major generals: William Howe, Sir Henry Clinton, and John Burgoyne. On the day before the battle, Americans began to fortify the high ground of Charlestown peninsula, overlooking Boston. Breed's Hill was the battle location, nearer to Boston than Bunker Hill, the site first chosen (and the source of the battle's erroneous name).

With civilians looking on from rooftops and church steeples, the British attacked in the blistering heat, with 2,400 troops moving in tight formation through tall grass. The Americans, pounded by naval guns, watched from behind hastily built earthworks as the waves of brightly uniformed British troops advanced up the hill. Ordered not to fire until they could see "the whites of their eyes," the militiamen waited until the attackers had come within fifteen to twenty paces, then loosed a shattering volley. Through the cloud of oily smoke, the Americans could see fallen bodies "as thick as sheep

View of the Attack on Bunker's Hill

The Battle of Bunker Hill and the burning of Charlestown peninsula.

in a fold." The militiamen cheered as they watched the greatest soldiers in the world retreating in panic.

Within a half hour, however, the British had re-formed and attacked again. Another sheet of flames and lead greeted them, and the vaunted redcoats retreated a second time. Still, the proud British generals were determined not to be humiliated by the ragtag rustics. On the third attempt, when the colonials began to run out of gunpowder and were forced to throw stones, a bayonet charge ousted them. The British took the high ground, but at the cost of 1,054 casualties. Colonial losses were about 400. "A dear bought victory," recorded General Clinton, "another such would have ruined us."

The Battle of Bunker Hill had two profound effects. First, the high number of British casualties made the English generals more cautious in subsequent encounters with the Continental army. Second, Congress recommended that all able-bodied men enlist in a militia. This tended to divide the male population into Patriot and Loyalist camps. A middle ground was no longer tenable.

While Boston remained under siege, the Continental Congress held to the dimming hope of a compromise. On July 5 and 6, 1775, the delegates issued two major documents: an appeal to the king, thereafter known as the Olive Branch Petition, and a Declaration of the Causes and Necessity of

Taking Up Arms. The Olive Branch Petition, written by John Dickinson, professed continued loyalty to George III and begged him to restrain further hostilities pending a reconciliation. The declaration, also largely Dickinson's work, traced the history of the controversy, denounced the British for the unprovoked assault at Lexington, and rejected independence but affirmed the colonists' purpose to fight for their rights rather than submit to slavery. "Our cause is just," he declared. "Our Union is perfect." Such impassioned rhetoric failed to impress George III. On August 22 he declared the defiant colonists "open and avowed enemies." The next day he issued a proclamation of rebellion.

Before the end of July 1775, the Congress had authorized an ill-fated attack against British troops in the walled Canadian city of Quebec. One force, under General Richard Montgomery, advanced toward Quebec by way of Lake Champlain; another, under General Benedict Arnold, struggled through the Maine woods. The American units arrived outside Quebec in September, exhausted and hungry. Then they were ambushed by a silent killer: smallpox. "The small pox [is] very much among us," wrote one soldier. As the deadly virus raced through the American camp, General Montgomery faced a brutal dilemma. Most of his soldiers had signed up for short tours of duty, many of which were scheduled to expire at the end of the year. He could not afford to wait until spring for the smallpox to subside. Seeing little choice but to fight, Montgomery ordered a desperate attack on the British forces at Quebec during a blizzard, on December 31, 1775. The assault was a disaster. Montgomery was killed early in the battle and Benedict Arnold wounded. Over 400 Americans were taken prisoner. The rest of the Patriot force retreated to its camp outside the walled city and appealed to the Continental Congress for reinforcements.

The smallpox virus continued attacking both the Americans in the camp and their comrades taken captive by the British. As fresh troops arrived, they, too, fell victim to the deadly virus. Benedict Arnold warned George Washington in February 1776 that the runaway disease would soon lead to "the entire ruin of the Army." By May there were only 1,900 American soldiers left outside Quebec, and 900 of them were infected with smallpox. Sensing the weakness of the American force, the British attacked and sent the ragtag Patriots on a frantic retreat up the St. Lawrence River to the American-held city of Montreal and eventually back to New York and New England. The sick were left behind, but the smallpox virus traveled with the fleeing soldiers. Major General Horatio Gates later remarked that "every thing about this Army is infected with the Pestilence; The Clothes, The Blankets, the Air & the Ground they Walk on."

Quebec was the first military setback for the Revolutionaries. It would not be the last. And smallpox would continue to bedevil the American war effort. The veterans of the failed Canadian campaign brought home both smallpox and demoralizing stories about the disease, thus spreading the epidemic to civilians and making the recruitment of new soldiers more difficult. Men who might risk British gunfire balked at the more terrifying thought of contracting smallpox in a military camp.

As the fighting spread north into Canada and south into Virginia and the Carolinas, the Continental Congress appointed commissioners to negotiate peace treaties with Indian tribes, organized a Post Office Department, and formed a navy and marine corps.

When George Washington arrived outside Boston to take charge of the American forces after the Battle of Bunker Hill, the military situation was stalemated, and so it remained through the winter, until early March 1776. At that time American forces occupied Dorchester Heights, to the south of Boston, bringing the city under threat of bombardment with cannon and mortars. General William Howe, who had long since replaced Gage as British commander, reasoned that discretion was the better part of valor and retreated with his forces by water to Halifax. The last British troops, along with fearful American Loyalists, embarked from Boston on March 17, 1776. By that time British power had collapsed nearly everywhere, and the British faced not the suppression of a rebellion but the reconquest of a continent.

COMMON SENSE   In early 1776 Thomas Paine's pamphlet *Common Sense* was published anonymously in Philadelphia, transforming the revolutionary controversy. Born of Quaker parents, Paine had distinguished himself in England chiefly as a drifter, a failure in marriage and business. At age thirty-seven he had sailed for America with a letter of introduction from Benjamin Franklin and the purpose of setting up a school for young ladies. When the school did not work out, he moved into the political controversy as a freelance writer and, with *Common Sense,* proved himself the consummate Revolutionary rhetorician. Until his pamphlet appeared, the squabble had been mainly with Parliament, but Paine directly attacked allegiance to the monarchy, the last frayed connection to Britain. The common sense of the matter, to Paine, was that King George III and his advisers bore the responsibility for the malevolence toward the colonies. Americans should consult their own interests, abandon George III, and declare their independence: "The blood of the slain, the weeping voice of nature cries, 'TIS TIME TO PART."

INDEPENDENCE

Within three months more than 100,000 copies of Thomas Paine's pamphlet were in circulation across the colonies. "*Common Sense* is working a powerful change in the minds of men," George Washington noted. One by one the provincial governments authorized their delegates in the Continental Congress to take the final step. On June 7, 1776, Richard Henry Lee of Virginia moved "that these United Colonies are, and of right ought to be, free and independent states." South Carolina and Pennsylvania, however, initially opposed severing ties with England. After feverish lobbying by radical Patriots, the dissenters changed their minds and the resolution passed on July 2, a date that "will be the most memorable epoch in the history of America," John Adams wrote to his wife, Abigail. The memorable date, however, became July 4, 1776, when Congress adopted the Declaration of Independence, an eloquent statement of political philosophy that still retains its dynamic force.

JEFFERSON'S DECLARATION   Although Thomas Jefferson is often called the author of the Declaration of Independence, he is more accurately termed its draftsman. In June 1776 the Continental Congress appointed a committee of five men—Jefferson, Benjamin Franklin, John Adams, Robert Livingston of New York, and Roger Sherman of Connecticut—to develop a public explanation of the reasons for colonial discontent and to provide a rationale for independence. John Adams convened the committee on June 11. The group asked Adams and Jefferson to produce a first draft, whereupon Adams deferred to Jefferson because of the thirty-three-year-old Virginian's reputation as a superb writer.

During two days in mid-June 1776, in his rented lodgings in Philadelphia, Jefferson wrote the first statement of American grievances and principles. He drew primarily upon two sources: his own draft preamble to the Virginia Constitution, written a few weeks earlier, and George Mason's draft of Virginia's Declaration of Rights, which had appeared in Philadelphia newspapers in mid-June.

Jefferson shared his draft with the committee members, and they made several minor revisions to the opening paragraphs and to his listing of the charges against King George III. They submitted the document to the entire Congress on June 28, whereupon it was tabled until July 1. Over the next three days the legislators made eighty-six changes in Jefferson's declaration, including shortening its overall length by one fourth. Jefferson regretted many of the changes, but the legislative editing improved the declaration,

The Coming Revolution

The Continental Congress votes for independence on July 2, 1776.

making it more concise, accurate, and coherent—and, as a result, more powerful.

The Declaration of Independence is grounded in John Locke's contract theory of government—the theory, in Jefferson's words, that governments derived "their just Powers from the consent of the people," who were entitled to "alter or abolish" those that denied their "unalienable rights" to "life, Liberty, and the pursuit of Happiness." The appeal was no longer simply to "the rights of Englishmen" but to the broader "laws of Nature and Nature's God." The document set forth "a history of repeated injuries and usurpations, all having in direct object the establishment of an absolute Tyranny over these States." The "Representatives of the United States of America," therefore, declared the thirteen "United Colonies" to be "Free and Independent States."

"WE ALWAYS HAD GOVERNED OURSELVES"   So it had come to this, thirteen years after Britain had won domination of North America. Historians have advanced numerous explanations of what caused the Revolutionary controversy: "unfair" regulation of trade, the restrictions on settling western lands, the tax controversy, the debts to British merchants, the growth of a national consciousness, the lack of representation in Parliament, ideologies of Whiggery and the Enlightenment, and the abrupt shift from a mercantile to an "imperial" policy after 1763.

Each factor contributed something to the collective colonial grievances that rose to a climax in a gigantic failure of British statesmanship. A conflict between British sovereignty and American rights had come to a point of confrontation that adroit statesmanship might have avoided, sidestepped, or outflanked. Irresolution and vacillation in the British ministry finally gave way to the stubborn determination to force an issue long permitted to drift. The colonists saw these developments as the conspiracy of a corrupted oligarchy—and finally, they decided, of a despotic king—to impose an "absolute Tyranny."

Perhaps the last word on how the Revolution came about should belong to an obscure participant, Levi Preston, a Minuteman from Danvers, Massachusetts. Asked sixty-seven years after Lexington and Concord about British oppressions, the ninety-one-year-old veteran responded: "What were they? Oppressions? I didn't feel them." When asked about the hated Stamp Act, he claimed that he "never saw one of those stamps" and was "certain I never paid a penny for one of them." Nor had he ever heard of John Locke or his theories. "We read only the Bible, the Catechism, Watts's Psalms and Hymns, and the Almanack." When his exasperated interviewer asked why, then, he had support the Revolution, Preston replied, "Young man, what we meant in going for those redcoats was this: we always had governed ourselves, and we always meant to. They didn't mean we should."

MAKING CONNECTIONS

- The American Revolutionary rhetoric was important not only for fighting the Revolution: it also provided the framework for the creation of state and national governments after independence was won. This framework will be discussed in the next two chapters.

- The discussion of "Discontent on the Frontier" showed the tension between colonists in the more urban eastern areas of several states and those on the western frontier. These tensions will reappear in several chapters—for example, in the Federalist–anti-Federalist debate over ratification of the Constitution (in Chapter 7).

FURTHER READING

For a narrative survey of the events leading to the Revolution, see Edward Countryman's *The American Revolution*, rev. ed. (2003). For Great Britain's perspective on the imperial conflict, see Sir Lewis Bernstein Namier's *England in the Age of the American Revolution,* 2nd ed. (1961) and Ian R. Christie, *Crisis of Empire* (1966).

The intellectual foundations of revolt are traced in Bernard Bailyn's *The Ideological Origins of the American Revolution,* enlarged ed. (1992) and in John Phillip Reid's *Constitutional History of the American Revolution: The Authority of Rights* (1987). To understand how these views were connected to organized protest, see Pauline Maier's *From Resistance to Revolution: Colonial Radicals and the Development of American Opposition to Britain, 1765–1776* (1972).

A number of books deal with specific events in the crisis. Oliver M. Dickerson's *The Navigation Acts and the American Revolution* (1951) stresses the change from trade regulation to taxation in 1764. Edmund S. Morgan and Helen M. Morgan's *The Stamp Act Crisis: Prologue to Revolution,* rev. ed. (1962) gives the colonial perspective on that crucial event. Also valuable are Hiller B. Zobel's *The Boston Massacre* (1970), Benjamin Woods Labaree's *The Boston Tea Party, 1773: Catalyst for Revolution* (1964), and David Ammerman's *In the Common Cause: American Response to the Coercive Acts of 1774* (1974).

Events west of the Appalachian Mountains are chronicled concisely by Jack M. Sosin in *The Revolutionary Frontier, 1763–1783* (1967). Pauline Maier's *American Scripture: Making the Declaration of Independence* (1997) is the best analysis of the framing of that crucial document.

Part Two

BUILDING

A

NATION

1776

States initiate their own constitutions (1776–1787)

Battle of Saratoga (1777)

British occupy Philadelphia; George Washington's troops winter at Valley Forge, Pennsylvania (1777–1778)

Americans sign the Treaty of Alliance with France (1778)

British attack French ships, drawing France into the American Revolution (1778)

Spain enters the American Revolution as an ally of France (1779)

1780

Federalists and anti-Federalists debate the role of the federal government (1780s–1790s)

Americans and French defeat British at Yorktown (1781)

U.S. operates under the Articles of Confederation (1781–1789)

Treaty of Paris ends the American Revolution (1783)

Constitutional Convention (1787)

Shays's Rebellion pits a debtor army against the republic's elite, leading to a victory for conservatism (1787)

Alexander Hamilton, John Jay, and James Madison publish The Federalist, defending the idea of a strong central government (1787–1788)

George Washington serves as the first U.S. president (1789–1797)

Industrial Revolution begins in England (ca. 1780)

James Watt installs a steam engine powered loom in an English cotton-spinning factory (1785)

British iron production increases from 17,000 tons (1740) to 68,000 tons (1788)

British prisoners are first transported to Australia (1788)

French Revolution begins (1789)

1790

Debate over national bank spawns the first national political parties, the Federalists and the Republicans (1790s)

Bill of Rights is adopted (1791)

Jay's Treaty settles most major issues between U.S. and England (1795)

Pinckney's Treaty challenges Spain's presence in North America (1795)

Treaty of Greenville opens up white settlement in the Northwest Territory (1795)

George Washington's farewell address advises against permanent foreign entanglements (1796)

John Adams serves as U.S. president (1797–1801)

Congress creates the Department of the Navy and a new army (1798)

Alien and Sedition Acts limit freedom of speech and the press (1798)

French national convention declares France a republic (1792)

French Revolution results in the execution of King Louis XVI (1793)

England and France fight a prolonged war (1793–1815)

England announces its orders in council, allowing the British navy to seize the cargo of ships bound for, or coming from, French Caribbean possessions (1793)

XYZ affair brings U.S. and France to the brink of war (1797–1798)

SOCIAL

100,000 colonists (more than 3 percent of the population) remain loyal to the crown and flee America during the Revolutionary War (1770s–1780s)

The war disrupts life in the colonies, destroying crops and livestock and making family life more difficult (1770s–1780s)

55,000 slaves flee to freedom during the war (1770s–1780s)

John Trumbull, Charles Willson Peale, and other American artists depict events of the war and its leaders (1770s–1780s)

17 colleges are established in the colonies (1770s–1780s)

Independence Day becomes the most important public ritual in the U.S. (1780s)

Indian tribes lose huge parcels of land to U.S. expansion (1780s)

Women emerge from the Revolution with no political rights (1783)

Congress reserves income from land sales for support of schools (1785)

Virginia Statute of Religious Freedom (1786)

Delegates to the Constitutional Convention make no formal mention of women's rights, nor do they use the word *slavery* in the Constitution (1787)

U.S. extends from the Atlantic Ocean to the Mississippi River and has a population of nearly 4 million (1789)

Women's rights activist Judith Sargent Murray calls for "mutuality in marriage," reflecting a new sense of women's role in society (1790)

Free Slave Act protects freed slaves from kidnapping or seizure (1793)

Shawnee, Ottawa, Chippewa, and Potawatomi warriors are defeated at the Battle of Fallen Timbers (1794)

Naturalization Act lengthens the residency requirement for citizenship (1798)

Alien Act and Alien Enemies Act empower the president to deport or imprison dangerous aliens (1798)

ECONOMIC

1776

British occupy major colonial ports, disrupting trade (1776–1781)

Continental Congress has difficulty financing and supplying the Continental army (1776–1781)

Price for a bushel of wheat in the colonies rises from less than $1 (1777) to $80 (1779) as a result of the war

1780

Land reforms and new political rights establish the basis for greater social and political equality and for a middle class (1780s–1800s)

U.S. suffers acute economic downturn (1770s–1790s)

U.S. resumes trade with England (1783)

Trade with China begins (1784–1785)

Land Ordinance of 1785 outlines procedures for land surveys and sale (1785)

Seven states issue paper currency to increase available credit (1785–1786)

Agricultural crisis leads to a revolt against high taxes and a demand for debt and tax relief (1787)

Northwest Ordinance sets a precedent for future U.S. expansion (1787)

Congress grants land as payment to Revolutionary War veterans (1787)

U.S. has heavy federal debt and almost no federal revenue (1789)

1790

U.S. commerce and exports far surpass colonial trade (1790)

Hamilton's "Report on Manufactures" recommends protective tariffs to foster and protect U.S. industries (1791)

Bank of the United States is established (1791)

Vigilantes in Pennsylvania lead the Whiskey Rebellion in opposition to Hamilton's 1791 excise tax (1794)

Land Act doubles the price of land, benefiting speculators (1796)

1800

Thomas Jefferson and Aaron Burr are tied in vote for the president; the election is thrown into the House of Representatives (1800)

Judiciary Act is passed by lame-duck Congress to ensure Federalist control of the judiciary (1801)

Thomas Jefferson serves as U.S. president (1801–1809)

Marbury v. Madison establishes that the Supreme Court can invalidate federal laws (1803)

U.S. purchases Louisiana Territory from France; Lewis and Clark depart St. Louis to explore the West (1803)

Jefferson claims executive privilege and withholds documents from the Burr conspiracy trial (1807)

James Madison serves as U.S. president (1809–1817)

1810 War of 1812 (1812–1815)

U.S. troops occupy West Florida (1813)

British burn the White House and the Capitol (1814)

Treaty of Ghent ends War of 1812 (1814)

U.S. defeats England at the Battle of New Orleans (1815)

Barbary pirates hold U.S. ships for ransom; Jefferson blockades Tripoli (1801–1805)

Slave rebellion overturns French rule in Haiti (1801)

Napoleonic Empire (1804–1815)

Napoléon defeats Russia and Austria and controls western Europe (1805)

England defeats French and Spanish fleets in the Battle of Trafalgar, securing British control of the high seas (1805)

England sets up a "paper blockade" of European ports (1806)

British steel production reaches 260,000 tons (1806)

England again begins to interfere with U.S. shipping and resumes the practice of impressment (1807)

French enact the continental system and blockade English ports (1806–1807)

Latin America gains independence from Europe (1810–1824)

George Stephenson invents the first locomotive (1814)

Congress of Vienna establishes the diplomatic principle of the balance of power (1814–1815)

Foreign slave trade is outlawed (1808)
300,000 slaves are illegally smuggled into
the U.S. (1808–1861)

U.S. shipping and Treasury revenues increase as a result of wars in Europe
(early 1800s)
Land Act reduces minimum sale of land,
allowing purchases by ordinary settlers
(1800)
Jefferson repeals the whiskey tax and other
Federalist excises (1802)
Enticed by the Lewis and Clark expedition,
trappers and traders travel west of the
Mississippi River to exploit the region's
abundance of pelts (1806 and after)

1800

Embargo Act (1807) causes exports to
plummet from $108 million in 1806 to
$22 million in 1808
Nonintercourse Act reopens trade with all
countries except France and Great
Britain (1809)

Tecumseh attempts to unite natives in an
Indian confederacy, loses the Battle of
Tippecanoe, and flees to Canada (1811)
Francis Scott Key pens "The Star-Spangled
Banner" (1814)

Macon's bill reopens trade with Britain and
France (1810)
Improved transportation and more readily
available credit spawn industrialization,
expressed in a shift to commercial farm-
ing and manufacturing (1810–1840s)
Construction of the National Road (Cum-
berland Road) begins (1811)
Charter of the Bank of the United States
expires (1811)
First fully mechanized U.S. factory opens at
Waltham, Massachusetts (1813)

1810

While it was one thing for Patriot leaders to declare American independence from British authority, it was quite another to win it on the battlefield. Barely one third of the colonists actively supported the Revolution, the political stability of the new nation was uncertain, and George Washington found himself in command of a poorly supplied, untested army.

But the Revolutionary movement would persevere and prevail. The skill and fortitude of Washington and his lieutenants enabled the Americans to exploit their geographic advantages. Equally important was the intervention of the French on behalf of the Revolutionary cause. The Franco-American alliance proved decisive. In 1783, after eight years of sporadic fighting and heavy human and financial losses, the British gave up the fight and their American colonies.

Amid the Revolutionary turmoil the Patriots faced the daunting task of forming new governments for themselves. Their deeply engrained resentment of British imperial rule led them to grant considerable powers to the individual states. As Thomas Jefferson declared, "Virginia, Sir, is my country." Such powerful local ties help explain why the colonists focused their attention on creating new state constitutions rather than a national government. The Articles of Confederation, ratified in 1781, provided only the semblance of national authority. All power to make and execute laws remained with the states.

After the end of the Revolutionary War, the flimsy government authorized by the Articles of Confederation proved inadequate to the needs of the new—and expanding—nation. This realization led to the Constitutional Convention of 1787. The process of drafting and ratifying the new constitution prompted a debate on the relative significance of national power, local control, and individual freedom that has provided the central theme of American political thought ever since.

The American Revolution involved much more than the apportionment of political power, however. It also unleashed social forces and posed social questions that would help reshape the very fabric of American culture. What would be the role of women African Americans, and Native Americans in the new republic? How would the contrasting economies of the various regions of the new United States be developed? Who would control the vast territories to the west of the original thirteen states? How would the new republic relate to the other nations of the world?

These controversial questions helped foster the first national political parties in the United States. During the 1790s Federalists, led by Alexander Hamilton, and Republicans, led by Thomas Jefferson and James Madison, engaged in a heated debate about the political and economic future of the new nation. With Jefferson's election as president in 1800, the Republicans gained the upper hand in national politics for the next quarter century. In the process they presided over a maturing society that aggressively expanded westward at the expense of the Native Americans, ambivalently embraced industrial development, fitfully engaged in a second war with Great Britain, and ominously witnessed a growing sectional controversy over slavery.

6

THE AMERICAN
REVOLUTION

FOCUS QUESTIONS

· What were the American and British military strategies and the Revolutionary War's major turning points?

· What was the effect of the war on the home front?

· Why is the American Revolution considered a "social revolution" in matters of social equality, slavery, the rights of women, and religious freedom?

· How did the Revolution mark the beginnings of a distinctive American culture?

To answer these questions and access additional review material, please visit www.wwnorton.com/studyspace.

ew foreign observers thought the upstart American Revolutionaries could win a war against the world's greatest empire. The Americans lost most of the battles in the Revolutionary War but eventually forced the British to sue for peace and grant the colonists their independence. The surprising result testified to the tenacity of the Patriots, to the importance of the French alliance, and to the peculiar difficulties facing the British as they tried to conduct a demanding military campaign thousands of miles from home.

The American Revolution had unexpected consequences affecting political, economic, and social life. While securing American independence, it generated a new sense of nationalism and created a unique system of self-governance; it also began a process of societal definition and change that has yet to run its course. The turmoil of revolution upset traditional class and social relationships and helped transform the lives of people who had long been relegated to the periphery of historical concern—African Americans, women, and Indians. In important ways, then, the Revolution was much more than simply a war for independence. It was an engine for political experimentation and social transformation.

1776: WASHINGTON'S NARROW ESCAPE

On July 2, 1776, the day that Congress voted for independence, British redcoats landed on Staten Island, across New York Harbor from Manhattan. By mid-August, Major General William Howe had some 32,000 men at his disposal, including 9,000 Hessians (German soldiers hired by the British), the largest force mustered by the British in the eighteenth century. General Washington transferred most of his men from New York to Boston, but he could muster only about 19,000 poorly trained soldiers and militiamen. Such a force could not defend New York, but Congress wanted it held. This meant that Washington had to expose his men to entrapments from which they escaped more by luck and Howe's caution than by any strategic genius of the American commander. The inexperienced George Washington was still learning the art of generalship, and the New York campaign afforded some costly lessons.

FIGHTING IN NEW YORK AND NEW JERSEY By invading and occupying New York, the British sought to sever New England from the rest of the rebellious colonies. In late August the British inflicted heavy losses and forced Washington to evacuate Long Island in order to reunite his divided forces. Only a timely rainstorm kept the British fleet out of the East River and made possible a nighttime withdrawal of American forces to Manhattan.

Had the British moved quickly, they could have trapped Washington's army in lower Manhattan. But the main American force of 6,000 men withdrew northward to the mainland of New York, crossed the Hudson River, and retreated across New Jersey and over the Delaware River into Pennsylvania. In the retreating army marched a volunteer from England, Thomas Paine. Having opened an eventful year with his inspiring pamphlet *Common Sense,* he would now compose *The American Crisis,* in which he exhorted Americans with the immortal line "These are the times that try men's souls." The eloquent pamphlet, ordered read in the American army camps, helped restore shaken morale—as events would soon do more decisively.

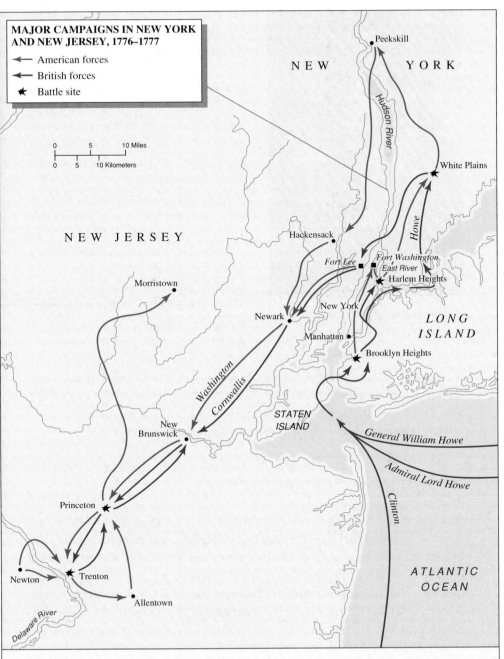

MAJOR CAMPAIGNS IN NEW YORK AND NEW JERSEY, 1776–1777

← American forces

← British forces

★ Battle site

Why did Washington lead his army from Brooklyn Heights to Manhattan and from there to New Jersey? How could Howe have ended the rebellion in New York? What is the significance of the battle at Trenton?

George Washington at Princeton

By Charles Willson Peale.

General Howe, firmly—and comfortably—based in New York City (which the British held throughout the war), followed conventional practice by settling down with his army to wait out the winter. But George Washington was not yet ready to hibernate; instead, he seized the initiative. On Christmas night 1776 American soldiers crossed the icy Delaware River into New Jersey. Near dawn at Trenton, the Americans surprised a garrison of 1,500 Hessians. The daring raid was a total rout, from which only 500 royal soldiers escaped death or capture. Washington's men suffered only six casualties, one of whom was Lieutenant James Monroe, the future president. A week later, at nearby Princeton, the Americans repelled three regiments of redcoats before taking refuge in winter quarters at Morristown, in the hills of northern New Jersey. After repeated American defeats the campaigns of 1776 had ended with two minor but uplifting victories. Howe had missed his great chance—indeed, several chances—to bring the rebellion to a speedy end.

AMERICAN SOCIETY AT WAR

DIVIDED LOYALTIES After the British army occupied New York, many civilians assumed that the rebellion was collapsing, and thousands hastened to sign an oath of allegiance to the crown. But the events at Trenton and Princeton reversed the outlook. With the British withdrawal, New Jersey quickly reverted to rebel control. Nonetheleas, many colonists remained Tory in outlook. During or after the war roughly 100,000 of them, more than 3 percent of the total population, left America for Canada or Britain. American opinion concerning the Revolution divided in three ways: Patriots, or Whigs (as the Revolutionaries called themselves), Tories, and an indifferent middle group swayed by the better organized and more energetic radicals.

Tories were concentrated mainly in the seaport cities, but they came from all walks of life. Almost all governors, judges, and other royal officials were loyal to Britain; most Anglican ministers also preferred the mother country. Where planter aristocrats tended to be Whigs, as in North Carolina, back-country farmers (many of them recently Regulators) leaned toward the Tories. When Patriots took control of an area, Loyalists faced a difficult choice: accompany the British and leave behind their property, or stay behind and face the wrath of the Patriots. In this sense the War for Independence was also very much a civil war that divided families and communities. The fratricidal hatred that often goes with civil war gave rise to bloodcurdling atrocities in the backcountry of New York and Pennsylvania and in Georgia, where Tory militiamen and their Indian allies went marauding against frontier Whigs. Whigs responded in kind against the Loyalists.

MILITIA AND ARMY Since the end of the French and Indian War, the colonies had required all adult males between the ages of fifteen and sixty to enroll in their local militia company, attend monthly drills, and turn out on short notice for emergencies. When fighting erupted between the British and the Revolutionaries, members of community militias had to choose sides.

American militiamen served two purposes. They were a home guard, defending their community, and they augmented the Continental army. Dressed in hunting shirts and armed with muskets, they preferred to ambush their opponents or engage them in hand-to-hand combat rather than fight in

American Militia

This sketch of the militiamen by a French soldier at Yorktown shows "one of those ubiquitous American frontiersman-turned-soldier" (second from right).

traditional formations. They also tended to kill unnecessarily and to torture prisoners. To repel an attack, the militia somehow materialized; the danger past, it evaporated, for there were chores to do at home.

The Continental army was on the whole better trained and more motivated than the militias. Although many soldiers were attracted by bounties of land or cash and some deserted, most of those who persevered were animated by genuine patriotic fervor and a thirst for adventure that enabled them to survive the horrors of combat and the tedium of camp life. Unlike the full-time professional soldiers in the British army, George Washington's Continental army, which fluctuated in size from 5,000 to 20,000, was populated mostly by citizen-soldiers, poor native-born Americans or immigrants who had been indentured servants or convicts.

FINANCIAL STRAINS AND SMALLPOX The new Continental Congress struggled to provide the army with adequate supplies. None of the states contributed more than a part of its share, and Congress reluctantly let army agents take supplies directly from farmers in return for certificates promising future payment. To pay for the war, Congress and the states printed paper money. With goods scarce, prices in terms of paper dollars, or "Continentals," rose sharply.

During the harsh winter at Morristown, New Jersey (1776–1777), George Washington's army nearly disintegrated as terms of enlistment expired and deserters fled the hardships of brutally cold weather, inadequate food, and widespread disease. Smallpox continued to wreak havoc among the American armies. "The small Pox! The small Pox!" John Adams wrote to his wife, Abigail. "What shall We do with it?" By 1777 George Washington had come to view the virus with greater dread than "the Sword of the Enemy." On any given day, one fourth of the American troops were deemed unfit for duty, usually because of smallpox. Some Americans suspected that the British were practicing biological warfare by sending infected civilians and clothing behind the American lines.

The threat of smallpox to the war effort was so great that in early 1777 Washington ordered a mass inoculation, which he managed to keep secret from British intelligence. Inoculating an entire army was an enormous and risky undertaking. Each soldier had to be interviewed to determine whether he had ever had smallpox. Then those who believed they had never been infected were inoculated. The virus was implanted in an incision, usually on the arm or hand. For unknown reasons the resulting smallpox produced less severe symptoms than natural infections—fewer pustules, less scarring, and far fewer deaths. Inoculated soldiers had to be quarantined while the virus ran its course, but the infected soldiers were thereafter immune to the disease. Washington's daring gamble paid off. One of the 400 Connecticut soldiers who was inoculated in the summer of 1777 reported its success: "We lost none. I had the smallpox favorably as did the rest." The successful inoculation of the American army marks one of Washington's greatest strategic accomplishments of the war.

Only about 1,000 soldiers stuck out the winter in New Jersey. With the spring thaw, however, recruits began arriving to claim the bounty of $20 and 100 acres of land offered by Congress to those who would enlist for three years or for the duration of the conflict, if less. With some 9,000 regular troops, George Washington began sparring and feinting with British forces in northern New Jersey.

BEHIND THE LINES   Civilians saw their lives profoundly changed by the Revolutionary War. British forces occupied the major cities (Boston, New York, Philadelphia, Charleston, Savannah), towns and villages were destroyed, crops and livestock confiscated, families disrupted, and husbands and fathers killed or maimed.

While some civilians viewed the hardships as a patriotic duty, others saw in the Revolution a means of self-aggrandizement rather than self-sacrifice. The inflation in prices for basic foods and products created new opportunities for quick profits and entrepreneurial chicanery. Robert Morris, a prominent Philadelphia merchant who became treasurer of the Congress upon the condition that he continue his private ventures, told a colleague that "there never has been so fair an opportunity for making a large fortune since I have been conversant in the world."

The poor suffered most amid the disruptions and skyrocketing prices. A bushel of wheat that sold for less than $1 in 1777 brought $80 two years later. Many consumers appealed to authorities to institute price controls so they could afford basic necessities. Others took more direct action. In Boston, women paraded through the streets a merchant accused of hoarding while "a large concourse of men stood amazed." The poor saw themselves as victims of gouging merchants and retailers. No longer willing to defer quietly to the discrimination, they grabbed the opportunity afforded by the Revolution to claim new economic and political rights. To Revolutionary leaders such as John Adams, the "democratical" demands put forward by the laboring classes were as odious as British regulatory measures. The specter of mechanics and laborers exercising political power horrified him. The American people, he and others insisted, must accept social inequality as a fact of human existence and defer to the leadership of their betters. The "one thing" absolutely required of a new republic was "a decency, and respect, and veneration introduced for persons of authority."

1777: SETBACKS FOR THE BRITISH

Indecision, overconfidence, and poor communications plagued British military planning in the campaigns of 1777. The profoundly confident "Gentleman Johnny" Burgoyne proposed to bisect the colonies. His men would advance southward from Canada to the Hudson River while another force moved eastward from Fort Oswego, on Lake Ontario, down the Mohawk Valley. The British general Howe decided to move against the Patriot capital, Philadelphia, expecting the Pennsylvania Tories to rally to the crown and secure the colony.

Washington, sensing Howe's purpose, withdrew most of his men from New Jersey to meet the new threat. At Brandywine Creek, south of Philadelphia, the British outmaneuvered and routed Washington's forces on September 11, and fifteen days later British troops occupied Philadelphia. Washington counterattacked in a dense fog at Germantown on October 4, but British reinforcements from Philadelphia under General Lord Charles Cornwallis arrived in time to repulse the Americans. Washington's army retired to winter quarters at Valley Forge, Pennsylvania, while Howe and his men remained for the winter in the relative comfort of Philadelphia, twenty miles away. Howe's plan had succeeded, up to a point. He had taken Philadelphia—or as Benjamin Franklin put it, Philadelphia had taken him. But the Tories there proved fewer than Howe had expected, and his decision to move on Philadelphia from the south, by way of Chesapeake Bay, put his forces even farther from Burgoyne's army in the north. Meanwhile, Burgoyne was stumbling into disaster in northern New York.

SARATOGA   General Burgoyne moved south toward Lake Champlain in 1777 with about 7,000 men, his mistress, and a baggage train that included some thirty carts carrying his personal trappings and a large supply of champagne. A powerful force on paper, the expedition was in fact much too cumbersome to be effective in the dense forests and rugged terrain of upstate New York. Burgoyne sent part of his army down the St. Lawrence River with Lieutenant Colonel Barry St. Leger, and at Fort Oswego they were joined by a force of Iroquois allies. The combined group headed east toward Albany. When they met the more mobile Americans, the British suffered two serious reversals.

At Oriskany, New York, on August 6, 1777, a band of militiamen thwarted an ambush by Tories and Indians and gained time for Benedict Arnold to bring 1,000 soldiers to the relief of Fort Stanwix, which had been under siege by St. Leger. Convinced they faced an even greater force than they actually did, the Indians deserted, and the Mohawk Valley was secured for the Patriot forces. To the east, at Bennington, Vermont, on August 16, New England militiamen

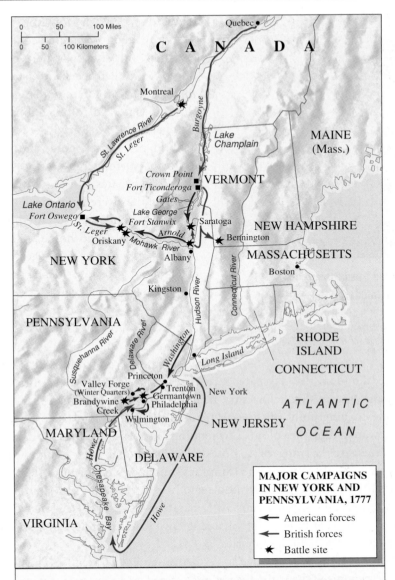

MAJOR CAMPAIGNS IN NEW YORK AND PENNSYLVANIA, 1777

← American forces

← British forces

★ Battle site

What were the consequences of Burgoyne's strategy of dividing the colonies with two British forces? How did life in Washington's camp at Valley Forge transform the American army? Why was Saratoga a turning point in the American Revolution?

General John Burgoyne

Commander of England's northern forces. Burgoyne and most of his British troops surrendered to the Americans at Saratoga on October 17, 1777.

repulsed a British foraging party. American reinforcements continued to gather, and after two sharp clashes Burgoyne pulled back to Saratoga, where American forces under General Horatio Gates surrounded him. On October 17, 1777, Burgoyne, resplendent in his scarlet, gold, and white uniform, surrendered to the plain-blue-coated Gates. Most of Burgoyne's 5,700 soldiers were imprisoned in Virginia, but Gentleman Johnny himself was permitted to go home, where he received an icy reception. The victory at Saratoga proved critically important to the American cause.

ALLIANCE WITH FRANCE On December 2, 1777, news of the surprising American triumph at Saratoga reached London; two days later it reached Paris, where it was celebrated almost as if it were a French victory. Its impact on the French made Saratoga a decisive turning point of the war. In 1776 the French had taken their first step toward aiding the colonists by sending fourteen ships with military supplies crucial to the Americans; most of the Continental army's gunpowder in the first years of the war came from that source. Besides arms, artillery, and ammunition, the French had also secretly sent clothing, shoes, and other supplies to help the Americans. After Saratoga the French saw their chance to strike a sharper blow at their hated enemy, Britain, and entered into serious negotiations with the Americans.

On February 6, 1778, France and America signed two treaties. The first officially recognized the United States and offered trade concessions, including important privileges to American shipping. The second agreed, first, that if France entered the war, both countries would fight until American independence was won; second, that neither would conclude a "truce or peace" without the consent of the other; and third, that each guaranteed the other's possessions in America "from the present time and forever against all other powers." France further bound itself to seek neither Canada nor other British possessions on the mainland of North America.

By June 1778 British vessels had fired on French ships, and the two nations were at war. In 1779, after extracting promises from the French to help it regain territories taken by the British in the previous war, including Gibraltar, Spain entered the war as an ally of France but not of the United States. The following year, Britain declared war on the Dutch, who persisted in carrying on a profitable trade with the French and shot Americans. The rebel farmers at Concord had indeed fired a shot "heard round the world." The American fight for independence had expanded into a world war, and the fighting now spread to the Mediterranean, Africa, India, the West Indies, and the high seas.

1778: BOTH SIDES REGROUP

THE REVOLUTIONARY ARMY AT VALLEY FORGE   For George Washington's army, bivouacked at Valley Forge, near Philadelphia, the winter of 1777–1778 was a season of intense suffering. The American force, encamped in crowded, lice-infested huts, endured cold, hunger, and disease. Some troops lacked shoes and blankets. Their makeshift log-and-mud huts offered little protection from the howling winds and bitter cold. Most of the army's horses died of exposure or starvation. By February 7,000 troops were too ill for duty. More than 2,500 soldiers died at Valley Forge; another 1,000 deserted. Fifty officers resigned on one December day. Several hundred more left before winter's end. By March the once-gaunt troops at Valley Forge saw their strength restored. Their improved health enabled Washington to begin a rigorous training program designed to bring unity and order to his motley force. By the end of March 1778, the ragtag soldiers were beginning to resemble a professional army. Moreover, as winter drew to an end, the army's morale gained strength from congressional promises of extra pay and bonuses after the war and from the news of the French alliance.

PEACE OVERTURES AND THE EVACUATION OF PHILADELPHIA After Saratoga, Lord North, the British prime minister, knew that winning the war was unlikely, but the king refused to let him either resign or make peace. On March 16, 1778, the House of Commons adopted a program that in effect granted all the American demands prior to independence. Parliament repealed the Townshend tea duty, the Massachusetts Government Act, and the Prohibitory Act, which had closed the colonies to commerce. It then dispatched a peace commission to negotiate an end to the war, but its members did not reach Philadelphia until after Congress had ratified the French treaties. Congress refused to begin any negotiations until American independence was recognized or British forces withdrawn, neither of which the royal commissioners could promise.

Unbeknownst to the British negotiators, the crown had already authorized the evacuation of British troops from Philadelphia, a withdrawal that further weakened what little bargaining power the commissioners had. After Saratoga, General Howe resigned his command, and Sir Henry Clinton replaced him. Fearing a blockade by the French fleet that had sailed from France in June 1778, Clinton pulled his troops out of Philadelphia and sent them to New York.

As General Clinton's forces marched eastward toward New York, Washington pursued them across New Jersey. On June 28 he engaged the British in an indecisive battle at Monmouth Court House. Clinton's forces then slipped away to New York City while Washington's army took up a position at White Plains, north of the city. From that time on, the northern theater, scene of the major campaigns and battles in the first years of the war, settled into a long stalemate.

ACTIONS ON THE FRONTIER   The one major American success of 1778 occurred far from the New Jersey battlefields. Out to the west, at Forts Niagara and Detroit, the British under Colonel William Hamilton had incited frontier Tories and Indians to raid western settlements and had offered to pay for American scalps. To end the attacks, young George Rogers Clark took 175 frontiersmen on flatboats down the Ohio River in early 1778. They marched through the woods and on the evening of July 4 surprised the British at Kaskaskia (in present-day Illinois). At the end of the year, Clark marched his men (almost half of them French volunteers) through icy rivers and flooded prairies, sometimes in water neck deep, and captured an astonished British garrison at Vincennes (in present-day Indiana).

Meanwhile, Tories and Iroquois in western Pennsylvania continued to terrorize frontier settlements through the summer of 1778. In response, General Washington dispatched an expedition of 4,000 men to the area. At Newton, New York (near Elmira), the American force defeated the only serious opposition on August 29, 1779, and proceeded to carry out Washington's instruction that the Iroquois country be not "merely overrun but destroyed." The American troops burned about forty Indian villages, together with their orchards and food stores. The destruction broke the power of the Iroquois federation for all time, but sporadic encounters with various tribes of the region continued to the end of the war.

In the Kentucky territory, Daniel Boone and his small band of settlers risked constant attack by the Shawnees and their British and Tory allies. During the Revolution they survived frequent ambushes, at least seven skirmishes, and three pitched battles. In 1778 Boone and some thirty men, aided by their wives and children, held off an assault by more than 400 Indians at Boonesborough.

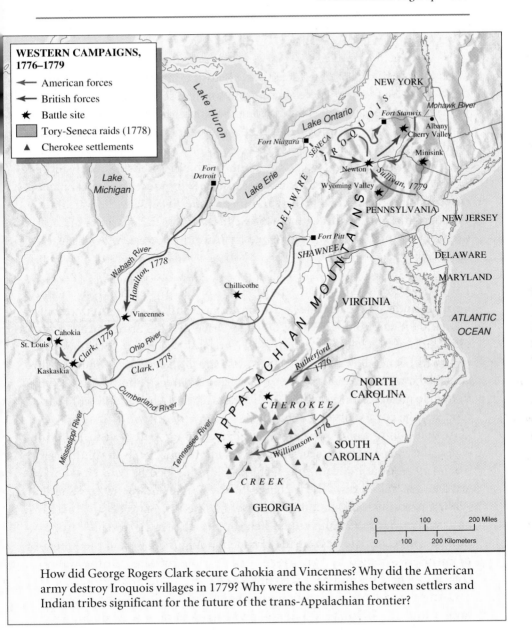

WESTERN CAMPAIGNS, 1776–1779

◄━━ American forces

◄━ British forces

✱ Battle site

▨ Tory-Seneca raids (1778)

▲ Cherokee settlements

How did George Rogers Clark secure Cahokia and Vincennes? Why did the American army destroy Iroquois villages in 1779? Why were the skirmishes between settlers and Indian tribes significant for the future of the trans-Appalachian frontier?

Despite such ferocious fighting and dangerous circumstances, the white settlers refused to leave Kentucky. By thus weakening the major Indian tribes along the frontier, the American Revolution cleared the way for rapid settlement of the trans-Appalachian West after the war ended.

THE WAR IN THE SOUTH

At the end of 1778, the focus of the British military action shifted suddenly to the South. The whole region from Virginia southward had been free of major action since 1776. Now it would become the focus of the war as the British tested King George's belief that a sleeping Tory power in the South needed only the presence of a few redcoats to be awakened. From the point of view of British imperial goals, the southern colonies were ultimately more important than the northern ones because they produced valuable staple crops such as tobacco, indigo, tar, and turpentine. Eventually the war in the Carolinas not only involved opposing British and American armies but also degenerated into brutal guerrilla-style civil conflicts between Loyalists and Patriots.

THE CAROLINAS   In November 1778 British forces took Savannah, Georgia, and then headed toward Charleston, South Carolina, plundering plantation manors along the way. Outside Charleston the British awaited additional naval and land forces from New York and New Jersey. After their arrival with Generals Clinton and Cornwallis in February 1780, the British launched a massive assault against the Patriot defenders, and on May 12, in the single greatest American loss of the war. General Benjamin Lincoln surrendered the city and its 5,500 soldiers.

At that point, against Washington's advice, Congress turned to Horatio Gates, the victor of Saratoga, giving him command of the Revolutionary troops in the South. Meanwhile, General Clinton sailed back to New York, leaving General Cornwallis in charge of the British troops in the South. While Cornwallis was subduing the Carolina interior, Gates began a march on Camden, South Carolina, then held by the British. Cornwallis's troops clashed with Gates's forces outside Camden in August 1780, and the American army was routed by the British. The Patriots retreated all the way to Hillsborough, North Carolina, 160 miles away.

Cornwallis had South Carolina just about under British control, but his cavalry leaders, Sir Banastre Tarleton and Patrick Ferguson, who mobilized Tory militiamen, overreached themselves in their effort to subdue the Whigs. "Bloody Tarleton" ordered rebels killed after they surrendered. Ferguson sealed his doom when he threatened to march over the mountains and hang the Revolutionary leaders there. Instead, the feisty "overmountain men" went after Ferguson. They caught him and his Tories on Kings Mountain, along the border between North Carolina and South Carolina. There, on October 7, 1780, they routed his force. Kings Mountain was the turning point of the war in the South. By proving that the British were not invincible, the American victory emboldened small farmers to join guerrilla bands under such partisan leaders as Francis Marion, "the Swamp Fox," and Thomas Sumter, "the Carolina Gamecock."

While the overmountain men were closing in on Ferguson, Congress chose a new commander for the southern theater, General Nathanael Greene, "the fighting Quaker" of Rhode Island. Greene shrewdly lured Cornwallis and his troops, making them chase the Americans across the Carolinas, thus taxing British energy and supplies. Splitting his army, Greene sent out about 700 men under General Daniel Morgan to engage Tarleton's 1,000 men at Cowpens, South Carolina, on January 17, 1781. The Americans routed the British; Tarleton and a handful of cavalry escaped, but more than 100 of his men were killed, and more than 700 were taken prisoner. Morgan and his men then linked up with Greene's main force, and the combined army offered battle at Guilford Courthouse, North Carolina (near what became Greensboro), on March 15, 1781. After inflicting heavy losses, Greene withdrew, and Cornwallis was left in possession of the field, but at a cost of nearly 100 men killed and more than 400 wounded.

Cornwallis's army marched off toward Wilmington, on the North Carolina coast, to take on supplies. Greene returned to South Carolina in the hope of drawing Cornwallis after him or forcing the British to give up the state. There he joined forces with the local guerrillas and in a series of brilliant actions kept losing battles while winning the war. By September 1781 he had narrowed British control in the Deep South to Charleston and Savannah, although for more than a year longer Whigs and Tories slashed at each other "with savage fury" in the backcountry.

Meanwhile, Cornwallis's army had headed north, away from Greene's forces, reasoning that Virginia must be eliminated as a source of reinforcement before the Carolinas could be subdued. In 1781 Cornwallis met up with the traitor Benedict Arnold, now a *British* general, who had been engaged in a war of maneuver against the American forces. Arnold, from July until September 1780, had been the American commander at West Point, New York. Overweening in ambition, lacking in moral scruples, and a reckless spender on his fashionable wife, he had nursed a grudge against Washington over an official reprimand for his extravagances as commander of reoccupied Philadelphia. Arnold crassly plotted to sell out the American garrison at West Point to the British, even suggesting how they might capture George Washington himself. The American seizure of the British go-between, Major John André, ended Arnold's plot. Forewarned that his plan had been discovered, Arnold joined the British in New York, and the Americans hanged André as a spy.

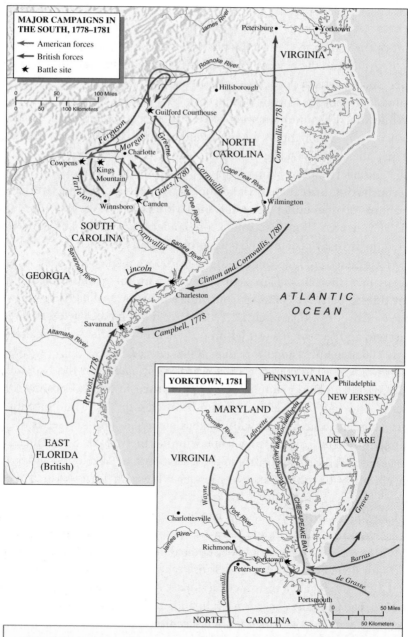

MAJOR CAMPAIGNS IN THE SOUTH, 1778–1781

← American forces
← British forces
★ Battle site

0   50   100 Miles
0   50   100 Kilometers

James River
Petersburg
Yorktown
VIRGINIA
Roanoke River
Hillsborough
Guilford Courthouse
Ferguson
Morgan
Charlotte
NORTH CAROLINA
Greene
Cornwallis, 1781
Cowpens
Kings Mountain
Cornwallis
Cape Fear River
Tarleton
Gates, 1780
Winnsboro
Camden
Pee Dee River
Wilmington
SOUTH CAROLINA
Cornwallis
Santee River
Clinton and Cornwallis, 1780
Savannah River
Lincoln
GEORGIA
Charleston
ATLANTIC OCEAN
Savannah
Campbell, 1778
Altamaha River
Prevost, 1778
EAST FLORIDA (British)

YORKTOWN, 1781

PENNSYLVANIA
Philadelphia
NEW JERSEY
MARYLAND
Potomac River
Lafayette
Washington and Rochambeau
DELAWARE
VIRGINIA
Wayne
Charlottesville
York River
James River
CHESAPEAKE BAY
Graves
Richmond
Yorktown
Petersburg
Barras
Cornwallis
de Grasse
Portsmouth
NORTH   CAROLINA
0   50 Miles
0   50 Kilometers

Why did the British suddenly shift their campaign to the South? Why were the battles at Savannah and Charleston major victories for the British? How did Nathaniel Greene undermine British control of the Deep South? Why did Cornwallis march to Virginia and camp at Yorktown? How was the French navy crucial to the American victory? Why was Cornwallis forced to surrender?

YORKTOWN   When Lord Cornwallis linked up with Benedict Arnold at Petersburg, Virginia, their combined forces totaled 7,200, far more than the small American army they faced. The arrival of American reinforcements led Cornwallis to pick Yorktown, Virginia, as a defensible site. There appeared to be little reason to worry about a siege, since General Washington's main land force seemed preoccupied with attacking New York, and the British navy controlled American waters.

To be sure, there was a small American navy, but it was no match for the British fleet. The American fleet was little more than a nuisance to the British. But at a critical point, thanks to the French navy, the British lost control of the Chesapeake waters. Indeed, it is impossible to imagine an American victory in the Revolution without the assistance of the French. As long as the British navy maintained supremacy at sea, the Americans could not hope to force a settlement to their advantage.

Then, in 1781, the elements for a combined American-French action suddenly fell into place. As General Cornwallis moved his British army into Virginia in May, Washington persuaded the commander of the French army to join forces for an attack on New York. The two armies linked up in July, but before they could strike at New York, word came from the West Indies that an entire French fleet and some 3,000 soldiers under Admiral de Grasse were bound for Chesapeake Bay. Washington and his troops secretly slipped out of New York and met up with the French in Philadelphia; the combined American-French forces immediately set out toward Yorktown. Meanwhile, a French fleet that had been blockaded by the British at Newport evaded the barricade and sailed south toward Chesapeake Bay.

On August 30 Admiral de Grasse's fleet reached Yorktown, where his troops joined the American force already watching Cornwallis. On September 6, the day after a British fleet under Admiral Thomas Graves appeared, de Grasse gave battle and forced the British to abandon the effort to relieve Cornwallis, whose fate was quickly sealed. When the siege of Yorktown began, on September 28, the situation already looked bleak for Cornwallis. Washington commanded 16,000 soldiers, double the size of the British army. Unable to break the siege or escape, Cornwallis was forced to surrender. On October 17, 1781, four years to the day after Saratoga, a red-coated drummer boy climbed atop the British parapet and began beating the call for a truce. Cornwallis sued for peace, and on October 19, their colors cased (that is, sheathed in a cloth covering), the British force marched out to the tune of "The World Turned Upside Down." Cornwallis himself claimed to be too "ill" to appear.

Surrender of Lord Cornwallis

The pivotal British surrender at Yorktown in 1794.

NEGOTIATIONS

Whatever lingering hopes of victory the British may have harbored vanished at Yorktown. "Oh God, it is all over," Lord North groaned at news of the surrender. On February 27, 1782, the House of Commons voted against continuing the war and on March 5 authorized the crown to make peace. Peace negotiations between the American diplomats—Ben Franklin, John Jay, and John Adams—and the British began in Paris, but their difficult task was immediately complicated by the French commitment to Spain. Both the United States and Spain were allied with France but not with each other. America was bound by its French alliance to fight on until the French made peace, and the French were bound to help the Spanish recover Gibraltar from England. Unable to deliver Gibraltar, or so the tough-minded Jay reasoned, the French might try to bargain off American land west of the Appalachians in its place. Fearful that the French were angling for a separate peace with the British, Jay persuaded Franklin to play the same game. Ignoring their instructions to consult fully with the French, they agreed to further talks with the British. On November 30, 1782, the talks produced a preliminary treaty with

Great Britain. If it violated the spirit of the alliance, it did not violate the strict letter of the treaty with France, for the French minister was notified the day before it was signed, and final agreement still depended on a Franco-British settlement.

THE TREATY OF PARIS   Early in 1783 France and Spain gave up trying to acquire Gibraltar and reached an armistice with Britain. The Treaty of Paris was finally signed on September 3, 1783. In accord with the bargain already struck, Great Britain recognized the independence of the United States and agreed to a Mississippi River boundary to the west. Both the northern and the southern borders left ambiguities that would require further definition. Florida, as it turned out, passed back to Spain. The British further granted the Americans the "liberty" of fishing off Newfoundland and in the Gulf of St. Lawrence and the right to dry their catch on the unsettled coast of Canada. On the matter of pre–Revolutionary War debts owed by Americans, the best the British could get was a promise that British merchants should "meet with no legal impediment" in seeking to collect them. And on the tender point of Loyalists whose property had been confiscated, the negotiators agreed that Congress would "earnestly recommend" to the states the restoration of confiscated property. Each of the last two points was little more than a face-saving gesture to the British.

THE POLITICAL REVOLUTION

REPUBLICAN IDEOLOGY   The Americans had won their War of Independence. Had they undergone a political revolution as well? John Adams offered an answer: "The Revolution was effected before the war commenced. The Revolution was in the minds and hearts of the people. . . . This radical change in the principles, opinions, sentiments, and affections of the people, was the real American Revolution."

Yet Adams's observation ignores the fact that the Revolutionary War itself served as the catalyst for a prolonged debate about what forms of government would best serve the new American republic. The conventional British model of mixed government sought to balance the monarchy, the aristocracy, and the common people so as to protect individual liberty. Because of the more fluid and democratic nature of their new society, however, Americans knew that they must develop new political assumptions and institutions. They had no monarchy or aristocracy. Yet how could sovereignty reside in the common people? How could Americans ensure the survival of a

NORTH AMERICA, 1783

England
United States
Spain

How did France's treaties with Spain complicate the peace-treaty negotiations with the British? What were the terms of the Peace of Paris? Why might the ambiguities in the treaty have led to conflicts among the Americans, the Spanish, and the English?

republican form of government, long assumed to be the most fragile? The war thus provoked a flurry of state constitution making that remains unique in history. Ideas such as the contract theory of government, the sovereignty of the people, the separation of powers, and natural rights found their way quickly, almost automatically, into the frames of government that were devised while the fight went on—amid other urgent business.

The very idea of republican government—a balanced polity animated by civic virtue—was a far more radical departure in that day than it would seem to later generations. Through the lens of republican thinking, Americans began to see themselves in a new light. As free citizens of a republic, Americans would cast off the aristocratic corruptions of the Old World and usher in a new reign of individual liberty and public virtue. The new American republic, in other words, would endure as long as the majority of the people were virtuous and willingly placed the good of society above the self-interest of individuals. Herein lay the hope and the danger of the American experiment in popular government: even as leaders enthusiastically fashioned new state constitutions, they feared that their experiments in republicanism would fail because of a lack of civic virtue among the people.

STATE CONSTITUTIONS Most political experimentation between 1776 and 1787 occurred at the state level. At the onset of the fighting, every colony experienced the departure of its governor and other officials and usually the expulsion of Loyalists from its assembly, which then assumed power as a provincial "congress" or "convention." But those legislatures were acting as revolutionary bodies without any legal basis for the exercise of authority. In two states this presented little difficulty. Connecticut and Rhode Island, which as corporate colonies had been virtually little republics, simply purged their charters of any reference to colonial ties. Massachusetts followed their example until 1780.

In the other states the prevailing notions of social contract and popular sovereignty led to written constitutions that specified the framework and powers of government. Constitution making began even before independence. In May 1776 Congress advised the colonies to set up new governments "under the authority of the people." The first state constitutions varied mainly in detail. They formed governments much like the colonial administrations, but with elected governors and senates instead of appointed governors and councils. Generally they embodied, sometimes explicitly, a separation of powers as a safeguard against abuses. Most of them also included a bill of rights that protected the time-honored rights of petition, freedom of speech, trial by jury, freedom from self-incrimination, and the like. Most tended to limit the powers of governors and increase the powers of the legislatures, which had led the people in their quarrels with the colonial governors.

THE ARTICLES OF CONFEDERATION The new central American government, like the state governments, grew out of an extralegal revolutionary body. The Continental Congress exercised government powers without any constitutional sanction before 1781. Plans for a permanent national government emerged very early, however, when a committee headed by John Dickinson produced a draft constitution, the Articles of Confederation and Perpetual Union, which was adopted in November 1777.

The central government envisaged by the Articles of Confederation had little authority. Congress was intended not as a legislature, nor as a sovereign entity unto itself, but as a collective substitute for the monarch. In essence it was to be a plural executive rather than a parliamentary body. For all the weaknesses of the central government proposed by the Articles of Confederation, it represented the most appropriate structure for the new nation. After all, the Revolution on the battlefields had yet to be won, and the statesmen did not have the luxury of engaging in prolonged and perhaps fratricidal debates over the distribution of power that proposals for other systems would have provoked. There would be time later for modifications.

THE SOCIAL REVOLUTION

Political revolutions often spawn social revolutions, and the turmoil of the Revolution allowed outlets for long-festering frustrations among the lower ranks. What did the Revolution mean to those workers, servants, farmers, and freed slaves who participated in the Stamp Act demonstrations, supported the boycotts, idolized Tom Paine, and fought with Washington and Greene? The more conservative Patriots would have been content to replace royal officials with the rich, the wellborn, and the able and let it go at that. But more radical revolutionaries, in the apt phrase of one historian, raised the question not only of home rule but also of who shall rule at home.

EQUALITY AND ITS LIMITS   This spirit of equality weakened old habits of deference. Participation in the army or militia activated men who had taken little interest in politics. The new political opportunities afforded by the creation of state governments thus led more ordinary citizens to participate than ever before. The social base of the new legislatures was much broader than that of the old assemblies.

Men fighting for their liberty found it difficult to justify denying other white men the rights of suffrage and representation. The property qualifications for voting, which already admitted an overwhelming majority of white men, were lowered still further in some states. In Pennsylvania, Delaware, North Carolina, and Georgia, any male taxpayer could vote, although officeholders had to meet

Social Democracy

In this watercolor by Benjamin Latrobe, a gentleman plays billiards with artisans, suggesting that "the spirit of independence was converted into equality."

more stringent property requirements. In the state legislatures younger men often replaced older men, some of whom had been Loyalists. More often than not, the newcomers were men with less property and little education. Some states concentrated much power in a legislature chosen by a wide suffrage, but not even Pennsylvania, which adopted the most radical state constitution, went quite so far as to grant universal male suffrage.

New developments in land tenure that grew out of the Revolution extended the democratic trends of suffrage requirements. The state legislatures seized Tory estates. This land was of small consequence, however, in comparison to the unsettled land that had been at the disposal of the crown and proprietors. Now in the hands of state assemblies, much of this land was distributed as bonuses to veterans of the war. Western lands, formerly closed by the Royal Proclamation of 1763 and the Quebec Act of 1774, were soon thrown open to settlers.

THE PARADOX OF SLAVERY   The Revolutionary generation of leaders was the first to confront slavery and consider abolishing it. The principles of liberty and equality so crucial to the rebellion against England had clear implications for America's enslaved blacks. Thomas Jefferson's draft of the Declaration of Independence had indicted the king for having violated the "most sacred rights of life and liberty of a distant people" by encouraging the slave trade in the colonies, but Jefferson had deleted the clause "in complaisance to

South Carolina and Georgia." After independence all the states except Georgia stopped the importation of African slaves, although South Carolina later reopened it.

African-American soldiers or sailors were present at most major Revolutionary battles, from Lexington to Yorktown, most of them serving on the Loyalist side. Slaves who served in the cause of independence got their freedom and in some cases land bounties. But the British army, which freed tens of thousands of slaves during the war, was a greater instrument of emancipation than the American forces. Most of the freed blacks found their way to Canada or to British colonies in the Caribbean. American Whigs showed no mercy to blacks caught aiding or abetting the British cause. A Charleston mob hanged and then burned Thomas Jeremiah, a free black man who was convicted of telling slaves that the British "were come to help the poor Negroes."

In the northern states, which had fewer slaves than the southern states, the doctrines of liberty led swiftly to emancipation for all, either during the fighting or shortly afterward. South of Pennsylvania the potential consequences of emancipation were so staggering—South Carolina had a black majority—that whites refused to extend the principle of liberty to their slaves. Although some southern slaveholders were troubled, most could not bring themselves to free their own slaves. Anti-slavery sentiment in the southern states went only so far as to relax the manumission laws under which owners might voluntarily free their slaves. Some 10,000 enslaved Virginians were manumitted during the 1780s. By the outbreak of the Civil War, in 1861, approximately half the blacks living in Maryland were free.

Slaves, especially in the upper South, also earned their freedom through their own actions during the Revolutionary era, frequently by running away. They often gravitated to the growing number of African-American communities in the North. Because of emancipation laws in the northern states, and with the formation of free black neighborhoods in the North and in several southern cities, runaways found refuge and the opportunities for new lives. It is estimated that 55,000 slaves fled to freedom during the Revolution.

THE STATUS OF WOMEN   The logic of liberty applied to the status of women as much as to that of African Americans. Women had remained essentially confined to the domestic sphere during the eighteenth century. They could not vote or preach or hold office. Few had access to formal education. Although in some colonies women could own property and execute contracts, in other colonies they could not legally own even their own clothes, and they had no legal rights over their children. Divorces were extremely difficult to obtain.

The Revolution offered women new opportunities and engendered in many a new outlook. The war also drew women at least temporarily into new roles. They plowed fields and melted down pots and pans to make shot. Women also served the armies in various roles—by handling supplies and serving as spies or couriers. Wives often followed their husbands to army camps, where they nursed the wounded and sick, cooked and washed for the able, and frequently buried the dead. On occasion, women took their place in the firing line.

To be sure, most women retained the domestic outlook that had long been imposed upon them, but a few free-spirited reformers demanded equal treatment. In an essay titled "On the Equality of the Sexes," written in 1779 and published in 1790, Judith Sargent Murray of Gloucester, Massachusetts, stressed that women were perfectly capable of excelling outside the domestic sphere.

Elizabeth Freeman

Also known as Mum Bett, was born around 1742 and sold as a slave to a Massachusetts family. She won her freedom by claiming in court that the Bill of Rights and the new state constitution gave liberty to all, and her case contributed to the eventual abolition of slavery in Massachusetts. One of Freeman's great-grandchildren was scholar and civil rights leader W.E.B. Du Bois.

Early in the Revolutionary struggle, Abigail Adams, one of the most learned women of the time, wrote her husband, John: "In the new Code of Laws which I suppose it will be necessary for you to make I desire you would remember the Ladies. . . . Do not put such unlimited power into the hands of the Husbands." Since men were "Naturally Tyrannical," she stressed, "why then, not put it out of the power of the vicious and the Lawless to use us with cruelty and indignity." Otherwise, "the Ladies" would "foment a Rebellion, and will not hold ourselves bound by any Laws in which we have no voice, or Representation."

John Adams expressed surprise that women might be discontented, but he clearly knew the privileges enjoyed by males and was determined to retain them: "Depend upon it, we know better than to repeal our Masculine systems." The supposedly more liberal Thomas Jefferson agreed with John Adams on the matter. When asked about women's voting rights, he replied that "the tender breasts of ladies were not formed for political convulsion." The legal status of women thus did not benefit dramatically from the egalitarian doctrine unleashed by the Revolution. Married women in most states still forfeited control of their own property to their husbands, and women gained no political rights.

FREEDOM OF RELIGION   The Revolution also set in motion a transition from the toleration of religious dissent to a complete freedom of religion in the separation of church and state. The Anglican Church, established as the official state religion in five colonies and parts of two others, was especially vulnerable because of its association with the crown and because non-Anglicans outnumbered Anglicans in all states except Virginia. And all but Virginia eliminated tax support for the church before the fighting was over. In 1776 the Virginia Declaration of Rights (a bill of rights) guaranteed the free exercise of religion, and in 1786 the Virginia Statute of Religious Freedom (written by Thomas Jefferson) declared that "no man shall be compelled to frequent or support any religious worship, place or ministry whatsoever" and "that all men shall be free to profess and by argument to maintain,

Religious Development

The Congregational Church developed a national presence in the early nineteenth century, and Lemuel Haynes, depicted here, was its first African-American preacher.

their opinions in matters of religion." These statutes and the Revolutionary ideology that justified them helped shape the course that religion would take in the new United States: pluralistic and voluntary rather than monolithic and state supported.

In churches as in government, the Revolution set off a period of constitution making as some of the first national church bodies emerged. In 1784 the Methodists, who at first were an offshoot of the Anglicans, came together in a general conference at Baltimore. The Anglican Church, rechristened Episcopal, gathered in a series of meetings that by 1789 had united the various dioceses in a federal union; in 1789 the Presbyterians also held their first general assembly, in Philadelphia. That same year the Catholic Church got its first higher official in the United States when John Carroll was named bishop of Baltimore.

THE EMERGENCE OF AN AMERICAN CULTURE

The Revolution generated among some Americans a sense of common nationality. One of the first ways in which to forge a national consciousness was through the annual celebration of the new nation's independence from Great Britain. On July 2, 1776, when the Second Continental Congress had resolved "that these United Colonies are, and of right ought to be, free and independent states," John Adams had written his wife, Abigail, that future generations would remember that date as their "day of deliverance."

As it turned out, however, Americans fastened not upon July 2 but upon July 4 as their Independence Day. To be sure, it was on the Fourth that Congress formally adopted the Declaration of Independence and ordered it to be printed and distributed throughout the states, but America by then had been officially independent for two days. Independence Day quickly became the most popular and most important public ritual in the United States. Huge numbers of people from all walks of life suspended their normal routine in order to devote a day to parades, formal orations, and fireworks displays. In the process the infant republic began to create its own myth of national identity that transcended local or regional concerns and forged a feeling of national unity.

AMERICA'S "DESTINY" In a special sense, American nationalism embodied an idea of divine mission. Many people, at least since the time of the Pilgrims, had thought of America as singled out by God for a special identity, a special mission. John Winthrop referred to the Puritan commonwealth as representing a "city upon a hill," and Jonathan Edwards believed that God had singled out America as "the glorious renovator of the world." This sense of mission was neither limited to New England nor rooted solely in Calvinism. From the democratic rhetoric of Thomas Jefferson to the pragmatism of George Washington to heady toasts bellowed in South Carolina taverns, patriots everywhere articulated a special role for American leadership in history. The mission was now a call to lead the way toward liberty and equality. Meanwhile, however, Americans had to address more immediate problems created by their new nationhood. The Philadelphia patriot, doctor, and scientist Benjamin Rush issued a prophetic statement in 1787: "The American war is over: but this is far from being the case with the American Revolution. On the contrary, but the first act of the great drama is closed."

MAKING CONNECTIONS

- The American Revolution was the starting point for the foreign policy of the United States. Many of the specific foreign concerns that will be discussed in Chapters 8 and 9 sprang from issues directly relating to the Revolution.

- Much of what became Jacksonian democracy (introduced in Chapter 10) can be traced to social and political movements associated with the American Revolution.

- The innovations set forth in the new state constitutions during the Revolution created a reservoir of ideas and experience that formed the basis for the creation of the federal Constitution in 1787, as we will see in Chapter 7.

FURTHER READING

The Revolutionary War is the subject of Colin Bonwick's *The American Revolution* (1991), Theodore Draper's *A Struggle for Power: The American Revolution* (1996), Gordon S. Wood's *The Radicalism of the American Revolution* (1991), Benson Bobrick's *Angel in the Whirlwind: The Triumph of the American Revolution* (1997), and Jeremy Black's *War for America: The Fight for Independence, 1775–1783* (1991).

On the social history of the Revolutionary War, see John W. Shy's *A People Numerous and Armed: Reflections on the Military Struggle for American Independence,* rev. ed. (1990), Charles Royster's *A Revolutionary People at War: The Continental Army and American Character, 1775–1783* (1979), Lawrence Delbe Cress's *Citizens in Arms: The Army and the Militia in American Society to the War of 1812* (1982), and E. Wayne Carp's *To Starve the Army at Pleasure: Continental Army Administration and American Political Culture, 1775–1783* (1984). Colin G. Calloway tells the neglected story of the Indian experiences in the Revolution in *The American Revolution in Indian Country: Crisis and Diversity in Native American Communities* (1995).

Why some Americans remained loyal to the crown is the subject of Bernard Bailyn's *The Ordeal of Thomas Hutchinson* (1974), Robert M. Calhoon's *The Loyalists in Revolutionary America, 1760–1781* (1973), and Mary Beth Norton's *The British-Americans: The Loyalist Exiles in England, 1774–1789* (1972).

The definitive study of African Americans during the Revolutionary era remains Benjamin Quarles's *The Negro in the American Revolution* (1961). Mary Beth Norton's *Liberty's Daughters: The Revolutionary Experience of American Women, 1750–1800,* new ed. (1996) and Linda K. Kerber's *Women of the Republic: Intellect and Ideology in Revolutionary America* (1980) document the role women played in securing independence. Joy Day Buel and Richard Buel Jr.'s *The Way of Duty: A Woman and Her Family in Revolutionary America* (1984) shows the impact of the Revolution on one New England family.

The standard introduction to the diplomacy of the Revolutionary era is Jonathan R. Dull's *A Diplomatic History of the American Revolution* (1985).

7

SHAPING A FEDERAL UNION

FOCUS QUESTIONS

- What were the achievements and weaknesses of the Confederation government?
- What were the issues involved in writing the Constitution?
- What were the debates surrounding the ratification of the Constitution?

To answer these questions and access additional review material, please visit www.wwnorton.com/studyspace.

In an address to fellow graduates at the Harvard commencement ceremony in 1787, young John Quincy Adams, the son of John and Abigail Adams, lamented "this critical period" when the United States was struggling to establish itself as a new nation. Historians thereafter used his phrase to designate the years when the infant republic operated under the Articles of Confederation, 1781 to 1787. Fear of centralized government power dominated the period and limited the scope and effectiveness of the new government. Yet while there were weaknesses of the Confederation, there were also major achievements during the so-called critical period. Moreover, lessons learned under the Confederation would prompt the formulation of a national constitution intended to balance central and local authority.

THE CONFEDERATION

The Confederation Congress had little authority. It could only request money from the states; it could make treaties with foreign countries but could not enforce them; it could borrow money but lacked the means to ensure repayment. Congress was virtually helpless to cope with the postwar problems of diplomacy and economic depression, problems that would have challenged the resources of a much stronger government. Yet in spite of its handicaps, the Confederation Congress somehow managed to keep afloat and to lay important foundations. It concluded the Treaty of Paris in 1783, created the first federal executive departments, and formulated principles of land distribution and territorial government that guided westward expansion all the way to the Pacific coast.

THE ARTICLES OF CONFEDERATION   When the Articles of Confederation took effect, in 1781, they did little more than legalize the status quo. Congress had full power over foreign affairs and questions of war and peace; it could decide disputes between the states; it had authority over coinage, the postal service, and Indian affairs and responsibility for the government of the western territories. But it had no courts and no power to enforce its resolutions and ordinances. It also had no power to levy taxes, but had to rely on requests submitted to the states, which state legislatures could ignore—and usually did.

The states, after their battles with Parliament, were in no mood for a strong central government. Congress could not regulate interstate and foreign commerce and for certain important acts a "special majority" was required. Nine states had to approve measures dealing with war, privateering, treaties, coinage, finances, or the army and navy. Unanimous approval by the states was needed to levy tariffs (often called duties) on imports. Amendments to the articles also required unanimous ratification by the states.

The Confederation had neither an executive nor a judicial branch; there were no administrative head of government (only the president of the Congress, chosen annually) and no federal courts. In 1781, however, anticipating ratification of the Articles of Confederation, Congress set up three government departments: Foreign Affairs, Finance, and War. Each was to have a single head responsible to Congress. Given time and stability, Congress and the department heads might have evolved into something like the parliamentary cabinet system. As it turned out, these agencies were the forerunners of the government departments to be established under the Constitution.

FINANCE   Since there was neither president nor prime minister, but only the presiding officer of Congress and its secretary, the closest thing to an executive head of the Confederation was Robert Morris, who was superintendent of finance in the final years of the war. Morris wanted to make both himself and the Confederation more powerful. He envisioned a coherent program of taxation and debt management to make the government financially stable.

As the foundation of his plan, Morris secured in 1781 a congressional charter for the Bank of North America, which would hold government cash, lend money to the government, and issue currency. But his program depended ultimately upon a secure income for the Confederation government, and it proved impossible to win the unanimous approval of the states for the necessary amendments to the Articles of Confederation. As a consequence the Confederation never did put its finances in order. The Continental currency quickly proved worthless and was never redeemed. The government debt, domestic and foreign, grew from $11 million to $28 million as Congress paid off citizens' and soldiers' claims. Each year, Congress ran a deficit in its operating expenses.

LAND POLICY   Congress might ultimately have hoped to draw an independent income from the sale of western lands, but throughout the Confederation period little acreage was sold. The Confederation nevertheless dealt more effectively with the western lands than with anything else. There Congress had direct authority, at least on paper. Thinly populated by Indians, French settlers, and a growing number of American squatters, the region north of the Ohio River and west of the Appalachian Mountains had long been the site of overlapping claims by colonies and speculators.

Between 1784 and 1787 policies for western development emerged in three major ordinances of the Confederation Congress. These documents, which rank among its greatest achievements —and among the most important in American history—set precedents that the United States would follow in its future expansion. Thomas Jefferson's inclination was to grant self-government to western territories at an early stage, allowing settlers to meet and choose their own officials. Under Jefferson's proposed ordinance of 1784, when a territory's population equaled that of the smallest existing state, the territory would achieve full statehood.

In the Land Ordinance of 1785, the delegates outlined a plan of surveys and sales that eventually stamped a rectangular pattern on much of the nation's surface. Wherever Indian titles had been extinguished, the Northwest was to be surveyed and six-mile-square townships established along east-west and north-south lines. Each township was in turn to be divided into thirty-six sections, each one mile square (or 640 acres). The 640-acre sections were to be auctioned for no less than $640. Such terms favored land speculators, of course, since few common folk had that much money or were able to work that much land. In later years new land laws would make smaller lots available at lower prices, but in 1785 Congress confronted an empty Treasury, and delegates believed this system would raise the needed funds.

Spurred by the plans for land sales and settlement, Congress drafted the Northwest Ordinance of 1787. The new plan abandoned the commitment to early self-government in the territories. Because of the trouble that might be expected from squatters who were clamoring for free land, the Northwest Ordinance transition required a period of colonial. At first the territory fell subject to a governor, a secretary, and three judges, all chosen by Congress. When any territory in the region had a population of 5,000 free male adults, it could choose an assembly, and Congress would name a governing council. The governor would have a veto, and so would Congress.

The resemblance of these territorial governments to the old royal colonies is clear, but there were three significant differences. For one, the Northwest Ordinance anticipated statehood when any territory's population reached 60,000 "free inhabitants." At that point a convention could be called to draft a state constitution and apply to Congress for statehood. For another, it included a bill of rights that guaranteed religious freedom, proportional representation, trial by jury, habeas corpus, and the application of common law. Finally, the ordinance excluded slavery permanently from the Northwest. This decision proved fateful. As the progress of emancipation in the existing states gradually freed all slaves in the North, the Ohio River boundary of the Old Northwest extended the line between freedom and slavery all the way to the Mississippi River, encompassing what would become the states of Ohio, Indiana, Illinois, Michigan, and Wisconsin.

The Northwest Ordinance had an importance larger than establishing a formal procedure for transforming territories into states. It represented a sharp break with the imperialistic assumption behind European expansion into the Western Hemisphere. The new states were to be admitted to the American republic as equals rather than be treated as subordinate colonies.

The lands south of the Ohio River followed a different process of development. Title to the western lands remained with Georgia, North Carolina, and Virginia for the time being, but settlement proceeded at a far more rapid pace during and after the Revolution with substantial population centers growing up in Kentucky and Tennessee.

The Iroquois and Cherokees, battered during the Revolution, were in no position to resist encroachments. During the mid-1780s the Iroquois were forced to cede land in western New York and Pennsylvania, and the Cherokees gave up all claims in South Carolina, much of western North Carolina, and large portions of present-day Kentucky and Tennessee. At the same time the major Ohio tribes dropped their claim to most of Ohio, except for a segment bordering the western part of Lake Erie. The Creeks, pressed by Georgia to cede portions of their lands in 1784–1785, went to war in the summer of 1786 with covert aid from Spanish Florida. When Spanish support lapsed, however, the Creek chief struck a bargain in 1791 that gave the Creeks favorable trade arrangements with the United States but did not restore the lost land.

TRADE AND THE ECONOMY   The American economy after the Revolution went through a turbulent transition. Although farmers enmeshed in local markets maintained their livelihood during the Revolutionary era, commercial agriculture dependent upon trade with foreign markets suffered a severe downturn. In New England and much of the backcountry, fighting seldom interrupted the tempo of farming, and the producers of foodstuffs for local markets benefited in particular from rising prices and wartime demands. Virginia suffered a loss of enslaved workers, most of them carried off by the British. The British decision to close its West Indian colonies to American trade devastated what had been a thriving commerce in timber, wheat, and other foodstuffs.

Merchants suffered far more wrenching adjustments during the Revolution than farmers. Cut out of the British mercantile system, they had to find new markets. Circumstances that impoverished some enriched those who financed privateers, supplied the armies on both sides, and hoarded precious goods while demand and prices soared. By the end of the war, a strong sentiment for free trade had developed in both Britain and America. In the memorable year 1776 the Scottish economist Adam Smith published *The Wealth of Nations,* a classic manifesto against mercantilism. Some British statesmen embraced the new gospel of free trade, but the public and Parliament would cling to mercantilism for years to come.

British trade with the United States resumed after 1783. American ships were allowed to deliver American products and return to the United States with British goods, but they could not carry British goods anywhere else. The pent-up demand for consumer goods created a vigorous market in exports to America, fueled by British credit and the hard money that had come into the new nation with foreign aid, the expenditures of foreign armies, and

Merchants' Counting House

Americans involved in overseas trade, such as the merchants depicted here, had been sharply affected by the dislocations of war.

wartime trade and privateering. The result was a quick cycle of postwar boom and bust, a buying spree followed by a money shortage and economic troubles that lasted several years.

In colonial days the chronic trade deficit with Britain had been offset by the influx of coins from trade with the West Indies. Now American ships found themselves legally excluded from the British West Indies. But the islands still demanded wheat, fish, lumber, and other products from the mainland, and American shippers had not lost their talent for smuggling. By 1787 Americans were also trading with the Dutch, the Swedes, the Prussians, the Moroccans, and the Chinese, and American seaports were flourishing more than ever. By 1790 the value of American commerce and exports had far exceeded the trade of the colonies. Although most of the exports were the products of American forests, fields, and fisheries, during and after the war more workers had turned to small-scale manufacturing—shoes, textiles, soap—mainly for domestic markets.

DIPLOMACY   The achievements of the energetic young nation are more visible in hindsight than they were at the time. Until 1787 the shortcomings and failures of the Confederation government remained far more apparent— and the advocates of a stronger central government were extremely vocal on the subject. In diplomacy there remained the nagging problems of relations with Great Britain and Spain, both of which still kept military posts on American soil and conspired with Indians and white settlers in the West. The British, despite the peace treaty of 1783, held on to a string of forts along the Canadian border. From these outposts they kept a hand in the lucrative fur trade and maintained a degree of influence with the Indian tribes, whom they were suspected of stirring up to make sporadic attacks on American settlers.

Another major irritant was the confiscation of Loyalist property. The peace treaty with Britain had obligated Congress to end confiscations of Tory property, to guarantee immunity to Loyalists for twelve months, during which they could return and wind up their affairs, and to recommend that the states return confiscated property. Persecutions, even lynchings, of Loyalists occurred even after the end of the war. After 1783 some Loyalists returned unmolested, however, and resumed their lives in their former homes. By the end of 1787, moreover, all the states had rescinded laws discriminating against former Tories.

With Spain the chief issues were the southern boundary and the right to navigate the Mississippi River. According to the preliminary treaty with Britain, the United States claimed as its boundary a line running eastward from the mouth of the Yazoo River in what is now Mississippi. The treaty ending the war with Britain had also given Americans the right to navigate the Mississippi River to its mouth, near New Orleans, but the river was entirely within Spanish Louisiana in its lower reaches. The right to navigate the Mississippi River was crucial because of the growing American settlements upriver in Kentucky and Tennessee, but in 1784 Louisiana's Spanish governor closed the river to American commerce. In 1785 the Spanish government sent to America an ambassador who entered into long but fruitless negotiations with John Jay, the secretary for foreign affairs, over navigation of the Mississippi River and the southern border of the United States. The issue of American access to the lower Mississippi would remain unsettled for nearly another decade.

THE CONFEDERATION'S PROBLEMS   Of greatest concern to most Americans after the Revolution were protection of infant American industries from foreign competition and the currency shortage. Merchants and artisans were frustrated by British policies excluding them from British markets, and in retaliation they sought from the states tariffs on foreign goods (taxes on imports) that competed with theirs. The country would be on its way to economic independence, they argued, if only the money that flowed into the country were invested in domestic manufactures instead of being paid out for foreign goods. Nearly all the states gave some preference to American goods, but the lack of consistency in their laws put them at cross purposes, and so urban mechanics, along with merchants, were drawn into the movement for a stronger central government in the interest of uniform regulation of trade.

Domestic Industry

American craftsmen, such as this cabinet-maker, favored tariffs against foreign goods that competed with theirs.

The shortage of cash and other economic difficulties gave rise to more immediate demands for paper currency as legal tender, for postponement of tax and debt payments, and for laws to "stay" the foreclosure of mortgages. Farmers who had profited during the war found themselves squeezed afterward by depressed crop prices and mounting debts while merchants sorted out and opened up new trade routes. Creditors demanded hard money, but it was in short supply—and paper money was both scarce and virtually worthless after the depreciation of the Continental currency. The result was an outcry among debtor groups for relief, and around 1785 the demand for new paper money became the most divisive issue in state politics. In 1785–1786 seven states (Pennsylvania, New York, New Jersey, South Carolina, Rhode Island, Georgia, and North Carolina) issued paper money. In spite of the cries of calamity, the money served positively as a means of extending credit to hard-pressed farmers through state loans on farm mortgages. It was also used to fund state debts and to pay off the claims of veterans.

SHAYS'S REBELLION But many Americans—especially bankers and merchants—were horrified by such inflationary policies. An event in Massachusetts provided the final proof (some said) that the country was on the brink of anarchy: Shays's Rebellion. After 1780 Massachusetts had remained in the grip of a rigidly conservative regime. The state levied high poll and land taxes to pay off a heavy war debt, held mainly by wealthy creditors in Boston. The taxes fell most heavily upon beleaguered farmers and the poor in general.

When the legislature adjourned in 1786 without providing paper money or any other relief from taxes and debts, three western agricultural counties revolted. Armed bands closed the courts and prevented foreclosures, and a ragtag "army" of some 1,200 disgruntled farmers led by Captain Daniel Shays, a destitute farmer and war veteran, advanced upon the federal arsenal at Springfield in 1787. Shays and his followers sought a more flexible monetary policy, laws allowing them to use corn and wheat as money, and the right to postpone paying taxes until the depression lifted.

A small militia scattered Shays's men with a single volley that left four dead. The rebels nevertheless had a victory of sorts. The new state legislature included members sympathetic to the agricultural crisis. The legislators omitted direct taxes the following year, lowered court fees, and exempted clothing, household goods, and tools from the debt process. But a more important consequence was the impetus the rebellion gave to conservatism and nationalism.

CALLS FOR A STRONGER GOVERNMENT   Shays's Rebellion convinced many political leaders that the Articles of Confederation were inadequate. Self-interest led many bankers, merchants, and mechanics to promote a stronger central government as the only alternative to anarchy. Gradually Americans were losing the ingrained fear of a powerful central authority as they saw evidence that tyranny might come from other quarters, including the common people themselves.

Such developments led many of the Revolutionary leaders to revise their assessment of the American character. "We have, probably," concluded George Washington in 1786, "had too good an opinion of human nature in forming our confederation." People were stretching the meaning of liberty far beyond what he and others had envisioned. He found a "spirit of *locality*" rampant in the state legislatures that was destroying the "aggregate interests of the community." Even worse, he saw people taking the law and other people's property into their own hands. James Madison and other so-called Federalists concluded that the new republic must now depend for its success upon the constant virtue of the few rather than the public-spiritedness of the many.

ADOPTING THE CONSTITUTION

For these reasons, well before Shays's Rebellion nationalists were demanding a convention to revise the Articles of Confederation. After stalling for several months, Congress in 1787 passed a resolution endorsing a convention "for the sole and express purpose of revising the Articles of Confederation." By then five states had already named delegates; before the meeting six more states had acted. Rhode Island kept aloof throughout, leading critics to label it Rogue Island.

THE CONSTITUTIONAL CONVENTION Twenty-nine delegates began work in Philadelphia on May 25. Altogether fifty-five attended at one time or another, and after four months thirty-nine signed the Constitution. The document's durability and flexibility testify to the remarkable qualities of its creators. The delegates were surprisingly young: forty-two was the average age. Most were planters, merchants, lawyers, judges, bankers, many of them widely read in history, law, and political philosophy. At the same time they were practical, experienced, and tested in the fires of the Revolution. Twenty-one had fought in the conflict, seven had been state governors, most had served in the Continental Congress, and eight had signed the Declaration of Independence.

The magisterial George Washington served as presiding officer but participated little in the debates. Eighty-one-year-old Benjamin Franklin, the oldest delegate, also said little from the floor but provided a wealth of experience, wit, and common sense. More active in the debates were the thirty-six-year-old James Madison, the ablest political philosopher in the group;

Drafting the Constitution

George Washington presides over a session of the Constitutional Convention.

George Mason, the prickly author of the Virginia Declaration of Rights and a slaveholding planter who was burdened by gout, chronic indigestion, and a deep-rooted suspicion of all government; the witty, eloquent, and arrogant New York aristocrat Gouverneur Morris; James Wilson of Pennsylvania, one of the shrewdest lawyers in the new nation and next in importance at the convention only to Washington and Madison; and Roger Sherman of Connecticut, a self-trained lawyer adept at negotiating compromises. John Adams, like Jefferson, was serving abroad on a diplomatic mission. Also conspicuously absent during most of the convention was Alexander Hamilton, who regretfully went home when the two other New York delegates walked out to protest the loss of states' rights.

The delegates spent four sweltering months fighting flies, the humidity, and one another. However, on certain fundamentals they generally agreed: that government derives its just powers from the consent of the people but that society must be protected from the tyranny of the majority; that the people at large must have a voice in their government but that checks and balances must be provided to keep any one group from dominating; that a stronger central authority was essential but that all power is subject to abuse. Even the best of people are naturally selfish, they believed, and therefore government could not be founded upon a trust in goodwill and virtue. Yet by carefully checking power with countervailing power, the Founding Fathers hoped to devise institutions that could somehow constrain individual sinfulness and channel individual self-interest on behalf of the public good. Madison proved to be the energizing force at the convention, persuading others by the convincing eloquence of his arguments.

THE VIRGINIA AND NEW JERSEY PLANS   James Madison drafted the proposals that came to be called the Virginia Plan, presented on May 29, 1787. This plan called for separate legislative, executive, and judicial branches and a truly national government whose laws would be binding upon individual citizens as well as states. Congress would be divided into two houses: a lower house to be chosen by popular vote and an upper house of senators elected by the state legislatures. Congress could disallow state laws under the plan and would itself define the extent of its and the states' authority.

On June 15 William Paterson submitted the "New Jersey Plan," which kept the existing equal representation of the states in a unicameral Congress but gave the Congress power to levy taxes, regulate commerce, and name a plural executive (with no veto) and a supreme court. The plans presented the convention with two major issues: whether to amend the Articles of Confederation or draft an entirely new document and whether to apportion congressional representation by population or by state.

On the first point the convention voted to design a national government as envisioned by the Virginians. Experience had persuaded the delegates that an effective central government, as distinguished from a loose confederation of states needed the power to levy taxes, regulate commerce, raise an army and navy, and make laws binding upon individual citizens. The lessons of the 1780s suggested to them, moreover, that in the interest of order and uniformity the states must be denied certain powers: to issue money, void contracts, make treaties or wage war, and levy tariffs.

But other issues sparked furious disagreements. The first clash in the

James Madison

Madison was only thirty-six when he assumed a major role in the drafting of the Constitution. This miniature (ca. 1783) is by Charles Willson Peale.

convention involved the issue of representation, and it was solved by the Great Compromise, (sometimes called the Connecticut Compromise, as it was proposed by Roger Sherman). In the House of Representatives, apportionment would be by population, which pleased the more populous states; in the Senate there would be equal representation of each state (although the vote would be by individuals, not by states), which appeased the smaller states.

An equally contentious struggle ensued between northern and southern delegates over slavery. Few if any of the framers considered the possibility of abolishing slavery in those states—mostly southern—where it was still legal. In this respect they reflected the prevailing attitude of their time. Most agreed with South Carolina's John Rutledge when he asserted, "Religion and humanity [have] nothing to do with this [slavery] question. Interest alone is the governing principle of nations."

The "interest" of southern delegates, with enslaved African Americans so numerous in their states, dictated that slaves be counted as part of the population in determining the number of a state's representatives. Northerners were willing to count slaves when deciding each state's share of direct taxes but not for purposes of representation in Congress. The delegates, with little dissent, agreed in a compromise to count three fifths of the slaves as a basis for apportioning both representatives and direct taxes.

A more sensitive issue involved an effort to prevent the new central government from stopping the slave trade with Africa. Some state governments had already outlawed the practice, and several delegates demanded that the national government do the same. Southern delegates quickly protested. Eventually a compromise was reached whereby Congress could not prohibit the traffic until 1808 but could levy a tax of $10 a head on imported slaves. In drafting both provisions, a sense of delicacy—and hypocrisy—dictated the use of euphemisms. The Constitution thus spoke of "free persons" and "all other persons." The odious word *slavery* did not appear in the Constitution until the Thirteenth Amendment (1865) abolished the practice.

If the delegates found the slavery issue distracting, they considered irrelevant any discussion of the legal or political role of women under the new constitution. The Revolutionary rhetoric of liberty prompted a few women to demand political equality. "The men say we have no business [with politics]," Eliza Wilkinson of South Carolina observed, "but I won't have it thought that because we are the weaker sex as to bodily strength we are capable of nothing more than domestic concerns. They won't even allow us liberty of thought, and that is all I want." Her complaint, however, fell on deaf ears. There was never any formal discussion of women's rights at the convention. The new political framework still defined politics and government as outside the realm of female endeavor.

THE SEPARATION OF POWERS   The details of the government structure generated less debate in Philadelphia than the basic issues pitting the large states against the small and the northern states against the southern. Existing state constitutions, several of which already separated powers among legislative, executive, and judicial branches, set an example that reinforced the convention's resolve to disperse power with checks and balances. Some delegates displayed a thumping disdain for any democratizing of the political system. Hamilton called the people "a great beast," and Elbridge Gerry asserted that most of the nation's problems "flow from an excess of democracy."

Those elitist views were incorporated into the Constitution's mixed legislative system, which allowed the direct popular choice of just one chamber of Congress. The lower house was designed to be closest to the voters, who elected its delegates every two years. The upper house, or Senate, was elected by the state legislatures rather than directly by the voters. Staggered six-year terms prevent the choice of a majority in any given year and thereby further isolate senators from the passing fancies of public passion.

The decision that a single person be made the chief executive caused the delegates "considerable pause," according to James Madison. George Mason protested that this would create a "fetus of monarchy." Indeed, although subject to election every four years, the chief executive would wield powers that would exceed those of the British king. The president could veto acts of Congress, subject to being overridden by a two-thirds vote in each house, was commander in chief of the armed forces, and was responsible for the execution of the laws. The chief executive could make treaties with the advice and consent of two thirds of the Senate and appoint diplomats, judges, and other officers with the consent of a majority of the Senate. The president was instructed to report annually on the state of the nation and was authorized to recommend legislation.

But the president's powers were limited in certain key areas. The chief executive could neither declare war nor make peace; those powers were reserved for Congress. Unlike the British monarch, moreover, the president could be removed from office. The House could impeach (indict) the chief executive—and other civil officers—on charges of treason, bribery, or "other high crimes and misdemeanors"; the president could then be removed by the Senate with a two-thirds vote to convict. The presiding officer at the trial of a president would be the chief justice, since the usual presiding officer of the Senate (the vice president) would have a personal stake in the outcome.

The leading nationalists—men like James Madison, James Wilson, and Alexander Hamilton—wanted to strengthen the independence of the president by entrusting the choice to popular election. But an elected executive was still too far beyond the American experience. Besides, a national election would have created enormous problems of organization and voter qualification. James Wilson suggested instead that the people of each state choose presidential electors equal to the number of their senators and representatives. Others proposed that the legislators make the choice. Finally the convention voted to let the legislature decide the method in each state. Before long nearly all the states were choosing their electors by popular vote, and the electors were acting as agents of the party will, casting their votes as they had pledged them before the election. This method diverged from the original expectation that the electors would deliberate and make their own choices.

The third branch of government, the judiciary, caused surprisingly little debate. Both the Virginia and the New Jersey Plans had called for a supreme court, which the Constitution established, providing specifically for a chief justice of the United States and leaving up to Congress the number of other justices. Although the Constitution nowhere authorizes the courts to declare laws void when they conflict with the Constitution, the power of judicial review is implied and was soon exercised in cases involving both state and federal laws. Article VI declares the federal constitution, federal laws, and treaties to be the "supreme Law of the Land," state laws or constitutions "to the Contrary notwithstanding."

Although the Constitution extended vast new powers to the national government, the delegates' mistrust of unchecked power is apparent in repeated examples of countervailing forces: the separation of the three branches of government, the president's veto, the congressional power of impeachment and removal, the Senate's power to approve treaties and appointments, and the courts' implied right of judicial review. In addition, the new form of government specifically forbade Congress to pass ex post facto laws (laws adopted after an event to criminalize deeds already committed). It also reserved to the states large areas of sovereignty—a reservation soon made explicit by the Tenth Amendment. By dividing sovereignty between the people and the government, the framers of the Constitution provided a distinctive contribution to political theory. That is, by vesting ultimate authority in the people, they divided sovereignty *within* the government. This constituted a dramatic break with the colonial tradition. The British had always insisted that the sovereignty of the king-in-Parliament was indivisible.

The most glaring defect of the Articles of Confederation, the rule of state unanimity that defeated every effort to amend them, led the delegates to

Signing the Constitution, September 17, 1787

Thomas Pritchard Rossiter's painting shows George Washington presiding over what Thomas Jefferson called an assembly of demigods.

provide a less forbidding though still difficult method of amending the new constitution. Amendments can be proposed either by a two-thirds vote of each house or by a national convention specially called by two thirds of the state legislatures. Amendments can be ratified by approval of three fourths of the states acting through their legislatures or in special conventions.

THE FIGHT FOR RATIFICATION   The final article of the Constitution provided that it would become effective upon ratification by nine states (not quite the three-fourths majority required for amendment). The Congress submitted the convention's work to the states on September 28, 1787. In the ensuing political debate, advocates of the Constitution, who might properly have been called Nationalists because they preferred a strong central government, assumed the more reassuring name of Federalists. Opponents, who favored a more decentralized federal system, became anti-Federalists.

The Federalists were better prepared and better organized. They were usually clustered in or near cities and tended to be more cosmopolitan, urbane, and well educated. Anti-Federalists tended to be small farmers and frontiersmen who saw little to gain from the promotion of interstate commerce and much to lose from prohibitions on paper money and "stay" laws, which prevented foreclosure proceedings against farmers. Many of them also feared that an expansive land policy was likely to favor speculators.

THE FEDERALIST   Among the supreme legacies of the debate over the Constitution was a collection of essays called *The Federalist,* originally published in New York newspapers between 1787 and 1788. Initiated by Alexander Hamilton, the eighty-five articles published under the name Publius included about thirty by James Madison, nearly fifty by Hamilton, and five by John Jay. Written to promote state ratification of the Constitution, the essays defended the principle of a supreme national authority but sought to reassure doubters that there was little reason to fear tyranny by the new government.

In perhaps the most famous essay, Number 10, Madison argued that the country's very size and diversity would make it impossible for any single faction to form a majority that could dominate the government. This contradicted the prevailing notion that republics could work only in small countries like Switzerland and the Netherlands. In larger countries republican government would descend into anarchy and tyranny through the influence of factions. Quite the contrary, Madison argued. A republic with a balanced federal government could survive in a large and diverse country better than in a smaller country. "Extend the sphere," he wrote, "and you take in a greater variety of parties and interests; you make it less probable that a majority of the whole will have a common motive to invade the rights of other citizens."

The Federalists insisted that the new union would contribute to prosperity. The anti-Federalists, however, highlighted the dangers of power. They noted the absence of a bill of rights to protect individuals and states, and they found the ratification process highly irregular, which it was—indeed, it was illegal under the Articles of Confederation. Maryland's Luther Martin, who had walked out of the Constitutional Convention, urged his state not to ratify the Constitution by rejecting "those chains which are forged for it." The Anti-Federalist leaders—Martin, Patrick Henry, Richard Henry Lee of Virginia, George Clinton of New York, and Samuel Adams and Elbridge Gerry of Massachusetts—were often men whose careers and reputations had been established well before the Revolution. The Federalist leaders, on the other hand, were more likely to be younger men whose careers had begun in the Revolution and who had been "nationalized" in the fires of battle—men like Hamilton, Madison, and Jay.

The two groups disagreed more over means than ends, however. Both sides for the most part agreed that a stronger national government was needed and that it required an independent income to function properly. Both were convinced that the people must erect safeguards against tyranny, even the tyranny of the majority. Once the new government had become an accomplished fact, few diehards were left who wanted to undo the work of the Philadelphia convention.

THE DECISION OF THE STATES   Ratification of the new federal Constitution gained momentum before the end of 1787, and several of the smaller states were among the first to act, apparently satisfied that they had gained all the safeguards they could hope for in equality of representation in the Senate. New Hampshire was the ninth state to ratify the Constitution, on June 21, 1788, enabling it to be put into effect, but the Union could hardly succeed without the approval of Virginia, the most populous state, or New York, which had the third highest population and occupied a key position geographically.

There was strong opposition in both states. In Virginia, Patrick Henry became the chief spokesman for backcountry farmers who feared the powers of the new government, but wavering delegates were won over by a proposal that the convention should recommend a bill of rights. Virginia's convention voted for ratification on June 25, 1788. In New York, Alexander Hamilton and the other Federalists delayed a vote in the hope that action by Virginia would persuade the delegates that the new framework would go into effect

RATIFICATION OF THE CONSTITUTION

Order of Ratification	State	Date of Ratification
1	Delaware	December 7, 1787
2	Pennsylvania	December 12, 1787
3	New Jersey	December 18, 1787
4	Georgia	January 2, 1788
5	Connecticut	January 9, 1788
6	Massachusetts	February 6, 1788
7	Maryland	April 28, 1788
8	South Carolina	May 23, 1788
9	New Hampshire	June 21, 1788
10	Virginia	June 25, 1788
11	New York	July 26, 1788
12	North Carolina	November 21, 1789
13	Rhode Island	May 29, 1790

with or without New York. On July 26, 1788, they carried the day by the closest margin thus far, thirty to twenty-seven. North Carolina stubbornly withheld action until November 1789, when amendments comprising a bill of rights were submitted by Congress. Rhode Island, true to form, did not relent until May 29, 1790, by the closest margin of all—two votes.

Upon notification that New Hampshire had become the ninth state to ratify the Constitution, the Confederation Congress began to draft plans for an orderly transfer of power. On September 13, 1788, it selected New York City as the seat of the new government and fixed the date for elections. On October 10, 1788, the Confederation Congress transacted its last business and passed into history. "Our constitution is in actual operation," the elderly Benjamin Franklin wrote to a friend; "everything appears to promise that it will last; but in this world nothing is certain but death and taxes." George Washington was even more uncertain about the future under the new plan of government. He had told a fellow delegate as the convention adjourned, "I do not expect the Constitution to last for more than twenty years."

"A More Perfect Union"

The Constitution has lasted much longer, of course, and in the process it has provided a model of republican government whose features have been repeatedly borrowed by other nations through the years. Yet what makes the

8

THE FEDERALIST ERA

FOCUS QUESTIONS

· How did the new government operate?

· What was Alexander Hamilton's Federalist program?

· What characterized the beginnings of the first party system (composed of Federalists and Republicans)?

· What were the elements of the Federalists' foreign policy?

To answer these questions and access additional review material, please visit www.wwnorton.com/studyspace.

The new American republic was a sprawling nation of energetic individuals eager to test the limits of their freedom and exploit the nation's vast natural resources and economic opportunities. The new Constitution created a more powerful central government to deal with the problems of the vast new nation, but several foreign and domestic crises did not allow for an easy transition.

A NEW NATION

In 1789 the United States and the western territories reached from the Atlantic Ocean to the Mississippi River and was inhabited by almost 4 million people. The new nation harbored distinct regional differences. Although still characterized by small farms and bustling seaports, New

A New Society

An engraving from the title page of *The Universal Asylum and Columbian Magazine*, (published in Philadelphia in 1790). America is represented as a woman laying down her shield to engage in education, art, commerce, and agriculture.

England was on the verge of developing a small-scale manufacturing sector. The middle Atlantic states boasted the most well-balanced economy, the largest cities, and the most diverse collection of ethnic and religious groups. The South, a more ethnically homogeneous agricultural region, was increasingly dependent upon slave labor. By 1790 the southern states were exporting as much tobacco as they had been before the Revolution. Most important, however, was the surge in cotton production. Between 1790 and 1815 the annual production of cotton rose from less than 3 million pounds to 93 million pounds.

The United States in 1790 was predominantly a rural society. Eighty percent of households were involved in agricultural production. Only a few cities had more than 5,000 residents. The first national census, taken in 1790, counted 750,000 African Americans, almost one fifth of the population. Most of them lived in the five southernmost states; less than 10 percent lived outside the South. Most African Americans, of course, were enslaved, but there were many free blacks as a result of the Revolutionary turmoil. In fact, the proportion of free to enslaved blacks was never higher than in 1790.

The 1790 census did not even count the many Indians still living east of the Mississippi River. It is estimated that there were over eighty tribes numbering perhaps as many as 150,000 persons in 1790. In the Old Northwest along the Great Lakes, the British continued to arm the Indians and encouraged them to resist American encroachments. Between 1784 and 1790 Indians killed or captured some 1,500 settlers in Kentucky alone. Such bloodshed generated a ferocious reaction among settlers eager to eradicate the Indians. In the South the five most powerful tribes—the Cherokees, Chickasaws, Choctaws, Creeks, and Seminoles—numbered between 50,000 and 100,000. They steadfastly refused to recognize U.S. authority and used Spanish-supplied weapons to thwart white settlement.

Only about 125,000 whites and blacks lived west of the Appalachian Mountains in 1790. But that was soon to change. Rapid population growth, cheap land, and new economic opportunities fueled the westward migration. The average white woman gave birth to eight children, and the white population doubled approximately every twenty-two years. This made for a very young population on average. In 1790 almost half of all white Americans were under sixteen.

A NEW GOVERNMENT   The new Congress of the United States opened with a whimper rather than a bang. On March 4, 1789, the appointed date of its first session in bustling New York City, only eight senators and thirteen representatives took their seats. A month passed before both chambers gathered a quorum. Only then could the temporary presiding officer of the Senate count the ballots and certify the foregone conclusion that George Washington, with sixty-nine votes, was the unanimous choice of the Electoral College for president. John Adams, with thirty-four votes, the second-highest number, became vice president. Washington was a reluctant president. Yet he felt compelled to serve because he had been "summoned by my country." A self-made man with little formal education, Washington had a remarkable capacity for moderation and mediation that helped keep the infant republic from disintegrating.

THE GOVERNMENT'S STRUCTURE   The president and the Congress had to create a government anew. During the summer of 1789, Congress created executive departments corresponding to those already formed under the Confederation. To head the Department of State, Washington named Thomas Jefferson, recently back from his diplomatic duties in France. Leadership of the Department of the Treasury went to Washington's wartime aide, Alexander Hamilton, who had since become a prominent lawyer in

New York. Tall, graceful Edmund Randolph, former governor of Virginia and owner of a 7,000-acre debt-ridden plantation worked by 200 slaves, assumed the new position of attorney general. Almost from the beginning, Washington routinely called these men to sit as a group to discuss and advise on policy matters. This was the origin of the president's cabinet, an advisory body for which the Constitution made no formal provision.

Washington named John Jay as the first chief justice of the Supreme Court, and Jay served until 1795. Born in New York City in 1745, Jay had graduated from King's College (now Columbia University). His distinction as a lawyer led New York to send him as its representative to the First and Second Continental Congresses. After serving as president of the Continental Congress in 1778–1779, Jay became the American minister in Spain. While in Europe he helped John Adams and Benjamin Franklin negotiate the Treaty of Paris in 1783. After the Revolution, Jay served as secretary of foreign affairs. He joined Madison and Hamilton as co-author of *The Federalist* and became one of the most effective champions of the Constitution.

THE BILL OF RIGHTS   In the new House of Representatives, James Madison made a bill of rights one of the first items of business. The lack of provisions protecting individuals' and states' rights had been one of the anti-Federalists' major objections to the Constitution. In May 1789 Madison drew the first eight amendments to the Constitution from the Virginia Declaration of Rights, which George Mason had written in 1776. They provided safeguards for certain fundamental individual rights: freedom of religion, press, speech, and assembly; the right to keep and bear firearms; the right to refuse to house soldiers in private homes; protection from unreasonable searches and seizures; the right to refuse to testify against oneself; the right to a speedy public trial, with legal counsel present before an impartial jury; and protection against cruel and unusual punishment. The Ninth and Tenth Amendments declared that the enumeration of rights in the Constitution "shall not be construed to deny or disparage others retained by the people" and that "powers not delegated to the United States by the Constitution . . . are reserved to the States respectively, or to the people." The states voted separately on each proposed amendment, and the Bill of Rights became effective on December 15, 1791.

Madison viewed the Bill of Rights as "the most dramatic single gesture of conciliation that could be offered the remaining opponents of the government." Those "opponents" included prominent Virginians George Mason and Richard Henry Lee as well as artisans, small traders, and backcountry farmers who expressed a profound egalitarianism. These "poor and middling" folk were skeptical that even the "best men" were capable of subordinating self-interest to the good of the republic. They believed that all people were prone to corruption; no one could be trusted. Therefore, a bill of rights was necessary to protect the liberties of all against the encroachments of a few. Yet the Bill of Rights provided no rights or legal protection to African Americans or Indians.

HAMILTON'S VISION

Revenue was the new federal government's most critical need, and Congress quickly enacted a tariff intended to raise money and protect America's new manufacturers from foreign competition by raising prices on imported goods. Yet tariffs resulted in higher prices on imported goods bought by Americans, most of whom were tied to the farm economy. This circumstance raised a basic and perennial question: should rural consumers be forced to subsidize the nation's infant manufacturing sector?

The tariff launched the effort to get the country on a sound financial footing. In finance, with all its broad implications for policy in general, it was the thirty-four-year-old Alexander Hamilton who seized the initiative in 1789.

Alexander Hamilton

Secretary of the Treasury from 1789 to 1795.

The first secretary of the Treasury was born out of wedlock on a Caribbean island, deserted by his ne'er-do-well Scottish father, and left an orphan at thirteen by the death of his mother. With the help of friends and relatives, he found his way, at seventeen, to New York, attended King's College, and entered the Continental army, where he became a favorite of George Washington's. Hamilton distinguished himself at the siege of Yorktown, and he remained a frustrated military genius, hungry for greater glory on the field of battle. He studied law, passed the bar examination, established a legal practice in New York, and became a self-made aristocrat, serving as a collector of revenues and as a member of the Confederation Congress. An early convert to nationalism, he played a crucial part in promoting the Constitutional Convention and defending its work in *The Federalist.*

During the Revolutionary War, Colonel Hamilton had witnessed the near-fatal weaknesses of the Confederation Congress. Its lack of authority and money almost lost the war. Now, as the nation's first secretary of the Treasury, he was determined to transform an economically weak and fractious nation. To flourish in a warring world, Hamilton believed, the United States needed to unleash the energy and ambition of its citizens so as to create a vibrant economy driven by the engines of capitalism. He wanted to nurture the hustling, bustling, aspiring spirit that he believed distinguished Americans from others. Just as he had risen from poverty and shame to become immensely successful, he wanted to ensure that Americans would always have such opportunities. To do so, he envisioned a limited but assertive government that encouraged new fields of enterprise and fostered investment and entrepreneurship. Thriving markets and new industries would best ensure the fate of the republic, and a secure federal debt would give investors a stake in the success of the new national government. The young Hamilton was supremely confident in his ability to shape fiscal policies that would provide economic opportunity and ensure government stability. His success in minting a budget, a funded debt, a federal tax system, a national bank, a customs service, and a coast guard provided the foundations for American capitalism and American government.

The new government needed Hamilton's ambition and brilliance. In a series of reports submitted to Congress in 1790 and 1791, he outlined his program for government finances and the economic development of the United States.

ESTABLISHING THE PUBLIC CREDIT   Hamilton's first of two "Reports on Public Credit" dealt with the vexing issue of war-generated debt. Both the federal government and the individual states had emerged from the Revolution with substantial debts. France, Spain, and Holland had lent the United States money and supplies to fight the war, and Congress had incurred more debt by printing paper money and selling government bonds. State governments had also accumulated huge obligations. After the war some states had set about paying off their debts, but the efforts were uneven. Only the federal government could wipe the slate clean. Hamilton insisted that the debts from the Revolution were a *national* responsibility because all Americans had benefited from independence. He also knew that federal assumption of state debts would enhance a sense of nationalism by helping the people see the benefits of a strong central government. Finally, the Treasury secretary was determined to shore up the federal government's finances because he believed that preserving individual freedom and the sanctity of property went hand in hand.

Hamilton's controversial report on public credit made two key recommendations: first, it called for funding the federal debt at face value, which meant that citizens holding government securities could exchange them for new interest-bearing bonds of the same face value; second, it declared that the federal government should assume state debts from the Revolution. Holders of state bonds would exchange them for new national bonds. The funding scheme was controversial because many farmers and ex-soldiers in need of immediate money had sold their securities for a fraction of their value to speculators. Spokesmen for the sellers argued that they should be reimbursed for their losses; otherwise, the speculators would gain a windfall. Hamilton sternly resisted. The speculators, he argued, had "paid what the commodity was worth in the market, and took the risks." Therefore, they should reap the benefits. In fact, Hamilton insisted, the government should favor the financial community because it represented the bedrock of a successful nation.

Payment of the national debt, Hamilton believed, would be not only a point of national honor and sound finance, ensuring the country's credit for the future; it would also be an occasion to assert the federal power of taxation and thus instill respect for the authority of the national government. It was on this point, however, that Madison, who had been Hamilton's close ally in the movement for a stronger government, broke with him. Madison did not question whether the debt should be paid, but he was troubled that speculators would become the chief beneficiaries. Also disturbing was the fact that northerners held most of the debt. Madison's opposition touched off a vigorous debate that deadlocked the question of debt funding and assumption through much of 1790.

The stalemate finally ended in the summer of 1790, when Hamilton, Jefferson, and Madison reached a compromise. In return for northern votes in favor of locating the permanent national capital on the Potomac River along the Virginia border, Madison pledged to seek enough southern votes to pass the debt-assumption bill, with the further arrangement that those states with smaller debts would get in effect outright grants from the federal government to equalize the difference. These arrangements secured enough votes to carry Hamilton's funding and assumption plans. The national capital would be moved from New York City to Philadelphia for ten years, after which it would be located in a new federal city bordering northern Virginia. In August 1790 Congress finally passed the legislation for Hamilton's plan. Jefferson later claimed to have been "duped" by Hamilton into agreeing to the "Compromise of 1790" because he did not fully understand the implications of the debt-assumption plan. It is more likely that Jefferson had been outsmarted. He only later realized how relatively insignificant the location of the national capital was when compared with the far-reaching effects of Hamilton's economic program.

A NATIONAL BANK   Alexander Hamilton's vast program of funding federal and state debts generated, as if by magic, a great sum of capital for the new nation. Having established the federal government's creditworthiness, the relentless Hamilton moved on to a related measure essential to his vision of national greatness: a national bank, which by issuance of bank notes (paper money) might provide a uniform national currency as well as a source of expanding capital for the developing economy. Government bonds held by the bank would back up the currency. The Bank of the United States, chartered by Congress, would remain under government oversight, but private investors would supply four fifths of the $10 million capital and name twenty of the twenty-five directors; the government would purchase the other one fifth of the capital and name five directors. Government bonds would be received in payment for three fourths of the stock in the bank, and the other fourth would be payable in gold and silver.

Once again James Madison rose to lead the opposition, arguing that he could find no basis in the Constitution for a national bank. That was enough to raise in President Washington's mind serious doubts as to the constitutionality of the measure, which Congress passed over Madison's objections.

The vote in Congress revealed the growing sectional division in the young United States. Representatives from the northern states voted thirty-three to one in favor of the national bank; southern congressmen opposed the bank nineteen to six. Before signing the bill into law, President Washington sought the advice of his cabinet and found an equal division of opinion. This resulted in the first great debate on constitutional interpretation. Should there be a strict or a broad construction of the Constitution? Were the powers of Congress only those explicitly stated in the document, or were others implied? The argument turned chiefly on Article I, Section 8, which authorizes Congress to "make all Laws which shall be necessary and proper for carrying into execution the foregoing Powers."

Such language left room for disagreement and led to a colossal confrontation between Jefferson and Hamilton. Secretary of State Jefferson pointed to the Tenth Amendment, which reserves to the states and the people powers not delegated to Congress. A bank might be a convenient aid to Congress in collecting taxes and regulating the currency, but it was not, as Article I,

Section 8, specified, *necessary*. Hamilton insisted that the power to charter corporations was included in the sovereignty of any government, whether or not expressly stated. George Washington accepted Hamilton's argument and signed the bill. By doing so, in Jefferson's words, the president had opened up "a boundless field of power," which in coming years would lead to a further broadening of implied powers with the approval of the Supreme Court.

ENCOURAGING MANUFACTURES Alexander Hamilton's fertile imagination and his audacious ambitions for the new country were not yet exhausted. At the end of 1790, he submitted the second of his "Reports on Public Credit," which included a proposal for an excise tax on alcoholic beverages to help raise federal revenue to cover the nation's debts. Six weeks later Hamilton proposed a national mint, which was established in 1792 to provide money for the new nation. And on December 5, 1791, as the culmination of his financial program, he proposed, in his "Report on Manufactures," an extensive program of federal aid to promote the development of manufacturing enterprises.

Certificate of the New York Mechanick Society

An illustration of the growing diversification of labor, by Abraham Godwin (ca. 1785).

In the "Report on Manufactures," Hamilton argued for active government encouragement of manufacturing to provide productive uses for the new capital he had created by his funding, assumption, and banking schemes. Multiple advantages would flow from the aggressive development of manufactures: the diversification of labor in a country given over too exclusively to farming; improved productivity through the greater use of machinery; work for those not ordinarily employed, such as women and children; the promotion of immigration; a greater scope for the diversity of talents in business; and a better domestic market for agricultural products.

To secure his ends, Hamilton advocated protective tariffs, some of which were enacted in 1792, to protect young American industries from foreign competitors. Tariffs were, in essence, taxes on imported goods. The rest of Hamilton's manufacturing program was filed away—but not forgotten: it provided an arsenal of arguments for the manufacturing sector in years to come. Hamilton denied that his scheme favored the northern states. If, as seemed likely, the northern and middle Atlantic states should become the chief sites for manufacturing, he claimed, they would create robust markets for agricultural products, some of which the southern states were peculiarly qualified to produce. The nation as a whole would benefit, he argued, as commerce between North and South increased, supplanting the trade across the Atlantic Ocean with Britain and Europe.

HAMILTON'S ACHIEVEMENT   Largely because of the skillful Hamilton, the Treasury Department during the 1790s began retiring the Revolutionary War debt, enhanced the value of the Continental paper dollar, secured the government's credit, and attracted foreign capital. Prosperity, so elusive in the 1780s, began to flourish at the end of the century.

Hamilton professed a truly nationalist outlook, and he focused his energies on the rising power of commercial capitalism. Tying the government closely to the rich and the wellborn, Hamilton believed, promoted the government's financial stability and guarded the public order against the potential social turbulence that he feared would emerge in a republic.

But many Americans then and since have interpreted such views as elitist and self-serving. To be sure, Hamilton never understood the people of the villages and farms, the people of the frontier. They were foreign to his world, despite his own humble beginnings. And they, along with the planters of the South, would be at best only indirect beneficiaries of his programs. There were, in short, vast numbers of people who saw little gain from the Hamiltonian economic program and thus were drawn into opposition against it. Indeed, Jefferson claimed that he and Hamilton were "pitted against each other every day in the cabinet like two fighting-cocks."

The Republican Alternative

Opposition to the Hamiltonian economic program spawned the first national political parties. Alexander Hamilton emerged as the embodiment of the Federalists; James Madison and Thomas Jefferson led those who took the name Republicans (also called the Democratic Republicans) and thereby implied that the Federalists aimed at a monarchy. Neither side in the disagreement over national policy deliberately set out to create formal political parties. But there were growing differences of both philosophy and self-interest that simply would not subside.

The crux of the debate centered on the relative power of the federal government and the states. At the outset, Madison assumed leadership of Hamilton's opponents in Congress, and he argued that Hamilton was trampling upon states' rights in forging a powerful central government. After the Compromise of 1790, which assured the funding of state debts, Jefferson and Madison resolutely opposed Hamilton's policies. They opposed his move to place an excise tax on whiskey, which would especially burden the trans-Appalachian farmers whose livelihood depended upon the sale of the beverage, and they opposed his proposal for a national bank and his "Report on Manufactures." As these differences developed, the personal hostility between Jefferson and Hamilton festered within the cabinet, much to the distress of President Washington.

Thomas Jefferson

A portrait by Charles Willson Peale (1791).

JEFFERSON'S AGRARIAN VIEW Thomas Jefferson, twelve years Hamilton's senior, was in most respects his opposite. In contrast to the self-made Hamilton, Jefferson was an agrarian aristocrat, the son of a successful surveyor and land speculator. Jefferson read or spoke seven languages. He was an architect of some distinction (Monticello, the Virginia state capitol, and the University of Virginia are monuments to his talent), a man who understood mathematics and engineering, an inventor, and an agronomist.

Hamilton and Jefferson had contrasting perspectives on America's future. Hamilton was a hardheaded realist who foresaw a diversified capitalist economy, with agriculture balanced by commerce and industry, and was thus the better prophet. Jefferson was an agrarian idealist who feared that the growth of crowded cities would divide society into a capitalist aristocracy on the one hand and a deprived working class on the other. Hamilton feared anarchy and loved order; Jefferson feared tyranny and loved liberty.

Hamilton championed a strong central government run by a wealthy elite actively engaged in encouraging capitalist enterprise. Jefferson desired a decentralized agrarian republic. Jefferson's ideal America was one in which small farmers predominated. He did not oppose all forms of manufacturing; he feared that the unlimited expansion of commerce and industry would produce a large class of propertyless wage laborers dependent upon others for their livelihood and therefore subject to political manipulation and economic exploitation.

CRISES FOREIGN AND DOMESTIC

As the disputes between Jefferson and Hamilton intensified, George Washington proved ever more adept at transcending party differences and holding things together with his unmatched prestige. In 1792 he won unanimous reelection, and no sooner had his second term begun than problems of foreign relations leaped to center stage, delivered by the consequences of the French Revolution, which had begun in 1789, during the first months of his presidency. Americans supported the popular revolt against the French monarchy, up to a point. By the spring of 1792, the idealistic experiment in liberty, equality, and fraternity had turned into a monster that plunged France into war with Austria and Prussia and began devouring its own children, along with its enemies, in the Terror of 1793–1794.

After the execution of King Louis XVI, early in 1793, Great Britain joined with the monarchies of Spain and Holland in a war against the French republic. For the next twenty-two years, Britain and France were at war, with only a brief respite, until the final defeat of the French forces under Napoléon in 1815. The war presented George Washington, just beginning his second term, with an awkward problem. By the 1778 Treaty of Alliance, the United States was a perpetual ally of France, obligated to defend her possessions in the West Indies.

Americans, however, wanted no part of the European war. They were determined to maintain their lucrative trade with both sides. For their part, Hamilton and Jefferson found in the neutrality policy one issue on which they could agree. Where they differed was in how best to implement it. President Washington issued a neutrality proclamation on April 22, 1793, that declared the United States "friendly and impartial toward the belligerent powers."

CITIZEN GENET   At the same time, President Washington had accepted Thomas Jefferson's argument that the United States should recognize the new French government (becoming the first country to do so) and receive its new ambassador, Edmond-Charles Édouard Genet. Early in 1793, Genet landed at Charleston, South Carolina, where he received a hero's welcome, and made his way northward to Philadelphia. En route he brazenly engaged in quite nonneutral activities. He outfitted privateers to capture British ships, and he conspired with frontiersmen and land speculators to launch an attack on Spanish Florida and Louisiana in retaliation for Spain's opposition to the French Revolution.

After arriving in Philadelphia, Genet quickly became an embarrassment even to his Republican friends. The cabinet finally agreed unanimously that he had to go, and George Washington demanded his recall. The behavior of the French made it hard even for Republicans to retain sympathy for the French Revolution, but Jefferson and others maintained their support. Jefferson was so disgusted by Washington's refusal to support the French Revolution and by his own ideological warfare with Alexander Hamilton that he would resign as secretary of state at the end of 1793. Nor did the British make it easy for Federalists to rally to their side. Near the end of 1793, they announced orders in council allowing them to seize the cargo of American ships with provisions for or exports from French islands in the Caribbean. By 1794 a prolonged foreign-policy crisis between the United States and Great Britain threatened to renew warfare between the two old enemies.

JAY'S TREATY   Early in 1794 Republican leaders in Congress were gaining support for commercial retaliation to end British trade abuses when the British gave George Washington a timely opening for a settlement. They stopped seizing American ships, and on April 16, 1794, Washington named Chief Justice John Jay as a special envoy to Great Britain. Jay left with instructions to settle all major issues: to get the British out of their forts along the northwestern frontier, win reparations for the losses of American shippers, secure compensation to planters for southern slaves carried away in 1783, and negotiate a commercial treaty that would legalize American commerce with the British West Indies.

The pro-British Jay had little leverage with which to wring concessions from the British, however, and after seven months of negotiations he won only two pledges: the British promised to evacuate the northwestern posts by 1796 and to pay damages for the seizure of American ships and cargo in 1793–1794. In exchange for those concessions, Jay agreed to the British definition of neutral rights. He accepted the principles that naval stores (tar, pitch, and turpentine), food, and war supplies headed to enemy ports on neutral ships were contraband and that trade with enemy colonies prohibited in peacetime could not be opened in wartime (the "rule of 1756"). Britain also gained most-favored-nation treatment in American commerce and a promise that French privateers would not be outfitted in American ports. Finally, Jay conceded that the British need not compensate U.S. citizens for the enslaved people who had escaped during the war, and he promised that the pre-Revolutionary American debts to British merchants would be paid by the U.S. government. Perhaps most important, he failed to gain unrestricted access for American commerce to the British West Indies.

Public outrage greeted the terms of Jay's Treaty. The public debate was so intense that some Americans feared civil war might erupt. Even Federalist shippers, ready for a settlement with the British on almost any terms, criticized Jay's failure to fully open up the British West Indies to American commerce. Much of the outcry, however, came from disappointed Republican partisans who had sought an escalation of the conflict with the hated England. In the end, moderation prevailed. George Washington worried that his opponents were prepared to separate "the Union into Northern & Southern." Once he endorsed Jay's Treaty, there were even calls for his impeachment. Yet the president, while acknowledging that the proposed agreement was imperfect, concluded that adopting it was the only way to avoid war with Britain. Without a single vote to spare, Jay's Treaty won the necessary two-thirds majority on June 24, 1795. Washington hesitated but signed the treaty as the best he was likely to get. The major votes in Congress were again aligned by region; 80 percent of the votes for the treaty came from New England or the middle Atlantic states; 74 percent of those voting against the treaty were cast by southerners.

THE FRONTIER   Other events also had an important bearing on Jay's Treaty, adding force to the importance of its settlement of the Canadian frontier. While Jay was haggling in London, frontier conflict with Indians escalated, with U.S. troops twice crushed by northwestern Indians. At last, General Wayne, known as Mad Anthony, led an expedition into the Northwest Territory in the fall of 1793. The following year, on August 4, Indians representing eight tribes and reinforced by some Canadian militias, attacked

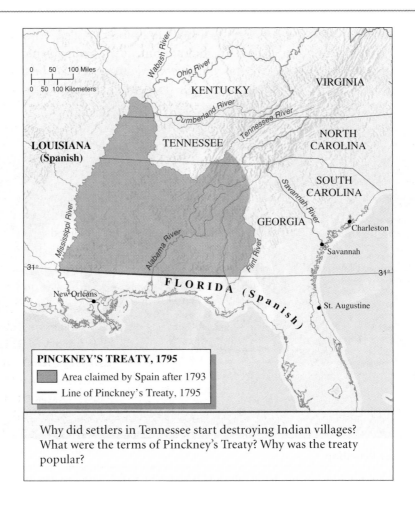

0 50 100 Miles
0 50 100 Kilometers

Wabash River

Ohio River

KENTUCKY

VIRGINIA

Cumberland River

Tennessee River

LOUISIANA
(Spanish)

TENNESSEE

NORTH
CAROLINA

SOUTH
CAROLINA

Savannah River

GEORGIA

Charleston

Mississippi River

Alabama River

Savannah

31°

31°

Flint River

FLORIDA (Spanish)

New Orleans

St. Augustine

PINCKNEY'S TREATY, 1795

Area claimed by Spain after 1793
—— Line of Pinckney's Treaty, 1795

Why did settlers in Tennessee start destroying Indian villages?
What were the terms of Pinckney's Treaty? Why was the treaty
popular?

Republicans, however, and Jefferson's party scored heavily in the next
Pennsylvania elections.

PINCKNEY'S TREATY   While these stirring events were transpiring in
Pennsylvania, Spain was suffering setbacks to its schemes to consolidate its
control over Florida and the Louisiana territory. Spain had refused to recognize the legitimacy of America's southern boundary established by the Treaty
of Paris in 1783, and its agents thereafter sought to thwart American expansion southward. Spanish intrigues among the Creeks, Choctaws, Chickasaws,
and Cherokees were keeping up the same sort of turmoil the British had fomented along the Ohio River.

In the mid-1790s, however, the shifting balance of power in Europe led Spain to end its designs on America. This change of heart resulted in Pinckney's Treaty, by which the U.S. ambassador, Thomas Pinckney, pulled off a diplomatic triumph in 1795 when he won Spanish acceptance of an American boundary at the 31st parallel, free navigation of the Mississippi River, the right to deposit goods at New Orleans without having to pay customs duties for a period of three years (with promise of renewal), a commission to settle American claims against Spain, and a promise on each side to refrain from inciting Indian attacks on the other. Ratification of Pinckney's Treaty was immensely popular, especially among westerners eager to use the Mississippi River to transport crops to market.

SETTLEMENT OF NEW LAND

Now that John Jay and Thomas Pinckney had settled matters with Britain and Spain and General Anthony Wayne in the Northwest had suppressed Indian resistance, a renewed surge of settlers headed for the West. New lands, ceded by the Indians in the Treaty of Greenville, revealed a Congress once again divided on the issue of federal land policy. There were two basic viewpoints on the matter: that the public domain should serve mainly as a source of revenue and that it was more important to get the country settled, an endeavor that required low land prices. Policy would evolve from the first to the second viewpoint, but for the time being the federal government's need for revenue took priority.

LAND POLICY Opinions on land policy, like opinions on other issues, separated Federalists from Republicans. Federalists involved in real-estate speculation might prefer lower land prices, but the more influential Federalists, like Hamilton and Jay, preferred to build the population of the eastern states first, lest the East lose political influence and a labor force important to the growth of manufactures. Men of their persuasion favored high federal land prices to enrich the Treasury and the sale of relatively large parcels of land to speculators rather than small tracts to settlers. Jefferson and Madison were reluctantly prepared to go along with such a land policy for the sake of reducing the national debt, but Jefferson yearned for a plan by which the land could be settled more readily. In any case, he suggested, frontiersmen would do as they had done before: "They will settle the lands in spite of everybody." The pioneers of the West, always moving out beyond the settlers and the surveyors, were already proving him right.

The Federalist land policy prevailed in the Land Act of 1796, which retained the 640-acre minimum size mandated by the Northwest Ordinance of 1787 while doubling the price per acre to $2 and requiring that the full amount be paid within a year. Such terms were well beyond the means of most settlers and even many speculators. As a result, by 1800 federal land offices had sold fewer than 50,000 acres. Continuing demands for cheaper land led to the Land Act of 1800, which reduced the minimum unit to 320 acres and spread payments over four years. The Land Act of 1804 further reduced the minimum parcel to 160 acres, which became the traditional homestead, and the price per acre went down to $1.64.

THE WILDERNESS ROAD   The lure of western lands led thousands of settlers to follow Daniel Boone into the territory known as Kentucky or Kaintuck, from the Cherokee name Ken-Ta-Ke (Great Meadow). In the late eighteenth century, Kentucky was a farmer's fantasy and a hunter's paradise, with its fertile soil and abundant forests teeming with buffalo, deer, and wild turkeys.

Boone himself was the product of a pioneer background. Born on a small farm in 1734 in central Pennsylvania, the son of hardworking Quakers, he moved with his family to western North Carolina in 1750. There Daniel emerged as the region's greatest hunter, trading animal skins for salt and other household goods. After hearing numerous reports about the territory over the mountains, Boone set out alone in 1769 to find a trail into Kentucky. Armed with a long rifle, tomahawk, and hunting knife and dressed in a hunting shirt, deerskin leggings, and moccasins, he found what was called the Warriors' Path, a narrow foot trail that buffalo, deer, and Indians had worn along the steep ridges. It took him through the Cumberland Gap, in southwestern Virginia. For two years thereafter, Boone explored the region, living off the plentiful game. He returned to North Carolina with exciting stories about the riches of Kentucky.

In 1773 Boone led the first group of settlers through the Appalachian Mountains at the Cumberland Gap. Two years later Boone and thirty woodsmen used axes to widen the Warriors' Path into what became known as the Wilderness Road, a passage that more than 300,000 settlers would use over the next twenty-five years. At a point where a branch of the Wilderness Road intersected with the Kentucky River, near what is now Lexington, Boone built a settlement that was named Boonesborough.

A steady stream of settlers, mostly Scotch-Irish from Pennsylvania, Virginia, and North Carolina, poured into Kentucky during the last quarter of the eighteenth century. The backcountry settlers came on foot or horseback, often leading a mule or a cow that carried their few tools and other possessions. On a good day they might cover fifteen miles. Near a creek or spring they would buy a parcel or stake out a claim and mark its boundaries by chopping notches into "witness trees." They would then build a lean-to for temporary shelter and clear the land for planting. The pioneers grew melons, beans, turnips, and other vegetables, but corn was the preferred crop because it kept well and had so many uses. Pigs provided pork, and cows supplied milk, butter, and cheese. Many of

The Wilderness Trail

Daniel Boone Escorting Settlers through the Cumberland Gap by George Caleb Bingham.

the frontier families also built crude stills to manufacture a potent whiskey they called corn likker.

TRANSFER OF POWER

By 1796 President Washington had decided that two terms in office were enough. Weary of increasingly bitter political quarrels and the venom of the partisan press, he was ready to retire to Mount Vernon. He would leave behind a formidable record of achievement: the organization of a national government with demonstrated power, the establishment of the national credit and a growing economy, the settlement of territory previously held by Britain and Spain, the stabilization of the northwestern frontier, and the admission of three new states: Vermont (1791), Kentucky (1792), and Tennessee (1796).

WASHINGTON'S FAREWELL   President George Washington's farewell address to the nation focused on domestic policy and, in particular, on the need for unity among Americans in backing their new government. Washington decried the "baneful effects" of sectionalism and partisanship while acknowledging that parties were "useful checks upon the administration of the government, and serve to keep alive the spirit of liberty."

In foreign relations, he asserted, the United States should display "good faith and justice toward all nations" and avoid either "an habitual hatred or an habitual fondness" for other countries. The young nation should also "steer clear of permanent alliances with any portion of the foreign world." This statement drew little notice at the time, but it proved profoundly important in shaping American attitudes toward foreign policy for generations thereafter. Later spokesmen for such an isolationist policy would distort Washington's position by claiming that he had opposed any "entangling alliances." On the contrary, Washington was not preaching isolationism; he was instead warning against any further permanent arrangements like the one with France, still technically in effect. Washington recognized that "we may safely trust to temporary alliances for extraordinary emergencies." Washington's warning against permanent foreign entanglements served as a fundamental principle in U.S. foreign policy until the early twentieth century.

THE ELECTION OF 1796   With George Washington out of the race, the United States in 1796 held its first partisan election for president. The logical choice of the Federalists would have been Washington's protégé, Alexander Hamilton, the chief architect of their programs. But Hamilton's policies had left scars and made enemies. In Philadelphia a caucus of Federalist congressmen chose John Adams as their heir apparent, with Thomas Pinckney of South Carolina, fresh from his treaty negotiations in Spain, as the nominee for vice president. As expected, the Republicans drafted Thomas Jefferson and added geographic balance to the ticket with Aaron Burr of New York.

The growing strength of the Republicans, fueled by the smoldering resentment of Jay's Treaty, very nearly swept Jefferson into office and perhaps would have but for the public appeals of the French ambassador for Jefferson's election—an action that backfired. The Federalists won a majority among the electors, but Alexander Hamilton hatched an impulsive scheme that nearly threw the election away after all. Thomas Pinckney, Hamilton thought, would be easier to influence than the strong-minded Adams. He therefore sought to have the South Carolina Federalists withhold a few votes for Adams and bring Pinckney in first. The Carolinians cooperated, but New Englanders got wind of the scheme and dropped Pinckney. The upshot of Hamilton's failed scheme was to cut Pinckney out of both the presidency and the vice presidency and elect Jefferson vice president with sixty-eight electoral votes, to Adams's seventy-one.

THE ADAMS YEARS

Vain and cantankerous, short and paunchy, John Adams had crafted a distinguished career as a Massachusetts lawyer; a leader in the Revolutionary movement and the hardest-working member of the Continental Congress; a diplomat in France, Holland, and Britain; and George Washington's vice president. His political philosophy fell somewhere between Jefferson's and Hamilton's. He shared neither the one's faith in the common people nor the other's fondness for an aristocracy of "paper wealth." He favored the classic republican balance of aristocratic, democratic, and monarchical elements in government. A man of powerful intellect and forthright convictions, Adams was haunted by the feeling that he was never properly appreciated—and he may have been right. On the overriding issue of his administration, war and peace, he kept his head when others about him were losing theirs—probably at the cost of his reelection.

WAR WITH FRANCE John Adams faced the daunting task of succeeding the most popular man in America. He inherited from George Washington his divided cabinet—there was as yet no precedent for changing personnel at the start of each new administration. Adams also inherited a menacing quarrel with France, a byproduct of Jay's Treaty. When John Jay had accepted the British position that food and naval stores, as well as war supplies, bound for enemy ports were contraband subject to seizure, the French reasoned that American cargo headed for British ports was subject to the same interpretation. The French loosed their corsairs with even more devastating effect than the British had in 1793–1794. By the time of Adams's inauguration, in 1797, the French had plundered some 300 American ships and broken diplomatic relations with the United States.

John Adams

Political philosopher and politician. Adams was the first president to take up residence in the White House, in 1800.

President Adams immediately acted to restore relations with France. In 1797 Charles Cotesworth Pinckney (brother of Thomas) sailed for

Paris with John Marshall, a Virginia Federalist, and Elbridge Gerry, a Massachusetts Republican, for further negotiations. After long, nagging delays the three commissioners were accosted by three French counterparts (whom Adams labeled X, Y, and Z in his report to Congress), agents of the French foreign minister, Charles-Maurice de Talleyrand. The French diplomats said that negotiations could begin only if the Americans paid a bribe of $250,000 to the French government.

Such bribes were common eighteenth-century diplomatic practice, but Talleyrand's price was high for a mere promise to negotiate. The American answer, according to the commissioners' report, was "no, no, not a sixpence." When the XYZ affair was reported in Congress and the press, the response was translated into the more stirring slogan "millions for defense but not one cent for tribute." Even the most partisan Republicans, except for Thomas Jefferson, were hard put to make any more excuses for the French, and many of them joined the chorus for war. An undeclared naval war in fact raged from 1798 to 1800, but Adams resisted a formal declaration of war.

Conflict with France

A cartoon indicating the anti-French sentiment generated by the XYZ affair. The three American ministers (at left) reject the "Paris Monster's" demand for money.

Congress, however, authorized the capture of armed French ships, suspended commerce with France, and renounced the 1778 Treaty of Alliance, which was already defunct.

Adams used the French crisis to strengthen American defenses. In 1798 Congress created a Department of the Navy, and by the end of 1799 the number of naval ships had increased from three to thirty-three. By then American ships had captured eight French vessels and secured America's overseas commerce.

By the fall of 1798, even before the naval war was fully under way, Talleyrand began to make peace overtures. Adams named three peace commissioners, who arrived in Paris to find themselves confronting a new government under First Consul Napoléon Bonaparte. They sought two objectives: $20 million to pay for the American ships seized by the French and the formal cancellation of the 1778 Treaty of Alliance. By the Convention of 1800, ratified in 1801, the French agreed only to terminate the alliance and the quasi war.

THE WAR AT HOME   The simmering naval conflict with France mirrored an ideological war at home between Federalists and Republicans. Already-heated partisan politics had begun boiling over during the latter years of Washington's administration. The rhetoric grew so personal that opponents commonly resorted to duels. Federalists and Republicans saw each other as traitors to the principles of the American Revolution. Thomas Jefferson, for example, decided that Alexander Hamilton, George Washington, John Adams, and other Federalists were suppressing individual liberty in order to promote selfish interests. He adamantly opposed Jay's Treaty because it was pro-British and anti-French, and he was disgusted by the army's suppression of the Whiskey Rebellion.

Such volatile issues forced Americans to take sides, and the Revolutionary generation of leaders, a group that John Adams had called the band of brothers, began to fragment into die-hard factions. Long-standing political friendships disintegrated amid the venomous partisan attacks and sectional divisions between North and South. Jefferson observed that a "wall of separation" had come to divide the nation's political leaders. "Politics and party hatreds," he wrote his daughter from the nation's capital, "destroy the happiness of every being here."

Jefferson was no innocent in the matter; his no-holds-barred tactics contributed directly to the partisan tensions. As vice president under Adams, he displayed a gracious deviousness. He led the Republican faction opposed to Adams and schemed to embarrass him. In 1797 Jefferson secretly hired a rogue journalist, James Callender, to produce a scurrilous pamphlet that described President Adams as a deranged monarchist intent upon naming himself king.

For his part the combative Adams refused to align himself completely with the Federalists, preferring instead to mimic George Washington and retain his independence as chief executive. He was too principled and too prickly to toe a party line. Soon after his election he invited Jefferson to join with him in creating a bipartisan administration. After all, they had worked well together in the Continental Congress and in France, and they harbored great respect for each other. After consulting with James Madison, however, Jefferson refused to accept the new president's offer. Within a year he and Adams were at each other's throats.

The conflict with France deepened the partisan divide emerging in the young United States. The real purpose of the French crisis all along, the more ardent Republicans suspected, was to provide Federalists with an excuse to put down domestic political opposition. The infamous Alien and Sedition Acts of 1798 lent credence to their suspicions. These and two other measures, passed amid the wave of patriotic war fever, limited freedom of speech and the press and the liberty of aliens. Proposed by extreme Federalists in Congress, the legislation did not originate with John Adams but had his blessing. Goaded by his wife, Abigail, his primary counselor, Adams signed the controversial statutes and in doing so made the greatest mistake of his presidency. By succumbing to the partisan hysteria and enacting the vindictive acts, Adams bore out what Benjamin Franklin had said about him years before: he "means well for his country, is always an honest man, often a wise one, but sometimes and in some things, absolutely out of his senses."

Three of the four repressive acts reflected native hostility to foreigners, especially the French and the Irish, a large number of whom had become active Republicans and were suspected of revolutionary intent. The Naturalization Act extended from five to fourteen years the residency requirement for citizenship. The Alien Act empowered the president to deport "dangerous" aliens at his discretion. The Alien Enemies Act authorized the president in time of declared war to expel or imprison enemy aliens at will. Finally, the Sedition Act defined as a high misdemeanor any conspiracy against legal measures of the government, including interference with federal officers and insurrection or rioting. What is more, the law forbade writing, publishing, or speaking anything of "a false, scandalous and malicious" nature against the government.

The purpose of such laws was transparently partisan, designed to punish Republicans. Of the ten convictions under the act, all were directed at Republicans, some for trivial matters. In the very first case a drunk Republican was fined $100 for wishing out loud that the wad of a salute cannon might hit President Adams in his rear. The few convictions under the act only created martyrs to the cause of freedom of speech and the press and exposed the vindictiveness of Federalist judges.

To offset the "reign of witches" unleashed by the Alien and Sedition Acts, Jefferson and Madison drafted the Kentucky and Virginia Resolutions. These passed the legislatures of their respective states in late 1798. The resolutions, much alike in their arguments, denounced the Alien and Sedition Acts as "alarming infractions" of constitutional rights and advanced the state-compact theory. Since the Constitution arose as a compact among the states, the resolutions argued, it followed logically that the states retained the right to say when Congress had exceeded its powers. The states could "interpose" their judgment on acts of Congress and "nullify" them if necessary.

These doctrines of interposition and nullification, reworked by later theorists, were destined to be used for causes unforeseen by their authors. At the time, it seems, both Jefferson and Madison intended the resolutions to serve chiefly as propaganda, the opening guns in the presidential campaign of 1800. Neither Kentucky nor Virginia took steps to nullify or interpose its authority in the enforcement of the Alien and Sedition Acts. Instead, both called upon the other states to help them win a repeal in Congress. In Virginia, citizens talked of armed resistance to the federal government.

REPUBLICAN VICTORY   As the presidential election of 1800 approached, civil unrest boiled over. Grievances were mounting against Federalist policies: taxation to support an unneeded army, the Alien and Sedition Acts, the lingering fears of John Adams's affinity for "monarchism," the hostilities aroused by Alexander Hamilton's economic programs, the suppression of the Whiskey Rebellion, and Jay's Treaty. When Adams opted for peace with France in 1800, he probably doomed his one chance for reelection. Only a wave of patriotic war fever with a united party behind him could have gained him victory at the polls. His decision for peace gained him much goodwill among Americans but left the Hamiltonians angry and his party divided.

In 1800 the Federalists summoned enough unity to name Adams and Charles Cotesworth Pinckney as their candidates. But the Hamiltonian Federalists continued to snipe at the president and his policies, and soon after his renomination Adams removed two of them from his cabinet. A furious Hamilton struck back with a pamphlet questioning Adams's fitness to be president, citing his "disgusting egotism." Intended for private distribution among Federalist leaders, the pamphlet reached the hands of Aaron Burr, who circulated it widely.

Jefferson and Burr, as the Republican presidential candidates, once again represented the alliance of Virginia and New York. Jefferson, perhaps even more than Adams, became the target of vitriolic abuse. Opponents labeled him an atheist and a supporter of the excesses of the French Revolution. Jefferson refused to answer the attacks and directed the campaign from his Virginia home at Monticello. He was portrayed as a friend to farmers and a champion of states' rights, frugal government, liberty, and peace.

John Adams proved more popular than his party, whose candidates generally fared worse than the president, but the Republicans edged him out by seventy-three electoral votes to sixty-five. The decisive states were New York and South Carolina, either of which might have given the victory to Adams. But in New York former senator Aaron Burr's organization won control of the legislature, which cast the electoral votes. In South Carolina, Charles Pinckney (cousin of the Federalist Pinckneys) won over the legislature with well-placed promises of Republican patronage. Still, the result was not final, for Jefferson and Burr had tied with seventy-three votes each, and the choice of the president was thrown into the House of Representatives, where Federalist diehards tried vainly to give the election to Burr. This was too much for Hamilton, who opposed Jefferson but held a much lower opinion of Burr. The stalemate in the House continued for thirty-five ballots. The deadlock was broken only when a Jefferson supporter assured a Federalist congressman from Delaware that Jefferson would refrain from the wholesale removal of Federalists appointed to federal offices and would uphold Hamilton's financial policies. The representative resolved to vote for Jefferson, and several other Federalists agreed simply to cast blank ballots, permitting Jefferson to win without any of them having to vote for him.

Before the Federalists relinquished power to the Jeffersonian Republicans on March 4, 1801, their lame-duck Congress passed the Judiciary Act of 1801. Intended to ensure Federalist control of the judicial system, this act created sixteen circuit courts with a new judge for each and increased the number of federal attorneys, clerks, and marshals. Before he left office, Adams named John Marshall to the vacant office of chief justice of the Supreme Court and appointed Federalists to all the new positions in the federal judiciary, including forty-two justices of the peace for the new District of Columbia. The Federalists, defeated and destined never to regain national power, had in the words of Jefferson "retired into the judiciary as a stronghold."

The election of 1800 marked a major turning point in American political history. It was the first time that one political party, however ungracefully, relinquished power to the opposition party. Jefferson's victory signaled the

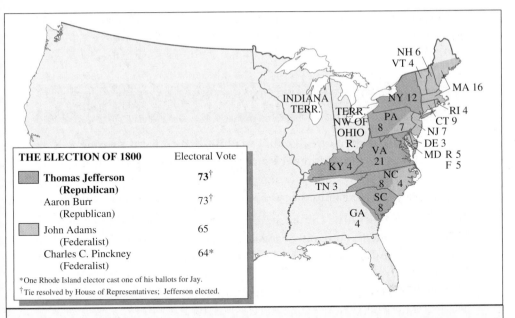

THE ELECTION OF 1800	Electoral Vote
Thomas Jefferson (Republican)	**73†**
Aaron Burr (Republican)	73†
John Adams (Federalist)	65
Charles C. Pinckney (Federalist)	64*

*One Rhode Island elector cast one of his ballots for Jay.
†Tie resolved by House of Representatives; Jefferson elected.

Why was the election of 1800 a key moment in American history? How did the Republicans win New York and South Carolina? How did Congress break the tie between Jefferson and Burr?

emergence of a new, more democratic political system, dominated by parties, partisanship, and wider public participation—at least among white men. Before and immediately after independence, politics was a popular but undemocratic activity: people took a keen interest in public affairs, but socially prominent families, the "rich, the able, and the wellborn," dominated political life. However, the fierce political battles of the late 1790s, culminating in 1800 with Jefferson's election, wrested control of politics from the governing elite and established the right of more people to play an active role in governing the young republic. With the gradual elimination of property qualifications for voting and the proliferation of newspapers, pamphlets, and other publications, the "public sphere" in which political issues were debated and decided expanded enormously in the early nineteenth century.

John Adams regretted the democratization of politics and the rise of fractious partisanship. "Jefferson had a party, Hamilton had a party, but the commonwealth had none," he sighed. The defeated president was so distraught at the turn of events that he decided not to participate in Jefferson's inauguration in the new capital of Washington, D.C. Instead, he boarded a stagecoach for the 500-mile trip to his home in Quincy, Massachusetts. He and Jefferson would not communicate for the next twelve years.

MAKING CONNECTIONS

- Thomas Jefferson's Republican philosophy offered a strong alternative to Alexander Hamilton's Federalism. As the next chapter shows, however, once the Republicans got into power, they adopted a number of Federalist principles and positions.

- The Bank of the United States and the protective tariff continued to be controversial. The bank's charter was renewed for another twenty years in 1816, the same year in which the first truly protective tariff was passed (Chapter 10), but in the 1830s the bank was eliminated, and the tariff became a major source of sectional conflict (Chapter 11).

- The foreign-policy crises with England and France described in this chapter will lead to the War of 1812, discussed in Chapter 9.

FURTHER READING

The best introduction to the early Federalists remains John C. Miller's *The Federalist Era, 1789–1801* (1960). Other works analyze the ideological debates among the nation's first leaders. Richard Buel Jr.'s *Securing the Revolution: Ideology in American Politics, 1789–1815* (1972), Joyce Appleby's *Capitalism and a New Social Order: The Republican Vision of the 1790s* (1984), Drew R. McCoy's *The Last of the Fathers: James Madison and the Republican Legacy* (1989), and Stanley Elkins and Eric McKitrick's *The Age of Federalism: The Early American Republic, 1788–1800* (1993) trace the persistence and transformation of ideas first fostered during the Revolutionary crisis. John F. Hoadley's *Origins of American Political Parties, 1789–1803* (1986) is superb.

Federalist foreign policy is explored in Jerald A. Comb's *The Jay Treaty: Political Battleground of the Founding Fathers* (1970), William Stinchcombe's *The XYZ Affair* (1980), and Felix Gilbert's *To the Farewell Address: Ideas of Early American Foreign Policy* (1961).

For specific domestic issues, see Thomas P. Slaughter's *The Whiskey Rebellion: Frontier Epilogue to the American Revolution* (1986) and Harry Ammon's *The Genet Mission* (1973). Patricia Watlington's *The Partisan Spirit: Kentucky Politics, 1779–1792* (1972) examines the Kentucky Resolutions. The treatment of Indians in the Old Northwest is explored in Richard H. Kohn's *Eagle and Sword: The Federalists and the Creation of the Military Establishment in America, 1783–1802* (1975). For the Alien and Sedition Acts, consult James Morton Smith's *Freedom's Fetters: The Alien and Sedition Laws and American Civil Liberties* (1956). Daniel Sisson's *The American Revolution of 1800* (1974) is useful for its treatment of that important election.

Several books focus on social issues of the post-Revolutionary period, including *Keepers of the Revolution: New Yorkers at Work in the Early Republic* (1992), edited by Paul A. Gilje and Howard B. Rock; Ronald Schultz's *The Republic of Labor: Philadelphia Artisans and the Politics of Class, 1720–1830* (1993); and Peter Way's *Common Labour: Workers and the Digging of North American Canals, 1780–1860* (1993).

The African-American experience in the Revolutionary era is detailed in Mechal Sobel's *The World They Made Together: Black and White Values in Eighteenth-Century Virginia* (1987) and Gary B. Nash's *Forging Freedom: The Formation of Philadelphia's Black Community, 1720–1840* (1988).

9

THE EARLY REPUBLIC

FOCUS QUESTIONS

- What were the domestic policies of the Republicans once they were in power?
- How did politics divide the early republic?
- What were the causes and effects of the War of 1812?

To answer these questions and access additional review material, please visit www.wwnorton.com/studyspace

The early years of the new republic laid the foundation for the nation's development as the first society in the world organized around the promise of equal opportunity for all—except African-American slaves, Indians, and women. White American men in the fifty years after independence were on the move and on the make. Their prospects seemed unlimited, their optimism unrestrained. Land sales west of the Appalachian Mountains soared in the early nineteenth century as aspiring farmers shoved Indians aside in order to establish homesteads of their own. Enterprising, mobile, and increasingly diverse in religion and national origin, thousands of ordinary folk uprooted themselves from settled communities and went in search of personal advancement, occupying more territory in a single generation than had been settled in the 150 years of colonial history. Between 1800 and 1820 the trans-Appalachian population soared from 300,000 to 2 million. By 1840 over 40 percent of Americans lived west of the mountains in eight new states.

The migrants flowed westward in three streams between 1780 and 1830. One ran from the Old South—Virginia, Maryland, and the Carolinas—through Georgia into the newer states of Alabama and Mississippi. Another wave traversed the Blue Ridge Mountains from Maryland and Virginia, crossing into Kentucky and Tennessee. The third route was in the North, taking New Englanders westward across the Berkshires into New York, Pennsylvania, Ohio, and Michigan. Many of the pioneers stayed only a few years before continuing westward in search of cheaper and more fertile land.

The spirit of opportunistic independence affected free blacks as well as whites, Indians as well as immigrants. Free blacks were the fastest growing segment of the population during the early nineteenth century. Many slaves had gained their freedom during the Revolutionary War, by escaping, joining British forces, or serving in American units. Every state except South Carolina promised freedom to slaves who fought the British. Afterward state after state in the North outlawed slavery, and anti-slavery societies blossomed, exerting increasing pressure on the South to end the degrading practice.

The westward migration of whites brought incessant conflict with Native Americans. Indians fiercely resisted but ultimately succumbed to a federal government and a federal army determined to displace them. Most white Americans, however, were less concerned about Indians and slavery than they were about seizing their own opportunities. Politicians suppressed the volatile issue of slavery; their priorities were elsewhere. Westward expansion, economic growth, urban development, and the democratization of politics fostered a pervasive entrepreneurial spirit among the generation of Americans born after 1776—especially outside the South. In 1790 nine out of ten Americans lived on the land and engaged in what is called household production; their sphere of activity was local. But with each passing year, farmers increasingly focused on producing surplus crops and livestock to be sold in regional markets. Cotton prices soared, and in the process the Deep South grew ever more committed to a plantation economy dependent upon slave labor, world markets, and New England shippers and merchants. The burgeoning market economy produced boom-and-bust cycles, but overall the years from 1790 to 1830 were quite prosperous, with young Americans experiencing a "widening scope of opportunity."

While most Americans after the Revolution continued to work as farmers, a growing number of young adults found employment in new or greatly expanded enterprises: textiles, banking, transportation, publishing, retailing, teaching, preaching, medicine, law, construction, and engineering.

Technological innovations (steam power, power tools, and new modes of transportation) and their social applications (mass communication turnpikes, the postal service, banks, and corporations) fostered an array of new industries and businesses. The emergence of a factory system transformed the nature of work for many Americans. Proud apprentices, journeymen, and master craftsmen, who controlled their labor and invested their work with an emphasis on quality rather than quantity, resented the proliferation of mills and factories populated by "half-trained" workers dependent upon an hourly wage and subject to the sharp fluctuations of the larger economy.

Young America was rapidly changing. The decentralized agrarian republic of 1776, nestled along the Atlantic seaboard, had become by 1830 a sprawling commercial nation connected by networks of roads and canals and cemented by economic relationships—all animated by a restless spirit of enterprise, experimentation, and expansion.

JEFFERSONIAN SIMPLICITY

On March 4, 1801, the soft-spoken, brilliant, and charming Thomas Jefferson became the first president to be inaugurated in the new federal city. Washington, District of Columbia, was then an array of undistinguished buildings clustered around two centers, Capitol Hill and the executive mansion. Congress, having met in eight towns since 1774, had at last found a permanent home but enjoyed few amenities. There were two places of amusement, a racetrack and a theater thick with "tobacco smoke, whiskey breaths, and other stenches." Practically deserted much of the year, the nation's new capital came to life only when Congress assembled.

Jefferson's inauguration befitted the simple surroundings. The new president walked two blocks from his lodgings to the unfinished Capitol, entered the Senate chamber, took the oath administered by the recently appointed chief justice John Marshall, read his address in a barely audible voice, and returned to his boardinghouse for dinner. A tone of simplicity and conciliation ran through Jefferson's inaugural address. "We are all Republicans—we are all Federalists," he assured the nation. He then presented a ringing affirmation of republican government: "I know, indeed, that some honest men fear that a republican government cannot be strong; that this government is not strong enough. I believe this, on the contrary, the strongest government on earth. I believe it is the only one where every man . . . would meet invasions of the public order as his own personal concern."

JEFFERSON IN OFFICE

The deliberate display of republican simplicity at Jefferson's inauguration set the style of his administration. Although a man of expensive personal tastes, he took pains to avoid the monarchical trappings of his Federalist predecessors. Jefferson, a widower, discarded the coach and six in which Washington and Adams had traveled to state occasions and rode about the city on horseback, often by himself. He continued to wear plain clothes. White House dinners were held at a circular table so that no one should take precedence. This practice infuriated several European diplomats accustomed to aristocratic formalities, and they boycotted White House affairs.

Jefferson liked to think of his election as the "revolution of 1800," but the electoral margin had been razor thin, and the policies that he followed were more conciliatory than revolutionary. Jefferson placed in policy-making positions men of his own party, and he was the first president to pursue the role of party leader, cultivating congressional support at his dinner parties and elsewhere. In the cabinet the leading figures were Secretary of State James Madison, a longtime neighbor and political ally, and Swiss-born secretary of the Treasury Albert Gallatin, a Pennsylvania Republican whose financial skills had won him the respect of the Federalists. In an effort to cultivate Federalist New England, Jefferson chose men from that region for the positions of attorney general, secretary of war, and postmaster general.

The Executive Mansion

A watercolor of the president's house during Jefferson's term in office. Jefferson called it "big enough for two emperors, one pope, and the grand lama in the bargain."

In lesser offices, Jefferson resisted the wholesale removal of Federalists, preferring to wait until vacancies appeared. But pressure from Republicans often forced him to remove the Federalists. In one area, however, he managed to remove the offices rather than the appointees. In 1802 Congress repealed the Judiciary Act of 1801 and so abolished the circuit judgeships and other offices to which John Adams had made his "midnight appointments" before leaving office. A new judiciary act restored to six the number of Supreme Court justices and set up six circuit courts, each headed by a justice.

MARBURY V. MADISON The "midnight appointments" that President Adams made just before he left office sparked the important case of *Marbury v. Madison* (1803), the first in which the Supreme Court asserted its right to declare an act of Congress unconstitutional. The case involved the appointment of the Maryland Fedaralist William Marbury as justice of the peace in the District of Columbia. Marbury's official letter of appointment, or commission, signed by President Adams just two days before he left office, remained undelivered when James Madison became secretary of state, and President Jefferson directed him to withhold it. Marbury then sued for a court order (a writ of mandamus) directing Madison to deliver his commission. Chief Justice John Marshall, a distant Virginia cousin of Jefferson's, wrote the Court's opinion. He held that Marbury deserved his commission but denied that the Court had jurisdiction in the case. Marshall and the court ruled that Section 13 of the Federal Judiciary Act of 1789, which gave the Court original jurisdiction in mandamus proceedings, was unconstitutional because the Constitution specified that the Court should have original jurisdiction only in cases involving ambassadors or states. The Court, therefore, could issue no order in the case. With one bold stroke, the Federalist Marshall had chastised the Jeffersonians while avoiding an awkward confrontation with an administration that might have defied his order. At the same time he established the stunning precedent of the Court's declaring a federal law invalid on the grounds that it violated provisions of the Constitution.

DOMESTIC REFORMS Jefferson's first term was a succession of triumphs in both domestic and foreign affairs. The president did not set out to discard Alexander Hamilton's Federalist economic program. Under the tutelage of Treasury Secretary Gallatin, he learned to accept the national bank as an essential convenience. It was too late, of course, to undo Hamilton's funding and debt-assumption operations but none too soon, in the opinion of both Jefferson and Gallatin, to begin retiring the resultant federal debt. Jefferson detested

Hamilton's belief that a regulated federal debt was a national "blessing" because it gave the bankers and investors who lent money to the U.S. government a direct stake in the success of the new republic. Jefferson believed that a large federal debt would bring only high taxes and government corruption, so he set about reducing government expenses and paying down the debt. In 1802 Jefferson won the repeal of the whiskey tax and other Federalist excises, much to the relief of backwoods distillers, drinkers, and grain farmers.

Without the revenue from excise taxes, frugality was all the more necessary to a federal government chiefly dependent upon its tariffs and the sale of western lands for revenue. Happily for the Treasury, both trade and land sales flourished. The European war continually increased American shipping traffic, and thus tariff revenues padded the Treasury. At the same time, settlers flocked to the western land purchased from the federal government. Ohio's admission to the Union in 1803 increased the number of states to seventeen.

By the "wise and frugal government" that the president promised in his inaugural address, Jefferson and Gallatin reasoned, the United States could live within its income, like a prudent farmer. The basic formula was simple: cut back on military expenses. A standing army menaced a free society anyway. It therefore should be kept to a minimum, with defense left primarily to state militias. The navy, which the Federalists had already reduced, ought to be reduced further. Coastal defense, Jefferson argued, should rely upon land-based fortifications and a "mosquito fleet" of small gunboats.

In 1807 Jefferson crowned his reforms by signing an act that outlawed the foreign slave trade as of January 1, 1808, the earliest date possible under the Constitution. At the time, South Carolina was the only state that still permitted the trade, but for years to come an illegal traffic in Africans would continue. By one informal estimate perhaps 300,000 enslaved blacks were smuggled into southern states between 1808 and 1861.

THE LOUISIANA PURCHASE In 1803 events produced the greatest single achievement of Jefferson's administration. The Louisiana Purchase of 1803 more than doubled the territory of the United States by bringing into its borders the entire Mississippi River valley west of the river itself.

The French had settled Louisiana in the early eighteenth century, but after their defeat by England in the Seven Years' War they had ceded the territory to Spain in exchange for West Florida. Soon after taking power in France in 1799, however, Napoléon had forced the Spanish to return the territory and expressed his intention of creating a North American empire. When word of the deal reached Washington, D.C. in 1801, Jefferson dispatched the New Yorker Robert R. Livingston, as the new American minister to France. Spain

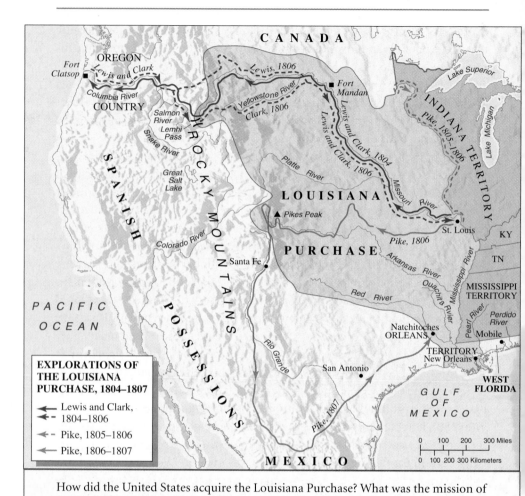

EXPLORATIONS OF
THE LOUISIANA
PURCHASE, 1804–1807

← Lewis and Clark,
←- 1804–1806

←- Pike, 1805–1806

← Pike, 1806–1807

How did the United States acquire the Louisiana Purchase? What was the mission of Lewis and Clark's expedition? What were the consequences of Lewis and Clark's reports about the Western territory?

in control of the Mississippi River outlet was bad enough, but Napoléon in control could mean serious trouble.

Livingston engaged the French in a series of long and frustrating negotiations. In April 1803 Napoléon's foreign minister, Talleyrand, suddenly asked if the United States would like to buy the whole of Louisiana. Livingston, once he regained his composure, snapped up the offer. Disease again played an important role in shaping history. Napoléon was willing to sell the territory because his French army on Hispaniola had been decimated not only by a slave revolt but also by yellow fever. Having failed to conquer the sugar-rich island and eager to renew his struggle against England, Napoléon had apparently decided simply to cut his losses in the New World, turn a quick profit, please the Americans, and go back to reshaping the map of Europe.

By the treaty of cession, dated April 30, 1803, the United States paid about $15 million for the huge territory. The treaty was vague in defining the boundaries of Louisiana. Its language could be stretched to provide a tenuous claim on Texas and a much stronger claim on West Florida, from Baton Rouge on the Mississippi River past Mobile to the Perdido River on the east. When Livingston asked about the boundaries, Talleyrand responded: "I can give you no direction. You have made a noble bargain for yourselves, and I suppose you will make the most of it."

The surprising turn of events presented Jefferson with a great new "empire of liberty"—and a constitutional dilemma. Nowhere did the Constitution mention the purchase of territory. Jefferson at first suggested a constitutional amendment, but his advisers argued against delay lest Napoléon change his mind. The power to purchase territory, they reasoned, resided in the power to make treaties. In the end, Jefferson relented, trusting, he said, "that the good sense of our country will correct the evil of loose construction when it shall produce ill effects." New England Federalists boggled at the prospect of new western states that would probably strengthen the Jeffersonian party. In a reversal that foreshadowed many similar reversals on constitutional issues, Federalists found themselves arguing for strict construction of the Constitution while Republicans brushed aside such scruples. Gaining over 800,000 square miles trumped any legal concerns. The Senate ratified the treaty by an overwhelming vote of twenty-six to six, and on December 20, 1803, U.S. representatives took formal possession of the vast Louisiana Territory.

The Spanish kept West Florida, but within a decade it would be ripe for the plucking. American settlers in 1810 staged a rebellion in Baton Rouge and proclaimed the republic of West Florida, which was quickly annexed and occupied by the United States as far east as the Pearl River. In 1812 the state of Louisiana absorbed the region. The following year, with Spain itself a battlefield for French and British forces, U.S. troops took over the rest of West Florida, now the Gulf coast of the states of Mississippi and Alabama. The United States had truly made the most of a shrewd bargain.

THE LEWIS AND CLARK EXPEDITION   An amateur scientist long before he became president, Thomas Jefferson asked Congress to finance a mapping and scientific expedition to explore the far Northwest in 1803, beyond the Mississippi, in what was still foreign territory. Congress approved, and Jefferson assigned as commanders the twenty-nine-year-old Meriwether Lewis, his former private secretary, and another Virginian, a former army officer, William Clark.

In 1804 the "Corps of Discovery," numbering nearly fifty, set out from the small village of St. Louis to ascend the muddy Missouri River. Local Indians introduced them to clothes made from deer hides and taught them hunting techniques. Lewis and Clark kept detailed journals of their travels and drew maps of the unexplored regions. As they moved up the Missouri, the landscape changed from forest to prairie grass. They saw huge herds of bison and other large game animals, which had become more abundant after a smallpox epidemic had wiped out most of the Indian villages in the area. The expedition passed trappers and traders headed south with rafts and boats laden with furs. Six months after leaving St. Louis, near the Mandan Sioux villages in what is now North Dakota, they built a fort and wintered in relative comfort, sending back a barge loaded with maps, soil samples, and plant and animal specimens. In the spring they added to their main party a French guide and his remarkable Shoshone wife, Sacagawea, and they set out once again upstream. At the head of the Missouri River, they took the north fork, thenceforth named the Jefferson River, crossed the rugged Rocky Mountains, braved attacks by grizzly bears, and in dugout canoes descended the Snake and Columbia rivers to the Pacific. The following spring they split

Exploring the Far Northwest

Captain Clark and his men shooting bears, from a book of engravings of the Lewis and Clark expedition (ca. 1810).

into two parties, with Lewis heading back east by almost the same route and Clark going by way of the Yellowstone River. They reunited at the juncture of the Missouri and Yellowstone rivers, returning together to St. Louis in 1806, having been gone nearly two and a half years and having traversed over 8,000 miles. No longer was the Far West unknown country. Their reports of friendly Indians and abundant beaver pelts attracted traders and trappers to the region and gave the United States a claim to the Oregon Country by right of discovery and exploration.

POLITICAL SCHEMES President Jefferson's policies, including the Louisiana Purchase, brought him solid support in the South and the West. Even New Englanders were moving to his side. By 1809 John Quincy Adams, the son of the second president, would become a Republican. Die-hard Federalists read the handwriting on the wall. The acquisition of vast new territories in the West would reduce New England and the Federalist party to insignificance in political affairs. Under the leadership of Timothy Pickering, secretary of state under Washington and Adams and now a U.S. senator, a group of bitter Massachusetts Federalists called the Essex Junto considered seceding from the Union, an idea that would simmer in New England for another decade.

Timothy Pickering and other Federalists also hatched a scheme that involved Vice President Aaron Burr, who had been on the outs with the Jeffersonians. Their plan, which would link New York with New England and depended upon Burr's election as governor of New York, could not win the support of even the extreme Federalists: Alexander Hamilton bitterly opposed it on the grounds that Burr was "a dangerous man, and one who ought not to be trusted with the reins of government."

Those remarks led to a duel between Hamilton and Burr in July 1804 at Weehawken, New Jersey, across the Hudson River from New York City. Hamilton personally opposed dueling, but his romantic streak and sense of manly honor compelled him to meet the vice president's challenge and demonstrate his courage—he was determined not to kill his opponent. Burr had no such scruples. On a grassy ledge above the Hudson River, he shot Hamilton through the heart. Hamilton went to his death, as his son had gone to his in a similar duel, also settled in Weehawken, the previous year. Hamilton's death ended both Pickering's scheme and Burr's political career—but not Burr's intrigues.

Burr would lose the gubernatorial election. In the meantime, the presidential campaign of 1804 began when a Republican congressional caucus renominated Jefferson. Opposed by the Federalist Charles C. Pinckney, Jefferson won 162 of the 176 electoral votes. It was the first landslide election in American history.

DIVISIONS IN THE REPUBLICAN PARTY

JOHN RANDOLPH AND THE OLD REPUBLICANS   Freed from a strong opposition—Federalists made up only one quarter of the new Congress—the Republican majority began to lose its cohesion as the nineteenth century progressed. The Virginia congressman known as John Randolph of Roanoke, initially a Jefferson supporter, became the most conspicuous of the dissidents. A brilliant, witty, but erratic and unyielding Virginia planter-philosopher, he was a powerful combination of principle, intelligence, wit, arrogance, and rancor.

Randolph became the crusty spokesman for a shifting group of "Old Republicans," whose adherence to party principles had rendered them more Jeffersonian than Jefferson himself. The Old Republicans were mostly southerners who defended states' rights and strict construction of the Constitution. They opposed any compromise with the Federalists and promoted an agrarian way of life. The Jeffersonian, or moderate, Republicans tended to be more pragmatic and nationalist in their orientation. As Thomas Jefferson himself demonstrated, they were willing to go along with tariffs and national banks. Randolph broke with Jefferson in 1806, when the president sought an appropriation of $2 million for a thinly disguised bribe to win French influence in persuading Spain to give up the Floridas. Thereafter he resisted Jefferson's initiatives almost reflexively. Randolph and his colleagues were sometimes called Quids, or the Tertium Quid (Third Something), and their dissent gave rise to talk of a third party, neither Republican nor Federalist. But they never got together, and their failure would typify the experience of almost all third-party movements thereafter.

THE BURR CONSPIRACY   Sheer brilliance and shrewdness had carried Aaron Burr to the vice presidency, and he might have become Jefferson's heir apparent but for his taste for intrigue. Caught up in the dubious schemes of Federalist diehards in 1800 and again in 1804, he ended his political career when he killed Alexander Hamilton. Indicted in New York and New Jersey for murder and heavily in debt, Burr fled first to Spanish-held Florida. Once the furor subsided, the vice president boldly returned to Washington in November to preside over the Senate. As long as he stayed out of New York and New Jersey, he was safe.

But Burr focused his attention less on the Senate than on a cockeyed scheme to carve out a personal empire for himself in the West. The so-called Burr conspiracy originated when Burr met with General James Wilkinson, an old friend with a tainted Revolutionary War record who was a spy for the

Spanish and had a penchant for easy money, a taste for rum, and an eye for intrigue. Just what Wilkinson and Burr were up to will probably never be known. The most likely explanation is that they sought to organize a secession of the Louisiana territory and set up an independent republic. Wilkinson developed cold feet, however, and sent a letter to President Jefferson warning of "a deep, dark, wicked and wide-spread conspiracy." Traveling south to recruit adventurers, Burr was apprehended and taken to Richmond, Virginia, for a trial that, like the conspiracy, had a stellar cast. Charged with treason, Burr was brought before Chief Justice John Marshall.

The case established two major constitutional precedents. The first came about when Jefferson, on the grounds of executive privilege, ignored a subpoena requiring him to appear in court with certain papers. He believed that the independence of the executive branch would be compromised if the president were subject to a court writ. The second was Marshall's rigid definition of treason. Treason under the Constitution, Marshall concluded, consisted of "levying war against the United States or adhering to their enemies" and required "two witnesses to the same overt act." Since the prosecution failed to produce two witnesses to an overt act of treason by Burr, the jury found him not guilty. To avoid further legal entanglements, Burr left the country for France. He returned unmolested in 1812 to practice law in New York and died at the age of eighty.

WAR IN EUROPE

Oppositionists of whatever stripe were more an annoyance than a threat to Jefferson. The more intractable problems of his second term involved the renewal of the European war in 1803, which helped resolve the problem of Louisiana but put more strains on Jefferson's desire to avoid "entangling alliances" and the quarrels of Europe. In 1805 Napoléon's defeat of Russian and Austrian forces gave him control of western Europe. That same year the British

Preparation for War to Defend Commerce

In 1806 and 1807 American shipping was caught in the crossfire of the war between Britain and France.

defeat of the French and Spanish fleets in the Battle of Trafalgar secured Britain's control of the seas. The war turned into a battle of elephant and whale, Napoléon dominant on land, the British dominant on the water, neither able to strike a decisive blow at the other, and neither restrained by concerns over neutral rights or international law.

HARASSMENT BY BRITAIN AND FRANCE   For two years after the renewal of European warfare, American shippers reaped the benefits, taking over trade with the French and Spanish West Indies. But in the case of the *Essex* (1805), a British court ruled that the practice of shipping French and Spanish goods through U.S. ports on their way elsewhere did not neutralize enemy goods. The practice violated the British rule of 1756, under which trade closed in time of peace remained closed in time of war. Goods shipped in violation of the rule, the British held, could be seized at any point under the doctrine of continuous voyage. After 1807 British interference with American shipping increased, not just to keep supplies from Napoléon's continent but also to hobble competition with British merchant ships.

In 1806 the British ministry adopted orders in council, which set up a paper blockade of Europe. Vessels headed for European ports had to get British licenses and accept British inspection or be liable to seizure. It was a paper blockade because even the powerful British navy was not large enough to monitor every European port. Napoléon retaliated with his "Continental System," proclaimed in the Berlin Decree of 1806 and the Milan Decree of 1807. In the first he declared his own paper blockade of the British Isles; in the second he ruled that neutral ships that complied with British regulations were subject to seizure when they reached Continental ports. The situation presented American shippers with a dilemma: if they complied with the demands of one side, they were subject to seizure by the other.

The risks were daunting, but the prospects for profits were so great that American shippers ran the risk. Seamen faced a more dangerous risk: a renewal of the practice of impressment. The use of press-gangs to kidnap men in British (and colonial) ports was a long-standing method of recruitment used by the British navy. The seizure of British subjects from American vessels became a new source of recruits, justified on the principle that British subjects remained British subjects for life: "Once an Englishman, always an Englishman."

In the summer of 1807, the British frigate, *Leopard* accosted a U.S. vessel, the *Chesapeake,* just outside territorial waters off the coast of Virginia. After the *Chesapeake*'s captain refused to allow his ship to be searched, the *Leopard* opened fire, killing three and wounding eighteen. The *Chesapeake,* unready for battle, was forced to strike its colors (that is, to lower its flag as a sign of surrender). A British search party seized four men, one of whom was later hanged for desertion from the British navy. Public wrath was so aroused that Jefferson could have had war on the spot. Like Adams before him, however, he resisted war fever and suffered politically as a result.

THE EMBARGO   Jefferson resolved to use public indignation at the British to promote "peaceable coercion." In December 1807, in response to his request, Congress passed the Embargo Act, which stopped all exports of American goods and prohibited American ships from leaving for foreign ports. It also effectively ended imports, since it was unprofitable for foreign ships to return from America empty. The constitutional basis of the embargo was the power to regulate commerce, which in this case Republicans interpreted broadly as the power to prohibit commerce.

Jefferson's embargo failed from the beginning, however, because few Americans were willing to make the necessary sacrifices. Trade remained profitable despite the risks, and violating the embargo was almost laughably easy. While American ships sat idle in ports, their crews laid off and unpaid, smugglers flourished and the British enjoyed a near monopoly of legitimate trade. Neither France nor Great Britain was significantly hurt by Jefferson's policy.

But Jefferson was injured. The unpopular embargo revived the languishing Federalist party in New England, which renewed the charge that Jefferson was in league with the French. At the same time, agriculture in the South and the West suffered for want of foreign outlets for grain, cotton, and tobacco. After fifteen months, Jefferson accepted failure, and on March 1, 1809, he signed a repeal of the embargo shortly before he relinquished the "splendid misery" of the presidency. In the election of 1808, the presidency passed to another Virginian, Secretary of State James Madison.

THE DRIFT TO WAR   Madison was entangled in foreign affairs from the beginning of his presidency. Still insisting on neutral rights and freedom of the seas, he pursued Jefferson's policy of "peaceful coercion" by different but equally ineffective means. In place of the embargo, Congress had substituted the Nonintercourse Act, which reopened trade with all countries except France and Great Britain and authorized the president to reopen trade with whichever nation gave up its restrictions. Nonintercourse proved as impotent as the embargo. In the vain search for an alternative, Congress in 1810, reversed itself and adopted a measure introduced by Nathaniel Macon of North Carolina. Macon's bill reopened trade with the warring powers but provided that if either dropped its restrictions, nonintercourse would be restored with the other.

Napoléon's foreign minister, the duke de Cadore, informed the U.S. minister in Paris that he had withdrawn the Berlin and Milan Decrees, but the carefully worded Cadore letter had strings attached: revocation of the decrees depended upon withdrawal of the British orders in council. The strings were plain to see, but Madison either misunderstood or, more likely, went along in the hope of putting pressure on the British. The British initially refused to give in, and on June 1, 1812, Madison reluctantly asked Congress for a declaration of war. On June 16, 1812, however, the British foreign minister, facing economic crisis, revoked the orders in council. Britain preferred not to risk war with the United States on top of its war with Napoléon. But it was too late. On June 18, 1812, Congress, unaware of the British repeal, granted Madison's request for war. With more time, more patience, or a transatlantic cable, Madison's policy would have been vindicated without resort to war.

THE WAR OF 1812

CAUSES   The main cause of the war—the violation of neutral shipping rights—seems clear enough. Neutral rights dominated Madison's war message and provided the salient reason for mounting public hostility toward the British. Yet the geographic distribution of the congressional vote raised a troubling question. Most votes for war came from the farm regions that stretched from Pennsylvania southward and westward. The maritime states of New York and New England, the region that bore the brunt of British attacks on U.S. trade, voted against the declaration. One explanation for this seeming anomaly is simple enough. The farming regions suffered damage to their markets for grain, cotton, and tobacco while New England shippers made profits from smuggling in spite of the British restrictions.

Other plausible explanations for the sectional vote, however, include frontier Indian attacks that were blamed on the British, western land hunger, and the American desire for territory in British Canada and Spanish Florida. The constant pressure to open new lands repeatedly forced or persuaded Indians to sign treaties they did not always understand, causing stronger resentment among tribes that were losing more and more of their land. It was an old story, dating from the Jamestown settlement, but one that took a new turn with the rise of a powerful Shawnee leader, Tecumseh.

Tecumseh recognized the consequences of Indian disunity and set out to form a confederation of tribes to defend Indian hunting grounds, insisting that no land cession was valid without the consent of all tribes, since they held the land in common. By 1811 Tecumseh had matured his plans and headed south from the Indiana Territory to win the Creeks, Cherokees, Choctaws, and Chickasaws to his cause. His speeches were filled with emotion and anger. "The white race is a wicked race," he declared. "They seize your land; they corrupt your women." Only by driving them out "upon a trail of blood" would the Indians survive.

General William Henry Harrison, governor of the Indiana Territory, learned of Tecumseh's plans and met with him twice. In the fall of 1811, however, Harrison decided that Tecumseh must be stopped. He gathered 1,000 troops near the Shawnees' capital on the Tippecanoe River while the Indian leader was away. Although Tecumseh had warned the Shawnees against fighting in his absence, they attacked Harrison's encampment. One quarter of Harrison's men died or were wounded, yet the Shawnees lost the Battle of Tippecanoe; their town was burned, their supplies destroyed. Tecumseh's dreams of an Indian confederacy went up in smoke, and the Shawnee leader sought British protection in Canada.

The Battle of Tippecanoe reinforced suspicions that the British were inciting the Indians. Frontier settlers believed that a U.S. conquest of Canada would end British influence among the Indians and open a new empire for land-hungry Americans. It was also one place where the British, in case of war, were vulnerable to an American attack. Madison and others acted on the mistaken assumption that the Canadians were eager to be liberated from British control. Thomas Jefferson had told Madison that the U.S. "acquisition of Canada" was "[a] matter of marching [north with a military force]." The British were vulnerable in Florida as well. East Florida, still under Spanish

Tecumseh

The Shawnee leader who tried to unite Indian tribes in defense of their land. He was killed in 1813 at the Battle of the Thames.

control, also posed a threat to the Americans, since Spain allowed sporadic Indian attacks across the frontier. Moreover, the British were suspected of smuggling goods through Florida and intriguing with the Indians on the southwestern border.

Such concerns helped generate war fever. In the Congress that assembled in 1811, several new members from southern and western districts clamored for war in defense of "national honor" and demanded an invasion of Canada. Among them were Henry Clay and Richard Mantor Johnson of Kentucky, Felix Grundy of Tennessee, and John C. Calhoun of South Carolina. John Randolph of Roanoke christened these "new boys" the "war hawks." The young senator Henry Clay, a tall, rawboned westerner know for his combative temperament and propensity for dueling, yearned for war. "I am for resistance by the *sword*," he vowed. He promised that the Kentucky militia stood ready to march on Canada and acquire its lucrative fur trade.

PREPARATIONS As it turned out, the war hawks would get neither Canada nor Florida, for in 1812 James Madison had carried into war a nation that was ill prepared both financially and militarily. The Republican program of small federal budgets and military cutbacks was not an effective way to win a war. And Madison, a studious, soft-spoken man, lacked anything resembling martial qualities. He was no George Washington.

The year before, despite urgent pleas from Treasury Secretary Albert Gallatin, Congress had let the twenty-year charter of the Bank of the United States expire. A combination of strict-constructionist Republicans and Anglophobes, who feared the large British interest in the bank, caused its demise. Meanwhile, trade had collapsed, and tariff revenues had declined. Loans were needed to cover about two thirds of the war costs, but northeastern opponents of the war were reluctant to lend money.

The military situation was almost as bad. War had been likely for nearly a decade, but Republican budgetary constraints had prevented preparations. When the War of 1812 began, the army numbered only 6,700 men, ill trained, poorly equipped, and led by aging officers. The navy, on the other hand, was in comparatively good shape, with able officers and trained men. Its ships were well outfitted and seaworthy—all sixteen of them. In the first year of the war, the navy produced the only U.S. victories in isolated duels with British vessels, but their effect was mainly an occasional boost to morale. Within a year the British had blockaded the U.S. coast, except for New England, where they hoped to cultivate anti-war feeling, and most of the little American fleet was bottled up in port.

THE WAR IN THE NORTH   The only place where the United States could effectively strike at the British was Canada. Madison's best hope was a quick attack on Quebec or Montreal to cut Canada's lifeline, the St. Lawrence River. The Madison administration opted for a three-pronged drive against Canada: along the Lake Champlain route toward Montreal, with General Henry Dearborn in command; along the Niagara River, with forces under General Stephen Van Rensselaer; and into Upper Canada (north of Lake Erie and Lake Ontario) from Detroit, with General William Hull and some 2,000 men. In Detroit the sickly and senile Hull procrastinated while his position worsened and the news arrived that an American fort isolated at the head of Lake Huron had surrendered. The British commander cleverly played upon Hull's worst fears. Gathering what redcoats he could to parade in view of Detroit's defenders, he announced that thousands of Indian allies were at the rear and he would be unable to control them once fighting began. Fearing a massacre, Hull, without consulting his officers and without a shot being fired, surrendered his entire force.

Along the Niagara River front, General Van Rensselaer was more aggressive. An advance party of 600 Americans crossed the river and worked their way up the bluffs on the Canadian side to occupy Queenstown Heights. The stage was set for a major victory, but the New York militia refused to reinforce Van Rensselaer's men, claiming that their military service did not obligate them to leave the country. They complacently remained on the New York side and watched their outnumbered countrymen fall to a superior force across the river.

On the third front, the old invasion route via Lake Champlain, the incompetent General Dearborn led his army north from Plattsburgh toward Montreal. He marched his men up to the border, where the state militia once again stood on its alleged constitutional rights and refused to cross, and then marched them back to Plattsburgh.

Madison's navy secretary now pushed vigorously for American control of inland waters. At Presque Isle (near Erie), Pennsylvania, in 1813, the twenty-eight-year-old Oliver Hazard Perry, already a fourteen-year veteran who had seen action against Tripoli, was busy building ships from green timber. At the end of the summer, Commodore Perry set out in search of the British, whom he found at Lake Erie's Put-in-Bay on September 10. After completing the preparations for battle, Perry told an aide, "This is the most important day of my life."

Two British warships used their superior weapons to pummel the *Lawrence,* Perry's flagship, from a distance. Blood flowed on the deck so

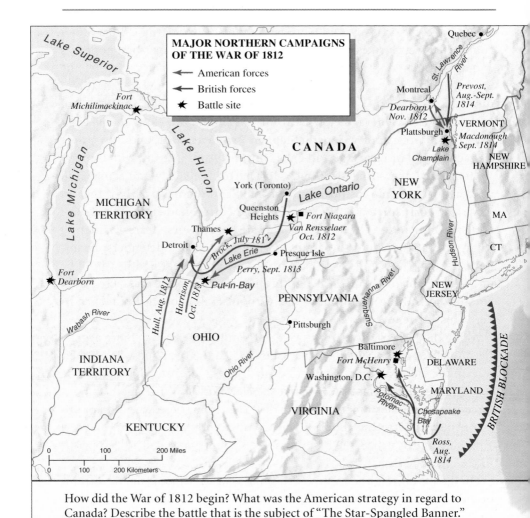

MAJOR NORTHERN CAMPAIGNS OF THE WAR OF 1812

← American forces

← British forces

★ Battle site

How did the War of 1812 begin? What was the American strategy in regard to Canada? Describe the battle that is the subject of "The Star-Spangled Banner."

freely that the sailors slipped and fell as they wrestled with the cannon. After four hours of intense shelling, none of the *Lawrence*'s guns was working, and most crew members were dead or wounded. The British expected the Americans to turn tail, but Perry refused to quit. He had himself rowed to another vessel, carried the battle to the enemy, and finally accepted surrender of the entire British squadron. Hatless, begrimed, and bloodied, Perry sent General William Henry Harrison the long-awaited message: "We have met the enemy and they are ours."

More good news followed. At the Battle of the Thames, on October 5, in Canadian territory east of Detroit, General Harrison eliminated British

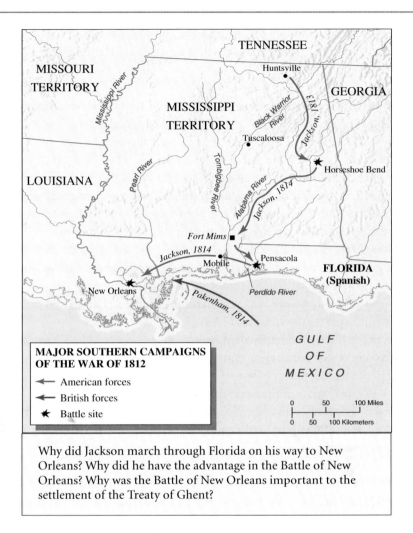

MAJOR SOUTHERN CAMPAIGNS
OF THE WAR OF 1812

◄── American forces

◄── British forces

★ Battle site

Why did Jackson march through Florida on his way to New
Orleans? Why did he have the advantage in the Battle of New
Orleans? Why was the Battle of New Orleans important to the
settlement of the Treaty of Ghent?

power in Upper Canada and released the Northwest from any further threat.
In the course of the battle, the great Indian leader Tecumseh was killed, his
dream of Indian unity dying with him.

THE WAR IN THE SOUTH   In the South, too, the war flared up in
1813. On August 30 Creeks allied with the British attacked Fort Mims, on
the Alabama River above Mobile, killing almost half the people in the fort.
As major general of the Tennessee militia, Andrew Jackson summoned about
2,000 volunteers and set out on a vengeful campaign that crushed Creek resistance. The decisive battle occurred in eastern Alabama on March 27, 1814,
at Horseshoe Bend, on the Tallapoosa River, in the heart of the Upper Creek

country. With the Treaty of Fort Jackson, the Indians ceded two thirds of their land to the United States, including part of Georgia and most of Alabama.

BRITISH STRATEGY   Four days after the Battle of Horseshoe Bend, Napoléon's French Empire collapsed. Now free to deal solely with America, the British developed a threefold plan of operations for 1814: they would launch a two-pronged invasion of America via Fort Niagara and Lake Champlain to increase the clamor for peace in the Northeast; extend the naval blockade to New England, subjecting coastal towns to raids; and seize New Orleans and take control of the Mississippi River, lifeline of the West. Uncertainties about the peace settlement in Europe prevented the release of British veterans for a full-scale assault upon the New World, however. And after a generation of conflict, war-weariness countered the British thirst for revenge against the former colonials. British plans were also stymied by the more resolute young American commanders Madison had placed in charge of strategic areas by the summer of 1814.

The main British effort focused on the invasion via Lake Champlain. A land assault might have taken Plattsburgh and forced American troops out of their protected positions nearby, but England's army, led by General George Prevost, governor general of Canada, bogged down while its flotilla engaged a U.S. naval squadron, led by Commodore Thomas Macdonough, on Lake Champlain. The battle ended in September 1814 with the British flotilla destroyed or captured.

FIGHTING IN THE CHESAPEAKE   Meanwhile however, American forces suffered the most humiliating experience of the war, as the British captured and burned Washington, D.C. With attention focused on the Canadian front, the Chesapeake Bay offered the British several inviting targets, including Baltimore, then the fourth-largest city in America. On the evening of August 24, 1814, the British marched unopposed into Washington and straight to the White House, where officers ate a meal that had been prepared for President and Mrs. Madison, who had hastily joined other refugees in Virginia. The British then burned the White House, the Capitol, and all other government buildings except the Patent Office. A tornado the next day compounded the damage, but a violent thunderstorm dampened both the fires and the enthusiasm of the British forces, who left to prepare a new assault on Baltimore.

That attack was a different story. With some 13,000 men, chiefly militia, American units fortified the heights behind the city. About 1,000 men held Fort McHenry, on an island in the harbor. The British fleet bombarded the fort to no avail, and the invaders abandoned their attack. Francis Scott Key, a Washington lawyer, watched the siege from a vessel in the harbor. The sight of the flag still in place at dawn inspired him to draft the verses of what come to be called "The Star-Spangled Banner." Later revised and set to the tune of an English drinking song, it was immediately popular and eventually became America's national anthem.

THE BATTLE OF NEW ORLEANS   The British failure at Baltimore followed by three days their failure on Lake Champlain; their offensive against New Orleans, however, had yet to run its course. Along the Gulf coast, General Andrew Jackson had been shoring up the defenses of Mobile and New Orleans. In late 1814, without authorization, he invaded Spanish Florida and took Pensacola, putting an end to British intrigues there. Back in Louisiana by the end of November, he began to erect defenses on the approaches to New Orleans. But the British fleet, with some 8,000 soldiers under General Sir Edward Pakenham, cautiously took up positions on a plain near the Mississippi River just south of the city.

Pakenham's painfully careful approach—he waited until all his artillery was available—gave Jackson time to build earthworks bolstered by cotton bales. It was an almost invulnerable position, but Pakenham, contemptuous of Jackson's motley array of frontier militiamen, Creole aristocrats, free blacks, and pirates, ordered a frontal assault at dawn on January 8, 1815. His redcoats emerged out of the morning fog and ran into a murderous hail of artillery shells and deadly rifle fire. Before the British withdrew, about 2,000 had been killed or wounded, including Pakenham himself, whose body, pickled in a barrel of rum, was returned to the ship where his wife awaited news of the battle.

The slow pace of communication during the early nineteenth century meant that the Battle of New Orleans occurred after a peace treaty had been signed in Europe. But this is not to say that it was an anticlimax or that it had no effect on the outcome of the war, for the treaty was yet to be ratified, and the British might have exploited to advantage the possession of New Orleans had they won it. The battle ensured ratification of the treaty as it stood, and both governments acted quickly.

THE TREATY OF GHENT   Peace efforts had begun in 1812, even before hostilities commenced, but negotiations bogged down after the fighting started. The British were stalling, awaiting news of smashing victories to strengthen their hand. Word of the U.S. victory on Lake Champlain weakened the British resolve. The British will to fight was further eroded by a continuing power struggle in Europe, by the eagerness of British merchants to renew trade with America, and by the war-weariness of a tax-burdened public. The British finally decided that the war was not worth the cost. Envoys from both sides eventually agreed to end the fighting, return prisoners, restore previous boundaries, and settle nothing else. The Treaty of Ghent was signed on Christmas Eve of 1814.

THE HARTFORD CONVENTION   While the diplomats converged on a peace settlement, in Europe, an entirely different kind of meeting was taking place in Hartford, Connecticut. An ill-fated affair, the Hartford Convention represented the climax of New England's disaffection with "Mr. Madison's war." New England had managed to keep aloof from the war and extract a profit from illegal trading and privateering. After the fall of Napoléon, however, the British extended their blockade to New England, occupied part of Maine, and conducted several raids along the coast. Even Boston seemed threatened. Instead of rallying to the American flag, however, Federalists in the Massachusetts legislature voted to convene a meeting of New England states to plan independent action.

On December 15, 1814, the Hartford Convention assembled with delegates from Massachusetts, Rhode Island, Connecticut, Vermont, and New Hampshire. The convention proposed seven constitutional amendments designed to limit Republican influence, including the requirement of a two-thirds vote to declare war or admit new states, a prohibition on embargoes lasting more than sixty days, a one-term limit on the presidency, and a ban on successive presidents from the same state.

The Hartford Convention carried the unmistakable threat of secession if its demands were ignored. Yet the threat quickly evaporated. When messengers from Hartford reached Washington, D.C., they found the battered capital celebrating the good news from Ghent and New Orleans. The consequence was a fatal blow to the Federalist party, which never recovered from the stigma of disloyalty stamped on it by the Hartford Convention.

THE AFTERMATH   For all the ineptitude with which the War of 1812 was fought, it generated an intense patriotic feeling. Despite the standoff with which it ended at Ghent, the American public felt victorious, thanks to Andrew Jackson and his men at New Orleans, as well as to the heroic exploits of U.S. frigates in their duels with British ships. However, the war revealed America's desperate need for a more efficient system of internal transportation— roads, bridges, canals. Even more important, the conflict launched the United States toward economic independence, as the interruption of trade encouraged the birth of American manufactures. This was a profound development, for the emergence of a factory system would generate far-reaching social effects as well as economic growth. After forty years of fragile independence, it dawned on the world that the new republic might not only survive but flourish.

One of the strangest results of the War of 1812 was a reversal of roles by the Republicans and the Federalists. Out of the wartime experience the Republicans had learned some lessons in nationalism. The necessities of war had "Federalized" Madison or "re-Federalized" the Father of the Constitution. Perhaps, he reasoned, a peacetime army and navy were necessary. He also had come to see the value of a national bank and of higher tariffs to protect infant American industries from foreign competition. But while Madison was embracing such nationalistic measures, the Federalists were borrowing the Jeffersonian theory of states' rights and strict construction. It was yet another reversal of roles in constitutional interpretation. It would not be the last.

We Owe Allegiance to No Crown

The War of 1812 generated a renewed spirit of nationalism.

MAKING CONNECTIONS

- Jefferson's embargo and the War of 1812 encouraged the beginnings of manufacturing in the United States, an important subject to be discussed in Chapter 12.

- The Federalist party collapsed because of its opposition to the War of 1812. But as the next chapter shows, Republicans did not prosper as much as might have been expected in the absence of political opposition.

- The American success in the War of 1812 (a moral victory at best) led to a tremendous sense of national pride and unity, a spirit analyzed in the next chapter.

FURTHER READING

Marshall Smelser's *The Democratic Republic, 1801–1815* (1968) presents an overview of the Republican administrations. The standard biography of Jefferson is Joseph J. Ellis's *American Sphinx: The Character of Thomas Jefferson* (1996). On the life of Jefferson's friend and successor, see Drew R. McCoy's *The Last of the Fathers: James Madison and the Republican Legacy* (1989). Joyce Appleby's *Capitalism and a New Social Order: The Republican Vision of the 1790s* (1984) minimizes the impact of republican ideology.

Linda K. Kerber's *Federalists in Dissent: Imagery and Ideology in Jeffersonian America* (1970) explores the Federalists while out of power. The concept of judicial review and the courts can be studied in Richard E. Ellis's *The Jeffersonian Crisis: Courts and Politics in the Young Republic* (1971). On John Marshall, see G. Edward White's *The Marshall Court and Cultural Change, 1815–1835* (1988). Milton Lomask's two-volume *Aaron Burr: The Years from Princeton to Vice President, 1756–1805* (1979) and *The Conspiracy and the Years of Exile, 1805–1836* (1982) trace the career of that remarkable American.

For the Louisiana Purchase, consult Alexander De Conde's *This Affair of Louisiana* (1976). For a captivating account of the Lewis and Clark expedition, see Stephen Ambrose's *Undaunted Courage: Meriwether Lewis, Thomas Jefferson, and the Opening of the American West* (1996). Bernard W. Sheehan's *Seeds of Extinction: Jeffersonian Philanthropy and the American Indian* (1973) is more analytical in its treatment of the Jeffersonians' Indian policy and the opening of the West.

Burton Spivak's *Jefferson's English Crisis: Commerce, Embargo, and the Republican Revolution* (1979) discusses Anglo-American relations during Jefferson's administration; Clifford L. Egan's *Neither Peace Nor War: Franco-American Relations, 1803–1812* (1983) covers French-American relations. An excellent revisionist treatment of the events that brought on war in 1812 is J.C.A. Stagg's *Mr. Madison's War: Politics, Diplomacy, and Warfare in the Early American Republic, 1783–1830* (1983). The war itself is the focus of Donald R. Hickey's *The War of 1812: A Forgotten Conflict* (1989). See also David Curtis Skaggs and Gerard T. Altoff's *A Signal Victory: The Lake Erie Campaign, 1812–1813* (1997).

Part Three

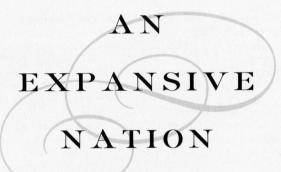

AN
EXPANSIVE
NATION

James Monroe serves as U.S. president (1817–1825)

McCulloch v. Maryland decision declares the federal government "supreme within its sphere of action" (1819)

1820 Missouri Compromise defuses sectional crisis over slavery (1820)

Election of 1824 is thrown into the House of Representatives; John Quincy Adams serves as U.S. president (1825–1829)

1828 Widespread labor organization leads to the formation of the Workingmen's party (1828)

John Calhoun writes *South Carolina Exposition and Protest,* which declares that states can nullify federal law (1828)

Andrew Jackson is elected U.S. president (1828)

Andrew Jackson serves as U.S. president (1829–1837)

1830

Expansion of suffrage for white adult males (1830s–1840s)

Webster-Hayne debate regarding states' rights (1830)

Indian Removal Act begins forced federal acquisition of tribal lands (1830)

In *Cherokee Nation v. Georgia,* the Supreme Court denies Cherokees the right to self-government (1831)

Jackson's entire cabinet resigns (1831)

The first national party conventions (1831)

A South Carolina state convention adopts a nullification ordinance declaring unconstitutional the tariff acts of 1828 and 1832 (1832)

Calhoun resigns as vice president to defend nullification in Senate (1832)

Jackson issues his Nullification Proclamation (1832)

The Anti-Masonic party is the first third party to run a candidate for president (1832)

The passage of the compromise tariff and the force bill averts crisis in the Union (1833)

A new two-party system pits Democrats against the Whig coalition (1836)

English defeat Napoléon at the Battle of Waterloo (1815)

Reactionaries take control of France (1815)

Spain cedes all of Florida to the U.S. (1819)

Peterloo Massacre of workers in England (1819)

Liberal revolts occur in Naples, northern Italy, Spain, and Brazil (1820)

French put down revolution in Spain (1822–1823)

Monroe Doctrine reaffirms U.S. hegemony in the Americas (1823)

Decembrist revolt of liberal army officers in Russia fails (1825)

Trade unionism in England promotes the interests of laborers (1820s–1830s)

Mexico controls former Spanish holdings in the American West and welcomes American merchants (1820s–1840s)

Greek independence from the Ottoman Empire (1829)

20,000 white settlers and 1,000 black slaves reside in the coastal region of East Texas, outnumbering the 5,000 Mexicans residing in the area (1830)

Revolution in France overthrows Restoration monarchy and brings Louis-Philippe and bourgeoisie to power (1830)

Revolutions in Belgium, the Rhineland, Italy, and Brazil (1830)

George Stephenson's locomotive speeds along the Liverpool-Manchester railway at sixteen miles per hour (1830)

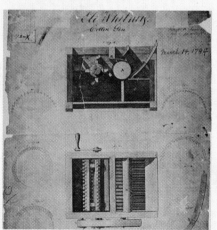

Mechanized cotton mills account for 22 percent of England's entire industrial production (1831)

Revolutions in Poland, Spain, and Italy are put down by conservatives (1831–1834)

The Reform Bill of 1832 expands suffrage in England by 50 percent and prevents revolution in Britain (1832)

American patriotism is greatly intensified by war with Great Britain (1815)

Andrew Jackson attacks Seminoles in Florida (1817)

American Colonization Society is founded to return blacks to Africa (1817)

Congressional report concludes that Indians should be "moralized or exterminated" (1818)

First free public secondary school opens (1821)

First freed slaves are returned to Africa (1822)

Over 200,000 people flee a drought in South Carolina (1820s–1830s)

U.S. population is nearly 13 million (1828)

Social and economic inequality abound, with 4 percent of New York City's population controlling 76 percent of its wealth (1828)

The Second Great Awakening occurs as religious revivals combine emotional fervor with a spirit of social equality (1820s–1830s)

The number of city dwellers doubles (1820s–1840)

The number of churches in New England increases by one third in one year (1830–1831)

The founding of the Mormon Church (1830)

Nativism surges as the immigration of Irish and German Catholics increases (1830s)

"Oregon Fever" draws thousands of migrants to the Oregon Trail in search of land to settle (1830s–1840s)

Nat Turner leads a slave uprising in Virginia (1831)

Roger B. Taney calls blacks "a separate but degraded people" (1831)

Technology improves diet, clothing, housing, and transportation (1830s–1840s)

Samuel Morse invents the telegraph machine, leading to a communications revolution (1832)

U.S. merchants resume trade with England (1815)

Congress reestablishes the Bank of the United States (1816)

Tariff protects U.S. industry but jeopardizes agriculture (1816)

Collapse of cotton prices in England triggers panic in U.S. (1819)

Trappers, traders, and Indians gather annually in Rocky Mountains to trade (1820s–1830s)

1820

Tariff favors manufacturing interests (1824)

Henry Clay's American System is defined (1824)

Erie Canal opens (1825)

Tariff further promotes manufacturing at the expense of agricultural interests (1828)

1828

The Industrial Revolution is in full bloom as textile mills and other factories sprout up around much of New England; the beginnings of labor organization (1820s–1840s)

State and private building of roads, canals, and railroads promotes growth of cities, further settlement, and commercial farming (1820s–1850s)

Jackson vetoes the Maysville Road bill and sets a precedent for limiting federal assistance for internal improvements (1830)

1830

The Preemption Acts allow squatters to stake out land claims prior to surveys and later to purchase that land at $1.25 per acre (1830, 1841)

American shipping companies set up trading offices and warehouses on the California coast to tap into that region's rich supply of animal hides (1830s)

Jackson vetoes the early renewal of Second Bank's charter, and his use of "pet banks" fuels a bank war (1832)

Cyrus Hall McCormick builds the first grain reaper, transforming the scale of American agriculture (1834)

National trade and craft unions are established (1834)

Sale of public land rises from 4 million acres to 20 million acres, an increase fueled by speculative investment spawned by state banks (1834–1836)

The Distribution Act and Specie Circular promote Jackson's hard currency theories and strain the economy (1836)

Jackson sets ten-hour workday at a Philadelphia naval yard (1836)

Charter expires on the Second Bank of the U.S.; Jackson wins bank war (1836)

1840

Martin Van Buren serves as U.S. president (1837–1841)

Van Buren calls a special session of Congress to deal with financial panic (1837)

Congress debates petitions to abolish slavery and slave trade in Washington, D.C. (1837–1841)

Parties organize down to the precinct level; the proportion of white male voters increases from 20 percent (1824) to 78 percent (1840)

William Henry Harrison is elected president (1840)

John Tyler serves as president when Harrison dies (1841–1845)

Tyler vetoes Henry Clay's bill for a new national bank; his entire cabinet (except for Daniel Webster) resigns (1842)

Congressional Whigs expell Tyler from their party (1842)

James Polk serves as president (1845–1849)

John L. O'Sullivan refers to U.S. expansion as "our manifest destiny" (1845)

Texas is formally annexed (1845)

The Mexican War with the United States heightens American nationalism (1845–1848)

The United States acquires Oregon (1846)

American troops capture Mexico City (1847)

1848

The Treaty of Guadalupe Hidalgo ends the Mexican War; the United States is awarded Texas north of the Rio Grande, California, and New Mexico (1848)

England's Factory Act limits the workday for children to eight hours (1833)

Abolition of slavery in the British Empire (1833)

Poor-law reform in England (1834)

Santa Anna's Mexican army defeats American forces at the Alamo (1836)

Santa Anna signs a treaty recognizing the independence of Texas (1836)

Depression in England (1837)

Canadian insurrection (1837)

The Chartist Movement in England seeks radical political reforms, including universal male suffrage (1838–1848)

The Opium War between China and Britain over trade in opium (1839–1842)

Lower and Upper Canada are united by an act of Parliament (1840)

The beginnings of socialism in Europe (1840s)

England claims the right to patrol the coast of Africa and to search American ships sailing there to see if they carry slaves (1841)

The Webster-Ashburton Treaty settles contested boundaries with British Canada and calls for joint British-American patrols of the African coast (1842)

China is forced to cede Hong Kong to Britain and to open up five ports to trade with the West (1842)

Railroad construction fuels the consumption of iron and coal (1840s)

Friedrich Engels publishes *The Condition of the Working Class* (1844)

The Irish potato famine (1845); similar crop failures in 1846, 1848, and 1851 in Ireland and Europe force 1 million people to flee, many to the United States

Approximately 800 Americans live in Mexican-controlled California (1846)

England repeals its Corn Laws, which had regulated the price of imported wheat (1846)

Ten Hours Act passed in England, limiting the workday to ten hours per day (1848)

John Stuart Mill publishes *Principles of Political Economy* (1848)

Karl Marx publishes *The Communist Manifesto* (1848)

The British complete the conquest of India (1848)

Revolutions in France, Prussia, Italy, and Austria; many refugees flee to America (1848–1849)

The American Temperance Union is founded (1833)

12,000 Cherokees are forced to migrate westward along the Trail of Tears (1835–1838)

Prosperity enables the urban middle class to hire maids and cooks, which creates additional free time (1830s–1860s)

Daily newspapers such as the *New York Herald* and *New York Tribune* make reading a form of popular entertainment (1830s–1860s)

One third of the labor force is jobless as a result of the depression (1837)

Mississippi becomes the first state to grant married women control over their own property (1839); by 1860, eleven other states do likewise

325,000 Indians (200 tribes) inhabit lands west of the Mississippi River (1840)

78 percent of total population, 91 percent of whites are literate (1840)

America has seventy-eight colleges and universities (1840)

Catharine Beecher publishes *A Treatise on Domestic Economy,* which becomes the "leading handbook for the cult of domesticity" (1841)

350,000 persons travel to California and Oregon, leading to tensions between settlers and Indians (1841–1867)

American writers including Dickinson, Hawthorne, Poe, Melville, and Whitman reexamine life in nineteenth-century America (1840s–1870s)

Urbanization leads to new forms of entertainment, including circuses, boxing, fraternal societies, theater, concerts, dances, lectures, etc. (mid-1800s)

Knickerbocker Base Ball Club becomes the first professional baseball team in America (1845)

2.4 million immigrants arrive in America (1845–1854)

The first professional baseball game is played (1846)

The Mormon Trek to Utah (1846–1851)

The Seneca Falls Convention promotes women's rights (1848)

Mass migration of young, unmarried men from every social class, state, territory, and from abroad, to disorderly mining shantytowns occurs (1848–1850)

The panic of 1837 leads to unemployment, wage cuts, and soaring prices (1837)

John Deere introduces the steel plow (1837)

3,000 miles of waterways link much of the nation to New York City (1837)

Port of New Orleans exports more than any other U.S. port (1830s–1840s)

Cotton accounts for more than half of the U.S.'s exports (1830s–1860)

The United States produces 60 percent of the world's cotton (1840)

The United States has 3,328 miles of railroads (1840), which soon increase to 30,626 (1860)

Independent Treasury Act (1840)

Van Buren extends the ten-hour workday to all government offices (1840)

Thirty-two mills and factories operate in Lowell, Massachusetts (1840)

Independent Treasury is repealed (1841)

The Supreme Court rules that labor unions are not illegal (1842)

Samuel Morse inaugurates the first telegraph line (1844)

Charles Goodyear patents stronger, improved (vulcanized) rubber (1844)

Fifty-two transatlantic shipping lines operate between New York and Europe (1845)

The advent of clipper ships doubles the speed of older merchant ships (1845)

Elias Howe invents the sewing machine (1846)

Independent Treasury is restored (1846)

1840

Gold is discovered at Sutter's Mill in California (1848)

1848

mericans during the early nineteenth century formed a relentless migratory stream that spilled over the Appalachian Mountains, spanned the Mississippi River, and in the 1840s reached the Pacific Ocean. Wagons, canals, flatboats, steamboats, and eventually railroads helped transport them. The feverish expansion of the United States into new western territories brought Americans into conflict with Native Americans, Mexicans, the British, and the Spanish. Only a few people, however, expressed moral reservations about displacing others. Most Americans believed it was the "manifest destiny" of the United States to spread across the entire continent—at whatever cost and at whomever's expense. Americans generally felt that they enjoyed the blessing of Providence in their efforts to consolidate the entire continent under their control.

While most people continued to earn their living from the soil, textile mills and manufacturing plants began to dot the landscape and transform the nature of work and the pace of life. By midcentury the United States was emerging as one of the world's major industrial powers. In addition, the lure of cheap land and plentiful jobs, as well as the promise of political equality and religious freedom, attracted millions of immigrants from Europe. The newcomers, mostly from Germany and Ireland, faced ethnic prejudices, religious persecution, and language barriers that made assimilation into American culture difficult.

These developments gave social life in the second quarter of the nineteenth century a dynamic and fluid quality. The United States, said the philosopher-poet Ralph Waldo Emerson, was "a country of beginnings, of projects, of designs, of expectations." A restless optimism characterized the period. People of a lowly social status who heretofore had accepted their lot in life now strove to climb the social ladder and enter the political arena. The patrician republic espoused by Jefferson and Madison gave way to the frontier democracy promoted by Andrew Jackson and his supporters. Americans were no longer content to be governed by a small, benevolent aristocracy of talent and wealth. They began to demand—and obtain—government of, by, and for the people.

The fertile economic environment during the antebellum era helped foster the egalitarian idea that individuals (except African Americans, Native Americans, and women) should have an equal opportunity to better themselves and should be granted political rights and privileges.

In America, observed a journalist in 1844, "one has as good a chance as another according to his talents, prudence, and personal exertions."

The exuberant individualism embodied in such mythic expressions of economic equality and political democracy spilled over into the cultural arena during the first half of the century. The so-called Romantic movement applied democratic ideals to philosophy, religion, literature, and the fine arts. In New England, Ralph Waldo Emerson and Henry David Thoreau joined other transcendentalists in espousing a radical individualism. Other reformers were motivated more by a sense of spiritual mission than by democratic individualism. Reformers sought to introduce public schools, abolish slavery, promote temperance, and improve the lot of the disabled, the insane, and the imprisoned. Their efforts ameliorated some of the problems created by the frenetic economic growth and territorial expansion. But the reformers made little headway against slavery. It would take a brutal civil war to dislodge America's "peculiar institution."

10

NATIONALISM AND SECTIONALISM

FOCUS QUESTIONS

· What were the characteristics of the "Era of Good Feelings"?

· How did economic policies, diplomacy, and judicial decisions reflect the nationalism of those years?

· What were the various issues that promoted sectionalism?

· What was the fate of the Republican party after the collapse of the Federalists?

To answer these questions and access additional review material, please visit www.wwnorton.com/studyspace.

Amid the jubilation that followed the War of 1812, Americans began to transform their young republic into a sprawling nation. Hundreds of thousands of people began to stream westward at the same time that the largely local economy was maturing into a national market. The spread of plantation slavery and the cotton culture into the Old Southwest—Georgia, Alabama, Mississippi, Louisiana, Arkansas, and Texas—disrupted family ties and changed social life. In the North and the West, meanwhile, a dynamic urban middle class began to emerge. Such dramatic changes prompted vigorous political debates over economic policies, transportation improvements, and the extension of slavery into the new territories. In the process the nation began to divide into three powerful regional blocs—North, South, and West—whose shifting coalitions would shape the political landscape until the Civil War.

ECONOMIC NATIONALISM

After the War of 1812, a new surge of economic prosperity generated a widespread sense of well-being and enhanced the prestige of the national government. The idea spread that the country needed a more balanced "national" economy of farming, commerce, and manufacturing, as well as a more muscular military. President James Madison, in his first annual message to Congress after the war, recommended several steps to strengthen the nation: better fortifications, a permanent national army and a strong navy, a new national bank, effective protection of the new industries against foreign competition through the use of tariffs, a system of canals and roads for commercial and military use, and to top it off, a great national university. "The Republicans have out-Federalized Federalism," one observer remarked.

THE BANK OF THE UNITED STATES   The trinity of economic nationalism—proposals for a second national bank, protective tariffs, and internal improvements—ignited the greatest controversies. After the national bank's charter expired in 1811, the country fell into a financial muddle. State-chartered banks mushroomed with little or no regulation, and their bank notes (paper money) flooded the channels of commerce with currency of uncertain value. Because hard money (coins) had been in such short supply during the war, many state banks had suspended specie (gold or silver) payments in exchange for paper notes, thereby further depressing their value.

To remedy this situation, Congress in 1816 created a new Bank of the United States, to be located in Philadelphia. Modeled on Alexander Hamilton's first national bank, its charter again ran for twenty years, and the government owned one fifth of the stock and named five of the twenty-five directors. The bank served as the depository for government funds, and its bank notes were accepted in payments to the government. In return for its privileges, the Bank of the United States had to keep the government's funds without charge, lend the government up to $5 million upon demand, and pay the government a cash bonus of $1.5 million.

The bitter debate over the bank set a pattern of regional alignment for most other economic issues. Missouri senator Thomas Hart Benton predicted that the currency-short western towns would be at the mercy of a centralized eastern bank. "They may be devoured by it any moment! They are in the jaws of the monster! A lump of butter in the mouth of a dog! One gulp, one swallow, and all is gone!"

The debate over the national bank was also noteworthy because of the leading roles played by the era's greatest statesmen: John C. Calhoun of South

Carolina, Henry Clay of Kentucky, and Daniel Webster of New Hampshire. Calhoun, as an economic nationalist, introduced the bank measure and pushed it through, justifying its constitutionality by citing the congressional power to regulate the currency. Clay, who had long opposed a central national bank, now asserted that new circumstances had made one indispensable. Webster, on the other hand, led the opposition of the New Englanders, who did not want Philadelphia to displace Boston as the nation's banking center. Later, after he had moved from New Hampshire to Massachusetts, Webster would return to Congress as the champion of a much stronger national government, whereas events would steer Calhoun toward a defiant embrace of states' rights.

A PROTECTIVE TARIFF   The shift of capital from commerce to manufactures, begun during Thomas Jefferson's embargo of 1807, had accelerated during the war. Peace in 1815 brought a sudden renewal of cheap British imports and generated pleas for tariffs (taxes on imports) to protect young American industries. The self-interest of the manufacturers, who as yet had little political power, was reinforced by a patriotic desire for economic independence from Britain.

The Tariff of 1816, the first intended more to protect industry against foreign competition than to raise revenue, easily passed in Congress. Both the South and New England split their votes, with New England supporting the tariff and the South opposing the bill, while the middle Atlantic states and the Old Northwest cast only five negative votes altogether. Led by John Calhoun, the minority of southerners who voted for the tariff had hoped that the South might itself become a manufacturing center. Although in 1810 the southern states had almost as many mills and factories as New England, within a few years New England would move ahead of the South in manufacturing, and Calhoun would turn against tariffs. The tariff would then become a sectional issue, with manufacturers and food growers favoring higher tariffs while cotton and tobacco planters and shipping interests favored lower duties.

INTERNAL IMPROVEMENTS   The third major economic issue of the time involved goverment financing of internal improvements: the building of roads and the development of water transportation. The war had highlighted the shortcomings of existing arteries. Troop movements through the western wilderness had proved very difficult, and settlers found that unless they located themselves near navigable waters, they were cut off from trade and limited to a frontier subsistence.

The Union Manufactories of Maryland in Patapsco Falls, Baltimore County (ca. 1815)

A textile mill established during the embargo of 1807, the Union Manufactories would employ over 600 people by 1825.

The federal government had entered the field of internal improvements under Thomas Jefferson. In 1803, when Ohio became a state, Congress decreed that 5 percent of the proceeds from state land sales would go to building a National Road from the Atlantic coast into Ohio and beyond as the territory developed. Construction of the National Road began in 1815. Originally called the Cumberland Road, it was the first federally financed interstate roadway. By 1818 it ran from Cumberland, Maryland, to Wheeling, Virginia, on the Ohio River. By 1838 it extended all the way to Vandalia, Illinois. By reducing transportation costs and opening up western markets, the National Road and privately financed turnpikes accelerated the commercialization of agriculture.

In 1817 John Calhoun put through the House a bill to place in a fund for internal improvements the $1.5 million bonus that the Bank of the United States had paid for its charter, as well as all future dividends on the government's bank stock. Opposition to federal spending on transportation projects centered in New England and the South, regions that expected to gain the least from western development. Support came largely from the West, which urgently needed good roads. On his last day in office, President Madison, bothered by questions about the bill's constitutionality, vetoed the proposed legislation. Internal improvements remained for another hundred years, with few exceptions, the responsibility of states and private enterprise.

Nonetheless, despite disagreements about who would pay for internal improvements, improved transportation and communication (daily newspapers, express mail service, and the telegraph) during the second quarter of the nineteenth century helped create a national market for goods and services. No longer limited to local or regional markets, farmers and manufacturers rapidly expanded production. Banks offered easy access to capital, and enterprising Americans rushed to take advantage of unprecedented entrepreneurial opportunities. Commercial agriculture and the factory system began to displace subsistence farming and household production during the second quarter of the nineteenth century. Mills and factories sprouted across the countryside. New technologies greatly increased productivity and in the process changed the rhythms of work and the relationships between laborers and employers. These first stirrings of an industrial revolution spawned a sustained economic expansion that would transform society and politics.

"GOOD FEELINGS"

JAMES MONROE   As James Madison approached the end of a turbulent presidency, he, like Jefferson, turned to a fellow Virginian, another secretary of state, to be his successor. For Madison that man would be James Monroe. At the outbreak of the Revolution, Monroe was just beginning his studies at the College of William and Mary. He joined the army at sixteen, was wounded at Trenton, and had been made a lieutenant colonel by the time the war ended. Later he studied law with Thomas Jefferson, absorbing Jeffersonian principles in the process.

Monroe had served in the Virginia assembly, as governor of Virginia, in the Confederation Congress and the U.S. Senate, and as minister (ambassador) to France, England, and Spain. Under Madison he had been secretary of state and secretary of war. In the 1816 presidential election he overwhelmed his Federalist opponent, Rufus King of New York. Monroe, with his powdered wig, cocked hat, and knee breeches, was the last of the Revolutionary generation to serve in the White House and the last president to dress in the old style.

Firmly grounded in Republican principles, Monroe was never able to keep up with the onrush of the "new nationalism," which advocated federal economic policies such as a central national bank and a tariff on imports so as to promote industrial growth and enhance economic independence from Europe. Monroe accepted as an accomplished fact the Bank of the United States and the protective tariff, but during his tenure there was no further extension of economic nationalism. Indeed, there was a minor setback: he permitted the National Road to be carried forward, but in his veto of the 1822 Cumberland Road bill, he denied the authority of Congress to collect tolls for its repair and maintenance. Instead, he urged a constitutional amendment, as had Jefferson and Madison, to remove all doubt about federal authority in the field of internal improvements.

Monroe surrounded himself with some of the ablest young Republican leaders: John Quincy Adams became secretary of state, William H. Crawford of Georgia continued as secretary of the Treasury, and John C. Calhoun headed the War Department. The new administration took power with America at peace and the economy flourishing. Soon after his inauguration, Monroe embarked on a goodwill tour of New England. In Boston, lately a hotbed of wartime dissent, a Federalist newspaper commented on the president's visit under the heading "Era of Good Feelings." The label became a popular catchphrase for Monroe's administration, one that historians would later seize upon. Yet the Era of Good Feeling was brief. The collapse of the Federalist party did not mean that the Republicans would grow more unified. They continued to suffer from rancorous internal tensions. Moreover, the social order began to show signs of increasing stratification as the nation experienced dramatic economic growth and rapid westward migration. A resurgence of sectionalism erupted just as the postwar prosperity collapsed in the panic of 1819.

For two years, however, general harmony in national politics reigned, and even when troubles arose, little of the blame fell on Monroe. In 1820 he was reelected without opposition, as the Federalists were too weak to put up a candidate. Monroe won all the electoral votes except three abstentions and one vote from New Hampshire for John Quincy Adams.

RELATIONS WITH BRITAIN   Fueling the contentment after the war was a growing rapprochement with England. American shippers resumed trade with Britain in 1815. The Treaty of Ghent had left unsettled a number of minor disputes, but two important compacts—the Rush-Bagot Agreement of 1817 and the Convention of 1818—removed several potential causes of irritation. In the first, resulting from an exchange of notes between Acting Secretary of State Richard Rush and the British minister to the United States, Charles Bagot, the threat of naval competition on the Great Lakes vanished with an arrangement to limit forces there to several federal ships collecting customs duties. Although the exchange made no reference to the disputed land boundary between the United States and Canada, its spirit gave rise to the tradition of an unfortified border, the longest in the world.

The Convention of 1818 covered three major points. The northern limit of the Louisiana Purchase was settled by extending the national boundary along the 49th parallel west from Lake of the Woods in what would become Minnesota to the crest of the Rocky Mountains. West of that point the Oregon Country would be open to joint U.S.-British occupation, but the boundary remained unsettled. The right of Americans to fish off Canada's Newfoundland and Labrador, granted in 1783, was acknowledged once again. The chief remaining problem was Britain's continuing exclusion of U.S. ships from the West Indies in order to reserve that lucrative trade for British ships. The rapprochement with Britain therefore fell short of perfection.

THE EXTENSION OF BOUNDARIES   The year 1819 was one of the more fateful in American history, a time when a whole sequence of developments came into focus. Controversial efforts to expand U.S. territory, an intense financial panic, a combative debate over the extension of slavery, and several landmark Supreme Court cases combined to bring an unsettling end to the Era of Good Feelings.

The aggressive new nationalism reached a climax with the acquisition of Florida. Spanish sovereignty over Florida was more a technicality than an actuality. The tenuously held province had been a thorn in the side of the United States during the War of 1812, when it had served as a center of British intrigue; a haven for Creek refugees, who were beginning to take the name Seminole (Runaway or Separatist); and a harbor for runaway slaves and criminals.

Spain, once the dominant power of the Americas, was now a nation in rapid decline, suffering from both internal decay and colonial revolts and unable to enforce its obligations under Pinckney's Treaty of 1795 to pacify the Florida frontier. In 1816 U. S. forces clashed with a group of escaped slaves who had taken over a British fort on the Appalachicola River. Seminoles were soon fighting white settlers in the area, and in 1817 Secretary of War Calhoun authorized a military campaign against the Seminoles and summoned General Andrew Jackson from Nashville to take command.

Jackson's orders allowed him to pursue Indians into Spanish territory but not to attack any Spanish post. A man of Jackson's tenacity naturally felt hobbled by such a restriction, since when it came to Spaniards or Indians, few white Tennesseans—certainly not Andrew Jackson—were likely to bother with technicalities. Jackson pushed his troops eastward through Florida, reinforced by Tennessee volunteers and friendly Creeks, taking a Spanish post and skirmishing with the Seminoles. He hanged two of their leaders without a trial. For two British agents in the area, he convened a court-martial, during

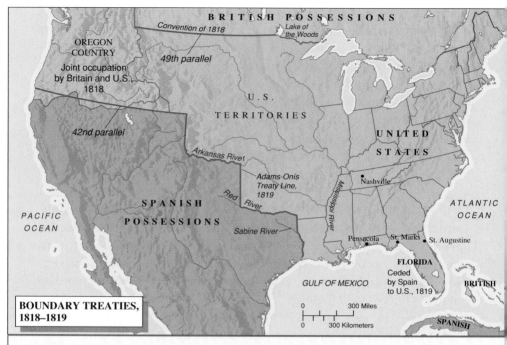

BRITISH POSSESSIONS

Convention of 1818

Lake of the Woods

OREGON COUNTRY

49th parallel

Joint occupation by Britain and U.S. 1818

U.S. TERRITORIES

42nd parallel

UNITED STATES

Arkansas River

Adams-Onís Treaty Line, 1819

Nashville

SPANISH

Red River

PACIFIC OCEAN

POSSESSIONS

Sabine River

ATLANTIC OCEAN

Pensacola St. Marks St. Augustine

FLORIDA
Ceded by Spain to U.S., 1819

BRITISH

GULF OF MEXICO

0   300 Miles
0   300 Kilometers

SPANISH

BOUNDARY TREATIES, 1818–1819

What territorial terms did the Convention of 1818 settle? How did Jackson's actions in Florida help Adams claim the territory from Spain? What were the terms of the treaty with Spain?

which it was revealed that they had befriended the Seminoles and offered them military training. Jackson had one hanged and the other shot. The Florida Panhandle was in American hands by the end of May 1818.

Jackson's exploits aroused anger in Madrid and concern in Washington. Spain demanded the return of its territory and the punishment of Jackson, but Spain's impotence was plain for all to see. Monroe's cabinet at first prepared to disavow Jackson's actions, especially his direct attack on Spanish posts. Calhoun, as secretary of war, wanted to discipline Jackson for disregard of orders—a stand that would later cause bad blood between the two men—but privately confessed a certain pleasure at the outcome. In any case a man as popular as Jackson was almost invulnerable. And he had one important friend in Washington, Secretary of State John Quincy Adams, who realized that Jackson's military actions had strengthened his own hand in negotiations already under way with the Spanish. U.S. forces withdrew from

Florida, but negotiations resumed with the knowledge that the United States could retake Florida at any time.

With Florida's fate a foregone conclusion, John Quincy Adams cast his eye toward a larger purpose, a final definition of the ambiguous western boundary of the Louisiana Purchase and—his boldest stroke—extension of its boundary to the Pacific coast. In lengthy negotiations, Adams gradually gave ground on claims to Texas but stuck to his demand for a transcontinental line. Agreement came early in 1819. With the Transcontinental Treaty, Spain ceded all of Florida to the United States in return for the U.S. government assumption of Spanish debts owed to U.S. merchants. The western boundary of the Louisiana Purchase would run along the Sabine River in Texas and then, in stair-step fashion, up to the Red River, along the Red, and up to the Arkansas River. From the source of the Arkansas, it would go north to the 42nd parallel and thence west to the Pacific coast. Florida became a U.S. territory, and its first governor was Andrew Jackson. In 1845 Florida finally achieved statehood.

CRISES AND COMPROMISES

THE PANIC OF 1819   John Quincy Adams's Transcontinental Treaty of 1819 was a diplomatic triumph and the climactic event of America's postwar nationalism. Even before it was signed, however, two thunderclaps signaled the end of the brief Era of Good Feelings and warned of stormy weather ahead: the financial panic of 1819 and the controversy over Missouri statehood. The panic resulted from a sudden collapse of cotton prices in the English market as British textile mills turned from American cotton to cheaper East Indian sources. The price collapse set off a decline in the demand for other American goods and revealed the fragility of the prosperity that had begun after the War of 1812.

Since 1815 much of the economic boom had been built upon a shaky foundation. Businessmen, bankers, farmers, and land speculators had caused a volatile expansion of credit, succumbing to the contagion of get-rich-quick fever that was sweeping the country. Even the directors of the second Bank of the United States engaged in the same reckless extension of loans that the state banks had pursued. In 1819, just as alert businessmen began to take alarm, a case of extensive fraud and embezzlement in the Baltimore branch of the Bank of the United States came to light. The disclosure led to the resignation of the director of the bank. His replacement, Langdon Cheves, a former congressman from South Carolina, established sounder policies.

Cheves reduced salaries and other costs, postponed the payment of dividends, restrained the extension of credit, and presented for redemption the state bank notes that came in, thereby forcing the state-chartered banks to keep specie (gold and silver) reserves. Cheves rescued the bank from near ruin, but only by putting pressure on the state banks. They in turn put pressure on their debtors, who found it harder to renew old loans or get new ones. In 1822, his job completed, Cheves retired and was succeeded in the following year by Nicholas Biddle of Philadelphia. The Cheves policies were the result rather than the cause of the panic, but they pinched debtors. Hard times lasted about three years, and in the popular mind the federal bank deserved much of the blame. The panic passed, but resentment of the national bank lingered in the South and the West.

THE MISSOURI COMPROMISE   Just as the financial panic was breaking over the country, another cloud appeared on the horizon: the onset of a fierce sectional controversy over slavery. By 1819 the country had an equal number of slave and free states—eleven of each. The line between them was defined by the southern and western boundaries of Pennsylvania and the Ohio River. Although slavery lingered in some places north of the line, it was on the way to extinction there. West of the Mississippi River, however, no move had been made to extend the dividing line across the Louisiana Territory, where slavery had existed from the days when France and Spain had colonized the area. At the time the Missouri Territory embraced all of the Louisiana Purchase except the state of Louisiana, which entered the Union in 1812, and the Arkansas Territory, organized in 1819. The old French town of St. Louis became the funnel through which settlers, largely southerners who brought their slaves with them, rushed westward beyond the Mississippi River.

In early 1819 the House of Representatives was asked to approve legislation enabling Missouri to draft a state constitution, its population having passed the minimum of 60,000. At that point, Representative James Tallmadge Jr., a New York congressman, proposed a resolution prohibiting the further introduction of slaves into Missouri, which already had some 10,000, and providing freedom at age twenty-five to those born after the territory's admission as a state. The House passed the amendment on an almost strictly sectional vote, and the Senate rejected it by a similar tally, but with several northerners joining in the opposition. With population growing faster in the North, a political balance between the free states and the slave states could be held only in the Senate.

Maine's application for statehood made it easier to arrive at an agreement. Since colonial times, Maine had been the northern province of Massachusetts.

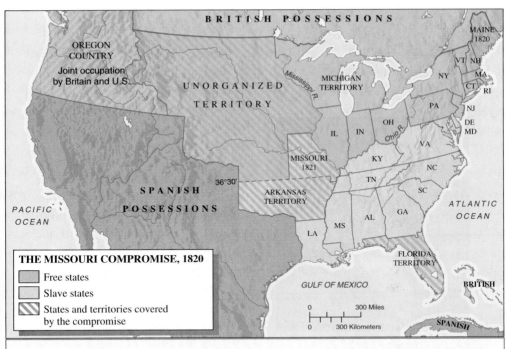

THE MISSOURI COMPROMISE, 1820

Free states

Slave states

States and territories covered by the compromise

What caused the sectional controversy over slavery in 1819? What were the terms of the Missouri Compromise? What was Henry Clay's solution to the Missouri constitution's ban on free blacks in that state?

The Senate linked its request for separate statehood with Missouri's and voted to admit Maine as a free state and Missouri as a slave state, thus maintaining the balance between free and slave states in the Senate. An Illinois senator further extended the compromise by an amendment to exclude slavery from the rest of the Louisiana Purchase north of 36°30', Missouri's southern border. Slavery thus would continue in the Arkansas Territory and in Missouri but would be excluded from the remainder of the area. People at that time presumed that what remained was the Great American Desert, unlikely ever to be settled. Thus the arrangement seemed to be a victory for the slave states. On August 10, 1821, President Monroe proclaimed the admission of Missouri as the twenty-fourth state. For the moment the controversy was settled. "But this momentous question," the aging Thomas Jefferson wrote to a friend, "like a firebell in the night awakened and filled me with terror. I considered it at once as the knell of the Union."

JUDICIAL NATIONALISM

JOHN MARSHALL   During the early nineteenth century many of the nation's leading attorneys and judges were nationalists. They believed that an expanding nation needed a central government with enough power and responsibility to override state and local interests. And they argued that an independent judiciary should have the authority to settle disputes between the states and the federal government. The leader among these judicial nationalists was John Marshall. A Virginia veteran of the Revolution, Marshall had served as secretary of state for John Adams. He had never been a judge before becoming chief justice in 1801. Yet he established the power of the Supreme Court by his force of mind and determination. During Marshall's early years on the Court (he served thirty-four years altogether), he affirmed the principle of judicial review of legislative acts. In *Marbury v. Madison* (1803) and *Fletcher v. Peck* (1810) the Court struck down first a federal law and then a state law as unconstitutional.

John Marshall

Chief justice and pillar of judicial nationalism.

EXPANDING THE POWER OF THE FEDERAL GOVERNMENT
In the fateful year of 1819, John Marshall and the Court made two decisions of major importance in checking the power of the states and expanding the power of the federal government: *Dartmouth College v. Woodward* and *McCulloch v. Maryland.*

The *Dartmouth College* case involved an attempt by the New Hampshire legislature to alter a charter granted the college by King George III in 1769, under which the governing body of trustees became a self-perpetuating board. In 1816 the state's Republican legislature, irritated by this residue of monarchical rule as well as by the fact that Federalists dominated the board of trustees, placed Dartmouth under the control of a board named by the governor. The original trustees sued and lost in the state courts but with Daniel Webster as their counsel gained a hearing before the Supreme Court.

The charter, declared Marshall, was a valid contract that the legislature had violated, an action expressly forbidden by the Constitution. This decision implied an enlarged definition of *contract* that seemed to put private corporations beyond the reach of the states that chartered them. "If business is to prosper," Marshall explained, "men must have the assurance that contracts will be enforced."

John Marshall's single most important interpretation of the constitutional system appeared in *McCulloch v. Maryland* (1819). In the unanimous decision the Court upheld the "implied powers" of Congress to charter the Bank of the United States and denied the state of Maryland's attempt to tax it. In a lengthy opinion, Marshall rejected Maryland's argument that the federal government was the creature of sovereign states. Instead, he insisted, it arose directly from the people acting through the conventions that had ratified the Constitution ("We, the people of the United States, . . . do ordain and establish"). Whereas sovereignty was divided between the states and the national government, the latter, "though limited in its powers, is supreme within its sphere of action."

The state's effort to tax the national bank conflicted with the supreme law of the land. One great principle that "entirely pervades the Constitution," Marshall wrote, was "that the Constitution and the laws made in pursuance thereof are supreme: . . . they control the Constitution and laws of the respective states, and cannot be controlled by them." Maryland's effort to tax a national bank was therefore unconstitutional, for "the power to tax involves the power to destroy"—which was precisely what the legislatures of Maryland and several other states had in mind with respect to the bank.

John Marshall's last great decision, *Gibbons v. Ogden* (1824), established national supremacy in regulating interstate commerce and thereby dealt another blow to proponents of states' rights. In 1808 the New York legislature had granted Aaron Ogden the exclusive ferry rights across the Hudson River between New York and New Jersey. A competitor, Thomas Gibbons, protested the state's right to grant such a monopoly. On behalf of a unanimous Court, Marshall ruled that the state's action conflicted with the federal Coasting Act, under which Gibbons operated. Congressional power to regulate commerce among the states, the Court said, "like all others vested in Congress, is complete in itself, may be exercised to its utmost extent, and acknowledges no limitations other than are prescribed in the Constitution." In striking down the monopoly created by the state, the nationalist Marshall had opened the way to extensive development of steamboat navigation and, soon afterward, railroads. Such judicial nationalism provided a crucial support for economic expansion.

NATIONALIST DIPLOMACY

THE PACIFIC NORTHWEST   In foreign affairs, too, nationalism continued to be an effective force. Within two years of final approval of John Quincy Adams's Transcontinental Treaty, the secretary of state was able to draw another important transcontinental line. In 1819 Spain had abandoned its claim to the Oregon Country above the 42nd parallel. Russia, however, had claims along the Pacific coast as well, including trading outposts from Alaska as far south as California. In 1823 Secretary of State Adams contested "the right of Russia to any territorial establishment on this continent." The U.S. government, he informed the Russian minister, assumed the principle "that the American continents are no longer subjects for any new European colonial establishments." The upshot of his protest was a treaty signed in 1824, whereby Russia, which had more pressing concerns in Europe, accepted the latitude line of 54°40′ as the southern boundary of its claim. The Oregon Territory, to the south of the line, remained subject to joint occupation by the United States and Great Britain under their agreement of 1818.

THE MONROE DOCTRINE   Secretary of State Adams's disapproval of further European colonization in the Western Hemisphere had clear implications for Latin America as well. One consequence of the Napoleonic Wars and the French occupation of Spain and Portugal was a series of wars of liberation in Latin America. Within little more than a decade after the flag of rebellion was first raised in 1811, Spain had lost almost its entire empire in the Americas. All that was left were the islands of Cuba and Puerto Rico and the colony of Santo Domingo on the island of Hispaniola.

That Spain could not regain her empire seems clear enough in retrospect. The British navy would not have permitted it because Britain's trade with the area was too important. For a time after Napoléon's defeat, however, European rulers were determined to restore monarchical "legitimacy" everywhere. In 1822, when the major European powers met in the Congress of Verona, they authorized France to suppress the constitutionalist movement in Spain and restore the authority of the monarchy. In 1823 French troops crossed the Spanish border, put down the rebels, and restored King Ferdinand VII to absolute authority. Rumors began to circulate that France would also try to restore Ferdinand's "legitimate" power over Spain's American empire. President Monroe and Secretary of War Calhoun were alarmed at the possibility, although John Quincy Adams took the more realistic view that any such action was unlikely. The British foreign minister, George Canning, was also worried about French and Spanish intentions, and he urged the

United States to protect Latin America. Monroe at first agreed, with the support of his sage advisers Jefferson and Madison.

Adams urged upon Monroe and the cabinet the independent course of proclaiming a unilateral policy against the restoration of Spain's colonies. "It would be more candid," Adams said, "as well as more dignified, to avow our principles explicitly to Russia and France, than to come in as a cockboat in the wake of the British man-of-war." Adams knew that the British navy would stop any action by a European power in Latin America. The British wanted the United States to agree not to acquire any more Spanish territory, including Cuba, Texas, and California, but Adams preferred to avoid such a commitment.

Monroe incorporated the substance of Adams's views into his annual message to Congress in 1823. The Monroe Doctrine, as it was later called, comprised four major points: (1) that "the American continents . . . are henceforth not to be considered as subjects for future colonization by any European powers"; (2) that the political system of European powers was different from that of the United States, which would "consider any attempt on their part to extend their system to any portion of this hemisphere as dangerous to our peace and safety"; (3) that the United States would not interfere with existing European colonies; and (4) that the United States would keep out of the internal affairs of European nations and their wars.

At the time the statement drew little attention either in the United States or abroad. Over the years, however, the Monroe Doctrine, not even so called until 1852, became one of the cherished principles of U.S. foreign policy. For the time being, however, it slipped into obscurity for want of any occasion to invoke it. In spite of Adams's affirmation, the United States came in as a cockboat in the wake of the British man-of-war after all, for the effectiveness of the doctrine depended upon British naval supremacy. The doctrine had no standing in international law. It was merely a statement of intent by an American president to Congress and did not even draw enough interest for the European powers to renounce it.

ONE-PARTY POLITICS

Almost from the start of Monroe's second term, in 1821, jockeying for the presidential succession in 1824 began. Three members of Monroe's cabinet were active candidates: Secretary of War John Calhoun, Secretary of the Treasury William H. Crawford, and Secretary of State John Quincy Adams.

Henry Clay

Clay entered the Senate at age twenty-eight despite the requirement that senators be at least thirty years old.

Henry Clay, longtime Speaker of the House, and an outspoken economic nationalist, also thirsted for the office. And on the fringes of the Washington scene, a new force appeared in the person of Andrew Jackson, the scourge of the British, Spanish, and Seminoles, who had became a senator from Tennessee in 1823. All were Republicans, for again no Federalist stood a chance, but they were competing in a new political world, complicated by the crosscurrents of nationalism and sectionalism. With only one party there was in effect no party, for there existed no generally accepted method for choosing a "regular" candidate.

State legislatures were free to nominate presidential candidates Tennessee and Pennsylvania supported Jackson, and Calhoun agreed to serve as his running mate. (The 1824 election was the first to feature paired presidential and vice-presidential candidates.) Kentucky named Clay, Massachusetts named Adams, and the amiable, hulking Crawford was selected by a poorly attended congressional caucus. Of the four candidates only two articulated defined programs, and the outcome was an early lesson in the danger of committing oneself on the issues too soon. Crawford's friends emphasized his devotion to states' rights and strict constitutional construction. Clay, on the other hand, took his stand for the "American System": the national bank, the protective tariff, and a national program of internal improvements to bind the country together and strengthen its economy. Adams was close to Clay, openly dedicated to internal improvements but less strongly committed to the tariff. Jackson, where issues were concerned, carefully avoided commitment. His managers hoped that by being all things to all voters, Jackson could capitalize on his popularity as the hero of New Orleans at the end of the War of 1812.

THE "CORRUPT BARGAIN" The election of 1824 turned on personalities and sectional allegiance more than issues. Adams, the only northern candidate, carried New England, the former bastion of the Federalist party, and won most of New York's electoral votes. Clay took Kentucky, Ohio, and Missouri, while Crawford carried Virginia, Georgia, and Delaware.

Jackson swept the Southeast plus Illinois and Indiana and, with Calhoun's support, the Carolinas, Pennsylvania, Maryland, and New Jersey.

The result was inconclusive in both the electoral vote and the popular vote. In the Electoral College, Jackson had ninety-nine votes, Adams eighty-four, Crawford forty-one, and Clay thirty-seven; in the popular vote the proportion ran about the same. Whatever else might have been said about the outcome, it was clearly a defeat for Clay's American System: New England and New York opposed him on internal improvements, the South and the Southwest on the protective tariff. Sectionalism had defeated the national economic program, yet the advocate of the American System now assumed the role of president maker, since the election was thrown into the House of Representatives, where Clay's influence as Speaker of the House was decisive. Clay had little trouble choosing, since he regarded Jackson as unfit for the office. "I cannot believe," he muttered, "that killing 2,500 Englishmen at New Orleans qualifies for the various, difficult and complicated duties of the Chief Magistracy." He eventually threw his support to Adams. The final vote in the House, which was by state, carried Adams to victory with thirteen votes to Jackson's seven and Crawford's four.

It was a costly and controversial victory, for it united Adams's foes and crippled his administration before it got under way. There is no evidence that Adams entered into any secret bargain with Clay to win his support, but the charge was widely believed after Adams made Clay his secretary of state, the office from which three successive presidents had risen. A campaign to elect Jackson next time was launched almost immediately after the 1824 decision. "The people have been cheated," Jackson growled. William Crawford's supporters, including Martin Van Buren, "the Little Magician" of New York politics, soon moved into the Jackson camp.

JOHN QUINCY ADAMS   Short, plump, peppery John Quincy Adams was one of the ablest men, one of the hardest workers, and one of the finest intellects ever to enter the White House, but he lacked the common touch and the politician's gift for maneuver. A stubborn man who saw two brothers and two sons die from alcoholism, he suffered from chronic bouts of depression that spawned a grim self-righteousness and self-pity, qualities that did not endear him to fellow politicians.

Adams's first annual message to Congress provided a grandiose blueprint for national development, set forth so bluntly that it became a political disaster. The central government, the president asserted, should finance internal improvements, set up a national university, fund scientific explorations, build

John Quincy Adams

A brilliant man but an ineffective leader.

astronomical observatories, and create a department of the interior. To refrain from using broad federal powers, Adams maintained, "would be treachery to the most sacred of trusts." In leading the nation, officers of the government should not be "palsied by the will of our constituents."

Such provocative language obscured whatever grandeur of conception the message to Congress had. For a minority president to demean the sovereignty of the voter was tactless enough, but for the son of John Adams to cite the example "of the nations of Europe and of their rulers" was downright suicidal. At one fell swoop he had revived all the Republican suspicions of the Adamses as closet monarchists.

Adams's presidential message hastened the emergence of a new party system. The minority who cast their lot with Adams and Clay were turning into National Republicans; the opposition, the growing party of Jacksonians, were the Democratic Republicans, who would eventually drop the name Republican and become Democrats.

Adams's headstrong plunge into nationalism and his refusal to play the game of politics condemned his administration to utter frustration. The popular mood was turning against federal authority. Congress ignored most of Adams's domestic proposals, and in foreign affairs the triumphs he had scored as secretary of state had no sequels.

The central political issue during Adams's presidency was a complex debate over tariff policy. The panic of 1819 had provoked calls in 1820 for a higher tariff, but the effort failed by one vote in the Senate. In 1824 those determined to protect American industry from foreign competition renewed the effort, with greater success. The Tariff of 1824 favored the middle Atlantic and New England manufacturers with higher duties on woolens, cotton, iron, and other finished goods. Henry Clay's Kentucky won a tariff on hemp, a fiber used for making rope, and a tariff on raw wool brought the wool-growing interests to the support of the measure. Additional federal revenues were provided by duties on sugar, molasses, coffee, and salt.

Four years later Andrew Jackson's supporters sought to advance their presidential candidate through an awkward scheme hatched by John Calhoun.

The plan was to present a bill with such outrageously high tariffs on imported raw materials that the eastern manufacturers would join the commercial interests there and, with the votes of the agricultural South and Southwest, combine to defeat the measure. In the process, Jacksonians in the Northeast could take credit for supporting the tariff, and other Jacksonians, wherever it fit their interests, could take credit for opposing it—while Jackson himself remained in the background. Virginia's John Randolph saw through the ruse. The tariff bill, he asserted, "referred to manufactures of no sort of kind, but the manufacture of a President of the United States."

The complicated scheme did help elect Jackson in 1828, but in the process John Calhoun became a victim of his own machinations. His tariff bill, to his chagrin, passed, thanks to the growing strength of manufacturing interests in New England and several crucial amendments that exempted certain raw materials needed by American industry. Daniel Webster, now a senator from Massachusetts, explained that he was ready to deny all he had said before against the tariff because New England had built up her manufactures on the understanding that the protective tariff was a settled policy.

When the tariff bill passed in May 1828, it was Calhoun's turn to explain his newfound opposition to the gospel of protection, and nothing so well illustrates the flexibility of constitutional principles as the switch in positions by Webster and Calhoun. Back in South Carolina, Calhoun prepared the *South Carolina Exposition and Protest* (1828), which was issued anonymously along with a series of resolutions by the state legislature. In that document, Calhoun set forth the right of a state to nullify an act of Congress that it found unconstitutional.

THE ELECTION OF JACKSON   Thus far the stage was set for the election of 1828, which might more truly be called a political revolution than that of 1800. But if the issues of the day had anything to do with the election, they were hardly visible in the campaign, in which politicians on both sides reached depths of scurrilousness that had not been plumbed since 1800. Those campaigning for Adams denounced Jackson as a hot-tempered, ignorant barbarian, a participant in repeated duels and frontier brawls, a man whose fame rested upon his reputation as a killer. In addition, Jackson's enemies dredged up the story that he had lived in adultery with his wife, Rachel, before they were married. In fact they had been married for two years before discovering that her divorce from her former husband had not been finalized. As soon as the divorce was official, Andrew and Rachel had remarried.

The Jacksonians, however, were also not averse to mudslinging. They lambasted Adams, condemning him as a man corrupted by foreigners in the courts of Europe. They called him a gambler and a spendthrift for having bought a billiard table and a chess set for the White House and a puritanical hypocrite for despising the common people and warning Congress to ignore the will of the people. The Jacksonians also attacked Adams for signing the Tariff of 1828 and for winning the 1824 election by backroom deals. Adams had gained the presidency, the Jacksonians claimed, by a "corrupt bargain" with Henry Clay.

In the campaign of 1828, Jackson held most of the advantages. As a military victor he stirred the patriotism of voters. As a son of the West and an Indian fighter, he was a hero to voters in the new states along the frontier. As a planter and slaveholder he had the trust of southern planters. Debtors and local bankers who hated the national bank also turned to Jackson. In addition, his vagueness on the issues protected him from attack by interest groups. Not least of all, Jackson benefited from a spirit of democracy in which the common folk were no longer satisfied to look to elites for leadership, as they had done in the past.

Since the Revolution and especially since 1800, more people were voting as more and more states expanded the suffrage from only those men with property to taxpaying white men and even, in some states, to universal male suffrage. After 1815 the new states of the West entered the Union with either white male suffrage or a low taxpaying requirement, and older states such as Connecticut (in 1818), Massachusetts (in 1821), and New York (in 1821) abolished their property requirements for voting. As more men voted and participated in political activities, the ideal of social equality took on more importance in the political culture.

Jackson embodied this new, more democratic political world. A tall, sinewy frontiersman born in South Carolina, he grew to be proud, gritty, and short-tempered. During the Revolution, when he was a young boy, his mother died, two of his brothers were killed by redcoats, and Jackson himself was wounded by a British officer's saber. He would carry this scar for life, along with the conviction that it was not enough for a man to be right; he had to be tough as well. His toughness inspired his soldiers to nickname him Old Hickory. During a duel with a man reputed to be the best shot in Tennessee, Jackson nevertheless let his opponent fire first. For his gallantry he received a bullet that lodged next to his heart. Unfazed, he straightened himself, patiently took aim, and killed his foe. "I should have hit him," Jackson claimed, "if he had shot me through the brain." As a fighter, horse

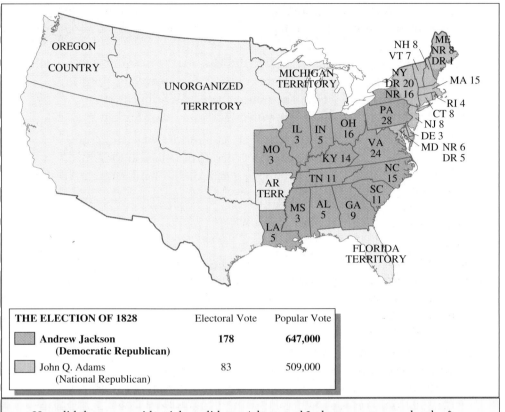

THE ELECTION OF 1828	Electoral Vote	Popular Vote
Andrew Jackson (Democratic Republican)	**178**	**647,000**
John Q. Adams (National Republican)	83	509,000

How did the two presidential candidates, Adams and Jackson, portray each other? Why did Jackson seem to have the advantage in the election of 1828? How did the broadening of suffrage affect the presidential campaign?

trader, land speculator, and frontier lawyer, Jackson symbolized the rugged western temperament. A fellow law student described him as a "most roaring, rollicking, game-cocking, horse-racing, card-playing, mischievous fellow." One of his campaign slogans announced, "Adams can write, Jackson can fight."

The 1828 election returns revealed that Jackson had won by a comfortable margin. The electoral vote was 178 to 83. Adams had won all of New England (except one of Maine's nine electoral votes) and a scattering of votes in New York and Maryland. All the rest belonged to Jackson. A convulsive new era in American politics was about to begin.

> ## MAKING CONNECTIONS
>
> · Thomas Jefferson referred to the Missouri Compromise as "a firebell in the night." He was right. The controversy over the expansion of slavery, introduced here, will reappear in Chapter 14, in the discussion of Texas and the Mexican War.
>
> · John Quincy Adams's National Republicans, who could trace some of their ideology to the Federalists, will be at the core of the Whig coalition that opposes Jackson in Chapter 11.
>
> · Several of the issues on which the nation united during the Era of Good Feelings—the bank and the protective tariff, for example—will become much more divisive, as will be discussed in the next chapter.

FURTHER READING

The standard overview of the Era of Good Feelings remains George Dangerfield's *The Awakening of American Nationalism, 1815–1828* (1965). The gathering sense of a national spirit can be traced in Daniel J. Boorstin's *The Americans: The National Experience* (1965).

For discussions of the American System, see Bray Hammond's *Banks and Politics in America from the Revolution to the Civil War* (1957) and George Rogers Taylor's *The Transportation Revolution, 1815–1860* (1951). A classic overview of the economic trends of the period is Douglass C. North's *The Economic Growth of the United States, 1790–1860* (1961).

A stimulating synthesis of economic, social, and political developments is Sean Wilentz's *Chants Democratic: New York City and the Rise of the American Working Class, 1788–1850* (1984). The emergence of slavery as the most divisive sectional issue is treated in Donald L. Robinson's *Slavery in the Structure of American Politics, 1765–1820* (1970).

On diplomatic relations during James Monroe's presidency, see William Earl Weeks's *John Quincy Adams and American Global Empire* (1992). For relations after 1812, see Ernest R. May's *The Making of the Monroe Doctrine* (1975).

Background on Andrew Jackson can be obtained from works cited in Chapter 11. The campaign that brought Jackson to the White House is analyzed in Robert Vincent Remini's *The Election of Andrew Jackson* (1963).

11

THE JACKSONIAN IMPULSE

FOCUS QUESTIONS

· What was the social and political context of the Jackson and Van Buren administrations?

· What were Andrew Jackson's attitudes and actions concerning the tariff (and nullification), Indian policy, and the Bank of the United States?

· Why did a new party system (of Democrats versus Whigs) arise?

To answer these questions and access additional review material, please visit www.wwnorton.com/studyspace.

The election of Andrew Jackson coincided with a distinctive new era in politics, economic development, and social change. Jackson was the first president not to come from a prominent colonial family. As a self-made soldier, politician, and land speculator from the backcountry, he symbolized a transformation in the nation's social structure and political temper.

Profound economic and social transformations were reshaping the young United States. In 1828 there were twenty-four states and almost 13 million people, many of them recent arrivals from Germany and Ireland. The national population was growing rapidly, doubling every twenty-three years. Surging foreign demand for cotton and other goods helped fuel a transportation revolution and an economic boom. Textile mills and shoe factories sprouted across the New England countryside, their spinning looms fed by cotton grown in the newly cultivated lands of Alabama and Mississippi.

Cities increasingly became the centers of the nation's commerce, industry, finance, and political activity. The urban population grew twice as fast as the rural population during the second quarter of the nineteenth century. A more urban society and a more specialized and speculative economy created more instability as people took greater risks to make money. A more stratified social order also emerged, with some people acquiring great wealth while most others worked for wages.

An agrarian economy that earlier had produced crops and goods for household use or local exchange expanded into a market-oriented economy engaged in national and international commerce. New canals and roads opened up eastern markets to western farmers in the Ohio River valley. The new economic order brought with it regional specialization and increasing division of labor. As more land was put into cultivation and commercial farmers came to rely upon banks for credit to buy land and seed, they were subject to greater risks and the volatility of the market. In the midst of periodic financial panics and sharp business depressions, farmers unable to pay their debts lost their farms to "corrupt" banks, which they believed had engaged in reckless speculative ventures and had benefited from government favoritism.

For many people the transition to cash-crop agriculture and capitalist manufacturing was painful and unsettling. A traditional economy of independent artisans and subsistence farmers was giving way to a system of centralized workshops, mills, and factories based on wage labor. Chartered corporations and commercial banks began to dominate local economies. With the onset of the factory system and urban commerce, people left farms and shops and became dependent upon others for their food, clothing, and livelihood. This transformation called into question the traditional assumption of Thomas Jefferson and others that a republic could survive only if most of its citizens were independent, self-reliant property owners, neither too rich to dominate other people nor too poor to become dependent and subservient.

A NEW POLITICAL CULTURE

At the same time that the urban population was increasing and more people were engaging in wage labor rather than agriculture, many states, especially those west of the Appalachian Mountains, were reducing or eliminating the property requirement for voting. This enabled white men with little or no property to participate in the political process. The easing of voting restrictions reflected the feeling on the parts of workers, artisans, and small merchants, as well as farmers, that a more democratic ballot would help combat the rising influence of commercial and manufacturing interests. By 1830 only six states continued to require voters to own a certain amount of property. The easing of such restrictions meant that four times as many men voted in the 1828 presidential election as had voted in the 1824 election.

By gaining access to the political process as voters, propertyless men encouraged a new type of politician, one who identified with the values and desires of the masses. To have been born in a log cabin and to be a "common man" wearing a coonskin cap rather than a powdered wig became great political advantages during the Jacksonian era. As Andrew Jackson himself declared, he governed on behalf of "the humble members of society—the farmers, mechanics, and laborers."

The mass-based Democratic party that ushered Jackson into the White House in early 1829 reflected the emergence of a new political culture during the 1820s. Up to that time well-organized national political parties had been virtually nonexistent. The Jacksonian era witnessed the crystallization of formal parties (the Democratic party and the Whig party), which took

Verdict of the People

George Caleb Bingham's painting depicts the increasingly democratic politics of the mid–nineteenth century.

particular stands on issues, held formal nominating conventions to select presidential and vice-presidential candidates, and had as members congressmen and senators who voted with their party on the issues.

The second quarter of the nineteenth century also witnessed a new style of politicking. It featured fierce polemics, colorful politicians, expensive campaigns, tightly controlled local party "machines," and intense partisan loyalties. Politics during the Jacksonian era was a vibrant public phenomenon that involved mass marches, vigorous debates, and high voter turnout. The local party machines used a partisan network of employers and landlords to help party members find jobs and housing; in return they could expect their members to vote without question for the candidates they designated. Citizens turned to local, state, and federal politicians to help relieve their distress and promote their prosperity. For example, they expected the government to settle the Indian "problem," open up new and cheaper land, and build roads and canals along which they could send their produce and goods.

The new Democratic party was an unstable coalition of northern workers (many of them Irish and German immigrants), owners of small farms, landless laborers, and aspiring entrepreneurs from all sections of the country. Their shared concern was the preservation of a "just" and "virtuous" society in which most people were small property holders jealous of their freedom from monopolists or corrupt politicians. Democrats therefore opposed tariffs and the central national bank, as well as any other efforts to centralize government power. At the same time frontier folk settling in the new states of the Old Northwest (Ohio, Indiana, and Illinois) and the Old Southwest were no longer willing to defer to traditional political and social elites.

Yet to call the Jacksonian era the age of the common man, as many historians have done, is misleading. While political participation increased during the Jacksonian era, the period never produced true economic and social equality. Power and privilege, for the most part, remained in the hands of an "uncommon" elite. Moreover, many Jacksonians in power proved to be as opportunistic and manipulative as the "corrupt" patrician politicians they displaced. And for all their egalitarian rhetoric, Jacksonian Democrats never embraced the principle of economic equality. "Distinctions in society will always exist under every just government," Andrew Jackson observed. "Equality of talents, or education, or of wealth cannot be produced by human institutions." He and his supporters wanted people to have an equal chance to compete in the economic marketplace and in the political arena, but they never sanctioned equality of income or status. "True republicanism," one commentator declared, "requires that every man shall have an equal chance—that every man shall be free to become as unequal as he can."

In the afterglow of Jackson's electoral victory, however, few observers troubled with such distinctions. It was time to celebrate the commoner's ascension to the presidency.

JACKSON TAKES OFFICE

APPOINTMENTS AND RIVALRIES   Andrew Jackson believed that government workers who stayed too long in office became corrupt. So he set about replacing John Quincy Adams's appointees with his own supporters. But his use of the "spoils system" has been exaggerated. During his first year in office, Jackson replaced only about 9 percent of the appointed officials in the federal government, and during his entire term he replaced fewer than 20 percent.

Jackson's administration was from the outset divided between the partisans of Secretary of State Martin Van Buren and those of Vice President John

All Creation Going to the White House

The scene following Jackson's inauguration as president, according to the satirist Robert Cruikshank.

C. Calhoun. Much of the political history of the next few years would turn upon the rivalry between the two statesmen as each jockeyed for position as Jackson's successor. Van Buren held most of the advantages, foremost among them his skill at timing and tactics. Jackson, new to political administration, leaned heavily upon him for advice and for help in soothing the ruffled feathers of rejected office seekers. Calhoun, a man of towering intellect, humorless outlook, and apostolic zeal, possessed a demonic sense of duty and a keen interest in political theory. As vice president he was determined to defend southern interests against the advance of northern industrialism and abolitionism.

THE EATON AFFAIR   In his battle for political power with Calhoun, Van Buren had luck as well as political skill on his side. Fate handed him a trump card: the succulent scandal known as the Peggy Eaton affair. The daughter of an Irish tavern owner, Margaret Eaton was a vivacious widow whose husband supposedly had committed suicide upon learning of her affair with Tennessee senator John Eaton. Her marriage to Eaton, three months before he entered Jackson's cabinet as secretary of war, had scarcely made a virtuous woman of her in the eyes of the proper ladies of Washington. Floride Calhoun, the vice president's wife, especially objected to Peggy Eaton's lowly origins and unsavory past. She pointedly snubbed her, and the cabinet wives followed suit.

Peggy's plight reminded Jackson of the gossip that had pursued his wife, Rachel, and he pronounced Peggy "chaste as a virgin." The cabinet members, however, were unable to cure their wives of what Van Buren dubbed "the Eaton Malaria." Van Buren was a widower, free to lavish on poor Peggy all the attention that Jackson thought was her due. Mrs. Eaton herself finally gave in to the chill and withdrew from society. The outraged Jackson came to link Calhoun with what he called a conspiracy against her and drew even closer to Van Buren.

INTERNAL IMPROVEMENTS   While Washington social life weathered the winter of 1829–1830, Van Buren delivered some additional blows to Calhoun. It was easy to bring Jackson into opposition to federally financed internal improvements and thus to programs with which Calhoun had long been identified. In 1830 the Maysville Road bill, passed by Congress, offered Jackson a happy chance for a dual thrust at his rivals John Calhoun and Henry Clay. The bill authorized the government to buy stock in a road from Maysville to Clay's hometown of Lexington. The road lay entirely within the state of Kentucky, and though part of a larger scheme to link up with the

National Road via Cincinnati it could be viewed as a purely local undertaking. On that ground, Jackson vetoed the bill, prompting widespread acclaim. Yet while Jackson continued to oppose federal aid to local projects, he supported such projects as the National Road, as well as road building in the territories and river and harbor bills, the "pork barrels" from which every congressman tried to pluck a morsel for his district. Even so, Jackson's attitude toward the Maysville Road set an important precedent, on the eve of the railroad age, for limiting federal initiative in internal improvements. Railroads would be built altogether by state funds and private capital at least until 1850.

NULLIFICATION

CALHOUN'S THEORY   There is a fine irony to John Calhoun's plight in the Jackson administration, for the South Carolinian was now midway between his early phase as an economic nationalist and his later phase as a states' rights sectionalist. Conditions in his home state had brought on the change. Suffering from agricultural depression, South Carolina lost almost 70,000 residents to emigration during the 1820s and would lose nearly twice that number in the 1830s. Most South Carolinians blamed the protective tariff, which tended to raise the prices of manufactured goods. Insofar as tariffs discouraged the sale of foreign goods in the United States, they reduced the ability of British and French traders to buy southern cotton. This situation worsened already existing problems of low cotton prices and exhausted land. The South Carolinians' malaise was compounded by the increasing criticism of slavery. Hardly had the nation emerged from the Missouri controversy when the city of Charleston, South Carolina, was thrown into panic by the thwarted Denmark Vesey slave insurrection of 1822.

The unexpected passage of the Tariff of 1828, called the tariff of abominations by its critics, left Calhoun no choice but to join the opposition or give up his home base. Calhoun's *South Carolina Exposition and Protest* (1828), written in opposition to the new tariff, contained a finespun theory of nullification, whereby a state could in effect repeal a federal law. This theory stopped just short of justifying secession from the Union. The unsigned statement accompanied resolutions of the South Carolina legislature protesting the tariff. Calhoun, however, had not entirely abandoned his earlier nationalism. He wanted to preserve the Union by protecting the minority rights that the agricultural and slaveholding South claimed. The fine balance he struck between states' rights and central authority was actually not far removed from Andrew Jackson's own philosophy, but growing tensions between the two men would complicate

John C. Calhoun

During the Civil War the Confederate government printed, but never issued, a one-cent postage stamp bearing Calhoun's likeness.

the issue. The flinty Jackson, in addition, was determined to prevent any state defiance of federal law.

THE WEBSTER-HAYNE DEBATE South Carolina's leaders hated the tariff, but they had postponed any action against its enforcement, hoping for a new tariff policy from the Jackson administration. There the issue stood until 1830, when the great Webster-Hayne debate sharpened the lines between states' rights and the Union. The immediate occasion for the debate, however, was the question of federally-owned land.

The federal government still owned immense tracts of land, and the question of how to dispose of the acreage dominated the sectional debate. Late in 1829 a Connecticut senator, fearing the continued drain of residents from New England, sought to restrict land sales in the West. When the resolution came before the Senate in 1830, Missouri's Thomas Hart Benton, who for years had been calling for lower land prices, denounced it as a sectional attack designed to impede the settlement of the West so that the East might maintain its supply of cheap factory labor.

Robert Y. Hayne of South Carolina took Benton's side. Senator Hayne saw in the public land issue a chance to strengthen the alliance of South and West reflected in the 1828 presidential vote for Jackson. Perhaps by endorsing a policy of cheap land in the West, southerners could win western support for lower tariffs. The government, said Hayne, endangered the Union by imposing a hardship upon one section to the benefit of another. The sale of public land as a source of revenue for the central government would create "a fund for corruption—fatal to the sovereignty and independence of the states."

Daniel Webster of Massachusetts rose to offer a dramatic defense of the East. Possessed of a thunderous voice and a theatrical flair, Webster was widely recognized as the nation's foremost orator. With the gallery hushed, the "God-like Daniel" denied that the East had ever sought to restrict development of the West. He then rebuked those southerners who "habitually speak of the Union in terms of indifference, or even of disparagement." Webster sought to lure Hayne into defending states' rights and upholding the doctrine of nullification instead of pursuing coalition with the West.

Hayne took the bait. Young, handsome, and himself an accomplished speaker, he defended Calhoun's *South Carolina Exposition,* arguing that the Union was a compact of the states, and that the federal government, which was their agent, could not be the judge of its own powers, else its powers would be unlimited. Rather, the states remained free to judge when the national government had overstepped the bounds of its constitutional authority. The right of state interposition, whereby a state could interpose its authority over a federal law in order to thwart an unjust federal statute, was "as full and complete as it was before the Constitution was formed."

In rebutting the idea that a state could thwart a federal law, Webster offered a nationalistic view of the Constitution. From the beginning, he asserted, the American Revolution had been a crusade of the united colonies rather than one of each separately. True sovereignty resided in the people as a whole, for whom both federal and state governments acted as agents in their respective spheres. If a single state could nullify a law of the federal government, then the Union would be a "rope of sand," a practical absurdity. A state could neither nullify a federal law nor secede from the Union. The practical outcome of nullification would be a confrontation leading to civil war.

Those sitting in the Senate galleries and much of the nation at large thrilled to Webster's eloquence. His closing statement has become justly famous: "Liberty and Union, now and forever, one and inseparable." In the practical world of coalition politics, Webster also had the better argument, for the Union and majority rule meant more to westerners, including Jackson, than the abstractions of state sovereignty and nullification promoted by Calhoun and other southerners. As for the public lands, the disputed resolution to restrict land sales was soon defeated anyway. And whatever one might argue about the origins of the Union, its evolution would more and more validate Webster's position.

THE RIFT WITH CALHOUN   As yet, however, Jackson had not spoken out on the issue. Like Calhoun he was a slaveholder, albeit a westerner, and he might be expected to sympathize with South Carolina, his native state. Soon all doubt was removed, at least on the point of nullification. On April 13, 1830, a Jefferson Day dinner, honoring the birthday of the former president, was held in Washington. Jackson and Van Buren agreed that the president should present a dinner toast that would indicate his opposition to nullification. When his turn came, Jackson rose, stood erect as a poplar, raised his glass, pointedly stared at Calhoun, and announced, "Our Union— it must be preserved!" Calhoun tried quickly to retrieve the situation with a toast to "the Union, next to our liberty most dear!" But Jackson had set off a bombshell that exploded the plans of the states' righters.

Nearly a month afterward, the final nail was driven into the coffin of Calhoun's presidential ambitions. On May 12, 1830, Jackson saw a letter confirming reports that in 1818 Calhoun, as secretary of war, had proposed disciplining him for his reckless behavior during the Florida invasion. This discovery prompted a tense correspondence between President Jackson and Calhoun and ended with a curt note from the president cutting off further communication.

The growing rift prompted Jackson to remove all Calhoun partisans from the cabinet. He then named Van Buren the U. S. minister to London, pending Senate approval. In the fall of 1831, Jackson announced his readiness for one more term as president, with the idea of returning Van Buren from London in time for the New Yorker to succeed him in 1836. But in 1832, when the Senate reconvened, Van Buren's enemies opposed his appointment as minister to England and gave Calhoun, as vice president, a chance to reject the nomination with a tie-breaking vote. "It will kill him, sir, kill him dead," Calhoun told Senator Thomas Hart Benton. Benton disagreed: "You have broken a minister, and elected a Vice-President." So, it turned out, he had. Calhoun's vote against Van Buren aroused popular sympathy for the New Yorker, who would soon be nominated to succeed Calhoun as vice president.

The Rats Leaving a Falling House

During his first term, Jackson was beset by dissension within his administration. Here "public confidence in the stability and harmony of this administration" is toppling.

His own presidential hopes blasted, Calhoun eagerly became the public leader of the South Carolina nullificationists, who believed that despite reductions supported by Jackson, tariff rates remained too high. By the end of 1831, Jackson was calling for further tariff reductions to take the wind out of the nullificationists' sails, and the Tariff of 1832 did cut revenues another $5 million, but mainly on unprotected items. Average tariff rates were about 25 percent, but rates on cottons, woolens, and iron remained around 50 percent. South Carolinians labeled such high rates an "abomination."

THE SOUTH CAROLINA ORDINANCE South Carolinians, living in the only state where slaves were a majority, feared that the federal authority to impose tariffs might eventually be used to end slavery. In the state elections of 1832, the advocates of nullification took the initiative in organization and agitation. A special legislative session called for the election of a state convention, which overwhelmingly adopted a nullification ordinance repudiating the tariff acts of 1828 and 1832 as unconstitutional and forbidding collection of the duties in the state after February 1, 1833. The legislature chose Robert Hayne as governor and elected Calhoun to succeed him as senator. Calhoun promptly resigned as vice president in order to defend nullification on the Senate floor.

In the crisis, South Carolina found itself standing alone. Other southern states expressed sympathy, but none endorsed nullification. Jackson's response was measured and firm—at least in public. In private he threatened to hang Calhoun and all other traitors—and later expressed regret that he had failed to hang at least Calhoun. In his annual message on December 4, 1832, Jackson announced his firm intention to enforce the tariff, but once again he urged Congress to lower the rates. On December 10 he followed up with his Nullification Proclamation, a document that characterized the doctrine of nullification as an "impractical absurdity." Jackson appealed to the people of his native state not to follow false leaders: "The laws of the United States must be executed. . . . Those who told you that you might peaceably prevent their execution, deceived you. . . . Their object is disunion. But be not deceived by names. Disunion by armed force is treason."

CLAY'S COMPROMISE Jackson then sent federal soldiers and ships to Charleston to enforce the tariff in South Carolina. The nullifiers mobilized the state militia while their local opponents, called Unionists, organized a volunteer force. In 1833 the president requested from Congress a "force bill" authorizing him to use the army to compel compliance with federal law in South Carolina. At the same time he endorsed a bill in Congress that would have lowered tariff duties.

When the force bill was introduced, Calhoun immediately rose in opposition, denying that either he or his state favored disunion. Calhoun claimed that he did not want the South to leave the Union; he wanted the region to regain its political dominance of the Union. Passage of the bill eventually came to depend upon the support of Kentucky senator Henry Clay, who finally yielded to those urging him to save the day. On February 12, 1833, he introduced a plan to reduce the tariff gradually until 1842, by which time no rate would be more than 20 percent. South Carolina would have preferred a greater reduction, but Clay's plan got the nullifiers out of the corner into which they had painted themselves.

On March 1, 1833, Congress passed the compromise tariff and the force bill, and Jackson signed both. The South Carolina convention then met and rescinded its nullification ordinance. In a face-saving gesture it nullified the force bill, for which Jackson no longer had any need. Both sides were able to claim victory. The president had upheld the supremacy of the Union, and South Carolina had secured a reduction of the tariff. Calhoun, worn out by the controversy, returned to his plantation. "The struggle, so far from being over," he ominously wrote, "is not more than fairly commenced."

RACIAL PREJUDICE IN THE JACKSONIAN ERA

The Jacksonian era was rife with contradictions. Many of the same social factors and economic forces that promoted the democratization of the political process during the 1820s also led Democrats, North and South, to justify white supremacy, slavery, and the removal of Indians from their ancestral lands. The same Democrats who demanded political equality for themselves denied social equality and political rights to African Americans, Indians, and women.

What explains such contradictory behavior? By emphasizing the racial inferiority of Indians and blacks, white wage earners could, in a tortuous sense, enhance their own self-esteem and justify their own economic interests. In addition, many northern workers feared for their own jobs if runaway slaves continued to stream northward or if all the enslaved workers in the South were freed.

ATTITUDES TOWARD BLACKS   Roger B. Taney, Andrew Jackson's attorney general, declared in 1831 that blacks were a "separate and degraded people" and therefore could be discriminated against by local and state governments. Free blacks in most northern states during the Jacksonian era were denied basic civil rights and forced to live under segregated conditions. In 1829 government officials in Cincinnati, a haven for runaway southern slaves, ordered all African Americans out of the city within thirty days. A mob of whites decided to hurry them on, destroying most of the city's black neighborhood in their fury.

Anti-black riots occurred in other northern cities as well. Whites who participated in an 1834 riot against African Americans in Philadelphia explained that they were simply defending themselves against the efforts of blacks and abolitionists "to break down the distinctive barrier between the colors [so] that the poor whites may gradually sink into the degraded condition of the Negroes—that, like them, they may be slaves and tools" of economic elites. Four years later, the state of Pennsylvania officially disenfranchised blacks. By 1860 almost every state, old and new, had disenfranchised free blacks while easing voting qualifications for white men.

The Democratic coalition that elected Jackson thus depended for its survival on a widely shared "white racism" and the ability to avoid potentially divisive discussions of slavery. In the South the majority of farmers who supported the slaveholding Jackson and identified with the Democrats did not own slaves, but they still embraced theories of racial superiority.

JACKSON'S INDIAN POLICY   During the 1820s and 1830s the United States was fast becoming a multicultural nation of people from many countries. Most whites, however, were as racist in their treatment of Indians as they were in their treatment of blacks. "Next to the case of the black race within our bosom," declared former president James Madison, "that of the red [race] on our borders is the problem most baffling to the policy of our country."

Andrew Jackson, however, saw nothing baffling about Indian policy. His attitude toward Indians was typically western: Native Americans were barbarians and better off out of the way. At the Battle of Horseshoe Bend in Alabama in 1814, General Jackson's federal troops had massacred nearly 900 Creeks. Jackson and most Americans on the frontier despised and feared Indians—and vice versa. Jackson believed that a "just, humane, liberal policy toward Indians" dictated moving all of them onto the plains west of the Mississippi River, to the Great American Desert, which white settlers would never covet since it was believed to be fit mainly for horned toads and rattlesnakes.

Most of the northern tribes were too weak to resist the offers of Indian commissioners who, if necessary, used bribery and alcohol to woo the chiefs. Only rarely did the tribes rebel. In Illinois and the Wisconsin Territory an armed clash known as the Black Hawk War erupted in 1832. Under Chief Black Hawk, bands of Sauk and Fox sought to reoccupy land they had abandoned the previous year. Facing famine and hostile Sioux west of the Mississippi River, they were simply seeking a place to raise a crop of corn. The Illinois militia mobilized to expel them, chased them into the Wisconsin Territory, and massacred women and children as they tried to escape across the Mississippi River. When Black Hawk surrendered, he confessed that his "heart is dead, and no longer beats quick in his bosom. He is now a prisoner to the white men; they will do with him as they wish. But he can stand torture and is not afraid of death. He is no coward. Black Hawk is an Indian." The Black Hawk War came to be remembered, however, less because of the atrocities inflicted on the Indians than because among the participants were two native Kentuckians later to be pitted against each other: Lieutenant Jefferson Davis of the regular army and Captain Abraham Lincoln of the Illinois volunteers.

In the South two proud Indian nations, the Seminoles and the Cherokees, put up a stubborn resistance to white encroachments. The Seminoles were in fact a group of different tribes that had gravitated to Florida in the eighteenth century. They fought a protracted guerrilla war in the Everglades from 1835 to 1842, but most of the vigor went out of their resistance after 1837, when their leader, Osceola, was seized by treachery under a flag of truce, imprisoned, and left to die. After 1842 only a few hundred Seminoles remained, hiding out in the swamps. Most of the rest had been banished to the West.

THE TRAIL OF TEARS   The Cherokees had, by the end of the eighteenth century, fallen back into the mountains of northern Georgia and western North Carolina, settling on land guaranteed them in 1791 by a treaty with the U. S. government. In 1827 the Cherokees, relying upon their treaty rights, adopted a constitution in which they pointedly declared that they were not subject to any other state or nation. The next year, Georgia declared that after June 1, 1830, the authority of state law would extend over the Cherokees living within the boundaries of the state.

The discovery of gold in 1829 brought bands of rough white prospectors onto Cherokee land. The Cherokees sought relief in the Supreme Court, but in *Cherokee Nation v. Georgia* (1831) John Marshall ruled that the Court lacked jurisdiction because the Cherokees were a "domestic dependent nation" rather than a foreign state in the meaning of the Constitution. Marshall added, however, that the Cherokees had "an unquestionable right" to their land until they wished to cede it to the United States.

In 1830 a Georgia law had required whites in the Cherokee territory to obtain licenses authorizing their residence there and to take an oath of allegiance to the state. Two New England missionaries among the Indians refused to abide by the law and were sentenced to four years at hard labor. On appeal their case reached the Supreme Court as *Worcester v. Georgia* (1832), and the court held that the Cherokee Nation was "a distinct political community" within which Georgia law had no force. The Georgia law was

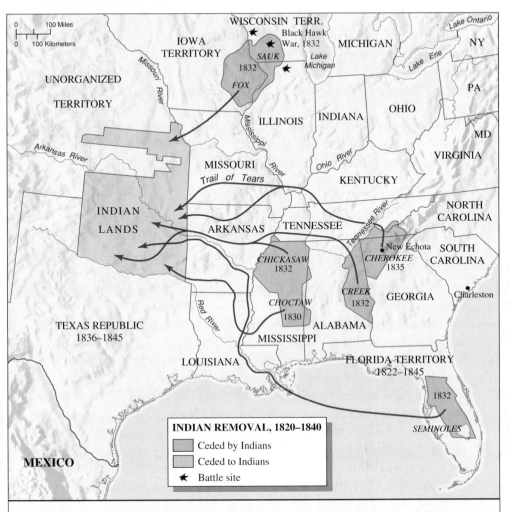

Why did Congress exile the Choctaws, Chickasaws, Creeks, Seminoles, and Chero-kees to the territory west of Arkansas and Missouri? How far did the tribes have to travel, and what were the conditions on the trip? Why were the Indians not forced to move earlier than the 1830s?

therefore unconstitutional. Now Georgia faced down the Supreme Court with the tacit consent of the president. Andrew Jackson is supposed to have said privately, "[Chief Justice John]Marshall has made his decision, now let him enforce it!" Whether or not he spoke so bluntly, Jackson did nothing to implement the Court's decision. Under the circumstances there was noth-ing for the Cherokees to do but give in and sign a treaty, which they did in

1835. They gave up their land in the Southeast in exchange for land in the Indian Territory west of Arkansas, $5 million from the federal government, and expenses for transportation.

By 1838 some 17,000 Cherokees, and some 2,000 African Americans they had enslaved, had departed westward, following other tribes on the 800-mile "Trail of Tears." It was a grueling journey. Four thousand Cherokees did not survive the trip. A few who never left their homeland held out in their native mountains and acquired title to land in North Carolina; thenceforth they were the "Eastern Band" of Cherokees.

THE BANK CONTROVERSY

THE BANK'S OPPONENTS   The overriding national issue in the presidential campaign of 1832 was neither Andrew Jackson's Indian policy nor South Carolina's obsession with the high tariff. It was the question of rechartering the Bank of the United States, whose legal mandate would soon lapse. Jackson had absorbed the West's hostility toward the bank after the panic of 1819. He insisted that the bank was unconstitutional no matter what Chief Justice John Marshall had said in *McCulloch v. Maryland*. Jackson, suspicious of all banks, especially disliked a central national bank.

Under the management of Nicholas Biddle, the second Bank of the United States had facilitated business expansion and supplied a stable currency by forcing state banks to keep a specie (gold or silver) reserve on hand to back up their paper currency. The bank also acted as the collecting and disbursing agent for the federal government, which held one fifth of the bank's $35 million capital stock. From the start this combination of private and public functions caused problems for the bank. As the government's revenues soared, the bank became the most powerful lending institution in the country, a central bank, in effect, whose huge size enabled it to determine the amount of available credit for the nation. Moreover, by issuing paper money of its own, the bank provided a stable, uniform currency for the expanding economy as well as a mechanism for regulating the pace of growth.

Arrayed against the bank were powerful enemies: some of the state and local banks that had been forced to reduce their volume of paper money, groups of debtors who had suffered from the reduction, and businessmen and speculators on the make, who disliked the bank's tight credit policies. States' rights groups questioned the bank's constitutionality. Financiers on New York's Wall Street resented the supremacy of the bank on Philadelphia's Chestnut Street. Like Jackson many westerners and workingmen believed that the bank was a powerful monopoly controlled by the wealthy few and was irreconcilable with a democracy. Biddle, born to wealth and social prestige, cultured, witty, and supremely self-confident, was an excellent banker but also a convenient symbol for those who saw the bank as the cozy friend of capitalists.

THE RECHARTER EFFORT   The bank's twenty-year charter would run through 1836, but Biddle could not afford the uncertainty of waiting until then for a renewal. He pondered whether to force the issue of recharter before the election of 1832 or after. On this point, leaders of the National Republicans, especially Henry Clay and Daniel Webster, argued that the time to move was before the election. Clay, already the candidate of the National Republicans, proposed making the bank the central issue of the presidential election. Friends of the bank held a majority in Congress, and Jackson would risk loss of support in the election if he vetoed renewal. But they failed to grasp the depth of public distaste for the bank and succeeded mainly in handing Jackson a charged issue on the eve of the election. "The Bank," Jackson told Martin Van Buren in May 1832, "is trying to kill me. But I will kill it."

Rechartering the Bank

Jackson Battling the Hydra-headed Bank of the United States

Both houses passed the recharter by a comfortable margin but without the two-thirds majority needed to override a presidential veto. On July 10, 1832, Jackson vetoed the bill, sending it back to Congress with a ringing denunciation of monopoly and special privilege. An effort to overrule the veto failed in the Senate. The stage was set for a nationwide financial crisis.

CAMPAIGN INNOVATIONS   In the 1832 presidential campaign a third party entered the field for the first time. The Anti-Masonic party had grown out of popular hostility toward the Masonic order, a fraternal organization whose members were suspected of having kidnapped and murdered a New Yorker for revealing the "secrets" of his lodge. Opposition to a fraternal order was hardly the foundation on which to build a lasting national political organization, but the Anti-Masonic party made three important contributions to national politics: in addition to being the first third party, it was the first party to hold a national nominating convention and the first to announce an official platform, all of which it accomplished in 1831 when it nominated William Wirt of Maryland for president.

The major parties followed its example by holding national conventions of their own. In 1831 delegates of the National Republican party assembled in Baltimore to nominate Henry Clay. Andrew Jackson endorsed the idea of a nominating convention for the Democratic party (the name Republican was now formally dropped) to demonstrate popular support for its candidates. To that purpose the convention first adopted the two-thirds rule for nomination (which prevailed until 1936) and then named Martin Van Buren as Jackson's running mate. The Democrats, unlike the other two parties, adopted no formal platform at their first convention and relied substantially upon hoopla and the president's popularity to carry the election.

The outcome was an overwhelming endorsement of Jackson in the Electoral College, with 219 votes to 49 for Clay, and a less overwhelming but solid victory in the popular vote, 688,000 to 530,000. William Wirt carried only Vermont. South Carolina, preparing for nullification and unable to stomach either Jackson or Clay, delivered its eleven votes to the governor of Virginia.

THE REMOVAL OF GOVERNMENT DEPOSITS   Andrew Jackson viewed the 1832 election as a mandate to further weaken the Bank of the United States, and he decided to remove all government deposits and distribute them to state banks. When Secretary of the Treasury Louis McLane opposed removal of the federal deposits and suggested a modified version of the bank, Jackson shook up his cabinet. In the reshuffling, Attorney General

Roger Taney moved to the Treasury, where he complied with the president's wishes.

Taney continued to draw on government accounts with the national bank, but deposited new government receipts in state banks. By the end of 1833, twenty-three state banks—"pet banks," as they came to be called—had the benefit of federal deposits. Transferring the government's deposits was a highly questionable action under the law, and the Senate voted to censure Jackson.

Biddle also rejected Jackson's efforts to cripple the bank. "This worthy President," he declared, "thinks that because he has scalped Indians and imprisoned judges, he is to have his way with the bank. He is mistaken." Biddle ordered that the bank curtail loans throughout the nation and demand the redemption of state bank notes in specie as quickly as possible. By tightening the nation's money supply, he sought to bring the economy to a halt, create a sharp depression, and reveal to the nation the importance of maintaining the bank. By 1834 the tightness of credit was creating widespread complaints of business distress.

The financial contraction resulting from the bank war quickly gave way to a speculative binge encouraged by the deposit of federal funds in state banks. With the restraint of the Bank of the United States removed, the state banks issued paper money without keeping sufficient gold reserves on hand. New banks proliferated, blissfully printing bank notes to lend to speculators. Sales of public land rose from 4 million acres in 1834 to 15 million in 1835 and 20 million in 1836. At the same time the states plunged heavily into debt to finance the building of roads and canals, inspired by the success of New York's Erie Canal in opening up the entire state's economy to the markets of the eastern seaboard and Europe. By 1837 the total indebtedness of the states had soared to $170 million, a very large sum for the time.

FISCAL MEASURES   Still, the federal surplus continued to mount as the widespread purchases of public land continued. Many westerners proposed simply to lower the price of land; southerners preferred to lower the tariff, but such action would upset the compromise achieved in the Tariff of 1833. Finally, in 1836, the Distribution Act was passed, a compromise that allowed the government to distribute most of the surplus as loans to the states. To satisfy Jackson's concerns, the funds were technically deposits, but they were never demanded. Distribution of the federal surplus was to be in proportion to each state's representation in Congress.

About a month after passage of the Distribution Act, Jackson's Treasury secretary issued the Specie Circular of July 11, 1836. With that document the president belatedly applied his hard-money convictions to the sale of public land. According to his order, the government after August 15 would accept only gold and silver in payment for land. Doing so would supposedly "repress frauds," withhold support "from the monopoly of the public lands in the hands of speculators and capitalists," and discourage the "ruinous extension" of bank notes and credit.

Irony dogged Jackson to the end on this matter. Since few settlers could get their hands on hard money, they were now left all the more at the mercy of speculators for land purchases. Both the Distribution Act and the Specie Circular put many state banks in jeopardy. The distribution of the federal surplus to the state governments entailed the removal of large deposits from state banks. In turn the state banks had to call in many of their loans in order to accumulate enough money to be able to transfer federal funds to the state governments. This situation caused greater dismay in the already chaotic state banking community. At the same time the new requirement that only hard money be accepted for federal land purchases put an added strain on the local supplies of gold and silver.

BOOM AND BUST   The boom-and-bust cycle of the 1830s had causes larger even than Andrew Jackson, causes that were beyond his control. The inflation of middecade was rooted not solely in a sudden expansion of bank notes, as it seemed at the time, but also in an increase of gold and silver flowing into the country from England and France and, especially, Mexico, for investment and for the purchase of American cotton and other products.

Contrary to appearances the gold and silver reserves in U. S. banks actually kept pace with the increase of bank notes, despite reckless behavior by some banks. By 1836, however, a tighter economy had caused a decline in both British investments abroad and British demand for American cotton just when the new western lands were creating a rapid increase in the cotton supply. Fortunately for Jackson the panic of 1837 did not erupt until he was out of the White House. His successor would serve as the scapegoat.

VAN BUREN AND THE NEW PARTY SYSTEM

THE WHIG COALITION   Before the depression set in, the Jacksonian Democrats reaped a political bonanza. Jackson had defeated nullification in South Carolina and eliminated the national bank, and the people loved him for it. The hard times following the contraction of the economy turned Americans against Nicholas Biddle and the national bank, but not against Jackson, the professed friend of "the people" and foe of the "selfish" interests of financiers and speculators.

By 1834 Jackson's opponents had begun to pull together a new coalition of diverse elements, united chiefly by their hostility to him. The imperious demeanor of the so-called champion of democracy had given rise to the name King Andrew I. Jackson's followers therefore were labeled Tories, supporters of the king, and his opponents Whigs, a name that linked them to the Patriots of the American Revolution. The diverse coalition of Whigs clustered around the National Republican party of John Quincy Adams, Henry Clay, and Daniel Webster. Into the combination streamed remnants of the Anti-Masons and the Democrats, who for one reason or another were alienated by Jackson's stand on the bank, Indian removal, hard money, or internal improvements. Of the forty-one Democrats in Congress who had voted to recharter the bank, twenty-eight had joined the Whigs by 1836.

Whiggery always had about it an atmosphere of social conservatism and elitism. The core Whigs were the supporters of Henry Clay, men who promoted a national economic policy. In the South the Whigs enjoyed the support of the urban banking and commercial interests, as well as their planter associates, holders of most of the slaves in the region. In the West, farmers who valued internal improvements joined the Whig ranks. Most states' rights supporters eventually dropped away, and by the early 1840s the Whigs were becoming the party of economic nationalism, even in the South. Unlike the Democrats, who attracted Catholic immigrants from Germany and Ireland, Whig voters tended to be native-born or British-American Protestants—Presbyterians, Baptists, and Congregationalists—who were active in promoting social reforms such as abolition and temperance.

THE ELECTION OF 1836   By 1836, a new two-party system was emerging from the Jackson and anti-Jackson forces, a system that would remain in fairly even balance for twenty years. In 1835, eighteen months before the election, the Democrats held their second national convention, nominating Jackson's handpicked successor, Vice President Martin Van Buren. The Whig coalition, united chiefly in its opposition to Jackson, held no convention but adopted a strategy of multiple candidacies, hoping to throw the election into the House of Representatives. The result was a free-for-all reminiscent of 1824, except that this time one candidate stood apart from the rest. It was Van Buren against the field. The Whigs put up three favorite sons: Daniel Webster, named by the Massachusetts legislature; Hugh Lawson White, chosen by anti-Jackson Democrats in the Tennessee legislature; and William Henry Harrison of Indiana, nominated by a predominantly Anti-Masonic convention in Harrisburg, Pennsylvania. In the popular vote, Van Buren outdistanced the entire Whig

Martin Van Buren

"The Little Magician."

field, with 765,000 votes to 740,000 votes for the Whigs, most of which were cast for Harrison.

Martin Van Buren, the eighth president, was the first of Dutch ancestry. The son of a tavern keeper in Kinderhook, New York, he had attended a local academy, read law, and entered politics. Although he kept up a limited legal practice, he had been primarily a professional politician, so skilled in the arts of organization and manipulation that he was dubbed the Little Magician. In 1824 he supported Crawford, then switched his allegiance to Jackson in 1828 but continued to look to the Old Republicans of Virginia as the southern anchor of his support. Elected governor of New York, Van Buren quickly resigned to join Jackson's cabinet and, because of Jackson's support, became minister to London and then vice president. Short and trim, Van Buren was also called the Red Fox for his long reddish sideburns, dominant forehead, and long, striking nose. His elegant attire, engaging personality, and constant political scheming gave further credence to his nicknames.

THE PANIC OF 1837   President Van Buren inherited a financial panic. An already precarious economy was tipped over by a depression in England, which resulted in a drop in the price of cotton and caused English banks and investors to contract their activities in the United States and refuse extensions of loans. This was a particularly hard blow since much of America's economic expansion depended upon European—and mainly English—investment capital. As creditors hastened to foreclose, the inflationary spiral went into reverse. States curtailed ambitious plans for roads and canals and in many cases felt impelled to repudiate their debts. In the crunch many of the state banks collapsed, and the federal government itself lost some $9 million it had deposited in pet banks.

The common folk, as always, were particularly hard hit during the economic slump and largely had to fend for themselves. By the fall of 1837, one third of the workforce was jobless. Those still fortunate enough to have jobs saw their wages cut by 30 to 50 percent within two years. At the same time, prices for food and clothing skyrocketed. As the winter of 1837 approached, a journalist reported that in New York City 200,000 people were "in utter and hopeless distress with no means of surviving the winter but those provided by charity." There was no government aid, only that provided by churches and voluntary societies.

Van Buren's advisers and supporters were inclined to blame speculators and bankers for the hard times. At the same time they expected the evildoers to get what they deserved in a healthy shakeout that would restore the economy. Van Buren did not believe that he or the government had any responsibility to rescue hard-pressed farmers or businessmen or to provide public welfare. But he did feel obliged to keep the government itself in a healthy financial situation. To that end he called a special session of Congress in 1837, which quickly voted to postpone indefinitely the distribution of the surplus because of a probable upcoming deficit and approved an issue of Treasury notes to cover immediate expenses.

AN INDEPENDENT TREASURY   Van Buren proposed that the federal government cease risking its deposits in shaky state banks and set up an independent Treasury. Under this plan the federal government would keep its funds in its own vaults and do business entirely in hard money. The Whigs preferred that the federal government promote economic development, perhaps in the form of tariff or currency legislation.

Van Buren's Independent Treasury Act aroused stiff opposition from a combination of Whigs and conservative Democrats who feared deflation, and it took the Red Fox several years of maneuvering to get what he wanted. John Calhoun signaled a return to the Democratic fold, after several years of flirting with the Whigs, when he came out in favor of the independent Treasury. Van Buren gained western support for the plan by backing a more liberal policy of federal land sales. Congress finally passed the Independent Treasury Act on July 4, 1840. Although the Whigs repealed it in 1841, it would be restored in 1846.

The protracted struggle over the Treasury was only one of several issues that occupied politicians' attention during the late 1830s. Petitions asking Congress to abolish slavery and the slave trade in the District of Columbia provoked tumultuous debate, especially in the House of Representatives. A dispute over the Maine boundary kept British-American animosity at a simmer. But basic to the spreading malaise was the depressed condition of the economy, which lasted through Van Buren's term. Fairly or not, the administration became the target of growing discontent. The president won renomination by the Democrats easily enough, but the general election was another matter.

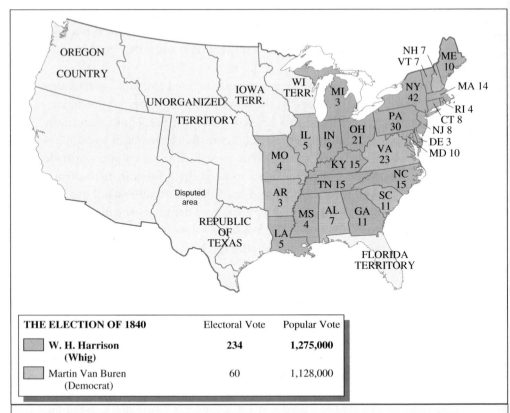

THE ELECTION OF 1840	Electoral Vote	Popular Vote
W. H. Harrison **(Whig)**	**234**	**1,275,000**
Martin Van Buren (Democrat)	60	1,128,000

Why did Van Buren carry several western states but few others? How did the Whigs achieve a decisive electoral victory over the Democrats? How was their strategy in 1840 different from their campaign in 1836?

THE "LOG CABIN AND HARD CIDER" CAMPAIGN   The Whigs got an early start on their election campaign when they met at Harrisburg, Pennsylvania, on December 4, 1839, to choose a candidate. Henry Clay, the legislative veteran who coupled the ideas of a visionary with shrewd political savvy, expected 1840 to be his year. He was wrong. Although Clay led on the first ballot, the Whig convention preferred a military hero who could enter the race with few known political convictions or enemies. So the delegates turned to William Henry Harrison, victor at the Battle of Tippecanoe against the Shawnees in 1811 while governor of the Indiana Territory and briefly a congressman and a senator from Ohio. To rally their states' rights wing, the Whigs chose for vice president John Tyler of Virginia, Clay's close friend.

The Whigs had no platform. A detailed platform would have risked dividing a coalition united chiefly by opposition to the Democrats. But they had a catchy slogan, "Tippecanoe and Tyler Too," and they soon had a rousing campaign theme, which a Democratic newspaper unwittingly supplied: it declared sardonically "that upon condition of his receiving a pension of $2,000 and a barrel of cider, General Harrison would no doubt consent to withdraw his pretensions, and spend his days in a log cabin on the banks of the Ohio." The Whigs seized upon the cider and log-cabin symbols to depict Harrison as a simple man sprung from the people. Actually, he sprang from one of the first families of Virginia, was a college graduate, and lived in an Ohio farmhouse.

The presidential campaign of 1840 produced the largest turnout of any election up to that time. To the Whigs, Van Buren symbolized the economic slump as well as aristocratic snobbery. "Van! Van! Is a Used-Up Man!" went one of their campaign slogans, and down he went by the thumping margin of 234 electoral votes to 60.

ASSESSING THE JACKSON YEARS

The Whigs may have won in 1840, but the Jacksonian movement had permanently altered American politics. Long-standing ambivalence about political parties had been purged in the fires of political conflict, and mass political parties had arrived to stay. They were now widely justified as a "positive good." By 1840 both parties were tightly organized down to the precinct level, and the proportion of adult white males who voted in the presidential election had nearly tripled, from 27 percent in 1824 to 78 percent in 1840. That much is beyond dispute, but the phenomenon of Andrew Jackson, the great symbol for an age, has inspired conflicts of interpretation as spirited as those among his supporters and opponents at the time. Was he the leader of a vast democratic movement that welled up in the West and mobilized a farmer-laborer alliance to sweep the "monster" bank into the dustbin of history? Or was he essentially a frontier tycoon, an opportunist for whom the ideal of democracy provided effective political rhetoric?

In the Jacksonian view the alliance of government and business always invited special favors and made for an eternal source of corruption. The central bank epitomized such evil. Good government policy, at the national level in particular, avoided the granting of special privileges and let free competition regulate the economy.

In the bustling world of the nineteenth century, Jackson's laissez-faire policies actually opened the way for a host of aspiring entrepreneurs eager to replace the established economic elite with a new order of free-enterprise capitalism. And in fact there was no great conflict in the Jacksonian mentality between the farmer or planter who delved in the soil and the independent speculator and entrepreneur who grew wealthy by other means. Jackson himself was both. The Jacksonian mentality did not foresee the degree to which, in a growing country, unrestrained enterprise could lead to new economic combinations, centers of economic power largely independent of government regulation. But history is forever producing unintended consequences. Here the ultimate irony would be that the laissez-faire rationale for preserving an agrarian republic eventually became the justification for the growth of unregulated corporate powers far greater than any ever wielded by Nicholas Biddle's hated central bank.

MAKING CONNECTIONS

- This chapter analyzed the political side of "Jacksonian democracy." Chapter 12 concludes with an assessment of the accuracy of that term from social and economic perspectives.

- John C. Calhoun, Henry Clay, and Daniel Webster, three of the statesmen considered in this chapter, continued for many years to be the major spokesmen for their positions. Their last great debate, over the Compromise of 1850, is discussed in Chapter 16.

FURTHER READING

A fine survey of events covered in this chapter is Daniel Feller's *The Jacksonian Promise: America, 1815–1840* (1995). A more political focus can be found in Harry L. Watson's *Liberty and Power: The Politics of Jacksonian America* (1990).

A still-valuable standard introduction to the development of the political parties of the 1830s is Richard Patrick McCormick's *The Second Party System: Party Formation in the Jacksonian Era* (1966). For an outstanding analysis of women in New York City during the Jacksonian period, see Christine Stansell's *City of Women: Sex and Class in New York, 1789–1860* (1986). John

F. Marszalek's *The Petticoat Affair: Manners, Mutiny, and Sex in Andrew Jackson's White House* (1997) assesses the Peggy Eaton controversy.

The best biography of Jackson remains Robert Vincent Remini's three-volume work: *Andrew Jackson: The Course of American Empire, 1767–1821* (1977), *Andrew Jackson: The Course of American Freedom, 1822–1832* (1981), and *Andrew Jackson: The Course of American Democracy, 1833–1845* (1984). On Jackson's successor, consult John Niven's *Martin Van Buren: The Romantic Age of American Politics* (1983).

The political philosophies of Jackson's opponents are treated in Daniel Walker Howe's *The Political Culture of the American Whigs* (1979) and William P. Vaughn's *The Antimasonic Party in the United States, 1826–1843* (1983).

Two studies of the impact of the bank controversy are William G. Shade's *Banks or No Banks: The Money Issue in Western Politics, 1832–1865* (1972) and James Roger Sharp's *The Jacksonians versus the Banks: Politics in the States after the Panic of 1837* (1970). Daniel Feller's *The Public Lands in Jacksonian Politics* (1984) is a good introduction to that important topic.

The outstanding book on the nullification issue remains William W. Freehling's *Prelude to Civil War: The Nullification Controversy in South Carolina, 1816–1836* (1965). John M. Belohlavek's *"Let the Eagle Soar!": The Foreign Policy of Andrew Jackson* (1985) is a thorough study of Jacksonian diplomacy. Ronald N. Satz's *American Indian Policy in the Jacksonian Era* (1974) surveys Jackson's Indian policy.

12

THE DYNAMICS
OF GROWTH

FOCUS QUESTIONS

- What caused the expansion of agriculture, industry, and transportation?
- How had patterns of immigration changed by the middle of the nineteenth century?
- What was the status of labor unions?

To answer these questions and access additional review material, please visit www.wwnorton.com/studyspace.

The Jacksonian-era political debate between democratic ideals and elitist traditions was rooted in a profound transformation of social and economic life. Between 1815 and 1850 the United States expanded all the way to the Pacific coast. An industrial revolution in the Northeast began to reshape the economy and propel an unrelenting process of urbanization. In the West an agricultural empire began to emerge, focused on corn, wheat, and cattle. In the South, cotton became king, and its reign came to depend upon the expanding institution of slavery. At the same time, innovations in transportation—canals, steamboats, and railroads—conquered time and space and knit together a transcontinental market. In sum, an eighteenth-century economy based upon small-scale farming and local commerce matured into a far-flung capitalist marketplace entwined with world trade. These economic developments in turn generated changes in every other area of life, from politics to the legal system, from the family to social values.

AGRICULTURE AND THE NATIONAL ECONOMY

The first stage of industrialization brought with it an expansive commercial and urban outlook that by the end of the century would supplant the agrarian philosophy espoused by Thomas Jefferson and many others. "We are greatly, I was about to say fearfully, growing," South Carolina's John Calhoun told his congressional colleagues in 1816, and many other statesmen shared his ambivalent outlook. Would the republic retain its virtue and cohesion amid the turmoil of chaotic commercial development? In the brief Era of Good Feelings after the War of 1812, such a troublesome question was easily brushed aside as economic opportunities seemed available to free Americans everywhere.

COTTON A major source of economic opportunity in the South was provided by the cultivation of cotton, the profitable staple crop that was spreading from South Carolina and Georgia into the new lands of Mississippi and Alabama. Cotton had been cultivated since ancient times, but the proliferation of English textile mills during the late eighteenth century created a rapidly growing market for the fluffy fiber. For many years, cotton had remained rare and expensive because of the need for hand labor to separate the lint from the tenacious green seeds. But that problem was solved in 1793 when Eli Whitney, a Yale graduate who had gone south to teach, devised a mechanism for removing the sticky seeds. The cotton gin (short for "engine") enabled a person to separate fifty times as much cotton as could be done by hand.

By inventing the cotton gin, Eli Whitney had spurred a revolution. Cotton production soared during the first half of the nineteenth century, and planters found a profitable new use for slavery. Planters and their enslaved workers migrated westward into Kentucky, Tennessee, Alabama, Mississippi, Louisiana, and Texas, and the cotton culture became a way of life that tied the Old Southwest to the coastal Southeast in a common interest.

Not the least of the cotton gin's revolutionary consequences was that cotton became a major export commodity for the United States. After Napoléon's defeat in 1815, European demand for cotton skyrocketed. From 1815 to 1819, cotton exports averaged 39 percent of the value of all exports, and from the mid-1830s to 1860 they accounted for more than half the total. Cotton precipitated a phenomenal expansion of the national economy. The South supplied the North with both raw materials and markets for manufactures. Income from the North's role in handling the cotton trade then provided surpluses for capital investment.

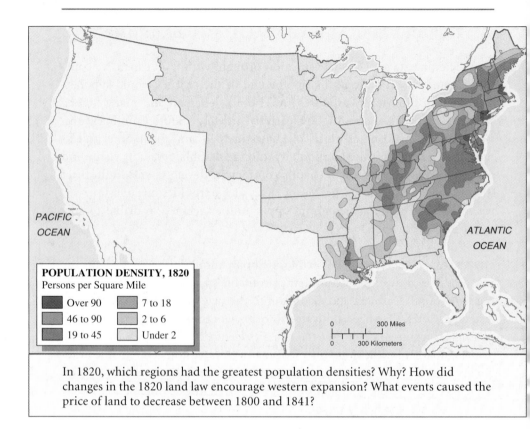

POPULATION DENSITY, 1820
Persons per Square Mile

- Over 90
- 46 to 90
- 19 to 45
- 7 to 18
- 2 to 6
- Under 2

In 1820, which regions had the greatest population densities? Why? How did changes in the 1820 land law encourage western expansion? What events caused the price of land to decrease between 1800 and 1841?

FARMING THE WEST The westward flow of planters and their slaves to Alabama and Mississippi during these flush times mirrored another migration: through the Ohio River valley and the Great Lakes region, where the Indians had been steadily pushed westward. By 1860 more than half the nation's expanded population resided west of the Appalachians, and the restless movement had long since spilled across the Mississippi River and touched the shores of the Pacific. North of the expanding cotton belt in the Gulf states, the fertile woodland soil, riverside bottomlands, and black loam of the prairies drew farmers from the rocky lands of New England and the exhausted soils of the Southeast. The development of effective iron plows greatly eased the grueling job of breaking the soil.

A new federal land law passed in 1820 reduced the minimum price per acre and reduced the minimum plot from 160 acres to 80. A settler could

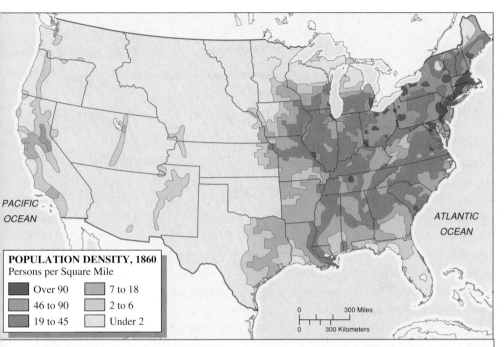

POPULATION DENSITY, 1860
Persons per Square Mile

- Over 90
- 46 to 90
- 19 to 45
- 7 to 18
- 2 to 6
- Under 2

In 1860, which regions had the greatest population densities? Why? How did new technologies allow farmers to grow more crops on larger pieces of land? What regions benefited most from the new technologies?

now buy a farm for as little as $100, and over the years the proliferation of state banks made it possible to continue buying land on credit. Even that was not enough for westerners, however, who began a long—and eventually victorious—agitation for further relaxation of the land laws. They favored "preemption," the right of squatters to purchase land at the minimum price, and graduation, the progressive reduction of the price on land that did not sell.

Congress eventually responded with two bills. Under the Preemption Act of 1830, squatters could stake out claims ahead of the land surveys and later get 160 acres at the minimum price of $1.25 per acre. In effect the law recognized a practice enforced more often than not by frontier vigilantes. Under the Graduation Act of 1854, the price of unsold land was to go down in stages until the land could sell for $1.25 per acre after thirty years.

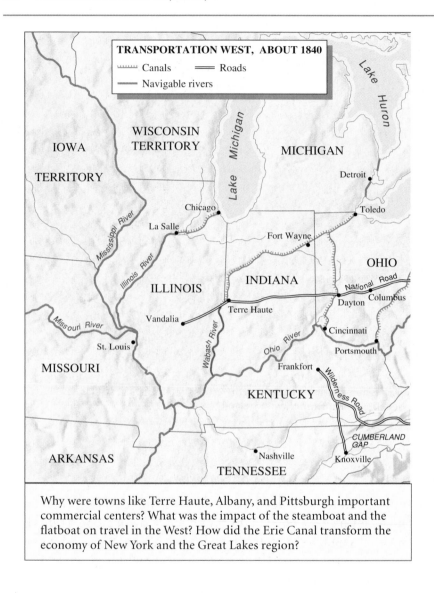

TRANSPORTATION WEST, ABOUT 1840

Why were towns like Terre Haute, Albany, and Pittsburgh important commercial centers? What was the impact of the steamboat and the flatboat on travel in the West? How did the Erie Canal transform the economy of New York and the Great Lakes region?

TRANSPORTATION, COMMUNICATION, AND THE NATIONAL ECONOMY

NEW ROADS Transportation improvements helped spur the development of a national market for goods and services. In 1795 the Wilderness Road, which followed the trail blazed by Daniel Boone twenty years before,

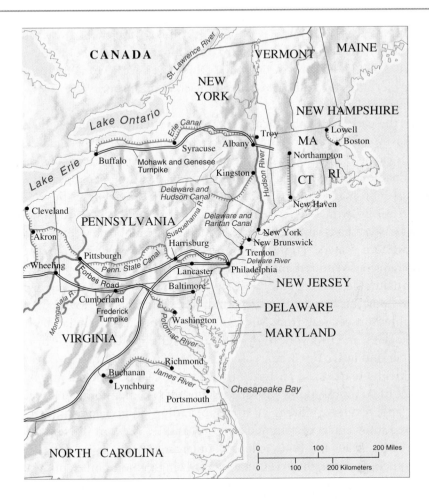

was opened to wagon and stagecoach traffic, thereby easing the route through the Cumberland Gap in Kentucky. In the Deep South there were no such major highways. South Carolinians and Georgians pushed westward on whatever trails or rutted roads had appeared.

To the northeast, public demand for graded and paved roads packed with crushed stones gathered momentum after completion of the Philadelphia-Lancaster Turnpike in 1794 (the term *turnpike*, derives from a pole, or pike, at the tollgate, which was turned to admit the traffic). By 1821 there were some 4,000 miles of turnpikes, mainly connecting eastern cities, but western traffic could move along the Frederick Turnpike to Cumberland and thence along the National Road to Wheeling, Virginia, on the Ohio River, in 1818, then to Columbus in the Northwest Territory and by about midcentury on to Vandalia, Illinois.

WATER TRANSPORTATION Once turnpike travelers had reached the Ohio River, they could float westward on flatboats. In the early 1820s an estimated 3,000 flatboats went down the Ohio River every year, and for many years thereafter the flatboat remained the chief means for conveying freight and people downstream.

By the early 1820s the turnpike boom was giving way to new developments in water transportation: the river steamboat and the canal barge, which carried goods far more cheaply than did Conestoga wagons on the National Road. The first commercially successful steamboat appeared when Robert Fulton and Robert R. Livingston sent the *Clermont* up the Hudson River to Albany in 1807. After that the use of steamboats spread rapidly to other eastern and western rivers. By 1836, 361 steamboats were navigating the western waters. During the next decade, the shallow-draft, steam-powered ships ventured into far reaches of the Mississippi River valley.

The durable flatboat still carried to market most of the western wheat, corn, flour, meal, port, whiskey, and soap and candles (byproducts of slaughterhouses), lead from Missouri, copper from Michigan, lumber from the Rockies, and ironwork from Pittsburgh. But the steamboat, by bringing cheaper and faster two-way traffic to the Mississippi River valley, created a continental market and an agricultural empire that became the new bread-basket of America. Along with the new farmers came promoters, speculators, and retailers. Villages at strategic trading points along the streams evolved into centers of commerce and urban life. The port of New Orleans grew in the 1830s and 1840s to lead all others in exports.

By then, however, the Erie Canal was drawing eastward much of the trade that had once gone down the Mississippi to the Gulf of Mexico. In 1817 the New York legislature had endorsed Governor DeWitt Clinton's dream of a canal connecting the Hudson River with Lake Erie. Eight years later, in 1825, the canal, forty feet wide and four feet deep, was open for the entire 363 miles from Albany west to Buffalo; branches soon put most of the state within its reach. The Erie Canal was an engineering marvel. The longest canal in the world, it traversed rivers and valleys, forests and marshes. It reduced travel time from New York City to Buffalo from twenty days to six, and the cost of moving a ton of freight plummeted from $100 to $5.

The speedy success of the New York waterways inspired a mania for canals in other states that lasted more than a decade. But no other canal ever matched the spectacular success of the Erie. It rendered the entire Great Lakes region an economic tributary to New York City and had major economic and political consequences, tying together West and East while further isolating the Deep South. With the addition of new canals spanning

The Erie Canal

Junction of the Northern and Western Canals (1825), an aquatint by John Hill.

Ohio and Indiana from north to south, much of the upper Ohio River valley was also drawn into New York's economic sphere.

RAILROADS The financial panic of 1837 and the subsequent depression cooled the canal fever. Meanwhile, a more versatile form of transportation was gaining on the canal: the railroad. In 1825, the year the Erie Canal was completed, the world's first commercial steam railway began operation in England, and soon the port cities of Baltimore, Charleston, and Boston were alive with schemes to penetrate the hinterlands by rail. By 1840 American railroads, with a total of 3,328 miles, had outdistanced the canals by just two miles. Over the next twenty years, though, railroads grew nearly tenfold, covering 30,626 miles; more than two thirds of that total was built in the 1850s. But it was still not until the eve of the Civil War that railroads surpassed canals in total haulage.

Travel on the early railroads tested the courage of passengers. Wood was used for fuel, and sparks often caused fires or damaged passengers' clothing. Invention of the "spark arrester" and the use of coal for fuel alleviated those problems. Yet land travel, whether by stagecoach or train, remained a jerky, bumpy, wearying ordeal.

Water travel, where available, offered far more comfort, but the railroad gained supremacy over other forms of transportation because of its economy, speed, and reliability. Trains averaged ten miles an hour, doubling the speed of stagecoaches. Railroads also provided indirect benefits, by encouraging frontier settlement and making farming more profitable. During the antebellum period the reduced shipping costs resulting from the growth of railroads aided the expansion of farming more than manufacturing, since manufacturers in the Northeast, especially in New England, had better access to water transportation. The railroads' demand for iron and equipment of various kinds did provide an enormous market for the industries that made those capital goods, however. And the ability of railroads to operate year-round in all kinds of weather gave them an advantage in carrying freight.

But the epic railroad boom had negative effects as well. By opening up possibilities for quick and often shady profits, it helped corrupt political life, and by opening up access to the trans-Appalachian West, it helped accelerate the decline of Indian culture. In addition, the railroad dramatically quickened the tempo and mobility of life. The writer Nathaniel Hawthorne spoke for many Americans when he charged that the locomotive "comes down upon you like fate, swift and inevitable." With its unsettling whistle it brought "the noisy world into the midst of our slumbrous peace."

OCEAN TRANSPORTATION For oceangoing traffic the start of regularly scheduled service was the most important change of the early 1800s. In the first week of 1818, ships of the New York–based Black Ball Line inaugurated weekly transatlantic service between New York and Liverpool, England. By 1845 some fifty-two transatlantic lines ran square-riggers on schedule from New York, with three regular sailings per week. Many other lines ran in the coastwise trade, to Charleston, Savannah, New Orleans, and elsewhere.

The same year, 1845, witnessed a great innovation with the launching of the first clipper ship, the *Rainbow*. Built for speed, the sleek clippers doubled the speed of the older merchant vessels, and trading companies rushed to purchase them. Long and lean, with tall masts and many sails, they cut dashing figures during their brief but colorful career, which lasted less than two decades. What prompted the clipper boom was the lure of Chinese tea, a drink long coveted in America but in scarce supply. Tea leaves were a perishable commodity that had to reach the market quickly, and the new clippers

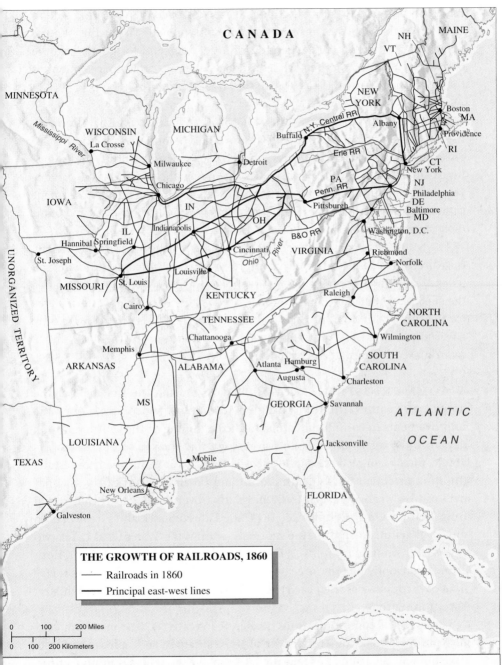

THE GROWTH OF RAILROADS, 1860

—— Railroads in 1860

—— Principal east-west lines

0   100   200 Miles

0   100   200 Kilometers

Why did railroads expand rapidly in the 1850s? What were the principal east-west lines? Why did many lines terminate in places like St. Louis and Chicago?

made this possible. Even more important, the discovery of California gold in 1848 lured thousands of prospectors and entrepreneurs from the Atlantic seaboard. The new settlers generated an urgent demand for goods, and the clippers met it. But clippers, while fast, lacked ample cargo space, and after the Civil War they would give way to the larger steamship.

THE ROLE OF THE GOVERNMENT The massive internal improvements of the antebellum era were the product of initiatives by both state governments and private ventures, undertaken sometimes jointly and sometimes separately. After the panic of 1837, however, the states left railroad development mainly to private corporations, the source of most investment capital. Still, several southern and western states built their own lines, and most states granted generous tax concessions.

The federal government helped, too, despite the belief of some politicians that direct involvement in internal improvements was unconstitutional. The federal government bought stock in turnpike and canal companies and after the success of the Erie Canal extended land grants to several western states for the support of canal projects. Congress provided for railroad surveys by government engineers, granted tracts of land, and reduced the tariff duties on iron used in railroad construction.

A COMMUNICATIONS REVOLUTION During the first half of the nineteenth century, the transportation revolution helped spark dramatic improvements in communications. At the beginning of the century, it took days or often weeks for news to travel along the Atlantic seaboard. For example, after George Washington died in 1799 at his Mount Vernon estate, the announcement of his death did not appear in New York City newspapers until a week later. Naturally news took even longer to travel to and from Europe. On December 24, 1814, the United States and Great Britain met in Belgium to sign the peace treaty ending the War of 1812. Yet two weeks later, on January 8, 1815, the Battle of New Orleans was fought. Both armies were oblivious to the cease-fire that had been declared. It took forty-nine days for news of the peace treaty ending the War of 1812 to reach New York from Europe.

The speed of communications accelerated greatly as the nineteenth century unfolded. The construction of turnpikes, canals, and railroads and the development of steamships and the telegraph generated a communications revolution. By 1830 Andrew Jackson's inaugural address could be "conveyed" from Washington, D.C., to New York City in sixteen hours, but it reached New Orleans in six days. Mail began to be delivered by "express," a system in which riders could mount fresh horses at relay stations. Still, even with such advances the states and territories west of the Appalachian Mountains struggled to get timely deliveries and news.

THE INDUSTRIAL REVOLUTION

While the South and the West developed the agricultural basis for a national economy, the Northeast was laying the foundation for an industrial revolution. Technology in the form of the cotton gin and the mechanical grain harvester and improvements in transportation had quickened agricultural development. But technology altered the economic landscape even more profoundly, by giving rise to the factory system.

EARLY TEXTILE MANUFACTURES At the end of the colonial period, manufacturing remained at the household, or handicraft, stage of development or, at most, at the "putting-out" stage, in which a merchant capitalist would distribute raw material (say, leather patterns for shoes) to be worked up at a laborer's home, collected, and sold. Eighteenth-century farm families had to produce much of what they needed in the way of crude implements, shoes, and clothing. The transition from home production to the factory was slow, but one for which a base had been laid before 1815.

In the eighteenth century, Great Britain had gotten a long head start in industrial production. Britain led the way in the development of iron smelting by coke (refined coal), the invention of the steam engine in 1705, its improvement by James Watt in 1765, and a series of inventions that mechanized textile production. Britain carefully guarded its hard-won secrets, forbidding the export of machines or even publication of descriptions of them, even preventing informed mechanics from leaving the country. But the secrets could not be kept. In 1789 Samuel Slater arrived in Rhode Island from England with the plan of a water-powered spinning machine in his head. He contracted with an enterprising merchant-manufacturer to build a mill in Pawtucket, and in that little mill, completed in 1790, nine children turned out a satisfactory cotton yarn.

Still, the progress of textile production faltered until Thomas Jefferson's embargo in 1807 and the War of 1812 restricted imports and encouraged New England merchant capitalists to transfer their resources to manufacturing. New England, it happened, had one distinct advantage: ample rivers near the coast, where water transportation was readily available. By 1815 New England textile mills numbered in the hundreds. The foundations of textile manufacture were laid, and they spurred the growth of garment trades and a machine-tool industry that built and serviced the mills.

AMERICAN TECHNOLOGY Meanwhile, Americans became famous for their "practical" inventiveness. In 1804 Oliver Evans developed a high-pressure steam engine that was adapted to a variety of uses in ships and factories. Among the other outstanding American originals was Cyrus Hall McCormick of Virginia. McCormick invented a primitive grain reaper in 1831, a development as significant to the agricultural economy of the Old Northwest as the cotton gin was to the South.

After tinkering with his machine for almost a decade, McCormick applied for a patent in 1841. Six years later he moved to Chicago and built a plant for manufacturing his reapers and mowers. Within just a few years, he had sold thousands of new machines, transforming the scale of agriculture. With a sickle a farmer could harvest half an acre of wheat a day; with a McCormick reaper two people could work twelve acres a day. McCormick's success attracted other manufacturers and inventors, and soon there were mechanical threshers to separate the grains of wheat from the straw. As the volume of agricultural products soared, prices dropped, income rose, and for many farm families in the Old Northwest the standard of living improved.

A spate of inventions in the 1840s generated profound changes. In 1844 Charles Goodyear patented a process for vulcanizing rubber, which made the product stronger and more elastic, and in the process created the fabric for rainproof coats. In the same year the first intercity telegraph message was transmitted, from Baltimore to Washington, D.C., on the device Samuel F. B. Morse had invented back in 1832. The telegraph was slow to catch on, but seventeen years after that demonstration, with the completion of connections to San Francisco, an entire continent had been wired for instant communication. In 1846 Elias Howe patented his design of the sewing machine, soon improved upon by Isaac Merrit Singer. The sewing machine, incidentally, was one invention that slowed the progress of the factory. Since it was adapted to use in the home, it gave the putting-out system a new life in the clothing industry.

It is hard to exaggerate the importance of science and technology in changing the way people were living by midcentury. For examples, improved transportation and a spreading market economy combined with innovations in canning and refrigeration allowed for a more healthful diet. Fruit and vegetables, heretofore available only during harvest season, could be shipped during much of the year. At the same time, the scientific breeding of cattle helped make meat and milk more abundant.

Technological advances also improved living conditions: houses could be larger, better heated, and better illuminated. Although working-class residences had few creature comforts, the affluent were able to afford indoor plumbing, central heating, gas lighting, bathtubs, iceboxes, and sewing machines. Even the lower classes were able to afford new coal-burning cast-iron cooking stoves, which facilitated more varied meals and improved heating. The first sewer systems helped cities begin to rid streets of human and animal waste, while underground water lines enabled fire companies to use hydrants rather than bucket brigades. Machine-made clothes fit better and were cheaper than clothes sewed by hand from homespun cloth; newspapers and magazines were more abundant and affordable, as were clocks and watches. Technology changed not only how people lived but also how they worked. The factory system would have profound effects on the nineteenth-century economic landscape, particularly in the Northeast.

THE LOWELL SYSTEM Modern industrialism appeared first in New England. At Lowell, Massachusetts, along the Merrimack River, the Merrimack Manufacturing Company in 1822 developed a water-powered plant similar to one in Waltham, Massachusetts, in which spinning and weaving by power machinery had been brought together under one roof for the first time in 1813. Lowell grew dramatically, and it soon provided the model for other mill towns in Massachusetts, New Hampshire, and Maine.

The chief features of the "Lowell system" were a large capital investment, the concentration of all production processes in one plant under unified management, and specialization in a relatively coarse cloth requiring minimum skill by workers. In the public mind, however, the system was associated above all with the conscious attempt by its founders to establish an industrial center compatible with republican virtues. Lowell's founders insisted that they could design model factory centers that would enhance rather than corrupt the social fabric. They would avoid the drab, crowded, and wretched life of the English mill villages by locating their mill in the countryside and then establishing an ambitious program of paternal supervision of the workers. The employees were mostly young women from New England farm families whose prospects for finding gainful employment or a husband were diminishing. With so many men migrating westward, New England had been left with a surplus of women. Employers also preferred to hire women because of their manual dexterity and their willingness to work for wages lower than those demanded by men. Many women were drawn to the mills by the chance to escape the wearying routine of farm life and earn money to help the family or improve their own circumstances. As one female mill

Merrimack Mills and Boarding Houses (1848)

Just one of the milling companies in Lowell, Massachusetts.

worker explained, she was working because of "a father's debts . . . to be paid, an aged mother to be supported, a brother's ambition to be aided."

Single girls flocked to Lowell. To reassure concerned parents, the mill owners promised to provide the "Lowell girls" with good wages, tolerable work, comfortable housing, moral discipline, and a variety of educational and cultural opportunities, such as lectures and evening classes. The carefully planned and supervised factory system was designed bring together the benefits of industrial capitalism and republican simplicity.

Initially visitors to Lowell praised the well-designed red-brick mills. The laborers appeared "healthy and happy." The female workers lived in dormitories staffed by matronly supervisors, church attendance was mandatory, and temperance regulations and curfews were rigidly enforced. Despite thirteen-hour days and six-day workweeks, one worker described Lowell's community life as approaching "almost Arcadian simplicity." But with mushrooming growth, Lowell lost its innocence. By 1840 Lowell had thirty-two mills and factories in operation, and the blissful rural town had become a bleak industrial city.

Other factory centers sprouted up across New England, displacing forests and farms and engulfing villages, filling the air with smoke, noise, and stench. Between 1820 and 1840 the number of Americans engaged in manufacturing increased eightfold, and the number of city dwellers more than doubled. During the 1830s, as textile prices and wages dropped, relations between workers and managers deteriorated. A new generation of owners and foremen stressed efficiency and profit margins over community values. The machines were worked at a faster pace, and workers organized strikes to protest conditions.

The "Lowell girls" drew attention less because they were typical than because they were special. Increasingly common was the family system, sometimes called the Rhode Island system or the Fall River system, which prevailed in textile companies outside northern New England. Factories that relied upon waterpower often appeared in unpopulated areas, along with tenements or mill villages that increasingly housed newly arrived foreign immigrants. Whole families might be hired, the men for heavy labor, the women and children for the lighter work. The system also promoted paternalism. Employers dominated the life of the mill villages. Employees worked from sunup to sunset and longer in winter. Such long hours were common on the farms of the time, but in factories the work was more intense and less varied and offered no seasonal letup.

Mill Girls

Massachusetts mill workers of the mid–nineteenth century, photographed holding shuttles. Although mill work initially provided women with an opportunity for independence and education, conditions soon deteriorated as profits took precedence.

INDUSTRIALIZATION AND THE ENVIRONMENT Textile mills along New England's rivers provided new jobs but in the process transformed the environment. The mills, fed by waterpower, led to deforestation,

Milling and the Environment

A mill dam on the Appomattox River near Petersburg, Virginia, in 1865.

air pollution, and a decline in the spring fish runs throughout New England's network of river valleys. They also provoked violent conflicts between farmers and mill owners.

Between 1820 and 1850 some forty textile and flour mills were built along the Merrimack River, which runs from New Hampshire through northeastern Massachusetts. In pre-industrial England and America the common-law tradition required that water be permitted to flow as it had always flowed; the right to use it was reserved to those who owned land adjoining streams and rivers. In other words, running water, by nature, could not be converted into private property. People living along rivers could divert water for domestic use or to water livestock but could not use naturally flowing water to irrigate land or drive machinery.

The rise of the water-powered textile industry challenged those long-standing assumptions. Entrepreneurs acquired water rights by purchasing land adjoining rivers and buying the acquiescence of nearby landowners; then, in the 1820s, they began renting the water that flowed to the textile mills. Water suddenly became a commodity independent of the land. It was then fully incorporated into the industrial process. Canals, locks, and dams were built to facilitate the needs of the proliferating mills. Flowing water was transformed from a societal resource to a private commodity.

The changing uses of water transformed the region's ecology. Rivers shape regions far beyond their banks, and the changing patterns of streams now affected marshlands, meadows, vegetation, and the game and other wildlife that depended upon those habitats. The dams built to harness water to turn the mill wheels that ground corn and wheat flooded pastures and decimated fish populations, spawned urban growth that in turn polluted the rivers, and aroused intense local resentment, particularly among the New Hampshire residents far upstream of the big Massachusetts textile factories. In 1859 angry farmers, loggers, and fishermen tried to destroy a massive dam in Lake Village, New Hampshire. But their axes and crowbars caused little damage. By then the Industrial Revolution could not be stopped. It was not only transforming lives and property; it was reshaping nature as well.

INDUSTRY AND CITIES In 1855 a journalist exclaimed that "the great phenomenon of the Age is the growth of cities." In terms of the census definition of *urban* as a place with 8,000 inhabitants or more, the proportion of urban to rural populations grew from 3 percent in 1790 to 16 percent in 1860. Because of their strategic locations and their importance as centers of trade and transportation, the Atlantic seaports of New York, Philadelphia, Baltimore, and Boston were the four largest U.S. cities throughout the pre–Civil War period. New York outpaced all its competitors. By 1860 it was the first American city to boast a population of more than 1 million, largely because of its superior harbor and its unique access to commerce afforded by the Erie Canal.

Pittsburgh, at the head of the Ohio River, was already a center of iron production by 1800, and Cincinnati, at the mouth of the Little Miami River, soon surpassed all other meatpacking centers. Louisville, because it stood at the falls of the Ohio River, became an important trade center. On the Great Lakes the leading cities—Buffalo, Cleveland, Detroit, Chicago, and Milwaukee—also stood at important breaking points in water transportation. Chicago was especially well located to become a hub of both water and rail transportation, connecting the Northeast, the South, and the trans-Mississippi West. During the 1830s St. Louis tripled in size, mainly because most of the trans-Mississippi grain and fur trade was funneled down the Missouri River. By 1860 St. Louis and Chicago were positioned to challenge Baltimore and Boston for third and fourth places on the list of the nation's largest cities.

THE POPULAR CULTURE

During the colonial era working Americans had little time for play or amusement. Their priority was sheer survival, and most adults worked from dawn to dusk six days a week. In rural areas, people participated in barn raisings and corn-husking parties, shooting matches and footraces, while residents of the seacoast sailed and fished. In colonial cities, people attended balls, went on sleigh rides and picnics, and played "parlor games" at home— billiards, cards, and chess. By the early nineteenth century, however, a more urban society could indulge in more diverse forms of recreation. As more people moved to cities in the first half of the nineteenth century, they began to create a distinctive urban culture. Laborers and shopkeepers sought new forms of leisure and entertainment as pleasant diversions from their long workdays.

URBAN RECREATION In working-class neighborhoods at midcentury, young men formed volunteer fire companies and fraternal societies whose primary activities were drinking and gambling. Social drinking was pervasive during the first half of the nineteenth century. Barn raisings, corn huskings, quilting parties, militia musters, church socials, court sessions, holidays, and political gatherings—all featured liquor, hard cider, or beer. In Mississippi, recalled Senator Henry Foote, heavy drinking on such social occasions had become so fashionable that "a man of strict sobriety" was considered "a cold-blooded and uncongenial wretch."

The more affluent and educated people viewed leisure time as an opportunity for self-improvement and so attended lectures by prominent figures such as Ralph Waldo Emerson and the minister Henry Ward Beecher. Circuses began touring the country. Footraces, horse races, and boat races began attracting thousands of spectators. Nearly 100,000 people attended a horse race at Union Track on Long Island.

So-called blood sports were also a popular form of amusement. Cockfighting and dogfighting at saloons attracted excited crowds and frenzied betting. Prizefighting, also known as boxing, eventually displaced the animal contests. Imported from Britain, boxing surged into prominence at midcentury and then, as now, proved popular with all social classes. The early contestants tended to be Irish or English immigrants, often sponsored by a neighborhood fire company, fraternal association, or street gang.

THE PERFORMING ARTS Theaters were the most popular form of indoor entertainment at midcentury. People flocked to opera houses and

Bare Knuckles

Blood sports emerged as popular urban entertainment for men of all social classes.

theaters to watch a wide spectrum of performances: Shakespeare's tragedies, "blood and thunder" melodramas, comedies, minstrel shows, operas, magic shows, acrobatics, and pageants. Audiences were predominantly young and middle-aged men. "Respectable" women rarely attended. Behavior in antebellum theaters was raucous and at times disorderly. Patrons were participants as well as spectators: audiences cheered the heroes and heroines and hissed at the villains. If an actor did not meet expectations, audiences hurled epithets, nuts, eggs, fruit, shoes, or chairs.

The 1830s witnessed the emergence of the first uniquely American form of mass entertainment: the blackface minstrel show. Rooted in a tradition of folk theatricals, minstrel shows featured white performers made up as blacks. "Minstrelsy" drew upon African-American subjects and reinforced prevailing racial stereotypes. It featured banjo and fiddle music, "shuffle" dances, and lowbrow humor. Between the 1830s and the 1870s minstrel shows were immensely popular throughout the nation, especially among northern working-class ethnic groups and southern whites.

Although antebellum minstrel shows usually portrayed slaves as loyal and happy and caricatured northern free blacks as superstitious buffoons who preferred slavery to freedom, minstrelsy represented more than an expression of virulent racism and white exploitation of black culture; it also

The Crow Quadrilles

This sheet-music cover, printed in 1837, shows eight vignettes caricaturing African Americans. Minstrel shows enjoyed nationwide popularity while reinforcing racial stereotypes.

provided a medium for the expression of authentic African-American dance and music.

IMMIGRATION

Throughout the nineteenth century, land in America remained plentiful and relatively cheap, while labor was scarce and relatively expensive. The United States in the nineteenth century thus remained a strong magnet for immigrants, offering them chances to take up farming or urban employment. Glowing reports from early arrivals who made good reinforced romantic views of American economic opportunity and political and religious freedom.

During the forty years from the outbreak of the Revolution to the end of the War of 1812, immigration had slowed to a trickle. Wars in Europe restricted travel from Europe until 1815. Within a few years, however, passenger ships had begun to cross the North Atlantic in large numbers. The years from 1845 to 1854 saw the greatest proportional influx of immigrants in U.S. history, 2.4 million, or about 14.5 percent of the total population in 1845. In 1860 the population was 31 million, with more than one of every eight resident foreign-born. The largest groups were the Irish (1.6 million), the Germans (1.2 million), and the British (588,000), mostly English.

THE IRISH What caused so many Irish to flee their homeland in the nineteenth century was the onset of a prolonged depression that brought immense social hardship. The most densely populated country in Europe, Ireland was so ravaged by its economic collapse that in rural areas the average age at death declined to nineteen. By the 1830s the number of Irish immigrants leaving for America was growing quickly, and after an epidemic of potato rot in 1845 brought to rural Ireland a famine that killed upward of 1 million peasants, the flow of Irish immigrants to Canada and the United States became a flood.

By 1850 the Irish constituted 43 percent of the foreign-born population of the United States. Unlike the German immigrants, who were predominantly male, the Irish newcomers were relatively evenly apportioned by sex; in fact a slight majority of them were women, most of whom were single young adults.

Most of the Irish arrivals had been tenant farmers, but their rural sufferings left them with little taste for farmwork and little money with which to buy land in America. Many Irish men hired on with the construction gangs building canals and railways—about 3,000 went to work on the Erie Canal as early as 1818. Others labored in iron foundries, steel mills, warehouses, and shipyards. Many

Irish Immigration

In 1847 nearly 214,000 Irish immigrated to the United States and Canada aboard ships of the White Star Line and other companies. Despite promises of spacious, well-lit, well-ventilated, and heated accommodations in steerage, 30 percent of these immigrants died on board.

Irish women found jobs as domestic servants, laundresses, or workers in New England textile mills. In 1845 the Irish constituted only 8 percent of the workforce in the Lowell mills; by 1860 they made up 50 percent. Relatively few immigrants during the Jacksonian era found their way to the South, where land was expensive and industries scarce. The widespread use of slavery also left few opportunities in the region for free manual laborers.

Too poor to move inland, most of the destitute Irish congregated in the eastern cities. By the 1850s the Irish made up over half the population of Boston and New York City and were almost as prominent in Philadelphia. Irish newcomers crowded into filthy, poorly ventilated buildings plagued by high rates of crime, infectious disease, prostitution, alcoholism, and infant mortality. The archbishop of New York at midcentury described the Irish as "the poorest and most wretched population that can be found in the world."

Many enterprising Irish immigrants forged remarkable careers, however. Twenty years after arriving in New York, Alexander T. Stewart became the owner of the nation's largest department store and thereafter accumulated vast real estate holdings in Manhattan. Michael Cudahy, who began work in a Milwaukee meatpacking business at age fourteen, became head of the Cudahy Packing Company and developed a process for the curing of meats using refrigeration. Dublin-born Victor Herbert emerged as one of America's most revered composers, and Irish dancers and playwrights came to dominate the stage.

These accomplishments did little to quell the anti-Irish sentiments prevalent in nineteenth-century America. Irish immigrants confronted demeaning stereotypes and violent anti-Catholic prejudices. It was commonly assumed that the Irish were ignorant, filthy, clannish folk incapable of assimilation. Many employers posted signs saying "No Irish Need Apply." But the Irish could be equally contemptuous of other groups, such as free blacks, who competed with them for low-status jobs. In 1850 the *New York Tribune* expressed concern that the Irish, having themselves escaped from "a galling, degrading bondage" in their homeland, typically voted against any proposal for equal rights for African Americans. For their part, many blacks viewed the Irish with equal disdain.

The Irish, after becoming citizens, formed powerful voting blocs. Drawn mainly to the party of Andrew Jackson, they set a crucial example of identification with the Democrats, one that other ethnic groups by and large followed. In Jackson the Irish immigrants found a hero. Himself the son of Irish colonists, he was also popular for having defeated the hated English at New Orleans. In addition, the Irish immigrants' loathing of aristocracy, which they associated with English rule, attracted them to the party claiming to represent "the common man."

Although property requirements initially kept most Irish Americans from voting, a New York State law extended the franchise in 1821, and five years later the state removed the property qualification altogether. In the 1828 election, Irish voters made the difference between Jackson and John Quincy Adams. With African Americans, women, and Native Americans still years away from gaining voting rights, Irish men became the first "minority group" to exert a remarkable political influence.

Perhaps the greatest collective achievement of the Irish immigrants was their stimulating the growth of the Catholic Church in the United States. Years of persecution had instilled in Irish Catholics a fierce loyalty to the doctrines of the church as the supreme authority over all the affairs of the world. Such passionate attachment to Catholicism generated both community cohesion among Irish Americans and fear among American Protestants.

GERMAN AND OTHER IMMIGRANTS During the eighteenth century, Germans had responded to William Penn's offer of religious freedom and cheap, fertile land by coming in large numbers to America. As a consequence, when a new wave of German migration formed in the 1830s, there were still many Germans in Pennsylvania and Ohio who had preserved their language and rural culture.

The new wave of German migration took on a markedly different cast. It peaked in 1854, just a few years after the crest of Irish arrivals, when 215,000 Germans disembarked in U.S. ports. These immigrants included a large number of learned, cultured professional people—doctors, lawyers, teachers, engineers—some of them refugees from the failed German revolution of 1848. In addition to an array of political opinions ranging from laissez-faire conservatism to Marxism, the Germans brought with them a variety of religious preferences. One third of the new arrivals were Catholic, most were Protestants (usually Lutherans), and a significant number were Jews, free thinking atheists, or agnostics.

Unlike the Irish many Germans were independent farmers, skilled workers, or shopkeepers who arrived with enough money to establish themselves as skilled laborers or in farm jobs. They often migrated in families and groups rather than individually, and this clannish quality helped them sustain elements of their language and culture in the New World.

Among those who prospered in America were Ferdinand Schumacher, who began peddling flaked oatmeal in Ohio and whose company became eventually the Quaker Oats Company; Heinrich Steinweg, a piano maker who changed his name to Steinway and became famous for the quality of his pianos; and Levi Strauss, a Jewish tailor who followed the gold rushers to California and began making durable work pants that were later dubbed blue jeans, or Levi's. Major centers of German settlement developed in southwestern Illinois and Missouri (around St. Louis), Texas (near San Antonio), Ohio, and Wisconsin (especially around Milwaukee). The larger German communities developed traditions of bounteous food, beer, and music along with German turnvereins (gymnastic societies), sharpshooter clubs, fire-engine companies, and kindergartens.

Two other groups that began to arrive during the 1840s and 1850s were but the vanguard for greater numbers to come later. Annual arrivals from Scandinavia, most of them religious dissenters, did not exceed 1,000 until 1843, but by 1860 a total of 72,600 Scandinavians were living in the United States. The Norwegians and Swedes gravitated, usually in family groups, to Wisconsin and Minnesota, where the climate and woodlands reminded them of home.

By the 1850s the rapid development of California after the discovery of gold had attracted Chinese, who, like the Irish in the East, did the heavy work of construction. Most of the Chinese immigrants came from Kwang-tung (Guangdong)* Province, a region noted for its political turmoil, social violence, and economic hardship. The immigrants to the United States were mostly married, illiterate men desperate for work. Single women did not travel abroad, and married women usually stayed behind to raise their children. During the mid–nineteenth century a laborer in southern China might earn $5 a month; in California he could work for a railroad or a mine and make six times as much. After three or four years of such work, an immigrant could return to China with his savings and become a "big, very big gentleman."

NATIVISM Many native-born Americans resented those newcomers who brought with them alien languages, mysterious customs, and perhaps worst of all, feared religions. The flood of Irish and German Catholics aroused Protestant hostility to "popery." A militant Protestantism growing out of the early nineteenth-century revivals heated up the climate of suspicion. There were also fears that German communities were fomenting political radicalism and that the Irish were forming voting blocs, but above all hovered the menace of unfamiliar religious practices. Catholic authoritarianism was widely perceived as a threat to hard-won American liberties, religious and political.

By the 1830s nativism was conspicuously on the rise. In 1834 a series of anti-Catholic sermons by the leading New England minister of the era, revivalist and later abolitionist Lyman Beecher, incited a mob to burn a convent in Charlestown, Massachusetts. In 1844 armed clashes between Protestants and Catholics in Philadelphia caused numerous deaths and injuries. Sporadically the nativist spirit took organized form in groups that proved their patriotism by hating foreigners and Catholics.

In 1855 delegates from thirteen states gathered to form the American party, which had the trappings of a secret fraternal order. Members pledged never to vote for any foreign-born or Catholic candidate. When asked about the organization, they were to say "I know nothing," and in popular parlance the American party thus became the Know-Nothing party. In state and local campaigns during 1854, Know-Nothings had carried one election after another. They swept the Massachusetts legislature, winning all but two seats in the lower house. That fall they elected more than forty congressmen. For a while the Know-Nothings threatened to control New England, New York,

---

*Wade-Giles transliterations are used in this text with Pinyin transliterations, adopted by the Chinese government after the death of Mao Tse-tung (Mao Zedong) in 1976, in parentheses.

A Know-Nothing Cartoon

The Catholic Church attempts to control American religious and political life through Irish immigration.

and Maryland and showed strength elsewhere, but the movement subsided when slavery became the focal issue of the 1850s.

The Know-Nothings demanded the exclusion of immigrants and Catholics from public office and the extension of the period for naturalization (citizenship) from five to twenty-one years, but the American party never gathered the political strength to effect such legislation. Nor did Congress act during the period to restrict immigration in any way.

IMMIGRANT LABOR By meeting the need for cheap, unskilled labor, immigrants made a twofold contribution to economic growth: they moved into jobs vacated or bypassed by those who went to work in the factories, and they made up a pool of labor from which factory workers were eventually drawn.

In New England the large number of Irish workers, accustomed to harsh treatment and willing to work for what natives considered low wages, spelled the end of the "Lowell girls." By 1860 immigrants made up more than half the labor force in New England's mills. Even so their pay was generally higher than that of the women and children who worked to supplement family incomes. The flood of immigration never rose fast enough to stem the long-term rise in wages. Factory labor thus continued to draw laborers from the countryside. Work in the cities offered higher real wages than work on the farm. Labor costs encouraged factory owners to seek ever more efficient machines in order to increase production without hiring more workers. In addition, the owners' desire to control the upward pressure on wage rates accelerated the emphasis on mass production. By stressing high production and low prices, owners made it easier for workers to buy the items they made.

LABOR

Skilled workers in cities before and after the Revolution were called artisans, craftsmen, or mechanics. They made or repaired shoes, hats, saddles, ironware, silverware, jewelry, glass, ropes, furniture, tools, weapons, and an array of wooden products; printers published books, pamphlets, and newspapers. These skilled workers operated within a guild system, a centuries-old economic and social structure developed in medieval Europe.

The Shoemaker, from The Book of Trades (1807)

When Philadelphia boot makers and shoemakers went on strike in 1806, a court found them guilty of a "conspiracy to raise their wages."

The daily routine of urban workers engaged in the "finishing trades" was a mixture of labor, recreation, and fellowship. Their workday began at around six in the morning. At eight-thirty they would take a break to eat pastries. At eleven another break would feature a dram of beer or sugared rum. The workers ate lunch around one o'clock and took another break in late afternoon. During their breaks they would engage in animated discussions of political issues, social trends, and an array of other topics and ideas. Workers in several of the skilled trades, especially shoemaking and printing, formed their own professional associations. Like medieval guilds, which were organized by particular trades, these trade associations were local societies that promoted the interests of their members. The trade groups pressured politicians for tariffs to protect them from foreign imports, provided insurance benefits, and drafted regulations to improve working conditions, ensure quality control, and provide equitable treatment of apprentices and journeymen. They also sought to control the total number or tradesmen in their profession so as to maintain wage levels. The New York shoemakers, for instance, complained about employers taking on too many apprentices, insisting that "two was as many as one man can do justice by."

The use of slaves as skilled workers also caused controversy among tradesmen. White journeymen in the South objected to competing with enslaved laborers. Other artisans refused to take advantage of slave labor. The Baltimore Carpenters' Society, for example, admitted as members only those employers who refused to use forced labor.

EARLY UNIONS Early labor unions faced serious legal obstacles—they were prosecuted as unlawful conspiracies. In 1806, for instance, Philadelphia shoemakers were found guilty of a "combination to raise their wages." The decision broke the union. Such precedents were used for many years to hamstring labor organizations until the Massachusetts Supreme Judicial Court made a landmark ruling in *Commonwealth v. Hunt* (1842). In that case the court ruled that forming a trade union was not in itself illegal, nor was a demand that employers hire only members of the union.

Until the 1820s labor organizations took the form of local trade unions, confined to one city and one craft. From 1827 to 1837, however, organization on a larger scale began to take hold. In 1834 the National Trades' Union was set up to federate the city societies. At the same time, national craft unions were established by the shoemakers, printers, combmakers, carpenters, and handloom weavers, but all the national groups and most of the local ones vanished in the economic collapse of 1837.

LABOR POLITICS With the widespread removal of property qualifications for voting, labor politics flourished briefly in the 1830s. Workingmen's parties appeared in New York, Boston, Philadelphia, and about fifteen states. They admitted many who were not workers by any strict definition, and their leaders were mainly reformers and small businessmen. These labor parties faded quickly, for a variety of reasons: the inexperience of labor politicians left the parties prey to manipulation by political professionals; some of their issues were also espoused by the major parties; and they were vulnerable to attack on the grounds of extreme radicalism. In addition, they often splintered into warring factions, which limited their effectiveness.

Once the labor parties had faded, many of their supporters found their way into a radical wing of the Jacksonian Democrats, which acquired the name Locofocos in 1835 when their opponents from New York City's regular Democratic organization, Tammany Hall, turned off the gaslights at one of their meetings and they produced candles, lighting them with the new friction matches known as locofocos. The Locofocos soon faded as a separate group but endured as a radical faction within the Democratic party.

Though the labor parties elected few candidates, they did succeed in drawing notice to their demands, many of which attracted the support of middle-class reformers. Above all they called for free public education for all children and the abolition of imprisonment for debt, causes that won widespread popular support. The labor parties and unions also actively promoted the ten-hour workday. In 1836 President Jackson established the ten-hour workday at the Naval Shipyard in Philadelphia in response to a strike, and in 1840 President Van Buren extended the limit to all government offices and projects. In private jobs the ten-hour workday became increasingly common, although by no means universal, before 1860.

THE REVIVAL OF UNIONS During the first half of the nineteenth century, labor unions remained local and weak. Often they came and went with a single strike. The greatest single labor dispute before the Civil War occurred on February 22, 1860, when shoemakers at Lynn and Natick, Massachusetts, walked out after their requests for higher wages were denied. Before the strike ended, it had spread through New England, involving perhaps twenty-five towns and 20,000 workers. The strike stood out not just for its size but also because the workers won. Most of the employers agreed to wage increases, and some also agreed to recognize the union as a bargaining agent.

By the mid–nineteenth century the union movement was maturing. Workers sought union recognition and regular collective-bargaining agreements. They also shared a growing sense of solidarity. In 1852 the National Typographical Union revived the effort to organize skilled crafts on a national scale. Others followed, and by 1860 about twenty such organizations had appeared, although none was strong enough as yet to do much more than hold national conventions and pass resolutions.

THE RISE OF THE PROFESSIONS The dramatic social changes of the first half of the nineteenth century opened up an array of new professions. Bustling new towns required new services—retail stores, printing shops, post offices, newspapers, schools, banks, lawyers, doctors, and others—that created more high-status jobs than had ever existed before. By definition professional workers are those who have specialized knowledge and skills that ordinary people lack. To be a professional in Jacksonian America, to be a self-governing individual exercising trained judgment in an open society, was the epitome of the democratic ideal, an ideal that rewarded hard work, ambition, and merit.

The rise of the professions resulted in large measure from the expansion of education and the circulation of knowledge. In the half century after the Revolution, Americans became a distinctively literate people. The nation's passion for reading fueled a thirst for education. Teaching was one of the fastest growing vocations in the antebellum period. Public schools initially preferred men over women as teachers, usually hiring them at age seventeen or eighteen. The pay was so low that few stayed in the profession their entire career, but for many educated, restless young adults, teaching was a convenient first job that offered independence and stature, as well as an alternative to the rural isolation of farming. The New Englander Bronson Alcott remembered being attracted to teaching by "a curiosity to see beyond the limits of my paternal home and become acquainted with the great world."

Teaching was a common stepping-stone for men who became lawyers. In the decades after the Revolution, young men, often hastily or superficially trained, swelled the ranks of the legal profession. They typically would teach for a year or two before clerking for a veteran attorney, who would train them in the law in exchange for their labors. The absence of formal standards for legal training and the scarcity of law schools help explain why there were so many attorneys in the antebellum period. In 1820 eleven of the twenty-three states required no specific length or type of study for aspiring lawyers.

Like attorneys, physicians in the early nineteenth century often had little formal academic training. Healers of every stripe and motivation established a medical practice without regulation. Most of them were self-taught or had learned their profession by assisting a doctor for several years, occasionally supplementing such internships with a few classes at the handful of new medical schools, which in 1817 graduated a total of only 225 students. That same year there were almost 10,000 physicians in the nation. By 1860 there were 60,000 self-styled physicians, and quackery was abundant. As a result, the medical profession lost its social stature and the public's confidence. Yet despite the lack of the first-rate medical education, American physicians were responsible for many breakthroughs in the treatment of a variety of illnesses.

The physical and industrial expansion of the United States during the first half of the nineteenth century gave rise to the profession of engineering, a field that has since become the single largest professional occupation for men in the United States. Building canals and railroads, developing machine tools and steam engines, constructing roads and bridges—all required specialized expertise. Beginning in the 1820s, Americans gained access to technical knowledge in mechanics' institutes, scientific libraries, and special schools that sprouted up across the young nation. Rensselaer Polytechnic Institute was founded in Troy, New York, in 1824 to teach the "applications of science to the common purposes of life." The already existing Franklin Institute of Philadelphia shifted its emphasis in the 1830s to mechanical engineering. By the outbreak of the Civil War, engineering had become one of the largest professions in the nation.

WOMEN'S WORK Women during the first half of the nineteenth century still worked primarily in the home. The prevailing assumption was that women by nature were most suited to marriage, maternal duties, and household management. The only professions readily available to women were nursing (often midwifery, the delivery of babies) and teaching, both of which were extensions of the domestic roles of health care and child care. Teaching and nursing commanded lower status and pay than did the male-dominated professions.

Most middle-class or affluent women focused their time outside the home on religious and benevolent work. They were unstinting volunteers in churches and reform societies. A very few women, however, courageously pursued careers in male-dominated professions. Harriet Hunt of Boston was a teacher who, after nursing her sister through a serious illness, set up shop in 1835 as a self-taught physician and persisted in medical practice although she was twice rejected for admission by the Harvard Medical School. Elizabeth Blackwell of Ohio managed to gain admission to the Geneva Medical College of Western New York, despite the disapproval of the faculty. When she walked in to her first class, "a hush fell upon the class as if each member had been struck with paralysis." Blackwell had the last laugh when she finished at the head of her class in 1849, but thereafter the medical school refused to admit any more women. Blackwell went on to found the New York Infirmary for Women and Children and later had a long career as a professor of gynecology at the London School of Medicine for Women.

JACKSONIAN INEQUALITY

During the years before the Civil War, the American myth of rags to riches endured. The legend had just enough basis in fact to make it plausible. John Jacob Astor, the wealthiest man in America (worth more than $20 million at his death in 1848), came of humble if not exactly destitute origins. But his and similar cases were more exceptional than common. Those who started with the handicaps of poverty and ignorance seldom made it to the top. In 1828 the top 1 percent of New York's families (worth $34,000 or more) held 40 percent of the wealth, and the top 4 percent held 76 percent. Similar circumstances prevailed in Philadelphia, Boston, and other cities.

A supreme irony of the times was that the so-called age of the common man, the age of Jacksonian democracy, seems actually to have been an age of growing social and economic inequality. Years before, in the late eighteenth century, slavery aside, American society probably approached equality more closely than any other population of its size anywhere else in the world. During the last half of the 1700s, social mobility was higher than before or since. By the time popular egalitarianism caught up with reality, reality was moving back toward greater inequality.

Why that happened is difficult to say, except that the boundless wealth of the untapped frontier narrowed as the land was occupied and claims on various opportunities were staked out. Such developments took place in New England towns even before the end of the seventeenth century. But despite growing social distinctions, it seems likely that the white population of America, at least, was better off than the general run of Europeans. New frontiers, both geographic and technological, raised the level of material well-being for all. And religious as well as political freedoms continued to attract people eager for liberty in a new land.

MAKING CONNECTIONS

- Eli Whitney's invention of the cotton gin had a profound effect on southern economic and social development. Chapter 15 describes the economy and society of the Old South in greater detail.

- The westward migration traced in this chapter increased tremendously in the 1840s, a trend discussed in Chapter 14.

- As this chapter demonstrated, the birth and expansion of railroads in the first half of the nineteenth century was an important part of "the dynamics of growth." Chapter 16 shows how a proposal for the first transcontinental railroad had an unexpected side effect: it intensified the debate over the spread of slavery westward.

Further Reading

On economic development in the nation's early decades, see Stuart Bruchey's *Enterprise: The Dynamic Economy of a Free People* (1990). The classic study of transportation and economic growth is George Roger Taylor's *The Transportation Revolution, 1815–1860* (1951). A fresh view is provided in Sarah H. Gordon's *Passage to Union: How the Railroads Transformed American Life, 1829–1929* (1996). On the Erie Canal, see Carol Sheriff's *The Artificial River: The Erie Canal and the Paradox of Progress, 1817–1862* (1996).

The impact of technology is traced in David J. Jeremy's *Transatlantic Industrial Revolution: The Diffusion of Textile Technologies between Britain and America, 1790–1830s* (1981) and John Lauritz Larson's *Internal Improvement: National Public Works and the Promise of Popular Government in the Early United States* (2001). On the invention of the telegraph, see Kenneth Silverman's *Lightning Man: The Accursed Life of Samuel F. B. Morse* (2003). For the story of steamboats, see Andrea Sutcliffe's *Steam: The Untold Story of America's First Great Invention* (2004).

Paul E. Johnson's *A Shopkeeper's Millennium: Society and Revivals in Rochester, New York, 1815–1837* (1978) studies the role religion played in the emerging industrial order. The attitude of the worker during this time of transition is surveyed in Edward E. Pessen's *Most Uncommon Jacksonians: The Radical Leaders of the Early Labor Movement* (1967). Detailed case studies of working communities include Anthony F. C. Wallace's *Rockdale: The Growth of an American Village in the Early Industrial Revolution* (1978), Thomas Dublin's *Women at Work: The Transformation of Work and Community in Lowell, Massachusetts, 1826–1860* (1979), and Sean Wilentz's *Chants Democratic: New York and the Rise of the American Working Class* (1984). Walter Licht's *Working for the Railroad: The Organization of Work in the Nineteenth Century* (1983) is rich in detail.

For a fine treatment of urbanization, see Charles N. Glaab and A. Theodore Brown's *A History of Urban America* (1967). On immigration, see *The Irish in America*, edited by Michael Coffey with text by Terry Golway (1997).

13

AN AMERICAN RENAISSANCE: RELIGION, ROMANTICISM, AND REFORM

FOCUS QUESTIONS

- Why did new religious movements emerge during the early nineteenth century?
- How did a distinctive American literary culture develop?
- What were the goals of the different reform movements during the second quarter of the nineteenth century?

To answer these questions and access additional review material, please visit www.wwnorton.com/studyspace.

American thought and culture in the early nineteenth century remained rooted in two contrasting perspectives: Puritan piety and Enlightenment rationalism. America, it was widely believed, had a mission to stand as an example of republican virtue to the world. The concept of America's unique mission still carried spiritual overtones, for the religious fervor that quickened in the Great Awakening had reinforced the idea of a providential national destiny and had infused American idealism with an element of perfectionism. The combination of widespread religious belief and fervent social idealism brought major reforms and advances in human rights.

RATIONAL RELIGION

DEISM   The currents of the Enlightenment and the Great Awakening, now mingling, now parting, flowed on into the nineteenth century and in different ways eroded the remnants of Calvinist orthodoxy. As time passed, the image of a stern God promising predestined hellfire and damnation gave way to a more optimistic religious outlook. Enlightenment rationalism increasingly stressed humanity's inherent goodness rather than its depravity and encouraged a belief in social progress and the promise of individual perfectibility.

Many leaders of the Revolutionary War era, such as Thomas Jefferson and Benjamin Franklin, became Deists even while nominally attached to churches. Deism, which arose in eighteenth-century Europe, embraced Sir Isaac Newton's image of the world as a smoothly operating machine. The God of the Deist had planned the universe, built it, set it in motion, and then left it to its own fate. By the use of reason, people might grasp the natural laws governing the universe. Deists rejected the belief that every statement in the Bible was literally true. They were skeptical of miracles and questioned the divinity of Jesus. Deists also supported freedom from religious coercion of all sorts.

Orthodox Christians could hardly distinguish such a doctrine from atheism, but Enlightenment rationalism soon began to make deep inroads into American Protestantism. The Congregational churches around Boston proved most vulnerable. A strain of rationalism had run through Puritan belief in its stress on literacy and the need for "right reason" to interpret the Scriptures. Moreover, Boston's progress—some would say its degeneration—from Puritanism to prosperity had persuaded many affluent families that they were anything but sinners in the hands of an angry God. Drawn to more consoling and less strenuous religious doctrines, some went back to the traditional rites of the Episcopal Church. Others simply dropped or qualified their adherence to Calvinist theology while remaining in the Congregational churches.

UNITARIANISM AND UNIVERSALISM   By the end of the eighteenth century, many well-educated New Englanders were drifting into Unitarianism, a belief emphasizing the oneness and benevolence of God, the inherent goodness of people, and the primacy of the individual's reason and conscience over established creeds and scriptural literalism. Humans were not inherently depraved, Unitarianism stressed; people were capable of doing tremendous good, and all were eligible for salvation. Boston was very much the center of the Unitarian movement, and its notion of "rational religion" flourished chiefly within Congregational churches. During the early nineteenth century more and more of these "liberal" churches adopted the name *Unitarian*.

A parallel anti-Calvinist movement, Universalism, attracted a different social group: wage laborers and people of more humble means. Universalists stressed the salvation of all men and women, not just the predestined elect of the Calvinist doctrine. God, they taught, was too merciful to condemn anyone to eternal punishment; eventually all souls would come into harmony with God. "Thus, the Unitarians and Universalists were in fundamental agreement," wrote one historian of religion, "the Universalists holding that God was too good to damn man; the Unitarians insisting that man was too good to be damned." Although both religious groups remained relatively small in number, they exercised a powerful influence over intellectual life, especially in New England.

THE SECOND GREAT AWAKENING

Despite the inroads of rationalism, nineteenth-century Americans remained a profoundly religious people—as they have been ever since. There was, the perceptive French visitor Alexis de Tocqueville observed in the 1830s, "no country in the world where the Christian religion retains a greater influence over the souls of men than in America." Around 1800, however, fears that secularism was on the march sparked an intense revival that soon grew into the Second Great Awakening, sometimes called the Great Revival. The new wave of evangelical fervor fed upon the spreading notion of social equality. Methodists and Baptists, neither of whom featured an educated clergy, sought to democratize religious practices and congregational structures. Such "populist" tendencies were reinforced by the growing popularity of the concept of free will. Salvation was available to everyone.

FRONTIER REVIVALS   In its frontier phase the Second Great Awakening, like the first, generated great excitement and strange manifestations. It gave birth, moreover, to a new ritual, the camp meeting, in which the fires of faith were repeatedly rekindled. Preachers on horseback found ready audiences among lonely frontier folk hungry for spiritual meaning and a sense of community. In the backwoods and in small rural hamlets, the traveling revival was as welcome an event as the traveling circus.

The Baptists embraced a simplicity of doctrine and organization that appealed especially to the common people of the frontier. Their theology was grounded in the authority of the Bible and the recognition of a person's innate depravity. But they replaced the Calvinist notion of predestination with the concept of universal redemption and highlighted the ritual of adult baptism. They also stressed the equality of all before God, regardless of wealth, social standing, or education. Since each congregation was its own highest authority, a frontier church would choose a Baptist minister on its own. Sometimes whole congregations moved across the mountains as a body.

The Methodists, who shared with the Baptists an emphasis on salvation by free will, established a much more centralized organization. They also developed the most effective recruiting method of all: the minister on horseback, who sought out people in the most remote areas with the message of salvation as a gift free for the taking. The "circuit rider" system began with Francis Asbury, a tireless British-born revivalist who scoured the trans-Appalachian frontier for lost souls, preaching some 25,000 sermons while defying hostile Indians and suffering through harsh winters. Asbury's mobile evangelism perfectly suited the frontier environment and the new democratic age. By the 1840s the Methodists had grown into the largest Protestant denomination in the country.

During the early nineteenth century, the Great Revival spread through the West and into more settled regions back East. Camp meetings were held in late summer or fall, when farmwork slackened. People converged from far and wide, camping in wagons, tents, or crude shacks. The crowds often numbered in the thousands, and the unrestrained atmosphere made for chaos. If a particular hymn or sermon excited someone, he or she would cry, shout, dance, or repeat the phrase. Mass excitement swept up even the most skeptical onlookers, and infusions of the spirit elicited strange manifestations. Some participants went into cataleptic trances; others contracted the "jerks," laughed the "holy laugh," babbled in unknown tongues, or got down on all fours and barked like dogs to "tree the devil," as a hound might tree a raccoon.

But dwelling on the bizarre aspects of the camp meetings distorts a social institution that offered a meaningful outlet to isolated rural folk. For women the camp meetings provided an alternative to the rigors and isolation of frontier domesticity. Camp meetings also brought a more settled community life through the churches they spawned and helped spread a more democratic faith among the frontier people.

CHARLES FINNEY AND THE BURNED-OVER DISTRICT Regions swept by revival fevers have been compared to forests devastated by fire. In 1830–1831 alone the number of churches in New England grew by one third. Western New York from Lake Ontario to the Adirondacks experienced such intense levels of fiery evangelical activity that it was labeled the burned-over district.

The most successful northern evangelist was a lawyer named Charles Grandison Finney. In the winter of 1830–1831, he preached for six months in

Religious Revival

An aquatint of a Methodist camp meeting in 1819.

upstate New York and helped generate 100,000 conversions. Finney wrestled with an age-old question that had plagued Protestantism: What role can the individual play in earning salvation? Orthodox Calvinists had long argued that grace was a gift of God, a predetermined decision apart from human understanding or control. In contrast, Finney insisted that the individual could choose to be saved. Finney thus transformed revivals into collective conversions.

THE MORMONS   The burned-over district gave rise to several religious movements, of which the most important was the Church of Jesus Christ of Latter-day Saints, or the Mormons. The founder, Joseph Smith, was the child of wandering parents who finally settled in the village of Palmyra, New York. In 1820 young Smith, then fourteen, had a vision of "two Personages, whose brightness and glory defy all description." They identified themselves as the Savior and God the Father and cautioned him that all existing religious denominations were false. About three years later. Smith claimed, an angel named Moroni led him to a hill near his father's farm in upstate New York, where Smith claimed to have found the *Book of Mormon,* a lost section of the Bible. It told the story of ancient Hebrews who inhabited the New World and to whom Jesus had made an appearance.

On the basis of this revelation, the charismatic Smith began forming his own church in 1830, and after a few years he was gathering converts by the thousands. Mostly poor New England farmers who had migrated to western New York, these religious seekers found in Mormonism the promise of a pure kingdom of Christ in America and an alternative to the era's social turmoil and degrading materialism. From the outset the Mormon "saints" upset the "gentiles" with their close-knit sense of community and their assurance of righteousness. Mormons rejected the notion of original sin staining the human race. They instead professed an optimistic creed stressing human goodness.

In their search for a refuge from persecution, the Mormons moved from New York to Ohio, then to several places in Missouri and finally, in 1839, to Nauvoo, Illinois, where they settled for some five years. Nauvoo became a bustling city of 12,000, and Joseph Smith, "the Prophet," became the community's leading entrepreneur: he owned the hotel and general store, served as mayor and as general of the city's militia, and was the trustee for the church.

Smith practiced "plural marriage," and in 1844 a crisis arose when dissidents accused him of justifying polygamy. The upshot was a schism in the church, efforts by non-Mormons in the neighboring counties to attack

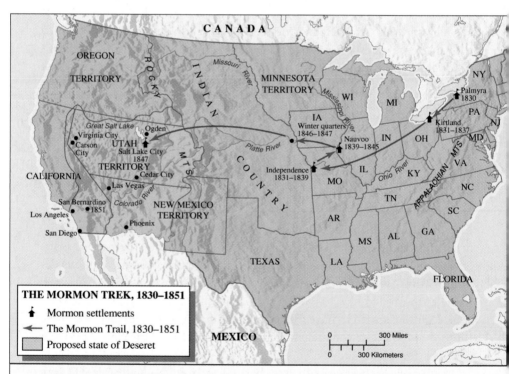

THE MORMON TREK, 1830–1851

† Mormon settlements
← The Mormon Trail, 1830–1851
▢ Proposed state of Deseret

Where were Mormon settlements established between 1830 and 1851? Why did Joseph Smith initially lead his congregation west? Why was the Utah Territory an ideal place for the Mormons to settle?

Nauvoo, and the arrest of Smith and his brother Hyrum. On June 27, 1844, an anti-Mormon lynch mob stormed the feebly defended Nauvoo jail and killed Joseph and Hyrum Smith.

In Brigham Young, the remarkable successor to Joseph Smith, the Mormons found a leader who was strong-minded, intelligent, and authoritarian. After the murder of Smith, Young patched up an unsure peace with the neighbors by promising that he and the Mormons would leave Illinois. Before the year was out, Young had chosen a new destination, near the Great Salt Lake in Utah, guarded by mountains to the east and north, deserts to the west and south, yet fed by mountain streams of melted snow. Despite its isolation, the Utah site was close enough to the Oregon Trail for the "saints" to prosper by trade with passing "gentiles."

The epic Mormon trek to Utah was better organized and less arduous than most of the overland migrations of the time. By the fall of 1846, in wagons and on foot, 15,000 migrants had reached winter quarters on the Missouri River, where they paused until the first bands set out the next spring for "the Promised Land." The first arrivals at Salt Lake in July 1847 found only "a broad and barren plain hemmed in by mountains . . . the paradise of the lizard, the cricket and the rattlesnake." By the end of 1848, however, the Mormons had developed an efficient irrigation system, and over the next decade, by cooperative labor, they brought about a spectacular greening of the desert. At first they organized their own state of Deseret (meaning "Land of the Honeybee," according to Young), but their independence was short-lived. In 1849 Congress incorporated the Utah Territory, including the Mormons' Salt Lake settlement, into the United States. Nevertheless, with Brigham Young named the territorial governor, the new arrangement afforded the Mormons virtual independence. By 1869 some 80,000 Mormons had settled in Utah.

ROMANTICISM IN AMERICA

The revival of emotional piety and the founding of new religions during the early 1800s represented a widespread tendency in the Western world to accentuate the stirrings of the spirit rather than the dry logic of reason. Another great victory of heart over head was the Romantic movement in thought, literature, and the arts. By the 1780s a revolt was brewing in Europe against the well-ordered world of Enlightenment thinkers. Were there not, many wondered, more activities that reason and logic could explain: moods, impressions, feelings; mysterious, unknown, and half-seen things? Americans took readily to the Romantics' emphasis on a realm beyond reason, individual freedom, and the inspiring beauties of nature.

TRANSCENDENTALISM   The most intense expression of such Romantic ideals in America was the transcendentalist movement of New England, which drew its name from its emphasis on transcending (or rising above) the limits of reason. American transcendentalism was largely inspired by the German philosopher Immanuel Kant and the British poet Samuel Taylor Coleridge, but it was rooted in New England Puritanism, to which it owed a pervasive moralism and profound spirituality. It also had a close affinity with the Quaker doctrine of the inner light. The inner light, a gift from God's grace, was transformed by transcendentalists into intuition, a faculty of the mind capable of perceiving things inaccessible to reason.

In 1836 an informal discussion group known as the Transcendental Club began to meet in Boston and Concord, Massachusetts. It was a loose association of freethinkers. The club included liberal clergymen such as Theodore Parker and George Ripley; writers such as Henry David Thoreau, Bronson Alcott, and Orestes Brownson; and learned women such as Margaret Fuller and Elizabeth Peabody and her sister Sophia, who married Nathaniel Hawthorne in 1842. Fuller edited the group's quarterly review, the *Dial* (1840–1844), before the duty fell to Ralph Waldo Emerson, soon to become the acknowledged high priest of transcendentalism.

EMERSON AND THOREAU   More than any other person, Emerson spread the transcendentalist gospel. Sprung from a line of New England ministers, he set out to be a Unitarian parson but quit the "cold and cheerless" denomination because of growing doubts about its emotional vitality. After travel to Europe, where he met England's great literary romantics, Emerson settled in Concord to take up the life of an essayist, poet, and popular speaker on the lecture circuit, preaching the good news of optimism, self-reliance, and the individual's unlimited potential. Having found reason "cold as a cucumber," he was determined to *transcend* the limitations of inherited conventions and rationalism in order to penetrate the inner recesses of the self.

Ralph Waldo Emerson

Transcendental poet and essayist.

Emerson's young friend and Concord neighbor Henry David Thoreau practiced the introspective self-reliance that Emerson preached. "I like people who can do things," Emerson stressed, and Thoreau, fourteen years his junior, could do many things well: carpentry, masonry, painting, surveying, sailing, and gardening. Thoreau, Emerson noted, was "as ugly as sin, long-nosed, queer-mouthed" and possessed of "uncouth and somewhat rustic manners." But he displayed a sense of uncompromising integrity, outdoor vigor, and tart individuality that Emerson found captivating.

Thoreau was also a thoroughgoing individualist. "If a man does not keep pace with his companion," he wrote, "perhaps it is because he hears a different drummer." After graduating from Harvard, Thoreau settled down in Concord to eke out a living as a part-time surveyor and maker of pencils. But he yearned to be a writer and a philosophical naturalist, and he took daily saunters in the woods and fields to drink in the beauties of nature and reflect upon the mysteries of life. The scramble for wealth among his neighbors disgusted rather than tempted him. "The mass of men," he wrote, "lead lives of quiet desperation."

Determined to practice "plain living and high thinking," Thoreau embarked on an experiment in self-reliant simplicity. On July 4, 1845, he took to the woods to live in a cabin he had built on Emerson's land beside Walden Pond, about a mile outside Concord. He wanted to free himself from the complexities and hypocrisies of society so as to devote his time to reflection and writing. His purpose was not to lead a hermit's life. He frequently walked the mile or so to town to dine with his friends and often welcomed guests at his cabin. "I went to the woods because I wished to live deliberately," he wrote in *Walden, or Life in the Woods* (1854), ". . . and not, when I came to die, discover that I had not lived."

Thoreau saw the Mexican War, which erupted while he was at Walden Pond, as a corrupt attempt to advance the cause of slavery. He refused to pay his poll tax as a gesture of opposition, for which he was put in jail (for only one night; an aunt paid the tax). Out of the incident grew the classic essay "Civil Disobedience" (1849), which

Henry David Thoreau

Author of the American classics *Walden* and "Civil Disobedience."

would influence the passive-resistance movements of Mahatma Gandhi in India and Martin Luther King Jr., in the American South. "If the law is of such a nature that it requires you to be an agent of injustice to another," Thoreau wrote, "then, I say, break the law."

The influence of Thoreau's ideas more than a century after his death shows the impact a contemplative individual can have on the world of action. For the most part, Thoreau and the transcendentalists avoided organized reform or political activities. They prized their individual freedom and distrusted all institutions—even those promoting causes they deemed worthy. The transcendentalists taught a powerful lesson: people must follow their conscience. In doing so, they inspired reform movements and were the quickening force for a generation of writers who produced the first age of classic American literature.

The Flowering of American Literature

Ever since gaining independence, the United States had suffered from a cultural inferiority complex. The Old World continued to set the standards in philosophy, literature, and the fine arts. As a British literary critic sneered in 1819, "Americans have no national literature." That may have been true, but during the early nineteenth century American culture began to flower.

A New England renaissance featured four poets who shaped the American imagination in a day when poetry was still read by a wide public: Henry Wadsworth Longfellow, John Greenleaf Whittier, Oliver Wendell Holmes Sr., and James Russell Lowell. Emily Dickinson was probably the most original of the writers contributing to this renaissance, but few of her poems were published at the time. Two New York writers, Washington Irving and James Fenimore Cooper, began to draw wide notice in Britain as well as in America. Irving's *The Sketch Book* (1819–1820) introduced such captivating stories as "Rip Van Winkle" and "The Legend of Sleepy Hollow." Cooper wrote about the frontiersman Natty Bumppo (also known as Hawkeye) in *The Pioneers* (1823), the first of the five *Leather-Stocking Tales*, novels of people pitted against nature in the backwoods. Virginian Edgar Allan Poe emerged as the master of horrifying stories and profound poetry. Then in the half decade of 1850–1855 came the publication of such works as *The Scarlet Letter* and *The House of the Seven Gables* by Nathaniel Hawthorne, *Moby-Dick* by Herman Melville, and *Leaves of Grass* by Walt Whitman. The literary historian F.O. Mathiessen wrote in his book *American Renaissance*, "You might search all the rest of American literature without being able to collect a group of books equal to these in imaginative quality."

The most provocative writer during the antebellum period was Walt Whitman, a remarkably vibrant personality who disdained inherited social conventions and artistic traditions. There was something elemental in Whitman's character, something bountiful and generous and compelling—even his faults and inconsistencies were ample. Born on a Long Island farm, he moved with his family to Brooklyn and from the age of twelve worked mainly as a handyman and journalist, frequently taking the ferry across the harbor to booming, bustling Manhattan.

Whitman remained relatively obscure until the first edition of his poems, *Leaves of Grass* (1855), caught the eye and aroused the ire of readers. Emerson found it "the most extraordinary piece of wit and wisdom that America has

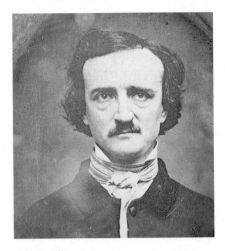

Edgar Allan Poe

Perhaps the most inventive American writer of the period.

yet contributed," but more conventional critics shuddered at Whitman's explicit sexual references and groused at his indifference to rhyme and meter as well as his buoyant egotism. The jaunty Whitman refused to conform to genteel notions of art, however, and he spent most of his career working on *Leaves of Grass*, enlarging and reshaping it in successive editions. He identified the growth of his gargantuan collection of poems with the growth of the country, which he celebrated in all its variety. Thoreau described Whitman as the "greatest democrat the world has seen."

NEWSPAPERS The flowering of American literature during

Politics in an Oyster House **(1848) by Richard Caton Woodville**

A newspaper reader engages in eager discussion.

the first half of the nineteenth century came at a time of massive expansion in newspaper readership. In 1847 Richard Hoe of New York invented the rotary press, which printed 20,000 sheets an hour. Like many technological advances this one was a mixed blessing. The high cost of the press made it harder for someone of small means to break into publishing. On the other hand, it expedited production of cheap newspapers as well as magazines and books. The availability of newspapers costing only a penny apiece transformed daily reading into a form of popular entertainment. Newspaper circulation soared in every city. The "penny dailies," explained one editor, "are to be found in every street, lane, and alley; in every hotel, tavern, counting-house, [and] shop." The United States had more newspapers than any other nation in the world. As readership grew, the content of the papers expanded beyond political news and commentary to include society gossip, sports, and reports of sensational crimes and accidents.

EDUCATION

Literacy in nineteenth-century America was surprisingly widespread, given the condition of public education. In 1840, according to census data, some 78 percent of the total population and 91 percent of the white population could read and write. Since the colonial period, in fact, Americans had enjoyed the highest literacy rate in the Western world. Most children learned to read in church or private schools, from formal tutors, or from their families.

EARLY PUBLIC SCHOOLS   During the 1830s the demand for government-supported public schools peaked. Workers wanted free public schools to give their children an equal chance at economic and social success. Education, it was also argued, would be a means of social reformeled, by improving manners and reducing crime and poverty.

Horace Mann of Massachusetts led the drive for statewide school systems. Trained as a lawyer, he shepherded through the legislature in 1837 a bill that created a state board of education, then served as head of the new agency. Mann went on to sponsor many reforms in Massachusetts, including the first state-supported training for teachers, a state association of teachers, and a minimum school year of six months. Mann defended the public- school system as the best conduit to social stability and equal economic opportunity: "Education then, beyond all other devices of human origin, is a great equalizer of the conditions of men—the balance wheel of the social machinery."

While the North had made great strides in public education by 1850, the educational pattern in the South continued to reflect the region's aristocratic pretensions and rural isolation: the South had a higher percentage of college students than any other region but a lower percentage of public-school students. And the South had some 500,000 white illiterates, more than half the total number in the young nation.

Nationwide, most students going beyond the elementary grades went to private academies, often subsidized by church and public funds. Such schools, begun in colonial days, multiplied until there were more than 6,000 of them in 1850. Public high schools became well established in school systems only after the Civil War; in 1860 there were barely 300 in the whole country.

HIGHER EDUCATION   The post-Revolutionary proliferation of colleges continued after 1800 with the spread of small denominational colleges and state universities. Nine colleges had been founded in the colonial

The George Barrell Emerson School, Boston (ca. 1850)

Although higher education for women initially met with some resistance, seminaries like this one, started in the 1820s and 1830s, taught women mathematics, physics, and history, as well as music, art, and the social graces.

period, all of which survived; but not many of the fifty that sprang up between 1776 and 1800 lasted. Of the seventy-eight colleges and universities in 1840, fully thirty-five had been founded after 1830, almost all affiliated with a Christian denomination. A post-Revolutionary movement for state-supported universities flourished in those southern states that had had no colonial university. Federal policy abetted the spread of universities in the West. When Congress granted statehood to Ohio in 1803, it set aside two townships for the support of a state university and kept up that policy in other new states.

Colleges and universities during the nineteenth century were tiny when compared with today's institutions of higher learning. Most enrolled 100 students or fewer, and the largest rarely had more than 600. Virtually all of those students were men. Elementary education for girls was generally accepted, but training beyond that level was not. Progress began with the academies, some of which taught boys and girls alike. Good "female seminaries," like those founded by Emma Willard at Troy, New York (1821), and Mary Lyon at South Hadley, Massachusetts (1837), paved the way for women's colleges.

The curricula in female seminaries usually differed from the courses in men's schools, giving more attention to the social amenities and such "embellishments" as music and art. Vassar, opened at Poughkeepsie, New York, in 1861, is usually credited with being the first women's college to give priority to conventional academic subjects and standards. In general the West gave the greatest impetus to coeducation, with state universities in the lead. But once admitted, female students remained in a subordinate status. At Oberlin College in Ohio, for instance, women were expected to clean male students' rooms and were not allowed to speak in class or recite at graduation exercises. Coeducation did not mean equality.

Antebellum Reform

The United States in the antebellum period was awash in reform movements. The urge to eradicate evil had its roots in the American sense of spiritual zeal and moral mission, which in turn drew upon increasing faith in the perfectibility of humankind. The revival fever of the Second Great Awakening helped generate a widespread belief that people could eradicate many of the evils afflicting society. Transcendentalism, the spirit of which infected even those unfamiliar with its philosophical roots, offered a romantic faith in the individual and the belief that human intuition led to right thinking.

Such a perfectionist bent found outlet in diverse reform movements and activities during the first half of the nineteenth century. Few areas of life escaped the concerns of the reformers: observance of the Sabbath, dueling, crime and punishment, the hours and conditions of work, poverty, vice, care of the handicapped, pacifism, foreign missions, temperance, women's rights, and the abolition of slavery. Some crusaders challenged a host of evils; others focused on pet causes. One Massachusetts reformer, for example, insisted that "a vegetable diet lies at the basis of all reforms."

While a perfectionist impulse helped excite the reform movements of the Jacksonian era, social and economic changes helped supply the reformers themselves, most of whom were women. The rise of an urban middle class offered affluent women greater time to devote to social concerns. Material prosperity enabled them to hire maids and cooks, often Irish immigrants, who in turn freed them from household chores. Many women joined charitable organizations, most of which were led by men. Some reformers proposed legislative remedies for social ills; others stressed personal conversion or private philanthropy. Whatever the method or approach, social reformers mobilized in great numbers during the second quarter of the nineteenth century.

TEMPERANCE   The temperance crusade was perhaps the most widespread of the reform movements. The census of 1810 reported some 14,000 distilleries producing 25 million gallons of alcoholic beverages each year. William Cobbett, an English reformer who traveled in the United States, noted in 1819 that one could "go into hardly any man's house without being asked to drink wine or spirits, even *in the morning.*"

The temperance movement during the first half of the nineteenth century rested on a number of arguments. Foremost was the religious demand that "soldiers of the cross" lead blameless lives. Others stressed the economic implications of sottish workers. The dynamic new economy, with factories and railroads moving on strict schedules, made tippling by the labor force a far greater problem than it had been in a simpler agrarian economy. Humanitarians also emphasized the relations between drinking and poverty. Much of the movement's propaganda focused on the sufferings of innocent mothers and children. "Drink," said a pamphlet from the Sons of Temperance, "is the prolific source (directly or indirectly) of nearly all the ills that afflict the human family."

In 1826 a group of Boston ministers organized the American Society for the Promotion of Temperance. The society pursued its objectives through lectures, press campaigns, an essay contest, and the formation of local and state societies. A favorite device was to ask each person who took the pledge to put by his signature a *T* for "total abstinence." With that a new word entered the language: *teetotaler*.

In 1833 the society called a national convention in Philadelphia, where the American Temperance Union was formed. It passed a resolution that the sale of liquor was morally wrong and ought to be prohibited by law. The Temperance Union, at its spring convention in 1836, called for abstinence from all alcoholic beverages, a decision that caused moderates to abstain from the movement instead. Still, between 1830 and 1860 the temperance agitation drastically reduced per capita consumption of alcohol.

PRISONS AND ASYLUMS   The Romantic era's belief that people are innately good and capable of improvement brought about major changes in the treatment of prisoners, the disabled, and dependent children. If removed from society, it was believed, the needy and deviant could be made whole again. Unhappily, this ideal kept running up against the dictates of convenience and economy. The institutions for people with problems had a way of turning into breeding grounds of brutality and neglect.

In the colonial period, prisons were usually places for brief confinement before punishment, which was either death or some kind of pain or humiliation: whipping, mutilation, confinement in stocks, branding, and the like. A new attitude began to emerge after the Revolution, and gradually the idea of the penitentiary developed. It would be a place where the guilty experienced penitence and underwent rehabilitation, not just punishment.

An early model of the new system, widely copied, was the Auburn Penitentiary, commissioned by New York in 1816. The prisoners at Auburn had separate cells and gathered for meals and group labor. Discipline was severe. The men were marched out in lockstep and never put face-to-face or allowed to talk. But prisoners were at least reasonably secure from abuse by other prisoners. The system, its advocates argued, had a beneficial effect on the prisoners and saved money, since the workshops supplied prison needs and produced goods for sale at a profit. By 1840 there were twelve prisons of the Auburn type scattered across the nation.

The reform impulse also found an outlet in the care of the insane. The Pennsylvania Hospital (1751), one of the first in the country, had a provision in its charter that it should care for "lunaticks," but before 1800 few other hospitals provided care for the mentally ill. There were in fact few hospitals of any kind. The insane were usually confined at home with hired keepers or in jails and almshouses. After 1815, however, public asylums that separated the disturbed from criminals began to appear.

The most important figure in arousing public concern about the plight of the mentally ill was Dorothea Dix. A pious Boston schoolteacher, she was called upon to instruct a Sunday-school class at the East Cambridge House of Correction in 1841. She found there a roomful of insane persons completely neglected, fed slop, and left without heat on a cold March day. In a report to the state legislature in 1843, Dix told of persons confined "*in cages, closets, cellars, stalls, pens! Chained, naked, beaten with rods, and lashed into obedience.*" Wardens charged Dix with "slanderous lies," but she won the support of leading reformers as well as a large state appropriation for improving the treatment of the insane. From Massachusetts she carried her campaign throughout the country and abroad. By 1860 she had persuaded twenty states to heed her advice to develop programs to improve the conditions in prisons and asylums.

WOMEN'S RIGHTS   Whereas Dorothea Dix stood out as an example of the opportunity that reform activities gave middle-class women to enter public life, Catharine Beecher, a founder of women's schools in Connecticut and Ohio, published a guide prescribing the domestic sphere for women. *A Treatise on Domestic Economy* (1841) became the leading handbook of what historians have labeled the cult of domesticity. While Beecher upheld high standards in women's education, she also accepted the prevailing view that a "woman's sphere" was the home and argued that young women should be primarily trained in the domestic arts of housework and child rearing.

The official status of women during this period remained much as it had been in the colonial era. Legally a woman was unable to vote, and after marriage she was denied legal control of her property and even of her children. Women could not be ministers or pursue most other professions. Higher education was rarely an option. A wife could not make a will, sign a contract, or bring suit in court without her husband's permission. Gradually, however, more and more women began to complain about their status. The organized movement for women's rights in the United States had its origins in 1840, when the anti-slavery movement split over the question of women's right to participate. Women decided then that they needed to organize on behalf of their own emancipation, too.

In 1848 two prominent moral reformers and advocates of women's rights, Lucretia Mott, a Philadelphia Quaker, and Elizabeth Cady Stanton, a graduate of Troy Female Seminary who refused to be merely "a household drudge," called a convention to discuss "the social, civil, and religious condition and rights of women." The hastily organized Seneca Falls Convention, the first of its kind, issued on July 19, 1848, the Declaration of Sentiments.

The document proclaimed the self-evident truth that "all men and women are created equal," and the attendant resolutions said that all laws placing women "in a position inferior to that of men, are contrary to the great precept of nature, and therefore of no force or authority." Such language was too strong for most of the 1,000 delegates, and only about one third of them signed the document. Yet the Seneca Falls gathering represented an important first step in the evolving campaign for women's rights.

From 1850 until the Civil War, the women's rights leaders held annual conventions and carried on a program of organizing, lecturing, and petitioning. The movement had to struggle in the face of meager funds and anti-feminist women and men. The movement owed its success to the work of a few courageous women who refused to be intimidated by the odds against them. Susan B. Anthony, an ardent Quaker already active in temperance and anti-slavery groups, joined the crusade in the 1850s. Unlike Stanton and Mott, she was unmarried and therefore able to devote most of her attention to the women's crusade. As one observer put it, Stanton "forged the thunderbolts and Miss Anthony hurled them." Both were young when the movement started, and both lived into the twentieth century, focusing after the Civil War on demands for women's suffrage. Although women did not win voting rights until much later, they did make some legal gains. The state of Mississippi, seldom regarded as a hotbed of reform, was the first to grant married women control over their property, in 1839; by the 1860s eleven more states had such laws.

Elizabeth Cady Stanton and Susan B. Anthony

Stanton (*left*) "forged the thunderbolts and Miss Anthony hurled them."

UTOPIAN COMMUNITIES

The pervasive climate of reform during and after the Jacksonian era also excited a quest for utopia. Plans for ideal communities had long been an American passion, at least since the Puritans set out to build a wilderness Zion. Over 100 utopian communities sprang up between 1800 and 1900. Among the most durable were the Shakers, officially the United Society of Believers in Christ's Second Appearing, founded by Ann Lee (Mother Ann Lee). She arrived in New York State from England with eight followers in 1774. Believing religious fervor to be a sign of inspiration from the Holy Ghost, they had strange fits in which they saw visions and prophesied. These manifestations later evolved into a ritual dance—hence the name Shakers. Mother Ann claimed that God was genderless and that she was the female incarnation, as Jesus had been the male. She preached celibacy to prepare Shakers for the perfection that was promised them in Heaven.

Mother Ann died in 1784, but the group found new leaders. From the first community at New Lebanon, New York, the movement spread into New England, Ohio, and Kentucky. By 1830 about twenty groups of Shakers were flourishing. In these communities all property was held in common, and strict celibacy was practiced. Men and women not only slept separately but also worked and ate separately. Governance of the colonies was concentrated in the hands of select elders chosen by the ministry. To outsiders this might seem almost despotic, but the Shakers emphasized equality of labor and reward, and members were free to leave at will. The superbly managed Shaker farms yielded a surplus for the market. They were among the nation's leading sources of garden seed and medicinal herbs, and many of their manufactures, including clothing, household items, and especially furniture, were prized for their simple beauty. By the mid–twentieth century, however, few members remained alive; the Shakers reached the peak of activity between 1830 and 1860.

John Humphrey Noyes, founder of the Oneida Community, developed a quite different ideal community. Educated at Dartmouth and Yale Divinity School, he was converted at one of Charles G. Finney's revivals and entered the ministry. He was forced out, however, when he declared that with true conversion came perfection and a complete release from sin. In 1836 he gathered a group of a dozen or so "Perfectionists" around his home in Putney, Vermont. Ten years later Noyes announced a new doctrine of "complex marriage," which meant that every man in the community was married to every woman and vice versa. "In a holy community," he claimed, "there is no more reason why sexual intercourse should be restrained by law, than why eating and drinking should be." To outsiders such theology smacked of "free love," and Noyes was arrested. He fled to New York State and in 1848 established the Oneida Community, which numbered more than 200 by 1851.

The communal group at Oneida eked out a living with farming and logging until the mid-1850s, when the inventor of a new steel animal trap joined the community. Oneida traps were soon known as the best in the country. The community then branched out into sewing silk, canning fruit, and making silver spoons. The spoons were so popular that, with the addition of knives and forks, tableware became the Oneida specialty. In 1879, however, the community faced a crisis when Noyes fled to Canada to avoid prosecution for adultery. The members then abandoned the practice of universal marriage, and in 1881 they converted the community to a joint-stock company, the Oneida Community, Ltd., which today remains a successful flatware company.

In contrast to these religious-based communities, Robert Owen's New Harmony was based upon a secular principle. A British capitalist who worried about the degrading social effects of the factory system, Owen bought the town of Harmonie, Indiana, promptly christening it New Harmony. In 1825 a varied group of about 900 colonists gathered in New Harmony for a period of transition from Owen's ownership to the new system of cooperation. The high proportion of learned participants generated a certain intellectual electricity about the place. There were frequent lectures and social gatherings with music and dancing. For a time, New Harmony looked like a brilliant success, but it soon fell into discord. The problem, it seems, was one common to most reform groups: every idealist wanted his own patented plan put into practice. In 1827 Owen returned from a visit to England to find New Harmony insolvent. The following year he dissolved the project and sold or leased the land.

Brook Farm was the most celebrated of all the utopian communities, because it had the support of Ralph Waldo Emerson and other well-known literary figures of New England. George Ripley, a Unitarian minister and transcendentalist, conceived of Brook Farm as a combination of high thinking and plain living. Most Brook Farmers found considerable fulfillment in the new community. Said one, "We were happy, contented, well-off and carefree; doing a great work in the world, enthusiastic and faithful, we enjoyed every moment of every day." The place survived financially, however, mainly because of an excellent community school that drew tuition-paying students from outside. But when a new central building burned down on the day of its dedication in 1846, the community spirit expired in the embers.

Like Brook Farm most of the utopian communities were short-lived. While such experiments had little effect on the larger society, they did express the deeply ingrained desire for perfectionism inherent in the American character, a desire that would continue to spawn such noble, if frequently naive, experiments thereafter. Among all the targets of the reformers' wrath, however, one great evil would finally take precedence over the others: human bondage. The paradox of American slavery coupled with American freedom, of "the world's fairest hope linked with man's foulest crime," in the novelist

Herman Melville's words, would inspire the climactic crusade of the age, abolitionism, one that would ultimately move to the center of the political stage and sweep the nation into an epic—and tragic—civil war.

MAKING CONNECTIONS

- The anti-slavery campaign, especially its abolitionist aspect, was related to the reform movements discussed in this chapter. It is discussed again in Chapter 15.

- Chapter 17 will show how the Civil War had a significant impact on the status of women in society, a continuation of a theme discussed here.

FURTHER READING

Russel Blaine Nye's *Society and Culture in America, 1830–1860* (1974) provides a wide-ranging survey. On the reform impulse, consult Ronald G. Walter's *American Reformers, 1815–1860,* rev. ed. (1997). Revivalist religion is treated in Nathan O. Hatch's *The Democratization of American Christianity* (1989) and Christine Leigh Heyrman's *Southern Cross: The Beginnings of the Bible Belt* (1997). On the Mormons, see Leonard Arrington's *Brigham Young: American Moses* (1985).

The best introduction to transcendentalist thought is Paul F. Boller's *American Transcendentalism, 1830–1860: An Intellectual Inquiry.* (1974). A more recent treatment is Carlos Baker's *Emerson among the Eccentrics: A Group Portrait* (1996). Several books describe various aspects of the antebellum reform movement. For temperance, see W. J. Rorabaugh's *The Alcoholic Republic: An American Tradition* (1979) and Barbara Leslie Epstein's *The Politics of Domesticity: Women, Evangelism, and Temperance in Nineteenth-Century America* (1981). Stephen Nissenbaum's *Sex, Diet, and Debility in Jacksonian America: Sylvester Graham and Heath Reform* (1980) looks at a pioneering reformer concerned with diet and lifestyle. On prison reform and other humanitarian projects, see David J. Rothman's *The Discovery of the Asylum: Social Order and Disorder in the New Republic,* rev. ed. (2002), Gerald N. Grob's *Mental Institutions in America: Social Policy to 1875* (1973), Charles E. Rosenberg's *The Care of Strangers: The Rise of America's Hospital*

System (1987), and Thomas J. Brown's biography *Dorothea Dix: New England Reformer* (1998).

Lawrence A. Cremin's *American Education: The National Experience, 1783–1876* (1980) traces early school reform. For other views, see Stanley K. Schultz's *The Culture Factory: Boston Public Schools, 1789–1860* (1973) and Carl F. Kaestle and Eric Foner's *Pillars of the Republic: Common Schools and American Society, 1780–1860* (1983).

On women during the antebellum period, see Nancy F. Cott's *The Bonds of Womanhood: "Woman's Sphere" in New England, 1780–1835*, 2nd ed. (1997) and Ellen C. DuBois's *Feminism and Suffrage: The Emergence of an Independent Women's Movement in America, 1848–1869* (1978). Also valuable are Shirley Samuels's *The Culture of Sentiment: Race, Gender, and Sentimentality in Nineteenth-Century America* (1992), Jeanne Boydston, Mary Kelley, and Anne Margolis's *The Limits of Sisterhood: The Beecher Sisters on Women's Rights and Woman's Sphere* (1988), and Mary P. Ryan's *Women in Public: Between Banners and Ballots, 1825–1880* (1989).

Michael Fellman's *The Unbounded Frame: Freedom and Community in Nineteenth-Century American Utopianism* (1973) surveys the utopian movements.

14

MANIFEST DESTINY

FOCUS QUESTIONS

- What were the main issues in national politics in the 1840s?
- Why did settlers migrate west, and what conditions did they face?
- What were the causes and consequences of the Mexican War?

To answer these questions and access additional review material, please visit www.wwnorton.com/studyspace.

During the 1840s the quest for better economic opportunities and more space in the West continued to excite the American imagination. People frustrated by the growing congestion and rising cost of living along the Atlantic seaboard saw in the West a bountiful source of personal freedom, business potential, social democracy, and adventure. "If hell lay to the west," one pioneer declared, "Americans would cross heaven to get there."

Millions of Americans in the nineteenth century crossed the Mississippi River and endured unrelenting hardships in order to fulfill their "providential destiny" to subdue and settle the entire continent. Economic depressions in 1837 and 1841 intensified the appeal of starting anew out West. Texas, Oregon, and Utah were the favored destinations until the discovery of gold in California in 1848 sparked a stampede that threatened to depopulate New England of its young men. Trappers and farmers, miners and merchants, hunters, ranchers, teachers, house servants, and prostitutes, among others, also headed west seeking their fortune. Others sought religious freedom or new converts to Christianity. Whatever the reason, the pioneers formed an unceasing migratory stream flowing across the Great Plains and the Rocky Mountains. The Indian and Mexican inhabitants of the region soon found themselves swept aside by successive waves of American settlers.

THE TYLER YEARS

When President William Henry Harrison took office in 1841, elected, like Andrew Jackson, mainly on the strength of his military record and his lack of a public stand on major issues, observers expected him to be a tool in the hands of Whig leaders Daniel Webster and Henry Clay. Webster became secretary of state, and although Clay preferred to stay in the Senate, his friends filled the cabinet. As it turned out, however, Harrison's administration would never prove itself, for Harrison served the shortest term of any president. At the inauguration, held on a chilly, rainy day, he caught cold. On April 4, 1841, exactly one month after the inauguration, he died of pneumonia at age sixty-eight.

John Tyler, the first vice president to succeed upon the death of a president, served practically all of Harrison's term. At age fifty-one, the Virginia slaveholder was the youngest president to date. He already had a long career behind him as legislator, governor, congressman, and senator, and his positions on all the important issues had been forcefully stated. Although a Whig, he favored a strict construction of the Constitution and was a stubborn defender of states' rights. When someone asked if he was a nationalist, Tyler retorted that he had "no such word in my political vocabulary." He opposed Henry Clay's American system—protective tariffs, a national bank, and internal improvements at national expense. Originally a Democrat, Tyler had broken with the party over Andrew Jackson's condemnation of South Carolina's effort to nullify a federal law and Jackson's imperious use of executive authority. Thus Tyler, the states' rights Whig, had been chosen to "balance" the ticket by party leaders in 1840; no one expected that he would actually wield power. After Tyler become president, some critics called him His Accidency.

DOMESTIC AFFAIRS   Given more finesse by Henry Clay, the powerful senator might have bridged the policy divisions between him and the president. But for once, driven by his own presidential ambition, the Great Compromiser lost his instinct for compromise. When Congress met in a special session in 1841, Clay introduced a series of resolutions designed to supply the platform that the party had evaded in the previous election. The chief points were repeal of the Independent Treasury Act, establishment of a third

Bank of the United States, distribution to the states of money from federal land sales, and higher tariffs. The imperious Clay then set out to push his program through Congress. "Tyler dares not resist. I will drive him before me," Clay predicted.

Tyler, it turned out, was not easily driven. Although he agreed to the repeal of the Independent Treasury Act and signed a higher tariff bill in 1842, Tyler vetoed Clay's bill for a new national bank. This prompted his entire cabinet to resign with the exception of Secretary of State Daniel Webster, an unprecedented action. Tyler replaced the defectors with anti-Jackson Democrats who, like him, had become Whigs. Irate congressional Whigs expelled Tyler from the party, and Democrats viewed him as an untrustworthy renegade. Henry Clay assumed leadership of the Whig party, and the stubborn Tyler became a president without a party.

FOREIGN AFFAIRS   In foreign relations, tensions with Great Britain captured Tyler's attention. A major issue involved the suppression of the African slave trade, which both countries had outlawed in 1808. In 1841 the British prime minister asserted the right to patrol off the coast of Africa and search American vessels for slaves. But the U.S. government refused to accept such intrusions. Relations were further strained late in 1841 when enslaved Africans on the *Creole*, bound from Hampton Roads, Virginia, to New Orleans, mutinied and sailed to the Bahamas, where the British set them free. Secretary of State Webster demanded that the slaves be returned as American property, but the British refused.

At this point a new British government accepted Webster's overtures for negotiations and sent Lord Ashburton to Washington, D.C. Ashburton was widely known to be friendly to Americans, and the talks proceeded smoothly. The negotiations settled the disputed Maine boundary as well as other border disputes with Great Britain by accepting the existing line between the Connecticut and St. Lawrence rivers and compromising on the line between Lake Superior and Lake of the Woods along the border between the future state of Minnesota and Canada. The Webster-Ashburton Treaty (1842) also provided for joint naval patrols off the African coast to suppress the slave trade.

THE WESTERN FRONTIER

In the 1840s most Americans were no more stirred by the quarrels of John Tyler and Henry Clay over such issues as the banking system and tariffs than students of history would be at a later date. What aroused public interest was the contining migration westward across the Great American Desert and the Rocky Mountains to the Pacific coast. In 1845 a magazine editor labeled this bumptious spirit of expansion. "Our manifest destiny," he wrote, "is to overspread the continent allotted by Providence for the free development of our yearly multiplying millions." God, in other words, felt that the United States should extend itself from the Atlantic to the Pacific—and beyond. At its best this much-trumpeted notion of Manifest Destiny offered a moral justification for American expansion, a prescription for what an enlarged United States could and should be. At its worst it was a cluster of flimsy rationalizations for naked greed and imperial ambition. Whatever the case, settlers began streaming into the Far West during the 1840s in the aftermath of the panic of 1837 and the prolonged economic depression.

As they crossed the Mississippi River and made their way westward, pioneers entered not only a new environment but a new culture as well. The Great Plains and the Far West were already occupied by Indians and Mexicans, who had lived in the region for centuries and had established their own distinctive customs and ways of life. Now they were joined by Americans of diverse ethnic origins and religious persuasions. It made for a volatile mix.

WESTERN INDIANS   Historians estimate that over 325,000 Indians inhabited the Southwest, the Great Plains, California, and the Pacific Northwest in 1840, when the flood of white settlers began to pour into the region. The Native Americans often warred against one another. They were divided into more than 200 tribes, each with its own language, religion, economic base, kinship practices, and system of governance. Some were primarily farmers; others were nomadic hunters who preyed upon game animals.

Some twenty-three tribes resided on the Great Plains, a vast grassland stretching from the Mississippi River west to the Rocky Mountains and from Canada south to Mexico. Plains Indians such as the Arapaho, Blackfoot, Cheyenne, Kiowa, and Sioux were horse-borne nomads; they migrated across the grasslands with the buffalo herds, carrying their tepees with them. Disputes over buffalo and hunting grounds sparked clashes between rival tribes, events that help explain the cult of the warrior among the Plains Indians. Scalping or killing an enemy would earn praise from elders and feathers for ceremonial headdresses.

Quite different Indian tribes lived to the south and west of the Plains Indians. In the arid region including what is today Arizona, New Mexico, and southern Utah were the peaceful Pueblo tribes: Acoma, Hopi, Laguna, Taos, Zia, Zuni. They were sophisticated farmers who lived in adobe villages along rivers that irrigated their crops of corn, beans, and squash. Their rivals were the Apache and the Navajo, war-loving hunters who roamed the countryside in small bands and preyed upon the Pueblos. They, in turn, were periodically harassed by their powerful enemies, the Comanches.

To the north, in the Great Basin between the Rocky Mountains and the Sierra Nevadas, Paiutes and Gosiutes struggled to survive in the harsh, arid region of what is today Nevada, Utah, and eastern California. They traveled in family groups and subsisted on berries, pine nuts, insects, and rodents. West of the mountains, along the California coast, Indians lived in small villages. They gathered wild plants and acorns and were adept at fishing in the rivers and bays. The Indian tribes living in the Northwest—the Nisqually, Spokane, Yakama, Chinook, Klamath, and Nez Perce (Pierced Nose)— enjoyed the most abundant natural resources and the most temperate climate.

All the Indian tribes eventually felt the unrelenting pressure of white expansion. Because Indian life on the plains depended upon the buffalo, the influx of white settlers and buffalo hunters posed a dirct threat to the Indians' cultural survival. In an 1846 petition to President James Polk, the Sioux protested that "for several years past the Emigrants going over the Mountains from the United States have been the cause that Buffalo in great measure left our hunting grounds, thereby causing us to go into the Country of Our Enemies to hunt, exposing our lives daily for the necessary subsistence of our wives and children and getting killed on several occasions." But the

Buffalo Hunt, Chasing Back (1860s)

This painting by George Catlin shows a hunter outrunning a buffalo.

federal government turned a deaf ear to such pleas for assistance. It continued to build a string of frontier forts to protect the advancing settlers, and it sought to use treaties to gain control of more Indian land. When officials of the Bureau of Indian Affair could not coerce, cajole, or confuse Indian leaders into selling the title to their tribal land, fighting ensued. And after the discovery of gold in California in 1848, the tidal wave of white expansion flowed all the way to the West Coast.

THE SPANISH WEST AND MEXICAN INDEPENDENCE   As American settlers moved westward, they also encountered Spanish-speaking peoples. Many whites were as contemptuous of Latinos as they were of Indians. Senator Lewis Cass, an expansionist from Michigan, expressed the sentiment of many Americans during a debate over the annexation of New Mexico. "We do not want the people of Mexico," he declared, "either as citizens or as subjects. All we want is a portion of territory." The vast majority of the Spanish-speaking people in what is today called the American Southwest resided in New Mexico. Most of them were mestizos (of mixed Indian and Spanish blood), and they were usually poor ranch hands or small farmers and herders.

The Spanish efforts at colonization had been less successful in Arizona and Texas than in New Mexico and Florida. The Yuma and Apache Indians in Arizona and the Comanches and Apaches in Texas had thwarted their efforts to establish Catholic missions. In eastern Texas during the first half of the eighteenth century, French traders from Louisiana undermined the authority and influence of the Spanish missions that were established. The French supplied the Indians with guns, ammunition, and promises of protection. Several of the Texas missions were abandoned and reestablished near San Antonio in 1731. By 1750 the Pawnees, Wichitas, Comanches, and Apaches were using Spanish horses and French rifles to raid Spanish settlements in Texas. By 1790 the Latino population in Texas numbered only 2,510, while in New Mexico it exceeded 20,000.

In 1807 French forces had occupied Spain and imprisoned the king, creating chaos throughout Spain's colonial possessions, including Mexico. Miguel Hidalgo y Costilla, a creole priest (born in the New World of European ancestry), took advantage of the fluid situation to organize a revolt of Indians and mestizos against Spanish rule in Mexico. The poorly organized uprising failed miserably. In 1811 Spanish troops captured Hidalgo and executed him. Other Mexicans, however, continued to yearn for independence. In 1820 Mexican creoles again tried to liberate themselves from Spanish authority. By then the Spanish forces in Mexico had lost much of their cohesion and

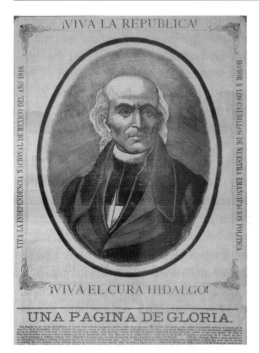

¡Viva El Cura Hidalgo!

This patriotic broadside celebrating Mexican independence shows Father Miguel Hidalgo in an oval medallion.

dedication. Facing a growing revolt, the last Spanish officials withdrew in 1821, and Mexico became an independent nation.

Mexican independence from Spain unleashed tremors throughout the Southwest. American fur traders streamed into New Mexico and Arizona and developed a lucrative commerce in beaver pelts. Soon thereafter wagon trains carrying American settlers were leaving Missouri and heading west to Santa Fe. American entrepreneurs flooded into the western Mexican province of California and soon became a powerful force for change; by 1848 Americans made up half the non-Indian population. In Texas, American adventurers decided to promote their own independence from a newly independent—and chaotic—Mexican government. Suddenly, it seemed, the Southwest was a frontier ripe for American exploitation and settlement.

THE ROCKY MOUNTAINS AND OREGON COUNTRY During the early nineteenth century, the Northwest frontier consisted of the Nebraska, Washington, and Oregon territories. Fur traders especially were drawn to the Missouri River, with its many tributaries. During the 1820s and 1830s the fur trade had inspired a uniquely reckless breed of "mountain men" who relished life in the wilderness. They were the first whites to find their way around the Rocky Mountains, and they pioneered the trails that settlers by the 1840s were beginning to traverse as they flooded the Oregon Country and trickled across the border into California.

Beyond the mountains the Oregon Country stretched from the 42nd parallel north to 54°40. Between those parallels, Spain and Russia had given up their right of settlement, leaving Great Britain and the United States as the only claimants. By the Convention of 1818, the two countries had agreed to southern cotton plantations, but the death rate among Indian workers was twice as high as that of enslaved blacks in the Deep South.

Few accounts of life in California took note of the brutalities inflicted upon the Indians, however. Instead, they portrayed the region as a proverbial land of milk and honey, ripe for development. Such a natural paradise could not long remain a secret, and already Americans had been visiting the Pacific coast in search of profits and land. By the mid-1830s shippers had begun setting up agents to buy cowhides and store them until a company ship arrived. One of the traders, John A. Sutter, had tried the Santa Fe trade first, then found his way to California. At the juncture of the Sacramento and American rivers (later the site of Sacramento), he built an enormous enclosure that guarded an entire village of settlers and shops. Completed in 1843, the enclosure became the mecca for Americans bent on settling the Sacramento country. It stood at the end of what became the most traveled route through the Sierra Navadas, the California Trail, which forked off from the Oregon Trail and ran through the mountains near Lake Tahoe. By 1846 there were perhaps 800 Americans in California, along with some 8,000 to 12,000 Californians of Mexican descent.

MOVING WEST

Most of the western pioneers during the second quarter of the nineteenth century were American-born whites from the upper South and the Midwest. Only a few African Americans joined in the migration. Although some emigrants traveled by sea to California, most went overland. Between 1841 and 1867 some 350,000 men, women, and children made the arduous trek to California or Oregon, while hundreds of thousands of others settled along the way in Colorado, Texas, Arkansas, and other areas.

THE SANTA FE TRAIL   After gaining its independence from Spain in 1821, the government of Mexico was much more interested in trade with the United States than Spain had been. In Spanish-controlled Santa Fe, in fact, all commerce with the United States had been banned. After 1821, however, trade flourished. Hundreds of entrepreneurs made the 1,000-mile trek from St. Louis to Santa Fe, forging a route that became known as the Santa Fe Trail. Soon Mexican traders began leading caravans east to Missouri. By the 1830s there was so much commercial activity between Mexico and St. Louis that the Mexican silver peso had become the primary medium of exchange in Missouri. The traders pioneered more than a new territory. They also showed that heavy wagons could cross the plains and the mountains, and they developed the technique of organized caravans for common protection.

southern cotton plantations, but the death rate among Indian workers was twice as high as that of enslaved blacks in the Deep South.

Few accounts of life in California took note of the brutalities inflicted upon the Indians, however. Instead, they portrayed the region as a proverbial land of milk and honey, ripe for development. Such a natural paradise could not long remain a secret, and already Americans had been visiting the Pacific coast in search of profits and land. By the mid-1830s shippers had begun setting up agents to buy cowhides and store them until a company ship arrived. One of the traders, John A. Sutter, had tried the Santa Fe trade first, then found his way to California. At the juncture of the Sacramento and American rivers (later the site of Sacramento), he built an enormous enclosure that guarded an entire village of settlers and shops. Completed in 1843, the enclosure became the mecca for Americans bent on settling the Sacramento country. It stood at the end of what became the most traveled route through the Sierra Navadas, the California Trail, which forked off from the Oregon Trail and ran through the mountains near Lake Tahoe. By 1846 there were perhaps 800 Americans in California, along with some 8,000 to 12,000 Californians of Mexican descent.

MOVING WEST

Most of the western pioneers during the second quarter of the nine-teenth century were American-born whites from the upper South and the Midwest. Only a few African Americans joined in the migration. Although some emigrants traveled by sea to California, most went overland. Between 1841 and 1867 some 350,000 men, women, and children made the arduous trek to California or Oregon, while hundreds of thousands of others settled along the way in Colorado, Texas, Arkansas, and other areas.

THE SANTA FE TRAIL   After gaining its independence from Spain in 1821, the government of Mexico was much more interested in trade with the United States than Spain had been. In Spanish-controlled Santa Fe, in fact, all commerce with the United States had been banned. After 1821, however, trade flourished. Hundreds of entrepreneurs made the 1,000-mile trek from St. Louis to Santa Fe, forging a route that became known as the Santa Fe Trail. Soon Mexican traders began leading caravans east to Missouri. By the 1830s there was so much commercial activity between Mexico and St. Louis that the Mexican silver peso had become the primary medium of exchange in Missouri. The traders pioneered more than a new territory. They also showed that heavy wagons could cross the plains and the mountains, and they developed the technique of organized caravans for common protection.

religious rituals. Once inside the missions, the Indians were baptized as Catholics, taught the Spanish language, and stripped of their Indian heritage. They were forced to wear Spanish clothes, abandon their native rituals, and obey the friars. Soldiers living in the missions enforced the will of the friars.

The California mission served multiple roles. It was church, fortress, home, town, farm, and imperial agent. The missions were economic as well as religious and cultural institutions; they quickly became substantial agricultural enterprises. Missions produced crops, livestock, clothing, and household goods, both for profit and to supply the neighboring presidios. Indians provided the labor.

The Franciscans used overwhelming force to maintain the labor system in the missions. Rebellious Indians were whipped or imprisoned; soldiers hunted down runaways. Mission Indians died at an alarming rate. One Franciscan friar reported that "of every four Indian children born, three die in their first or second year, while those who survive do not reach the age of twenty-five." Infectious disease was the primary threat, but the intensive labor regimen took a high toll as well. The Indian population along the California coast declined from 72,000 in 1769 to 18,000 by 1821. Saving souls cost many lives.

EARLY DEVELOPMENT IN CALIFORNIA   For all of its rich natural resources, California remained thinly populated by Indians and mission friars well into the nineteenth century. It was a simple, almost feudal agrarian society without schools, industry, or defenses. In 1821, when Mexico wrested its independence from Spain, Californians took comfort in the fact that Mexico City was so far away that it would exercise little effective control over its most distant state. During the next two decades, Californians, including many recent American arrivals, staged ten revolts against the Mexican governors dispatched to lord over them.

Yet Mexican rule did produce a dramatic change in California history. In 1824 Mexico passed a colonization act that granted hundreds of huge "rancho" estates to Mexican settlers. With free labor extracted from Indians, who were treated like slaves, the rancheros lived a life of self-indulgent luxury, gambling, horse racing, bull baiting, and dancing. They soon cast covetous eyes on the vast estates controlled by the Franciscan missions. In 1833–1834 they persuaded the Mexican government to confiscate the missions, exile the friars, release the Indians from Church control, and make the mission lands available to new settlement. Within a few years some 700 new rancho grants of 4,500 to 50,000 acres were issued along the coast from San Diego to San Francisco. Organized like feudal estates, these California ranches resembled "joint occupation" of the region. Until the 1830s, however, joint occupation had been a legal technicality because the only American presence was the occasional mountain man who wandered across the Sierra Nevadas or the infrequent trading vessel from Boston or New York City. Word of Oregon's fertile soil, plentiful rain, and magnificent forests gradually spread eastward. By the late 1830s a stream of emigrants began flowing along the Oregon Trail. Soon "Oregon fever" swept the nation. By 1845 there were about 5,000 settlers in Oregon's Willamette Valley.

THE SETTLEMENT OF CALIFORNIA   California was also an alluring attraction for new settlers and entrepreneurs. It first felt the influence of European culture in 1769, when Spain grew concerned about Russian fur traders moving south along the Pacific coast from their base in Alaska. To thwart Russian intentions, Spain sent a naval expedition to explore and settle the region. The Spanish discovered San Francisco Bay and constructed presidios (military garrisons) at San Diego and Monterey. Even more important, Franciscan friars, led by Junípero Serra, established a Catholic mission at San Diego.

Over the next fifty years, Franciscans built twenty more California missions, spaced a day's journey apart along the coast from San Diego to San Francisco. There they converted Indians and established thriving agricultural estates. As in Mexico the Spanish monarchy awarded huge land grants in California to a few ex-soldiers and colonists, who turned the grants into profitable cattle ranches. The Indians were left with the least valuable land, and most of them subsisted as farmers or artisans serving the missions. The mission-centered culture created by the Hispanic settlers who migrated to California from Mexico was quite different from the patterns of conquest and settlement in Texas and New Mexico. In those more settled regions the original missions were converted into secular parishes and the property divided among the Indians. In California the missions were much larger, more influential, and longer lasting.

Franciscan missionaries, aided by Spanish soldiers, gathered most of the coastal Indian population in California under their control: the number of "mission Indians" more than doubled between 1776 and 1784. The Spanish saw the Indians as ignorant and indolent heathens who must be converted to Catholicism and made useful members of the Spanish Empire. Viewing the missions as crucial imperial outposts, the Spanish government provided military support, annual cash grants, and supplies from Mexico. The Franciscan friars enticed the local Indians into the adobe-walled, tile-roofed missions by offering them gifts or impressing them with their "magical"

¡Viva El Cura Hidalgo!

This patriotic broadside celebrating Mexican independence shows Father Miguel Hidalgo in an oval medallion.

dedication. Facing a growing revolt, the last Spanish officials withdrew in 1821, and Mexico became an independent nation.

Mexican independence from Spain unleashed tremors throughout the Southwest. American fur traders streamed into New Mexico and Arizona and developed a lucrative commerce in beaver pelts. Soon thereafter wagon trains carrying American settlers were leaving Missouri and heading west to Santa Fe. American entrepreneurs flooded into the western Mexican province of California and soon became a powerful force for change; by 1848 Americans made up half the non-Indian population. In Texas, American adventurers decided to promote their own independence from a newly independent—and chaotic—Mexican government.

Suddenly, it seemed, the Southwest was a frontier ripe for American exploitation and settlement.

THE ROCKY MOUNTAINS AND OREGON COUNTRY During the early nineteenth century, the Northwest frontier consisted of the Nebraska, Washington, and Oregon territories. Fur traders especially were drawn to the Missouri River, with its many tributaries. During the 1820s and 1830s the fur trade had inspired a uniquely reckless breed of "mountain men" who relished life in the wilderness. They were the first whites to find their way around the Rocky Mountains, and they pioneered the trails that settlers by the 1840s were beginning to traverse as they flooded the Oregon Country and trickled across the border into California.

Beyond the mountains the Oregon Country stretched from the 42nd parallel north to 54°40. Between those parallels, Spain and Russia had given up their right of settlement, leaving Great Britain and the United States as the only claimants. By the Convention of 1818, the two countries had agreed to

THE OVERLAND TRAILS   Like travelers on the Santa Fe Trail, people bound for Oregon and California rode in wagon caravans. But on the Overland Trails to the West Coast, most of them were settlers rather than traders. They traveled mostly in family groups and came from all over the United States. The wagon trains followed the trail west from Independence, Missouri, along the North Platte River into what is now Wyoming, through South Pass down to Fort Bridger, then down the Snake River to the Columbia River, and along the Columbia to their goal in Oregon's fertile Willamette Valley. They usually left Missouri in late spring, completing the grueling 2,000-mile trek in six months. Traveling in ox-drawn canvas-covered wagons nicknamed prairie schooners, they jostled their way across the dusty or muddy trails and traversed rugged mountains. By 1845 some 5,000 people were making the arduous journey annually. The discovery of gold in California in 1848 brought some 30,000 pioneers along the Oregon Trail in 1849. By 1850, the peak year of travel along the trail, the annual count had risen to 55,000.

The journey west was extraordinarily difficult. Cholera claimed many lives. On average there was one grave every eighty yards along the trail between the Missouri River and the Willamette Valley. The trail's grinding routine of chores and physical labor took its toll on once-buoyant spirits. This was especially true for women, who worked throughout the day and into the night. Women cooked, washed, sewed, and monitored the children while men drove the wagons, tended the horses and cattle, and did the heavy labor. But the unique demands of the trail soon dissolved such neat distinctions and posed new tasks. Women found themselves gathering buffalo dung for fuel, pitching in to dislodge a wagon mired in mud, helping to construct an impromptu bridge, or performing a variety of other "unlady-like" tasks.

Wagon-wheel Ruts near Guernsey, Wyoming

The wheels of thousands of wagons traveling to Oregon cut into solid rock as oxen strained up hillsides, leaving indentations that are still visible today.

THE INDIANS AND THE WAGON TRAINS   Contrary to the mythology, Indians rarely attacked wagon trains. Less than 4 percent of the fatalities associated with the Overland Trails experience resulted from Indian raids. More often Indians either allowed the settlers to pass through their tribal lands

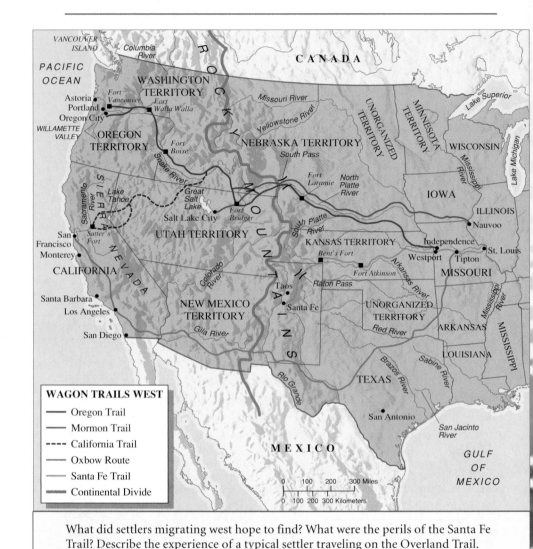

WAGON TRAILS WEST
—— Oregon Trail
—— Mormon Trail
---- California Trail
—— Oxbow Route
—— Santa Fe Trail
▓▓▓ Continental Divide

What did settlers migrating west hope to find? What were the perils of the Santa Fe Trail? Describe the experience of a typical settler traveling on the Overland Trail.

unmolested or demanded payment. Many wagon trains never encountered a single Indian, and others received generous aid from Indians who served as guides, advisers, or traders. The Indians, one woman pioneer noted, "proved better than represented." To be sure, as the number of pioneers increased dramatically during the 1850s, clashes between overlanders and Indians over water and land increased, but never to the degree portrayed in Western novels and films.

In 1851 U.S. officials invited the Indian tribes from the northern plains to a conference in the grassy valley, along the North Platte River, near Fort Laramie in what is now southeastern Wyoming. Almost 10,000 Indians— men, women, and children—attended the treaty council. What made the huge gathering even more remarkable is that so many of the tribes were at war with one another. After nearly three weeks of heated discussions, during which the chiefs were presented with a mountain of gifts, federal negotiators and tribal leaders agreed to the Fort Laramie Treaty. The government promised to provide an annual cash payment to the Indians as compensation for the damage caused by wagon trains traversing their hunting grounds. In exchange the Indians agreed to stop harassing white caravans, to allow federal forts to be built, and to confine themselves to a specified area "of limited extent and well-defined boundaries." Specifically, the Indians were restricted to land north and south of a corridor through which the Overland Trails passed.

Several tribes, however, refused to accept the provisions. The most powerful, the Lakota Sioux, reluctantly signed the agreement but thereafter failed to abide by its restrictions. "You have split my lands and I don't like it," declared Black Hawk, a Sioux chief at Fort Laramie. "These lands once belonged to the Kiowas and Crows, but we whipped these nations out of them, and in this we did what the white men do when they want the lands of the Indians." Despite the dissension the agreement was significant, in part because it foreshadowed the "reservation" concept of Indian management that would be instituted after the Civil War.

GREAT PLAINS ECOLOGY The massive migrations along the Santa Fe and Overland trails wreaked havoc on the environment of the Great Plains. Hundreds of thousands of settlers and traders brought with them millions of animals—horses, cattle, oxen, and sheep—all of which consumed huge amounts of prairie grass. The wagons and herds trampled vegetation and gouged ruts in the landscape that survive to this day. With the onset of the California gold rush in 1849, Plains Indians, led by Cheyennes, seized the opportunity to supply buffalo meat and skins to the white pioneers. Tracking and killing buffalo required a great many horses, and the four-legged creatures added to the strain on the prairie grasslands and river bottoms. A major climatic change coincided with the mass migrations sparked by the discovery of gold in California. In 1849 a prolonged drought struck the region west of the Mississippi River and produced widespread suffering. Starving Indians demanded or begged for food from passing wagon trains. Tensions between Native Americans and white travelers brought additional federal cavalry units to the plains, exacerbating the shortage of forage grasses.

THE PATHFINDER: JOHN FRÉMONT   The most aggressive champion of American settlement in Mexican California and the Far West was John Charles Frémont, "the Pathfinder." Frémont, born in Savannah, Georgia, and raised in the South, became the consummate explorer and romantic adventurer. Possessed of boundless energy and reckless courage, a robust love of the outdoors, and an exuberant, self-promoting personality, he inspired both respect and awe.

Frémont was commissioned a second lieutenant in the U.S. Topographical Corps in 1838. In 1842 he mapped the Oregon Trail beyond South Pass—and met Christopher "Kit" Carson, one of the most knowledgeable of the mountain men. Carson became Frémont's frequent associate and the most famous frontiersman after Daniel Boone. In 1843–1844 Frémont, typically clad in a deerskin shirt, blue army trousers, and moccasins, launched a second expedition. He moved on to Oregon, then swept down the eastern slopes of the Sierra Nevadas, headed southward through the central valley of California, bypassed the mountains in the south, and returned via the Great Salt Lake. His excited reports on both expeditions, published together in the 1845, gained a wide national circulation and helped arouse the interest of easterners.

ANNEXING TEXAS

AMERICAN SETTLEMENTS   America's lust for new land focused on the most accessible of all the Mexican borderlands, Texas. By the 1830s Texas was rapidly turning into a province of the United States, for Mexico in 1823 had begun welcoming American settlers into the region as a means of stabilizing the border.

Foremost among the promoters of the American colonization of Texas was Stephen F. Austin, a Missouri resident who gained from Mexico a huge land grant originally given to his father by Spanish authorities. Before Spain finally granted Mexican independence, Austin had started a colony on the lower Brazos River in central Texas, and by 1824 more than 2,000 hardy souls had settled on his land. Most of the newcomers were southern farmers drawn to rich new cotton land selling for only a few cents an acre. By 1830 the coastal region of Texas had approximately 20,000 white settlers and 1,000 African-American slaves brought in to work the cotton. The newcomers quickly outnumbered the Mexicans in the area and showed little interest in Catholicism or other aspects of Mexican culture.

The Mexican government, opposed to slavery, grew alarmed at the flood of strangers engulfing the Texas province and in 1830 forbade further immigration. But illegal immigrants from the United States crossed the long border as easily as illegal Mexican immigrants would later cross in the opposite direction. By 1835 the American population in Texas had mushroomed to around 30,000, about ten times the Mexican population. Friction mounted in 1832 and 1833 as Americans demanded greater representation and power from the Mexican government. Instead of granting the request, General Antonio López de Santa Anna, who had seized power in Mexico, dissolved the national congress late in 1834, abolished the federal system of government, and became dictator.

In the fall of 1835, Texans rebelled against Santa Anna's "despotism." Delegates from all the towns and settlements met in November and drafted a Declaration of Causes explaining the rebellion. It forcefully expressed their grievances against the Mexican government but stopped short of declaring independence. A furious Santa Anna ordered all Americans expelled, all Texans disarmed, and all rebels arrested. As fighting erupted, volunteers from southern states rushed to assist the 30,000 Texans in their revolution against a Mexican nation of 7 million people. On March 2, 1836, as Santa Anna approached with an army to oust them, the Texans declared their independence.

TEXAS INDEPENDENCE   At San Antonio the Mexican army assaulted a small garrison of Texans and American volunteers holed up in an abandoned mission, the Alamo. Among the most celebrated of the volunteers was Davy Crockett, the Tennessee frontiersman who had fought Indians under Andrew Jackson and served as a congressman. He was indeed a colorful character, full of spunk and brag and thoroughly expert at killing with his trusty rifle, Old Betsy.

On February 23, 1836, General Santa Anna demanded that the Alamo's defenders surrender, only to be answered with a cannon shot. Thousands of Mexican soldiers then launched a series of frontal assaults. For twelve days the Mexicans were repulsed and suffered fearful losses. Then, on March 6, the defenders of the Alamo, fewer than 200, were awakened by the sound of Mexican bugles playing the dreaded "Deguello" ("No Mercy to the Defenders"). Soon thereafter Santa Anna's men attacked from every side. They were twice repulsed, but on the third try, as the defenders ran low on ammunition, the Mexicans broke through the battered north wall and swarmed through the breach.

The frontiersmen used their muskets as clubs, but soon most were slain. Santa Anna ordered the wounded Americans killed and their bodies burned with the rest. The only survivors were sixteen women, children, and servants. It was a complete victory for Santa Anna, but a costly one. The defenders of the Alamo gave their lives at the price of 1,544 Mexicans, and their heroic stand inspired the rest of Texas to fanatic resistance. While Santa Anna dictated a "glorious" victory declaration, his aide wrote in his diary, "One more such 'glorious victory' and we are finished."

On March 2, 1836, while the siege of the Alamo continued, delegates from all fifty-nine Texas towns met at the village of Washington-on-the-Brazos and signed a declaration of independence. Over the next seventeen days the delegates drafted a constitution for the Republic of Texas and established an interim government. The delegates then hastily adjourned as Santa Anna's troops, fresh from their victory at the Alamo, bore down upon them.

The commander in chief of the gathering Texas forces was Sam Houston, a flamboyant Tennessee frontiersman. Houston was born into a military family in Virginia in 1793. His father died when Sam was fourteen, and his mother took the children to live on a farm in eastern Tennessee. As a youth, Houston befriended the Cherokee Indians and developed close ties with them, learning their customs and language. He joined the army in 1813, serving under Andrew Jackson in the Creek War. After receiving three near-mortal wounds, Houston rose to the rank of first lieutenant before resigning in 1818 to practice law. He later served two terms in Congress and in 1827 was elected governor of Tennessee. In 1835 Houston moved to Texas and soon thereafter was named commanding general of the revolutionary army.

After the Mexican victory at the Alamo, Sam Houston beat a strategic retreat eastward from Gonzales, gathering reinforcements as he went, including volunteers from the United States. Just west of the San Jacinto River he paused near the site of the city that would later bear his name and on April 21, 1836, surprised a Mexican encampment there. The 800 Texans and American volunteers charged, yelling "Remember the Alamo," and overwhelmed the panic-stricken Mexican force. They killed 630 Mexican soldiers while losing only 9 of their own, and they took

Sam Houston

Commander in chief of the Texas forces.

Santa Anna prisoner. The Mexican dictator bought his freedom by signing a treaty recognizing the independence of Texas. The Mexican Congress repudiated the treaty and refused to recognize the loss of its northern province, but the war was at an end.

NEGOTIATIONS FOR ANNEXATION   Residents of the Lone Star Republic drafted a constitution that legalized slavery and banned free blacks. They made Sam Houston their first president and voted for annexation to the United States as soon as the opportunity arose. The U.S. president then was Houston's old friend Andrew Jackson, but even Old Hickory could put politics ahead of friendship and be discreet when delicacy demanded it. The addition of Texas as a new slave state in 1836 threatened to ignite a fractious sectional quarrel that might endanger Martin Van Buren's election as Jackson's successor. Worse than that, it raised the specter of war with Mexico. Concerned about such repercussions, Jackson delayed official recognition of the Republic of Texas until his last day in office, and his successor, Van Buren, avoided the issue of annexation during his term as president.

Rebuffed in Washington, Texans focused on building their separate republic. They began to talk of expanding Texas to the Pacific, creating a new nation rivaling the United States. France and Britain extended official recognition to the nation of Texas and began to develop trade relations with the republic. Meanwhile, thousands of Americans poured into the new republic. The population grew from 40,000 in 1836 to 150,000 in 1845. Many settlers were attracted by low land prices. And most were eager to see Texas join the Union.

Reports of growing British influence in Texas during the early 1840s created anxieties in the U.S. government and among southern slaveholders, who became the chief advocates of annexation. The United States began secret negotiations with Texas in 1843, and in April, John C. Calhoun, President Tyler's secretary of state, completed an annexation treaty that went to the Senate for ratification.

Calhoun chose this moment to send the British minister (ambassador) to the United States a letter instructing him on the blessings of slavery and stating that the annexation of Texas was needed to foil the British abolitionists. Publication of the note fostered the claim that Calhoun and Tyler wanted Texas as a means to promote the expansion of slavery. It was so worded, one newspaper editor wrote Andrew Jackson, as to "drive off every northern man from the support of the measure." Sectional division, plus fear of a war with Mexico, contributed to the Senate's overwhelming rejection of Calhoun's Texas annexation treaty. Solid Whig opposition contributed more than anything else to its defeat.

POLK'S PRESIDENCY

THE ELECTION OF 1844   Although adding Texas to the Union was a popular idea among the citizenry, prudent leaders in both political parties had hoped to keep the divisive issue out of the 1844 presidential campaign. Whig Henry Clay and Democrat Martin Van Buren, the leading candidates, opposed annexation of pro-slavery Texas on the grounds that it might spark civil war. Whigs embraced Clay's stance, and the convention nominated him unanimously. The Whig platform omitted any reference to Texas.

The Democratic Convention was a different story. Former President Van Buren's southern supporters, including Andrew Jackson, abandoned his effort to gain the nomination because of his opposition to Texas annexation. With the convention deadlocked, expansionist forces nominated James Knox Polk of Tennessee. The party platform promoted territorial expansion, and to win support in the North and the West as well as in the South, it called for "the re-occupation of Oregon and the re-annexation of Texas."

The Democratic combination of southern and western expansionism constituted a winning strategy that forced Whig nominee Henry Clay to hedge his statement on Texas. While he still believed the integrity of the Union to be the chief consideration, he had "no personal objection to the annexation" if it could be achieved "without dishonor, without war, with the common consent of the Union, and upon just and fair terms." His explanation seemed clear enough, but prudence was no match for spread-eagle oratory and the emotional pull of Manifest Destiny. Clay's divisive stand turned more Whig votes to the new Liberty party, an anti-slavery party begun by a group of abolitionists in 1840. In the western counties of New York, the Liberty party drew enough votes away from the Whigs to give the state to Polk. Had he carried New York, the overconfident Clay would have won the election by seven electoral votes. Instead, Polk won a narrow plurality of 38,000 popular votes nationwide but a clear majority of the Electoral College, 170 to 105. At forty-nine, Polk was the youngest president the nation had seen.

POLK AND HIS PROGRAM   Born near Charlotte, North Carolina, James Polk moved to Tennessee as a young man. After studying at the University of North Carolina, he had become a successful lawyer and planter and entered politics early, serving fourteen years in Congress (four as Speaker of the House) and two as governor of Tennessee. Young Hickory, as his partisans liked to call him, was a short, slender man with a shock of grizzled hair, probing gray eyes, and a seemingly permanent grimace. Humorless and dogmatic, he had none of Andrew Jackson's charisma but

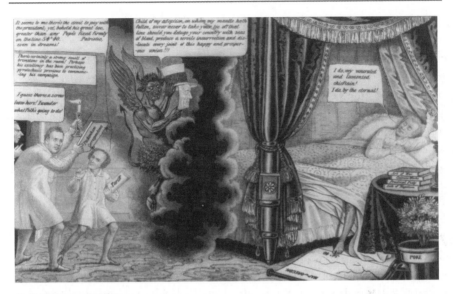

Polk's Dream (1846)

The devil advises Polk to claim all of disputed Oregon even if "you deluge your country with seas of blood, produce a servile insurrection, and dislocate every joint of this happy and prosperous union."

shared Jackson's strong prejudices and his stubborn determination. Polk had a penchant for eighteen-hour workdays, which destroyed his health during his four years in the White House. He would die just three months after leaving office.

On domestic policies, Polk adhered to Jackson's principles, but he and the new Jacksonians subtly reflected the growing influence of the slaveholding South on the Democratic party. Abolitionism, Polk warned, could destroy the Union, but his pro-slavery stance further fragmented public opinion. Anti-slavery northerners had already begun to drift away from the Democratic party, which was increasingly perceived as representing the slaveholding interest in the South.

Single-mindedly committed to the tasks at hand, Polk was a poor diplomat but a formidable leader. His major objectives were reduction of the tariff, reestablishment of the federal independent Treasury, settlement of the Oregon boundary dispute with Britain, and the acquisition of California from Mexico. He got them all. The Walker Tariff of 1846, in keeping with Democratic tradition, lowered the tariff, and in the same year, Polk persuaded Congress to restore the independent Treasury, which the Whigs had eliminated. Twice Polk vetoed internal-improvement bills, leading critics to charge that he was determined to further the South's interests at the expense of the national interest.

Polk's chief concern remained geographic expansion. The acquisition of slaveholding Texas was already under way before he took office. President Tyler, taking Polk's election as a mandate to act, had asked Congress to accomplish annexation by joint resolution, which required only a simple majority in each house and avoided the two-thirds Senate vote needed to ratify a treaty. Congress had read the election returns, too, and after a bitter debate over slavery, the resolution passed by votes of 27 to 25 in the Senate and 120 to 98 in the House. Tyler signed the resolution on March 1, 1845, offering to admit Texas to the Union, just three days before Polk was inaugurated. Texas voters ratified the action in October, and the new state formally entered the Union on December 29, 1845. A furious Mexico dispatched troops to the Texas border.

OREGON   Meanwhile, the Oregon boundary issue heated up as American expansionists insisted that the newly elected president abandon previous offers to settle with Britain on the 49th parallel and stand by the Democrats' platform pledge to take all of Oregon. In his inaugural address, President Polk claimed that the American title to Oregon was "clear and unquestionable," but privately he favored a prudent compromise. The British, however, refused his offer to extend the boundary along the 49th parallel. Polk then withdrew the offer and renewed his demand for all of Oregon. In the annual message to Congress at the end of 1845, he asked permission to give Britain notice that joint occupation of Oregon would end in one year. After a long and bitter debate, Congress adopted the provocative resolution.

Fortunately for Polk the British government had no enthusiasm for war over a distant territory at the cost of profitable trade relations with the United States. In early June 1846 the British government submitted a draft treaty to extend the Canadian-American border along the 49th parallel and through the main channel south of Vancouver Island. On June 18 the Senate ratified the treaty. Most of the country was satisfied. Southerners cared less about Oregon than Texas, and northern business interests valued British trade more than Oregon. Besides, the country was by then at war with Mexico.

THE MEXICAN WAR

THE OUTBREAK OF WAR   On March 6, 1845, two days after Polk took office, the Mexican government broke off relations with the United States. When an effort at negotiation failed, Polk ordered troops under General

Zachary Taylor to take up positions along the Rio Grande. These positions lay in territory that was doubly disputed: Mexico recognized neither the U.S. annexation of Texas nor the Rio Grande boundary between itself and Texas. Polk's intention was clear: he wanted to goad the Mexicans into a conflict in order to secure Texas and also obtain California and New Mexico. Ulysses S. Grant, then a young officer serving under Taylor, later admitted, "We were sent to provoke a fight, but it was essential that Mexico commence it."

Polk resolved that he could achieve his purposes only by force, and he won the cabinet's approval of a war message to Congress. That very evening, May 9, 1846, the news arrived that Mexicans had attacked U.S. soldiers north of the Rio Grande. Eleven Americans were killed, five wounded, and the remainder taken prisoner. Polk's provocative scheme had worked. In his war message the president seized the high ground, declaring that the use of force was a response to Mexican aggression, a recognition that war had been forced upon the United States. Mexico, he claimed, "has invaded our territory, and shed American blood upon the American soil." The House and Senate quickly passed the resolution, and Polk signed the declaration of war on May 13, 1846.

OPPOSITION TO THE WAR In the Mississippi River valley, where expansion fever ran high, the war with Mexico was immensely popular. Whig opinion in the North, however, ranged from lukewarm to hostile. Massachusetts congressman John Quincy Adams, who voted against participation, called it "a most unrighteous war." An obscure congressman from Illinois named Abraham Lincoln, upon taking his seat in 1847, began introducing "spot resolutions," calling upon President Polk to name the spot where American blood had been shed on American soil, implying that the troops may in fact have been in Mexico when fired upon. Once again, as in 1812, New England was a hotbed of opposition. Some New Englanders were ready to separate from the slave states, and the Massachusetts legislature called the conflict a war of conquest.

PREPARING FOR BATTLE However flimsy the justification for conflict, both the United States and Mexico were ill prepared for war. The U.S. military was small and inexperienced. At the outset of war, the regular army numbered barely over 7,000, in contrast to the Mexican force of 32,000. Many of the Mexicans, however, had been pressed into service or recruited from prisons and thus made less than enthusiastic fighters. Before the war ended, the American force had grown to 104,000, of whom about 31,000 were regular army troops and marines. The rest were six- and twelve-month volunteers.

Among the volunteers were sons of Henry Clay and Daniel Webster, but most of the soldiers came from coarser backgrounds. Volunteer militia companies, often filled with frontier toughs, lacked uniforms, standard equipment, and discipline. Repeatedly, despite the best efforts of the commanding generals, these undisciplined forces engaged in plunder, rape, and murder. Nevertheless, these rough-and-tumble Americans consistently defeated the larger Mexican forces, which had their own problems with training, discipline, and munitions.

The United States entered the war without even a tentative plan of action, and politics complicated the task of devising one. President Polk sought to manage every detail of the conflict. What Polk wanted, Senator Thomas Hart Benton wrote later, was "a small war, just large enough to require a treaty of peace, and not large enough to make military reputations, dangerous for the presidency." Winfield Scott, general in chief of the army, was both a Whig and a politically ambitious officer. Polk nevertheless put him in charge of the Rio Grande front, but when Scott quarreled with Polk's secretary of war, the exasperated president withdrew the appointment.

There now seemed a better choice for commander. General Zachary Taylor's men had scored two victories over Mexican forces north of the Rio Grande, and on May 18, 1846, they crossed the river border and occupied Matamoros, which a demoralized and bloodied Mexican army had abandoned. These quick victories brought Taylor instant popularity, and the president responded willingly to the public demand that he be made overall commander for the conquest of Mexico. "Old Rough and Ready" Taylor, a bowlegged and none-too-handsome man of sixty-one, seemed unlikely stuff from which to fashion a hero, but he had achieved Polk's main objective, the conquest of Mexico's northern provinces. Taylor became an immediate folk hero to his troops and to Americans back home, so much so that Polk began to see him as a political threat.

THE ANNEXATION OF CALIFORNIA   President Polk had long coveted the valuable Mexican territory along the Pacific coast and had tried buying it, but to no avail. He then sought to engineer a Texas-style revolt against Mexican rule among the American settlers in California. To that purpose, near the end of 1845, John C. Frémont brought out a band of sixty frontiersmen, including Kit Carson, ostensibly on another exploration of California and Oregon. In 1846 Frémont and his men moved into the Sacramento Valley in northern California. Soon thereafter, Americans in the area fell upon Sonoma on June 14, proclaimed the independent Republic of California, and hoisted the hastily designed Bear flag, a California grizzly bear and star painted on white cloth, a version of which would become the state flag.

By the end of June, Frémont had endorsed the Bear Flag Republic and set out for Monterey on the coast. Before he arrived, the commander of the Pacific Fleet, having heard of the outbreak of hostilities, sent a party ashore to raise the U.S. flag and proclaim California part of the United States. The Republic of California had lasted less than a month, and most Californians of whatever origin welcomed a change that promised order instead of the confusion of the unruly Bear Flaggers. Sporadic clashes with Mexicans continued until 1847, when they finally capitulated. Meanwhile, Colonel Stephen Kearny's army, having earlier captured Santa Fe, ousted the Mexican forces from southern California and occupied Los Angeles.

TAYLOR'S BATTLES   Both California and New Mexico had been taken before General Zachary Taylor fought his first major battle in northern Mexico. Having waited for more men and munitions, Taylor and his troops finally headed southward, in September 1846, toward the heart of Mexico. His first goal was the fortified city of Monterrey, which he took after a five-day siege. President Polk was growing increasingly unhappy with Taylor's popularity, however, and with what he considered Taylor's excessive passivity.

But Polk's grand strategy was itself flawed. Having never seen the Mexican desert, the president wrongly assumed that Taylor's men could live off the land and need not depend upon resupply. Polk therefore misunderstood the general's reluctance to strike out across several hundred miles of barren desert north of Mexico City. On another point the president was simply duped. The old Mexican General Santa Anna, forced out of power in 1845, got word to Polk from his exile in Cuba that in return for the right considerations he would bring about a settlement of the war. Polk in turn assured the Mexican leader that Washington would pay well for any territory taken through such a settlement. In 1846 U.S. forces allowed Santa Anna to return to his homeland. Soon he was again in command of the Mexican army and was named president once more. But instead of carrying out his pledge to Polk to negotiate an end to the war, Santa Anna prepared to fight Taylor's army. Polk's blundering intrigue had put the ablest Mexican general back in command of the enemy army.

In October 1846, Polk and his cabinet decided to order an assault of Mexico City from the south by way of Vera Cruz, which left General Taylor's forces idle. Polk would have preferred a Democratic general to lead the new offensive, but for want of a better choice he named Winfield Scott to the field command. Zachary Taylor, miffed at his reduction to a minor role and harboring a "violent disregard" for Scott's abilities, disobeyed orders and took the offensive himself.

Near the hacienda of Buena Vista, Santa Anna's large but ill-trained army met Taylor's untested volunteers. The Mexican general invited the vastly outnumbered Americans to surrender. "Tell him to go to hell," Taylor replied. In the hard-fought Battle of Buena Vista (February 22–23, 1847), Taylor's son-in-law, Colonel Jefferson Davis, the future president of the Confederacy, led a regiment that broke up a Mexican cavalry charge. Neither side could claim victory. Buena Vista was the last major action on the northern front, and Taylor was granted leave to return home.

SCOTT'S TRIUMPH   Meanwhile, the long-planned southern assault on Mexico City began on March 9, 1847, when Winfield Scott's army landed on the beaches south of Vera Cruz. It was the first major amphibious operation by U.S. forces and was carried out without loss. The Mexican commander at Vera Cruz surrendered on March 27 after a week-long siege. Scott and some 14,000 soldiers then retraced the 260-mile route to Mexico City taken by Cortés and the Spanish more than 300 years earlier. Santa Anna tried to set a trap for the Americans at the mountain pass of Cerro Gordo, but Scott's men did the trapping, taking more than 3,000 Mexican prisoners.

Scott then waited until reinforcements and new supplies arrived from the coast. After three months, with his numbers almost doubled, Scott and his army set out on August 7 through the mountain passes into the valley of Mexico. The general directed a brilliant flanking operation around the lakes and marshes that guard the eastern approaches to Mexico City, then another around the Mexican defenses at San Antonio. On September 13, 1847, U.S. forces entered Mexico City. At the national palace a battalion of marines raised the flag and occupied the "halls of Montezuma."

After the fall of the Mexican capital, Santa Anna resigned and fled the country. By the Treaty of Guadalupe Hidalgo, signed on February 2, 1848, Mexico gave up all claims to Texas above the Rio Grande and ceded California and New Mexico to the United States. In return the United States agreed to pay Mexico $15 million and assume the claims of U.S. citizens against Mexico up to $3.25 million. The Senate ratified the treaty on March 10, 1848. By the end of July, the last remaining U.S. soldiers had boarded ship for home.

THE WAR'S LEGACIES   The seventeen-month-long war cost the United States 1,733 killed, 4,152 wounded, and far more—11,550—dead of disease, mostly dysentery and chronic diarrhea ("Montezuma's revenge"). It remains the deadliest war in American history in terms of the percentage of combatants killed. Out of every 1,000 U.S. soldiers in Mexico, some 110 died. The

Why did Frémont initially settle in the Salinas Valley before marching north, only to march south to San Francisco? How did Polk's fear of Taylor's popularity undermine the Americans' military strategy? What was the significance of Scott's assault on Mexico City?

next highest death rate would be in the Civil War, with 65 killed out of every 1,000 participants.

The military and naval expenditures were $98 million. For that price, and payments made under the treaty, the United States acquired more than 500,000 square miles of territory (more than 1 million, counting Texas), including the great Pacific harbors of San Diego, Monterey, and San Francisco.

Except for a small addition made by the Gadsden Purchase in 1853, these annexations rounded out the continental United States.

Several important firsts are associated with the Mexican War: the first successful offensive American war, the first major amphibious military operation, and the nation's first war covered by correspondents. It was also the first significant combat experience for a group of junior officers who would serve as leading generals during the Civil War: Robert E. Lee, Ulysses S. Grant, Thomas "Stonewall" Jackson, George B. McClellan, George Pickett, Braxton Bragg, George Meade, and others.

Initially the victory in Mexico unleashed a surge of national pride, but as the years passed, the Mexican War was increasingly seen as a war of conquest. The acquisition of Oregon, Texas, California, and the new Southwest made the United States a transcontinental nation. Extending authority over this vast new land greatly expanded the scope of the federal government. In 1849, for example, Congress created the Department of the Interior to supervise the distribution of land, the creation of new territories and states, and the "protection" of the Indians and their land. President Polk naively assumed that the dramatic expansion of American territory to the Pacific would strengthen "the bonds of Union." He was wrong. No sooner was Texas annexed than a violent debate erupted over the extension of slavery into the new territories. That debate would culminate in a war that would nearly destroy the Union.

MAKING CONNECTIONS

- This chapter opened with an account of the brief administration of William Henry Harrison, the first Whig president. The collapse of the Whig party is detailed in Chapter 16.

- The West developed quickly after the expansionist policies of the 1840s. Chapter 19 takes the story to the 1890s.

- This chapter ended by noting that the debate over slavery "would culminate in a war that would nearly destroy the union." Chapter 16's discussion of "The Crisis of Union" traces the relationship between the Mexican War and the Civil War more explicitly.

FURTHER READING

For background on Whig programs and ideas, see Richard Patrick McCormick's *The Second American Party System: Party Formation in the Jacksonian Era* (1966). Frederick Merk's *Manifest Destiny and Mission in American History* (1963) remains a classic. Another treatment of expansionist ideology is Thomas R. Hietala's *Manifest Design: Anxious Aggrandizement in Late Jacksonian America* (1985).

The best survey of western expansion is Richard White's *"It's Your Misfortune and None of My Own": A New History of the American West* (1991). Robert M. Utley's *A Life Wild and Perilous: Mountain Men and the Paths to the Pacific* (1997) tells the dramatic story of the rugged frontiersmen who discovered corridors over the Rocky Mountains. The movement of settlers to the West is ably documented in John Mack Faragher's *Women and Men on the Overland Trail*, 2nd ed. (2001) and David Dary's *The Santa Fe Trail: Its History, Legends, and Lore* (2000). The best account of the California gold rush is Malcolm J. Rohrbough's *Days of Gold: The California Gold Rush and the American Nation* (1997).

Gene M. Brack's *Mexico Views Manifest Destiny, 1821–1846: An Essay on the Origins of the Mexican War* (1975) describes Mexico's viewpoint on U.S. designs on the West. On the siege of the Alamo, see William C. Davis's *Three Roads to the Alamo: The Lives and Fortunes of David Crockett, James Bowie, and William Barret Travis* (1998). An excellent biography related to the emergence of Texas is Gregg Cantrell's *Stephen F. Austin: Empresario of Texas* (1999). On James K. Polk and the war, see John H. Schroeder's *Mr. Polk's War: American Opposition and Dissent, 1846–1848* (1973). The best survey of the military conflict is John S. D. Eisenhower's *So Far from God: The U.S. War with Mexico, 1846–1848* (1989). An excellent analysis of the diplomatic aspects of Mexican-American relations is David M. Pletcher's *The Diplomacy of Annexation: Texas, Oregon, and the Mexican War* (1973).

Part Four

A HOUSE
DIVIDED
AND REBUILT

	POLITICAL	GLOBAL
1846	Wilmot Proviso attempts to ban slavery in former Mexican lands (1846)	Liberals demand reforms in Britain, Austria, Hungary, the German states, and the Italian states (1848)
	The Calhoun resolutions counter the Wilmot Proviso (1847)	Revolutions erupt in France, Prussia, Italy, and Austria (1848–1849)
	"Free soil" becomes focus of the 1848 presidential campaign (1848)	Counterrevolutions take place in France, Prussia, Italy, and Austria (1849)
	Zachary Taylor serves as president (1849–1850)	
1850	California (1849) and New Mexico (1850) adopt free-state governments	
	Compromise of 1850 temporarily defuses the slavery issue	Taiping Rebellion in China (1850–1864)
	Fugitive Slave Act heightens racial tensions in the North (1850)	Expansion of European banking system promotes investment in railroads, industry, and commerce (1850s–1870s)
	Millard Fillmore serves as president following Taylor's death (1850–1853)	Industry fuels growth of middle class in Britain, France, and Germany (1850s–1870s)
	Franklin Pierce serves as president (1853–1857)	French acquire Indochina (1850–1890s)
	Gadsden Purchase renews debate regarding slavery in the territories (1853)	Louis Napoléon assumes the throne in France, taking the name Napoléon III (1852–1870)
1854	Kansas-Nebraska Act repeals portions of the Missouri Compromise and allows settlers to determine whether new territories will be slave or free (1854)	France is governed by the Second Republic (1852–1870)
		Commodore Matthew Perry arrives in Japan (1853)
	Republican party is formed (1854)	Crimean War (1853–1856)
	Dred Scott ruling declares that slaves, even if freed, cannot be citizens (1857)	Panama Railroad is completed, shortening the water route from New York to California by 8,000 nautical miles (1855)
	James Buchanan serves as president (1857–1861)	Following the Indian Mutiny, power in India is transferred from the East India Company to the British government (1857–1858)
	Lincoln-Douglas debates highlight the issue of slavery (1858)	
1860	South Carolina secedes from Union after election of Abraham Lincoln (1860)	Harris Convention opens Japan to American trade (1858)
	Abraham Lincoln serves as president (1861–1865)	Treaty of Tientsin ends the Anglo-Chinese War and opens some Chinese ports to U.S. commerce (1858)
	Mississippi, Florida, Alabama, Georgia, Louisiana, and Texas secede from the Union (1861)	Italy is unified (1859–1870)
	The seceded states form the Confederate States of America and name Jefferson Davis its president (1861)	England receives shipment of 23 billion pounds of southern cotton, resulting in 50 percent oversupply (1861)
	Confederates attack Fort Sumter; Lincoln blockades southern ports, and both sides call up armies (1861)	British allow Confederate agents to acquire British gunships for use against northern vessels (1861–1865)
	Battle of Bull Run becomes first major land battle of the war (1861)	Serfs in Russia are emancipated (1861)
1862	Robert E. Lee takes command of the Army of Northern Virginia (1862)	England's cotton surplus runs out, closing mills and leaving tens of thousands of mill workers unemployed; many emigrate to the U.S. (1862)
	Battles of Shiloh, Antietam, and Fredericksburg (1862)	
	Lincoln issues a preliminary Emancipation Proclamation (1862)	French install Austrian archduke Maximilian as emperor of Mexico (1862)

Frederick Douglass, a former slave, provides focused leadership for the abolition campaign in the North (1840s–1850s)

U.S. population is 23 million, including 3.2 million enslaved African Americans (1850)

Most of southern society consists of yeoman farmers (1850s–1860s)

Plains tribes agree to tribal borders in the Fort Laramie Treaty (1851)

Harriet Beecher Stowe's *Uncle Tom's Cabin* is published (1852)

135,000 SETS, 270,000 VOLUMES SOLD.

UNCLE TOM'S CABIN

FOR SALE HERE.

AN EDITION FOR THE MILLION, COMPLETE IN 1 Vol, PRICE 37 1-2 CENTS.
IN GERMAN, IN 1 Vol., PRICE 50 CENTS.
IN 2 Vols., CLOTH, 6 PLATES, PRICE $1.50.
SUPERB ILLUSTRATED EDITION, IN 1 Vol., WITH 153 ENGRAVINGS.
PRICES FROM $2.50 TO $5.00.

The Greatest Book of the Age.

Henry David Thoreau writes *Walden, or Life in the Woods* in response to the complexities of modern life (1854)

Pottawatomie Massacre pits pro- and anti-slavery factions against each other in "bleeding" Kansas (1856)

John Brown leads a raid on Harpers Ferry, Virginia, to protest slavery (1859)

25 percent of southerners hold slaves (1860)

Wealthy planters owning considerable land and 100 or more slaves are the elite of southern society (1860)

U.S. population reaches 31 million, of which 16 percent is urban (1860)

New York City becomes the first U.S. city with a population of 1 million (1860)

The Union has a population of 23 million, the Confederacy, 9 million (1860)

180,000–200,000 African Americans serve in the Union army (1861–1865)

All southern white men aged 18 to 35 are conscripted into the Confederate army (1862)

Thousands of women assume roles previously filled by men (1861–1865)

South continues to use slaves to grow staple crops, such as cotton, for export (1840s–1850s)   **1846**

1850

Mining camps crowded with prospectors dot the California landscape (1850s)

"Prime field hands" are sold for $1,500 to $2,000 (1850s)

Democratic tariff decreases rates to their lowest levels since 1816 (1857)

Financial panic leads to depression (1857)   **1854**

Edwin Drake drills America's first oil well near Titusville, Pennsylvania (1859)

Record cotton crops are harvested (1859–1860)

Union states produce 97 percent of firearms and 96 percent of railroad equipment in the U.S. (1860)   **1860**

Confederacy produces just 7 percent of manufactured goods (1860)

Union has 20,000 miles of railroad; the Confederacy has 10,000 miles (1860)

The South produces 4 million bales of cotton (1860)

The South has 60 percent of the nation's pigs and half its cattle (1860)

The Confederacy prints $1 billion in currency, causing runaway inflation (1861–1865)

Wheat replaces cotton as the nation's chief export (1861–1865)

First U.S. paper currency is issued (1862)   **1862**

Congress approves Homestead Act, transcontinental railroad project, and Morrill Land Grant Act to expand the economy (1862)

Battles of Chancellorsville, Vicksburg, Gettysburg, and Chattanooga (1863)

Lincoln issues a Proclamation of Amnesty and Reconstruction (1863)

Ulysses S. Grant becomes supreme commander of the Union armies (1864)

Wade-Davis bill outlines a radical plan for Reconstruction (1864)

1865 Robert E. Lee surrenders to Ulysses S. Grant at Appomattox Court House (1865)

Bureau of Refugees, Freedmen, and Abandoned Lands is established (1865)

Andrew Johnson serves as president after Lincoln is assassinated (1865–1869)

Civil Rights Act is passed (1866)

Southern states are readmitted to the Union (1866–1870)

With "Seward's folly," Alaska formally becomes a U.S. possession (1867)

Congress enacts Military Reconstruction Act, Command of the Army Act, and Tenure of Office Act (1867)

Johnson violates Tenure of Office Act by firing the secretary of war (1867)

House votes to impeach Johnson; Senate votes not to convict (1868)

Fourteenth Amendment grants citizenship to all persons born or naturalized in the U.S. (1868)

1870 Ulysses S. Grant serves as president (1869–1877)

Fifteenth Amendment forbids governments to deny vote to any person based on race, color, or previous condition of servitude (1870)

Department of Justice is created (1870)

Crédit Mobilier scandal breaks, rocking the Grant administration (1872)

Civil Rights Act prohibits discrimination in public places (1875)

1877 Compromise of 1877 gives election to Ohioan Rutherford B. Hayes

Reconstruction ends (1877)

Forced to find other sources of raw cotton, English manufacturers turn to Egypt, India, and Brazil (1862–1864)

International Workingmen's Association (First International) is founded (1864)

Prussia and Austria declare war on Denmark (1864)

Otto von Bismarck unites Germany under Prussian leadership (1866–1871)

Prussian-Italian alliance forms against Austria, leading to war (1866–1867)

French withdraw from Mexico (1866–1867)

British North America Act makes Canada a united confederation with its own government (1867)

Karl Marx publishes *Das Kapital* (1867)

Reform Act expands suffrage in England (1867)

Japanese shogunate is abolished; Meiji restoration begins (1867–1868)

Suez Canal opens (1869)

Prussia wins decisive victory in Franco-Prussian War (1870–1871)

Defeat of the Paris Commune leads to declaration of the Third Republic in France (1871)

England legalizes labor unions (1871)

German Empire is declared at Versailles (1871)

All northern men aged 20 to 45 are conscripted into the Union army; announcement of draft lottery causes rioting and $2 million in damages in New York (1863)

Thirteenth Amendment frees 4 million slaves (1865)

White women's roles are redefined in the South as women do tasks previously assigned to slaves (1865)

600 blacks serve in state legislatures and U.S. Congress (1865–1870)

"Black codes" establish a distinct set of laws for African Americans in the South (1865–1866)

Freed slaves reaffirm their families and establish schools and communities (1865–1870)

Ku Klux Klan is established in Pulaski, Tennessee (1866)

Enforcement Acts are passed to protect southern blacks (1870–1871)

Terrorism of Molly Maguires reaches its peak (1874–1875)

Higher taxes, new currency, and sale of bonds help North finance its war effort, providing over $2 billion (1862–1865)

National Banking Act provides uniform system of banking (1863)

Severe food shortages leave the Confederate army competing with civilians for the few surviving crops (1863)

Contract Labor Act allows employers to bind immigrant laborers by paying for their passage to the U.S. (1864)

Sherman's troops leave the southern economy in ruins (1864–1865)

Emancipation results in widespread unemployment and $4 billion in lost revenue (1865)

Wartime changes enable northern industrialists to further develop the North's economy (1865)

Congress begins trying to retire paper currency issued during the war (1866)

National Labor Union (NLU) convenes in Baltimore (1866)

Freed blacks take up sharecropping, become wage laborers, and otherwise integrate themselves into the postwar economy (1865–1870)

Knights of Labor is formed (1869)

Financial panic sets off depression (1873)

U.S. Treasury reissues $26 million to offset deflationary spiral (1874)

1865

1870

600,000 African-American students attend southern schools (1877)

Repression of southern blacks escalates with the Compromise of 1877

Specie Resumption Act allows paper currency to be exchanged for gold (1875)

Great Railroad Strike of 1877

1877

O f all the regions of the United States during the first half of the nineteenth century, the South was the most distinctive. Southern society remained fundamentally rural and agricultural long after the rest of the nation embraced urban-industrial development. Likewise, the planter elite's tenacious desire to preserve and expand the institution of slavery muted social-reform impulses in the South and ignited a prolonged political controversy that would end in civil war.

The relentless settlement of the western territories set in motion a ferocious competition between North and South for political influence in the burgeoning West. Would the new western states be "slave" or "free"? The issue of allowing slavery into the new territories involved more than humanitarian concern for the plight of enslaved blacks. By the 1840s the North and the South had developed quite different economic interests. The North wanted high tariffs on imported products to "protect" its industries from foreign competition. Southerners, on the other hand, favored free trade because they wanted to import British goods in exchange for the cotton they provided British textile mills.

A series of political compromises glossed over the fundamental differences between the regions during the first half of the nineteenth century. But abolitionists refused to give up their crusade against slavery. Moreover, a new generation of politicians emerged in the 1850s, leaders from both North and South who were less willing to seek political compromises. The continuing debate over allowing slavery into the western territories kept sectional tensions at a fever pitch. By the time Abraham Lincoln was elected president in 1860, many people had decided that the nation could not survive half-slave and half-free; something had to give.

In a last-ditch effort to preserve the institution of slavery, eleven southern states seceded from the Union and created a separate Confederate nation. That, in turn, prompted northerners such as Lincoln to support a civil war to preserve the Union. No one realized in 1861 how prolonged and costly the War between the States would become. Over 630,000 soldiers and sailors would die of wounds or disease. The colossal carnage caused even the most seasoned observers to blanch in disbelief. As President Lincoln confessed in his second inaugural address, no one expected the war to become so "fundamental and astonishing."

Nor did anyone envision how sweeping the war's effects would be on the future of the country. The northern victory in 1865 restored the Union and in the process helped accelerate America's transformation into a modern nation-state. National power and a national consciousness began to displace the sectional emphases of the antebellum era. A Republican-led Congress enacted federal legislation to foster industrial and commercial development and western expansion. In the process the United States began to leave behind the Jeffersonian dream of a decentralized agrarian republic.

The Civil War also ended slavery, yet the status of the freed African Americans remained precarious. The former slaves found themselves legally free, but most were without property, homes, education, or training. Although the Fourteenth Amendment (1868) set forth guarantees for the civil rights of African Americans and the Fifteenth Amendment (1870) provided that black men could vote, local authorities found ingenious—and often violent—ways to avoid the spirit and letter of the new laws.

The restoration of the former Confederate states to the Union did not come easily. Much bitterness and resistance remained among the vanquished. Although Confederate leaders were initially disenfranchised, they continued to exercise considerable authority in political and economic matters. Indeed, in 1877 the last federal troops were removed from the occupied South, and former Confederates declared themselves "redeemed" from the stain of occupation. By the end of the nineteenth century, most states of the former Confederacy had devised a system of legal discrimination that re-created many aspects of slavery.

15

THE OLD SOUTH

FOCUS QUESTIONS

· What were the dominant industries and forms of agriculture in the Old South?

· How did the dependence upon agriculture and slavery shape southern society?

· How did the anti-slavery movement emerge, and how did the South respond to it?

To answer these questions and access additional review material, please visit www.wwnorton.com/studyspace.

Southerners, a North Carolina newspaper editor once wrote, are "a mythological people, created half out of dream and half out of slander, who live in a still legendary land." Most Americans, including southerners themselves, harbor a cluster of myths and stereotypes about the South. Perhaps the most enduring myths come from novels and movies such as *Gone with the Wind* (1939). The South portrayed in romanticized Hollywood productions is a stable agrarian society led by paternalistic white planters and their families, who live in white-columned mansions and represent a "natural" aristocracy of virtue and talent within their community. In these accounts, southerners are kind to their slaves and devoted to the rural values of independence and chivalric honor, values celebrated by Thomas Jefferson.

By contrast, a much darker image of the Old South emerged from abolitionist pamphlets and Harriet Beecher Stowe's best-selling novel, *Uncle*

Tom's Cabin (1852). Those exposés of southern culture portrayed planters as arrogant aristocrats who raped enslaved women, brutalized enslaved workers, and lorded over their community with haughty disdain for the rights and needs of others. They bred slaves like cattle, broke up slave families, and sold slaves "down the river" to certain death in the Louisiana sugar mills and rice plantations.

Such contrasting images die hard, in large part because each one is rooted in reality. Nonetheless, efforts to determine what really set the Old South apart from the rest of the nation generally pivot on two lines of thought: the impact of the environment (climate and geography) and the effects of human decisions and actions. The South's warm, humid climate was ideal for the cultivation of commercial crops such as tobacco, cotton, rice, and sugarcane. The growth of those lucrative cash crops helped foster the plantation system and the expansion of slavery. In the end those developments brought about the civil war that shook the foundations of a republic rooted in the principles of freedom and equality.

THE DISTINCTIVE FEATURES OF THE OLD SOUTH

While geography was a key determinant of the South's economy and culture, many observers have located the origins of southern distinctiveness in the institution of racial slavery. The resolve of whites to maintain and expand such a labor system in turn led to a sense of racial unity that muted class conflict among whites. Yet the biracial character of the population exercised an even greater influence over southern culture, as it has since that time. In shaping patterns of speech, folklore, music, and literature, black southerners immeasurably influenced and enriched the region's culture.

The South differed from other sections of the country in its high proportion of native-born Americans in its population, both white and black. Unlike the North, the South drew few European immigrants after the Revolution. One reason was that the main shipping lines went from Britain to northern ports; another, that the prospect of competing with slave labor deterred immigrants. After the Missouri controversy of 1819–1821, the South increasingly became a consciously minority region, its population growth lagging behind that of other sections of the country, and its defiant dependence upon slavery more and more an isolated and odious anachronism.

AGRICULTURAL DIVERSITY The preponderance of farming also remained a distinctive southern characteristic, whether pictured as the Jeffersonian yeoman living by the sweat of his brow or the lordly planter

Southern Agriculture

Planting sweet potatoes on James Hopkinson's plantation, Edisto Island, South Carolina, April 1862.

dispatching his slave gangs. The focus on King Cotton and other cash crops such as rice and sugarcane has obscured the degree to which the South fed itself from its own fields. The upper South in many areas practiced general farming in much the same way as the Old Northwest. Corn grew everywhere, but it went less to the market than for local consumption, as feed for herds and food for people. Livestock added to the diversity of the farm economy. In 1860 the South had half the nation's cattle, over 60 percent of the hogs, nearly 45 percent of the horses, 52 percent of the oxen, nearly 90 percent of the mules, and about 33 percent of the sheep, the last mostly in the upper South.

Yet the story of the antebellum southern economy was hardly one of unbroken prosperity. The South's cash crops quickly exhausted the soil. Planting cotton or tobacco year after year leached the fertility from the fields. By 1860 much of eastern Virginia had long ago abandoned tobacco and in some places had turned to growing wheat for the northern market. The older farming lands had trouble competing with the newer soil farther west, in Alabama, Mississippi, and Louisiana, but these lands, too, began to show wear and tear. So first the Southeast and then the Old Southwest faced a growing sense of economic crisis as the nineteenth century advanced.

MANUFACTURING AND TRADE By 1840 many thoughtful southerners had concluded that the agrarian region desperately needed to develop its own manufacturing and trade. After the War of 1812, as cotton growing swept everything before it, the South became increasingly dependent upon the northern economy. Cotton and tobacco were exported mainly in northern vessels, and southerners also relied upon connections in the North for goods imported from Europe. The South became a kind of colonial dependency of the North.

Two major explanations were given for the lag in southern industrial development. First, blacks were presumed unsuited to factory work, perhaps because they supposedly could not adjust to the discipline of work by the clock. Second, the ruling elites of the Old South were said to have developed a lordly disdain for industrial activity, because a certain aristocratic prestige derived from owning plantations and holding slaves. But any argument that black labor was incompatible with industry flew in the face of the evidence, since factory owners bought or hired enslaved workers for just about every kind of manufacture.

Nor should one take at face value the legendary indifference of aristocratic planters to profits and losses. More often than not by the second quarter of the nineteenth century the successful planter was an acquisitive entrepreneur bent on maximizing profits. Economic historians have concluded that enslaved workers on the average supplied a hefty 10 percent return on their cost. By a strictly economic calculation, investment in slaves and land was the most profitable investment available in the antebellum South.

WHITE SOCIETY IN THE SOUTH

If an understanding of the Old South must begin with a knowledge of potent social myths, it must end with a sense of tragedy. White southerners had won short-term economic gains at the cost of both lagging social development and moral isolation in the eyes of the world. The concentration on slave-based agriculture as well as the paucity of cities and immigrants deprived the South of dynamic sources of economic growth and social innovation. The slaveholding South hitched its wagon not to a star but to the growing British demand for cotton. During the late 1850s southern agricultural prosperity seemed endless. Yet end it did. The heyday of expansion in British textiles was over by 1860, but by then the Deep South had become locked into large-scale cotton production that would endure for generations to come.

PLANTERS AND PLANTATION MISTRESSES During the first half of the nineteenth century, wealth in the South was increasingly concentrated

King Cotton Captured

An engraving showing cotton being trafficked in Louisiana.

in the hands of the planter elite. Although great plantations were relatively few in number, they set the tone for economic and social life. What distinguished the plantation from the farm, in addition to its size, was the use of a large enslaved labor force, managed by overseers, to grow primarily staple crops (cotton, rice, tobacco, and sugarcane) for profit.

If to be called a planter one had to hold twenty slaves, only 1 out of every 30 whites in the South in 1860 was a planter. Fewer than 11,000 planters held 50 or more slaves, and the owners of over 100 slaves numbered only 2,300. The census listed just 11 planters with 500 slaves and only 1 with as many as 1,000 slaves. Yet this privileged elite tended to think of its class interests as synonymous with the interests of the entire South and to perceive of its members as "natural aristocrats."

The planter group, making up under 4 percent of the adult white men in the South, held more than half the slaves and produced most of the cotton and tobacco and all of the sugar and rice. In a white population numbering just over 8 million in the states and territories that allowed slavery in 1860, the total number of slaveholders was only 383,637. But assuming that each family numbered five people, then whites with some proprietary interest in slavery constituted 1.9 million, or roughly one fourth of the South's white population. While most southern whites belonged to the small-farmer class, they often deferred to the planter elite. In part such deference reflected the desire of many small farmers to become planters themselves. Over time, however, land and slave prices soared, thereby narrowing prospects for upward social mobility. Between 1830 and 1860 the cotton belt witnessed a growing concentration of wealth in the hands of a slaveholding elite.

The mistress of the plantation supervised the domestic household in much the same way that the planter took care of the business outdoors. She oversaw the preparation of food and linens, the housecleaning, the care of the sick, and a hundred other details. While plantation wives enjoyed entertaining and being entertained, they owed their genteel circumstances to the domestic services provided by enslaved blacks, often women and girls.

One of the most frustrating realities for the plantation mistress was the lack of personal freedom occasioned by the complex demands of her "separate sphere" of genteel domesticity. White women living in a slaveholding culture confronted a double standard in terms of moral and sexual behavior. While they were expected to be models of Christian piety and sexual discretion, their husbands, brothers, and sons enjoyed greater latitude. Many white planters and their sons viewed slave women not only as sources of labor but also as sources of sexual satisfaction. They often rationalized the rape of a slave woman as no crime at all, for slaves had no rights in their eyes.

THE MIDDLE CLASS Overseers on the largest plantations generally came from the middle class of small farmers or skilled workers (artisans) or were younger sons of planters. Most wanted to become slaveholders themselves, but others were constantly on the move in search of more lucrative opportunities. Occasionally there were black overseers, but the highest management position to which a slave could aspire was usually that of "driver," or leader, placed in charge of a small group of slaves with the duty of getting them to work without creating dissension.

The most numerous white southerners were the yeoman farm families, who lived in modest two-room cabins rather than columned mansions. They raised a few hogs and chickens, grew some corn and cotton, and traded with neighbors more than they bought from stores. The men in the family focused their energies on outdoor labors. Women and children worked in the fields during harvest time but spent most of their days attending to domestic chores. Many of these "middling" farmers held a handful of slaves, but most had none. Most of the South's small farms were located in the midst of the plantation economy.

Southern farmers were typically mobile folk, willing to pull up stakes and move west or southwest in pursuit of better land. They tended to be fiercely independent and suspicious of government authority, and they overwhelmingly embraced the Democratic party and evangelical Protestantism. Even though only a minority of the middle-class farmers held slaves, most of them supported the slave system. They feared that the slaves, if freed, would compete with them for land, and they enjoyed the social status that racially based slavery afforded them. Such sentiments pervaded the border states as well as the Deep South. Kentucky, for example, held a referendum on the issue of slavery in 1849, and the voters, most of whom owned no slaves, resoundingly endorsed the slave system.

"POOR WHITES" Stereotyped views of southern society had prepared many visitors to the Old South to see only planters and "poor whites," and many a yeoman farmer living in crude comfort, his wealth concealed in cattle and swine off foraging in the woods, was mistaken for "white trash," a degraded class relegated to the least desirable land and given over to hunting and fishing, hound dogs and moonshine whiskey. Speculation had it that the "poor whites" were descended from indentured servants or convicts transported to the colonies from Britain. The problem, however, was less heredity than environment, the consequence of a trilogy of "lazy diseases": hookworm, malaria, and pellagra, all of which produced an overpowering lethargy. Around 1900 modern medicine discovered cures for these diseases. By 1930 the regional diseases had practically disappeared, taking with them many of the stereotypes about "poor whites."

HONOR AND VIOLENCE From colonial times most southern white men had prided themselves on adhering to a moral code centered on a prickly sense of honor that included a combative sensitivity to slights; loyalty to family, locality, state, and region; deference to elders and social "betters"; and an almost theatrical hospitality. Duels constituted the ultimate public expression of personal honor and manly courage. Although not confined to the South, dueling was much more common there than in the rest of the young nation, a fact that gave rise to the observation that southerners will be polite until they are angry enough to kill you. Dueling was outlawed in the northern states after Aaron Burr killed Alexander Hamilton in 1804, and a number of southern states and counties banned the practice as well—but the prohibition was rarely enforced. Many of the most prominent southern leaders engaged in duels—congressmen, senators, governors, newspaper editors, and planters. The roster of participants included Andrew Jackson, Henry Clay, Sam Houston, and Jefferson Davis.

BLACK SOCIETY IN THE SOUTH

Slavery was one of the fastest growing elements of American life during the first half of the nineteenth century. In 1790 there were less than 700,000 enslaved blacks in the United States. By 1830 there were more than 2 million, and by 1860 there were almost 4 million.

"FREE PERSONS OF COLOR" African Americans had diverse experiences in the United States, depending upon their geographic location and the nature of their working and living conditions. In the Old South "free persons of color" occupied an uncertain status, balanced somewhere between slavery and freedom, subject to racist legal restrictions not imposed upon whites. Free blacks gained liberty in several ways. Over the years some slaves were able to purchase their freedom, and some gained it as a reward for wartime military service. Others were freed by conscientious masters.

By 1830 there were 319,000 free blacks in the United States, about 150,000 of whom lived in the South. The free persons of color included a large number of mulattoes, people of mixed racial ancestry. The census of 1860 reported 412,000 such persons in the United States, or about 10 percent of the black population, probably a drastic undercount. In urban centers like Charleston and especially New Orleans, "colored" society became virtually a third caste, made up of people who occupied a status somewhere between that of blacks and that of whites. Some of them built substantial fortunes and even became slaveholders.

Black slaveholders were a tiny minority, however. The 1830 census revealed that 3,775 free blacks held 12,760 slaves. Most often black slaveholders were free blacks who bought their own family members with the express purpose of freeing them. But some African Americans engaged in slavery for purely selfish reasons.

Free blacks were often skilled artisans (blacksmiths, carpenters, cobblers), farmers, or common laborers. The increase in their numbers slowed as legislatures put more and more restrictions on the right to free slaves,

Free Blacks

This badge, issued in Charleston, South Carolina, was worn by a free black so that he would not be mistaken for someone's "property."

but by 1860 there were 262,000 free blacks in the slave states, a little over half the national total of 488,000. They were most numerous in the upper South and tended to live in urban areas.

Free blacks suffered widespread discrimination. All southern states required them to carry a pass. Whites often fraudulently claimed that a free black was in fact one of their runaway slaves, and if the African American did not have an official certificate of freedom, he could be enslaved. In many other ways as well, free blacks were not truly free. In North Carolina, blacks could not travel farther than one county away from their home. Most southern states prohibited them from voting. Blacks were not allowed to testify in court against whites, nor could they hold church services without the presence of a white minister.

PLANTATION SLAVERY Most slaves worked on plantations. The preferred jobs were as household servants and skilled workers, such as blacksmiths and carpenters. Field hands were usually housed in one- or two-room wooden shacks with dirt floors, some without windows. Based upon detailed records from eleven plantations in the lower South, scholars have calculated that more than half of all slave babies died in the first year of life, a mortality rate more than twice that of white infants.

Field hands worked from dawn to dusk. The slave codes adopted by the southern states subjected slaves not only to the slaveholder's governance but to surveillance by patrols of county militiamen, who abused slaves found at large. A majority of both planters and small farmers whipped slaves, at least occasionally. The difference between a good owner and a bad one, according to one ex-slave, was the difference between one who did not "whip too much" and one who "whipped till he bloodied you and blistered you."

Organized slave revolts were rare in the face of overwhelming white authority and firepower. In the nineteenth century only three major slave insurrections were attemped, two of which were betrayed before they got under way. Only the Nat Turner insurrection of August 1831, in rural Virginia, got beyond the planning stage. Turner, a black overseer, was also a religious exhorter who professed a divine mission in leading the movement. The revolt began when a small group of slaves killed Turner's master's family and set off down the road, repeating the process at other farmhouses, where other slaves joined in. Before it ended, at least fifty-five whites had been killed. Eventually trials resulted in seventeen hangings and seven deportations. The Virginia militia, for its part, killed large numbers of slaves indiscriminately in the process of putting down the rebels.

There were very few Nat Turners, however. Slaves more often retaliated against oppression by malingering or engaging in outright sabotage. Yet slaves

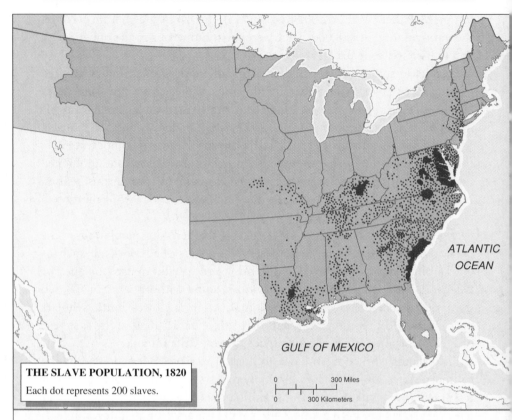

THE SLAVE POPULATION, 1820

Each dot represents 200 slaves.

ATLANTIC OCEAN

GULF OF MEXICO

Consider where the largest populations of slaves were clustered in the South in 1820. Why were most slaves clustered in these regions of the South and not in others? What were the limitations on the spread of slavery? How was the experience of plantation slavery different for men and women?

also knew that they would likely eat better on a prosperous plantation than on one they had reduced to poverty, and the shrewdest slaveholders knew that they would more likely benefit by holding out rewards than by inflicting pain. Plantations based upon the profit motive fostered mutual dependency between slaves and slaveholders, as well as natural antagonism. And in an agrarian society in which personal relations counted for much, blacks could win concessions that moderated the harshness of slavery, permitting them a certain degree of individual and community development.

THE EXPERIENCE OF SLAVE WOMEN Although black men and women often performed similar labors, they did not experience slavery in the same way. Slaveholders had different expectations for the men and women they

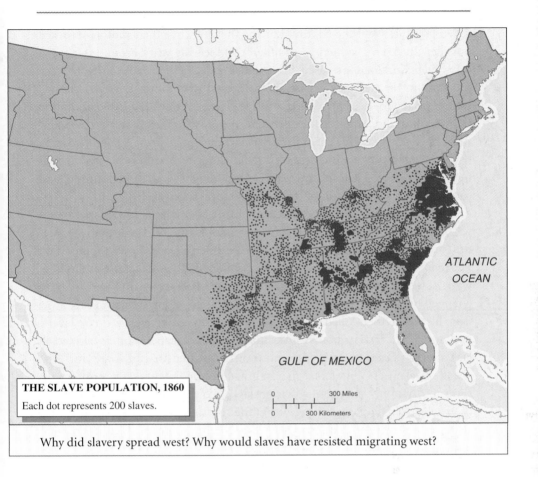

THE SLAVE POPULATION, 1860

Each dot represents 200 slaves.

ATLANTIC OCEAN

GULF OF MEXICO

0   300 Miles

0   300 Kilometers

Why did slavery spread west? Why would slaves have resisted migrating west?

controlled. During the colonial period male slaves vastly outnumbered females. By the mid–eighteenth century, however, the gender ratio had come into balance. Once slaveholders owners realized how profitable a fertile female slave could be over time, giving birth every two and a half years to a child who eventually could be sold, they began to encourage reproduction through a variety of incentives. Pregnant slaves were given less work to do and more food. Owners on some plantations rewarded new mothers with dresses and silver dollars.

But if motherhood endowed enslaved women with stature and benefits, it also entailed exhausting demands. Within days after childbirth the mother was put to work spinning, weaving, or sewing. A few weeks thereafter mothers were sent back to the fields; breast-feeding mothers were often forced to take their babies to the fields with them. On larger plantations elderly women, called grannies, kept the children during the day while their mothers worked outside. Once slave women passed their childbearing years, around the age of forty, their workload increased. Slaveholders put middle-aged women to work full-time in the fields or performing other outdoor labor. Enslaved women were expected to do "man's work" outside. They cut trees, hauled logs, plowed fields with mules, dug ditches, spread fertilizer, slaughtered and dressed animals, hoed corn, and picked cotton. Slave women of all ages usually worked in sex-segregated gangs, which enabled them to form close bonds with one another. To enslaved African Americans, developing a sense of community and camaraderie meant emotional and psychological survival.

Enslaved women faced the constant threat of sexual abuse. Sometimes a white master or overseer would rape a woman in the fields or cabins. Sometimes the owner would lock a woman in a cabin with a male slave whose task was to impregnate her. Female slaves responded to the sexual abuse in different ways. Often they fiercely resisted the sexual advances—and were usually whipped or even killed for their disobedience. Some seduced their master away from his wife. Others killed their babies rather than see them grow up in slavery.

Women had fewer opportunities than men to escape. Women tended to lack the physical strength and endurance required to run away and stay ahead of relentless pursuers. An even greater impediment was a mother's responsibility to her children. A few enslaved women did escape, but most of them learned to cope and resist within the confines of captivity. For them resistance to slavery took forms other than flight. Some engaged in truancy, hiding for days at a time. Many feigned illness to avoid work. Others sabotaged food or crops or stole from their master. Several slave women started fires. A few killed their masters, most often by poison.

FORGING A SLAVE COMMUNITY To generalize about slavery is to miss elements of diversity from place to place and time to time. The experience was as varied as people are. Enslaved African Americans were victims, but to stop at so obvious a perception would be to miss an important story of endurance and achievement. If ever there was an effective melting pot in American history, it may have been that in which Africans with a variety of ethnic, linguistic, and tribal origins fused to form a new community and a new culture as African Americans. Slave culture incorporated many African customs, especially in areas with few whites. Among the Gullah of the South Carolina and Georgia coast, for example, a researcher found as late as the 1940s more than 4,000 words still in use from the languages of twenty-one African tribes. Elements of African culture not only have survived but have interacted with those of the other cultures with which they came in contact.

SLAVE RELIGION Among the most important manifestations of slave culture was its dynamic religion, a mixture of African and Christian elements. Most Africans brought with them to the Americas a concept of a Creator, or Supreme God, whom they could recognize in the Christian Jehovah, and lesser gods, whom they might identify with Christ, the Holy Ghost, and the saints, thereby reconciling their African beliefs with Christianity. Alongside the church they retained beliefs in spirits, magic spells and herbs, and conjuring (the practice of healing by warding off evil spirits). Belief in magic is in fact a common response to conditions of danger or helplessness. Masters sought to instill lessons of Christian humility and obedience, but African Americans identified their plight with that of the Israelites in Egypt. And the ultimate hope of a better world gave solace in this one.

THE SLAVE FAMILY Slave marriages had no legal status, but slaveholders generally accepted marriage as a stabilizing influence on the plantation.

Plantation of J. J. Smith, Beaufort, South Carolina, 1862

Several generations of a family raised in slavery.

Sometimes they performed the marriages themselves or had a minister celebrate a formal wedding with all the trimmings. But whatever the formalities, the norm for the slave community, as for the white, was the nuclear family, with the father regarded as head of the household. Most slave children were socialized by means of the nuclear family, a process that afforded some degree of independence from white influence.

Childhood was short for slaves. At five or six years of age, children were given work assignments: they collected trash and kindling, picked cotton, scared away crows, weeded, and ran errands. By age ten they were full-time field hands. Children were often sold to new masters. In Missouri an enslaved woman saw six of her seven children, aged one to eleven, sold to six separate masters.

THE CULTURE OF THE SOUTHERN FRONTIER

There was substantial social and cultural diversity in the South during the three decades before the Civil War. The region known as the Old Southwest, for example, is perhaps the least well known. It included the states and territories west of the Georgia-Alabama border—Alabama, Mississippi, and Texas, Arkansas, Louisiana—as well as the frontier areas of Tennessee, Kentucky, and Florida.

Largely unsettled until the 1820s, this region bridged the South and the West, exhibiting characteristics of both areas. Raw and dynamic, marked by dangers, uncertainties, and opportunities, it served as a powerful magnet, luring thousands of settlers from Virginia and the Carolinas. By the 1830s most cotton production was centered in the lower South. The migrating southerners carved out farms, built churches, estabilished towns, and eventually brought culture and order to a raw frontier. As they took up new lives and occupations, the southern pioneers transplanted many practices and institutions from the coastal states. But they also fashioned a distinctly new set of values and customs.

THE DECISION TO MIGRATE During the 1820s the agricultural economy of the upper South suffered from depressed commodity prices and soil exhaustion. Hard times in the Carolinas and Virginia led many to migrate to the Old Southwest. Women were underrepresented among these migrants. Most dreaded the thought of taking up life in such a disease-ridden, violent, and primitive region, one that offered them neither independence nor adventure. They would remain part of a patriarchal culture in either area. Many women feared that life on the frontier would produce a "dissipation" of morals. They heard vivid stories of frontier lawlessness, drunkenness, gambling, and miscegenation.

Enslaved blacks had many of the same reservations about moving west. Almost 1 million captive African Americans were taken to the Old Southwest during the antebellum era, most of them in the 1830s. Like white women, they feared the region's harsh working conditions and torpid heat and humidity. They were also despondent at the breakup of their family ties. As the former slave turned abolitionist Frederick Douglass observed, the "removal" of a slave to the Southwest was considered a form of psychological "death."

THE JOURNEY AND SETTLEMENT Once in the Old Southwest, the pioneers bought land that had been appropriated from Indians. Parcels of 640 acres sold for as little as $2 an acre; land in Alabama's fertile black belt (named for the color of the soil) brought higher prices. As cotton prices soared in the 1830s, aspiring planters invested in as much land and as many slaves as possible. As a result, the average size of farms and plantations in the Old Southwest was larger than that in the Carolinas and Virginia.

But the Old Southwest was much more unhealthy than the Carolina Piedmont. The hot climate, contaminated water, and poor sanitation combined to unleash an epidemic of disease. Malaria was especially common. Life in tents and crude log cabins made many newcomers yearn for the material comforts they had left behind. A male settler reported that "all the men is very well pleased but the women is not very satisfied."

A MASCULINE CULTURE The southern frontier prompted important changes in sex roles, and relations between men and women became uncreasingly inequitable. Young men in the Old Southwest indulged in activities that would have generated disapproval in the Carolinas and Virginia. They drank, gambled, fought, and indulged their sexual desires. Alcohol consumption reached new heights along the southwestern frontier. Most plantations had their own stills for manufacturing whiskey, and alcoholism ravaged frontier families. Violence was also commonplace. The frequency of fights, stabbings, shootings, and murders shocked visitors. Equally disturbing was the propensity of white men to take sexual advantage of slave women. An Alabama woman married to a lawyer-politician was outraged by the "beastly passions" of the white men who fathered slave children and then sold them like livestock. She also recorded in her diary instances of men regularly beating their wives with whips and drinking to excess. Wives, it seems, had little choice but to endure the mistreatment because, as one woman wrote about a friend whose husband abused her, she was "wholly dependent upon his care."

ANTI-SLAVERY MOVEMENTS

EARLY OPPOSITION TO SLAVERY Scattered criticism of slavery developed in the North and the South in the decades after the Revolution, but the emancipation movement accelerated with the formation, in 1817, of the American Colonization Society, which proposed to resettle freed slaves in Africa. Its supporters included such prominent figures as James Madison, James Monroe, Henry Clay, John Marshall, and Daniel Webster, and its appeal was broad. Some backed it because of their opposition to slavery, while others saw it as a way to uphold slavery, by ridding the country of potentially troublesome free blacks. Articulate elements of the free African-American community denounced it from the start. A group of free blacks in Philadelphia, for example, stressed that they had "no wish to separate from our present homes for any purpose whatever." America, they insisted, was their native land.

Nevertheless, in 1821 agents of the Colonization Society acquired a parcel of land in West Africa that became the nucleus of a new country. In 1822 the first freed slaves arrived there from the United States, and twenty-five years later the society relinquished control to the Free and the Independent Republic of Liberia. But given its uncertain purpose, the colonization movement received only meager support from either anti-slavery or pro-slavery elements. By 1860 only about 15,000 blacks had emigrated, approximately 12,000 with the help of the Colonization Society. The number was infinitesimal compared with the number of slave births in the United States.

FROM GRADUALISM TO ABOLITION Meanwhile, in the early 1830s the anti-slavery movement went in a new direction. In Boston in 1831, William Lloyd Garrison began publication of an anti-slavery newspaper, the *Liberator*. Garrison, who rose from poverty in Newburyport, Massachusetts, had been apprenticed to a newspaperman and had edited several anti-slavery newspapers, but he had grown impatient with the strategy of moderation. In the first issue of his new paper, he renounced "the popular but pernicious doctrine of gradual emancipation" and vowed: "I *will be* as harsh as truth, and as uncompromising as justice. On this subject, I do not wish to think, to speak, or write, with moderation."

Garrison's combative language provoked outraged retorts from slaveholders. Their anger at abolitionists soared after the Nat Turner insurrection in 1831. Garrison, they assumed, bore a large part of the responsibility for the affair, but there is no evidence that Nat Turner had ever heard of him, and Garrison said that his newspaper had not a single subscriber in the South at the time. However violent his language, Garrison was in fact a pacifist, opposed to the use of force.

William Lloyd Garrison

Vocal abolitionist and advocate for immediate emancipation.

During the 1830s Garrison became the nation's most fervent foe of slavery. In 1831 he and his followers set up the New England Anti-Slavery Society. Two years later, with the help of Garrison and other abolitionists, two wealthy New York merchants, Arthur and Lewis Tappan, founded the American Anti-Slavery Society. They hoped to build on the publicity gained by the British anti-slavery movement, which had just induced Parliament to end slavery throughout the British Empire.

The American Anti-Slavery Society sought to convince people "that Slaveholding is a heinous crime in the sight of God, and that the duty, safety, and best interests of all concerned, require its *immediate abandonment,* without expatriation." The society went beyond the issue of emancipation to argue that blacks should "share an equality with the whites, of civil and religious privileges." The group issued a barrage of propaganda for its cause, including periodicals, tracts, lecturers, organizers, and fund-raisers.

FRACTIOUS TENSIONS As the anti-slavery movement spread, debates over tactics intensified. The Garrisonians, mainly New Englanders, were radicals who believed that American society had been corrupted from top to bottom and needed universal reform. Garrison embraced just about every important reform movement of the day: abolition, temperance, pacifism, and women's rights. He broke with the organized church, which to his mind was in league with slavery. The federal government was all the more so. The Constitution, he said, was "a covenant with death and an agreement with hell." Garrison therefore refused to vote.

Other reformers were less dogmatic. They saw American society as fundamentally sound and concentrated on purging it of slavery. Most of these abolitionists were evangelical Christians, and they promoted pragmatic political organization as the best instrument to end slavery. Garrison struck them as an impractical fanatic.

A showdown came in 1840 on the issue of women's rights. Women had joined the abolition movement from the start, but the activities of the Grimké sisters brought the issue of women's rights to center stage. Sarah and Angelina Grimké, daughters of a prominent slaveholding family in South Carolina, had broken with their parents and moved north to embrace Quakerism, abolitionism, and feminism. They set out speaking first to women in New England and eventually to audiences of both men and women.

Male leaders chastised the Grimkés and other female activists for engaging in "unfeminine" activity. The chairman of the Connecticut Anti-Slavery Society declared, "No woman will speak or vote where I am a moderator. It is enough for women to rule at home." He refused to "submit to PETTICOAT GOVERNMENT." Angelina Grimké stoutly rejected the conventional arguments. "It is a woman's right," she insisted, "to have a voice in all laws and regulations by which she is to be governed, whether in church or in state."

The debate over the role of women in the anti-slavery movement crackled and simmered until it finally exploded in 1840. At the American Anti-Slavery Society's annual meeting, the Garrisonians insisted upon the right of women to participate equally in the organization, and they carried their point. They did not commit the group to women's rights in any other way, however. Contrary opinion, mainly from the Tappans' New York group, ranged from outright anti-feminism to the simple fear of scattering their energies over too many reforms. The New Yorkers thus broke away to form the American and Foreign Anti-Slavery Society.

BLACK ANTI-SLAVERY ACTIVITY White male abolitionists also balked at granting full recognition to black abolitionists of either sex. Often blindly patronizing, white abolitionists expected free blacks to take a backseat in the movement. Despite the invitation to form separate black groups, black leaders were active in the white societies from the beginning. Three attended the organizational meeting of the American Anti-slavery Society in 1833, and some, notably former slaves, who could speak from firsthand experience, became outstanding agents for the movement.

One of the most effective black abolitionists was Sojourner Truth. Born to slaves in New York in 1797, she was given the name Isabella, but she renamed herself in 1843 after experiencing a mystical conversation with God, who told her "to travel up and down the land" preaching against the sins of slavery. She did just that, crisscrossing the country during the 1840s and 1850s, exhorting

Frederick Douglass (left) and Sojourner Truth (right)

Leading abolitionists.

audiences to support abolition and women's rights. Having been a slave until she fled to freedom in 1827, Sojourner Truth spoke with conviction and knowledge about the evils of the "peculiar institution" and the inequality of women. As she reportedly told a gathering of the Women's Rights Convention in Ohio in 1851, "I have plowed, and planted, and gathered into barns, and no man could head me—and ar'n't I a woman? I have borne thirteen children, and seen 'em mos' all sold off into slavery, and when I cried out with a mother's grief, none but Jesus heard—and ar'n't I a woman?" Through such compelling testimony, Sojourner Truth demonstrated the powerful intersection of abolitionism and women's rights agitation, and in the process she tapped the distinctive energies that women brought to reformist causes.

An equally gifted black abolitionist was Frederick Douglass, originally of Maryland. Blessed with an imposing appearance and a simple eloquence, he became the best-known black man in America. "I appear before the immense assembly this evening as a thief and a robber," he told a Massachusetts group in 1842. "I stole this head, these limbs, this body from my master, and ran off with them." Fearful of capture after publishing his influential

Narrative of the Life of Frederick Douglass (1845), he left for an extended lecture tour of the British Isles and returned two years later with enough money to purchase his freedom. He then started an abolitionist newspaper for blacks, the *North Star,* in Rochester, New York.

Douglass's *Narrative* was the best known of hundreds of accounts of enslavement and the escape to freedom, many of which described the Underground Railroad, a network of people who helped runaways escape and start new lives, often over the Canadian border. A few intrepid black refugees ventured back into slave states to organize additional escapes. Harriet Tubman, the most celebrated liberator, returned nineteen times. Born a slave on a Maryland plantation in about 1820, Tubman escaped when her master died. She fled north, eventually arriving in Philadelphia. There she met William Still, an African-American clerk for the Pennsylvania Anti-Slavery Society who served as a "conductor" on the Underground Railroad. Tubman soon became a conductor herself. Slipping back into the slave states, she would shepherd runaways northward, traveling at night and sleeping by day in the barns or attics of sympathizers along the way. A feisty, determined woman, she threatened to kill any slave who wanted to turn back. Among the 300 slaves Tubman helped liberate were her parents, her sister, and her two children.

REACTIONS TO ABOLITION Even in the North, blacks encountered widespread racial discrimination and segregation. Garrison, Douglass, and other abolitionists often confronted hostile white crowds who disliked blacks or found anti-slavery agitation bad for business. In 1837 an Illinois mob killed the anti-slavery newspaper editor Elijah P. Lovejoy, giving the movement a martyr to the causes of both abolition and freedom of the press.

In the 1830s abolition took a political turn, focusing at first on Congress. One shrewd strategy was to deluge Congress with petitions calling for the abolition of slavery in the nation's capital, the District of Columbia. Most such petitions were presented by former president John Quincy Adams, elected to the House from Massachusetts in 1830. In 1836, however, the House adopted a rule to lay abolition petitions automatically on the table, in effect ignoring them. Adams, "Old Man Eloquent," stubbornly fought this "gag rule" as a violation of the First Amendment and hounded its supporters until the rule was repealed in 1844.

Meanwhile, in 1840, the year of the schism in the anti-slavery movement, a small group of abolitionists called a national convention in Albany, New York, and launched the Liberty party, with James G. Birney, a one-time slaveholder from Alabama and Kentucky, as its candidate for president. In the 1840 presidential election, Birney polled only 7,000 votes, but in 1844 he won 60,000, and from that time forth an anti-slavery party contested every national election until Abraham Lincoln won the presidency in 1860.

THE DEFENSE OF SLAVERY James Birney was but one among a number of southerners propelled north during the 1830s by the South's growing hostility to emancipationist ideas. The anti-slavery movement in the upper South had its last stand in 1831–1832, when the Virginia legislature rejected a plan of gradual emancipation and African colonization. Thereafter southern partisans worked out an elaborate intellectual defense of slavery, presenting it in a positive light.

The evangelical Christian churches, which had widely condemned slavery at one time, gradually turned pro-slavery, at least in the South. Ministers of all denominations joined in the argument. Had not the patriarchs of the Hebrew Bible held bondsmen? Had not Saint Paul advised servants to obey their masters and told a fugitive servant to return to his master? And had not Jesus remained silent on the subject, at least insofar as the Gospels reported his words? In 1845 disputes over slavery split two great denominations along sectional lines and led to the formation of the Southern Baptist Convention and the Methodist Episcopal Church, South. Presbyterians, the only other major denomination to split, did not do so until the Civil War.

A more fundamental feature of the pro-slavery argument stressed the racial inferiority of blacks. Other arguments took a more "practical" view. Not only was slavery profitable, one argument went, but it was also a matter of social necessity. Thomas Jefferson, for instance, in his *Notes on the State of Virginia* (1785), had argued that emancipated slaves and whites could not live together without the risk of a race war growing out of the recollection of past injustices. What is more, it seemed clear to some defenders of slavery that blacks could not be expected to work if freed. They were too shiftless and improvident, the argument went. White workers, on the other hand, feared the competition in the job market if slaves were freed.

In his books *Sociology for the South; or, The Failure of Free Society* (1854) and *Cannibals All! or, Slaves without Masters* (1857), George Fitzhugh of Virginia argued that slavery provided security for African Americans in sickness and old age, whereas workers in the North were exploited for profit and then cast aside. People were not born equal, he insisted. Fitzhugh argued for an organic, hierarchical society, much like the family, in which each member had a place with both rights and obligations.

Within one generation such ideas had triumphed in the white South. Opponents of the faith in slavery as a "positive good" were either silenced or exiled. Freedom of thought in the Old South had become a victim of the region's growing obsession with the preservation and expansion of slavery.

MAKING CONNECTIONS

- The abolition movement never represented the majority of northerners. As Chapter 16 shows, however, by the end of the 1850s most voters in the North supported the idea of limiting the expansion of slavery westward, if not the abolition of it in the southern states.

- The Civil War brought great changes to southerners, both black and white. Chapter 17 describes the effect of the war on southern society.

- There are striking contrasts between the Old South of this chapter and the New South of Chapter 19.

FURTHER READING

Those interested in the problem of distinguishing myth and reality in the southern experience should consult William R. Taylor's *Cavalier and Yankee: The Old South and American National Character* (1961). Two assessments of the mind of the Old South and its defense of slavery are Eugene D. Genovese's *The Slaveholders' Dilemma: Freedom and Progress in Southern Conservative Thought, 1820–1860* (1992) and Eric H. Walther's *The Fire-Eaters* (1992).

Contrasting analyses of the plantation system are Eugene D. Genovese's *The World the Slaveholders Made: Two Essays in Interpretation* (1988) and Gavin Wright's *The Political Economy of the Cotton South: Households, Markets, and Wealth in the Nineteenth Century* (1978). Stephanie McCurry's *Masters of Small Worlds: Yeoman Households, Gender Relations, and the Political Culture of the Antebellum South Carolina Low Country* (1995) greatly enriches our understanding of southern households, religion, and political culture.

Other essential works on southern culture and society include Bertram Wyatt-Brown's *Honor and Violence in the Old South* (1986), Elizabeth Fox-Genovese's *Within the Plantation Household: Black and White Women of the Old South* (1988), Catherine Clinton's *Plantation Mistress: Woman's World in the Old South* (1982), Joan E. Cashin's *A Family Venture: Men and Women on the Southern Frontier* (1991), and Theodore Rosengarten's *Tombee: Portrait of a Cotton Planter* (1986).

A provocative discussion of the psychology of African-American slavery can be found in Stanley M. Elkins's *Slavery: A Problem in American Institutional and Intellectual Life,* 3rd ed. (1976). John W. Blassingame's *The Slave Community: Plantation Life in the Antebellum South,* rev. and enlarged ed. (1979); Eugene D. Genovese's *Roll, Jordan, Roll: The World the Slaves Made* (1974), and Herbert G. Gutman's *The Black Family in Slavery and Freedom, 1750–1925* (1976) all stress the theme of a persisting slave culture. On the question of slavery's profitability, see Robert William Fogel and Stanley L. Engerman's *Time on the Cross: The Economics of American Negro Slavery* (1974).

Other works on slavery include Lawrence W. Levine's *Black Culture and Black Consciousness: Afro-American Folk Thought from Slavery to Freedom* (1977); Albert J. Raboteau's *Slave Religion: The "Invisible Institution" in the Antebellum South* (1978); *We Are Your Sisters,* edited by Dorothy Sterling (1984); Deborah Gray White's *Ar'n't I a Woman? Female Slaves in the Plantation South,* rev. ed., (1999); and Joel Williamson's *The Crucible of Race: Black-White Relations in the American South since Emancipation* (1984). Charles Joyner's *Down by the Riverside: A South Carolina Slave Community* (1984) offers a vivid reconstruction of one community.

Useful surveys of abolitionism include James Brewer Stewart's *Holy Warriors: The Abolitionists and American Slavery,* rev. ed. (1997) and Julie Roy Jeffrey's *The Great Silent Army of Abolitionism: Ordinary Women in the Antislavery Movement* (1998). On William Lloyd Garrison, see Henry Mayer's *All on Fire: William Lloyd Garrison and the Abolition of Slavery* (1998). For the pro-slavery argument as it developed in the South, see Larry E. Tise's *Proslavery: A History of the Defense of Slavery in America, 1701–1840* (1987) and James Oakes's *The Ruling Race: A History of American Slaveholders* (1982). The problems southerners had in justifying slavery are explored in Kenneth S. Greenberg's *Masters and Statesmen: The Political Culture of American Slavery* (1985).

16

THE CRISIS OF UNION

FOCUS QUESTIONS

- How was slavery politicized?
- How did the Compromise of 1850 and the Kansas-Nebraska Act reflect sectional tensions?
- What led to the rise of a third-generation party system, dominated by Republicans and Democrats?
- What were the specific events that led to the secession of the southern states?

To answer these questions and access additional review material, please visit www.wwnorton.com/studyspace.

Wars have a way of corrupting ideals and breeding new wars, often in unforeseen ways. America's victory over Mexico in 1848 and its acquisition of vast new territories gave rise to quarrels over the newly acquired land. Those quarrels set in motion a series of disputes that would culminate in a crisis of union.

SLAVERY IN THE TERRITORIES

THE WILMOT PROVISO   The Mexican War was less than three months old when the seeds of a new conflict began to sprout. On August 8, 1846, a freshman Democrat from Pennsylvania, David Wilmot, stood up in the House of Representatives to discuss President Polk's request for $2 million to support the war effort against Mexico. Wilmot favored expansion, he explained, even the annexation of Texas as a slave state. But slavery had come to an end in Mexico, and if the United States should acquire Mexican territory, "God forbid that we should be the means of planting this institution upon it." Drawing upon the words of the Northwest Ordinance, he proposed that in land acquired from Mexico, "neither slavery nor involuntary servitude shall ever exist in any part of said territory."

The Wilmot Proviso politicized slavery finally and definitively. For a generation, since the Missouri controversy of 1819–1821, the issue had been lurking in the wings, kept there most of the time by politicians who feared its disruptive force. For the two decades following Wilmot's proposal, however, the question of extending slavery into new territories would never be far from center stage.

The House adopted the Wilmot Proviso, but the Senate balked. When Congress reconvened in December 1846, Polk persuaded Wilmot to withhold his amendment, but by then others were ready to take up the cause of prohibiting slavery in the new territories. When a New York congressman revived the proviso, the House again approved the amendment; again the Senate refused to endorse it. The House finally gave up, but in one form or another Wilmot's idea kept being revived.

John C. Calhoun devised a thesis to counter the proviso, which he set before the Senate in four resolutions on February 19, 1847. The Calhoun resolutions, which never came to a vote, argued that since the territories were the common possession of the states, Congress had no right to prevent any citizen from taking slaves into them. To do so would violate the Fifth Amendment, which forbids Congress to deprive any person of life, liberty, or property without due process of law, and slaves were property. By this clever stroke of logic, Calhoun took the basic guarantee of liberty, the Bill of Rights, and turned it into a basic guarantee of slavery. Calhoun's logic became established southern dogma, echoed by his colleagues and formally endorsed by the Virginia legislature.

POPULAR SOVEREIGNTY   To bypass the brewing conflict, President Polk suggested extending the Missouri Compromise, dividing free and slave territory at the latitude of 36°30′ all the way to the Pacific. Senator Lewis Cass of Michigan, an ardent Whig expansionist, offered a different solution. He argued that the citizens of a territory "regulate their own internal concerns," like the citizens of a state. Such an approach would combine the merits of expediency and democracy. It would take the issue of slavery in the territories out of the national arena and put it in the hands of those directly affected.

Popular sovereignty, or "squatter sovereignty," as Cass's idea was also called, had much to commend it. Without directly challenging the slaveholders' access to the new territories, it promised to open them quickly to nonslaveholding farmers, who would almost surely become the majority. With this tacit understanding the idea prospered in Cass's Old Northwest, where Stephen A. Douglas of Illinois and other prominent Democrats soon endorsed it.

When the Mexican War ended in 1848, the question of slavery in the new territories was no longer hypothetical. Nobody doubted that Oregon would become "free soil," but it, too, was drawn into the growing controversy. Territorial status for Oregon, pending since 1846, was delayed because its provisional government had excluded slavery. To concede that provision would imply an authority drawn from the powers of Congress, since a territory was created by Congress. After much wrangling, an exhausted Congress let Oregon settlers organize their territorial status without slavery but postponed a decision on the Southwest territories. Polk signed the bill on the principle that Oregon was north of 36°30′, the Missouri Compromise line of latitude.

Polk had promised to serve only one term, and having accomplished his major goals, he refused to run again. At the 1848 Democratic Convention, Lewis Cass, the author of "squatter sovereignty," won the presidential nomination, but the platform simply denied the power of Congress to interfere with slavery in the states and criticized all efforts to bring the question before Congress. The Democrats hoped that the voters would reward their party for winning the war against Mexico. The Whigs devised an even more artful shift. Once again, as in 1840, they passed over Henry Clay, their party leader, for a general, Zachary Taylor, whose popularity had grown since the Battle of Buena Vista. A resident of Louisiana and holder of more than 100 slaves, Taylor was an apolitical figure who had never voted in a national election. Once again, as in 1840, the party adopted no platform at all.

THE FREE-SOIL COALITION   The anti-slavery impulse was not easily squelched, however. David Wilmot had raised a standard to which a broad coalition could rally. People who shied away from the militant abolitionism of William Lloyd Garrison could more readily endorse the exclusion of slavery from all the territories. By doing so, moreover, they could strike a blow for liberty without caring about slavery itself, or about the slaves. One might simply want free soil for white farmers while keeping the unwelcome blacks far away in the South, where they supposedly belonged. Free soil in the new territories, therefore, rather than abolition in the South itself, became the rallying point for many Americans—and also the name of a new party.

Three major groups entered the new free-soil coalition: rebellious Democrats, anti-slavery Whigs, and members of the anti-slavery Liberty party. In 1848 they organized the Free-Soil party at a convention in Buffalo, New York. Its presidential nomination went to the former Democratic president,

Martin Van Buren. The party platform pledged the government to abolish slavery whenever such action became constitutional, but its main principle was the Wilmot Proviso, and it entered the campaign with the catchy slogan of "free soil, free speech, free labor, and free men."

The impact of the new party on the 1848 election was mixed. The Free-Soilers split the Democratic vote enough to throw New York's thirty-six electoral votes to Taylor and split the Whig vote enough to give Ohio to Lewis Cass, but Van Buren's total of 291,000 votes was far below the totals of 1,361,000 for Taylor and 1,222,000 for Cass. Taylor won with 163 to 127 electoral votes for Cass, and both major parties retained a national following.

THE CALIFORNIA GOLD RUSH   Meanwhile, a new dimension had been introduced into the vexing question of slavery in the territories. On January 24, 1848, gold was discovered in California. The word spread quickly, and gold fever became a worldwide epidemic. During 1849 more than 80,000 gold-seeking adventures reached California, with 55,000 traveling overland and the rest going by ship. The influx quickly reduced the Mexicans there to a minority, and sporadic conflicts with the Indians of the Sierra Nevada foothills decimated California's Native Americans.

Of all the frontiers in the American experience, the mining frontier was perhaps the most unstable. Unlike the land-hungry pioneers who traversed the overland trails, the miners were mostly unmarried young men with greatly diverse ethnic and cultural backgrounds. Few miners were interested in permanent settlement. They wanted to strike it rich quickly and return home. The mining camps in California's valleys and canyons and along its creek beds thus sprang up like mushrooms and disappeared almost as rapidly.

After touring the gold region, the territorial governor reported that the surge of newcomers had "entirely changed the character of Upper California." The mining shantytowns were disorderly, unsanitary, and often lawless communities where vigilante justice prevailed and leisure time revolved around saloons. One newcomer reported that "in the short space of twenty-four days, we have had murders, fearful accidents, bloody deaths, a mob, whippings, a hanging, an attempt at suicide, and a fatal duel." Within six months of arriving in California in 1849, one in every five gold seekers was dead. The gold fields and mining towns were so dangerous that nearly everyone carried a weapon—usually a pistol or bowie knife. Suicides were common, and disease was rampant.

Women were as rare in the mining camps as liquor was abundant. In 1850 less than 8 percent of California's total population was female, and even fewer women hazarded life in the camps. Racial and ethnic prejudice

Gold Miners, ca. 1850

Daguerreotype of miners panning for gold at their claim.

abounded in the mining camps. White Americans in the camps often looked with disdain upon the Latinos and Chinese, who were most often employed as wage laborers to help in the panning process, separating gold from sand and gravel. But the white Americans focused their contempt on the Indians. In the mining culture it was not a crime to kill Indians or to work them to death. American miners tried several times to outlaw foreigners in the mining country but had to settle for a tax on foreign miners, which was applied to Mexicans in express violation of the treaty ending the Mexican War.

CALIFORNIA STATEHOOD   California's civic leaders grew frustrated by the inability of military authorities to maintain law and order in the mining communities. In this context the new president, Zachary Taylor, thought he saw an ideal opportunity to use California statehood as a lever to end the stalemate in Congress brought about by the slavery issue.

Born in Virginia and raised in Kentucky, Taylor had been a soldier most of his adult life. Constantly on the move, he had acquired a home in Louisiana and a plantation in Mississippi. Southern Whigs had rallied to his support, expecting him to uphold the cause of slavery. Instead, he turned out to be a southern man who upheld Union principles and had no more use for John Calhoun's pro-slavery abstractions than Jackson had for his nullification doctrine. Slavery should be upheld where it existed, Taylor believed, but he had little patience with abstract theories about slavery in territories where it probably could not exist. Why not make the California and New Mexico territories, acquired from Mexico, into free states immediately, Taylor reasoned, and bypass the whole issue?

But the Californians, in desperate need of organized government, were ahead of him. In December 1849, without consulting Congress, California organized a free-state government. New Mexico responded more slowly, but by 1850 Americans there had adopted a free-state constitution. In his annual message on December 4, 1849, Taylor endorsed immediate statehood for California and enjoined Congress to avoid injecting slavery into the issue.

THE COMPROMISE OF 1850

The spotlight fell on the Senate, where the Compromise of 1850, one of the great dramas of American politics, was enacted by a stellar cast: the great triumvirate of Henry Clay, John C. Calhoun, and Daniel Webster. Seventy-three-year-old Henry Clay once again took the role of the Great Compromiser.

THE GREAT DEBATE   In January 1850 Clay presented a package of eight resolutions designed to solve all the disputed issues. He proposed to (1) admit California as a free state, (2) organize the remainder of the Southwest territories without restrictions on slavery, (3) deny Texas its extreme claim to much of New Mexico, (4) compensate Texas by assuming its debt, (5) uphold slavery in the District of Columbia, but (6) abolish the slave trade across its boundaries, (7) adopt a more effective fugitive slave act, and (8) deny congressional authority to interfere with the interstate slave trade. His proposals, in substance, became the Compromise of 1850, but only after a prolonged debate, the most celebrated, if not the greatest, in the annals of Congress—and the final great debate for Calhoun, Clay, and Webster.

On February 5–6 Clay summoned all his eloquence in defending his proposed settlement. In the interest of "peace, concord and harmony," he called for an end to "passion, passion—party, party—and intemperance." Otherwise, continued sectional bickering would lead to a "furious, bloody, implacable, exterminating" civil war. To avoid that catastrophe, he stressed, California should be admitted on the terms that its own citizens had approved.

The debate continued sporadically through February, with the Texan Sam Houston rising to support Clay's compromise, Mississippi's Jefferson

Davis defending the slavery cause on every point, and none endorsing President Taylor's straightforward plan. Taylor believed that slavery in the South could best be protected if southerners avoided injecting the issue into the dispute over new territories. Unlike Calhoun, he did not believe the new western territories were suitable for slave-based agriculture. Because Taylor believed the issue of bringing slaves into the territories was moot, he continued to urge Congress to admit California and New Mexico without reference to slavery. But few others embraced such a simple solution. In fact, a rising chorus of southern leaders threatened to secede from the Union if slavery were not allowed in California.

Then, in a dramatic move on March 4, Calhoun, desperately ill with tuberculosis, from which he would die in a few weeks, left his sickbed to sit in the Senate chamber. A colleague read his defiant remarks. "I have, Senators, believed from the first that the agitation on the subject of slavery would, if not prevented by some timely and effective measure, end in disunion," wrote Calhoun. Neither Clay's compromise nor Taylor's efforts, he declared, would serve the Union. The South needed simply an acceptance of its rights: to take slaves into the territories, to receive federal assistance in capturing and returning fugitive slaves, and to receive some guarantee of "an equilibrium between the sections."

Three days later Calhoun returned to hear Daniel Webster. The "godlike Daniel" no longer possessed the thunderous voice of his youth, nor did his shrinking frame project its once magisterial aura, but he remained a formidable presence. For his address to the Senate, he chose as his central theme the preservation of the Union: "I wish to speak today, not as a Massachusetts man, not as a Northern man, but as an American . . . I speak today for the preservation of the Union." The extent of slavery was already determined, he insisted, by the Northwest Ordinance, by the Missouri Compromise, and in the new lands by the law of nature. Both sections, to be sure, had legitimate grievances: on the one hand the excesses of "infernal fanatics and abolitionists" in the North and on the other hand southern efforts to expand slavery. But instead of threatening secession, he declared, let everyone "enjoy the fresh air of liberty and union."

Webster's March 7 speech was a supreme gesture of conciliation, but the famed senator had knowingly brought down a storm upon his head. New England abolitionists lambasted this "Benedict Arnold" for not aggressively supporting the free-soil cause and for endorsing the new fugitive slave law. On March 11 William H. Seward, a freshman Whig senator from New York, gave the anti-slavery reply to Webster. Compromise with slavery, he argued, was "radically wrong and essentially vicious." Seward insisted that a "higher law than the Constitution" demanded the abolition of slavery.

In mid-April a select committee of thirteen senators bundled Clay's suggestions into one comprehensive bill. Taylor continued to oppose Clay's compromise, and their feud threatened to split the Whig party. Another crisis loomed when word came that a convention in New Mexico was applying for statehood, with Taylor's support and on the basis of boundaries that conflicted with the Texas claim to the east bank of the Rio Grande.

TOWARD A COMPROMISE   On July 4, 1850, supporters of the Union staged a rally at the base of the unfinished Washington Monument. President Taylor attended the ceremonies in the hot sun. Five days later he died of a gastrointestinal affliction caused by tainted food or water. Taylor's sudden death strengthened the chances of compromise. The soldier in the White House was followed by a politician, Millard Fillmore. The son of a poor farmer in upstate New York, Fillmore had made his way as a lawyer and then as a candidate in the rough-and-tumble world of New York politics. Experience had taught him caution, which some interpreted as indecision, but he had made up his mind to support Henry Clay's compromise and had so informed Taylor. It was a strange switch. Taylor, the Louisiana slaveholder, had stoutly opposed the expansion of slavery and was ready to make war on his native region if it pressed the issue; Fillmore, whom southerners thought was anti-slavery, was ready to make peace.

At this point the young Senator Stephen A. Douglas of Illinois, a rising star of the Democratic party, rescued Clay's faltering compromise. Short and stocky, brash and brilliant, Douglas adopted the same strategy that Clay had used to pass the Missouri Compromise thirty years before. Reasoning that nearly everybody objected to one or another provision of Clay's proposal, Douglas worked on the principle of breaking it up into six (later five) separate measures. Few members were prepared to vote for all of them, but from different elements Douglas hoped to mobilize a majority for each.

Millard Fillmore

His support of the Compromise of 1850 helped the Union muddle through the crisis.

The plan worked. By September 1850 President Fillmore had signed the last of the five measures into law. The Union had muddled through, and the settlement went down in history as the Compromise of 1850. For a time it defused an explosive situation and settled each of the major points at issue.

First, California entered the Union as a free state, ending forever the old balance of free and slave states. Second, the Texas–New Mexico Act made New Mexico a territory and set the Texas boundary at its present location. In return for giving up its claims east of the Rio Grande, Texas was paid $10 million. Third, the Utah Act set up that future state's territory. The territorial act in each case omitted reference to slavery except to give the territorial legislature authority over "all rightful subjects of legislation" with provision for appeal to federal courts. For the sake of agreement, the deliberate ambiguity of the statement was its merit. Northern congressmen could assume that territorial legislatures might act to exclude slavery on the unstated principle of popular sovereignty. Southern congressmen assumed that they could not do so.

Fourth, a new Fugitive Slave Act put the matter of retrieving runaways wholly under federal jurisdiction and stacked the cards in favor of slave catchers. Fifth, as a gesture to anti-slavery forces, the slave trade, but not slavery itself, was abolished in the District of Columbia. Millard Fillmore pronounced the five measures making up the Compromise of 1850 "a final settlement" of the issues dividing the nation. Events would soon prove him wrong.

THE FUGITIVE SLAVE ACT Northern abolitionists were determined to keep the issue of slavery's evils in the forefront of public concerns. Southern intransigence in demanding the Fugitive Slave Act had presented abolitionists with an emotional new focus for agitation. The law offered a strong temptation to kidnap free blacks by denying alleged fugitives a jury trial and by providing a reward of $10 for each fugitive delivered to federal authorities. In addition, federal marshals could require citizens to help in its enforcement; violators could be imprisoned for up to six months and fined $1,000. Trouble followed. In Detroit, for example, authorities used military force to stop the rescue of an alleged fugitive slave by an outraged mob in October 1850.

There were relatively few such incidents, however. In the first six years of the Fugitive Slave Act, only three runaways were forcibly rescued from slave catchers. On the other hand, probably fewer than 200 were returned to bondage during those years. More than that were rescued by stealth. Still, the Fugitive Slave Act excited the anti-slavery impulse in the North.

UNCLE TOM'S CABIN Antislavery forces found their most persuasive appeal not in opposition to the Fugitive Slave Act but in the fictional drama of Harriet Beecher Stowe's *Uncle Tom's Cabin* (1852). The novel depicts a combination of unlikely saints and sinners, social stereotypes, and melodramatic escapades, and it was a smashing commercial success. Slavery, seen through Stowe's eyes, subjected its victims to callous brutality or, at the hands of indulgent masters, to the indignity of extravagant ineptitude and bankruptcy. Stowe poignantly portrayed the evils of the interstate slave trade, especially the breaking up of slave families, and she highlighted the

"The Greatest Book of the Age"

Uncle Tom's Cabin, as this advertisement indicates, was a tremendous commercial success.

horrors of the Fugitive Slave Act. It took time for the novel to work its effect on public opinion, however. The country was enjoying a surge of prosperity, and the course of the presidential campaign in 1852 reflected a common desire to lay sectional quarrels to rest.

THE ELECTION OF 1852 The Democrats chose as their presidential candidate Franklin Pierce of New Hampshire, a personable veteran of the Mexican War with little political experience. Soon they had a catchy slogan to aim at the Whigs: "We Polked you in 1844, we shall Pierce you in 1852." The platform pledged the Democrats to "abide by and adhere to a faithful execution of the acts known as the Compromise measures." Pierce rallied both the southern rights' partisans and the Van Burenite Democrats. The Free-Soilers, as a consequence, mustered only half as many votes as they had won in 1848.

The Whigs were less fortunate. They repudiated the lackluster Fillmore, who had faithfully supported the compromise, and tried to exploit martial glory by finally choosing General Winfield Scott, the hero of Mexico City, a native of Virginia backed mainly by northern Whigs. The Whig convention dutifully endorsed the Compromise of 1850, but with some opposition from the North. Scott, an able field commander but an inept politician, had gained a reputation for anti-slavery and nativist sentiments, alienating German-American and Irish-American voters. In the end, Scott carried only four states. The popular vote was closer: 1.6 million to 1.4 million.

Pierce, an undistinguished but sincere, boyishly handsome figure, a former congressman, senator, and soldier, was, like Polk, touted as another Young Hickory. But the youngest president yet was unable to unite the warring factions of his party. By the end of President Pierce's first year in office, Democratic leaders had decided he was a failure. By trying to be all things to all people, Pierce looked more and more like a "Northern man with Southern principles."

FOREIGN ADVENTURES

CUBA   Foreign diversions now distracted attention from domestic quarrels. Cuba, one of Spain's earliest possessions in the New World, had long been an object of U.S. desire, especially to southerners determined to expand slavery into new areas. In 1854 the Pierce administration offered Spain $130 million for the island, which Spain spurned. The U.S. ministers to Spain, France, and Britain then drafted the Ostend Manifesto, which declared that if Spain, "actuated by stubborn pride and a false sense of honor refused to sell," the United States must ask itself, "Does Cuba, in the possession of Spain, seriously endanger our internal peace and existence of our cherished Union?" If so, "we shall be justified in wresting it from Spain." Publication of the supposedly confidential dispatch left the administration no choice but to disavow what northern opinion widely regarded as a slaveholders' plot to acquire Cuba.

DIPLOMATIC GAINS IN ASIA   In Asia, American diplomacy scored some important achievements. In 1844 China signed an agreement with the United States that opened four ports, including Shanghai, to U.S. trade. A later treaty opened eleven more ports and granted Americans the right to travel and trade throughout China. About fifty American Protestant missionaries were in China by 1855, and for nearly a century China remained the most active field for missionaries.

Japan, meanwhile, had remained closed to U.S. trade for two centuries. Moreover, American whalers wrecked on the shores of Japan had been forbidden to leave the country. Mainly in their interest, President Fillmore entrusted a special Japanese expedition to Commodore Matthew Perry, who arrived in Tokyo in 1853. Perry sought to impress—and intimidate—the Japanese with U.S. military and technological superiority. He demonstrated the cannons on his steamships and presented the Japanese with gifts of rifles, pistols, telegraph instruments, and a working miniature locomotive. For their part the Japanese presented Perry with silk and ornate furnishings. Negotiations followed, and Japan eventually agreed to allow a U.S. consulate, treat castaways cordially, and permit American ships to visit certain ports to take on supplies and make repairs. Broad commercial relations began after the first American envoy, Townsend Harris, negotiated the Harris Convention of 1858, which opened five Japanese ports to U.S. trade. Japan continued to ban emigration but found the law increasingly difficult to enforce, and by the 1880s the Japanese government had abandoned its efforts to prevent Japanese from seeking work abroad.

THE KANSAS-NEBRASKA CRISIS

American commercial interests in Asia helped spark a growing interest in constructing a transcontinental railroad that would link the eastern seaboard to the Pacific coast. Railroad developers and land speculators also promoted this link, as did slaveholders who were eager to see the reach of slavery extended. During the 1850s the idea of building a transcontinental railroad, though a great national goal, reignited sectional rivalries and reopened the slavery issue.

Stephen Douglas, ca. 1852

Initiator of the Kansas-Nebraska Act.

DOUGLAS'S PROPOSAL   In 1852 and 1853 Congress debated and dropped several likely proposals for the route of the transcontinental rail line. For various reasons, including terrain, climate, and sectional interests, Secretary of War Jefferson Davis favored a southern route and encouraged what became known as the Gadsden Purchase, a barren stretch of

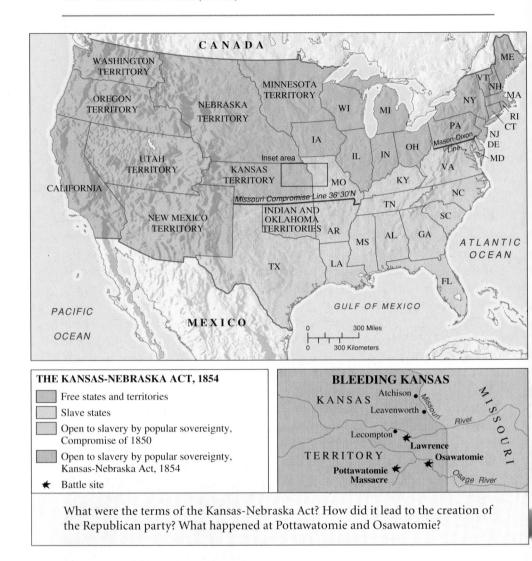

THE KANSAS-NEBRASKA ACT, 1854

- Free states and territories
- Slave states
- Open to slavery by popular sovereignty, Compromise of 1850
- Open to slavery by popular sovereignty, Kansas-Nebraska Act, 1854
- ★ Battle site

BLEEDING KANSAS

What were the terms of the Kansas-Nebraska Act? How did it lead to the creation of the Republican party? What happened at Pottawatomie and Osawatomie?

land in present-day New Mexico and Arizona. In 1853, at a cost of $10 million, the United States acquired the area from Mexico as a likely route for a Pacific railroad.

But midwestern spokesmen had other ideas concerning the path of the railroad. Since 1845 Illinois senator Stephen A. Douglas and others had been pushing for a route through a new territory west of Missouri and Iowa, bearing the Indian name Nebraska. In 1854, as chairman of the Committee on Territories, Douglas put forward a bill dealing with the entire unorganized portion of the Louisiana Purchase to the Canadian border. To carry his point, Douglas needed the support of southerners, and to win that support he needed to make some concession on slavery in the new territories. This he did by writing the concept of popular sovereignty into the bill, allowing voters in each territory to decide the issue themselves.

It was a clever dodge since the Missouri Compromise would exclude slaves until a territorial government had made a decision, thereby preventing slaveholders from getting established before the decision was reached. Southerners quickly spotted the barrier, and Douglas just as quickly made two more concessions. He supported an amendment for repeal of the Missouri Compromise insofar as it excluded slavery north of 36°30′, and he agreed to organize two territories: Kansas, west of Missouri, and Nebraska, west of Iowa and Minnesota.

Douglas's motives remain unclear. Railroads were surely foremost in his mind, but he may also have been influenced by the desire to win support for his bill in the South, by the hope that the principle of popular sovereignty would quiet the slavery issue and open the Great Plains, or by a chance to split the Whigs. But he had blundered by failing to appreciate the depth of anti-slavery feelings, thus damaging his presidential chances and setting the country on the road to civil war. Douglas himself preferred that the territories become free. Their climate and geography excluded plantation agriculture, he reasoned, and he could not comprehend how people could get so wrought up over abstract rights to take slaves into the territories. Yet he had in fact opened the possibility that slavery might gain a foothold in Kansas.

Douglas's proposal to repeal the Missouri Compromise was less than a week old when six anti-slavery congressmen published a protest, the "Appeal of the Independent Democrats." Their moral indignation quickly spread among those who opposed Douglas. Across the North, editorials, sermons, speeches, and petitions denounced Douglas's bill as a conspiracy to extend slavery. But Douglas had the votes in Congress for his Kansas-Nebraska Act and, once committed, he forced the issue with tireless energy. President Pierce impulsively added his support, and the bill passed in May 1854 by a vote of 37 to 14 in the Senate and 113 to 100 in the House.

Very well, many in the North reasoned, if the Missouri Compromise was not a sacred pledge and could be scrapped, then neither was the Fugitive Slave Act. On June 2, 1854, Boston witnessed the most dramatic demonstration against the act. After several attempts had failed to rescue a slave named Anthony Burns from being returned south, soldiers dispatched by President

Pierce marched him to a waiting ship through streets lined with people shouting "Kidnappers!" Burns was the last fugitive slave to be returned from Boston and was soon freed through purchase by Boston's African-American community.

THE EMERGENCE OF THE REPUBLICAN PARTY The cords that John C. Calhoun had said were holding the Union together were beginning to fray. The national church organizations of Baptists and Methodists, for instance, had split over slavery by 1845. The national political parties, which had mutual interests transcending sectional issues, were beginning to unravel under the strain of slavery. The Democrats managed to postpone disruption for yet a while, but their congressional delegation lost heavily in the North, enhancing the influence of the southern wing.

The strain of the Kansas-Nebraska Act soon destroyed the Whig party, however. Southern Whigs now tended to abstain from voting, while northern Whigs gravitated toward two new parties. One was the new American (Know-Nothing) party, which had raised the banner of nativism and the hope of serving the patriotic cause of Union. More northern Whigs joined with independent Democrats and Free-Soilers in spontaneous anti-slavery coalitions with a confusing array of names, including Anti-Nebraska, Fusion, and People's party. These coalitions finally converged in 1854, choosing the name Republican.

BLEEDING KANSAS After passage of the Kansas-Nebraska Act, attention swung to the plains of Kansas, where opposing elements gathered to stage what would turn out to be a dress rehearsal for civil war. All agreed that Nebraska would be a free state, but Kansas soon exposed the potential for mischief in Douglas's concept of popular sovereignty. The ambiguity of the law, useful to Douglas in getting it passed, only added to the chaos. The people of Kansas were "perfectly free to form and regulate their domestic institutions in their own way, subject only to the Constitution." That in itself invited conflicting interpretations, but the law failed to specify the time of any decision, adding to each side's sense of urgency in getting control of the territory.

The settlement of Kansas therefore differed from the typical pioneering efforts. Groups sprang up in North and South to hurry right-minded settlers westward, mostly from Missouri and the surrounding states. Although few of them held slaves, they were not sympathetic to militant abolitionism; racism was prevalent even among nonslaveholding whites. Many of the

Kansas settlers wanted to keep all blacks, enslaved or free, out of the territory. By 1860 there were only 627 African Americans in the territory.

When Kansas's first territorial governor arrived, in 1854, he found several thousand settlers already in place. He ordered that a census be taken and scheduled an election for a territorial legislature in 1855. On election day several thousand "border ruffians" crossed over from Missouri, illegally cast pro-slavery votes, and pledged to kill every "God-damned abolitionist in the Territory." The governor denounced the vote as a fraud but did nothing to alter the results, for fear of being killed. The new legislature expelled the few anti-slavery members, adopted a drastic slave code, and made it a capital offense to aid a fugitive slave.

Free-state advocates rejected this "bogus" government and quickly formed their own. In 1855 a constitutional convention, the product of an election of dubious legality, met in Topeka, drafted a state constitution excluding both slavery and free blacks from Kansas, and applied for admission to the Union. By 1856 a free-state "governor" and "legislature" were functioning in Topeka. Thus the territory had two illegal governments vying for recognition and control. The prospect of getting any government to command authority in Kansas seemed dim, and both sides began to arm. Once armed, they began to fight. In May 1856, 700 pro-slavery thugs entered the free-state town of Lawrence and smashed newspaper presses, set fire to the free-state governor's home, stole property, and destroyed the Free-State Hotel.

The "sack of Lawrence" resulted in just one casualty, but the incident aroused a fanatic Kansas Free-Soiler named John Brown, who had a history of mental instability. Two days after the sack of Lawrence, Brown, the father of twenty children, set out with four of his sons and three other men toward Pottawatomie, site of a pro-slavery settlement. There they dragged five men from their houses and hacked them to death in front of their screaming wives and children, ostensibly as revenge for the deaths of free-state men.

The Pottawatomie Massacre (May 24–25, 1856) set off a guerrilla war in the Kansas Territory that lasted through the fall. On August 30 Missouri ruffians raided the free-state settlement at Osawatomie. They looted the houses, burned them to the ground, and shot John Brown's son Frederick through the heart. The elder Brown, who barely escaped, swore to his surviving sons and followers, "I have only a short time to live—only one death to die, and I will die fighting for this cause." Altogether, by the end of 1856, about 200 settlers had been killed in Kansas and $2 million in property destroyed during the territorial civil war.

VIOLENCE IN THE SENATE   The violence in Kansas spilled over into Congress itself. On May 22, 1856, the day after the sack of Lawrence and two days before Brown's Pottawatomie Massacre, a flash of savagery on the Senate floor electrified the country. Just two days earlier Senator Charles Sumner of Massachusetts had finished an inflammatory speech in which he described the treatment of Kansas as "the rape of a virgin territory" and blamed it on the South's "depraved longing for a new slave State." Sumner made the elderly senator Andrew Pickens Butler of South Carolina a special target of his censure. He called Butler a liar and implied that he kept a slave mistress. Sumner also teased him about a speech impediment, the result of a stroke.

Sumner's rudeness might well have backfired had it not been for Butler's kinsman Preston S. Brooks, a fiery-tempered South Carolina congressman. For two days Brooks brooded over the insults to his relative, knowing that Sumner would refuse a challenge to a duel. On May 22 a vengeful Brooks confronted Sumner at his Senate desk, accused him of libel against South Carolina and Butler, and began beating him about the head with a cane. Sumner, struggling to rise, wrenched the desk from the floor and collapsed.

Brooks had satisfied his rage but in the process had created a martyr for the anti-slavery cause. Like so many other men in those years, he betrayed the zealot's gift for snatching defeat from the jaws of victory. For two and a half years, Sumner's empty Senate seat was a solemn reminder of the violence done to him. When the House censured Brooks, he resigned, but he was triumphantly reelected. His admirers presented him with new canes. The *Richmond Enquirer* urged Brooks to cane Sumner again: "These vulgar abolitionists in the Senate—must be lashed into submission."

SECTIONAL POLITICS   Within the span of five days in May of 1856, "Bleeding Kansas," "Bleeding Sumner," and "Bully Brooks" had fragmented the political landscape. The major parties could no longer evade the slavery issue. Already it had split the hopeful American party wide open. Southern delegates, with help from New York, killed a resolution to restore the Missouri Compromise and nominated Millard Fillmore for president. Later what was left of the Whig party endorsed him as well.

At its first national convention the new Republican party followed the Whig tradition by seeking out a military hero, John C. Frémont, "the Pathfinder" and leader in the conquest of California. The Republican platform also owed much to the Whigs. It favored a transcontinental railroad and, in general, more internal improvements. It condemned the repeal of the Missouri Compromise and the Democratic policy of territorial expansion.

The campaign slogan echoed that of the Free-Soilers: "Free soil, free speech, and Frémont." It was the first time a major-party platform had taken a stand against slavery.

The Democrats, meeting two weeks earlier, had rejected Pierce, the hapless victim of so much turmoil. They also spurned Douglas, because of the damage done by his Kansas-Nebraska Act. The party therefore turned to James Buchanan of Pennsylvania, who had long sought the nomination. The Democratic platform endorsed the Kansas-Nebraska Act and urged Congress not to interfere with slavery in either states or territories. The party reached out to its newly acquired Irish Catholic and German Catholic voters by condemning nativism and endorsing religious liberty.

The campaign of 1856 resolved itself into a contest in which the parties vied for northern or southern votes. The Republicans had few southern supporters and only a handful in the border states, where fear of disunion held many Whigs in line. Buchanan thus went into the campaign as the candidate of the only remaining national party. Frémont swept the northernmost states with 114 electoral votes, but Buchanan added five free states to his southern majority for a total of 174.

Buchanan, the only unmarried president then or since, brought to the White House a portfolio of impressive achievements in politics and diplomacy. He had been in Congress, had served as minister to Russia and Britain, and had been Polk's secretary of state in between. His long quest for the presidency had been built upon a southern alliance, and his political debts reinforced his belief that saving the Union depended upon concessions to the South. Republicans charged that he lacked the backbone to stand up to the southerners who dominated the Democratic majorities in Congress. To them his choice of four slave-state and only three free-state men for his cabinet seemed a bad omen.

THE DEEPENING SECTIONAL CRISIS

During James Buchanan's first six months in office, he encountered three crises in succession: the *Dred Scott* decision, new troubles in Kansas, and a business panic. These and other challenges proved his undoing.

THE *DRED SCOTT* CASE   On March 6, 1857, two days after Buchanan's inauguration, the Supreme Court rendered a decision in the long-pending case of *Dred Scott v. Sandford*. Dred Scott, born a slave in Virginia in about 1800, had been taken to St. Louis in 1830 and sold to an

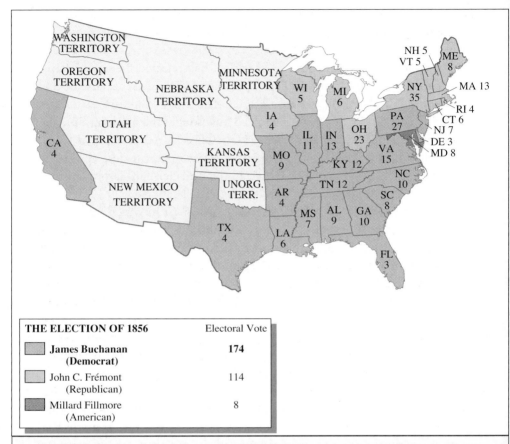

THE ELECTION OF 1856	Electoral Vote
James Buchanan (Democrat)	**174**
John C. Frémont (Republican)	114
Millard Fillmore (American)	8

What was the platform of the new Republican party? Why did Democrats pick Buchanan? What were the key factors that decided the election?

army surgeon, who took him as his servant to Illinois, then to the Wisconsin Territory (later Minnesota), where slavery was prohibited, and finally returned him to St. Louis in 1842. While in the Wisconsin Territory, Scott had met and married Harriet Robinson, and they eventually had two daughters.

After his master's death, in 1843, Scott apparently tried unsuccessfully to buy his freedom. In 1846 Harriet Scott persuaded her husband to file suit in the Missouri courts, claiming that residence in Illinois and the Wisconsin Territory had made them free. A jury decided in their favor, reaffirming the widespread notion that "once free, forever free." But the state supreme court ruled against the Scotts, arguing that a slave state did not have to

honor freedom granted to slaves by free states. When the case rose on appeal to the Supreme Court, the country anxiously awaited its opinion on the issue of whether freedom once granted could be lost by returning to a slave state.

Eight of the justices filed a separate opinion, and one concurred with Chief Justice Roger B. Taney. By different lines of reasoning, seven justices ruled that Scott had reverted to slave status upon his return to Missouri. Taney ruled that Scott lacked standing in the courts because he lacked citizenship. At the time the Constitution was adopted, Taney added, blacks "had for more than a century been regarded as . . . so far inferior, that they had no rights which the white man was bound to respect."

To clarify the definition of Scott's status, Taney moved to a second major question. He argued that the Missouri Compromise, by ruling that certain new territories were to exclude slaves, had deprived citizens of property by prohibiting slavery, an action "not warranted by the Constitution." The Supreme Court had declared an act of Congress unconstitutional for the first time since *Marbury v. Madison* (1803). Congress had repealed the Missouri Compromise in the Kansas-Nebraska Act three years earlier, but the decision now challenged the concept of popular sovereignty. If Congress itself could not exclude slavery from a territory, then presumably neither could a territorial government created by an act of Congress.

Pro-slavery elements, of course, greeted the court's opinion with glee. Many northerners denounced Taney's ruling, however. Little wonder that Republicans protested: the Court had declared their free-soil program unconstitutional. It had also reinforced the suspicion that the slavocracy was hatching a conspiracy. Were not all but one of the justices who joined Taney southerners? And had not Buchanan chatted with the chief justice at the inauguration and then urged the people to accept the decision as a final settlement?

And what of Dred Scott? Ironically his owner, now a widow, married a prominent Massachusetts abolitionist, who saw to it that Scott and his family were freed in 1857. A year later Dred Scott died of tuberculosis.

THE LECOMPTON CONSTITUTION   Out in Kansas, meanwhile, the struggle over slavery continued through 1857. The contested politics in the territory now resulted in an anti-slavery legislature and a pro-slavery constitutional convention. The convention, meeting at Lecompton, drew up a constitution under which Kansas would become a slave state. A referendum on the document was set for December 21, 1857, with rules and officials chosen by the convention.

Although Kansas had only about 200 slaves at the time, free-state men boycotted the election, claiming that it was rigged. At that point, President Buchanan took a fateful step. Influenced by southern advisers and politically dependent upon southern congressmen, he supported the pro-slavery Lecompton Convention. The election went according to form: 6,226 votes for the constitution with slavery, 569 for the constitution without slavery. Meanwhile, the acting governor had convened the anti-slavery legislature, which called for another election to vote on the Lecompton Constitution. Most of the pro-slavery settlers boycotted this election, and the result, on January 4, 1858, was overwhelming: 10,226 against the constitution, 138 for the constitution with slavery, 24 for the constitution without slavery.

The results suggested a clear majority against slavery, but Buchanan stuck to his support of the Lecompton Constitution, driving another wedge into the Democratic party. Senator Douglas, up for reelection in Illinois, could not afford to run as a champion of Lecompton. He broke dramatically with the president in a tense confrontation, but Buchanan persisted in trying to drive Lecompton "naked" through Congress. In the Senate, administration forces held firm, and in 1858 Lecompton was passed. In the House enough anti-Lecompton Democrats combined to put through an amendment for a new and carefully supervised popular vote in Kansas. Enough senators went along to pass the House bill. Southerners were confident the vote in Kansas would favor slavery, because to reject it the voters would have to reject the constitution, an action that would postpone statehood until the population reached 90,000. On August 2, 1858, Kansas voters nevertheless rejected Lecompton, 11,300 to 1,788. With that vote, Kansas, now firmly in the hands of its anti-slavery legislature, largely ended its role in the sectional controversy.

THE PANIC OF 1857   The third crisis of Buchanan's first half year in office, a financial panic, occurred in August 1857. It was brought on by a reduction in Europe's demand for American grain, a surge in manufacturing that outran the growth of markets, and the continued weakness and confusion of the state bank-note system. Failure of the Ohio Life Insurance and Trust Company precipitated the panic, which brought on a depression from which the country did not emerge until 1859.

Everything in those years seemed to get drawn into the vortex of sectional conflict, and business troubles were no exception. Northern businessmen tended to blame the depression on the Democratic tariff of 1857, which had put rates at their lowest level since 1816. The agricultural South weathered the crisis better than the North. Cotton prices fell, but slowly, and world markets for cotton quickly recovered. The result was an exalted notion of King Cotton's importance to the world and apparent confirmation of the growing argument that the southern system of slave-based agriculture was superior to the free-labor system of the North.

DOUGLAS VERSUS LINCOLN   Amid the recriminations over the *Dred Scott* decision, Kansas, and the depression, the center could not hold. The Lecompton battle put severe strains on the most substantial cord of Union that was left, the Democratic party. To many, Douglas seemed the best hope for unity and union, one of the few remaining Democratic leaders with support in both the North and the South. But now Douglas was being whipsawed by the extremes. The Kansas-Nebraska Act had cast him in the role of a doughface, a southern sympathizer. Yet his opposition to Lecompton, the fraudulent fruit of popular sovereignty, had alienated him from Buchanan's southern junta. For all his flexibility and opportunism, however, Douglas had convinced himself that popular sovereignty was a point of principle, a bulwark of democracy and local self-government. In 1858 he faced reelection to the Senate against the opposition of both Buchanan Democrats and Republicans. The year 1860 would give him a chance for the presidency, but first he had to secure his home base in Illinois.

To oppose him, Illinois Republicans named Abraham Lincoln of Springfield, a former Whig state legislator, one-term congressman, and small-town lawyer. Born in a Kentucky log cabin in 1809 and raised on farms in Indiana and Illinois, the young Lincoln had the wit and will to rise above his coarse beginnings. With less than twelve months of sporadic schooling, he learned to read, studied such books as came to hand, and eventually developed a prose style as lean and muscular as the man himself. He worked at various farm tasks, operated a ferry, and made two trips down to New Orleans as a flatboatman. Striking out on his own, he managed a general store in New Salem, Illinois, learned

Abraham Lincoln

Republican candidate for president, June 1860.

surveying, served in the Black Hawk War in 1832, won election to the legislature in 1834 (at the age of twenty-five), read law, and was admitted to the
bar in 1836.

Lincoln abhorred slavery but was no abolitionist. He did not believe the
two races could coexist as equals. But he did oppose any further extension of
slavery into new territories, assuming that over time it would die a "natural
death." Slavery, he said in the 1840s, was a vexing but "minor question on its
way to extinction." Lincoln stayed in the Illinois legislature until 1842 and in
1846 won a seat in Congress. After a single term he retired from active politics to cultivate his law practice in Springfield.

In 1854 the Kansas-Nebraska debate drew Lincoln back into the political
arena. At first he held back from the rapidly growing Republicans, but in 1856
he joined the new party, and by 1858 he was the obvious Republican choice to
oppose Douglas for the Senate. Candidate Lincoln resorted to the classic ploy
of the underdog: he challenged the favorite to a debate. Douglas knew he was
up against a formidable foe and had little relish for drawing attention to his
opponent, but he agreed to meet Lincoln in seven sites around the state. The
legendary Lincoln-Douglas debates took place that summer and fall.

The two men could not have presented a more striking contrast. Lincoln
was well over six feet tall, sinewy and craggy featured with a long neck and
deep-set, brooding eyes. Unassuming in manner, dressed in homely, well-
worn clothes and walking with a shambling gait, he lightened his essentially
serious demeanor with a refreshing sense of humor. To sympathetic observers, Lincoln conveyed an air of simplicity, sincerity, and common sense.
Douglas, on the other hand, was short, rotund, stern, and cocky, attired in
the finest custom-tailored suits. A man of considerable abilities and even
greater ambition, he strutted to the platform with the pugnacious air of a
predestined champion.

At the time and since, much attention focused on the second debate, at
Freeport, where Lincoln asked Douglas how he could reconcile popular sovereignty with the *Dred Scott* ruling that citizens had the right to carry slaves
into any territory. Douglas's answer, thenceforth known as the Freeport
Doctrine, was to state the obvious: whatever the Supreme Court might say
about slavery, it could not exist anywhere unless supported by local police
regulations. Thus, if settlers did not want slavery, they should simply refuse
to adopt a local code protecting it.

Douglas then tried to set some traps of his own. He accused Lincoln of ad-
vocating racial equality. Lincoln countered by affirming white supremacy.
There was, he asserted, a "physical difference between the white and black
races," and it would "forever forbid the two races living together on terms of

social and political equality." Lincoln did insist that blacks had an "equal" right to their freedom and the fruits of their labor. But the basic difference between the two men, Lincoln insisted, lay in Douglas's professed indifference to the moral question of slavery.

If Lincoln had the better of the argument, at least in the long view, Douglas had the better of the election, which he won in a vote by the Illinois legislature. Across the nation the elections recorded one loss after another for Buchanan Democrats. The administration had lost control of the House.

JOHN BROWN'S RAID   The gradual return of prosperity in 1859 offered hope that the political storms of the 1850s might yet pass. But the sectional issue of slavery still haunted the nation, and like lightning on the horizon it warned that a storm was brewing. In 1859 John Brown surfaced again, this time in the East. Since the Pottawatomie Massacre in 1856, he had led a furtive existence, engaging in fund-raising, recruiting, and occasional bushwhacking. His commitment to abolish the "wicked curse of slavery" had intensified, meanwhile, to a fever pitch.

On October 16, 1859, Brown launched his supreme gesture. From a Maryland farm he crossed the Potomac River with about twenty men, including five blacks, and occupied the federal arsenal in Harpers Ferry, Virginia (now West Virginia). He intended to arm the Maryland slaves he assumed would flock to his cause, set up a black stronghold in the mountains of western Virginia, and provide a nucleus of support for slave insurrections across the South.

What Brown actually did was to take the arsenal by surprise, seize a few hostages, and hole up in the fire-engine house. There he and his band were quickly surrounded by militiamen and town residents. The next morning, Brown sent his son Watson and another supporter out under a white flag, but the enraged crowd shot them both. Intermittent shooting broke out, and another Brown son was wounded.

John Brown

Although his anti-abolition efforts were based in Kansas, Brown was a native of Connecticut.

That night Lieutenant Colonel Robert E. Lee arrived with his aide, Lieutenant J.E.B. Stuart, and a force of marines. The following morning, October 18, Stuart and his troops broke down the barricaded doors and rushed into the fire-engine house. A young lieutenant found Brown kneeling with his rifle cocked. Before Brown could fire, however, the marine used the hilt of his sword to beat him unconscious. By then the siege was over. Altogether Brown's men had killed four people (including one marine) and wounded nine. Of their own force, ten died (including two of Brown's sons), five escaped, and seven were captured.

Brown, who survived his wounds, was quickly tried for treason, convicted, and sentenced to be hanged. "Let them hang me," he exulted. "I am worth inconceivably more to hang than for any other purpose." He was never more right. If Brown had failed in his purpose—whatever it was—he had become a martyr for the anti-slavery cause, and he had set off a panic throughout the slaveholding South. At his sentencing he delivered one of America's classic speeches: "Now, if it is deemed necessary that I should forfeit my life for the furtherance of the ends of justice, and mingle my blood further with the blood of my children and with the blood of millions in this slave country whose rights are disregarded by wicked, cruel, and unjust enactments, I say, let it be done."

When Brown, still unflinching, met his end, northern sympathizers held solemn observances. "That new saint," Ralph Waldo Emerson predicted, ". . . will make the gallows glorious like the Cross." William Lloyd Garrison, the lifelong pacifist, now wished "success to every slave insurrection at the South and in every slave country." By far the gravest effect of Brown's raid was to leave pro-slavery southerners in no mood to distinguish between John Brown and the Republican party. All through the fall and winter of 1859–1860, rumors of conspiracy and insurrection swept the region. Every northern visitor, commercial traveler, or schoolteacher came under suspicion, and many were driven out. "We regard every man in our midst an enemy to the institutions of the South," said an Atlanta newspaper editor, "who does not boldly declare that he believes African slavery to be a social, moral, and political blessing."

THE CENTER COMES APART

THE DEMOCRATS DIVIDE   Amid such hysteria unleashed by John Brown's assault at Harper's Ferry, the nation approached a presidential election destined to be the most fateful in its history. The Democrats gathered in Charleston, South Carolina, for their 1860 convention. Douglas's supporters

PROGRESSIVE DEMOCRACY—PROSPECT OF A SMASH UP.

Prospect of a Smash Up (1860)

This cartoon shows the Democratic Party—the last remaining national party—about to be split by sectional differences and the onrush of Republicans, led by Lincoln.

reaffirmed the platform of 1856, which simply promised congressional non-interference with slavery. Southern firebrands, however, now demanded a federal law protecting slavery in the territories. Buchanan supporters, hoping to stop Douglas, encouraged the strategy. When the southern planks lost in the ensuing debate, Alabama's delegation walked out of the convention, followed by delegates from the other Gulf states. The convention then decided to leave the overwrought atmosphere of Charleston and reassemble in Baltimore on June 18. The Baltimore convention finally nominated Douglas. The Charleston seceders met first in Richmond and then in Baltimore, where they adopted the slave-code platform defeated in Charleston and named Vice President John C. Breckinridge of Kentucky for president. Another cord of union had snapped: the last remaining national party.

LINCOLN'S ELECTION The Republicans, meanwhile, gathered in Chicago in the summer of 1860. There everything suddenly came together for "Honest Abe" Lincoln, the uncommon common man. Lincoln had emerged on the national scene during his unsuccessful senatorial campaign two years before and had since taken a stance on the containment of slavery strong enough to satisfy the abolitionists yet moderate enough to seem less threatening than they were.

Lincoln won the Republican nomination on the third ballot. The party platform denounced John Brown's raid as "among the gravest of crimes" and affirmed that each state should "control its own domestic institutions." The party repeated its resistance to the extension of slavery and, in an effort to gain broader support, endorsed a higher protective tariff for manufacturers, free homesteads for farmers, a more liberal naturalization law for immigrants, and internal improvements, including a Pacific railroad. With this platform, Republicans made a strong appeal to eastern businessmen, western farmers, and the large immigrant population.

Both major conventions revealed that opinions about slavery tended to become more radical in the upper North and the Deep South. Attitude seemed to follow latitude. In the border states between North and South—Missouri, Kentucky, Delaware, and Maryland—a sense of moderation aroused the diehard Whigs there to make one more try at reconciliation. Meeting in Baltimore a week before the Republicans met in Chicago, they organized the Constitutional Union party and named John Bell of Tennessee for president. Their platform simply called for the preservation of the Constitution and the Union.

Of the four candidates not one generated a national following, and the campaign devolved into a choice between Lincoln and Douglas in the North, Breckinridge and Bell in the South. One consequence of these campaigns was that each section gained a false impression of the other. The South never learned to distinguish Lincoln from the radicals; the North failed to gauge the force of southern intransigence. Lincoln stubbornly refused to offer the South assurances or to explain his position on slavery, which he insisted was a matter of public record.

The one man who tried to break through the barrier that was falling between the North and the South was Douglas, who attempted to mount a national campaign. Only forty-seven but already weakened by excessive drink, ill health, and disappointments, he wore himself out in one final glorious campaign. Down through the hostile areas of Tennessee, Georgia, and Alabama, he carried appeals on behalf of the Union.

By midnight on November 6, however, Lincoln's victory was clear. In the final count he had about 39 percent of the total popular vote but a clear electoral majority, with 180 votes in the Electoral College. He carried all eighteen free states by a wide margin. Among all the candidates only Douglas had electoral votes from both slave and free states, but his total of 12 was but a pitiful remnant of Democratic unionism. Bell took Virginia, Kentucky, and Tennessee, and Breckinridge swept the other slave states to come in second with 72 electoral votes.

SECESSION OF THE DEEP SOUTH   Lincoln's election panicked Southerners. Soon after the election, South Carolina set a special election for December 6 to choose delegates to a state convention. In Charleston

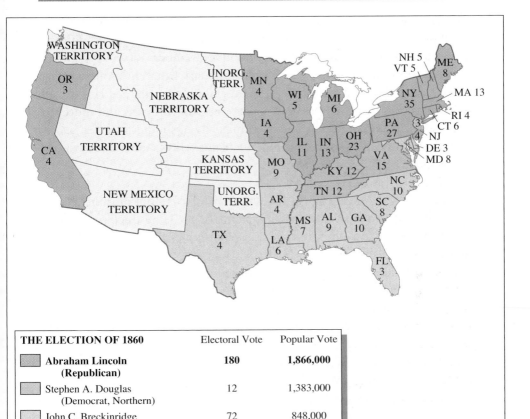

THE ELECTION OF 1860	Electoral Vote	Popular Vote
Abraham Lincoln **(Republican)**	**180**	**1,866,000**
Stephen A. Douglas (Democrat, Northern)	12	1,383,000
John C. Breckinridge (Democrat, Southern)	72	848,000
John Bell (Constitutional Union)	39	593,000

What caused the division in the Democratic party? How did Lincoln position himself to win the Republican nomination? What were the major factors that led to Lincoln's electoral victory?

on December 20, 1860, the convention unanimously endorsed an Ordinance of Secession, repealed the state's ratification of the Constitution, and severed its ties to the Union. By February 1, 1861, Mississippi, Florida, Alabama, Georgia, Louisiana, and Texas had declared themselves out of the Union. On February 4 a convention of those seven states met in Montgomery, Alabama, and on February 7 it adopted a provisional constitution for a new nation, the Confederate States of America. Two days later the delegates elected Jefferson Davis as its president. He was inaugurated February 18, with Alexander Stephens of Georgia as vice president.

In all seven states of the southernmost tier, a solid majority had voted for secessionist convention delegates, but their combined vote would not have been a majority of the presidential vote in November. What happened, it seemed, was what often happens in revolutionary situations: a determined and decisive minority acted quickly in an emotionally charged climate and carried its program over the weak objections of a confused and indecisive opposition. Trying to decide whether a majority of southern whites favored secession is probably beside the point—a majority was vulnerable to the decisive action of the secessionists.

BUCHANAN'S WAITING GAME   History is full of might-have-beens. A bold stroke, even a bold statement, by the lame-duck president at this point might have defused the crisis, but James Buchanan waffled. As Ulysses S. Grant recognized, Buchanan was a "granny of an Executive." Besides, a bold stroke might simply have hastened the conflict. No bold stroke came from president-elect Lincoln either, nor would he consult with the Buchanan administration during the long months before his inauguration on March 4, 1861. He inclined all too strongly to the belief that secession was just another bluff and kept his silence.

In his annual message on December 3, 1860, President Buchanan declared that secession was illegal but that he lacked authority to coerce a state to rejoin the Union. "Seldom have we known so strong an argument come to so lame and impotent a conclusion," the *Cincinnati Enquirer* editorialized. There was, however, a hidden weapon in the president's reaffirmation of a duty to "take care that the laws be faithfully executed" insofar as he was able. If the president could enforce the law upon all citizens, he would have no need to "coerce" a state. Indeed, Buchanan's position became the policy of the Lincoln administration, which fought a war on the theory that individuals, but not states, were in rebellion.

Buchanan held firm to his resolve, with some slight stiffening by the end of 1860, when secession became a fact, but he refrained from forceful action. On the day after Christmas, the small federal garrison at Charleston's Fort Moultrie had been moved into the nearly completed Fort Sumter by Major Robert Anderson, a Kentucky Unionist. South Carolina authorities exploded at this provocative act. Commissioners of the newly "independent" state demanded withdrawal of all federal forces, but they had overplayed their hand. Buchanan sharply rejected the South Carolina ultimatum to withdraw and dispatched a steamer, *Star of the West,* to Fort Sumter with reinforcements and provisions. On January 9, as the ship approached Charleston Harbor, Confederate batteries at Fort Moultrie and Morris Island opened fire and drove it away. It was in fact an act of war, but Buchanan chose to ignore the challenge. He decided instead to hunker down and ride out the remaining weeks of his term, hoping against hope that one of several compromise efforts would yet prove fruitful.

FINAL EFFORTS AT COMPROMISE   Desparate efforts at compromise continued in Congress until dawn on the day of Lincoln's inauguration. On December 18 Senator John J. Crittenden of Kentucky had proposed a series of resolutions that recognized slavery in the territories south of 36°30′ and guaranteed to maintain it where it already existed. The fight for a compromise was carried to the floor of each house of Congress and subjected to intensive but inconclusive debate during January and February.

Meanwhile, a peace conference met in a Washington hotel in February 1861. Twenty-one states sent delegates, and former president John Tyler presided, but the convention's proposal, substantially the same as the Crittenden Compromise, failed to win the support of either house of Congress. The only compromise proposal that met with any success was an amendment guaranteeing slavery where it existed. Many Republicans, including Lincoln, were prepared to go that far to save the Union, but they were unwilling to repudiate their stand against slavery in the territories. As it happened, after passing the House, the amendment passed the Senate without a vote to spare, twenty-four to twelve, on the dawn of inauguration day. It would have become the Thirteenth Amendment, with the first use of the word *slavery* in the Constitution, but the states never ratified it. When a Thirteenth Amendment was ratified in 1865, it did not guarantee slavery—it abolished it.

MAKING CONNECTIONS

- Through the 1850s most of the debate over slavery concerned its expansion into the territories; with Lincoln's Emancipation Proclamation, discussed in the next chapter, the issue would shift to slavery itself.

- Many of the Radical Republicans who designed Reconstruction (Chapter 18) had been anti-slavery Republicans before the war.

- The proposed transcontinental railroad that had brought about the Kansas-Nebraska crisis would finally be completed in 1869 (Chapter 20).

FURTHER READING

The best surveys of the forces and events leading to the Civil War include James M. McPherson's *Battle Cry of Freedom: The Civil War Era* (1988), Stephen B. Oates's *The Approaching Fury: Voices of the Storm, 1820–1861* (1997), and Bruce Levine's *Half Slave and Half Free: The Roots of Civil War* (1992). An excellent narrative of the political debate leading to secession is Michael A. Morrison's *Slavery and the American West: The Eclipse of Manifest Destiny and the Coming of the Civil War* (1997).

Mark J. Stegmaier's *Texas, New Mexico, and the Compromise of 1850: Boundary Dispute and Sectional Crisis* (1996) probes that crucial dispute while Michael F. Holt's *The Political Crisis of the 1850s* (1978) traces the demise of the Whigs. Eric Foner, in *Free Soil, Free Labor, Free Men: The Ideology of the Republican Party before the Civil War* (1970), shows how events and ideas combined in the formation of a new political party. A more straightforward study of the rise of the Republicans is William E. Gienapp's *The Origins of the Republican Party, 1852–1856* (1987). The economic, social, and political crises of 1857 are examined in Kenneth M. Stampp's *America in 1857: A Nation on the Brink* (1990).

Robert W. Johannsen's *Stephen A. Douglas* (1973) analyzes the issue of popular sovereignty. A more national perspective is provided in James A. Rawley's *Race and Politics: "Bleeding Kansas" and the Coming of the Civil War* (1969). On the role of John Brown in the sectional crisis, see Stephen B. Oates's *To Purge This Land with Blood: A Biography of John Brown* (1970). An excellent study on the South's journey to secession is William W. Freehling's *The Road to Disunion: Secessionists at Bay, 1776–1854*, (1990).

On Lincoln's role in the coming crisis of war, see Don E. Fehrenbacher's *Prelude to Greatness: Lincoln in the 1850s* (1962). Harry V. Jaffa's *Crisis of the House Divided: An Interpretation of the Issues in the Lincoln-Douglas Debate* (1959) details the debates, and Maury Klein's *Days of Defiance: Sumter, Secession, and the Coming of the Civil War* (1997) treats the Fort Sumter controversy.

17

THE WAR OF THE UNION

FOCUS QUESTIONS

· What were the major miltary strategies of the Civil War?

· How did the war affect the home front in the North and the South?

· What were the reasons for, and the results of, Lincoln's Emancipation Proclamation?

To answer these questions and access additional review material, please visit www.wwnorton.com/studyspace.

In mid-February 1861 Abraham Lincoln left Springfield, Illinois, and began a long, roundabout rail trip to Washington, D.C. At the end of the journey, reluctantly yielding to warnings of a plot to assassinate him, he secretly passed through Baltimore in the middle of the night and slipped into Washington before daybreak. As Lincoln prepared to take office and the possibility of civil war captured the attention of a divided nation, no one imagined the horrendous scope and intensity of the conflict that was to come. On both sides, people believed that any fighting would be over in little more than a month and that their daily lives would go on as usual.

END OF THE WAITING GAME

LINCOLN AND SECESSION   In his inaugural address on March 4, 1861, Lincoln reassured southerners that he had no intention of interfering with "slavery in the States where it exists." But secession was another matter. He insisted that the "Union of these States is perpetual," and he promised to "hold, occupy, and possess" areas belonging to the federal government. He pledged that the federal government would use force only if attacked, and he concluded with an appeal for harmony, saying: "We are not enemies, but friends. We must not be enemies. Though passion may have strained, it must not break our bonds of affection."

The momentum of secession took control of events, however. The day after the inauguration, word arrived from Charleston that time was running out at the federal garrison at Fort Sumter. The commander, Major Robert Anderson, had enough supplies for only a month, and the fort was surrounded by a Confederate "ring of fire." On April 4 Lincoln decided to resupply Anderson's garrison. Hoping to avoid a confrontation, he informed the governor of South Carolina that he was sending provisions but no guns, ammunition, or soldiers. The Confederate government was not willing to avoid a showdown, however, and it ordered the Confederate general Pierre G. T. Beauregard to demand that his former West Point professor surrender Fort Sumter. Anderson refused, and just before dawn on April 12 Confederate batteries opened fire. After thirty-three hours, Anderson, his ammunition exhausted, surrendered.

The attack on Fort Sumter signaled the end of the tense waiting game. On April 15 Lincoln issued a war proclamation calling upon the loyal states to supply 75,000 militiamen to put down the rebellion. Volunteers in both the North and the South crowded into recruiting stations, and huge new armies began to take shape. On April 19 Lincoln proclaimed a blockade of southern ports, which, as the Supreme Court later ruled, confirmed the existence of a state of war.

TAKING SIDES   Lincoln's war proclamation led four states of the upper South to join the Confederacy: Virginia, Arkansas, Tennessee, and North Carolina. Each had areas (mainly in the mountains) where both slaves and secessionists were scarce and Union sentiment ran strong. In fact, Unionists in western Virginia, bolstered by a Union army from Ohio under General George B. McClellan, formed a new state. In 1863 Congress admitted West Virginia with a state constitution that provided for emancipation of the few slaves there.

Of the other slave states, Delaware remained firmly in the Union, but Maryland, Kentucky, and Missouri went through bitter struggles to decide which side to support. The secession of Maryland would have encircled Washington, D.C., with Confederate states. To hold on to the state, Lincoln took drastic measures: he suspended the writ of habeas corpus (under which judges can require arresting officers to produce their prisoners and justify their arrest) and jailed pro-Confederate leaders. The fall elections ended the threat of Maryland's secession by returning a solidly Unionist majority in the state.

Kentucky, native state of both Abraham Lincoln and Jefferson Davis, harbored divided loyalties. Its fragile neutrality lasted until September 3, 1861, when a Confederate force captured several towns. General Ulysses S. Grant then moved Union troops into Paducah. Thereafter, Kentucky for the most part remained with the Union. It joined the Confederacy, some have said, only after the war.

Robert E. Lee's decision to join the confederacy epitomized the agonizing choice facing many Americans in 1861. Son of a Revolutionary War hero, Lee had graduated second in his class from West Point, had fought with distinction during the Mexican War, and had served in the U.S. Army for thirty years. When Fort Sumter was attacked, he was summoned by Lincoln's seventy-five-year-old general in chief, Winfield Scott, another Virginian, and offered command of the Union forces. After a sleepless night spent pacing the floor, he told Scott he could not go against his "country," meaning Virginia. Although Lee failed to "see the good of secession," he could not "raise my hand against my birthplace, my home, my children." Lee resigned his commission, retired to his estate, and soon answered a call to command the Virginia—later the Confederate—military forces.

On the other hand many southerners made great sacrifices to remain loyal to the Union. Some left their native region once the fighting began. Others who remained in the South found ways to support the Union. In every Confederate state except South Carolina, whole regiments were organized to fight for the Union, and at least 100,000 men from the southern states fought against the Confederacy. Many of the southern loyalists were Irish or German immigrants who had no love for slavery or the planter elite. Whatever their motives, they and other southern loyalists played a significant role in helping the Union cause.

NORTHERN AND SOUTHERN ADVANTAGES   The South seceded in part out of a growing awareness of its minority status in the nation: a balance sheet of the sections in 1861 shows the accuracy of that perception.

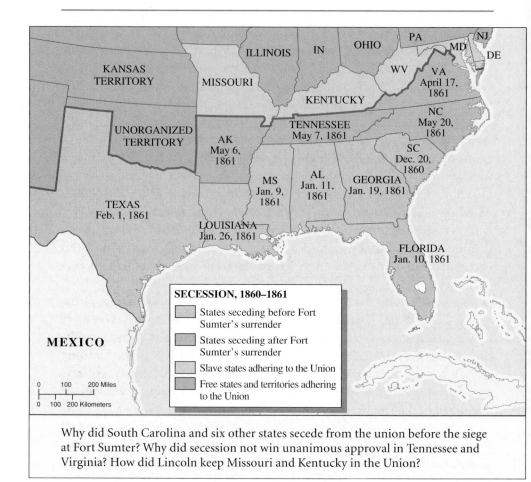

Why did South Carolina and six other states secede from the union before the siege at Fort Sumter? Why did secession not win unanimous approval in Tennessee and Virginia? How did Lincoln keep Missouri and Kentucky in the Union?

The Union held twenty-three states, including four border slave states, while the Confederacy had eleven. The population count was about 22 million in the Union to 9 million in the Confederacy, and about 4 million of the latter were enslaved. The Union therefore had an edge of about four to one in potential human resources. To help redress the imbalance, the Confederacy mobilized 80 percent or more of its military-age white, men, one third of whom would die during the prolonged war.

An even greater advantage for the North was its industry. The states that joined the Confederacy produced just 7 percent of the nation's manufactures on the eve of the war. The Union states produced 97 percent of the firearms and 96 percent of the railroad equipment. They had most of the trained mechanics and engineers, most of the shipping and mercantile firms, and the bulk of the banking and financial resources. The North's advantage in transportation weighed heavily as the war went on. The Union had more wagons, horses, and ships than the Confederacy and an impressive edge in railroads.

The South had the advantage of geography: the Confederates could fight a defensive war on their own territory. In addition, the South initially had more experienced military leaders. A number of circumstances had given rise to a strong military tradition in the South: the frequent skirmishes with Indians, the fear of slave insurrection, and a history of territorial expansion. Military careers had prestige, and military schools multiplied in the antebellum years, the most notable West Points of the South being the Citadel and Virginia Military Institute. West Point itself had drawn many southerners, producing a cadre of officers dominated by men from the region. By the end of the war, however, the Union had developed the better commanders.

BULL RUN   Caught up in the frothy excitement of military preparation, both sides predicted quick victory. Nowhere was this naive optimism more clearly displayed than at the First Battle of Bull Run (or Manassas).*An impatient public pressured both sides to strike quickly. Jefferson Davis allowed the battle-hungry General Pierre G. T. Beauregard to hurry the main Confederate army to Manassas Junction, Virginia, about twenty-five miles west of Washington. Lincoln decided that General Irvin McDowell's hastily assembled Union army of some 37,000 might overrun the outnumbered Confederates and quickly march on to Richmond, Virginia, the Confederate capital. With buoyant assumptions of victory, Johnny Reb and Billy Yank breezily stumbled into an entangling web of horror. The mood was so breezy, in fact, that hundreds of civilians had ridden out from Washington to picnic and watch the entertaining spectacle of what they thought would be a one-battle war. Instead, they witnessed a chaotic defeat.

It was a dry summer day on July 21, 1861, when General McDowell's raw recruits encountered Beauregard's army dug in behind a meandering, log-strewn little stream called Bull Run. The two generals, former classmates at West Point, adopted markedly similar plans: each would try to turn the other's left flank. The Union forces almost achieved their purpose early in the afternoon, but Confederate reinforcements, led by General Joseph E. Johnston, poured in to check the Union offensive. Amid the fury a South Carolina general rallied his men by pointing to Thomas Jackson's brigade of

---

*The Union most often named battles for natural features; the Confederacy, for nearby towns—thus Bull Run (Manassas), Antietam (Sharpsburg), Stons River (Murfresboro), and the like.

Union Soldiers at Harpers Ferry, Virginia, in 1862

Neither side in the Civil War was prepared for the magnitude of this first "modern" war.

Virginians: "Look at Jackson standing there like a damned stone wall." The analogy captured Jackson's fortitude, and the general was called Stonewall thereafter.

Their attack blunted, the exhausted northern troops eventually broke, and their frantic retreat turned into a panic as fleeing soldiers and terrified civilians clogged the Washington road. Lincoln read a gloomy dispatch from the front: "The day is lost. Save Washington and the remnants of this army. The routed troops will not re-form." Stonewall Jackson had hoped to pursue the fleeing Union troops into Washington. But the Confederates were almost as disorganized and exhausted as the Yankees, and they failed to give chase. It would have been futile anyway, for the next day a summer downpour turned roads into quagmires. The Battle of Bull Run was a sobering experience for both sides. Much of the romance—the splendid uniforms, bright flags, fervent songs—gave way to the agonizing realization that this would be a long, costly struggle.

THE WAR'S EARLY PHASE

The Battle of Bull Run demonstrated that the war would not be decided with one sudden stroke. General Winfield Scott had predicted as much, and now Lincoln fell back upon the three-pronged "anaconda" strategy that Scott had proposed. It called first for the Army of the Potomac to defend Washington D.C., and exert constant pressure on the Confederate capital at Richmond. At the same time the navy would blockade the southern coast and dry up the Confederacy's access to foreign goods and weapons. The final component of the plan would divide the Confederacy by sending navy gunboats and transports to invade the South along the main water routes: the Mississippi, Tennessee, and Cumberland rivers. While newspapers derided the anaconda strategy as far too slow, indicative of General Scott's old age and caution, it was intended to entwine and crush the southern resistance.

The Confederate strategy was simpler. If the Union forces could be stalemated, Jefferson Davis and others hoped, then the British or the French might be persuaded to join their cause, or perhaps public sentiment in the North would force Lincoln to seek a negotiated settlement. So at the same time that armies were forming in the South, Confederate diplomats were seeking assistance in London and Paris, and Confederate sympathizers in the North were urging an end to the North's war effort.

NAVAL ACTIONS   After the Battle of Bull Run and for the rest of 1861 and early 1862, the most important military actions involved naval war and a Union blockade of key southern ports. The Union navy never completely sealed off the South, but it greatly constricted the flow of goods and supplies into the region. The one great threat to the Union navy proved to be short-lived. The Confederates in Norfolk, Virginia, had fashioned an ironclad ship from an abandoned Union steam frigate, the *Merrimack*. Rechristened the *Virginia*, it ventured out on March 8, 1862, and wrought havoc among the Union ships at the entrance to Chesapeake Bay. But as luck would have it, a new Union ironclad, the *Monitor*, arrived from New York in time to engage the *Virginia* on the next day. They fought to a draw, and the *Virginia* returned to port, where the Confederates destroyed it when they had to give up Norfolk soon afterward. Thereafter the North tightened its grip on the South. The navy extended its bases down the Carolina coast in the late summer and fall of 1862. In the spring of 1862, Admiral David Farragut's ships forced open the lower Mississippi River and captured New Orleans and took Baton Rouge upriver.

FORMING ARMIES   While the Union navy was blockading southern ports and building new ships, the armies on both sides were recruiting men to form regiments to fight the land battles of the war. After Lincoln's initial

The U.S. Army Recruiting Office in City Hall Park, New York City

The sign advertises the money offered those willing to serve: $677 to new recruits, $777 to veteran soldiers, and $15 to anyone who brought in a recruit.

call for 75,000 ninety-day militiamen, Congress enlisted 500,000 more men, and after the Battle of Bull Run it added another 500,000. The typical nineteenth-century army often organized its units along community and ethnic lines. The Union army, for example, included a Scandinavian regiment (the 15th Wisconsin Infantry), a Highland Scots unit (the 79th New York Infantry), a French regiment (the 55th New York Infantry), and a mixed unit of Poles, Hungarians, Germans, Spaniards, and Italians (the 39th New York Infantry).

In the Confederacy, Jefferson Davis initially requested 100,000 twelve-month volunteers. Once the fighting started, he was authorized to raise up to 400,000 three-year volunteers. By early 1862 most of the veteran Confederate soldiers were nearing the end of their enlistment without having encountered much significant action. They were also resisting the incentives of bonuses and furloughs for reenlistment. The Confederate government then turned to conscription. On April 16, 1862, all white male citizens aged eighteen to thirty-five were declared members of the army for three years, and those already in service were required to serve out three years. In 1862 the upper age was raised to forty-five, and in 1864 the age limit was further extended from seventeen to fifty, with those under eighteen and over forty-five reserved for state defense.

The conscription law included two loopholes, however. First, a draftee might escape service either by providing an able-bodied substitute not of draft age or by paying $500 in cash. Second, exemptions, designed to protect key civilian work, were subject to abuse by men seeking "bombproof" jobs. The exemption of one white man for each plantation with twenty or more slaves led to bitter complaints about "a rich man's war and a poor man's fight."

The Union took nearly another year to begin drafting men into service. In 1863 the government began to draft men aged twenty to forty-five. Exemptions were granted to specified federal and state officeholders and to others on medical or compassionate grounds. By paying $300 one could avoid service. Conscription spurred men to volunteer, either to collect bounties or to avoid the disgrace of being drafted.

The Civil War draft flouted an American tradition of voluntary service and was widely held to be arbitrary and unconstitutional. Widespread public opposition impeded its enforcement in the North and the South. In New York City the announcement of a draft lottery on July 11, 1863, incited a week of rioting in which roving bands of working-class toughs took control of the streets. Although provoked by opposition to the draft, the riots exposed racial and ethnic tensions. The mobs, mostly Irish Catholic immigrants, set upon conscription offices, factories, docks, and the homes of prominent Republicans. But they directed their wrath most furiously at African Americans. They blamed blacks for causing the war and for threatening to take their own unskilled jobs. Over 100 people died before soldiers brought from Gettysburg restored order.

CONFEDERATE DIPLOMACY While the Union and Confederate armies mobilized, Confederated diplomacy focused on gaining help from foreign governments in the form of supplies, formal recognition, and perhaps even armed intervention. The Confederates indulged the unrealistic hope that official foreign recognition would prove decisive, when in fact it more likely would have followed a decisive victory in the field, which never came.

The first Confederate emissaries to England and France took hope when the British foreign minister received them informally after their arrival in London in 1861. In Paris, Napoléon III even promised them that he would recognize the Confederacy if Britain would lead the way. When the agents returned to London, however, the government refused to see them, partly because of Union pressure and partly out of British self-interest.

Confederate negotiators were far more successful at getting European supplies than gaining official recognition as a new nation. The most spectacular feat was the procurement of raiding ships. Although British law prohibited the sale of warships to belligerents, a southern agent was able to have ships built in Britain and then, on trial runs, escape to be outfitted with guns. In all, eighteen such ships were activated and saw action in the Atlantic, Pacific, and Indian oceans, where they sank hundreds of Union ships and instilled terror in the rest.

THE WEST AND THE CIVIL WAR During the Civil War western settlement continued. New discoveries of gold and silver along the eastern slopes of the Sierra Nevadas and in Montana and Colorado lured thousands of prospectors and their suppliers. Dakota, Colorado, and Nevada gained territorial status in 1861, Idaho and Arizona in 1863, and Montana in 1864. Silver-rich Nevada gained its statehood in 1864.

With the firing on Fort Sumter, many of the regular army units assigned to frontier outposts in the West began to head east to meet the Confederate threat. In Texas, the Indian Territory (Oklahoma), and southern New Mexico, Union soldiers left altogether. Elsewhere they left behind skeleton units. Texas was the only western state to join the Confederacy. For the most part, the federal government maintained its control of the other western territories during the war.

The most intense fighting in the West during the war occurred along the Kansas-Missouri border. There the disputes between the pro-slavery and anti-slavery settlers of the 1850s turned into brutal guerrilla warfare. The most prominent pro-Confederate leader in the area was William Quantrill. He and his pro-slavery followers, mostly teenagers, fought under a black flag, meaning that they gave no quarter. In destroying Lawrence, Kansas, in 1863, Quantrill ordered his forces to "kill every male and burn every house." By the end of the day, 182 boys and men had been killed. Their opponents, the Jayhawkers, responded in kind. They tortured and hanged pro-Confederate prisoners, burned houses, and destroyed livestock.

Many Indian tribes found themselves caught up in the war. Indian regiments fought on both sides, and in the Indian Territory they fought against each other. Indians among the "Five Civilized Tribes" held African-American slaves and felt a natural bond with southern whites. Oklahoma's proximity to Texas influenced the Choctaws and Chickasaws to support the Confederacy. The Cherokees, Creeks, and Seminoles were more divided in their loyalties.

ACTIONS IN THE WESTERN THEATER Little military activity happened in the eastern theater (east of the Appalachian Mountains) before

May 1862. The western theater (from the mountains to the Mississippi River), on the other hand, flared up with several clashes and an important penetration of the Confederate states. In western Kentucky the Confederate general Albert Sidney Johnston, a strapping Texan whom Davis considered the South's best general, had perhaps 40,000 men stretched over some 150 miles.

Early in 1862 General Ulysses S. Grant made the first Union thrust against the weak center of Johnston's overextended lines. Grant had graduated from West Point in the lower half of his class and in 1854 had resigned from the army in disgrace for drunkenness. Volunteering to serve in the Union army in 1861, he was assigned as an officer in the western theater. Moving out of Cairo, Illinois, and Paducah, Kentucky, with a gunboat flotilla, Grant swung southward up the Tennessee River and captured Fort Henry on February 6. He then moved overland to attack Fort Donelson and on February 16 captured its 12,000 men. Grant's blunt demand of "immediate and unconditional surrender" and his quick success sent a thrill through the dispirited North. The short, slouching, disheveled Grant was now a national hero—but not for long.

SHILOH   After defeats in Kentucky and Tennessee, General Johnston regrouped the Confederate forces in Corinth, Mississippi, in hopes of retaking control of the Mississippi River valley. As Grant moved his forces southward along the Tennessee River during the early spring of 1862, he made a costly mistake. While planning his attack on Corinth, he clumsily placed his troops on a rolling plateau between two creeks and failed to dig defensive trenches. Johnston shrewdly recognized Grant's oversight, and on the morning of April 6 the Confederate leader ordered an attack on the vulnerable Union soldiers.

The 44,000 Confederates struck suddenly at Shiloh, the site of a log church in the center of the Union camp in southwestern Tennessee. They found most of Grant's troops still sleeping or eating breakfast. Some died in their bedrolls. After a day of bloody carnage and confusion, Grant's men were pinned against the river. They may well have been annihilated had General Johnston not been mortally wounded at the peak of the battle; his second in command called off the attack. Grant and a brilliant general from Ohio, William Tecumseh Sherman, rallied their troops. Reinforcements arrived that night during a torrential rainstorm, and the next day Grant took the offensive. The Confederates glumly withdrew to Corinth, leaving the Union army too battered to pursue. Throughout the Civil War winning armies would fail to pursue their retreating foe, thus allowing the wounded opponent to slip away and fight again.

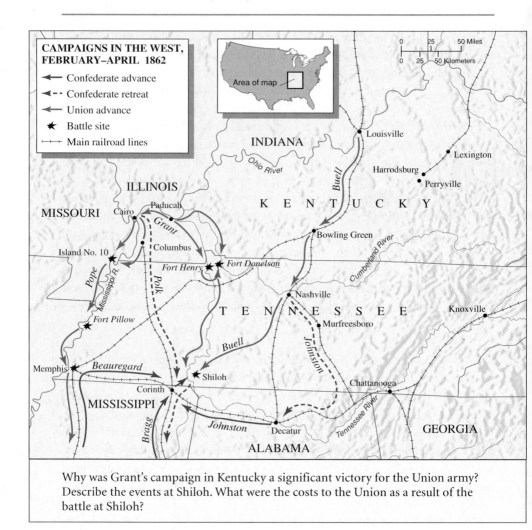

CAMPAIGNS IN THE WEST, FEBRUARY–APRIL 1862

← Confederate advance
◄- - Confederate retreat
← Union advance
★ Battle site
⊢⊢⊢ Main railroad lines

Area of map

0 · 25 · 50 Miles
0 · 25 · 50 Kilometers

INDIANA

Ohio River

Louisville

Lexington

ILLINOIS

Harrodsburg

Perryville

MISSOURI · Cairo · Paducah

K E N T U C K Y

Buell

Grant

Columbus

Bowling Green

Cumberland River

Island No. 10

Pope

Mississippi R.

Polk

Fort Henry · Fort Donelson

Nashville

Knoxville

T E N N E S S E E

Fort Pillow

Murfreesboro

Johnston

Buell

Memphis · Beauregard

Shiloh

Chattanooga

Corinth

MISSISSIPPI

Bragg

Johnston · Decatur

Tennessee River

GEORGIA

ALABAMA

Why was Grant's campaign in Kentucky a significant victory for the Union army? Describe the events at Shiloh. What were the costs to the Union as a result of the battle at Shiloh?

Shiloh, a Hebrew word meaning "Place of Peace," was the costliest battle in American history up to that point, although worse was to come. Combined casualties of nearly 20,000 exceeded the total dead and wounded of the Revolution, the War of 1812, and the Mexican War. After Shiloh, Confederate and Union leaders realized there would not be a quick end to the war. Moreover, after this battle the Union lost for a while the leadership of its finest general. Grant had blundered badly. Some critics charged that he had been drinking and called upon Lincoln to replace him. But the president, faced with the dithering of his other generals (especially George McClellan in the eastern theater), declined: "I can't spare this man; he fights." Grant's superior, General Henry Halleck, was not as forgiving, however. He relieved Grant of his command for several months, and as a result the Union thrust southward ground to a halt.

MCCLELLAN'S PENINSULAR CAMPAIGN   The eastern theater remained fairly quiet for nine months after Bull Run. After the Union defeat, Lincoln had replaced McDowell with the brilliant if theatrical and hesitant general George B. McClellan, Stonewall Jackson's classmate at West Point. As head of the Army of the Potomac, McClellan instituted a rigid training regimen, determined to build a powerful force that would be ready for its next battle. When General Winfield Scott retired in November 1861, McClellan became general in chief. On the surface, McClellan exuded confidence and poise, but his innate caution would prove crippling. Fearing failure, McClellan procrastinated as long as possible to avoid meeting the enemy in battle. After nine months of agonizing preparation, Lincoln and much of the public had grown impatient. The exasperated president finally ordered McClellan to begin moving by Washington's Birthday, February 22, 1862. McClellan brashly predicted, "I will be in Richmond in ten days."

In mid-March 1862, McClellan's army finally embarked, and before the end of May his advance units sighted the church steeples in Richmond. Thousands fled the city in panic, and President Jefferson Davis sent his family to a safe haven. But McClellan failed to capitalize on his situation. On May 31 the Confederate general Joseph E. Johnston struck at the Union forces, which were isolated by floodwaters on the south bank of the Chickahominy River. In the Battle of Seven Pines (Fair Oaks), only the arrival of reinforcements prevented a disastrous Union defeat. Both sides took heavy casualties, and Johnston was severely wounded.

At this point the fifty-five-year-old Robert E. Lee assumed command of the Army of Northern Virginia, changing the course of the war. Tall, erect, and broad shouldered, Lee was a slashing, daring leader. Unlike Johnston he enjoyed Jefferson Davis's trust and assembled a galaxy of superb field commanders: Stonewall Jackson, James Longstreet, D. H. Hill, Ambrose P. Hill, and J.E.B. Stuart.

Once in command, Lee assaulted the Union forces east of Richmond on June 26, 1862. But heavy losses prevented the Confederates from sustaining their momentum. Lee launched a final desperate attack at Malvern Hill (July 1), where the Confederates were riddled by artillery. As D. H. Hill observed, "It was not war, it was murder." This week of intense fighting, lumped together as the Seven Days Battles, failed to dislodge the Union forces.

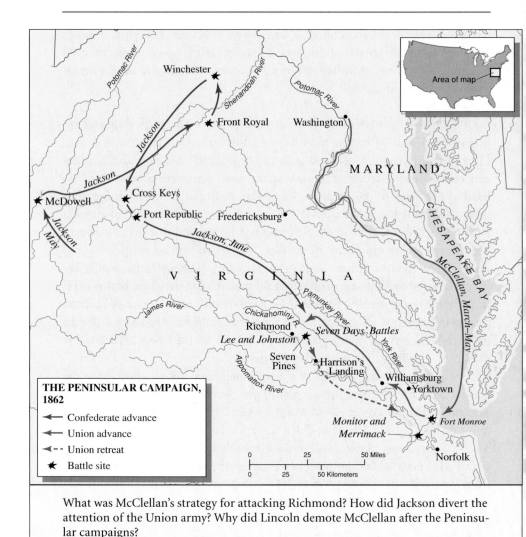

THE PENINSULAR CAMPAIGN, 1862

← Confederate advance

← Union advance

◄-- Union retreat

✳ Battle site

What was McClellan's strategy for attacking Richmond? How did Jackson divert the attention of the Union army? Why did Lincoln demote McClellan after the Peninsular campaigns?

On July 9 Lincoln visited the front, where McClellan lectured him on the correct strategy. Such insubordination was ample reason to remove the cocky general, but Lincoln recognized that doing so would demoralize the soldiers, who were still intensely loyal to McClellan. Instead, Lincoln returned to Washington and on July 11 called Henry Halleck from the west to take charge as general in chief, a post that McClellan had temporarily vacated. Thus began what would become Lincoln's frustrating search for a capable and consistent military leader.

SECOND BULL RUN   Lincoln and Halleck ordered McClellan to join forces with the bombastic John Pope for a new assault against Richmond from the north. Lee decided to attack Pope's army before the Union forces could be joined. At Cedar Mountain, Stonewall Jackson pushed back an advance party of Union troops and then seized supplies and destroyed the Union supply base at Manassas Junction.

At the Second Battle of Bull Run (or Manassas), fought on almost the same site as the earlier battle, the Confederates thoroughly confused Pope. J.E.B. Stuart's horsemen raided his headquarters, taking Pope's dress uniform and strategy book, which outlined the position of his units. Pope then exhausted his own men as he frantically tried to find the elusive Jackson. By the time they made contact with what they thought were only Jackson's forces, Lee's main army had joined in.

The trap was baited, and the Union army was lured in. On August 30, 1862, as Pope's troops engaged Jackson's line, James Longstreet's corps of 30,000 Confederates, screaming the Rebel yell "like demons emerging from the earth," drove the Union forces from the field. One New York regiment lost 124 of its 490 men, the highest percentage of deaths in any battle of the war. In the next few days the whipped Union forces pulled back to the fortifications around Washington, where McClellan once again took command and reorganized. He displayed his unflagging egotism in a letter to his wife: "Again I have been called upon to save the country." The disgraced Pope was dispatched to Minnesota to fight in the Indian wars.

ANTIETAM   Still on the offensive, Lee determined to move the battlefield out of the South and perhaps thereby gain foreign recognition of the Confederacy as a new nation. In September 1862 he led his troops into western Maryland and headed for Pennsylvania. As luck would have it, however, Lee's bold strategy was uncovered when a Union soldier picked up a bundle of cigars and discovered a secret order from Lee wrapped around them. The paper revealed that Lee had again divided his army, sending Jackson off to take Harpers Ferry, West Virginia.

McClellan boasted upon seeing the captured document, "Here is a paper with which, if I cannot whip Bobby Lee, I will be willing to go home." But instead of leaping at his unexpected opportunity, he delayed for sixteen crucial hours, still worried—as always—about enemy strength, and Lee was thereby able to reassemble most of his tired army behind Antietam Creek. Still, McClellan was optimistic, and Lincoln, too, relished the chance for a truly decisive blow. "God bless you and all with you," he wired McClellan. "Destroy the rebel army if possible."

In the midst of this second-guessing and carping, the deeper currents of the war were in fact turning in favor of the Union: in the lengthening war the Union's superior resources began to tell on the morale of the Confederacy. In both the eastern and the western theaters the Confederate counterattack had been repulsed. And while the armies clashed, Lincoln, by the stroke of a pen, changed the conflict from a war to restore the Union into a revolutionary struggle for the abolition of slavery: on January 1, 1863, he signed the Emancipation Proclamation.

EMANCIPATION

The Emancipation Proclamation was the product of long and painful deliberation, as opinion was divided even in the North as to whether all slaves should be freed. A deep-seated racial prejudice in the North had prevented the formation of a unified position. While most abolitionists favored both complete emancipation and social integration of the races, many anti-slavery activists wanted to prohibit slavery only in new territories and states. They were willing to allow slavery to continue in the South in order to avoid racial integration.

Lincoln had insisted that the purpose of the conflict was to restore the Union and that he did not have the authority to free the slaves. Yet the expanding war forced the issue. Fugitive slaves had begun to turn up in Union army camps, and generals did not know whether to declare them free. Some generals put the "contrabands" to work building fortifications; others liberated those slaves who had been held by Confederate owners, thus running the risk of upsetting border-state slaveholders. Lincoln himself edged toward emancipation.

As the war continued, Lincoln eventually concluded that complete emancipation was required for several reasons: slave labor was bolstering the Confederate cause, sagging morale in the North needed the boost of a transcendent moral ideal, and public opinion was swinging that way. Proclaiming a war on slavery, moreover, would end forever any chance that France or Britain would support the Confederacy.

The time to act came after the Battle of Antietam. On September 22, 1862, Lincoln issued a preliminary Emancipation Proclamation, warning that on January 1, 1863, all slaves in Confederate states or in areas still under active rebellion would be "thenceforward and forever free." The Emancipation Proclamation, with few exceptions, freed only those slaves still under Confederate control, as cynics noted then and later. But critics missed a point that slaves readily grasped. "In a document proclaiming liberty," wrote an African-Americans historian, "the unfree never bother to read the fine print."

Two Views of the Emancipation Proclamation

The Union view (top) shows a thoughtful Lincoln composing the proclamation, the Constitution and the Holy Bible in his lap. The Confederate view (bottom) shows a demented Lincoln, his foot on the Constitution and his inkwell held by the devil.

BLACKS IN THE MILITARY   Lincoln's Emancipation Proclamation reaffirmed the policy that African Americans could enroll in the armed services and sparked efforts to organize all-black military units. The War Department authorized general recruitment of blacks all over the country, thus making more concrete Lincoln's transformation of a war to preserve the Union into a revolution to overthrow the social, economic, and racial status quo in the South. The first challenge for black troops, however, was to overcome embedded racial fears of northern whites and to prove themselves in battle. By mid-1863 African-American soldiers were finally involved in significant combat in both the eastern and western theaters. Lincoln reported that several of his commanders believed that "the use of colored troops constitutes the heaviest blow yet dealt to the rebels."

Altogether almost 180,000 African Americans served in the Union army, around 10 percent of the total. Some 38,000 gave their lives. Blacks accounted for about one fourth of all enlistments in the navy, and of those almost 3,000 died. As the war entered its final months, freedom emerged more fully as a legal reality. The Thirteenth Amendment, which abolished slavery, was ratified by three fourths of the reunited states and became part of the Constitution on December 18, 1865, thus removing any lingering doubts about the legality of emancipation. By then, in fact, slavery remained only in the border states of Kentucky and Delaware.

WOMEN AND THE WAR

While breaking the bonds of slavery, the Civil War also loosened traditional restraints on female activity. Women on both sides played prominent roles in the conflict. Initially the call to arms revived heroic images of female self-sacrifice and domesticity. Women in the North and the South sewed uniforms, composed uplifting poems and songs, and raised money and supplies. Thousands of northern women worked with the U.S. Sanitary Commission, which organized medical relief and other services for soldiers. Others supported the freedmen's aid movement to help impoverished freed slaves.

In the North alone some 20,000 women served as nurses or other health-related volunteers. The most famous nurses were Dorothea Dix and Clara Barton, both untiring volunteers in service to the wounded and dying. Dix, the veteran reformer of the nation's insane asylums, became the Union army's first superintendent of women nurses. Barton was a schoolteacher and then one of the nation's first female patent clerks, but she remained frustrated by her desire to find "something to do that *was* something." She discovered fulfilling work at last as a nurse in the Civil War. Instead of accepting an assignment to a general hospital, she followed the troops on her own, working in makeshift field hospitals. At Antietam she came so close to the fighting that as she worked on a wounded soldier, a Confederate bullet ripped through the sleeve of her dress and killed the man.

The departure of hundreds of thousands of men for the battlefield forced women to assume the public and private roles the men left behind. In many southern towns and counties the home front became a world of white women, children, and slaves. But not all women willingly accepted the new roles required by the war. Many among the slaveholding elite found themselves woefully unprepared: they could not cook, sew, or knit, and they balked at the idea of daily chores.

Women in the North and the South found themselves farmers or plantation managers, clerks, munitions-plant workers, and schoolteachers. Some 400 women disguised themselves as men and fought in the war; dozens served as spies; others traveled with the armies, cooking meals and writing letters, and assisting with amputations. The number of widows, spinsters, and orphans mushroomed. Many bereaved women on both sides came to look on the war with what the poet Emily Dickinson called a "chastened stare."

GOVERNMENT DURING THE WAR

Freeing 4 million slaves and loosening the restraints on female activity constituted a monumental social and economic revolution. But an even broader revolution developed as political power shifted from South to North. Before the war southern congressmen exercised a great deal of influence. Once the secessionists had abandoned Congress to the Republicans, however, dramatic change occurred. Without congressional opposition from the South, Republicans were able to pass a new protective tariff, approve a transcontinental railroad that would run through Omaha, Nebraska, to Sacramento, California, and enact a homestead act, which granted free homesteads of 160 acres to settlers who occupied the land for five years—all acts that had been stalled by sectional controversy and were adopted before the end of 1862. That year also saw the passage of the Morrill Land Grant

Act, which provided federal aid to state colleges focused on the "agricultural and mechanic arts." The National Banking Act, which created a uniform system of banking and bank-note currency, followed in 1863 and helped the Union address a critical problem: how to finance the war.

UNION FINANCES   Congress had three options for solving the problem of financing the war: raising taxes, printing paper money, and borrowing. The taxes came chiefly in the form of the Morrill Tariff and excise taxes on manufacturers and nearly every profession. A butcher, for example, had to pay 30¢ for every head of beef he slaughtered, 10¢ for every hog, 5¢ for every sheep. An income tax rounded out the revenue measures.

But federal tax revenues trickled in so slowly that Congress in 1862 ordered the printing of paper money. Eventually $450 million in greenbacks was printed, enough to pay the bills without unleashing the kind of runaway inflation that burdened the Confederacy after Jefferson Davis allowed the unlimited issue of paper money. The congressional decision to allow the Treasury to print paper money was a profoundly important development for the U.S. economy, then and since. Unlike previous paper currencies issued by local banks, the federal greenbacks could not be exchanged for gold or silver. Instead, their value relied upon public trust in the government. Many bankers were outraged by the advent of the greenbacks. "Gold and silver are the only true measure of value," one financier declared. "These metals were prepared by the Almighty." But the crisis of the Union and the desperate need to finance the expanding war demanded such a solution.

Still, paper money and taxes provided only about two thirds of the money that financed the war. The rest came chiefly from the sale of bonds. A Philadelphia banker named Jay Cooke mobilized a nationwide network of agents and propaganda for the sale of government war bonds. It worked well, and over $2 billion was raised in the process.

CONFEDERATE FINANCES   Confederate finances were a disaster from the start. Tariffs were tried, but imports were low and therefore raised little revenue. In 1863 the Confederate Congress passed a measure that, like the Union's excises, taxed nearly everything. A 10 percent tax on all agricultural products did more to outrage farmers and planters than to supply the army. Enforcement was so lax and evasion so easy that the taxes produced only negligible income. The last resort, printing paper money, was in fact resorted to early. Beginning in 1861, the new Confederate government began an extended inflationary binge. Altogether the Confederacy turned out more than $1 billion in paper money, creating a dramatic spike in prices. By 1864 a wild turkey sold in a Richmond market for $100, flour went for $425 a barrel, and bacon for $10 a pound. Those living on a fixed income were caught in a merciless inflationary squeeze.

UNION POLITICS AND CIVIL LIBERTIES   On the home fronts during the Civil War, there was no moratorium on partisan politics, northern or southern. Within his own party, Lincoln faced a Radical wing composed mainly of prewar abolitionists. The so-called Radical Republicans formed a Joint Committee on the Conduct of the War, which increasingly pressured Lincoln to emancipate the slaves, confiscate southern plantations, and prosecute the war more vigorously. The majority of Republicans, however, supported the president, and the party was virtually united on economic matters.

The Democratic party suffered the loss of its southern wing as well as the death of its leader, Stephen A. Douglas, in June 1861. By and large northern Democrats supported a war for the Union "as it was" before 1860, giving reluctant support to Lincoln's policies but opposing wartime constraints on civil liberties and the new economic legislation. "War Democrats," such as Senator Andrew Johnson from Tennessee and Secretary of War Edwin Stanton, fully supported Lincoln's policies, while a peace wing of the party preferred a negotiated end to the fighting, even if that meant risking the Union. An extreme fringe among the peace Democrats flirted with outright disloyalty. The Copperheads, as they were called, were strongest in Ohio, Indiana, and Illinois, states with many transplanted southerners, some of whom were pro-Confederate.

Such open sympathy for the enemy spurred Lincoln to crack down hard. Early in the war he assumed certain emergency powers, such as the suspension of the writ of habeas corpus, which guarantees arrested citizens a speedy hearing. When critics charged that this violated the Constitution, Lincoln's congressional supporters pushed through the Habeas Corpus Act of 1863, which authorized the suspension of the writ. Some 14,000 Confederate sympathizers were arrested under the terms of the act.

In the midterm elections of 1862, the Democrats exploited growing war-weariness and resentment of Lincoln's war measures to gain a startling recovery, though not control of Congress. When asked his reaction to the election results, Lincoln replied that he felt somewhat "like the boy in Kentucky who stubbed his toe while running to see his sweetheart. The boy said he was too big to cry, and far too badly hurt to laugh." In fact the political climate left Lincoln increasingly perplexed as time passed.

At their 1864 national convention the Democrats called for an immediate armistice and named General George McClellan as their candidate, but he distanced himself from the peace platform by declaring that the two sides must agree on the terms of reunion before the fighting could stop. Radical Republicans, who still regarded Lincoln as too soft on the traitorous southerners, tried to thwart his renomination, but Lincoln outmaneuvered them at every turn. In a shrewd move he named as his vice-presidential running mate Andrew Johnson, a "war Democrat" from Tennessee, and called the two of them the National Union ticket to minimize partisanship. As the war ground on through 1864, with Grant's army taking heavy losses in Virginia, Lincoln fully expected to lose the election, but key military victories in August and September turned the tide. McClellan carried only New Jersey, Delaware, and Kentucky.

Abraham's Dream

This cartoon depicts Lincoln having a nightmare about the election of 1864. Lady Liberty brandishes the severed head of a black man at the door of the White House as General McClellan walks up the steps and Lincoln runs away.

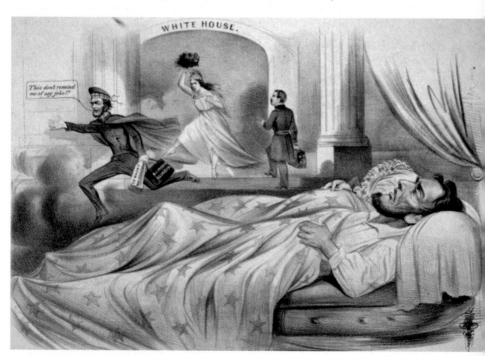

CONFEDERATE POLITICS   Unlike Lincoln, Jefferson Davis never had to face a presidential contest. He and his vice president, Alexander Stephens, were elected for a six-year term. But discontent flourished in the South as food grew scarce and prices skyrocketed. Starving women set off riots from Richmond to Mobile. A bread riot in Richmond in 1863, for example, ended only when Jefferson Davis threatened to shoot the demonstrators. After the Confederate congressional elections of 1863, about one third of the legislators were openly hostile toward the Davis administration. Although parties as such did not figure in the elections, it was noteworthy that many ex-Whigs and other opponents of secession were chosen.

Davis, like Lincoln, had to contend with dissenters. Especially troublesome were supporters of states' rights and secession who steadfastly opposed the centralizing tendencies of the Confederate government in Richmond. Georgia and North Carolina were strongholds of such sentiment. The states' rights champions challenged, among other things, the legality of conscription, taxes on farm produce, and above all the suspension of habeas corpus. Vice President Alexander Stephens himself carried on a running battle with Davis, accusing the president of trying to establish a "military despotism."

The internal bickering did not alone cause the Confederacy's defeat, but it certainly contributed to it. Whereas Lincoln was the consummate pragmatist, Davis was a brittle dogmatist with a waspish temper. Once he made a decision, nothing could change his mind. Nor could Davis ever admit a mistake. Such a personality was ill suited to serve as the chief executive of an infant nation.

THE CIVIL WAR AND THE ENVIRONMENT   Wars not only kill and maim people; they also transform the environment. While almost 750,000 soldiers died of wounds, disease, or accidents, equally appalling numbers of animals, especially horses and mules but also cattle and pigs, were killed in battle or for food. During the final year of the war, nearly 500 horses a day died of shell fire, starvation, overwork, or disease. Pork was the staple of the southern diet before the Civil War, and the region produced enough hogs to feed itself. After the war, however, the southern hog population was so devastated that the region had to import pigs and pork from the Midwest. Because midwestern hogs were bred for weight, their high fat content contributed to higher rates of heart disease and stroke in the postwar South.

Fighting during the Civil War also destroyed much of the Southern landscape. In 1864 a Confederate major wrote that near Chickamauga, Georgia,

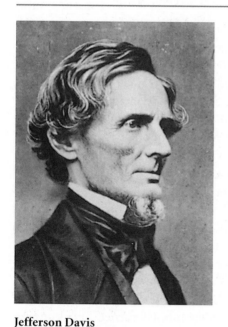

Jefferson Davis

President of the Confederacy.

just south of Chattanooga, Tennessee, the road was "covered with the skeletons of horses, and every tree bears the mark of battle. Many strong trunks were broken down by artillery fire." Hundreds of bridges and levees were also destroyed during the war, as were endless miles of fences, which foraging soldiers used for firewood. The loss of levees caused massive flooding; the loss of fencing meant that much of the postwar South would revert to open-range grazing. Craters gouged out by cannonballs pockmarked the landscape and provided breeding grounds for mosquitoes. The loss of so many animals meant that the mosquitoes focused on humans for their blood meal, thus increasing the spread of malaria. Hundreds of miles of trenches dug for military defense scarred the land and accelerated erosion. All told, the environment was as much a victim of the warfare as were the soldiers, and it would take years to heal nature's wounds across the South.

THE FALTERING CONFEDERACY

After the Union disaster at Fredericksburg, Lincoln's frustrating search for a capable general turned to one of Burnside's disgruntled lieutenants, Joseph Hooker, a handsome, ruddy-faced, hard-drinking character whose pugnacity had earned him the nickname Fighting Joe. But he was no more able to deliver the goods than Burnside.

CHANCELLORSVILLE With a force of 130,000 men, the largest Union army yet gathered, and a brilliant plan, Hooker failed his leadership test at Chancellorsville, Virginia, on May 1–5, 1863. Robert E. Lee, with perhaps half that number of troops, staged a textbook classic of daring and maneuver. Hooker's plan was to leave his base, opposite Fredericksburg, on a sweeping movement upstream across the Rappahannock and Rapidan rivers and flank Lee's position. A large diversionary force was to cross the Rappahannock below the town. Initially all went well, but Lee sniffed out the ruse. He moved his main force to meet Hooker and dispatched J.E.B. Stuart's cavalry to disrupt the Union lines of communication. Hooker suddenly lost sight of his opponent and panicked when rebel skirmishers fired on his advance columns. He then ordered his troops to pull back to the Chancellorsville crossroads. Lee quickly took advantage of Hooker's failure of nerve. He divided his army again, sending Stonewall Jackson with more than half the men on a long march to hit the enemy's exposed right flank.

On May 2 Jackson surprised Hooker's right flank at the edge of a densely wooded area called the Wilderness. The Confederates slammed into the Union lines with such furor that the defenders panicked and ran. The thick undergrowth made troop movements more chaotic than usual, and the fighting died out in confusion as darkness fell. The next day was Lee's, however, as his troops forced Hooker's army to recross the Rappahannock. It was the peak of Lee's career, but Chancellorsville was his last significant victory—and his costliest: the South lost 1,600 soldiers, among them Stonewall Jackson, mistakenly shot by his own men in the confused fighting. "I have lost my right arm," lamented Lee.

VICKSBURG While Lee's army held the Union forces at bay in the East, Ulysses Grant, his command now restored, had been groping his way down the Mississippi River toward the Confederate stronghold at Vicksburg, in western Mississippi. If Union forces could gain control of the Mississippi River, they could split the Confederacy in two. For months, Grant tried to discover a way to penetrate Vicksburg's heavily fortified defenses. The terrain complicated his task: Vicksburg was surrounded by bayous and marshes that made travel and resupply almost impossible. Torrential rains and widespread disease also hampered the army's movements. So in the spring of 1863, Grant finally decided to leave his supply base and live off the land. His soldiers crossed over to Louisiana, took a roundabout route to Jackson, Mississippi, where they routed the Confederates, and headed back to Vicksburg. The Union army pinned down 30,000 Confederates in Vicksburg, and Grant resolved to starve them out.

GETTYSBURG The plight of besieged Vicksburg put the Confederate high command in a quandary, in response to which Lee proposed a diversion. If he could win a great victory on northern soil, he might do more than just relieve the pressure on Vicksburg; he might bring an end to the war. In June 1863, therefore, he moved his forces into the Shenandoah Valley and again headed north across Maryland. Neither side chose Gettysburg, Pennsylvania,

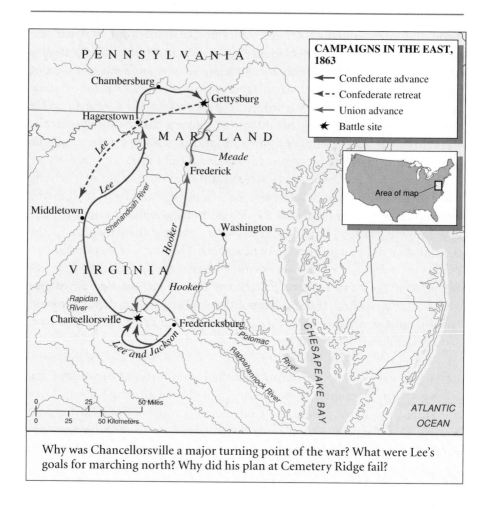

CAMPAIGNS IN THE EAST, 1863

◄—— Confederate advance
◄- - Confederate retreat
◄—— Union advance
★ Battle site

Area of map

Why was Chancellorsville a major turning point of the war? What were Lee's goals for marching north? Why did his plan at Cemetery Ridge fail?

as the site for the war's climactic battle. A Confederate foraging party entered the town in search of shoes and encountered units of Union cavalry on June 30, 1863. The main forces then quickly converged there.

On July 1, a hot, steamy day, the Confederates pushed the Union soldiers out of the town, but into stronger positions on high ground to the south. The new Union commander, George Meade, hastened reinforcements to the new lines along the heights. On July 2 Confederates launched furious assaults at the extreme flanks of Meade's army. The Union forces, who outnumbered their attackers almost two to one, fought just as bravely—and the assaults were repulsed.

The next day, Lee staked everything on a final attack on the Union center at Cemetery Ridge. At about two in the afternoon, General George Pickett's

15,000 Confederate troops emerged from the woods west of Cemetery Ridge and began their advance across rising open ground commanded by Union artillery. "Pickett's charge" was hopeless. At a distance of 700 yards, the Union artillery homed in on the advancing Virginians. Those who avoided the canister and grapeshot were devastated by a wall of musket fire. At the head of Pickett's division were the University Greys, thirty-one college students from Mississippi. Within an hour of their assault, every one of them was killed or wounded. As he watched the few survivers returning from the bloody field, General Lee muttered, "All this has been my fault."

With nothing left to do but retreat, Lee's dejected and mangled army began to slog south in a driving rain that "washed the blood from the grass." They left one third of their number behind on the ground, having had failed in all their purposes, not the least being to relieve the pressure on Vicksburg. On that same day, July 4, the entire Confederate garrison at Vicksburg surrendered after a forty-seven-day siege. The Confederacy was now irrevocably split. Had Meade aggressively pursued Lee, he might have delivered the final blow before the Rebels could get back across the flooded Potomac River, but again an army failed to capitalize on its advantage.

After the furious fighting at Gettysburg had ended, a group of northern states funded a military cemetery for the 6,000 soldiers killed in the battle. On

Harvest of Death

Timothy H. O'Sullivan's grim photograph of the dead at Gettysburg.

November 19,1863, the new cemetery was officially dedicated. In his brief re-marks, since known as the Gettysburg Address, President Lincoln eloquently expressed the pain and sorrow of the brutal civil war. The prolonged conflict was testing whether a nation "dedicated to the proposition that all men are created equal . . . can long endure." Lincoln declared that all Americans must ensure that the "honored dead" had not "died in vain." In stirring words that continue to inspire, Lincoln predicted that "this nation, under God, shall have a new birth of freedom—and that government of the people, by the peo-ple, and for the people, shall not perish from the earth."

CHATTANOOGA   The third great Union victory of 1863 occurred in fighting around Chattanooga, the railhead of eastern Tennessee and gateway to northern Georgia. On September 9 a Union army led by General William Rosecrans took Chattanooga and then rashly pursued General Braxton Bragg's forces into Georgia, where the two sides clashed at Chickamauga (an old Cherokee word ironically meaning "River of Death"). The battle (Sep-tember 19–20) had the makings of a Union disaster because it was one of the few times the Confederates had a numerical advantage (about 70,000 to 56,000). On the second day, Bragg smashed the Union's right flank, and only the stubborn stand on the left under the Virginia Unionist George H. Thomas (thenceforth known as the Rock of Chickamauga) prevented a rout. The battered Union forces fell back to Chattanooga while Bragg cut the rail-road and held the city virtually under siege.

Rosecrans seemed stunned and immobilized, but Lincoln urged him to hang on: "If we can hold Chattanooga, and East Tennessee, I think rebellion must dwindle and die." The president then dispatched reinforcements. Gen-eral Grant, given overall command of the western theater on October 16, re-placed Rosecrans with George Thomas. On November 24 the Union forces broke out of the city and captured Lookout Mountain in what was mainly a feat of mountaineering. The next day, Grant ordered Thomas's troops forward to positions at the foot of Missionary Ridge. But the men did not stop there. Still fuming because the Confederates had jeered them at Chickamauga, they charged toward the crest without orders. One of Thomas's aides explained to Grant, "When those fellows get started all hell can't stop them." The attackers could have been decimated, but the Confederates were unable to lower their big guns enough to hit the scrambling Yankees, and despite Bragg's "cursing like a sailor," his men fled as Thomas's troops reached the summit.

After the Confederate defeat, as the Union forces consolidated their con-trol of East Tennessee, already full of Unionist sympathizers, Jefferson Davis reluctantly replaced Bragg with Joseph Johnston. Lincoln, on the other hand, had finally found the general for whom he had been searching for almost three years. In March 1864 Ulysses S. Grant was brought to Washington and made general in chief.

THE CONFEDERACY'S DEFEAT

During the winter of 1863–1864, Confederates began to despair of victory. A War Department official in Richmond reported in his diary a spreading "sense of hopelessness." At the same time, Mary Chesnut of South Carolina reported that "gloom and despondency hang like a pall everywhere." Union leaders, sensing the momentum swinging their way, stepped up their pressure on Confederate forces.

The Union's main targets now were Lee's army in Virginia and General Joseph Johnston's forces in Georgia. Grant personally would accompany George Meade, who retained direct command over the Army of the Potomac; operations in the West were entrusted to Grant's longtime lieutenant, William T. Sherman. Grant brought with him a new strategy against Lee. Where his predecessors had hoped for the climactic single battle, he opted for a war of attrition. He would attack, attack, attack, keeping the pressure on the Confederates, grinding down their numbers and taking away their initiative and their will to fight. Victory, he had decided, would come to the side "which never counted its dead." Grant ordered his commanders to wage total war, confiscating or destroying civilian property of use to the Confederate war effort. It was a brutal, costly, but effective plan.

GRANT'S PURSUIT OF LEE   In May 1864 Grant's Army of the Potomac, numbering about 115,000 to Lee's 65,000, moved south across the Rappahannock River into the Wilderness of eastern Virginia, where Hooker had come to grief in the Battle of Chancellorsville. In the nightmarish Battle of the Wilderness (May 5–6), the armies fought blindly through the tangled brush and vines, the horror and agony of the wounded heightened by crackling brushfires. Grant's men suffered heavier casualties than Lee's, but the Confederates were running out of replacements.

Many of the officers in the Army of the Potomac were in awe of Lee. They especially feared another decisive counterattack on their flanks. When one of Grant's officers expressed concern about what Lee might do, Grant exploded:

> Oh, I am heartily tired of hearing what Lee is going to do. Some of you always seem to think he is suddenly going to turn a double somersault, and

Ulysses S. Grant

At his headquarters in City Point (now Hopewell), Virginia.

land in our rear and on both our flanks at the same time. Go back to your command, and try to think what we are going to do ourselves, instead of what Lee is going to do.

Always before, Lee's adversaries had retreated to lick their wounds, but Grant slid off to the left and continued his relentless advance southward, now toward Spotsylvania Court House. "Whatever happens," he assured Lincoln, "we will not retreat."

Along the Chickahominy River the two sides clashed at Cold Harbor (June 1–3). In twenty minutes 7,000 attacking Union soldiers were killed or wounded. Many of them had predicted as much. After the failed assault, Confederates retrieved a diary from a dead Massachusetts soldier. The final entry read: "June 3, 1864, Cold Harbor, Virginia. I was killed." Battered and again repulsed, Grant soon had his men moving again, headed for Petersburg, the junction of railroads running into Richmond from the south. "I shall take no backward steps," he declared.

Lee's army dug in around the town while Grant's forces laid siege. For nine months the two armies faced each other down while Grant kept trying to break the railroad arteries that were Lee's lifeline. Grant's men were generously supplied by vessels moving up the James River, while Lee's forces, beset by hunger, cold, and desertion, wasted away in their muddy trenches. Petersburg had become Lee's prison while disasters piled up elsewhere in the Confederacy. "From the summer of 1862," wrote a Confederate veteran, "the war became a war of wholesale devastation. From the spring of 1864, it seemed to have become nearly a war of extermination."

SHERMAN'S MARCH While Grant was besieging Lee in Virginia, the battle-hardened General William T. Sherman was doggedly pursuing Joseph Johnston's army through northern Georgia, toward Atlanta. Tightly strung, profane, and plagued by fits of depression, Sherman was one of the few generals to appreciate the concept of total war. He wanted to destroy Confederate

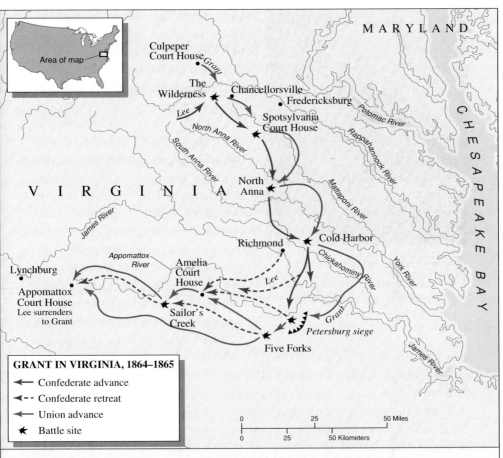

GRANT IN VIRGINIA, 1864–1865

◄— Confederate advance

◄-- Confederate retreat

◄— Union advance

★ Battle site

How were Grant's tactics in the Battle of the Wilderness different from the Union's previous encounters with Lee's army? Why did Grant have the advantage at Petersburg? How did Grant eventually force Lee to surrender?

morale as well as Confederate armies. Where Sherman loved a toe-to-toe fight, Johnston preferred retreat and evasion, determined not to risk a single life until the perfect conditions for fighting were obtained.

An impatient Jefferson Davis finally exploded at Johnston and replaced him with the towering, blond-bearded Texan John B. Hood, who did not know the meaning of retreat or evasion. As Lee once noted, Hood was "all lion, none of the fox." Having had an arm crippled by a bullet at Gettysburg and most of one leg shot off at Chickamauga, Hood had to be strapped to his horse. He was one of the most tenacious—and impetuous—fighters in the war, and during late July 1864 the army led by "the gallant Hood" struck

William Tecumseh Sherman

Sherman's campaign developed into a war of maneuver, but without the pitched battles of Grant's campaign.

three times from their base at Atlanta, each time fighting desperately but meeting a bloody rebuff. Sherman then circled the city and cut off the rail lines, forcing Hood to evacuate on September 1.

Sherman now resolved to make all of Georgia "howl" as his army embarked on its devastating march southeast from Atlanta through central Georgia. His intention was to "whip the rebels, to humble their pride, to follow them into their inmost recesses, and make them fear and dread us." Hood's Confederate army went in the other direction, cutting through northern Alabama and into Tennessee in the hope of luring Sherman away from the undefended Deep South. But Sherman refused to take the bait, although he did dispatch General George Thomas with 30,000 men to keep watch on Hood and his troops.

They did more than observe, however. In the Battle of Franklin (November 30), Hood sent his army across two miles of open Tennessee ground. Six waves of gray crashed against the entrenched Union lines but never broke through. A month later, on December 27, Hood suffered another devastating defeat, at Nashville, that effectively ended Confederate activity in Tennessee.

During all this Sherman and the main Union force were marching triumphantly through Georgia, waging war against the enemy's resources and will to resist. "War is war," Sherman bluntly declared, "not a popularity contest." On November 15, 1864, his men burned much of Atlanta and then spread out over a front twenty to sixty miles wide and headed southeast living off the land and destroying any crops, livestock, or supplies that might serve Confederate forces. Bands of stragglers and deserters from both armies joined in looting along the flanks.

When Sherman's army approached Savannah, Georgia, a month later, a swath of desolation 250 miles long lay behind them. Sherman's purpose was clear: he would keep the pressure on the Confederates "until they are not only ruined, exhausted, but humbled in pride and spirit." On December 21 Sherman rode into Savannah, and three days later he offered the city as a

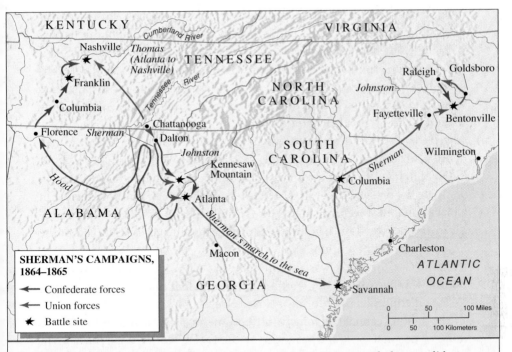

SHERMAN'S CAMPAIGNS, 1864–1865

⬅ Confederate forces
⬅ Union forces
✶ Battle site

What was Sherman's goal as he marched across Georgia? How much damage did Sherman do in Georgia and South Carolina? How did this affect the Confederate war effort?

Christmas gift to Lincoln. But Sherman paused only long enough to resupply his forces, who then moved on that "hell-hole of secession," South Carolina. There his men wrought even greater destruction. More than a dozen towns were torched, including the state capital of Columbia, which was captured on February 17, 1865. That same day the Confederates abandoned Charleston and headed north to join an army that Joseph Johnston was desperately trying to form.

During the late winter and early spring of 1865, the Confederacy found itself besieged. Defeat was in the air. Some Rebel leaders argued that it was time to negotiate a peace settlement. Confederate secretary of war John C. Breckinridge, the Kentuckian who had served as vice president under James Buchanan and had run for president in 1860, urged Robert E. Lee to negotiate an honorable end to the war. "This has been a magnificent epic," he said. "In God's name, let it not terminate in a farce." But Jefferson Davis dismissed any talk of surrender. If the Confederate armies should be defeated, he wanted the soldiers to disperse and fight a guerrilla war. "The war came and

now it must go on," he stubbornly insisted, "till the last man of this generation falls in his tracks, and his children seize his musket and fight our battle."

While Confederate forces made their last stands, Abraham Lincoln prepared for his second term as president. He was the first president since Andrew Jackson to have been reelected. The weary commander in chief had
weathered constant criticism during his first term, but with the war nearing
its end, Lincoln now garnered deserved praise. The *Chicago Tribune* observed that the president "has slowly and steadily risen in the respect, confidence, and admiration of the people."

On March 4, 1865, amid rumors of a Confederate attempt to abduct or assassinate the president, the six-foot-four-inch, rawboned Lincoln, dressed in
a black suit and stovepipe hat, his face weathered by prairie wind and political worry, delivered his brief but eloquent second inaugural address on the
East Portico of the Capitol. Not 100 feet away, looking down on Lincoln
from the Capitol porch, was a twenty-six-year-old actor named John Wilkes
Booth, who five weeks later would kill the president in a desperate attempt
to do something "heroic" for his beloved South.

The nation's capital had long before become an armed camp and a massive
military hospital. Sick and wounded soldiers were scattered everywhere: in
hotels, warehouses, schools, businesses, and private homes. Thousands of
Confederate deserters roamed the streets. After a morning of torrential rains,
the sun broke through the clouds just as Lincoln began to speak to the mud-
spattered audience of some 35,000, half of whom were African Americans.
While managing a terrible civil war, the president had experienced personal
tragedy (the loss of a second child, a wife plagued by mental instability) and
chronic depression. What kept him from unraveling was a principled pragmatism and godly foundation that endowed his life with purpose.

Lincoln's address was more sermon than speech, the reflections of a
somber statesman still struggling to understand the relation between divine
will and human endeavor. Rather than detailing the progress of the war effort or indulging in self-congratulatory celebration, Lincoln focused on the
origins and paradoxes of the war. Slavery, he said, had "somehow" caused the
war, and everyone bore some guilt for the national shame of racial injustice
and its bloody expiation. Both sides had known before the fighting began
that war was to be avoided at all costs, but "one of them would *make* war
rather than let the nation survive; and the other would *accept* war rather
than let it perish."

The weary but resolute commander in chief longed for peace. "Fondly do
we hope—fervently do we pray—that this mighty scourge of war may speed-
ily pass away." He wondered aloud why the war had lasted so long and been so

brutal. "The Almighty," he acknowledged, "has His own purposes." Lincoln noted the paradoxical irony of both sides in this civil war reading the same Bible, praying to the same God, and appealing for divine support in its fight against the other. The God of Judgment, however, would not be misled or denied. If God willed that the war continue until "every drop of blood drawn with the lash, shall be paid with another drawn by the sword, as was said three thousand years ago, so still it must be said 'the judgments of the Lord are true and righteous altogether.'" After four years of escalating combat, the war had grown "incomprehensible" in its scope and horrors. Now the president, looking gaunt and tired, urged the Union forces "to finish the work we are in," bolstered with "firmness in the right insofar as God gives us to see the right."

As Lincoln looked ahead to the end of the fighting and a "just and lasting peace," he stressed the need to "bind up the nation's wounds" by exercising the Christian virtues of forgiveness and mercy. Vengeance must be avoided at all costs. Reconciliation must be pursued "with malice toward none; with charity for all." Those eight words marvelously captured Lincoln's hopes for a restored Union. His simple but powerful and profound second inaugural speech, only 700 words long, endures because it manifests the extraordinary humility and complex faith of a president too humane to be vengeful or partisan. Redemption was his goal; victory was less important than peace. The sublime majesty of Lincoln's brief speech revealed how the rigors of war had transformed and elevated him from the obscure congressman who had entered the White House in 1861. The abolitionist leader Frederick Douglass proclaimed Lincoln's second inaugural address "a sacred effort."

APPOMATTOX During this final season of the Confederacy, Ulysses Grant kept pushing, probing, and battering General Lee's defenses around Petersburg, twenty miles south of Richmond. The Confederates were slowly starving, their trenches filled with rats and lice. Scurvy and dysentery were rampant. News of Sherman's devastating sweep through Dixie only added to the Confederates' gloom and the impulse to desert.

Under siege for almost ten months, the Confederate lines around Petersburg were becoming woefully thin, and Lee decided to sneak away to join Johnston's forces in North Carolina. In Richmond, President Davis, exhausted but still defiant, gathered what valuables he could carry and escaped by train. Torching everything of military and industrial value in Richmond, the retreating Confederate forces left the city on April 2, and the Union army entered, accompanied by Abraham Lincoln himself. Jefferson Davis would be captured in Georgia on May 10 by Union cavalry, but by then the Confederacy was already dead.

Robert E. Lee

Mathew Brady took this photograph in Richmond eleven days after Lee's surrender at Appomattox.

As Richmond lay burning, Lee pulled his shrunken army out of the trenches around nearby Petersburg with Grant's men in hot pursuit. Lee soon found his escape route cut by Union cavalry. Outnumbered six to one, surrounded, and out of food, Lee dismissed proposals to scatter his forces to wage guerrilla warfare. He instead told Grant he was prepared to surrender. Although his men shouted their willingness to keep fighting, Lee decided it was senseless to waste any more lives.

On April 9 (Palm Sunday), 1865, Lee donned a dress uniform and met the mud-spattered Grant in the parlor of Wilmer McLean's home at Appomattox Court House to tender his surrender. Grant, at Lee's request, let the Confederate officers keep their sidearms and permitted soldiers to keep their own horses and mules. Three days later the Confederate troops formed ranks for the last time as they prepared for the formal surrender. Deeply moved by the solemn splendor, Joshua Chamberlain, the Union general in charge, ordered his men to salute their foes as they paraded past. His Confederate counterpart signaled his troops to do likewise. General Chamberlain remembered that there was not a sound—no trumpets or drums, no cheers or jeers, simply "an awed stillness . . . as if it were the passing of the dead." On April 18 Johnston surrendered his forces to Sherman near Durham, North Carolina. The remaining Confederate forces surrendered during May.

A Modern War

The Civil War was in many respects the first modern war. Its scope was unprecedented. One out of every twelve men served in the war, and few families were unaffected by the event. Over 630,000 men died in the conflict from wounds or disease, 50 percent more than in World War II. Because battlefield surgeons were constantly overworked and frequently lacked equipment, supplies, and knowledge, almost any stomach or head wound proved fatal, and gangrene was rampant. Of the survivors, 50,000 returned home with one or more limbs amputated. Disease, however, was the greatest threat to soldiers, killing twice as many as were lost in battle.

The Civil War was also modern in that much of the killing was distant, impersonal, and mechanical. The opposing forces used an array of new weapons and instruments of war: artillery with "rifled," or grooved, barrels for geater accuracy, repeating rifles, ironclad ships, observation balloons, and wire entanglements. Men were killed without knowing who had fired the shot that felled them.

Historians have provided conflicting assessments of the reasons for the Union victory. Some have focused on the inherent weaknesses of the Confederacy: its lack of industry, the fractious relations between the states and the central government in Richmond, poor political and military leadership, faulty coordination and communication, the burden of slavery, and the disparities in population and resources compared with those of the North. Still others have highlighted the erosion of Confederate morale in the face of chronic food shortages and horrific human losses. The debate over why the North won and the South lost the Civil War will probably never end, but as in other modern wars, firepower and manpower were essential factors. Robert E. Lee's own explanation of the Confederate defeat retains an enduring legitimacy: "After four years of arduous service marked by unsurpassed courage and fortitude, the Army of Northern Virginia has been compelled to yield to overwhelming numbers and resources."

MAKING CONNECTIONS

- Certain fiscal measures enacted during the Civil War (when southerners were not in Congress to block them) helped fuel the postwar economic growth (discussed in Chapter 20).

- The Confederacy's defeat had a tremendous impact on all dimensions of life in the South, as Chapter 19 (on the New South) demonstrates.

FURTHER READING

The best one-volume overview of the Civil War period is James M. McPherson's *Battle Cry of Freedom: The Civil War Era* (1988). A good introduction to the military events is Herman Hattaway's *Shades of Blue and Gray* (1997). The outlook and experiences of the common soldier are explored in James M. McPherson's *For Cause and Comrades: Why Men Fought in the Civil War* (1997) and Earl J. Hess's *The Union Soldier in Battle: Enduring the Ordeal of Combat* (1997).

For emphasis on the South, turn first to Gary W. Gallagher's *The Confederate War* (1997). For a sparkling account of the birth of the Rebel nation, see William C. Davis's *"A Government of Our Own": The Making of the Confederacy* (1994). The same author provides a fine biography of the Confederate president in *Jefferson Davis: The Man and His Hour* (1991). On the best Confederate commander, see John M. Taylor's *Duty Faithfully Performed: Robert E. Lee and His Critics* (2000). On the key Union generals, see Lee Kennett's *Sherman: A Soldier's Life* (2001) and Josiah Bunting III's *Ulysses S. Grant* (2004).

Analytical scholarship on the military conflict includes Joseph L. Harsh's *Confederate Tide Rising: Robert E. Lee and the Making of Southern Strategy, 1861–1862* (1998), Steven E. Woodworth's *Jefferson Davis and His Generals: The Failure of Confederate Command in the West* (1990), and Paul D. Casdorph's *Lee and Jackson: Confederate Chieftains* (1992). Lonnie R. Speer's *Portals to Hell: Military Prisons of the Civil War* (1977) details the ghastly experience of prisoners of war.

The history of the North during the war is surveyed in Philip Sphaur Paludan's *A People's Contest: The Union and Civil War, 1861–1865,* 2nd ed. (1996) and J. Matthew Gallman's *The North Fights the Civil War: The Home Front* (1994).

The central northern political figure, Abraham Lincoln, is the subject of many books. See Harry V. Jaffa's *A New Birth of Freedom: Abraham Lincoln and the Coming of the Civil War* (2000). On Lincoln's great speeches, see Ronald C. White Jr.'s *The Eloquent President: A Portrait of Lincoln through His Words* (2005). The election of 1864 is treated in John C. Waugh's *Reelecting Lincoln: The Battle of the 1864 Presidency* (1997). On Lincoln's assassination, see William Hanchett's *The Lincoln Murder Conspiracies* (1983).

Concerning specific military campaigns, see Larry J. Daniel's *Shiloh: The Battle That Changed the Civil War* (1997), Thomas Goodrich's *Black Flag: Guerrilla Warfare on the Western Border, 1861–1865* (1995), Stephen W. Sears's

To the Gates of Richmond: The Peninsula Campaign (1992), James M. McPherson's *Crossroads of Freedom: Antietam* (2002), James Lee McDonough and James Pickett Jones's *War So Terrible: Sherman and Atlanta* (1988), Robert Garth Scott's *Into the Wilderness with the Army of the Potomac* (1985), Albert Castel's *Decision in the West: The Atlanta Campaign of 1864* (1992) and Ernest B. Furgurson's *Not War but Murder: Cold Harbor, 1864* (2000). On the final weeks of the war, see William C. Davis's *An Honorable Defeat: The Last Days of the Confederate Government* (2001).

The experience of the African-American soldier is surveyed in Joseph T. Glatthaar's *Forged in Battle: The Civil War Alliance of Black Soldiers and White Officers* (1990) and Ira Berlin, Joseph P. Reidy, and Leslie S. Rowland's *Freedom's Soldiers: The Black Military Experience in the Civil War* (1998). For the African-American woman's experience, see Jacqueline Jones's *Labor of Love, Labor of Sorrow: Black Women, Work, and the Family from Slavery to the Present* (1985).

Recent gender and ethnic studies include *Divided Houses: Gender and the Civil War*, edited by Catherine Clinton and Nina Silber (1992), Drew Gilpin Faust's *Mothers of Invention: Women of the Slaveholding South in the American Civil War* (1996), George C. Rable's *Civil Wars: Women and the Crisis of Southern Nationalism* (1989), and William L. Burton's *Melting Pot Soldiers: The Union's Ethnic Regiments,* 2nd ed. (1998).

18

RECONSTRUCTION: NORTH AND SOUTH

FOCUS QUESTIONS

· What were the different approaches to Reconstruction?

· How did Congress try to reshape southern society?

· What was the role of African Americans in the early postwar years?

· What were the main issues in national politics in the 1870s?

To answer these questions and access additional review material, please visit www.wwnorton.com/studyspace.

In the spring of 1865, the wearying war was over. At a frightful cost of over 600,000 lives and the destruction of the southern economy and much of its landscape, American nationalism had emerged triumphant, and some 4 million enslaved African-Americans were freed. Now the nation faced the imposing task of reuniting, providing for the freed slaves, and "reconstructing" a ravaged and resentful South.

THE WAR'S AFTERMATH

In the war's aftermath the victors faced important questions: Should the Confederate leaders be tried for treason? How should new governments be formed? How and at whose expense was the South's economy to be rebuilt? Should debts incurred by the Confederate state governments be honored?

Who should pay to rebuild the South's railroads and public buildings, dredge the clogged southern harbors, and restore damaged levees? What was to be done for the freed slaves? Were they to be given land? social equality? education? voting rights? Such complex questions required sober reflection and careful planning, but policy makers did not have the luxury of time or the benefit of consensus. Some wanted the former Confederate states returned to the Union with little or no changes in the region's social, political, and economic life. Others wanted southern society punished and transformed. At the end of 1865, the editors of the nation's foremost magazine, *Harper's Weekly,* expressed this vengeful attitude when they declared that "the forgive-and-forget policy . . . is mere political insanity and suicide."

ECONOMIC DEVELOPMENT IN THE NORTH   The Civil War was more truly a social revolution than the War of Independence, for it reduced the once-dominant power of the South's planter elite in national politics and elevated that of the northern "captains of industry." Government, both federal and state, grew more friendly to business leaders and more unfriendly to those who would probe into their activities. The wartime Congress had delivered on the major platform promises of the 1860 campaign, which had cemented the allegiance of northeastern businessmen and western farmers to the Republican party.

In the absence of southern members, Congress during the war had centralized national power and enacted the Republican economic agenda. It passed the Morrill Tariff, which doubled the average level of import duties. The National Banking Act created a uniform system of banking and banknote currency and helped finance the war. Congress also passed legislation confirming that the first transcontinental railroad would run along a north-central route, from Omaha to Sacramento, and donated public land and public bonds to ensure its financing. In the Homestead Act of 1862, moreover, Congress voted free federal homesteads of 160 acres to settlers, who had only to occupy the land for five years to gain title. The Morrill Land Grant Act of the same year conveyed to each state 30,000 acres of federal land per member of Congress from the state, the proceeds from the sale of which went to create colleges of "agriculture and mechanic arts." Such measures helped stimulate the North's economy in the years after the Civil War.

DEVASTATION IN THE SOUTH   The postwar South offered a sharp contrast to the victorious North. Along the path of General William T. Sherman's army, one observer reported in 1866, the countryside of Georgia and

A Street in the "Burned District"

Richmond, Virginia, Spring 1865.

South Carolina "looked for many miles like a broad black streak of ruin and desolation." Columbia, South Carolina, said another witness, was "a wilderness of ruins," Charleston a place of "vacant houses, of widowed women, of rotting wharves, of deserted warehouses, of weed-wild gardens, of miles of grass-grown streets, of acres of pitiful and voiceless barrenness."

Throughout the South, property values had collapsed. Confederate bonds and paper money were worthless; most railroads were damaged or destroyed. Cotton that had escaped destruction was seized as Confederate property or in forfeit of federal taxes. Emancipation wiped out $4 billion invested in human flesh and left the labor system in disarray. The great age of expansion in the cotton market was over. Not until 1879 would the cotton crop again equal the record harvest of 1860; tobacco production did not regain its prewar level until 1880; the sugar crop of Louisiana not until 1893; and the old rice industry of the Tidewater and the hemp industry of the Kentucky Bluegrass never regained their prewar status.

A TRANSFORMED SOUTH The defeat of the Confederacy transformed much of southern society. The liberation of slaves, the destruction of property, and the free fall in land values left many planters destitute and homeless. After the Civil War many former Confederates were so embittered that they abandoned their native region rather than submit to "Yankee rule." Some migrated to Canada, Europe, Mexico, South America, or Asia. Others preferred the western territories and states. Still others moved to northern and midwestern cities on the assumption that their educational and economic opportunities would be better among the victors.

Most of those who remained in the South found their farms, homes, and communities transformed. One Confederate army captain reported that on his father's plantation "our negroes are living in great comfort. They were delighted to see me with overflowing affection. They waited on me as before, gave me breakfast, splendid dinners, etc. But they firmly and respectfully informed me: 'We own this land now. Put it out of your head that it will ever be yours again.'"

LEGALLY FREE, SOCIALLY BOUND In the former Confederate states the newly freed slaves suffered most of all. According to the African-American abolitionist Frederick Douglass, the former slave remained dependent: "He had neither money, property, nor friends. He was free from the old plantation, but he had nothing but the dusty road under his feet. . . . He was turned loose, naked, hungry, and destitute to the open sky."

A few northerners argued that what the ex-slaves needed most was their own land. In 1865 Representative George Washington Julian of Indiana and Senator Charles Sumner of Massachusetts proposed to give freed slaves forty-acre homesteads carved out of Confederate lands taken under the Confiscation Act of 1862. But their plan for outright grants was replaced by a program of rentals, since under the law confiscation was effective only for the lifetime of the Confederate property owner. Discussions of land distribution, however, fueled rumors that freed slaves would get "forty acres and a mule," a slogan that swept the South at the end of the war. But even dedicated abolitionists shrank from taking land from whites to give to the freed slaves. Citizenship and legal rights were one thing, wholesale confiscation of property and land redistribution quite another.

Freedmen in Richmond, Virginia

According to a former Confederate general, freed blacks had "nothing but freedom."

Instead of land or material help, the freed slaves more often got advice about proper behavior.

THE FREEDMEN'S BUREAU   On March 3, 1865, while the war was still raging, Congress set up within the War Department the Bureau of Refugees, Freedmen, and Abandoned Lands to provide "provisions, clothing, and fuel" to relieve "destitute and suffering refugees and freedmen and their wives and children." Agents of the Freedmen's Bureau were entrusted with negotiating labor contracts (a new practice for both African Americans and planters), providing medical care, and setting up schools, often in cooperation with such northern agencies as the American Missionary Association and the Freedmen's Aid Society. The bureau had its own courts to deal with labor disputes and land titles, and its agents were authorized to supervise trials involving blacks in other courts.

The failure to grasp the intensity of white intransigence and racial prejudice thwarted the efforts of Freedmen's Bureau agents to protect and assist the former slaves, however. Congress was not willing to strengthen the powers of the bureau to deal with such problems. Beyond temporary relief measures, no program of Reconstruction ever incorporated much more than constitutional and legal rights for freedmen. These were important in themselves, of course, but the extent to which even they should go was very uncertain, to be settled more by the course of events than by any clear-cut commitment to social and economic equality.

THE BATTLE OVER RECONSTRUCTION

The problem of reconstructing the South centered on deciding what governments would constitute authority in the defeated states. This problem arose first in Virginia at the very beginning of the Civil War, when the state's thirty-five western counties refused to go along with secession. In 1861 a loyal state government of Virginia was proclaimed at Wheeling, and that government in turn formed a new state, called West Virginia, which was admitted to the Union in 1863. As Union forces advanced into the South, President Lincoln in 1862 named military governors for Tennessee, Arkansas, and Louisiana. By the end of the following year, he had formulated a plan for regular civilian governments in those states and any others that might be liberated from Confederate rule.

LINCOLN'S PLAN AND CONGRESS'S RESPONSE   In late 1863 President Lincoln had issued a Proclamation of Amnesty and Reconstruction, under which any Confederate state could form a Union government whenever a number equal to 10 percent of those who had voted in 1860 took an oath of allegiance to the Constitution and Union and received a presidential pardon. Participants also had to swear support for laws and proclamations dealing with emancipation. Excluded from the pardon, however, were certain groups: civil, diplomatic, and high military officers of the Confederacy; judges, congressmen, and military officers of the United States who had left their federal posts to aid the rebellion; and those accused of failure to treat captured black soldiers and their officers as prisoners of war.

Under this plan, governments loyal to the Union appeared in Tennessee, Arkansas, and Louisiana, but Congress refused to recognize them. In the absence of specific provisions for Reconstruction in the Constitution, politicians disagreed as to where authority properly rested. A few conservative and most moderate Republicans supported Lincoln's program of immediate restoration. A small but influential group, known as Radical Republicans, demanded a sweeping transformation of southern society that would include making the freed slaves full-fledged citizens. The Radicals hoped to reconstruct southern society so as to dismantle the planter elite and the Democratic Party.

The Radical Republicans were talented, earnest leaders who maintained that Congress, not the president, should supervise the Reconstruction program. To this end in 1864 they helped pass the Wade-Davis bill, sponsored by Senator Benjamin Franklin Wade of Ohio and Representative Henry Winter Davis of Maryland. In contrast to Lincoln's 10 percent plan, the Wade-Davis bill required that a *majority* of white male citizens declare their allegiance and that only those who swore an "ironclad" oath that they had always remained loyal to the Union could vote or serve in the state constitutional conventions. The conventions, moreover, would have to abolish slavery, deny political rights to high-ranking civil and military officers of the Confederacy, and repudiate Confederate war debts. Passed during the closing days of the 1864 session, the bill went unsigned by Lincoln, and that "pocket veto" led the bill's sponsors to issue the Wade-Davis Manifesto, a blistering statement accusing the president of usurping power and attempting to use readmitted states to ensure his reelection.

Lincoln issued his final statement on Reconstruction in his last public address, on April 11, 1865. Speaking from the White House balcony, he dismissed the theoretical question of whether the Confederate states had technically remained in the Union as "good for nothing at all—a mere pernicious abstraction." Those states were simply "out of their proper practical relation with the Union," and the object was to get them "into their proper practical relation" as quickly as possible. Lincoln hoped to get new southern state governments in operation before Congress met in December. He worried that Congress might push through a harsher Reconstruction program. Lincoln wanted "no persecution, no bloody work," no dramatic restructuring of southern social and economic life.

On the evening of April 14, Lincoln went to Ford's Theater and his rendezvous with death. Shot in the head by John Wilkes Booth, a crazed actor and Confederate zealot, the president died the next morning. Pursued into Virginia, Booth was trapped and shot in a burning barn. His last words were "Tell mother I die for my country. I thought I did for the best." Three collaborators were tried and hanged, along with Mary Surratt, at whose boardinghouse they had plotted. Three other conspirators received life sentences, including a Maryland doctor who set the leg Booth had broken when he jumped from Lincoln's box onto the stage.

JOHNSON'S PLAN   Lincoln's death elevated to the White House Vice President Andrew Johnson of Tennessee, a man who lacked most presidential virtues. When General Ulysses Grant learned that Lincoln had died and Johnson was president, he said that he "dreaded the change" because the new commander in chief was vindictive toward his native South. Essentially illiterate, Johnson was provincial and bigoted. He was also short-tempered and lacking in self-control. At the inaugural ceremonies in early 1865, he had drunkenly slurred his address, embarrasing Lincoln and the nation. Johnson was a War (pro-Union) Democrat who had been put on the National Union ticket in 1864 as a gesture of unity. Of origins as humble as Lincoln's, Johnson had moved as a youth from his birthplace in Raleigh, North Carolina, to Greeneville, Tennessee, where he became the proprietor of a tailor shop. Self-educated with the help of his wife, Johnson grew prosperous, acquiring several slaves in the process.

Beginning in the 1830s, Johnson emerged as a leading Jacksonian Democrat. A bitter critic of the "swaggering" planter aristocracy "who are too lazy and proud to work," he promoted free land for the poor, defended slavery, and championed white supremacy. A notoriously stubborn man, he became a self-righteous, hot-tempered orator who enjoyed strong drink and employed abusive language to belittle his opponents. His fiery speeches and firm principles helped him win election as mayor, congressman, governor, and senator.

Like many other whites living in mountainous eastern Tennessee, Johnson ardently believed in the Union. In 1861 he was the only southern senator from a Confederate state to vote against secession, leading critics to denounce him as a "traitor" to the region. Yet his devotion to the Union did not include opposition to slavery. He hated the Confederacy because he hated the planter elite. "Damn the Negroes," Johnson bellowed to a friend during the war, "I am fighting those traitorous aristocrats, their masters."

Some of the Radical Republicans at first thought President Johnson, unlike Lincoln, was one of them. Johnson had, for example, asserted that treason "must be made infamous and traitors must be impoverished." But the Radicals would soon find Johnson to be as unsympathetic as Lincoln had been to their sweeping agenda, if for different reasons. Johnson's loyalty to the Union sprang from a strict adherence to the Constitution and a fervent belief in

Andrew Johnson

A pro-Union Democrat from Tennessee.

limited government. He held that the rebellious states should be quickly brought back into their proper relation to the Union because the states and the Union were indestructible. In 1865 Johnson declared that "there is no such thing as Reconstruction. Those states have not gone out of the Union. Therefore Reconstruction is unnecessary."

Johnson's plan to restore the Union thus closely resembled Lincoln's. A new Proclamation of Amnesty, issued on May 29, 1865, excluded from pardon not only those Lincoln had excluded but also everybody with taxable property worth more than $20,000. Those wealthy planters and merchants were the people Johnson believed had led the South to secede. Those in the excluded groups might make special applications for presidential pardon, and before the year was out Johnson had issued some 13,000 pardons.

In each of the Rebel states not already organized by Lincoln, Johnson named a native Unionist provisional governor with authority to call a convention of men elected by loyal voters. Lincoln's 10 percent requirement was omitted. Johnson called upon the conventions to invalidate the secession ordinances, abolish slavery, and repudiate all debts incurred to aid the Confederacy. Each state, moreover, was to ratify the Thirteenth Amendment, which ended slavery. Like Lincoln, Johnson also endorsed limited voting rights for blacks. The state conventions for the most part met Johnson's requirements. Emboldened by the president's indulgence, however, southern whites ignored his advice to move cautiously in restoring their political and social traditions. Suggestions of black suffrage were scarcely raised in the state conventions and promptly squelched when they were.

SOUTHERN INTRANSIGENCE   When Congress met in December 1865, for the first time since the end of the war, it faced the fact that the new state governments in the former Confederacy were remarkably like the old ones. Among the new members presenting themselves to Congress were Georgia's Alexander Stephens, former vice president of the Confederacy, four Confederate generals, eight colonels, and six cabinet members. The Congress forthwith denied seats to all members from the eleven former Confederate states. It was too much to expect, after four bloody years, that the Unionists in Congress would welcome back ex-Confederates.

Furthermore, the new southern state legislatures, in passing repressive "black codes" restricting the freedom of blacks, baldly revealed that they intended to preserve the trappings of slavery as nearly as possible. As one southerner stressed, the "ex-slave was not a free man; he was a free Negro," and the black codes were intended to highlight the distinction.

The black codes varied from state to state, but some provisions were common. Existing black marriages, including common-law marriages, were recognized (although interracial marriages were prohibited), and testimony by blacks was accepted in legal cases involving them—in six states in all cases. Blacks could own property. They could sue and be sued in the courts. On the other hand, in Mississippi they could not own farmland, and in South Carolina they could not own city lots. They were required to enter into labor contracts with white employers, renewable annually, with provision for punishment in case of violation. Their dependent children were subject to compulsory apprenticeship and corporal punishment by the employer. "Vagrant" (unemployed) blacks were punished with severe fines, and if unable to pay, they were forced to work in the fields for whites who paid the courts for cheap labor. Slavery was thus revived in another guise.

THE RADICAL REPUBLICANS   Faced with such evidence of southern intransigence, moderate Republicans drifted more and more toward the Radical camp. The new Congress set up a Joint Committee on Reconstruction, with nine members from the House and six from the Senate, to gather evidence and submit proposals for reconstructing the Southern states. As a parade of witnesses testified to the Rebels' impenitence, initiative on the committee fell to determined Radicals: Benjamin Wade of Ohio, George Julian of Indiana, Henry Wilson of Massachusetts, and most conspicuously of all, Thaddeus Stevens of Pennsylvania and Charles Sumner of Massachusetts.

Stevens, a crusty old bachelor with a chiseled face, thin, stern lips, and brooding eyes, was the domineering floor leader in the House. Driven by a genuine if at times fanatical idealism, he angrily insisted that the "whole fabric of southern society *must* be changed." Sumner, Stevens's counterpart in the Senate, agreed. Now recovered from "Bully" Brooks's 1856 assault, Sumner strove to see the South *reconstructed* rather than simply restored. This put him at odds with President Johnson. After visiting the White House, Sumner found the president "harsh, petulant, and unreasonable." He was especially disheartened by President Johnson's "prejudice, ignorance, and perversity" regarding the treatment of African Americans. Sumner and other Radicals now grew determined to take matters into their own hands. He argued that "Massachusetts could govern Georgia better than Georgia could govern herself." The southern plantations, seedbeds of aristocratic pretension and secession, he later added, "must be broken up, and the freedmen must have the pieces."

Most of the Radical Republicans had long been connected with the antislavery cause, and they approached the question of African-American rights with a sincere humanitarian impulse. Yet the Republicans also had political reasons for promoting civil rights. The Republicans needed black votes to maintain their control of Congress and the White House. They also needed to disenfranchise former Confederates to keep them from helping to elect Democrats who would restore the old ruling class to power. In public, however, the Radical Republicans rarely disclosed such partisan self-interest. Instead, they asserted that the Republicans, the party of Union and freedom, could best guarantee the fruits of victory and that extending voting rights to African Americans would be the best way to promote their welfare.

The growing conflict of opinion over Reconstruction policy brought about an inversion in constitutional reasoning. Secessionists—and Andrew Johnson—were now arguing that the Confederate states had in fact technically remained in the Union, and some Radical Republicans were contriving arguments that they had left the Union after all. Thaddeus Stevens argued that the Confederate states had indeed seceded and were now conquered provinces, subject to the absolute will of the victors. He added that the "whole fabric of southern society must be changed." Charles Sumner maintained that the southern states, by their acts of secession, had in effect committed suicide and reverted to the status of unorganized territories and thus were subject to the will of Congress. Most congressmen, however, embraced the "forfeited-rights theory," which held that the states continued to exist but by the acts of secession and war had forfeited "all civil and political rights under the Constitution." And Congress, not the president, was the proper authority to determine how and when such rights might be restored.

JOHNSON'S BATTLE WITH CONGRESS   A long year of political battling remained, however, before this idea triumphed. By the end of 1865, the Radical Republicans' views had gained only a slight majority in Congress, insufficient to override presidential vetoes. The critical year of 1866 saw the gradual waning of Andrew Johnson's power, much of which was self-induced. Johnson first challenged Congress in February, when he vetoed a bill to extend the life of the Freedmen's Bureau. The measure, he said, assumed that wartime conditions still existed, whereas the country had returned "to a state of peace and industry." Since the Bureau was no longer valid as a war measure, Johnson believed it violated the Constitution. For the moment, Johnson's prestige remained sufficiently intact that the Senate upheld his veto.

Three days after the veto, however, on George Washington's Birthday, Johnson undermined his authority by launching an intemperate assault upon the Radical Republican leaders during an impromptu speech. From that point, moderate Republicans backed away from the president, and Radical Republicans went on the offensive.

In mid-March 1866 the Radical-led Congress passed the Civil Rights Act. A direct response to the black codes created by unrepentant state legislatures in the South, it declared that "all persons born in the United States . . . excluding Indians not taxed" were citizens entitled to "full and equal benefit of all laws." The granting of citizenship to native-born blacks, Johnson claimed, exceeded the scope of federal power. It would, moreover, "foment discord among the races." He vetoed the

The Cruel Uncle

A cartoon depicting Andrew Johnson leading two children, "Civil Rights" and "the Freedmen's Bureau," into the "Veto Wood."

measure, but this time, in April, Congress overrode the presidential veto. Then in July it enacted a revised Freedmen's Bureau bill, again overturning a veto. From that point on, Johnson's public and political support steadily eroded.

THE FOURTEENTH AMENDMENT   To remove all doubt about the validity of the new Civil Rights Act, the joint committee recommended a new constitutional amendment, which passed Congress in 1866 and was ratified by the states in 1868. The Fourteenth Amendment went far beyond the Civil Rights Act, however. The first section asserts four principles: it reaffirms the state and federal citizenship of all persons—regardless of race—born or naturalized in the United States, and it forbids any state (the word *state* would be important in later litigation) to "abridge the privileges and immunities of citizens," to deprive any *person* (again an important term) "of life, liberty, or property without due process of law," or to "deny any person . . . the equal protection of the laws."

These clauses have been the subject of lawsuits resulting in applications not foreseen at the time. The "due-process clause" has come to mean that state as well as federal power is subject to the Bill of Rights, and it has been used to protect corporations, as legal "persons," from "unreasonable" regulation by the states. Other provisions of the amendment had less far-reaching effects. One section specified that the debt of the United States "shall not be questioned" but declared "illegal and void" all debts contracted in aid of the Confederate rebellion. The final sentence specified the power of Congress to pass laws enforcing the amendment.

Johnson's home state was among the first to ratify the Fourteenth Amendment. In Tennessee, which had harbored more Unionists than any other Confederate state, the government had fallen under Radical Republican control. The rest of the South, however, steadfastly resisted the Radical challenge to Johnson's program. In 1866 bloody race riots in Memphis and New Orleans added fuel to the flames. Both incidents sparked indiscriminate massacres of blacks by local police and white mobs. The rioting, Radical Republicans argued, was the natural fruit of Johnson's foolish policy.

RECONSTRUCTING THE SOUTH

THE TRIUMPH OF CONGRESSIONAL RECONSTRUCTION   As 1866 drew to an end, the November congressional elections promised to be a referendum on the growing split between Johnson and the Radical Republicans. The president embarked on a speaking tour of the Midwest, a "swing around the circle," which provoked undignified shouting contests between the president and his audiences. In Cleveland he described the Radical Republicans as "factious, domineering, tyrannical" men. Various incidents tended to confirm his image as a "ludicrous boor," which Radical Republican newspapers eagerly promoted. When the election returns came in, the Republicans had more than a two-thirds majority in each house, a comfortable margin with which to override presidential vetoes.

Congress actually enacted a new reconstruction program even before the new members took office. On March 2, 1867, two days before the old Congress expired, it passed three basic laws of congressional Reconstruction over Johnson's vetoes: the Military Reconstruction Act, the Command of the Army Act, and the Tenure of Office Act.

The first of these acts prescribed conditions under which new southern state governments should be formed. The other two sought to block any effort by the president to obstruct the process. The Command of the Army Act required that all orders from the president as commander in chief go through the headquarters of the general of the army, then Ulysses Grant. The Tenure of Office Act required the Senate's permission for the president to remove any officeholder whose appointment the Senate had confirmed.

In large measure it was intended to retain Secretary of War Edwin Stanton, the one Radical Republican sympathizer in Johnson's cabinet. But an ambiguity crept into the wording of the act. Cabinet officers, it said, should serve during the term of the president who appointed them—and Lincoln had appointed Stanton, although, to be sure, Johnson was serving out Lincoln's term.

The Military Reconstruction Act was hailed—or denounced—as the triumphant victory of "Radical" Reconstruction. Originally intended by the Radical Republicans to give military commanders in the South ultimate control over law enforcement and to leave open indefinitely the terms of restoration, it was diluted by moderate Republicans until it boiled down to little more than a requirement that southern states accept African-American suffrage and ratify the Fourteenth Amendment.

Tennessee, which had already ratified the Fourteenth Amendment, was exempted from the application of the act. The other ten states were divided into five military districts, and the commanding officer of each was authorized to keep order and protect the "rights of persons and property." The Johnson governments remained intact for the time being, but new constitutions were to be framed "in conformity with the Constitution of the United States," in conventions elected by male citizens aged twenty-one and older "of whatever race, color, or previous condition." Each state constitution had to provide the same universal male suffrage. Then, once the constitution was ratified by a majority of voters and accepted by Congress, the state legislature had ratified the Fourteenth Amendment, and the amendment had become part of the Constitution, any given state would be entitled to renewed representation in Congress. Persons excluded from officeholding by the proposed amendment were also excluded from participation in the process. Before the end of 1867, new elections had been held in all the states but Texas.

Having clipped the president's wings, the Republican Congress moved a year later to safeguard its southern program from possible interference by the Supreme Court. On March 27, 1868, Congress simply removed the power of the Supreme Court to review cases arising under the Military Reconstruction Act, which Congress clearly had the constitutional right to do under its power to define the Court's appellate jurisdiction. The Court accepted this curtailment of its authority on the same day it affirmed the notion of an "indestructible Union" in *Texas v. White* (1869). In that case the Court also acknowledged the right of Congress to reframe state governments, thus endorsing the Radical Republican point of view.

THE IMPEACHMENT AND TRIAL OF JOHNSON By 1868 Radical Republicans were convinced not only that the power of the Supreme Court and the president needed to be curtailed but also that Andrew Johnson himself had to be removed from office. Johnson, though hostile to the congressional Reconstruction program, had gone through the motions required of him. He continued to pardon former Confederates, however, and transferred several of the district military commanders who had displayed Radical Republican sympathies. Johnson lacked Lincoln's resilience and pragmatism, and he allowed his temper to get the better of his judgment. He castigated the Radical Republicans as "a gang of cormorants and bloodsuckers who have been fattening upon the country." During 1867 newspapers reported that the differences between Johnson and the Republicans had grown irreconcilable.

The Radical Republicans unsuccessfully tried to impeach Johnson early in 1867, alleging a variety of flimsy charges, none of which represented an indictable crime. Then Johnson himself provided the occasion for impeachment when he deliberately violated the Tenure of Office Act in order to test its constitutionality. Secretary of War Edwin Stanton had become a thorn in Johnson's side, refusing to resign despite his disagreements with the president's Reconstruction policy. On August 12, 1867, during a congressional recess, Johnson suspended Stanton and named General Ulysses Grant in his place. When the Senate refused to confirm Johnson's action, however, Grant returned the office to Stanton.

The Radical Republicans now saw their chance to remove the president, and they were explicit about their political purpose. As Charles Sumner declared, "Impeachment is a political proceeding before a political body with a political purpose." The debate in the House was clamorous and vicious. On February 24, 1868, the House passed eleven articles of impeachment by a party-line vote of 126 to 47.

Eight of the articles focused on the charge that Johnson had unlawfully removed Stanton. Article 9 accused the president of issuing orders in violation of the Command of the Army Act. The last two articles in effect charged him with criticizing Congress by "inflammatory and scandalous harangues." Article 11 also accused him of "unlawfully devising and contriving" to violate the Reconstruction Acts, contrary to his obligation to execute the laws. At the very least, it stated, Johnson had tried to obstruct Congress's will while observing the letter of the law.

The Senate trial began on March 5, 1868, and continued until May 26, with Chief Justice Salmon P. Chase presiding. Debate eventually focused on

Stanton's removal, the most substantive impeachment charge. Johnson's lawyers argued that Lincoln, not Johnson, had appointed Stanton, so the Tenure of Office Act did not apply to him. At the same time they claimed (correctly, as it turned out) that the law was unconstitutional.

As the five-week trial ended and the voting began in May 1868, the Senate Republicans could afford only six defections from their ranks to ensure the two-thirds majority needed to convict. In the end seven moderate Republicans and all twelve Democrats voted to acquit. The final tally was thirty-five to nineteen for conviction, one vote short of the two thirds needed for removal from office. The renegade Republicans offered two primary reasons for their controversial votes: they feared damage to the separation of powers among the branches of government if Johnson were removed, and they were assured by Johnson's attorneys that the president would stop obstructing congressional policy in the South.

Although the Senate failed to remove Johnson, the trial crippled his already weak presidency. During the remaining ten months of his term, he initiated no other clashes with Congress. In 1868 Johnson sought the Democratic presidential nomination but lost to New York governor Horatio Seymour, who then lost to the Republican, Ulysses Grant, in the general election. A bitter Johnson refused to attend Grant's inauguration. His final act as president was to issue a pardon to former Confederate president Jefferson Davis. In 1874, after failed bids for the Senate and the House, Johnson won a measure of vindication with election to the Senate, the only former president ever to do so, but he died a few months later. He was buried with a copy of the Constitution placed under his head.

As for the impeachment trial, only two weeks after it ended, a Boston newspaper reported that Americans were amazed at how quickly "the whole subject of impeachment seems to have been thrown into the background and dwarfed in importance" by other events. Moreover, impeachment of Johnson was in the end a great political mistake, for the failure to remove the president damaged Radical Republican morale and support. Nevertheless, the Radical cause did gain something: Johnson's agreement not to obstruct the process of Reconstruction. Thereafter Radical Reconstruction began in earnest.

RADICAL RULE IN THE SOUTH   In June 1868 Congress agreed that seven southern states had met the conditions for readmission to the Union, all but Virginia, Mississippi, and Texas. Congress rescinded Georgia's admission, however, when the state legislature expelled twenty-eight African-American members and seated former Confederate leaders. The federal military commander in Georgia then forced the legislature to reseat the black members and remove the Confederates, and the state was compelled to ratify the Fifteenth Amendment before being readmitted in July 1870. Mississippi, Texas, and Virginia had returned earlier in 1870, under the added requirement that they, too, ratify the Fifteenth Amendment. That amendment, ratified in 1870, forbade the states to deny any citizen the right to vote on grounds of "race, color, or previous condition of servitude."

Long before the new governments had been established, partisan Republican groups began to spring up in the South, promoted by the Union League, an organization founded in 1862 to rally support for the federal government. Its representatives enrolled blacks and loyal whites as members, initiated them into the secrets and rituals of the order, and instructed them "in their rights and duties." These Union Leagues became a powerful source of Republican political strength in the South and as a result drew the ire of unreconstructed whites.

THE RECONSTRUCTED SOUTH

Throughout the South during Reconstruction, many former Confederates continued to harbor deeply ingrained racial prejudices. They adopted a militant stance against federally imposed changes in southern society. Whites used terror, intimidation, and violence to suppress black efforts to gain social and economic equality. In July 1866, for instance, a black woman in Clinch County, Georgia, was arrested and given sixty-five lashes for "using abusive language" in an encounter with a white woman. A month later another black woman suffered the same punishment. The Civil War had brought freedom to the enslaved, but it did not bring protection against exploitation or abuse.

THE FREED SLAVES   To focus solely on what white Republicans did to reconstruct the defeated South creates the false impression that the freed slaves were simply pawns in the hands of others. In fact, southern blacks were active agents in affecting the course of Reconstruction. Many former slaves found themselves liberated but destitute after the fighting ended. The mere promise of freedom, however, had raised their hopes for biracial democracy, equal justice, and economic opportunity. "Most anyone ought to know that a man is better off free than as a slave, even if he did not have anything," said the Reverend E. P. Holmes, a black Georgia preacher and former domestic servant. "I would rather be free and have my liberty."

Participation in the Union army or navy had provided many freedmen with training in leadership. Black military veterans would form the core of the first generation of African-American political leaders in the postwar South. Military service provided many former slaves with the first opportunities to learn to read and write. Army life also alerted them to alternative social choices and to new opportunities for economic advancement and social respectability. Fighting for the Union cause also instilled a fervent sense of nationalism. A Virginia freedman explained that the United States was "now *our* country—made emphatically so by the blood of our brethren."

Former slaves established independent churches after the war, churches that quickly formed the foundation of African-American community life. Blacks preferred Baptist churches over other denominations, in part because the decentralized structure allowed each congregation to worship in its own way. By 1890 over 1.3 million African Americans were worshipping in Baptist churches in the South, nearly three times as many as had joined any other denomination. In addition to forming viable new congregations, freed blacks organized thousands of fraternal, benevolent, and mutual-aid societies, clubs, lodges, and associations. Memphis, for example, had over 200 such organizations; Richmond boasted twice that number.

Freed slaves also hastened to reestablish and reaffirm their families. Marriages that had been prohibited were now legitimized through the assistance of the Freedmen's Bureau. By 1870 most former slaves were living in two-parent households.

Former slaves had little money or technical training and were thus faced with the prospect of becoming wage laborers to support themselves. To avoid this and retain as much autonomy as possible over their productive energies and those of their children, many freed slaves chose to become sharecroppers, tenant farmers who gained access to separate plots of land owned by whites. In payment for the use of the land and cabin, and sometimes even the tools, seed, and fertilizer needed to farm the land, they were required to give between one half and two thirds of the harvested crops to the white landowner. This arrangement gave them higher status than they would have had as wage laborers. It also gave them the freedom to set their own hours and work as much or as little as they pleased, and it enabled mothers and wives to devote time to domestic responsibilities while contributing to the family's income.

African-American communities in the postwar South also sought to establish schools. The antebellum planter elite had denied education to blacks because they feared that literate slaves would organize uprisings. After the war the white elite worried that formal education would encourage poor whites and poor blacks to leave the South in search of better social and economic opportunities. Economic leaders wanted to protect the competitive advantage afforded by the region's low-wage labor market. Yet white opposition to education for blacks made it all the more important to African Americans. South Carolina's Mary McLeod Bethune, the seventeenth child of former slaves and one of the first children in the household born after the Civil War, reveled in the opportunity to gain an education: "The whole world opened to me when I learned to read." She walked five miles to school as a child, earned a scholarship to college, and went on to become the first black woman to found a school that became a four-year college, Bethune-Cookman, in Daytona Beach, Florida.

The general resistance among the former slaveholding class to initiatives involving education forced the freed slaves to rely upon northern assistance or take their own initiative. African-American churches and individuals helped raise the money and often built the schools and paid the teachers. Soldiers who had acquired some literacy skills often served as the first teachers, and the classes included adults.

BLACKS IN SOUTHERN POLITICS   In the postwar South the new role of African Americans in politics caused the most controversy. If largely illiterate and inexperienced in the rudiments of politics, southern blacks were little different from the millions of whites enfranchised in the age of Jackson or immigrants herded to the polls by political bosses in New York and other cities after the war. Some freedmen frankly confessed their disadvantages. Beverly Nash, a black delegate to the South Carolina convention of 1868, told his colleagues: "I believe, my friends and fellow-citizens, we are not prepared for this suffrage. But we can learn. Give a man tools and let him commence to use them, and in time he will learn a trade. So it is with voting."

Several hundred African-American delegates participated in the statewide political conventions. Most had been selected by local political meetings or by churches, fraternal societies, Union Leagues, or black Federal army units, although a few simply appointed themselves. The African-American delegates "ranged all colors and apparently all conditions," but free mulattoes from the cities played the most prominent roles. At Louisiana's Republican state convention, for instance, nineteen of the twenty black delegates had been born free.

By 1867 former slaves had begun to gain political influence and vote in large numbers, and this development revealed emerging tensions within the African-American community. Some southern blacks resented the presence of northern brethren who moved south after the war, while others complained that few ex-slaves were represented in leadership positions. Northern blacks and the southern black elite, most of whom were urban dwellers, opposed efforts to redistribute land to the rural freedmen, and many insisted that political equality did not mean social equality. As an Alabama black leader stressed, "We do not ask that the ignorant and degraded shall be put on a social equality with the refined and intelligent." In general, however, unity rather than dissension prevailed, and African Americans focused on common concerns such as full equality under the law.

Brought suddenly into politics in times that tried the most skilled of statesmen, many African Americans served with distinction. Nonetheless, the derisive label "black Reconstruction" used by later critics exaggerates African-American political influence, which was limited mainly to voting, and overlooks the political clout of the large number of white Republicans, especially in the mountain areas of the upper South, who supported the congressional plan for Reconstruction. Only one of the new conventions, South

Freedmen Voting in New Orleans

The Fifteenth Amendment, passed in 1870, guaranteed at the federal level the right of citizens to vote regardless of "race, color, or previous condition of servitude." But former slaves had been registering to vote—and voting in large numbers—in state elections since 1867, as in this scene.

Carolina's, had a black majority, seventy-six to forty-one. Louisiana's was evenly divided racially, and in only two other conventions were more than 20 percent of the members black: Florida's, with 40 percent, and Virginia's, with 24 percent.

In the new state governments, any African-American participation was a novelty. Although some 600 blacks—most of them former slaves—served as state legislators, no black man was ever elected governor, and few served as judges. In Louisiana, however, Pinckney Pinchback, a northern black and former Union soldier, won the office of lieutenant governor and served as acting governor when the white governor was indicted for corruption. Several blacks were elected lieutenant governor, state treasurer, or secretary of state. There were two black senators in Congress during Reconstruction, Hiram Revels and Blanche K. Bruce, both from Mississippi, and fourteen black members of the House. Among them were some of the ablest congressmen of the time.

CARPETBAGGERS AND SCALAWAGS   The top positions in southern state governments went for the most part to white Republicans whom the opposition soon labeled carpetbaggers and scalawags, depending upon their place of birth. Northern opportunists who allegedly came south with all their belongings in carpetbags to reap political spoils were more often than not Union veterans who had arrived as early as 1865 or 1866, drawn south by the hope of economic opportunity. Others were lawyers, businessmen, editors, teachers, social workers, or preachers who came on missionary endeavors.

The scalawags, or southern white Republicans, were even more reviled and misrepresented. A Nashville newspaper editor called them the "merest trash that could be collected in a civilized community, of no personal credit or social responsibility." Most scalawags had opposed secession, forming a Unionist majority in mountain counties as far south as Georgia and Alabama and especially in the hills of eastern Tennessee. Though many were indeed crass opportunists who indulged in corruption at the public's expense, several were distinguished figures. They included the former Confederate general James Longstreet, who decided after Appomattox that the Old South must change its ways. To that end he became a successful cotton broker in New Orleans, joined the Republican party, and supported the Radical Reconstruction program. Others were former Whigs who found the Republican party's expansive industrial and commercial program in keeping with Henry Clay's earlier efforts to use the government to promote economic growth and industrial development.

THE RADICAL RECORD   Former Confederates not only resented carpetbaggers and scalawags, but they also objected to the new state constitutions, primarily because of their provisions allowing for black suffrage and civil rights. Nonetheless, most of the state constitutions remained in effect for some years after the end of Radical Republican control, and later constitutions incorporated many of their features. Conspicuous among the Radical innovations were steps toward greater democracy, such as requiring universal male suffrage, reapportioning legislatures more nearly according to population, and making more state offices elective.

Given the hostile circumstances in which the Radical Republican governments operated, their achievements were remarkable. They established the first state school systems, in which some 600,000 black pupils were enrolled by 1877. State governments under the Radical Republicans also paid more attention to the poor and to orphanages, asylums, and institutions for the disabled of both races. Public roads, bridges, railroads, and buildings were repaired or rebuilt. African Americans achieved new rights and opportunities that would never again be taken away, at least in principle: equality before the law and the right to own property, carry on business, enter professions, attend schools, and learn to read and write.

Yet several of the Republican state regimes also engaged on systematic corruption. Public money and public credit were often awarded to privately owned corporations, notably railroads, under conditions that invited influence peddling. Still, corruption was not invented by the Radical Republican regimes, nor did it die with them. In Mississippi the Republican Reconstruction governments were quite honest compared with those of their Democratic successors.

THE GRANT YEARS

THE ELECTION OF 1868   Ulysses S. Grant, who served as president during the collapse of Republican rule in the South, brought to the White House little political experience. But in 1868 northern voters supported the Lion of Vicksburg because of his brilliant record as a war leader. Both parties wooed Grant, but his falling-out with President Johnson pushed him toward the Republicans and built trust in him among the Radicals.

The Republican platform of 1868 endorsed Radical Reconstruction, cautiously defending black suffrage as a necessity in the South but a matter that each northern state should settle for itself. It also urged payment of the nation's war debt in gold rather than in the new "greenback" paper currency printed during the war. More important than the platform were the great expectations of a soldier-president, whose slogan was "Let us have peace."

The Democrats opposed the Republicans on both Reconstruction and the debt. The Republican Congress, the Democratic platform charged, had subjected ten states, "in the time of profound peace, to military despotism and Negro supremacy." As for the public debt the party endorsed the "Ohio idea" of Representative George H. Pendleton: since most war bonds had been bought with depreciated greenbacks, they should be paid off in greenbacks. With no conspicuously available candidate in sight, the convention turned to Horatio Seymour, wartime governor of New York and chairman of the convention. The Democrats ran a closer race than expected, attesting to the strength of traditional party loyalties. Although Grant swept the Electoral College by 214 to 80, his popular majority was only 307,000 out of 5.7 million votes. Over 500,000 African-American voters accounted for Grant's margin of victory.

Grant had proved himself a great leader in the war, but in the White House he was often blind to the political forces and influence peddlers around him. Shy and withdrawn, he was uncomfortable around intellectuals and impatient with idealists. Grant preferred watching horse races to reading about complex issues. Although personally honest, he was dazzled by men of wealth and unaccountably loyal to greedy subordinates who betrayed his trust. In the formulation of policy, he passively followed the lead of Congress. This approach initially endeared him to Republican party leaders, but it left him ineffective and caused others to grow disillusioned with his leadership. At the outset, Grant consulted nobody on his cabinet appointments. Some of his choices indulged personal whims; others simply reflected bad judgment. Secretary of State Hamilton Fish of New York turned out to be a fortunate exception; he masterfully guided foreign policy throughout the Grant presidency. Other than Fish, however, Grant's cabinet overflowed with incompetents.

THE GOVERNMENT DEBT   Financial issues dominated Grant's presidency. After the war the Treasury had assumed that the $432 million in greenbacks issued during the conflict would be retired from circulation and that the nation would revert to a "hard-money" currency—gold coins. Congress in 1866 granted the Treasury discretion to do so gradually. Many agrarian and debtor groups resisted this contraction of the money supply, believing that it would mean lower farm prices and harder-to-pay debts. They were joined by a large number of Radical Republicans who thought a combination of high tariffs and inflation would generate more rapid economic growth. In 1868 "soft-money" supporters in Congress halted the retirement of greenbacks, leaving $356 million outstanding. There matters stood when Grant took office.

The "sound-money" (or hard-money) advocates, mostly bankers, merchants, and other creditors, claimed that Grant's election was a mandate to save the country from the Democrats' "Ohio idea" of using greenbacks to repay government bonds. Quite influential in Republican circles, the sound-money advocates also had the benefit of agreeing with the deeply ingrained popular assumption that hard money was morally preferable to paper currency. Grant agreed as well, and in his inaugural address he endorsed payment of the national debt in gold as a point of national honor.

SCANDALS   Within less than a year of his election, Grant had fallen into a cesspool of scandal. In the summer of 1869, two railroad entrepreneurs, the crafty Jay Gould and the flamboyant con man James Fisk, connived with the president's brother-in-law to corner the nation's gold market. That is, they would create a public craze for gold by purchasing massive quantities and convincing traders that the price would keep climbing. As more buyers joined the frenzy, the value of gold would soar. The only danger was the federal Treasury's selling large amounts of gold. Gould concocted an argument that the government should refrain from selling gold on the market because the resulting rise in gold prices would raise temporarily depressed farm prices. Grant apparently smelled a rat from the start, but he was seen in public with the speculators. As the rumor spread on Wall Street, gold rose from $132 to $163 an ounce. Finally, on Black Friday, September 24, 1869, Grant ordered the Treasury to sell a large quantity of gold, and the bubble burst. Fisk got out by repudiating his agreements and hiring thugs to intimidate his creditors. "Nothing is lost save honor," he said.

The plot to corner the gold market was only the first of several scandals that rocked the Grant administration. In 1872 the public learned about the financial crookery of the Crédit Mobilier, a construction company that had milked the Union Pacific Railroad for exorbitant fees to line the pockets of insiders who controlled both firms. Union Pacific shareholders were left holding the bag. This chicanery had transpired before Grant's election in 1868, but it now touched a number of prominent Republicans who had been given shares of Crédit Mobilier stock in exchange for favorable votes. Of the thirteen congressmen involved, only two were censured.

Even more odious disclosures soon followed, some involving the president's cabinet. Grant's secretary of war, it turned out, had accepted bribes from merchants who traded with Indians at army posts in the West. He was impeached, but he resigned in time to elude trial. Post-office contracts, it was revealed, went to carriers who offered the highest kickbacks. In St. Louis a "whiskey ring" bribed tax collectors to bilk the government of millions of dollars in revenue. Grant's private secretary was enmeshed in that scheme, taking large sums of money and other valuables in return for inside information. There is no evidence that Grant himself participated in any of the scandals, but his poor choice of associates and his gullibility earned him widespread censure.

WHITE TERROR   President Grant initially fought hard to enforce the federal efforts to reconstruct the postwar South. By the time he became president, southern resistance had turned violent, as unrepentant whites organized vigilante groups to terrorize blacks. Most white southerners remained so conditioned by the social prejudices embedded in the institution of slavery that they were unable to conceive of blacks as citizens. In some places, hostility to the new regimes turned violent. Said one unreconstructed Mississippian in 1875, "Carry the election peaceably if we can, forcibly if we must."

The prototype of all the terrorist groups was the Ku Klux Klan (KKK), first organized in 1866 by some young men of Pulaski, Tennessee, as a social club, with the costumes and secret rituals common to fraternal groups. At first a group of pranksters, its members soon began to intimidate blacks and white Republicans, and the KKK spread rapidly across the South in answer to the Republican party's Union League. Klansmen rode about the countryside, hiding behind masks and under robes, spreading horrendous rumors, harassing blacks, and wreaking violence and destruction.

Worse Than Slavery

This Thomas Nast cartoon chides the Ku Klux Klan and the White League for promoting conditions "worse than slavery" for southern blacks after the Civil War.

At the urging of President Grant, Congress struck back with three Enforcement Acts (1870-1871) to protect black voters. The first of these measures levied penalties on persons who interfered with any citizen's right to vote. A second placed the election of congressmen under surveillance by federal election supervisors and marshals. The third (the Ku Klux Klan Act) outlawed the characteristic activities of the Klan—forming conspiracies, wearing disguises, resisting law officers, and intimidating government officials. In 1871 the federal government singled out nine counties in up-country South Carolina and pursued mass prosecutions that brought an abrupt halt to Klan terrorism. In general, however, the federal acts designed to protect African Americans suffered from weak and inconsistent enforcement. Moreover, the South's strong tradition of states' rights and local autonomy resisted federal force.

CONSERVATIVE RESURGENCE   The Klan in fact could not take credit for the overthrow of Republican control in any state. Perhaps its most important effect was to weaken the morale of African Americans and Republicans in the South and strengthen in the North a growing weariness with the whole "southern question." Republican control in the South gradually loosened as "Conservative" parties—a name used by Democrats to mollify former Whigs—mobilized the white vote. Scalawags and many carpetbaggers drifted away from the Radical Republican ranks under pressure from their white neighbors. Few of them had joined the Republicans out of concern for black rights in the first place. And where persuasion failed to work, Democrats were willing to use chicanery. As one enthusiastic Democrat boasted, "The white and black Republicans may outvote us, but we can outcount them."

Such factors led to the collapse of Republican control in Virginia and Tennessee as early as 1869 and in Georgia and North Carolina in 1870. Reconstruction lasted longest in states with the largest black population, where whites abandoned Klan hoods for barefaced intimidation in paramilitary groups like the Mississippi Rifle Club and the South Carolina Red Shirts. In the 1873 elections in Yazoo County, Mississippi, the Republicans cast 2,449 votes and the Democrats 638; two years later the Democrats polled 4,049 votes, the Republicans 7. By 1876 Radical Republican regimes survived only in Louisiana, South Carolina, and Florida, and those collapsed after the elections of that year.

The erosion of northern interest in promoting civil rights in the postwar South reflected weariness as well as interest in other activities. Western expansion, Indian wars, new economic opportunities, and political debates over the tariff and the currency distracted attention from southern outrages. In addition, a business panic in 1873 led to a sharp depression and created both social problems and new racial tensions in the North and the South

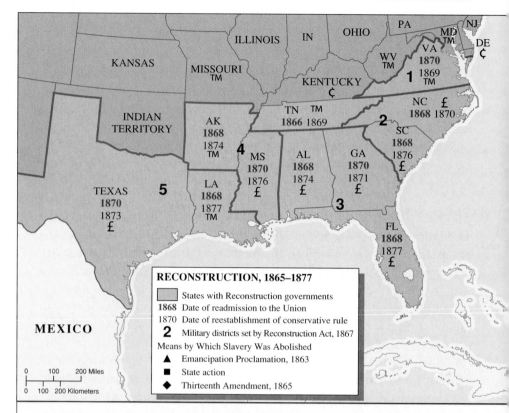

RECONSTRUCTION, 1865–1877

	States with Reconstruction governments
1868	Date of readmission to the Union
1870	Date of reestablishment of conservative rule
2	Military districts set by Reconstruction Act, 1867

Means by Which Slavery Was Abolished

▲ Emancipation Proclamation, 1863
■ State action
◆ Thirteenth Amendment, 1865

How did the Military Reconstruction Act reorganize government in the South in the late 1860s and 1870s? What did the former Confederate states have to do to be readmitted to the Union? How did "Conservative" parties gradually regain control of the South from the Republicans in the 1870s?

that helped undermine already inconsistent federal efforts to promote racial justice in the former Confederacy.

REFORM AND THE ELECTION OF 1872   Long before Grant's first term ended, Republicans broke ranks with the administration. Their alienation was a reaction to Radical Reconstruction and the incompetence and corruption in the administration. A new faction, called Liberal Republicans, favored free trade, the redemption of greenbacks with gold, the removal federal troops from the South, the restoration of the rights of former Confederates, and civil service reform. Open revolt first broke out in Missouri, where Carl Schurz, a German immigrant and war hero, led a group of Liberal

What I Know about Raising the Devil

With the tail and cloven hoof of the devil, Horace Greeley (center) leads a small band of Liberal Republicans in pursuit of incumbent president Ulysses S. Grant and his supporters in this 1872 cartoon.

Republicans who, with Democratic help, elected a governor in 1870 and sent Schurz to the Senate.

In 1872 the Liberal Republicans held their own national convention, which produced a compromise platform condemning the Republican party's "vindictive" southern policy and favoring civil service reform but remaining silent on the protective tariff. The delegates stampeded to endorse an anomalous presidential candidate: Horace Greeley, editor of the *New York Tribune* and an enthusiastic reformer. During his long journalistic career, Greeley had promoted vegetarianism, brown bread, free thinking, socialism, and spiritualism. His image as a visionary eccentric was complemented by his open hostility to the Democrats, whose support the Liberals needed. The Democrats gave the nomination to Greeley as the only hope of beating Grant and the Radical Republicans. Greeley's promise to end Radical Reconstruction and restore "self government" to the South won over Democrats who otherwise despised the man and his beliefs.

The 1872 election result surprised no one. Republican regulars duly endorsed Radical Reconstruction and the protective tariff. Grant still had seven southern states in his pocket, generous aid from business and banking interests, and the stalwart support of the Radical Republicans. Above all he still evoked the glory of military heroism. Greeley carried only six southern and border states, none in the North. Devastated by his crushing defeat and the death of his wife, Greeley entered a saniatorium and died three weeks later.

PANIC AND REDEMPTION   A paralyzing economic panic followed closely upon the public scandals besetting the Grant administration. A contraction of the nation's money supply resulting from the Treasury's postwar withdrawal of greenbacks and the reckless overexpansion of the railroads into sparsely settled areas helped precipitate a financial panic. During 1873 some twenty-five strapped railroads defaulted on their interest payments. A financial panic in Europe forced many financiers to unload American stocks and bonds. Caught short of cash, the prominent investment bank of Jay Cooke and Company went bankrupt on September 18, 1873. The event so frightened investors that the New York Stock Exchange had to close for ten days. The panic of 1873 set off a depression that lasted six years. It was the longest and most severe depression that Americans had yet suffered, marked by widespread bankruptcies, chronic unemployment, and a drastic slowdown in railroad building.

Hard times and political scandals hurt Republicans in the midterm elections of 1874, allowing the Democrats to win control of the House of Representatives and gain seats in the Senate. The new Democratic House immediately launched inquiries into the Grant scandals and unearthed further evidence of corruption in high places. The financial panic, meanwhile, focused attention once more on greenback currency. Since the value of greenbacks was lower than that of gold, paper money had become the chief circulating medium. Most people spent greenbacks first and held their gold or used it to settle foreign accounts, thereby draining much gold out of the country. To relieve this deflationary spiral and stimulate business expansion, the Treasury reissued $26 million in greenbacks that had previously been withdrawn.

For a time the advocates of paper money were riding high. But Grant vetoed an attempt to issue more greenbacks in 1874, and in his annual message he called for their gradual withdrawal and resumption of specie—redeeming greenbacks in gold. Congress obliged the president by passing the specie Resumption Act of 1875. The resumption of payments in gold to customers who turned in greenbacks began on January 1, 1879, after the Treasury had built a gold reserve for the purpose and reduced the value of the greenbacks in circulation. This act infuriated those promoting an inflationary monetary policy and led to the formation of the National Greenback party. The much debated and very complex "money question" would remain one of the most divisive issues in American politics until the end of the century.

THE COMPROMISE OF 1877 Grant yearned to run for president again in 1876, but his scandal-ridden administration cost him Republican support. James Gillespie Blaine of Maine, a former Speaker of the House, emerged as the Republican front-runner, but he, too, bore the taint of scandal. Letters in the possession of James Mulligan of Boston linked Blaine to dubious railroad dealings. Newspapers soon published the "Mulligan letters," and Blaine's candidacy was dealt a hefty blow.

The Republican Convention therefore eliminated Blaine and several other hopefuls in favor of Ohio's favorite son, Rutherford B. Hayes. Three times governor of Ohio and an advocate of hard money, Hayes had a sterling reputation and had been a civil service reformer. But his chief virtue, as a journalist put it, was that "he is obnoxious to no one."

The Democratic Convention was abnormally harmonious from the start. The nomination went on the second ballot to Samuel J. Tilden, a millionaire corporation lawyer and reform governor of New York who had directed a campaign to overthrow first the corrupt Tweed ring that controlled New York City politics and then the canal ring in Albany, which had bilked New York State of millions.

The 1876 election campaign generated no burning issues. Both candidates favored the trend toward relaxing federal authority and restoring white conservative rule in the South. In the absence of strong differences, Democrats waved the Republicans' dirty linen. In response, Republicans waved "the bloody shirt," which is to say that they engaged in verbal assaults on former Confederates and the spirit of rebellion, linking the Democratic party to secession and the outrages committed against Republicans in the South.

Early election returns pointed to a Tilden victory. Tilden had a 254,000-vote edge in the popular vote and won 184 electoral votes, just one short of a majority. Hayes had 165 electoral votes, but Republicans also claimed 19 disputed votes from Florida, Louisiana, and South Carolina. The Democrats laid a counterclaim to 1 of Oregon's 3 votes. The Republicans had clearly carried Oregon, but the outcome in the South was less certain, and given the fraud and intimidation perpetrated on both sides, nobody will ever know the truth of the matter. In all three of the disputed southern states, rival canvassing boards sent in different returns. The Constitution offered no guidance in this unprecedented situation. Even if Congress were empowered to sort things out, the Democratic House and the Republican Senate proved unable to reach an agreement.

The impasse dragged on for months, and there was even talk of partisan violence. Finally, on January 29, 1877, the two houses set up a special Electoral Commission that would investigate and report its findings. It had fifteen members, five each from the House, the Senate, and the Supreme Court. Members were chosen such that there were seven from each major party, with Justice David Davis of Illinois as the swing vote. Davis, though appointed to the Court by Lincoln, was no party regular and in fact was thought to be leaning toward the Democrats. Thus the panel appeared to be stacked in favor of Tilden.

As it turned out, however, the panel got restacked the other way. Short-sighted Democrats in the Illinois legislature teamed up with minority Greenbackers to name Davis their senator. Davis accepted, no doubt with a sense of relief. From the remaining justices, all Republicans, the panel chose Joseph P. Bradley to fill the vacancy. The decision on each state went by a vote of eight to seven along party lines, in favor of Hayes. After much bluster and the threat of a filibuster by the Democrats, the House voted on March 2 to accept the report and declared Hayes elected by an electoral vote of 185 to 184.

Critical to this outcome was the defection of southern Democrats who had made several informal agreements with the Republicans. On February 26, 1877, a bargain was struck at Wormley's Hotel in Washington, D.C., between prominent Ohio Republicans (including James A. Garfield) and powerful southern Democrats. The Republicans promised that if elected, Hayes would withdraw federal troops from Louisiana and South Carolina, letting the Republican governments there collapse. In return, the Democrats pledged to withdraw their opposition to Hayes, accept in good faith the Reconstruction amendments, and refrain from partisan reprisals against Republicans in the South.

Southern Democrats could now justify deserting Tilden. This so-called Compromise of 1877 brought a final "redemption" from the Radicals and a return to "home rule," which meant rule by white Democrats. As a former slave observed in 1877, "The whole South—every state in the south—has got [back] into the hands of the very men that held us as slaves." Other, more informal promises, bolstered the secret agreement. Hayes's friends pledged more support for rebuilding Mississippi River levees and other internal improvements, including a federal subsidy for a transcontinental railroad along a southern route. Southerners extracted a further promise that Hayes would name a white southerner as postmaster general, the cabinet position with the most patronage jobs to distribute. In return, southerners would let the Republicans make James Garfield the Speaker of the new House. Such a deal illustrates the relative weakness of the presidency compared with Congress during the postwar era.

THE END OF RECONSTRUCTION   In 1877 President Hayes withdrew federal troops from Louisiana and South Carolina, and the Republican governments there soon collapsed—along with Hayes's claim to legitimacy. Hayes chose a Tennessean as postmaster general. But after southern Democrats failed to permit the choice of James Garfield as Speaker of the House, Hayes expressed doubt about any further subsidy for railroad building, and none was voted. Most of the other promises made at Wormley's Hotel were renounced or forgotten.

As for southern promises regarding the civil rights of blacks, only a few Democratic leaders remembered them for long. Over the next three decades the federal protection of civil rights crumbled under the pressure of restored white rule in the South and the force of Supreme Court decisions narrowing the application of the Fourteenth and Fifteenth Amendments. Radical Reconstruction never offered more than an uncertain commitment to racial equality. Yet it left an enduring legacy, the Thirteenth, Fourteenth, and Fifteenth Amendments—not dead but dormant, waiting to be revived. If Reconstruction did not provide social equality or substantial economic opportunities for African Americans, it did create the opportunity for future transformation. It was a revolution, sighed former North Carolina governor Jonathan Worth, and "nobody can anticipate the action of revolutions."

MAKING CONNECTIONS

- The political, economic, and racial policies of the conservatives who overthrew the Republican governments in the southern states are described in Chapter 19.

- Several of the political scandals mentioned in this chapter were related to the railroads, a topic discussed in greater detail in Chapter 20.

- This chapter ended with the election of Rutherford B. Hayes; for a discussion of Hayes's administration, see Chapter 22.

Further Reading

The most comprehensive treatment of Reconstruction is Eric Foner's *Reconstruction: America's Unfinished Revolution, 1863-1877* (1988). On Andrew Johnson, see Hans L. Trefousse's *Andrew Johnson: A Biography* (1989). An excellent brief biography of Grant is Josiah Bunting III's *Ulysses S. Grant* (2004).

Scholars have been fairly sympathetic to the aims and motives of the Radical Republicans. See, for instance, Herman Belz's *Reconstructing the Union: Theory and Policy during the Civil War* (1969) and Richard Nelson Current's *Those Terrible Carpetbaggers: A Reinterpretation* (1988). The ideology of the Radical Republicans is explored in Michael Les Benedict's *A Compromise of Principle: Congressional Republicans and Reconstruction, 1863–1869* (1974).

The intransigence of southern white attitudes is examined in Michael Perman's *Reunion without Compromise* (1973) and Dan T. Carter's *When the War Was Over: The Failure of Self-Reconstruction in the South, 1865–1867* (1985). Allen W. Trelease's *White Terror: The Ku Klux and Southern Reconstruction* (1971) covers the various organizations that practiced vigilante tactics. The difficulties former laborers had in adjusting to the new labor system are documented in James L. Roark's *Masters without Slaves: Southern Planters to the Civil War and Reconstruction* (1977). Books on southern politics during Reconstruction include Michael Perman's *The Road to Redemption: Southern Politics, 1869–1879* (1984), Terry L. Seip's *The South Returns to Congress: Men, Economic Measures, and Intersectional Relationships, 1868–1879* (1983), and Mark W. Summer's *Railroads, Reconstruction, and the Gospel of Prosperity: Aid under Radical Republicans, 1865–1877* (1984).

Numerous works feature the freed blacks' experience in the South. Start with Leon F. Litwack's *Been in the Storm So Long: The Aftermath of Slavery* (1979), which covers the transition from slavery to freedom. Joel Williamson's *After Slavery: The Negro in South Carolina during Reconstruction, 1861–1877* (1965) argues that South Carolina blacks took an active role in pursuing their political and economic rights. The Freedmen's Bureau is explored in William S. McFeely's *Yankee Stepfather: General O. O. Howard and the Freedmen* (1968). The situation of freed slave women is discussed in Jacqueline Jones's *Labor of Love, Labor of Sorrow: Black Women, Work, and the Family, from Slavery to the Present* (1985).

The politics of corruption outside the South is depicted in William S. McFeely's *Grant: A Biography* (1981). The political maneuvers of the election of 1876 and the resultant crisis and compromise are explained in C. Vann Woodward's *Reunion and Reaction: The Compromise of 1877 and the End of Reconstruction* (1951) and in William Gillette's *Retreat from Reconstruction, 1869–1879* (1979).

GLOSSARY

Agricultural Adjustment Act (1933) New Deal legislation that established the Agricultural Adjustment Administration (AAA) to improve agricultural prices by limiting market supplies; declared unconstitutional in *United States v. Butler* (1936).

Alamo, Battle of the Siege in the Texas War for Independence, 1836, in which the San Antonio mission fell to the Mexicans, and Davy Crockett and Jim Bowie died.

***Alexander v. Holmes County Board of Education* (1969)** Case fifteen years after the *Brown* decision in which the U.S. Supreme Court ordered an immediate end to segregation in public schools.

Alien and Sedition Acts (1798) Four measures passed during the undeclared war with France that limited the freedoms of speech and press and restricted the liberty of noncitizens.

America First Committee Largely midwestern isolationist organization supported by many prominent citizens, 1940–41.

American Anti-Slavery Society National abolitionist organization founded in 1833 by New York philanthropists Arthur and Lewis Tappan, propagandist Theodore Dwight Weld, and others.

American Colonization Society Organized in 1816 to encourage colonization of free blacks to Africa; West African nation of Liberia founded in 1822 to serve as a homeland for them.

American Federation of Labor Founded in 1881 as a federation of trade unions, the AFL under president Samuel Gompers successfully pushed for the eight-hour workday.

American Protective Association Nativist, anti-Catholic secret society founded in Iowa in 1887 and active until the end of the century.

American System Program of internal improvements and protective tariffs promoted by Speaker of the House Henry Clay in his presidential campaign of 1824; his proposals formed the core of Whig ideology in the 1830s and 1840s.

Antietam, Battle of (Battle of Sharpsburg) One of the bloodiest battles of the Civil War, fought to a standoff on September 17, 1862, in western Maryland.

Anti-Federalists Forerunners of Thomas Jefferson's Democratic-Republican party; opposed the Constitution as a limitation on individual and states' rights, which led to the addition of a Bill of Rights to the document.

Appomattox Court House, Virginia Site of the surrender of Confederate general Robert E. Lee to Union general Ulysses S. Grant on April 9, 1865, marking the end of the Civil War.

Army-McCarthy hearings Televised U.S. Senate hearings in 1954 on Senator Joseph McCarthy's charges of disloyalty in the Army; his tactics contributed to his censure by the Senate.

Atlanta Compromise Speech to the Cotton States and International Exposition in 1895 by educator Booker T. Washington, the leading black spokesman of the day; black scholar W. E. B. Du Bois gave the speech its derisive name and criticized Washington for encouraging blacks to accommodate segregation and disenfranchisement.

Atlantic Charter Issued August 12, 1941, following meetings in Newfoundland between President Franklin D. Roosevelt and British prime minister Winston Churchill, the charter signaled the allies' cooperation and stated their war aims.

Atomic Energy Commission Created in 1946 to supervise peacetime uses of atomic energy.

Axis powers In World War II, the nations of Germany, Italy, and Japan.

Aztec Mesoamerican people who were conquered by the Spanish under Hernando Cortés, 1519–28.

baby boom Markedly higher birth rate in the years following World War II; led to the biggest demographic "bubble" in American history.

Bacon's Rebellion Unsuccessful 1676 revolt led by planter Nathaniel Bacon against Virginia governor William Berkeley's administration because it had failed to protect settlers from Indian raids.

Bakke v. Board of Regents of California **(1978)** Case in which the U.S. Supreme Court ruled against the California university system's use of racial quotas in admissions.

balance of trade Ratio of imports to exports.

Bank of the United States Proposed by the first secretary of the treasury, Alexander Hamilton, the bank opened in 1791 and operated until 1811 to issue a uniform currency, make business loans, and collect tax monies. The Second Bank of the United States was chartered in 1816 but was not renewed by President Andrew Jackson twenty years later.

barbary pirates Plundering pirates off the Mediterranean coast of Africa; President Thomas Jefferson's refusal to pay them tribute to protect American ships sparked an undeclared naval war with North African nations, 1801–1805.

barbed wire First practical fencing material for the Great Plains was invented in 1873 and rapidly spelled the end of the open range.

Battle of the Currents Conflict in the late 1880s between inventors Thomas Edison and George Westinghouse over direct versus alternating electric current; Westinghouse's alternating current (AC), the winner, allowed electricity to travel over long distances.

Bay of Pigs Invasion Hoping to inspire a revolt against Fidel Castro, the CIA sent 1,500 Cuban exiles to invade their homeland on April 17, 1961, but the mission was a spectacular failure.

Bill of Rights First ten amendments to the U.S. Constitution, adopted in 1791 to guarantee individual rights and to help secure ratification of the Constitution by the states.

Black Codes (1865–66) Laws passed in southern states to restrict the rights of former slaves; to combat the codes, Congress passed the Civil Rights Act of 1866 and the Fourteenth Amendment and set up military governments in southern states that refused to ratify the amendment.

Black Power Post-1966 rallying cry of a more militant civil rights movement.

Bland-Allison Act (1878) Passed over President Rutherford B. Hayes's veto, the inflationary measure authorized the purchase each month of 2 to 4 million dollars' worth of silver for coinage.

"Bleeding" Kansas Violence between pro- and antislavery settlers in the Kansas Territory, 1856.

Bloody Shirt, Waving the Republican references to Reconstruction-era violence in the South, used effectively in northern political campaigns against Democrats.

Bonus Expeditionary Force Thousands of World War I veterans, who insisted on immediate payment of their bonus certificates, marched on Washington in 1932; violence ensued when President Herbert Hoover ordered their tent villages cleared.

Boston Massacre Clash between British soldiers and a Boston mob, March 5, 1770, in which five colonists were killed.

Boston Tea Party On December 16, 1773, the Sons of Liberty, dressed as Indians, dumped hundreds of chests of tea into Boston harbor to protest the Tea Act of 1773, under which the British exported to the colonies millions of pounds of cheap—but still taxed—tea, thereby undercutting the price of smuggled tea and forcing payment of the tea duty.

Boxer Rebellion Chinese nationalist protest against Western commercial domination and cultural influence, 1900; a coalition of American, European, and Japanese forces put down the rebellion and reclaimed captured embassies in Peking (Beijing) within the year.

brain trust Group of advisers—many of them academics—that Franklin D. Roosevelt assembled to recommend New Deal policies during the early months of his presidency.

Branch Davidians Religious cult that lived communally near Waco, Texas, and was involved in a fiery 1993 confrontation with federal authorities in which dozens of cult members died.

Brook Farm Transcendentalist commune in West Roxbury, Massachusetts, populated from 1841 to 1847 principally by writers (Nathaniel Hawthorne, for one) and other intellectuals.

***Brown v. Board of Education of Topeka* (1954)** U.S. Supreme Court decision that struck down racial segregation in public education and declared "separate but equal" unconstitutional.

Budget and Accounting Act of 1921 Created the Bureau of the Budget and the General Accounting Office.

Bull Run, Battles of (First and Second Manassas) First land engagement of the Civil War took place on July 21, 1861, at Manassas Junction, Virginia, at which surprised Union troops quickly retreated; one year later, on August 29–30, Confederates captured the federal supply depot and forced Union troops back to Washington.

Bunker Hill, Battle of First major battle of the Revolutionary War; it actually took place at nearby Breed's Hill, Massachusetts, on June 17, 1775.

"Burned-Over District" Area of western New York strongly influenced by the revivalist fervor of the Second Great Awakening; Disciples of Christ and Mormons are among the many sects that trace their roots to the phenomenon.

Burr conspiracy Scheme by Vice-President Aaron Burr to lead the secession of the Louisiana Territory from the United States; captured in 1807 and charged with treason, Burr was acquitted by the U.S. Supreme Court.

***Bush v. Gore* (2000)** U.S. Supreme Court case that determined the winner of the disputed 2000 presidential election.

Calhoun Resolutions In making the proslavery response to the Wilmot Proviso, Senator John C. Calhoun argued that barring slavery in Mexican acquisitions would violate the Fifth Amendment to the Constitution by depriving slaveholding settlers of their property.

Calvinism Doctrine of predestination expounded by Swiss theologian John Calvin in 1536; influenced the Puritan, Presbyterian, German and Dutch Reformed, and Huguenot churches in the colonies.

Camp David Accords Peace agreement between Israeli prime minister Menachem Begin and Egyptian president Anwar Sadat, brokered by President Jimmy Carter in 1978.

carpetbaggers Northern emigrants who participated in the Republican governments of the Reconstruction South.

Chancellorsville, Battle of Confederate general Robert E. Lee won his last major victory and General "Stonewall" Jackson died in this Civil War battle in northern Virginia on May 1–4, 1863.

Chattanooga, Battle of Union victory in eastern Tennessee on November 23–25, 1863; gave the North control of important rail lines and cleared the way for General William T. Sherman's march into Georgia.

Chinese Exclusion Act (1882) Halted Chinese immigration to the United States.

Civil Rights Act of 1866 Along with the Fourteenth Amendment, guaranteed the rights of citizenship to freedmen.

Civil Rights Act of 1957 First federal civil rights law since Reconstruction; established the Civil Rights Commission and the Civil Rights Division of the Department of Justice.

Civil Rights Act of 1964 Outlawed discrimination in public accommodations and employment.

clipper ships Superior oceangoing sailing ships of the 1840s to 1860s that cut travel time in half; the clipper ship route around Cape Horn was the fastest way to travel between the coasts of the United States.

closed shop Hiring requirement that all workers in a business must be union members.

Coercive Acts/Intolerable Acts (1774) Four parliamentary measures in reaction to the Boston Tea Party that forced payment for the tea, disallowed colonial trials of British soldiers, forced their quartering in private homes, and set up a military government.

cold war Term for tensions, 1945–89, between the Soviet Union and the United States, the two major world powers after World War II.

***Commonwealth v. Hunt* (1842)** Landmark ruling of the Massachusetts supreme court establishing the legality of labor unions.

Compromise of 1850 Complex compromise mediated by Senator Henry Clay that headed off southern secession over California statehood; to appease the South it included a stronger fugitive slave law and delayed determination of the slave status of the New Mexico and Utah territories.

Compromise of 1877 Deal made by a special congressional commission on March 2, 1877, to resolve the disputed presidential election of 1876; Republican Rutherford B. Hayes, who had lost the popular vote, was declared the winner in exchange for the withdrawal of federal troops from the South, marking the end of Reconstruction.

Congress of Industrial Organizations (CIO) Umbrella organization of semi-skilled industrial unions, formed in 1935 as the Committee for Industrial Organization and renamed in 1938.

Congress of Racial Equality (CORE) Civil rights organization started in 1944 and best known for its "freedom rides," bus journeys challenging racial segregation in the South in 1961.

conspicuous consumption Phrase referring to extravagant spending to raise social standing, coined by Thorstein Veblen in *The Theory of the Leisure Class* (1899).

Constitutional Convention Meeting in Philadelphia, May 25–September 17, 1787, of representatives from twelve colonies—excepting Rhode Island—to revise the existing Articles of Confederation; convention soon resolved to produce an entirely new constitution.

containment General U.S. strategy in the cold war that called for containing Soviet expansion; originally devised in 1947 by U.S. diplomat George F. Kennan.

Continental Army Army authorized by the Continental Congress, 1775–84, to fight the British; commanded by General George Washington.

Continental Congress Representatives of a loose confederation of colonies met first in Philadelphia in 1774 to formulate actions against British policies; the Second Continental Congress (1775–89) conducted the war and adopted the Declaration of Independence and the Articles of Confederation.

convict leasing System developed in the post–Civil War South that generated income for the states and satisfied planters' need for cheap labor by renting prisoners out; the convicts, however, were often treated poorly.

Copperheads Northerners opposed to the Civil War.

Coral Sea, Battle of the Fought on May 7–8, 1942, near the eastern coast of Australia, it was the first U.S. naval victory over Japan in World War II.

cotton gin Invented by Eli Whitney in 1793, the machine separated cotton seed from cotton fiber, speeding cotton processing and making profitable the cultivation of the more hardy, but difficult to clean, short-staple cotton; led directly to the dramatic nineteenth-century expansion of slavery in the South.

counterculture "Hippie" youth culture of the 1960s, which rejected the values of the dominant culture in favor of illicit drugs, communes, free sex, and rock music.

court-packing plan President Franklin D. Roosevelt's failed 1937 attempt to increase the number of U.S. Supreme Court justices from nine to fifteen in order to save his Second New Deal programs from constitutional challenges.

Credit Mobilier scandal Millions of dollars in overcharges for building the Union Pacific Railroad were exposed; high officials of the Ulysses S. Grant administration were implicated but never charged.

Cuban missile crisis Caused when the United States discovered Soviet offensive missile sites in Cuba in October 1962; the U.S.-Soviet confrontation was the cold war's closest brush with nuclear war.

crop-lien system Merchants extended credit to tenants based on their future crops, but high interest rates and the uncertainties of farming often led to inescapable debts (debt peonage).

D-Day June 6, 1944, when an Allied amphibious assault landed on the Normandy coast and established a foothold in Europe from which Hitler's defenses could not recover.

Dartmouth College v. Woodward **(1819)** U.S. Supreme Court upheld the original charter of the college against New Hampshire's attempt to alter the board of trustees; set precedent of support of contracts against state interference.

Declaration of Independence Document adopted on July 4, 1776, that made the break with Britain official; drafted by a committee of the Second Continental Congress including principal writer Thomas Jefferson.

Deism Enlightenment thought applied to religion; emphasized reason, morality, and natural law.

Department of Homeland Security Created to coordinate federal antiterrorist activity following the 2001 terrorist attacks on the World Trade Center and Pentagon.

Depression of 1893 Worst depression of the century, set off by a railroad failure, too much speculation on Wall Street, and low agricultural prices.

Dixiecrats Deep South delegates who walked out of the 1948 Democratic National Convention in protest of the party's support for civil rights legislation and later formed the States' Rights (Dixiecrat) party, which nominated Strom Thurmond of South Carolina for president.

Dominion of New England Consolidation into a single colony of the New England colonies—and later New York and New Jersey—by royal governor Edmund Andros in 1686; dominion reverted to individual colonial governments three years later.

Donner Party Forty-seven surviving members of a group of migrants to California were forced to resort to cannibalism to survive a brutal winter trapped in the Sierra Nevadas, 1846–47; highest death toll of any group traveling the Overland Trail.

***Dred Scott v. Sandford* (1857)** U.S. Supreme Court decision in which Chief Justice Roger B. Taney ruled that slaves could not sue for freedom and that Congress could not prohibit slavery in the territories, on the grounds that such a prohibition would violate the Fifth Amendment rights of slaveholders.

due-process clause Clause in the Fifth and the Fourteenth amendments to the U.S. Constitution guaranteeing that states could not "deprive any person of life, liberty, or property, without due process of law."

Dust Bowl Great Plains counties where millions of tons of topsoil were blown away from parched farmland in the 1930s; massive migration of farm families followed.

Eighteenth Amendment (1919) Prohibition amendment that made illegal the manufacture, sale, or transportation of alcoholic beverages.

Ellis Island Reception center in New York Harbor through which most European immigrants to America were processed from 1892 to 1954.

Emancipation Proclamation (1863) President Abraham Lincoln issued a preliminary proclamation on September 22, 1862, freeing the slaves in the Confederate states as of January 1, 1863, the date of the final proclamation.

Embargo Act of 1807 Attempt to exert economic pressure instead of waging war in reaction to continued British impressment of American sailors; smugglers easily circumvented the embargo, and it was repealed two years later.

Emergency Banking Relief Act (1933) First New Deal measure that provided for reopening the banks under strict conditions and took the United States off the gold standard.

Emergency Immigration Act of 1921 Limited U.S. immigration to 3 percent of each foreign-born nationality in the 1910 census; three years later Congress restricted immigration even further.

encomienda System under which officers of the Spanish conquistadores gained ownership of Indian land.

ENIAC Electronic Numerical Integrator and Computer, built in 1944, the early, cumbersome ancestor of the modern computer.

Enlightenment Revolution in thought begun in the seventeenth century that emphasized reason and science over the authority of traditional religion.

Enola Gay American B-29 bomber that dropped the atomic bomb on Hiroshima, Japan, on August 6, 1945.

Environmental Protection Agency (EPA) Created in 1970 during the first administration of President Richard M. Nixon to oversee federal pollution control efforts.

Equal Rights Amendment Amendment to guarantee equal rights for women, introduced in 1923 but not passed by Congress until 1972; it failed to be ratified by the states.

Era of Good Feelings Contemporary characterization of the administration of popular Democratic-Republican president James Monroe, 1817–25.

Erie Canal Most important and profitable of the barge canals of the 1820s and 1830s; stretched from Buffalo to Albany, New York, connecting the Great Lakes to the East Coast and making New York City the nation's largest port.

Espionage and Sedition Acts (1917–18) Limited criticism of government leaders and policies by imposing fines and prison terms on those who acted out in opposition to in the First World War; the most repressive measures passed up to that time.

Fair Deal Domestic reform proposals of the second Truman administration (1949–53); included civil rights legislation and repeal of the Taft-Hartley Act, but only extensions of some New Deal programs were enacted.

Fair Employment Practices Commission Created in 1941 by executive order, the FEPC sought to eliminate racial discrimination in jobs; it possessed little power but represented a step toward civil rights for African Americans.

Family and Medical Leave Act (1993) Allowed certain workers to take twelve weeks of unpaid leave each year for family health problems, including birth or adoption of a child.

Farmers' Alliance Two separate organizations (Northwestern and Southern) of the 1880s and 1890s that took the place of the Grange, worked for similar causes, and attracted landless, as well as landed, farmers to their membership.

Federal Trade Commission Act (1914) Established the Federal Trade Commission to enforce existing antitrust laws that prohibited business combinations in restraint of trade.

The Federalist Collection of eighty-five essays that appeared in the New York press in 1787–88 in support of the Constitution; written by Alexander Hamilton, James Madison, and John Jay but published under the pseudonym "Publius."

Federalist party One of the two first national political parties, it favored a strong central government.

Fence-Cutters' War Violent conflict in Texas, 1883–84, between large and small cattle ranchers over access to grazing land.

"Fifty-four forty or fight" Democratic campaign slogan in the presidential election of 1844, urging that the northern border of Oregon be fixed at 54°40′ north latitude.

***Fletcher v. Peck* (1810)** U.S. Supreme Court decision in which Chief Justice John Marshall upheld the initial fraudulent sale contracts in the Yazoo Fraud cases; Congress paid $4.2 million to the original speculators in 1814.

Fort Laramie Treaty (1851) Restricted the Plains Indians from using the Overland Trail and permitted the building of government forts.

Fort McHenry Fort in Baltimore Harbor unsuccessfully bombarded by the British in September 1814; Francis Scott Key, a witness to the battle, was moved to write the words to "The Star-Spangled Banner."

Fort Sumter First battle of the Civil War, in which the federal fort in Charleston (South Carolina) Harbor was captured by the Confederates on April 14, 1861, after two days of shelling.

"forty-niners" Speculators who went to northern California following the discovery of gold in 1848; the first of several years of large-scale migration was 1849.

Fourteen Points President Woodrow Wilson's 1918 plan for peace after World War I; at the Versailles peace conference, however, he failed to incorporate all of the points into the treaty.

Fourteenth Amendment (1868) Guaranteed rights of citizenship to former slaves, in words similar to those of the Civil Rights Act of 1866.

franchise The right to vote.

"free person of color" Negro or mulatto person not held in slavery; immediately before the Civil War, there were nearly a half million in the United States, split almost evenly between North and South.

Free Soil party Formed in 1848 to oppose slavery in the territory acquired in the Mexican War; nominated Martin Van Buren for president in 1848, but by 1854 most of the party's members had joined the Republican party.

Free Speech Movement Founded in 1964 at the University of California at Berkeley by student radicals protesting restrictions on their right to demonstrate.

Freedmen's Bureau Reconstruction agency established in 1865 to protect the legal rights of former slaves and to assist with their education, jobs, health care, and landowning.

French and Indian War Known in Europe as the Seven Years' War, the last (1755–63) of four colonial wars fought between England and France for control of North America east of the Mississippi River.

Fugitive Slave Act of 1850 Gave federal government authority in cases involving runaway slaves; so much more punitive and prejudiced in favor of slaveholders than the 1793 Fugitive Slave Act had been that Harriet Beecher Stowe was inspired to write *Uncle Tom's Cabin* in protest; the new law was part of the Compromise of 1850, included to appease the South over the admission of California as a free state.

Fundamentalism Anti-modernist Protestant movement started in the early twentieth century that proclaimed the literal truth of the Bible; the name came from *The Fundamentals*, published by conservative leaders.

Gadsden Purchase (1853) Thirty thousand square miles in present-day Arizona and New Mexico bought by Congress from Mexico primarily for the Southern Pacific Railroad's transcontinental route.

Gentlemen's Agreement (1907) United States would not exclude Japanese immigrants if Japan would voluntarily limit the number of immigrants coming to the United States.

Gettysburg, Battle of Fought in southern Pennsylvania, July 1–3, 1863; the Confederate defeat and the simultaneous loss at Vicksburg spelled the end of the South's chances in the Civil War.

***Gibbons v. Ogden* (1824)** U.S. Supreme Court decision reinforcing the "commerce clause" (the federal government's right to regulate interstate commerce) of the Constitution; Chief Justice John Marshall ruled against the State of New York's granting of steamboat monopolies.

***Gideon v. Wainwright* (1963)** U.S. Supreme Court decision guaranteeing legal counsel for indigent felony defendants.

The Gilded Age Mark Twain and Charles Dudley Warner's 1873 novel, the title of which became the popular name for the period from the end of the Civil War to the turn of the century.

Glass-Owen Federal Reserve Act (1913) Created a Federal Reserve System of regional banks and a Federal Reserve Board to stabilize the economy by regulating the supply of currency and controlling credit.

Glass-Steagall Act (Banking Act of 1933) Established the Federal Deposit Insurance Corporation and included banking reforms, some designed to control speculation. A banking act of the Hoover administration, passed in 1932 and also known as the Glass-Steagall Act, was designed to expand credit.

Good Neighbor Policy Proclaimed by President Franklin D. Roosevelt in his first inaugural address in 1933, it sought improved diplomatic relations between the United States and its Latin American neighbors.

grandfather clause Loophole created by southern disfranchising legislatures of the 1890s for illiterate white males whose grandfathers had been eligible to vote in 1867.

Granger movement Political movement that grew out of the Patrons of Husbandry, an educational and social organization for farmers founded in 1867; the Grange had its greatest success in the Midwest of the 1870s, lobbying for government control of railroad and grain elevator rates and establishing farmers' cooperatives.

Great Awakening Fervent religious revival movement in the 1720s through the 1740s that was spread throughout the colonies by ministers like New England Congregationalist Jonathan Edwards and English revivalist George Whitefield.

Great Compromise (Connecticut Compromise) Mediated the differences between the New Jersey and Virginia delegations to the Constitutional Convention by providing for a bicameral legislature, the upper house of which would have equal representation and the lower house of which would be apportioned by population.

Great Depression Worst economic depression in American history; it was spurred by the stock market crash of 1929 and lasted until World War II.

Great Migration Large-scale migration of southern blacks during and after World War I to the North, where jobs had become available during the labor shortage of the war years.

Great Society Term coined by President Lyndon B. Johnson in his 1965 State of the Union address, in which he proposed legislation to address problems of voting rights, poverty, diseases, education, immigration, and the environment.

Greenback party Formed in 1876 in reaction to economic depression, the party favored issuance of unsecured paper money to help farmers repay debts; the movement for free coinage of silver took the place of the greenback movement by the 1880s.

habeas corpus, writ of An essential component of English common law and of the U.S. Constitution that guarantees that citizens may not be imprisoned without due process of law; literally means, "you must have the body."

Half-Breeds During the presidency of Rutherford B. Hayes, 1877–81, a moderate Republican party faction led by Senator James G. Blaine that favored some reforms of the civil service system and a restrained policy toward the defeated South.

Harlem Renaissance African-American literary and artistic movement of the 1920s and 1930s centered in New York City's Harlem district; writers Langston Hughes, Jean Toomer, Zora Neale Hurston, and Countee Cullen were among those active in the movement.

Harpers Ferry, Virginia Site of abolitionist John Brown's failed raid on the federal arsenal, October 16–17, 1859; he intended to arm the slaves, but ten of his compatriots were killed, and Brown became a martyr to his cause after his capture and execution.

Hartford Convention Meeting of New England Federalists on December 15, 1814, to protest the War of 1812; proposed seven constitutional amendments (limiting embargoes and changing requirements for officeholding, declaration of war, and admission of new states), but the war ended before Congress could respond.

Hawley-Smoot Tariff Act (1930) Raised tariffs to an unprecedented level and worsened the depression by raising prices and discouraging foreign trade.

Haymarket Affair Riot during an anarchist protest at Haymarket Square in Chicago on May 4, 1886, over violence during the McCormick Harvester Company strike; the deaths of eleven, including seven policemen, helped hasten the demise of the Knights of Labor, even though they were not responsible for the riot.

Hessians German soldiers, most from Hesse-Cassel principality (hence the name), paid to fight for the British in the Revolutionary War.

holding company Investment company that holds controlling interest in the securities of other companies.

Homestead Act (1862) Authorized Congress to grant 160 acres of public land to a western settler, who had only to live on the land for five years to establish title.

Homestead Strike Violent strike at the Carnegie Steel Company near Pittsburgh in 1892 that culminated in the disintegration of the Amalgamated Association of Iron and Steel Workers, the first steelworkers' union.

House Un-American Activities Committee (HUAC) Formed in 1938 to investigate subversives in the government; best-known investigations were of Hollywood no tables and of former State Department official Alger Hiss, who was accused in 1948 of espionage and Communist party membership.

Hundred Days Extraordinarily productive first three months of President Franklin D. Roosevelt's administration in which a special session of Congress enacted fifteen of his New Deal proposals.

impeachment Bringing charges against a public official; for example, the House of Representatives can impeach a president for "treason, bribery, or other high crimes and misdemeanors" by majority vote, and after the trial the Senate can remove the president by a vote of two-thirds.

implied powers Federal powers beyond those specifically enumerated in the U.S. Constitution; the Federalists argued that the "elastic clause" of Article I, Section 8, of the Constitution implicitly gave the federal government broad powers, while the Antifederalists held that the federal government's powers were explicitly limited by the Constitution.

"In God We Trust" Phrase placed on all new U.S. currency as of 1954.

indentured servant Settler who signed on for a temporary period of servitude to a master in exchange for passage to the New World; Virginia and Pennsylvania were largely peopled in the seventeenth and eighteenth centuries by English indentured servants.

Independent Treasury Act (1840) Promoted by President Martin Van Buren, the measure sought to stabilize the economy by preventing state banks from printing unsecured paper currency and establishing an independent treasury based on specie.

Indian Peace Commission Established in 1867 to end the Indian wars in the West, the commission's solution was to contain the Indians in a system of reservations.

Indian Removal Act (1830) Signed by President Andrew Jackson, the law permitted the negotiation of treaties to obtain the Indians' lands in exchange for their relocation to what would become Oklahoma.

Industrial Workers of the World Radical union organized in Chicago in 1905 and nicknamed the Wobblies; its opposition to World War I led to its destruction by the federal government under the Espionage Act.

internal improvements In the early national period the phrase referred to road building and the development of water transportation.

Interstate Commerce Commission Reacting to the U.S. Supreme Court's ruling in *Wabash Railroad* v. *Illinois* (1886), Congress established the ICC to curb abuses in the railroad industry by regulating rates.

Iran-Contra affair Scandal of the second Reagan administration involving sale of arms to Iran in partial exchange for release of hostages in Lebanon and use of the arms money to aid the Contras in Nicaragua, which had been expressly forbidden by Congress.

Iron Curtain Term coined by Winston Churchill to describe the cold war divide between western Europe and the Soviet Union's eastern European satellites.

Irreconcilables Group of isolationist U.S. senators who fought ratification of the Treaty of Versailles, 1919–20, because of their opposition to American membership in the League of Nations.

Jamestown, Virginia Site in 1607 of the first permanent English settlement in the New World.

Jay's Treaty Treaty with Britain negotiated in 1794 by Chief Justice John Jay; Britain agreed to vacate forts in the Northwest Territories, and festering disagreements (border with Canada, prewar debts, shipping claims) would be settled by commission.

Jim Crow Minstrel show character whose name became synonymous with post-Reconstruction laws revoking civil rights for freedmen and with racial segregation generally.

Judiciary Act of 1801 Enacted by the lame duck Congress to allow the Federalists, the losing party in the presidential election, to reorganize the judiciary and fill the open judgeships with Federalists.

Kansas-Nebraska Act (1854) Law sponsored by Illinois senator Stephen A. Douglas to allow settlers in newly organized territories north of the Missouri border to decide the slavery issue for themselves; fury over the resulting nullification of the Missouri Compromise of 1820 led to violence in Kansas and to the formation of the Republican party.

Kellogg-Briand Pact Representatives of sixty-two nations in 1928 signed the pact (also called the Pact of Paris) to outlaw war.

Kentucky and Virginia Resolutions (1798–99) Passed in response to the Alien and Sedition Acts, the resolutions advanced the state-compact theory that held states could nullify an act of Congress if they deemed it unconstitutional.

King William's War (War of the League of Augsburg) First (1689–97) of four colonial wars between England and France.

King's Mountain, Battle of Upcountry South Carolina irregulars defeated British troops under Patrick Ferguson on October 7, 1780, in what proved to be the turning point of the Revolutionary War in the South.

Knights of Labor Founded in 1869, the first national union picked up many members after the disastrous 1877 railroad strike but lasted, under the leadership of Terence V. Powderly, only into the 1890s; supplanted by the American Federation of Labor.

Know-Nothing (American) party Nativist, anti-Catholic third party organized in 1854 in reaction to large-scale German and Irish immigration; the party's only presidential candidate was Millard Fillmore in 1856.

Korean War Conflict touched off in 1950 when Communist North Korea invaded South Korea, which had been under U.S. control since the end of World War II; fighting largely by U.S. forces continued until 1953.

Ku Klux Klan Organized in Pulaski, Tennessee, in 1866 to terrorize former slaves who voted and held political offices during Reconstruction; a revived organization in the 1910s and 1920s stressed white, Anglo-Saxon, fundamentalist Protestant supremacy; the Klan revived a third time to fight the civil rights movement of the 1950s and 1960s in the South.

Land Ordinance of 1785 Directed surveying of the Northwest Territory into townships of thirty-six sections (square miles) each, the sale of the sixteenth section of which was to be used to finance public education.

League of Nations Organization of nations to mediate disputes and avoid war established after World War I as part of the Treaty of Versailles; President Woodrow Wilson's "Fourteen Points" speech to Congress in 1918 proposed the formation of the league.

Lecompton Constitution Controversial constitution drawn up in 1857 by proslavery Kansas delegates seeking statehood; rejected in 1858 by an overwhelmingly antislavery electorate.

Legal Tender Act (1862) Helped the U.S. government pay for the Civil War by authorizing the printing of paper currency.

Lend-Lease Act (1941) Permitted the United States to lend or lease arms and other supplies to the Allies, signifying increasing likelihood of American involvement in World War II.

Levittown Low-cost, mass-produced development of suburban tract housing built by William Levitt on Long Island in 1947.

Lexington and Concord, Battle of The first shots fired in the Revolutionary War, on April 19, 1775, near Boston; approximately 100 minutemen and 250 British soldiers were killed.

Leyte Gulf, Battle of Largest sea battle in history, fought on October 25, 1944, and won by the United States off the Philippine island of Leyte; Japanese losses were so great that they could not rebound.

Liberty party Abolitionist political party that nominated James G. Birney for president in 1840 and 1844; merged with the Free Soil party in 1848.

Lincoln-Douglas debates Series of senatorial campaign debates in 1858 focusing on the issue of slavery in the territories; held in Illinois between Republican Abraham Lincoln, who made a national reputation for himself, and incumbent Democratic senator Stephen A. Douglas, who managed to hold onto his seat.

Little Bighorn, Battle of Most famous battle of the Great Sioux War took place in 1876 in the Montana Territory; combined Sioux and Cheyenne warriors massacred a vastly outnumbered U.S. Cavalry commanded by Lieutenant Colonel George Armstrong Custer.

Lost Colony English expedition of 117 settlers, including Virginia Dare, the first English child born in the New World; colony disappeared from Roanoke Island in the Outer Banks sometime between 1587 and 1590.

Louisiana Purchase President Thomas Jefferson's 1803 purchase from France of the important port of New Orleans and 828,000 square miles west of the Mississippi River to the Rocky Mountains; it more than doubled the territory of the United States at a cost of only $15 million.

Lusitania British passenger liner sunk by a German U-boat, May 7, 1915, creating a diplomatic crisis and public outrage at the loss of 128 Americans (roughly 10 percent of the total aboard); Germany agreed to pay reparations, and the United States waited two more years to enter World War I.

Lyceum movement Founded in 1826, the movement promoted adult public education through lectures and performances.

maize Indian corn, native to the New World.

Manhattan Project Secret American plan during World War II to develop an atomic bomb; J. Robert Oppenheimer led the team of physicists at Los Alamos, New Mexico.

Manifest Destiny Imperialist phrase first used in 1845 to urge annexation of Texas; used thereafter to encourage American settlement of European colonial and Indian lands in the Great Plains and Far West.

Marbury v. Madison **(1803)** First U.S. Supreme Court decision to declare a federal law—the Judiciary Act of 1801—unconstitutional; President John Adams's "midnight appointment" of Federalist judges prompted the suit.

March on Washington Civil rights demonstration on August 28, 1963, where the Reverend Martin Luther King, Jr., gave his "I Have a Dream" speech on the steps of the Lincoln Memorial.

Marshall Plan U.S. program for the reconstruction of post–World War II Europe through massive aid to former enemy nations as well as allies; proposed by General George C. Marshall in 1947.

massive resistance In reaction to the *Brown* decision of 1954, U.S. senator Harry Byrd encouraged southern states to defy federally mandated school integration.

Maya Pre-Columbian society in Mesoamerica before about A.D. 900.

Mayflower Compact Signed in 1620 aboard the *Mayflower* before the Pilgrims landed at Plymouth, the document committed the group to majority-rule government; remained in effect until 1691.

Maysville Road Bill Federal funding for a Kentucky road, vetoed by President Andrew Jackson in 1830.

McCarran Internal Security Act (1950) Passed over President Harry S. Truman's veto, the law required registration of American Communist party members, denied them passports, and allowed them to be detained as suspected subversives.

McCulloch v. Maryland **(1819)** U.S. Supreme Court decision in which Chief Justice John Marshall, holding that Maryland could not tax the Second Bank of the United States, supported the authority of the federal government versus the states.

McNary-Haugen Bill Vetoed by President Calvin Coolidge in 1927 and 1928, the bill to aid farmers would have artificially raised agricultural prices by selling surpluses overseas for low prices and selling the reduced supply in the United States for higher prices.

Meat Inspection Act (1906) Passed largely in reaction to Upton Sinclair's *The Jungle,* the law set strict standards of cleanliness in the meatpacking industry.

mercantilism Limitation and exploitation of colonial trade by an imperial power.

Mestizo Person of mixed Native American and European ancestry.

Mexican War Controversial war with Mexico for control of California and New Mexico, 1846–48; the Treaty of Guadalupe Hidalgo fixed the border at the Rio Grande and extended the United States to the Pacific coast, annexing more than a half-million square miles of potential slave territory.

Midway, Battle of Decisive American victory near Midway Island in the South Pacific on June 4, 1942; the Japanese navy never recovered its superiority over the U.S. navy.

Military Reconstruction Act (1867) Established military governments in ten Confederate states—excepting Tennessee—and required that the states ratify the Fourteenth Amendment and permit freedmen to vote.

minstrel show Blackface vaudeville entertainment popular in the decades surrounding the Civil War.

Miranda v. Arizona (**1966**) U.S. Supreme Court decision required police to advise persons in custody of their rights to legal counsel and against self-incrimination.

Missouri Compromise Deal proposed by Kentucky senator Henry Clay to resolve the slave/free imbalance in Congress that would result from Missouri's admission as a slave state; in the compromise of March 20, 1820, Maine's admission as a free state offset Missouri, and slavery was prohibited in the remainder of the Louisiana Territory north of the southern border of Missouri.

Molly Maguires Secret organization of Irish coal miners that used violence to intimidate mine officials in the 1870s.

Monitor **and** *Merrimack,* **Battle of the** First engagement between ironclad ships; fought at Hampton Roads, Virginia, on March 9, 1862.

Monroe Doctrine President James Monroe's declaration to Congress on December 2, 1823, that the American continents would be thenceforth closed to colonization but that the United States would honor existing colonies of European nations.

Moral Majority Televangelist Jerry Falwell's political lobbying organization, the name of which became synonymous with the religious right—conservative evangelical Protestants who helped ensure President Ronald Reagan's 1980 victory.

Mormons Founded in 1830 by Joseph Smith, the sect (officially, the Church of Jesus Christ of Latter-Day Saints) was a product of the intense revivalism of the "Burned-Over District" of New York; Smith's successor Brigham Young led 15,000 followers to Utah in 1847 to escape persecution.

Montgomery bus boycott Sparked by Rosa Parks's arrest on December 1, 1955, a successful year-long boycott protesting segregation on city buses; led by the Reverend Martin Luther King.

Muckrakers Writers who exposed corruption and abuses in politics, business, meat-packing, child labor, and more, primarily in the first decade of the twentieth century; their popular books and magazine articles spurred public interest in progressive reform.

Mugwumps Reform wing of the Republican party which supported Democrat Grover Cleveland for president in 1884 over Republican James G. Blaine, whose influence peddling had been revealed in the Mulligan letters of 1876.

Munn v. Illinois **(1877)** U.S. Supreme Court ruling that upheld a Granger law allowing the state to regulate grain elevators.

NAFTA Approved in 1993, the North American Free Trade Agreement with Canada and Mexico allowed goods to travel across their borders free of tariffs; critics argued that American workers would lose their jobs to cheaper Mexican labor.

National Aeronautics and Space Administration (NASA) In response to the Soviet Union's launching of *Sputnik,* Congress created this federal agency in 1957 to coordinate research and administer the space program.

National Association for the Advancement of Colored People (NAACP) Founded in 1910, this civil rights organization brought lawsuits against discriminatory practices and published *The Crisis,* a journal edited by African-American scholar W. E. B. Du Bois.

National Defense Education Act (1958) Passed in reaction to America's perceived inferiority in the space race, the appropriation encouraged education in science and modern languages through student loans, university research grants, and aid to public schools.

National Industrial Recovery Act (1933) Passed on the last of the Hundred Days, it created public-works jobs through the Federal Emergency Relief Administration and established a system of self-regulation for industry through the National Recovery Administration, which was ruled unconstitutional in 1935.

National Organization for Women Founded in 1966 by writer Betty Friedan and other feminists, NOW pushed for abortion rights and nondiscrimination in the workplace, but within a decade it became radicalized and lost much of its constituency.

National Road First federal interstate road, built between 1811 and 1838 and stretching from Cumberland, Maryland, to Vandalia, Illinois.

National Security Act (1947) Authorized the reorganization of government to coordinate military branches and security agencies; created the

National Security Council, the Central Intelligence Agency, and the National Military Establishment (later renamed the Department of Defense).

National Youth Administration Created in 1935 as part of the Works Progress Administration, it employed millions of youths who had left school.

nativism Anti-immigrant and anti-Catholic feeling in the 1830s through the 1850s; the largest group was New York's Order of the Star-Spangled Banner, which expanded into the American, or Know-Nothing, party in 1854.

naval stores Tar, pitch, and turpentine made from pine resin and used in shipbuilding; an important industry in the southern colonies, especially North Carolina.

Navigation Acts Passed by the English Parliament to control colonial trade and bolster the mercantile system, 1650–1775; enforcement of the acts led to growing resentment by colonists.

Neutrality Acts Series of laws passed between 1935 and 1939 to keep the United States from becoming involved in war by prohibiting American trade and travel to warring nations.

New Deal Franklin D. Roosevelt's campaign promise, in his speech to the Democratic National Convention of 1932, to combat the Great Depression with a "new deal for the American people"; the phrase became a catchword for his ambitious plan of economic programs.

New England Anti-Slavery Society Abolitionist organization founded in 1832 by William Lloyd Garrison of Massachusetts, publisher of the *Liberator.*

New Freedom Democrat Woodrow Wilson's political slogan in the presidential campaign of 1912; Wilson wanted to improve the banking system, lower tariffs, and, by breaking up monopolies, give small businesses freedom to compete.

New Frontier John F. Kennedy's program, stymied by a Republican Congress and his abbreviated term; his successor Lyndon B. Johnson had greater success with many of the same concepts.

New Harmony Founded in Indiana by British industrialist Robert Owen in 1825, the short-lived New Harmony Community of Equality was one of the few nineteenth-century communal experiments not based on religious ideology.

New Left Radical youth protest movement of the 1960s, named by leader Tom Hayden to distinguish it from the Old (Marxist-Leninist) Left of the 1930s.

New Nationalism Platform of the Progressive party and slogan of former president Theodore Roosevelt in the presidential campaign of 1912; stressed government activism, including regulation of trusts, conservation, and recall of state court decisions that had nullified progressive programs.

New Orleans, Battle of Last battle of the War of 1812, fought on January 8, 1815, weeks after the peace treaty was signed but prior to its ratification; General Andrew Jackson led the victorious American troops.

New South *Atlanta Constitution* editor Henry W. Grady's 1886 term for the prosperous post–Civil War South he envisioned: democratic, industrial, urban, and free of nostalgia for the defeated plantation South.

Nineteenth Amendment (1920) Granted women the right to vote.

Nisei Japanese Americans; literally, "second generation."

normalcy Word coined by future president Warren G. Harding as part of a 1920 campaign speech—"not nostrums, but normalcy"—signifying his awareness that the public was tired of progressivism, war, and sacrifice.

North Atlantic Treaty Organization (NATO) Defensive alliance founded in 1949 by ten western European nations, the United States, and Canada to deter Soviet expansion in Europe.

Northwest Ordinance of 1787 Created the Northwest Territory (area north of the Ohio River and west of Pennsylvania), established conditions for self-government and statehood, included a Bill of Rights, and permanently prohibited slavery.

nullification Concept of invalidation of a federal law within the borders of a state; first expounded in the Kentucky and Virginia Resolutions (1798), cited by South Carolina in its Ordinance of Nullification (1832) of the Tariff of Abominations, used by southern states to explain their secession from the Union (1861), and cited again by southern states to oppose the *Brown* v. *Board of Education* decision (1954).

Nullification Proclamation President Andrew Jackson's strong criticism of South Carolina's Ordinance of Nullification (1832) as disunionist and potentially treasonous.

Office of Price Administration Created in 1941 to control wartime inflation and price fixing resulting from shortages of many consumer goods, the OPA imposed wage and price freezes and administered a rationing system.

Okies Displaced farm families from the Oklahoma dust bowl who migrated to California during the 1930s in search of jobs.

Old Southwest In the antebellum period, the states of Alabama, Mississippi, Louisiana, Texas, Arkansas, and parts of Tennessee, Kentucky, and Florida.

Oneida Community Utopian community founded in 1848; the Perfectionist religious group practiced universal marriage until leader John Humphrey Noyes, fearing prosecution, escaped to Canada in 1879.

OPEC Organization of Petroleum Exporting Countries.

Open Door Policy In hopes of protecting the Chinese market for U.S. exports, Secretary of State John Hay unilaterally announced in 1899 that Chinese trade would be open to all nations.

Operation Desert Storm Multinational allied force that defeated Iraq in the Gulf War of January 1991.

Operation Dixie CIO's largely ineffective post–World War II campaign to unionize southern workers.

Oregon fever Enthusiasm for emigration to the Oregon Country in the late 1830s and early 1840s.

Ostend Manifesto Memorandum written in 1854 from Ostend, Belgium, by the U.S. ministers to England, France, and Spain recommending purchase or seizure of Cuba in order to increase the United States' slaveholding territory.

Overland (Oregon) Trail Route of wagon trains bearing settlers from Independence, Missouri, to the Oregon Country in the 1840s through the 1860s.

overseer Manager of slave labor on a plantation.

Panic of 1819 Financial collapse brought on by sharply falling cotton prices, declining demand for American exports, and reckless western land speculation.

Panic of 1837 Major economic depression lasting about six years; touched off by a British financial crisis and made worse by falling cotton prices, credit and currency problems, and speculation in land, canals, and railroads.

Panic of 1857 Economic depression lasting about two years and brought on by falling grain prices and a weak financial system; the South was largely protected by international demand for its cotton.

Panic of 1873 Severe six-year depression marked by bank failures and railroad and insurance bankruptcies.

Peace of Paris Signed on September 3, 1783, the treaty ending the Revolutionary War and recognizing American independence from Britain also established the border between Canada and the United States, fixed the western border at the Mississippi River, and ceded Florida to Spain.

Pendleton Civil Service Act (1883) Established the Civil Service Commission and marked the end of the spoils system.

Pentagon Papers Informal name for the Defense Department's secret history of the Vietnam conflict; leaked to the press by former official Daniel Ellsberg and published in the *New York Times* in 1971.

Pequot War Massacre in 1637 and subsequent dissolution of the Pequot Nation by Puritan settlers, who seized the Indians' lands.

Personal Responsibility and Work Opportunity Act (1996) Welfare reform measure that mandated state administration of federal aid to the poor.

Philippine Sea, Battle of the Costly Japanese defeat of June 19–20, 1944; led to the resignation of Premier Tojo and his cabinet.

Pilgrims Puritan Separatists who broke completely with the Church of England and sailed to the New World aboard the *Mayflower,* founding Plymouth Colony on Cape Cod in 1620.

Pinckney's Treaty Treaty with Spain negotiated by Thomas Pinckney in 1795; established United States boundaries at the Mississippi River and the thirty-first parallel and allowed open transportation on the Mississippi.

planter In the antebellum South, the owner of a large farm worked by twenty or more slaves.

Platt Amendment (1901) Reserved the United States' right to intervene in Cuban affairs and forced newly independent Cuba to host American naval bases on the island.

Plessy v. Ferguson **(1896)** U.S. Supreme Court decision supporting the legality of Jim Crow laws that permitted or required "separate but equal" facilities for blacks and whites.

poll tax Tax that must be paid in order to be eligible to vote; used as an effective means of disenfranchising black citizens after Reconstruction, since they often could not afford even a modest fee.

popular sovereignty Allowed settlers in a disputed territory to decide the slavery issue for themselves.

Populist party Political success of Farmers' Alliance candidates encouraged the formation in 1892 of the National People's party (later renamed the Populist party); active until 1912, it advocated a variety of reform issues, including free coinage of silver, income tax, postal savings, regulation of railroads, and direct election of U.S. senators.

Pottawatomie Massacre Murder of five proslavery settlers in eastern Kansas led by abolitionist John Brown on May 24–25, 1856.

Potsdam Conference Last meeting of the major Allied powers, the conference took place outside Berlin from July 17 to August 2, 1945; United States president Harry Truman, Soviet dictator Joseph Stalin, and British prime minister Clement Atlee finalized plans begun at Yalta.

Proclamation of Amnesty and Reconstruction President Lincoln's plan for reconstruction, issued in 1863, allowed southern states to rejoin the Union if 10 percent of the 1860 electorate signed loyalty pledges, accepted emancipation, and had received presidential pardons.

Proclamation of 1763 Royal directive issued after the French and Indian War prohibiting settlement, surveys, and land grants west of the Appalachian Mountains; although it was soon overridden by treaties, colonists continued to harbor resentment.

Progressive party Created when former president Theodore Roosevelt broke away from the Republican party to run for president again in

1912; the party supported progressive reforms similar to the Democrats but stopped short of seeking to eliminate trusts.

Progressivism Broad-based reform movement, 1900–17, that sought governmental help in solving problems in many areas of American life, including education, public health, the economy, the environment, labor, transportation, and politics.

Protestant Reformation Reform movement that resulted in the establishment of Protestant denominations; begun by German monk Martin Luther when he posted his "Ninety-five Theses" (complaints of abuses in the Catholic church) in 1517.

Pullman Strike Strike against the Pullman Palace Car Company in the company town of Pullman, Illinois, on May 11, 1894, by the American Railway Union under Eugene V. Debs; the strike was crushed by court injunctions and federal troops two months later.

Pure Food and Drug Act (1906) First law to regulate manufacturing of food and medicines; prohibited dangerous additives and inaccurate labeling.

Puritans English religious group that sought to purify the Church of England; founded the Massachusetts Bay Colony under John Winthrop in 1630.

Quartering Act (1765) Parliamentary act requiring colonies to house and provision British troops.

Radical Republicans Senators and congressmen who, strictly identifying the Civil War with the abolitionist cause, sought swift emancipation of the slaves, punishment of the rebels, and tight controls over the former Confederate states after the war.

Railroad Strike of 1877 Violent but ultimately unsuccessful interstate strike, which resulted in extensive property damage and many deaths.

Reaganomics Popular name for President Ronald Reagan's philosophy of "supply side" economics, which combined tax cuts, less government spending, and a balanced budget with an unregulated marketplace.

Reconstruction Finance Corporation Federal program established in 1932 under President Herbert Hoover to loan money to banks and other institutions to help them avert bankruptcy.

Red Scare Fear among many Americans after World War I of Communists in particular and noncitizens in general, a reaction to the Russian Revolution, mail bombs, strikes, and riots.

Redcoats Nickname for British soldiers, after their red uniform jackets.

Redeemers/Bourbons Conservative white Democrats, many of whom had been planters or businessmen before the Civil War, who reclaimed control of the South following the end of Reconstruction.

Regulators Groups of backcountry Carolina settlers who protested colonial policies; North Carolina royal governor William Tryon retaliated at the Battle of Alamance on May 17, 1771.

Report on Manufactures First secretary of the treasury Alexander Hamilton's 1791 analysis that accurately foretold the future of American industry and proposed tariffs and subsidies to promote it.

Republican party Organized in 1854 by antislavery Whigs, Democrats, and Free Soilers in response to the passage of the Kansas-Nebraska Act; nominated John C. Frémont for president in 1856 and Abraham Lincoln in 1860.

Republicans Political faction that succeeded the Anti-Federalists after ratification of the Constitution; led by Thomas Jefferson and James Madison, it soon developed into the Democratic-Republican party.

Reservationists Group of U.S. senators led by Majority Leader Henry Cabot Lodge who would only agree to ratification of the Treaty of Versailles subject to certain reservations, most notably the removal of Article X of the League of Nations Covenant.

Revolution of 1800 First time that an American political party surrendered power to the opposition party; Jefferson, a Democratic-Republican, had defeated incumbent Adams, a Federalist, for president.

right-to-work State laws enacted to prevent imposition of the closed shop; any worker, whether or not a union member, could be hired.

Roe v. Wade (1973) U.S. Supreme Court decision requiring states to permit first-trimester abortions.

Roosevelt Corollary (1904) President Theodore Roosevelt announced in what was essentially a corollary to the Monroe Doctrine that the United States could intervene militarily to prevent interference from European powers in the Western Hemisphere.

Romanticism Philosophical, literary, and artistic movement of the nineteenth century that was largely a reaction to the rationalism of the previous century; romantics valued emotion, mysticism, and individualism.

Rough Riders The 1st U.S. Volunteer Cavalry, led in battle in the Spanish-American War by Theodore Roosevelt; they were victorious in their only battle near Santiago, Cuba, and Roosevelt used the notoriety to aid his political career.

Santa Fe Trail Beginning in the 1820s, a major trade route from St. Louis, Missouri, to Santa Fe, New Mexico Territory.

Saratoga, Battle of Major defeat of British general John Burgoyne and more than 5,000 British troops at Saratoga, New York, on October 17, 1777.

Scalawags Southern white Republicans—some former Unionists—who served in Reconstruction governments.

***Schenck v. U.S.* (1919)** U.S. Supreme Court decision upholding the wartime Espionage and Sedition Acts; in the opinion he wrote for the case, Justice Oliver Wendell Holmes set the now-familiar "clear and present danger" standard.

scientific management Analysis of worker efficiency using measurements like "time and motion" studies to achieve greater productivity; introduced by Frederick Winslow Taylor in 1911.

Scottsboro case (1931) In overturning verdicts against nine black youths accused of raping two white women, the U.S. Supreme Court established precedents in *Powell* v. *Alabama* (1932), that adequate counsel must be appointed in capital cases, and in *Norris* v. *Alabama* (1935), that African Americans cannot be excluded from juries.

Second Great Awakening Religious revival movement of the early decades of the nineteenth century, in reaction to the growth of secularism and rationalist religion; began the predominance of the Baptist and Methodist churches.

Second Red Scare Post–World War II Red Scare focused on the fear of Communists in U.S. government positions; peaked during the Korean War and declined soon thereafter, when the U.S. Senate censured Joseph McCarthy, who had been a major instigator of the hysteria.

Seneca Falls Convention First women's rights meeting and the genesis of the women's suffrage movement; held in July 1848 in a church in Seneca Falls, New York, by Elizabeth Cady Stanton and Lucretia Coffin Mott.

"separate but equal" Principle underlying legal racial segregation, which was upheld in *Plessy* v. *Ferguson* (1896) and struck down in *Brown* v. *Board of Education* (1954).

Servicemen's Readjustment Act (1944) The "GI Bill of Rights" provided money for education and other benefits to military personnel returning from World War II.

settlement houses Product of the late nineteenth-century movement to offer a broad array of social services in urban immigrant neighborhoods; Chicago's Hull House was one of hundreds of settlement houses that operated by the early twentieth century.

Seventeenth Amendment (1913) Progressive reform that required U.S. senators to be elected directly by voters; previously, senators were chosen by state legislatures.

Seward's Folly Secretary of State William H. Seward's negotiation of the purchase of Alaska from Russia in 1867.

Shakers Founded by Mother Ann Lee Stanley in England, the United Society of Believers in Christ's Second Appearing settled in Watervliet, New York, in 1774 and subsequently established eighteen additional communes in the Northeast, Indiana, and Kentucky.

sharecropping Type of farm tenancy that developed after the Civil War in which landless workers—often former slaves—farmed land in exchange for farm supplies and a share of the crop; differed from tenancy in that the terms were generally less favorable.

Shays's Rebellion Massachusetts farmer Daniel Shays and 1,200 compatriots, seeking debt relief through issuance of paper currency and lower taxes, stormed the federal arsenal at Springfield in the winter of 1787 but were quickly repulsed.

Sherman Anti-Trust Act (1890) First law to restrict monopolistic trusts and business combinations; extended by the Clayton Anti-Trust Act of 1914.

Sherman Silver Purchase Act (1890) In replacing and extending the provisions of the Bland-Allison Act of 1878, it increased the amount of silver periodically bought for coinage.

Shiloh, Battle of At the time it was fought (April 6–7, 1862), Shiloh, in western Tennessee, was the bloodiest battle in American history; afterward, General Ulysses S. Grant was temporarily removed from command.

single tax Concept of taxing only landowners as a remedy for poverty, promulgated by Henry George in *Progress and Poverty* (1879).

Sixteenth Amendment (1913) Legalized the federal income tax.

Smith-Connally War Labor Disputes Act (1943) Outlawed labor strikes in wartime and allowed the president to take over industries threatened by labor disputes.

***Smith v. Allwright* (1944)** U.S. Supreme Court decision that outlawed all-white Democratic party primaries in Texas.

Social Darwinism Application of Charles Darwin's theory of natural selection to society; used the concept of the "survival of the fittest" to justify class distinctions and to explain poverty.

social gospel Preached by liberal Protestant clergymen in the late nineteenth and early twentieth centuries; advocated the application of Christian principles to social problems generated by industrialization.

Social Security Act (1935) Created the Social Security system with provisions for a retirement pension, unemployment insurance, disability insurance, and public assistance (welfare).

Sons of Liberty Secret organizations formed by Samuel Adams, John Hancock, and other radicals in response to the Stamp Act; they impeded British officials and planned such harassments as the Boston Tea Party.

South Carolina Exposition and Protest Written in 1828 by Vice-President John C. Calhoun of South Carolina to protest the so-called Tariff of Abominations, which seemed to favor northern industry; introduced the concept of state interposition and became the basis for South Carolina's Nullification Doctrine of 1833.

Southeast Asia Treaty Organization (SEATO) Pact among mostly western nations signed in 1954; designed to deter Communist expansion and cited as a justification for U.S. involvement in Vietnam.

Southern Christian Leadership Conference (SCLC) Civil rights organization founded in 1957 by the Reverend Martin Luther King, Jr., and other civil rights leaders.

Southern renaissance Literary movement of the 1920s and 1930s that included such writers as William Faulkner, Thomas Wolfe, and Robert Penn Warren.

Spanish flu Unprecedentedly lethal influenza epidemic of 1918 that killed more than 22 million people worldwide.

spoils system The term—meaning the filling of federal government jobs with persons loyal to the party of the president—originated in Andrew Jackson's first term; the system was replaced in the Progressive Era by civil service.

Sputnik First artificial satellite to orbit the earth; launched October 4, 1957, by the Soviet Union.

Stalwarts Conservative Republican party faction during the presidency of Rutherford B. Hayes, 1877–81; led by Senator Roscoe B. Conkling of New York, Stalwarts opposed civil service reform and favored a third term for President Ulysses S. Grant.

Stamp Act (1765) Parliament required that revenue stamps be affixed to all colonial printed matter, documents, dice, and playing cards; the Stamp Act Congress met to formulate a response, and the act was repealed the following year.

Standard Oil Company Founded in 1870 by John D. Rockefeller in Cleveland, Ohio, it soon grew into the nation's first industry-dominating trust; the Sherman Anti-Trust Act (1890) was enacted in part to combat abuses by Standard Oil.

staple crop Important cash crop, for example, cotton or tobacco.

steamboats Paddlewheelers that could travel both up- and down-river in deep or shallow waters; they became commercially viable early in the nineteenth century and soon developed into America's first inland freight and passenger service network.

Stimson Doctrine In reaction to Japan's 1932 occupation of Manchuria, Secretary of State Henry Stimson declared that the United States would not recognize territories acquired by force.

Strategic Defense Initiative ("Star Wars") Defense Department's plan during the Reagan administration to build a system to destroy incoming missiles in space.

Student Non-violent Coordinating Committee Founded in 1960 to coordinate civil rights sit-ins and other forms of grassroots protest.

Students for a Democratic Society (SDS) Major organization of the New Left, founded at the University of Michigan in 1960 by Tom Hayden and A1 Haber.

Sugar Act (Revenue Act of 1764) Parliament's tax on refined sugar and many other colonial products; the first tax designed solely to raise revenue for Britain.

Taft-Hartley Act (1947) Passed over President Harry Truman's veto, the law contained a number of provisions to control labor unions, including the banning of closed shops.

tariff Federal tax on imported goods.

Tariff of Abominations (Tariff of 1828) Taxed imported goods at a very high rate; the South hated the tariff because it feared it would provoke Britain to reject American cotton.

Tariff of 1816 First true protective tariff, intended strictly to protect American goods against foreign competition.

Tax Reform Act (1986) Lowered federal income tax rates to 1920s levels and eliminated many loopholes.

Teapot Dome Harding administration scandal in which Secretary of the Interior Albert B. Fall profited from secret leasing to private oil companies of government oil reserves at Teapot Dome, Wyoming, and Elk Hills, California.

tenancy Renting of farmland by workers who owned their own equipment; tenant farmers kept a larger percentage of the crop than did sharecroppers.

Tennessee Valley Authority Created in 1933 to control flooding in the Tennessee River Valley, provide work for the region's unemployed, and produce inexpensive electric power for the region.

Tenure of Office Act (1867) Required the president to obtain Senate approval to remove any official whose appointment had also required Senate approval; President Andrew Johnson's violation of the law by firing Secretary of War Edwin Stanton led to the Radical Republicans retaliating with Johnson's impeachment.

Tertium Quid Literally, the "third something": states' rights and strict constructionist Republicans under John Randolph who broke with President Thomas Jefferson but never managed to form a third political party.

Tet Offensive Surprise attack by the Viet Cong and North Vietnamese during the Vietnamese New Year of 1968; turned American public opinion strongly against the war in Vietnam.

Tippecanoe, Battle of On November 7, 1811, Indiana governor William Henry Harrison (later president) defeated the Shawnee Indians at the Tippecanoe River in northern Indiana; victory fomented war fever against the British, who were believed to be aiding the Indians.

Title IX Part of the Educational Amendments Act of 1972 that required colleges to engage in "affirmative action" for women.

Tonkin Gulf Resolution (1964) Passed by Congress in reaction to supposedly unprovoked attacks on American warships off the coast of North Vietnam; it gave the president unlimited authority to defend U.S. forces and members of SEATO.

Tories Term used by Patriots to refer to Loyalists, or colonists who supported the Crown after the Declaration of Independence.

Townshend Acts (1767) Parliamentary measures (named for the chancellor of the exchequer) that punished the New York Assembly for failing to house British soldiers, taxed tea and other commodities, and established a Board of Customs Commissioners and colonial vice-admiralty courts.

Trail of Tears Cherokees' own term for their forced march, 1838–39, from the southern Appalachians to Indian lands (later Oklahoma); of 15,000 forced to march, 4,000 died on the way.

Transcendentalism Philosophy of a small group of mid-nineteenth-century New England writers and thinkers, including Ralph Waldo Emerson, Henry David Thoreau, and Margaret Fuller; they stressed "plain living and high thinking."

Transcontinental railroad First line across the continent from Omaha, Nebraska, to Sacramento, California, established in 1869 with the linkage of the Union Pacific and Central Pacific railroads at Promontory, Utah.

Truman Doctrine President Harry S. Truman's program of post–World War II aid to European countries—particularly Greece and Turkey—in danger of being undermined by communism.

trust Companies combined to control competition.

Twenty-first Amendment (1933) Repealed prohibition on the manufacture, sale, and transportation of alcoholic beverages, effectively nullifying the Eighteenth Amendment.

Twenty-second Amendment (1951) Limited presidents to two full terms of office or two terms plus two years of an assumed term; passed in reaction to President Franklin D. Roosevelt's unprecedented four elected terms.

Twenty-sixth Amendment (1971) Lowered the voting age from twenty-one to eighteen.

U.S.S. *Maine* Battleship that exploded in Havana Harbor on February 15, 1898, resulting in 266 deaths; the American public, assuming that the Spanish had mined the ship, clamored for war, and the Spanish-American War was declared two months later.

Uncle Tom's Cabin Harriet Beecher Stowe's 1852 antislavery novel popularized the abolitionist position.

Underground Railroad Operating in the decades before the Civil War, the "railroad" was a clandestine system of routes and safehouses through which slaves were led to freedom in the North.

Understanding clause Added to state constitutions in the late nineteenth century, it allowed illiterate whites to circumvent literacy tests for voting by demonstrating that they understood a passage in the Constitution; black citizens would be judged by white registrars to have failed.

Underwood-Simmons Tariff (1913) In addition to lowering and even eliminating some tariffs, it included provisions for the first federal income tax, made legal the same year by the ratification of the Sixteenth Amendment.

Unitarianism Late eighteenth-century liberal offshoot of the New England Congregationalist church; rejecting the Trinity, Unitarianism professed the oneness of God and the goodness of rational man.

United Farm Workers Union for the predominantly Mexican-American migrant laborers of the Southwest, organized by César Chavez in 1962.

United Nations Organization of nations to maintain world peace, established in 1945 and headquartered in New York.

Universal Negro Improvement Association Black nationalist movement active in the United States from 1916 to 1923, when its leader Marcus Garvey went to prison for mail fraud.

Universalism Similar to Unitarianism, but putting more stress on the importance of social action, Universalism also originated in Massachusetts in the late eighteenth century.

V-E Day May 8, 1945, the day World War II officially ended in Europe.

vertical integration Company's avoidance of middlemen by producing its own supplies and providing for distribution of its product.

veto President's constitutional power to reject legislation passed by Congress; a two-thirds vote in both houses of Congress can override a veto.

Vicksburg, Battle of The fall of Vicksburg, Mississippi, to General Ulysses S. Grant's army on July 4, 1863, after two months of siege was a turning point in the war because it gave the Union control of the Mississippi River.

Virginia and New Jersey Plans Differing opinions of delegations to the Constitutional Convention: New Jersey wanted one legislative body with equal representation for each state; Virginia's plan called for a strong central government and a two-house legislature apportioned by population.

Volstead Act (1919) Enforced the prohibition amendment, beginning January 1920.

Voting Rights Act of 1965 Passed in the wake of Martin Luther King's Selma to Montgomery March, it authorized federal protection of the right to vote and permitted federal enforcement of minority voting rights in individual counties, mostly in the South.

Wabash Railroad v. Illinois **(1886)** Reversing the U.S. Supreme Court's ruling in *Munn* v. *Illinois*, the decision disallowed state regulation of interstate commerce.

Wade-Davis Bill (1864) Radical Republicans' plan for reconstruction that required loyalty oaths, abolition of slavery, repudiation of war debts, and denial of political rights to high-ranking Confederate officials; President Lincoln refused to sign the bill.

Wagner Act (National Labor Relations Act of 1935) Established the National Labor Relations Board and facilitated unionization by regulating employment and bargaining practices.

War Industries Board Run by financier Bernard Baruch, the board planned production and allocation of war materiel, supervised purchasing, and fixed prices, 1917–19.

War of 1812 Fought with Britain, 1812–14, over lingering conflicts that included impressment of American sailors, interference with shipping, and collusion with Northwest Territory Indians; settled by the Treaty of Ghent in 1814.

War on Poverty Announced by President Lyndon B. Johnson in his 1964 State of the Union address; under the Economic Opportunity Bill signed later that year, Head Start, VISTA, and the Jobs Corps were created, and grants and loans were extended to students, farmers, and businesses in efforts to eliminate poverty.

War Production Board Created in 1942 to coordinate industrial efforts in World War II; similar to the War Industries Board in World War I.

War Relocation Camps Internment camps where Japanese Americans were held against their will from 1942 to 1945.

Warren Court The U.S. Supreme Court under Chief Justice Earl Warren, 1953–69, decided such landmark cases as *Brown v. Board of Education* (school desegregation), *Baker v. Carr* (legislative redistricting), and *Gideon v. Wainwright* and *Miranda v. Arizona* (rights of criminal defendants).

Washington Armaments Conference Leaders of nine world powers met in 1921–22 to discuss the naval race; resulting treaties limited to a specific ratio the carrier and battleship tonnage of each nation (Five-Power Naval Treaty), formally ratified the Open Door to China (Nine–Power Treaty), and agreed to respect each other's Pacific territories (Four-Power Treaty).

Watergate Washington office and apartment complex that lent its name to the 1972–74 scandal of the Nixon administration; when his knowledge of the break-in at the Watergate and subsequent coverup was revealed, Nixon resigned the presidency under threat of impeachment.

Webster-Ashburton Treaty Settlement in 1842 of U.S.-Canadian border disputes in Maine, New York, Vermont, and in the Wisconsin Territory (now northern Minnesota).

Webster-Hayne debate U.S. Senate debate of January 1830 between Daniel Webster of Massachusetts and Robert Hayne of South Carolina over nullification and states' rights.

Whig Party Founded in 1834 to unite factions opposed to President Andrew Jackson, the party favored federal responsibility for internal improvements; the party ceased to exist by the late 1850s, when party members divided over the slavery issue.

Whigs Another name for revolutionary Patriots.

Whiskey Rebellion Violent protest by western Pennsylvania farmers against the federal excise tax on corn whiskey, 1794.

Whitewater Development Corporation Failed Arkansas real estate investment that kept President Bill Clinton and his wife Hillary under investigation by Independent Counsel Kenneth Starr throughout the Clinton presidency; no charges were ever brought against either of the Clintons.

Wilderness, Battle of the Second battle fought in the thickly wooded Wilderness area near Chancellorsville, Virginia; in the battle of May 5–6, 1864, no clear victor emerged, but the battle served to deplete the Army of Northern Virginia.

Wilderness Road Originally an Indian path through the Cumberland Gap, it was used by over 300,000 settlers who migrated westward to Kentucky in the last quarter of the eighteenth century.

Wilmot Proviso Proposal to prohibit slavery in any land acquired in the Mexican War, but southern senators, led by John C. Calhoun of South Carolina, defeated the measure in 1846 and 1847.

Works Progress Administration (WPA) Part of the Second New Deal, it provided jobs for millions of the unemployed on construction and arts projects.

Wounded Knee, Battle of Last incident of the Indians Wars took place in 1890 in the Dakota Territory, where the U.S. Cavalry killed over 200 Sioux men, women, and children who were in the process of surrender.

writs of assistance One of the colonies' main complaints against Britain, the writs allowed unlimited search warrants without cause to look for evidence of smuggling.

XYZ Affair French foreign minister Tallyrand's three anonymous agents demanded payments to stop French plundering of American ships in 1797; refusal to pay the bribe led to two years of sea war with France (1798–1800).

Yalta Conference Meeting of Franklin D. Roosevelt, Winston Churchill, and Joseph Stalin at a Crimean resort to discuss the postwar world on February 4–11, 1945; Soviet leader Joseph Stalin claimed large areas in eastern Europe for Soviet domination.

Yazoo Fraud Illegal sale of the Yazoo lands (much of present-day Alabama and Mississippi) by Georgia legislators; by 1802 it had become a tangle of conflicting claims that the U.S. Supreme Court settled in *Fletcher* v. *Peck* (1810).

yellow journalism Sensationalism in newspaper publishing that reached a peak in the circulation war between Joseph Pulitzer's *New York World* and William Randolph Hearst's *New York Journal* in the 1890s; the papers' accounts of events in Havana Harbor in 1898 led directly to the Spanish-American War.

yeoman farmers Small landowners (the majority of white families in the South) who farmed their own land and usually did not own slaves.

Yorktown, Battle of Last battle of the Revolutionary War; General Lord Charles Cornwallis along with over 7,000 British troops surrendered at Yorktown, Virginia, on October 17, 1781.

Zimmermann telegram From the German foreign secretary to the German minister in Mexico, February 1917, instructing him to offer to recover Texas, New Mexico, and Arizona for Mexico if it would fight the United States to divert attention from Germany in case of war.

APPENDIX

THE DECLARATION
OF INDEPENDENCE

WHEN IN THE COURSE OF HUMAN EVENTS, it becomes necessary for one people to dissolve the political bands which have connected them with another, and to assume the Powers of the earth, the separate and equal station to which the Laws of Nature and of Nature's God entitle them, a decent respect to the opinions of mankind requires that they should declare the causes which impel them to the separation.

We hold these truths to be self-evident, that all men are created equal, that they are endowed by their Creator with certain unalienable rights, that among these are Life, Liberty, and the pursuit of Happiness. That to secure these rights, Governments are instituted among Men, deriving their just powers from the consent of the governed. That whenever any Form of Government becomes destructive of these ends, it is the Right of the People to alter or to abolish it, and to institute new Government, laying its foundation on such principles and organizing its powers in such form, as to them shall seem most likely to effect their Safety and Happiness. Prudence, indeed, will dictate that Governments long established should not be changed for light and transient causes; and accordingly all experience hath shown, that mankind are more disposed to suffer, while evils are sufferable, than to right themselves by abolishing the forms to which they are accustomed. But when a long train of abuses and usurpations, pursuing invariably the same Object evinces a design to reduce them under absolute Despotism, it is their right, it is their duty, to throw off such Government, and to provide new Guards for their future security.—Such has been the patient sufferance of these Colonies; and such is now the necessity which constrains them to alter their former Systems of Government. The history of the present King of Great Britain is a history of repeated injuries and usurpations, all having in direct object the establishment of an absolute Tyranny over these States. To prove this, let Facts be submitted to a candid world.

He has refused his Assent to Laws, the most wholesome and necessary for the public good.

He has forbidden his Governors to pass Laws of immediate and pressing importance, unless suspended in their operation till his Assent should be obtained; and when so suspended, he has utterly neglected to attend to them.

He has refused to pass other Laws for the accommodation of large districts of people, unless those people would relinquish the right of Representation in the Legislature, a right inestimable to them and formidable to tyrants only.

He has called together legislative bodies at places unusual, uncomfortable, and distant from the depository of their public Records, for the sole purpose of fatiguing them into compliance with his measures.

He has dissolved Representative Houses repeatedly, for opposing with manly firmness his invasions on the rights of the people.

He has refused for a long time, after such dissolutions, to cause others to be elected; whereby the Legislative powers, incapable of Annihilation, have returned to the People at large for their exercise; the State remaining in the mean time exposed to all dangers of invasion from without, and convulsions within.

He has endeavoured to prevent the population of these States; for that purpose obstructing the Laws of Naturalization of Foreigners; refusing to pass others to encourage their migrations hither, and raising the conditions of new Appropriations of Lands.

He has obstructed the Administration of Justice, by refusing his Assent to Laws for establishing Judiciary powers.

He has made Judges dependent on his Will alone, for the tenure of their offices, and the amount and payment of their salaries.

He has erected a multitude of New Offices, and sent hither swarms of Officers to harass our People, and eat out their substance.

He has kept among us, in times of peace, Standing Armies without the Consent of our legislatures.

He has affected to render the Military independent of and superior to the Civil Power.

He has combined with others to subject us to a jurisdiction foreign to our constitution, and unacknowledged by our laws; giving his Assent to their Acts of pretended Legislation:

For quartering large bodies of armed troops among us:

For protecting them, by a mock Trial, from Punishment for any Murders which they should commit on the Inhabitants of these States:

For cutting off our Trade with all parts of the world:

For imposing taxes on us without our Consent:

For depriving us of many cases, of the benefits of Trial by jury:

For transporting us beyond Seas to be tried for pretended offences:

For abolishing the free System of English Laws in a neighbouring Province, establishing therein an Arbitrary government, and enlarging its

Boundaries so as to render it at once an example and fit instrument for introducing the same absolute rule into these Colonies:

For taking away our Charters, abolishing our most valuable Laws, and altering fundamentally the Forms of our Governments:

For suspending our own Legislatures, and declaring themselves in vested with Power to legislate for us in all cases whatsoever.

He has abdicated Government here, by declaring us out of his Protection and waging War against us.

He has plundered our seas, ravaged our Coasts, burnt our towns, and destroyed the lives of our people.

He is at this time transporting large armies of foreign mercenaries to compleat the works of death, desolation, and tyranny, already begun with circumstances of Cruelty & perfidy scarcely paralleled in the most barbarous ages, and totally unworthy the Head of a civilized nation.

He has constrained our fellow Citizens taken Captive on the high Seas to bear Arms against their Country, to become the executioners of their friends and Brethren, or to fall themselves by their Hands.

He has excited domestic insurrections amongst us, and has endeavoured to bring on the inhabitants of our frontiers, the merciless Indian Savages, whose known rule of warfare, is an undistinguished destruction of all ages, sexes, and conditions.

In every stage of these Oppressions We have Petitioned for Redress in the most humble terms: Our repeated Petitions have been answered only by repeated injury. A Prince, whose character is thus marked by every act which may define a Tyrant, is unfit to be the ruler of a free people.

Nor have We been wanting in attention to our British brethren. We have warned them from time to time of attempts by their legislature to extend an unwarrantable jurisdiction over us. We have reminded them of the circumstances of our emigration and settlement here. We have appealed to their native justice and magnanimity, and we have conjured them by the ties of our common kindred to disavow these usurpations, which, would inevitably interrupt our connections and correspondence. They too must have been deaf to the voice of justice and of consanguinity. We must, therefore, acquiesce in the necessity, which denounces our Separation, and hold them, as we hold the rest of mankind, Enemies in War, in Peace Friends.

WE, THEREFORE, the Representatives of the UNITED STATES OF AMERICA, in General Congress, Assembled, appealing to the Supreme Judge of the world for the rectitude of our intentions, do, in the Name, and by Authority of the good People of these Colonies, solemnly publish and declare, That these United Colonies are, and of Right ought to be FREE AND INDEPENDENT STATES; that they are Absolved from all Allegiance to the

British Crown, and that all political connection between them and the State of Great Britain, is and ought to be totally dissolved; and that as Free and Independent States, they have full Power to levy War, conclude Peace, contract Alliances, establish Commerce, and to do all other Acts and Things which Independent States may of right do. And for the support of this Declaration, with a firm reliance on the Protection of Divine Providence, we mutually pledge to each other our Lives, our Fortunes, and our sacred Honor.

The foregoing Declaration was, by order of Congress, engrossed, and signed by the following members:

John Hancock

NEW HAMPSHIRE
Josiah Bartlett
William Whipple
Matthew Thornton

MASSACHUSETTS BAY
Samuel Adams
John Adams
Robert Treat Paine
Elbridge Gerry

RHODE ISLAND
Stephen Hopkins
William Ellery

CONNECTICUT
Roger Sherman
Samuel Huntington
William Williams
Oliver Wolcott

NEW YORK
William Floyd
Philip Livingston
Francis Lewis
Lewis Morris

NEW JERSEY
Richard Stockton
John Witherspoon
Francis Hopkinson
John Hart
Abraham Clark

PENNSYLVANIA
Robert Morris
Benjamin Rush
Benjamin Franklin
John Morton
George Clymer
James Smith
George Taylor
James Wilson
George Ross

DELAWARE
Caesar Rodney
George Read
Thomas M'Kean

MARYLAND
Samuel Chase
William Paca
Thomas Stone
Charles Carroll, of Carrollton

VIRGINIA
George Wythe
Richard Henry Lee
Thomas Jefferson
Benjamin Harrison
Thomas Nelson, Jr.
Francis Lightfoot Lee
Carter Braxton

NORTH CAROLINA
William Hooper
Joseph Hewes
John Penn

SOUTH CAROLINA
Edward Rutledge
Thomas Heyward, Jr.
Thomas Lynch, Jr.
Arthur Middleton

GEORGIA
Button Gwinnett
Lyman Hall
George Walton

Resolved, that copies of the declaration be sent to the several assemblies, conventions, and committees, or councils of safety, and to the several commanding officers of the continental troops; that it be proclaimed in each of the united states, at the head of the army.

ARTICLES OF CONFEDERATION

To all to whom these Presents shall come, we the undersigned Delegates of the States affixed to our Names send greeting.

Whereas the Delegates of the United States of America in Congress assembled did on the fifteenth day of November in the Year of our Lord One Thousand Seven Hundred and Seventy-seven, and in the Second Year of the Independence of America agree to certain articles of Confederation and perpetual Union between the States of Newhampshire, Massachusetts-bay, Rhodeisland and Providence Plantations, Connecticut, New York, New Jersey, Pennsylvania, Delaware, Maryland, Virginia, North-Carolina, South-Carolina and Georgia in the Words following, viz.

Articles of Confederation and perpetual Union between the States of Newhampshire, Massachusetts-bay, Rhodeisland and Providence Plantations, Connecticut, New-York, New-Jersey, Pennsylvania, Delaware, Maryland, Virginia, North-Carolina, South-Carolina and Georgia.

Article I. The stile of this confederacy shall be "The United States of America."

Article II. Each State retains its sovereignty, freedom and independence, and every power, jurisdiction and right, which is not by this confederation expressly delegated to the United States, in Congress assembled.

Article III. The said States hereby severally enter into a firm league of friendship with each other, for their common defence, the security of their liberties, and their mutual and general welfare, binding themselves to assist each other, against all force offered to, or attacks made upon them, or any of them, on account of religion, sovereignty, trade or any other pretence whatever.

ARTICLE IV. The better to secure and perpetuate mutual friendship and intercourse among the people of the different States in this Union, the free inhabitants of each of these States, paupers, vagabonds and fugitives from justice excepted, shall be entitled to all privileges and immunities of free citizens in the several States; and the people of each State shall have free ingress and regress to and from any other State, and shall enjoy therein all the privileges of trade and commerce, subject to the same duties, impositions and restrictions as the inhabitants thereof respectively, provided that such restrictions shall not extend so far as to prevent the removal of property imported into any State, to any other State of which the owner is an inhabitant; provided also that no imposition, duties or restriction shall be laid by any State, on the property of the United States, or either of them.

If any person guilty of, or charged with treason, felony, or other high misdemeanor in any State, shall flee from justice, and be found in any of the United States, he shall upon demand of the Governor or Executive power, of the State from which he fled, be delivered up and removed to the State having jurisdiction of his offence.

Full faith and credit shall be given in each of these States to the records, acts and judicial proceedings of the courts and magistrates of every other State.

ARTICLE V. For the more convenient management of the general interests of the United States, delegates shall be annually appointed in such manner as the legislature of each State shall direct, to meet in Congress on the first Monday in November, in every year, with a power reserved to each State, to recall its delegates, or any of them, at any time within the year, and to send others in their stead, for the remainder of the year.

No State shall be represented in Congress by less than two, nor by more than seven members; and no person shall be capable of being a delegate for more than three years in any term of six years; nor shall any person, being a delegate, be capable of holding any office under the United States, for which he, or another for his benefit receives any salary, fees or emolument of any kind.

Each State shall maintain its own delegates in a meeting of the States, and while they act as members of the committee of the States.

In determining questions in the United States, in Congress assembled, each State shall have one vote.

Freedom of speech and debate in Congress shall not be impeached or questioned in any court, or place out of Congress, and the members of Congress shall be protected in their persons from arrests and imprisonments, during the time of their going to and from, and attendance on Congress, except for treason, felony, or breach of the peace.

ARTICLE VI. No State without the consent of the United States in Congress assembled, shall send any embassy to, or receive any embassy from, or enter into any conference, agreement, alliance or treaty with any king, prince or state; nor shall any person holding any office of profit or trust under the United States, or any of them, accept of any present, emolument, office or title of any kind whatever from any king, prince or foreign state; nor shall the United States in Congress assembled, or any of them, grant any title of nobility.

No two or more States shall enter into any treaty, confederation or alliance whatever between them, without the consent of the United States in Congress assembled, specifying accurately the purposes for which the same is to be entered into, and how long it shall continue.

No State shall lay any imposts or duties, which may interfere with any stipulations in treaties, entered into by the United States in Congress assembled, with any king, prince or state, in pursuance of any treaties already proposed by Congress, to the courts of France and Spain.

No vessels of war shall be kept up in time of peace by any State, except such number only, as shall be deemed necessary by the United States in Congress assembled, for the defence of such State, or its trade; nor shall any body of forces be kept up by any State, in time of peace, except such number only, as in the judgment of the United States, in Congress assembled, shall be deemed requisite to garrison the forts necessary for the defence of such State; but every State shall always keep up a well regulated and disciplined militia, sufficiently armed and accoutred, and shall provide and constantly have ready for use, in public stores, a due number of field pieces and tents, and a proper quantity of arms, ammunition and camp equipage.

No State shall engage in any war without the consent of the United States in Congress assembled, unless such State be actually invaded by enemies, or shall have received certain advice of a resolution being formed by some nation of Indians to invade such State, and the danger is so imminent as not to admit of a delay, till the United States in Congress assembled can be consulted: nor shall any State grant commissions to any ships or vessels of war, nor letters of marque or reprisal, except it be after a declaration of war by the United States in Congress assembled, and then only against the kingdom or state and the subjects thereof, against which war has been so declared, and under such regulations as shall be established by the United States in Congress assembled, unless such State be infested by pirates, in which case vessels of war may be fitted out for that occasion, and kept so long as the danger shall continue, or until the United States in Congress assembled shall determine otherwise.

ARTICLE VII. When land-forces are raised by any State of the common defence, all officers of or under the rank of colonel, shall be appointed by the Legislature of each State respectively by whom such forces shall be raised, or in such manner as such State shall direct, and all vacancies shall be filled up by the State which first made the appointment.

ARTICLE VIII. All charges of war, and all other expenses that shall be incurred for the common defence or general welfare, and allowed by the United States in Congress assembled, shall be defrayed out of a common treasury, which shall be supplied by the several States, in proportion to the value of all land within each State, granted to or surveyed for any person, as such land and the buildings and improvements thereon shall be estimated according to such mode as the United States in Congress assembled, shall from time to time direct and appoint.

The taxes for paying that proportion shall be laid and levied by the authority and direction of the Legislatures of the several States within the time agreed upon by the United States in Congress assembled.

ARTICLE IX. The United States in Congress assembled, shall have the sole and exclusive right and power of determining on peace and war, except in the cases mentioned in the sixth article—of sending and receiving ambassadors—entering into treaties and alliances, provided that no treaty of commerce shall be made whereby the legislative power of the respective States shall be restrained from imposing such imposts and duties on foreigners, as their own people are subjected to, or from prohibiting the exportation or importation of and species of goods or commodities whatsoever—of establishing rules for deciding in all cases, what captures on land or water shall be legal, and in what manner prizes taken by land or naval forces in the service of the United States shall be divided or appropriated—of granting letters of marque and reprisal in times of peace—appointing courts for the trial of piracies and felonies committed on the high seas and establishing courts for receiving and determining finally appeals in all cases of captures, provided that no member of Congress shall be appointed a judge of any of the said courts.

The United States in Congress assembled shall also be the last resort on appeal in all disputes and differences now subsisting or that hereafter may arise between two or more States concerning boundary, jurisdiction or any other cause whatever; which authority shall always be exercised in the manner following. Whenever the legislative or executive authority or lawful agent of any State in controversy with another shall present a petition to Congress, stating the matter in question and praying for a hearing, notice thereof shall be given by order of Congress to the legislative or executive authority of the other State in controversy, and a day assigned for the appearance of the parties by their lawful agents, who shall then be directed to appoint by joint consent, commissioners or judges to constitute a court for hearing and determining the matter in question: but if they cannot agree, Congress shall name three persons out of each of the United States, and from the list of such persons each party shall alternately strike out one, the petitioners beginning, until the number shall be reduced to thirteen; and from that number not less than seven, nor more than nine names as Congress shall direct, shall in the presence of Congress be drawn out by lot, and the persons whose names shall be so drawn or any five of them, shall be commissioners or judges, to hear and finally determine the controversy, so always as a major part of the judges who shall hear the cause shall agree in the determination: and if either party shall neglect to attend at the day appointed, without reasons, which Congress shall judge sufficient, or being present shall refuse to strike, the Congress shall proceed to nominate three persons out of each State, and the Secretary of Congress shall strike in behalf of such party absent or refusing; and the judgment and sentence of the court to be appointed, in the manner before prescribed, shall be final and conclusive; and if any of the parties shall refuse to submit to the authority of such court, or to appear or defend their claim or cause, the court shall nevertheless proceed to pronounce sentence, or judgment, which shall in like manner be final and decisive, the judgment or sentence and other proceedings being in either case transmitted to Congress, and lodged among the acts of Congress for the security of the parties concerned: provided that every commissioner, before he sits in judgment, shall take an oath to be administered by one of the judges of the supreme or superior court of the State where the case shall be tried, "well and truly to hear and determine the matter in question, according to the best of his judgment, without favour, affection or hope of reward:" provided also that no State shall be deprived of territory for the benefit of the United States.

All controversies concerning the private right of soil claimed under different grants of two or more States, whose jurisdiction as they may respect such lands, and the states which passed such grants are adjusted, the said grants or either of them being at the same time claimed to have originated antecedent to such settlement of jurisdiction, shall on the petition of either party to the Congress of the United States, be finally determined as near as may be in the same manner as is before prescribed for deciding disputes respecting territorial jurisdiction between different States.

The United States in Congress assembled shall also have the sole and exclusive right and power of regulating the alloy and value of coin struck by their own authority, or by that of the respective States—fixing the standard of weights and measures throughout the United States—regulating the trade and managing all affairs with the Indians, not members of any of the States, provided that the legislative right of any State within its own limits be not infringed or violated—establishing and regulating post-offices from one State to another, throughout all of the United States, and exacting such postage on the papers passing thro' the same as may be requisite to defray the expenses of the said office—appointing all officers of the land forces, in the service of the United States, excepting regimental officers—appointing all the officers of the naval forces, and commissioning all officers whatever in the service of the United States—making rules for the government and regulation of the said land and naval forces, and directing their operations.

The United States in Congress assembled shall have authority to appoint a committee, to sit in the recess of Congress, to be denominated "a Committee of the States," and to consist of one delegate from each State; and to appoint such other committees and civil officers as may be necessary for managing the general affairs of the United States under their direction—to appoint one of their number to preside, provided that no person be allowed to serve in the office of president more than one year in any term of three years; to ascertain the necessary sums of money to be raised for the service of the United States, and to appropriate and apply the same for defraying the public expenses—to borrow money, or emit bills on the credit of the United States, transmitting every half year to the respective States an account of the sums of money so borrowed or emitted,—to build and equip a navy—to agree upon the number of land forces, and to make requisitions from each State for its quota, in proportion to the number of white inhabitants in such State; which requisition shall be binding, and thereupon the Legislature of each State shall appoint the regimental officers, raise the men and cloath, arm and equip them in a soldier like manner, at the expense of the United States; and the officers and men so cloathed, armed and equipped shall march to the place appointed, and within the time agreed on by the United States in Congress assembled: but if the United States in Congress assembled shall, on consideration of circumstances judge proper that any State should not raise men, or should raise a smaller number of men than the quota thereof, such extra number shall be raised, officered, cloathed, armed and equipped in the same manner as the quota of such State, unless the legislature of such State shall judge that such extra number cannot be safely spared out of the same, in which case they shall raise officer, cloath, arm and equip as many of such extra number as they judge can be safely spared. And the officers and men so cloathed, armed and equipped, shall march to the place appointed, and within the time agreed on by the United States in Congress assembled.

The United States in Congress assembled shall never engage in a war, nor grant letters of marque and reprisal in time of peace, nor enter into any treaties or alliances, nor coin money, nor regulate the value thereof, nor ascertain the sums and expenses necessary for the defence and welfare of the United States, or any of them, nor emit bills, nor borrow money on the credit of the United States, nor appropriate money, nor agree upon the number of vessels to be built or purchased, or the number of land or sea forces to be raised, nor appoint a commander in chief of the army or navy, unless nine States assent to the same: nor shall a question on any other point, except for adjourning from day to day be determined, unless by the votes of a majority of the United States in Congress assembled.

The Congress of the United States shall have power to adjourn to any time within the year, and to any place within the United States, so that no period of adjournment be for a longer duration than the space of six months, and shall publish the journal of their proceedings monthly, except such parts thereof relating to treaties, alliances or military operations, as in their judgment require secrecy; and the yeas and nays of the delegates of each State on any question shall be entered on the Journal, when it is desired by any delegate; and the delegates of a State, or any of them, at his or their request shall be furnished with a transcript of the said journal, except such parts as are above excepted, to lay before the Legislatures of the several States.

ARTICLE X. The committee of the States, or any nine of them, shall be authorized to execute, in the recess of Congress, such of the powers of Congress as the United States in Congress assembled, by the consent of nine States, shall from time to time think expedient to vest them with; provided that no power be delegated to the said committee, for the exercise of which, by the articles of confederation, the voice of nine States in the Congress of the United States assembled is requisite.

ARTICLE XI. Canada acceding to this confederation, and joining in the measures of the United States, shall be admitted into, and entitled to all the advantages of this Union: but no other colony shall be admitted into the same, unless such admission be agreed to by nine States.

ARTICLE XII. All bills of credit emitted, monies borrowed and debts contracted by, or under the authority of Congress, before the assembling of the United States, in pursuance of the present confederation, shall be deemed and considered as a charge against the United States, for payment and satisfaction whereof the said United States, and the public faith are hereby solemnly pledged.

ARTICLE XIII. Every State shall abide by the determinations of the United States in Congress assembled, on all questions which by this confederation are submitted to them. And the articles of this confederation shall be inviolably observed by every State, and the Union shall be perpetual; nor shall any alteration at any time hereafter be made in any of them; unless such alteration be agreed to in a Congress of the United States, and be afterwards confirmed by the Legislatures of every State.

And whereas it has pleased the Great Governor of the world to incline the hearts of the Legislatures we respectively represent in Congress, to approve of, and to authorize us to ratify the said articles of confederation and perpetual union. Know ye that we the undersigned delegates, by virtue of the power and authority to us given for that purpose, do by these presents, in the name and in behalf of our respective constituents, fully and entirely ratify and confirm each and every of the said articles of confederation and perpetual union, and all and singular the matters and things therein contained: and we do further solemnly plight and engage the faith of our respective constituents, that they shall abide by the determinations of the United States in Congress assembled, on all questions, which by the said confederation are submitted to them. And that the articles thereof shall be inviolably observed by the States we respectively represent, and that the Union shall be perpetual.

In witness thereof we have hereunto set our hands in Congress. Done at Philadelphia in the State of Pennsylvania the ninth day of July in the year of our Lord one thousand seven hundred and seventy-eight, and in the third year of the independence of America.

THE CONSTITUTION OF THE UNITED STATES

WE THE PEOPLE OF THE UNITED STATES, in order to form a more perfect Union, establish Justice, insure domestic Tranquility, provide for the common defence, promote the general Welfare, and secure the Blessings of Liberty to ourselves and our Posterity, do ordain and establish this Constitution for the United States of America.

ARTICLE. I.

Section. 1. All legislative Powers herein granted shall be vested in a Congress of the United States, which shall consist of a Senate and House of Representatives.

Section. 2. The House of Representatives shall be composed of Members chosen every second Year by the People of the several States, and the Electors in each State shall have the Qualifications requisite for Electors of the most numerous Branch of the State Legislature.

No Person shall be a Representative who shall not have attained to the Age of twenty five Years, and been seven Years a Citizen of the United States, and who shall not, when elected, be an Inhabitant of that State in which he shall be chosen.

Representatives and direct Taxes shall be apportioned among the several States which may be included within this Union, according to their respective Numbers, which shall be determined by adding to the whole Number of free Persons, including those bound to Service for a Term of Years, and excluding Indians not taxed, three fifths of all other Persons. The actual Enumeration shall be made within three Years after the first Meeting of the Congress of the United States, and within every subsequent Term of ten Years, in such Manner as they shall by Law direct. The Number of Representatives shall not exceed one for every thirty Thousand, but each State shall have at Least one Representative; and until such enumeration shall be made, the State of New Hampshire shall be entitled to chuse three, Massachusetts eight, Rhode-Island and Providence Plantations one, Connecticut five, New-York six, New Jersey four, Pennsylvania eight, Delaware one, Maryland six, Virginia ten, North Carolina five, South Carolina five, and Georgia three.

When vacancies happen in the Representation from any state, the Executive Authority thereof shall issue Writs of Election to fill such Vacancies.

The House of Representatives shall chuse their Speaker and other Officers; and shall have the sole Power of Impeachment.

Section. 3. The Senate of the United States shall be composed of two Senators from each State, chosen by the legislature thereof, for six Years; and each Senator shall have one Vote.

Immediately after they shall be assembled in Consequence of the first Election, they shall be divided as equally as may be into three Classes. The Seats of the Senators of the first Class shall be vacated at the Expiration of the second Year, of the second Class at the Expiration of the fourth Year, and of the third Class at the Expiration of the sixth Year, so that one third maybe chosen every second Year; and if Vacancies happen by Resignation, or otherwise, during the Recess of the Legislature of any State, the Executive thereof may make temporary Appointments until the next Meeting of the Legislature, which shall then fill such Vacancies.

No Person shall be a Senator who shall not have attained to the Age of thirty Years, and been nine Years a Citizen of the United States, and who shall not, when elected, be an Inhabitant of that State for which he shall be chosen.

The Vice President of the United States shall be President of the Senate, but shall have no Vote, unless they be equally divided.

The Senate shall chuse their other Officers, and also a President pro tempore, in the Absence of the Vice President, or when he shall exercise the Office of President of the United States.

The Senate shall have the sole Power to try all Impeachments. When sitting for that Purpose, they shall be on Oath or Affirmation. When the President of the United States is tried, the Chief Justice shall preside: And no Person shall be convicted without the Concurrence of two thirds of the Members present.

Judgment in Cases of Impeachment shall not extend further than to removal from Office, and disqualification to hold and enjoy any Office of honor, Trust or Profit under the United States: but the Party convicted shall nevertheless be liable and subject to Indictment, Trial, Judgment and Punishment, according to Law.

Section. 4. The Times, Places and Manner of holding Elections for Senators and Representatives, shall be prescribed in each State by the Legislature thereof; but the Congress may at any time by Law make or alter such Regulations, except as to the Places of chusing Senators.

The Congress shall assemble at least once in every Year, and such Meeting shall be on the first Monday in December, unless they shall by Law appoint a different Day.

Section. 5. Each House shall be the Judge of the Elections, Returns and Qualifications of its own Members, and a Majority of each shall constitute a Quorum to do Business; but a smaller Number may adjourn from day to day, and may be authorized to compel the Attendance of absent Members, in such Manner, and under such Penalties as each House may provide.

Each House may determine the Rules of its Proceedings, punish its Members for disorderly Behaviour, and, with the Concurrence of two thirds, expel a Member.

Each House shall keep a Journal of its Proceedings, and from time to time publish the same, excepting such Parts as may in their Judgment require Secrecy; and the Yeas and Nays of the Members of either House on any question shall, at the Desire of one fifth of those Present, be entered on the Journal.

Neither House, during the Session of Congress, shall, without the Consent of the other, adjourn for more than three days, not to any other Place than that in which the two Houses shall be sitting.

Section. 6. The Senators and Representatives shall receive a Compensation for their Services, to be ascertained by Law, and paid out of the Treasury of the United States. They shall in all Cases, except Treason, Felony and Breach of the Peace, be privileged from Arrest during their Attendance at the Session of their respective Houses, and in going to and returning from the same; and for any Speech or Debate in either House, they shall not be questioned in any other Place.

No Senator or Representative shall, during the Time for which he was elected, be appointed to any civil Office under the Authority of the United States, which shall have been created, or the Emoluments whereof shall have been encreased during such time; and no Person holding any Office under the United States, shall be a Member of either House during his Continuance in Office.

Section. 7. All Bills for raising Revenue shall originate in the House of Representatives; but the Senate may propose or concur with Amendments as on other Bills.

Every Bill which shall have passed the House of Representatives and the Senate shall, before it become a Law, be presented to the President of the United States; If he approve he shall sign it, but if not he shall return it, with his Objections to that House in which it shall have originated, who shall enter the Objections at large on their Journal, and proceed to reconsider it. If after such Reconsideration two thirds of that House shall agree to pass the Bill, it shall be sent, together with the Objections, to the other House, by which it shall likewise be reconsidered, and if approved by two thirds of that House, it shall become a Law. But in all such Cases the Votes of both Houses shall be determined by yeas and Nays, and the Names of the Persons voting for and against the Bill shall be entered on the Journal of each House respectively. If any Bill shall not be returned by the President within ten Days (Sundays excepted) after it shall have been presented to him, the Same shall be a Law, in like Manner as if he had signed it, unless the Congress by their Adjournment prevent its Return, in which Case it shall not be a Law.

Every Order, Resolution, or Vote to which the Concurrence of the Senate and House of Representatives may be necessary (except on a question of Adjournment) shall be presented to the President of the United States; and before the Same shall take Effect, shall be approved by him, or being disapproved by him, shall be repassed by two thirds of the Senate and House of Representatives, according to the Rules and Limitations prescribed in the Case of a Bill.

Section. 8. The Congress shall have Power To lay and collect Taxes, Duties, Imposts and Excises, to pay the Debts and provide for the common Defence and general Welfare of the United States; but all Duties, Imposts and Excises shall be uniform throughout the United States;

To borrow Money on the credit of the United States;

To regulate Commerce with foreign Nations, and among the several States, and with the Indian Tribes;

To establish an uniform Rule of Naturalization, and uniform Laws on the subject of Bankruptcies throughout the United States;

To coin Money, regulate the Value thereof, and of foreign Coin, and fix the Standard of Weights and Measures;

To provide for the Punishment of counterfeiting the Securities and current Coin of the United States;

To establish Post Offices and Post Roads;

To promote the Progress of Science and useful Arts, by securing for limited Times to Authors and Inventors the exclusive Right to their respective Writings and Discoveries;

To constitute Tribunals inferior to the supreme Court;

To define and punish Piracies and Felonies committed on the high Seas, and Offences against the Law of Nations;

To declare War, grant Letters of Marque and Reprisal, and make Rules concerning Captures on land and Water;

To raise and support Armies, but no Appropriation of Money to that Use shall be for a longer Term than two Years;

To provide and maintain a Navy;

To make Rules for the Government and Regulation of the land and naval Forces;

To provide for calling forth the Militia to execute the Laws of the Union, suppress Insurrections and repel Invasions;

To provide for organizing, arming, and disciplining, the Militia, and for governing such Part of them as may be employed in the Service of the United States, reserving to the States respectively, the Appointment of the Officers, and the Authority of training the Militia according to the discipline prescribed by Congress.

To exercise exclusive Legislation in all Cases whatsoever, over such District (not exceeding ten Miles square) as may, by Cession of Particular States, and the Acceptance of Congress, become the Seat of the Government of the United States, and to exercise like Authority over all Places purchased by the Consent of the Legislature of the State in which the Same shall be, for the Erection of Forts, Magazines, Arsenals, dock-Yards, and other needful Buildings;—And

To make all Laws which shall be necessary and proper for carrying into Execution the foregoing Powers, and all other Powers vested by this Constitution in the Government of the United States, or in any Department or Officer thereof.

Section. 9. The Migration or Importation of such Persons as any of the States now existing shall think proper to admit, shall not be prohibited by the Congress prior to the Year one thousand eight hundred and eight, but a Tax or duty may be imposed on such Importation, not exceeding ten dollars for each Person.

The Privilege of the Writ of Habeas Corpus shall not be suspended, unless when in Cases of Rebellion or Invasion the public Safety may require it.

No Bill of Attainder or ex post facto Law shall be passed.

No Capitation, or other direct, Tax shall be laid, unless in Proportion to the Census or Enumeration herein before directed to be taken.

No Tax or Duty shall be laid on Articles exported from any State.

No Preference shall be given by any Regulation of Commerce or Revenue to the Ports of one State over those of another: nor shall Vessels bound to, or from, one State, be obliged to enter, clear, or pay Duties in another.

No Money shall be drawn from the Treasury, but in Consequence of Appropriations made by Law; and a regular Statement and Account of the Receipts and Expenditures of all public Money shall be published from time to time.

No Title of Nobility shall be granted by the United States: And no Person holding any Office of Profit or trust under them, shall, without the Consent of the Congress, accept of any present, Emolument, Office, or Title, of any kind whatever, from any King, Prince, or foreign State.

Section 10. No State shall enter into any Treaty, Alliance, or Confederation; grant Letters of Marque and Reprisal; coin Money; emit Bills of Credit; make any Thing but gold and silver Coin a Tender in Payment of Debts; pass any Bill of Attainder, ex post facto Law, or Law impairing the Obligation of Contracts, or grant any Title of Nobility.

No State shall, without the Consent of the Congress, lay any Imposts or Duties on Imports or Exports, except what may be absolutely necessary for executing its inspection Laws: and the net Produce of all Duties and Imposts, laid by any State on Imports or Exports, shall be for the Use of the Treasury of the United States; and all such Laws shall be subject to the Revision and Controul of the Congress.

No State shall, without the Consent of Congress, lay any Duty of Tonnage, keep Troops, or Ships of War in time of Peace, enter into any Agreement or Compact with another State, or with a foreign Power, or engage in War, unless actually invaded, or in such imminent Danger as will not admit of delay.

ARTICLE. II.

Section. 1. The executive Power shall be vested in a President of the United States of America. He shall hold his Office during the term of four Years, and, together with the Vice President, chosen for the same Term, be elected, as follows:

Each State shall appoint, in such Manner as the Legislature thereof may direct, a Number of Electors, equal to the whole Number of Senators and Representatives to which the State may be entitled in the Congress: but no Senator or Representative, or Person holding an Office of Trust or Profit under the United States, shall be appointed an Elector.

The Electors shall meet in their respective States, and vote by Ballot for two Persons, of whom one at least shall not be an Inhabitant of the same State with themselves. And they shall make a List of all the Persons voted for, and of the Number of Votes for each; which List they shall sign and certify, and transmit sealed to the Seat of the Government of the United States, directed to the President of the Senate. The President of the Senate shall, in the Presence of the Senate and House of Representatives, open all the Certificates, and the Votes shall then be counted. The Person having the greatest Number of Votes shall be the President, if such Number be a Majority of the whole Number of Electors appointed; and if there be more than one who have such Majority, and have an equal Number of Votes, then the House of Representatives shall immediately chuse by Ballot one of them for President; and if no Person have a Majority, then from the five highest on the List the said House shall in like Manner chuse the President. But in chusing the President, the Votes shall be taken by States, the Representation from each State having one Vote; A quorum for this Purpose shall consist of a Member or Members from two thirds of the States, and a Majority of all the States shall be necessary to a Choice. In every Case, after the Choice of the President, the Person having the greatest Number of Votes of the Electors shall be the Vice President. But if there should remain two or more who have equal Votes, the Senate shall chuse from them by Ballot the Vice President.

The Congress may determine the Time of chusing the Electors, and the Day on which they shall give their Votes; which Day shall be the same throughout the United States.

No Person except a natural born Citizen, or a Citizen of the United States, at the time of the Adoption of this Constitution, shall be eligible to the Office of President; neither shall any Person be eligible to that Office who shall not have attained to the Age of thirty five Years, and been fourteen Years a Resident within the United States.

In Case of the Removal of the President from Office, or of his Death, Resignation, or Inability to discharge the Powers and Duties of the said Office, the Same shall devolve on the Vice President, and the Congress may by Law provide for the Case of Removal, Death, Resignation or Inability, both of the President and Vice President, declaring what Officer shall then act as

President, and such Officer shall act accordingly, until the Disability be removed, or a President shall be elected.

The President shall, at stated Times, receive for his Services, a Compensation, which shall neither be encreased or diminished during the Period for which he shall have been elected, and he shall not receive within that Period any other Emolument from the United States, or any of them.

Before he enters on the Execution of his Office, he shall take the following Oath or Affirmation:—"I do solemnly swear (or affirm) that I will faithfully execute the Office of President of the United States, and will to the best of my Ability, preserve, protect and defend the Constitution of the United States."

Section. 2. The President shall be Commander in Chief of the Army and Navy of the United States, and of the Militia of the several States, when called into the actual Service of the United States; he may require the Opinion, in writing, of the principal Officer in each of the executive Departments, upon any Subject relating to the Duties of their respective Offices, and he shall have Power to grant Reprieves and Pardons for Offences against the United States, except in Cases of Impeachment.

He shall have Power, by and with the Advice and Consent of the Senate, to make Treaties, provided two thirds of the Senators present concur; and he shall nominate, and by and with the Advice and Consent of the Senate, shall appoint Ambassadors, other public Ministers and Consuls, Judges of the supreme Court, and all other Officers of the United States, whose Appointments are not herein otherwise provided for, and which shall be established by Law; but the Congress may by Law vest the Appointment of such inferior Officers, as they think proper, in the President alone, in the Courts of Law, or in the Heads of Departments.

The President shall have Power to fill up all Vacancies that may happen during the Recess of the Senate, by granting Commissions which shall expire at the End of their next Session.

Section. 3. He shall from time to time give to the Congress Information of the State of the Union, and recommend to their Consideration such Measures as he shall judge necessary and expedient; he may, on extraordinary Occasions, convene both Houses, or either of them, and in Case of Disagreement between them, with Respect to the Time of Adjournment, he may adjourn them to such Time as he shall think proper; he shall receive Ambassadors and other public Ministers; he shall take Care that the Laws be faithfully executed, and shall Commission all the Officers of the United States.

Section. 4. The President, Vice President and all civil Officers of the United States, shall be removed from Office on Impeachment for, and Conviction of, Treason, Bribery, or other high Crimes and Misdemeanors.

ARTICLE. III.

Section. 1. The judicial Power of the United States, shall be vested in one supreme Court, and in such inferior Courts as the Congress may from time to time ordain and establish. The Judges, both of the supreme and inferior Courts, shall hold their Offices during good Behavior, and shall, at stated Times, receive for their Services, a Compensation, which shall not be diminished during their Continuance in Office.

Section. 2. The judicial Power shall extend to all Cases, in Law and Equity, arising under this Constitution, the Laws of the United States, and Treaties made, or which shall be made, under their Authority;—to all Cases affecting Ambassadors, other public Ministers and Consuls;—to all Cases of admiralty and maritime Jurisdiction;—the Controversies to which the United States shall be a Party;—to Controversies between two or more States;—between a State and Citizens of another State;—between Citizens of different States;—between Citizens of the same State claiming Lands under Grants of different States, and between a State, or the Citizens thereof, and foreign States, Citizens or Subjects.

In all cases affecting Ambassadors, other public Ministers and Consuls, and those in which a State shall be Party, the supreme Court shall have original Jurisdiction. In all the other Cases before mentioned, the supreme Court shall have appellate Jurisdiction, both as to Law and Fact, with such Exceptions, and under such Regulations as the Congress shall make.

The Trial of all Crimes, except in Cases of Impeachment, shall be by Jury; and such Trial shall be held in the State where the said Crimes shall have been committed; but when not committed within any State, the Trial shall be at such Place or Places as the Congress may by Law have directed.

Section. 3. Treason against the United States, shall consist only in levying War against them, or in adhering to their Enemies, giving them Aid and Comfort. No Person shall be convicted of Treason unless on the Testimony of two Witnesses to the same overt Act, or on Confession in open Court.

The Congress shall have Power to declare the Punishment of Treason, but no Attainder of Treason shall work Corruption of Blood, or Forfeiture except during the Life of the Person attainted.

Article. IV.

Section. 1. Full Faith and Credit shall be given in each State to the public Acts, Records, and judicial Proceedings of every other State. And the Congress may by general Laws prescribe the Manner in which such Acts, Records and Proceedings shall be proved, and the Effect thereof.

Section. 2. The Citizens of each State shall be entitled to all Privileges and Immunities of Citizens in the several States.

A Person charged in any State with Treason, Felony, or other Crime, who shall flee from Justice, and be found in another State, shall on Demand of the executive Authority of the State from which he fled, be delivered up, to be removed to the State having Jurisdiction of the Crime.

No Person held to Service or Labour in one State, under the Laws thereof, escaping into another, shall, in Consequence of any Law or Regulation therein, be discharged from such Service or Labour, but shall be delivered up on Claim of the Party to whom such Service or Labour may be due.

Section. 3. New States may be admitted by the Congress into this Union; but no new State shall be formed or erected within the Jurisdiction of any other State; nor any State be formed by the Junction of two or more States, or Parts of States, without the consent of the Legislatures of the States concerned as well as of the Congress.

The Congress shall have Power to dispose of and make all needful Rules and Regulations respecting the Territory or other Property belonging to the United States; and nothing in this Constitution shall be so construed as to Prejudice any Claims of the United States, or of any particular States.

Section. 4. The United States shall guarantee to every State in this Union a Republican Form of Government, and shall protect each of them against Invasion; and on Application of the Legislature, or of the Executive (when the Legislature cannot be convened) against domestic Violence.

Article. V.

The Congress, whenever two thirds of both Houses shall deem it necessary, shall propose Amendments to this Constitution, or, on the Application of the

Legislatures of two thirds of the several States, shall call a Convention for proposing Amendments, which, in either Case, shall be valid to all Intents and Purposes, as Part of this Constitution, when ratified by the Legislatures of three fourths of the several States, or by Conventions in three fourths thereof, as the one or the other Mode of Ratification may be proposed by the Congress; Provided that no Amendment which may be made prior to the Year One thousand eight hundred and eight shall in any Manner affect the first and fourth Clauses in the Ninth Section of the first Article; and that no State, without its Consent, shall be deprived of its equal Suffrage in the Senate.

ARTICLE. VI.

All Debts contracted and Engagements entered into, before the Adoption of this Constitution, shall be as valid against the United States under this Constitution, as under the Confederation.

This Constitution, and the Laws of the United States which shall be made in Pursuance thereof; and all Treaties made, or which shall be made, under the Authority of the United States, shall be the supreme Law of the Land; and the Judges in every State shall be bound thereby, any Thing in the Constitution or Laws of any State to the Contrary notwithstanding.

The Senators and Representatives before mentioned, and the Members of the several State Legislatures, and all executive and judicial Officers, both of the United States and of the several States, shall be bound by Oath or Affirmation, to support this Constitution; but no religious Test shall ever be required as a Qualification to any Office or public Trust under the United States.

ARTICLE. VII.

The Ratification of the Conventions of nine States, shall be sufficient for the Establishment of this Constitution between the States so ratifying the Same.

Done in Convention by the Unanimous Consent of the States present the Seventeenth Day of September in the Year of our Lord one thousand seven hundred and Eighty seven and of the Independence of the United States of America the Twelfth. In witness thereof We have hereunto subscribed our Names,

G⁰. WASHINGTON—Presdᵗ.
and deputy from Virginia.

New Hampshire	{ John Langdon { Nicholas Gilman		
		Delaware	{ Geo: Read { Gunning Bedford jun { John Dickinson { Richard Bassett { Jaco: Broom
Massachusetts	{ Nathaniel Gorham { Rufus King		
Connecticut	{ Wᵐ Samˡ Johnson { Roger Sherman		
		Maryland	{ James McHenry { Dan of St Thoˢ Jenifer { Danˡ Carroll
New York: . . .	Alexander Hamilton		
		Virginia	{ John Blair— { James Madison Jr.
New Jersey	{ Wil: Livingston { David A. Brearley. { Wᵐ Paterson. { Jona: Dayton		
		North Carolina	{ Wᵐ Blount { Richᵈ Dobbs Spaight. { Hu Williamson
Pennsylvania	{ B Franklin { Thomas Mifflin { Robᵗ Morris { Geo. Clymer { Thoˢ FitzSimons { Jared Ingersoll { James Wilson { Gouv Morris		
		South Carolina	{ J. Rutledge { Charles Cotesworth { Pinckney { Charles Pinckney { Pierce Butler.
		Georgia	{ William Few { Abr Baldwin

AMENDMENTS TO THE CONSTITUTION

ARTICLES IN ADDITION TO, and Amendment of the Constitution of the United States of America, proposed by Congress, and ratified by the Legislatures of the several States, pursuant to the fifth Article of the original Constitution.

AMENDMENT I.

Congress shall make no law respecting an establishment of religion, or prohibiting the free exercise thereof; or abridging the freedom of speech, or of the press; or the right of the people peaceably to assemble, and to petition the Government for a redress of grievances.

AMENDMENT II.

A well regulated Militia, being necessary to the security of a free State, the right of the people to keep and bear Arms, shall not be infringed.

AMENDMENT III.

No Soldier shall, in time of peace be quartered in any house, without the consent of the Owner, nor in time of war, but in a manner to be prescribed by law.

AMENDMENT IV.

The right of the people to be secure in their persons, houses, papers, and effects, against unreasonable searches and seizures, shall not be violated, and no Warrants shall issue, but upon probable cause, supported by Oath or affirmation, and particularly describing the place to be searched, and the persons or things to be seized.

AMENDMENT V.

No person shall be held to answer for a capital, or otherwise infamous crime, unless on a presentment or indictment of a Grand Jury, except in cases arising in the land or naval forces, or in the Militia, when in actual service in time of War or public danger; nor shall any person be subject for the same offence to be twice put in jeopardy of life or limb; nor shall be compelled in any criminal case to be a witness against himself, nor be deprived of life, liberty, or property, without due process of law; nor shall private property be taken for public use, without just compensation.

AMENDMENT VI.

In all criminal prosecutions, the accused shall enjoy the right to a speedy and public trial, by an impartial jury of the State and district wherein the crime shall have been committed, which district shall have been previously ascertained by law, and to be informed of the nature and cause of the accusation;

to be confronted with the witnesses against him; to have compulsory process for obtaining witnesses in his favor, and to have the Assistance of Counsel for his defence.

AMENDMENT VII.

In Suits at common law, where the value in controversy shall exceed twenty dollars, the right of trial by jury shall be preserved, and no fact tried by a jury, shall be otherwise re-examined in any Court of the United States, than according to the rules of the common law.

AMENDMENT VIII.

Excessive bail shall not be required, nor excessive fines imposed, nor cruel and unusual punishments inflicted.

AMENDMENT IX.

The enumeration in the Constitution, of certain rights, shall not be construed to deny or disparage others retained by the people.

AMENDMENT X.

The powers not delegated to the United States by the Constitution, nor prohibited by it to the States, are reserved to the States respectively, or to the people. [The first ten amendments went into effect December 15, 1791.]

AMENDMENT XI.

The Judicial power of the United States shall not be construed to extend to any suit in law or equity, commenced or prosecuted against one of the United States by Citizens of another State, or by Citizens or Subjects of any Foreign State. [January 8, 1798.]

Amendment XII.

The Electors shall meet in their respective states, and vote by ballot for President and Vice-President, one of whom, at least, shall not be an inhabitant of the same state with themselves; they shall name in their ballots the person voted for as President, and in distinct ballots the person voted for as Vice-President, and they shall make distinct lists of all persons voted for as President, and of all persons voted for as Vice President, and of the number of votes for each, which lists they shall sign and certify, and transmit sealed to the seat of the government of the United States, directed to the President of the Senate;—The President of the Senate shall, in the presence of the Senate and House of Representatives, open all the certificates and the votes shall then be counted;—The person having the greatest number of votes for President, shall be the President, if such number be a majority of the whole number of Electors appointed; and if no person have such majority, then from the persons having the highest numbers not exceeding three on the list of those voted for as President, the House of Representatives shall choose immediately, by ballot, the President. But in choosing the President, the votes shall be taken by states, the representation from each state having one vote; a quorum for this purpose shall consist of a member or members from two-thirds of the states, and a majority of all the states shall be necessary to a choice. And if the House of Representatives shall not choose a President whenever the right of choice shall devolve upon them, before the fourth day of March next following, then the Vice-President shall act as President, as in the case of the death or other constitutional disability of the President.—The person having the greatest number of votes as Vice-President, shall be the Vice-President, if such number be a majority of the whole number of Electors appointed, and if no person have a majority, then from the two highest numbers on the list, the Senate shall choose the Vice-President; a quorum for the purpose shall consist of two-thirds of the whole number of Senators, and a majority of the whole number shall be necessary to a choice. But no person constitutionally ineligible to the office of President shall be eligible to that of Vice-President of the United States. [September 25, 1804.]

Amendment XIII.

Section 1. Neither slavery nor involuntary servitude, except as a punishment for crime whereof the party shall have been duly convicted, shall exist within the United States, or any place subject to their jurisdiction.

Section 2. Congress shall have power to enforce this article by appropriate legislation. [December 18, 1865.]

AMENDMENT XIV.

Section 1. All persons born or naturalized in the United States, and subject to the jurisdiction thereof, are citizens of the United States and of the State wherein they reside. No State shall make or enforce any law which shall abridge the privileges or immunities of citizens of the United States; nor shall any State deprive any person of life, liberty, or property, without due process of law; nor deny to any person within its jurisdiction the equal protection of the laws.

Section 2. Representatives shall be apportioned among the several States according to their respective numbers, counting the whole number of persons in each State, excluding Indians not taxed. But when the right to vote at any election for the choice of electors for President and Vice President of the United States, Representatives in Congress, the Executive and Judicial officers of a State, or the members of the Legislature thereof, is denied to any of the male inhabitants of such State, being twenty-one years of age, and citizens of the United States, or in any way abridged, except for participation in rebellion, or other crime, the basis of representation therein shall be reduced in the proportion which the number of such male citizens shall bear to the whole number of male citizens twenty-one years of age in such State.

Section 3. No person shall be a Senator or Representative in Congress, or elector of President and Vice President, or hold any office, civil or military, under the United States, or under any State, who, having previously taken an oath, as a member of Congress, or as an officer of the United States, or as a member of any State legislature, or as an executive or judicial officer of any State, to support the Constitution of the United States, shall have engaged in insurrection or rebellion against the same, or given aid or comfort to the enemies thereof. But Congress may by a vote of two-thirds of each House, remove such disability.

Section 4. The validity of the public debt of the United States, authorized by law, including debts incurred for payment of pensions and bounties for services in suppressing insurrection or rebellion, shall not be questioned. But neither the United States nor any State shall assume or pay any debt or obligation incurred in aid of insurrection or rebellion against the United States, or any claim for the loss or emancipation of any slave; but all such debts, obligations and claims shall be held illegal and void.

Section 5. The Congress shall have power to enforce, by appropriate legislation, the provisions of this article. [July 28, 1868.]

AMENDMENT XV.

Section 1. The right of citizens of the United States to vote shall not be denied or abridged by the United States or by any State on account of race, color, or previous condition of servitude—

Section 2. The Congress shall have power to enforce this article by appropriate legislation.—[March 30, 1870.]

AMENDMENT XVI.

The Congress shall have power to lay and collect taxes on incomes, from whatever source derived, without apportionment among the several States, and without regard to any census or enumeration. [February 25, 1913.]

AMENDMENT XVII.

The Senate of the United States shall be composed of two senators from each State, elected by the people thereof, for six years; and each Senator shall have one vote. The electors in each State shall have the qualifications requisite for electors of the most numerous branch of the State legislature.

When vacancies happen in the representation of any State in the Senate, the executive authority of such State shall issue writs of election to fill such vacancies: *Provided,* That the legislature of any State may empower the executive thereof to make temporary appointments until the people fill the vacancies by election as the legislature may direct.

This amendment shall not be so construed as to affect the election or term of any senator chosen before it becomes valid as part of the Constitution. [May 31, 1913.]

Amendment XVIII.

After one year from the ratification of this article, the manufacture, sale, or transportation of intoxicating liquors within, the importation thereof into, or the exportation thereof from the United States and all territory subject to the jurisdiction thereof for beverage purposes is hereby prohibited.

The Congress and the several States shall have concurrent power to enforce this article by appropriate legislation.

This article shall be inoperative unless it shall have been ratified as an amendment to the Constitution by the legislatures of the several States, as provided in the Constitution, within seven years from the date of the submission thereof to the States by Congress. [January 29, 1919.]

Amendment XIX.

The right of citizens of the United States to vote shall not be denied or abridged by the United States or by any State on account of sex.

The Congress shall have power by appropriate legislation to enforce the provisions of this article. [August 26, 1920.]

Amendment XX.

Section 1. The terms of the President and Vice-President shall end at noon on the twentieth day of January, and the terms of Senators and Representatives at noon on the third day of January, of the years in which such terms would have ended if this article had not been ratified; and the terms of their successors shall then begin.

Section 2. The Congress shall assemble at least once in every year, and such meeting shall begin at noon on the third day of January, unless they shall by law appoint a different day.

Section 3. If, at the time fixed for the beginning of the term of the President, the President-elect shall have died, the Vice-President-elect shall become President. If a President shall not have been chosen before the time fixed for the beginning of his term, or if the President-elect shall have failed to qualify, then the Vice-President-elect shall act as President until a President shall have qualified; and the Congress may by law provide for the case wherein neither a President-elect nor a Vice-President-elect shall have qualified, declaring who shall then act as President, or the manner in which one who is to act shall be selected, and such person shall act accordingly until a President or Vice-President shall have qualified.

Section 4. The Congress may by law provide for the case of the death of any of the persons from whom the House of Representatives may choose a President whenever the right of choice shall have devolved upon them, and for the case of the death of any of the persons from whom the Senate may choose a Vice-President whenever the right of choice shall have devolved upon them.

Section 5. Sections 1 and 2 shall take effect on the 15th day of October following the ratification of this article.

Section 6. This article shall be inoperative unless it shall have been ratified as an amendment to the Constitution by the legislatures of three-fourths of the several States within seven years from the date of its submission. [February 6, 1933.]

Amendment XXI.

Section 1. The eighteenth article of amendment to the Constitution of the United States is hereby repealed.

Section 2. The transportation or importation into any State, Territory or possession of the United States for delivery or use therein of intoxicating liquors, in violation of the laws thereof, is hereby prohibited.

Section 3. This article shall be inoperative unless it shall have been ratified as an amendment to the Constitution by convention in the several States, as provided in the Constitution, within seven years from the date of the submission thereof to the States by the Congress. [December 5, 1933.]

Amendment XXII.

Section 1. No person shall be elected to the office of the President more than twice, and no person who has held the office of President, or acted as President, for more than two years of a term to which some other person was elected President shall be elected to the office of the President more than once. But this Article shall not apply to any person holding the office of President when this Article was proposed by the Congress, and shall not prevent any person who may be holding the office of President, or acting as President, during the term within which this Article becomes operative from holding the office of President or acting as President during the remainder of such term.

Section 2. This article shall be inoperative unless it shall have been ratified as an amendment to the Constitution by the legislatures of three-fourths of the several states within seven years from the date of its submission to the States by the Congress. [February 27, 1951.]

Amendment XXIII.

Section 1. The District constituting the seat of government of the United States shall appoint in such manner as the Congress may direct:

A number of electors of President and Vice-President equal to the whole number of Senators and Representatives in Congress to which the District would be entitled if it were a State, but in no event more than the least populous State; they shall be in addition to those appointed by the States, but they shall be considered, for the purposes of the election of President and Vice-President, to be electors appointed by a State; and they shall meet in the District and perform such duties as provided by the twelfth article of amendment.

Section 2. The Congress shall have the power to enforce this article by appropriate legislation. [March 29, 1961.]

Amendment XXIV.

Section 1. The right of citizens of the United States to vote in any primary or other election for President or Vice President, for electors for President or Vice President, or for Senator or Representative in Congress, shall not be denied or abridged by the United States or any State by reason of failure to pay any poll tax or other tax.

Section 2. The Congress shall have power to enforce this article by appropriate legislation. [January 23, 1964.]

AMENDMENT XXV.

Section 1. In case of the removal of the President from office or of his death or resignation, the Vice President shall become President.

Section 2. Whenever there is a vacancy in the office of Vice President, the President shall nominate a Vice President who shall take office upon confirmation by a majority vote of both Houses of Congress.

Section 3. Whenever the President transmits to the President pro tempore of the Senate and the Speaker of the House of Representatives his written declaration that he is unable to discharge the powers and duties of his office, and until he transmits to them a written declaration to the contrary, such powers and duties shall be discharged by the Vice President as Acting President.

Section 4. Whenever the Vice President and a majority of either the principal officers of the executive departments or of such other body as Congress may by law provide, transmit to the President pro tempore of the Senate and the Speaker of the House of Representatives their written declaration that the President is unable to discharge the powers and duties of his office, the Vice President shall immediately assume the powers and duties of the office as Acting President.

Thereafter, when the President transmits to the President pro tempore of the Senate and the Speaker of the House of Representatives his written declaration that no inability exists, he shall resume the powers and duties of his office unless the Vice President and a majority of either the principal officers of the executive departments or of such other body as Congress may by law provide, transmit within four days to the President pro tempore of the Senate and the Speaker of the House of Representatives their written declaration that the President is unable to discharge the powers and duties of his office. Thereupon Congress shall decide the issue, assembling within forty-eight hours for that purpose if not in session. If the Congress, within twenty-one days after receipt of the latter written declaration, or, if Congress is not in session, within twenty-one days after Congress is required to assemble, determines by two-thirds vote of both Houses that the President is unable to discharge the powers and duties of his office, the Vice President shall continue to discharge the same as Acting President; otherwise, the President shall resume the powers and duties of his office. [February 10, 1967.]

AMENDMENT XXVI.

Section 1. The right of citizens of the United States, who are eighteen years of age or older, to vote shall not be denied or abridged by the United States or by any State on account of age.

Section 2. The Congress shall have power to enforce this article by appropriate legislation [June 30, 1971.]

AMENDMENT XXVII.

No law, varying the compensation for the services of the Senators and Representatives shall take effect, until an election of Representatives shall have intervened. [May 8, 1992.]

PRESIDENTIAL ELECTIONS

Year	Number of States	Candidates	Parties	Popular Vote	% of Popular Vote	Electoral Vote	% Voter Participation
1789	11	**GEORGE WASHINGTON**	No party designations			69	
		John Adams				34	
		Other candidates				35	
1792	15	**GEORGE WASHINGTON**	No party designations			132	
		John Adams				77	
		George Clinton				50	
		Other candidates				5	
1796	16	**JOHN ADAMS**	Federalist			71	
		Thomas Jefferson	Democratic-Republican			68	
		Thomas Pinckney	Federalist			59	
		Aaron Burr	Democratic-Republican			30	
		Other candidates				48	
1800	16	**THOMAS JEFFERSON**	Democratic-Republican			73	
		Aaron Burr	Democratic-Republican			73	
		John Adams	Federalist			65	
		Charles C. Pinckney	Federalist			64	
		John Jay	Federalist			1	
1804	17	**THOMAS JEFFERSON**	Democratic-Republican			162	
		Charles C. Pinckney	Federalist			14	

Year	Number of States	Candidates	Parties	Popular Vote	% of Popular Vote	Electoral Vote	% Voter Participation
1808	17	**JAMES MADISON**	Democratic-Republican			122	
		Charles C. Pinckney	Federalist			47	
		George Clinton	Democratic-Republican			6	
1812	18	**JAMES MADISON**	Democratic-Republican			128	
		DeWitt Clinton	Federalist			89	
1816	19	**JAMES MONROE**	Democratic-Republican			183	
		Rufus King	Federalist			34	
1820	24	**JAMES MONROE**	Democratic-Republican			231	
		John Quincy Adams	Independent			1	
1824	24	**JOHN QUINCY ADAMS**	Democratic-Republican	108,740	30.5	84	26.9
		Andrew Jackson	Democratic-Republican	153,544	43.1	99	
		Henry Clay	Democratic-Republican	47,136	13.2	37	
		William H. Crawford	Democratic-Republican	46,618	13.1	41	
1828	24	**ANDREW JACKSON**	Democratic	647,286	56.0	178	57.6
		John Quincy Adams	National-Republican	508,064	44.0	83	

Year	Number of States	Candidates	Parties	Popular Vote	% of Popular Vote	Electoral Vote	% Voter Participation
1832	24	ANDREW JACKSON	Democratic	688,242	54.5	219	55.4
		Henry Clay	National-Republican	473,462	37.5	49	
		William Wirt	Anti-Masonic	101,051	8.0	7	
		John Floyd	Democratic			11	
1836	26	MARTIN VAN BUREN	Democratic	765,483	50.9	170	57.8
		William H. Harrison	Whig			73	
		Hugh L. White	Whig	739,795	49.1	26	
		Daniel Webster	Whig			14	
		W. P. Mangum	Whig			11	
1840	26	WILLIAM H. HARRISON	Whig	1,274,624	53.1	234	80.2
		Martin Van Buren	Democratic	1,127,781	46.9	60	
1844	26	JAMES K. POLK	Democratic	1,338,464	49.6	170	78.9
		Henry Clay	Whig	1,300,097	48.1	105	
		James G. Birney	Liberty	62,300	2.3		
1848	30	ZACHARY TAYLOR	Whig	1,360,967	47.4	163	72.7
		Lewis Cass	Democratic	1,222,342	42.5	127	
		Martin Van Buren	Free Soil	291,263	10.1		
1852	31	FRANKLIN PIERCE	Democratic	1,601,117	50.9	254	69.6
		Winfield Scott	Whig	1,385,453	44.1	42	
		John P. Hale	Free Soil	155,825	5.0		
1856	31	JAMES BUCHANAN	Democratic	1,832,955	45.3	174	78.9
		John C. Frémont	Republican	1,339,932	33.1	114	
		Millard Fillmore	American	871,731	21.6	8	

Year	Number of States	Candidates	Parties	Popular Vote	% of Popular Vote	Electoral Vote	% Voter Participation
1860	33	**ABRAHAM LINCOLN**	Republican	1,865,593	39.8	180	81.2
		Stephen A. Douglas	Democratic	1,382,713	29.5	12	
		John C. Breckinridge	Democratic	848,356	18.1	72	
		John Bell	Constitutional Union	592,906	12.6	39	
1864	36	**ABRAHAM LINCOLN**	Republican	2,206,938	55.0	212	73.8
		George B. McClellan	Democratic	1,803,787	45.0	21	
1868	37	**ULYSSES S. GRANT**	Republican	3,013,421	52.7	214	78.1
		Horatio Seymour	Democratic	2,706,829	47.3	80	
1872	37	**ULYSSES S. GRANT**	Republican	3,596,745	55.6	286	71.3
		Horace Greeley	Democratic	2,843,446	43.9	66	
1876	38	Rutherford B. Hayes	Republican	4,036,572	48.0	185	81.8
		Samuel J. Tilden	Democratic	4,284,020	51.0	184	
1880	38	**JAMES A. GARFIELD**	Republican	4,453,295	48.5	214	79.4
		Winfield S. Hancock	Democratic	4,414,082	48.1	155	
		James B. Weaver	Greenback-Labor	308,578	3.4		
1884	38	**GROVER CLEVELAND**	Democratic	4,879,507	48.5	219	77.5
		James G. Blaine	Republican	4,850,293	48.2	182	
		Benjamin F. Butler	Greenback-Labor	175,370	1.8		
		John P. St. John	Prohibition	150,369	1.5		
1888	38	**BENJAMIN HARRISON**	Republican	5,477,129	47.9	233	79.3
		Grover Cleveland	Democratic	5,537,857	48.6	168	
		Clinton B. Fisk	Prohibition	249,506	2.2		
		Anson J. Streeter	Union Labor	146,935	1.3		

Year	Number of States	Candidates	Parties	Popular Vote	% of Popular Vote	Electoral Vote	% Voter Participation
1892	44	**GROVER CLEVELAND**	Democratic	5,555,426	46.1	277	74.7
		Benjamin Harrison	Republican	5,182,690	43.0	145	
		James B. Weaver	People's	1,029,846	8.5	22	
		John Bidwell	Prohibition	264,133	2.2		
1896	45	**WILLIAM MCKINLEY**	Republican	7,102,246	51.1	271	79.3
		William J. Bryan	Democratic	6,492,559	47.7	176	
1900	45	**WILLIAM MCKINLEY**	Republican	7,218,491	51.7	292	73.2
		William J. Bryan	Democratic; Populist	6,356,734	45.5	155	
		John C. Wooley	Prohibition	208,914	1.5		
1904	45	**THEODORE ROOSEVELT**	Republican	7,628,461	57.4	336	65.2
		Alton B. Parker	Democratic	5,084,223	37.6	140	
		Eugene V. Debs	Socialist	402,283	3.0		
		Silas C. Swallow	Prohibition	258,536	1.9		
1908	46	**WILLIAM H. TAFT**	Republican	7,675,320	51.6	321	65.4
		William J. Bryan	Democratic	6,412,294	43.1	162	
		Eugene V. Debs	Socialist	420,793	2.8		
		Eugene W. Chafin	Prohibition	253,840	1.7		
1912	48	**WOODROW WILSON**	Democratic	6,296,547	41.9	435	58.8
		Theodore Roosevelt	Progressive	4,118,571	27.4	88	
		William H. Taft	Republican	3,486,720	23.2	8	
		Eugene V. Debs	Socialist	900,672	6.0		
		Eugene W. Chafin	Prohibition	206,275	1.4		

Year	Number of States	Candidates	Parties	Popular Vote	Percentage of Popular Vote	Electoral Vote	Percentage of Voter Participation
1916	48	**WOODROW WILSON**	Democratic	9,127,695	49.4	277	61.6
		Charles E. Hughes	Republican	8,533,507	46.2	254	
		A. L. Benson	Socialist	585,113	3.2		
		J. Frank Hanly	Prohibition	220,506	1.2		
1920	48	**WARREN G. HARDING**	Republican	16,143,407	60.4	404	49.2
		James M. Cox	Democratic	9,130,328	34.2	127	
		Eugene V. Debs	Socialist	919,799	3.4		
		P. P. Christensen	Farmer-Labor	265,411	1.0		
1924	48	**CALVIN COOLIDGE**	Republican	15,718,211	54.0	382	48.9
		John W. Davis	Democratic	8,385,283	28.8	136	
		Robert M. La Follette	Progressive	4,831,289	16.6	13	
1928	48	**HERBERT C. HOOVER**	Republican	21,391,993	58.2	444	56.9
		Alfred E. Smith	Democratic	15,016,169	40.9	87	
1932	48	**FRANKLIN D. ROOSEVELT**	Democratic	22,809,638	57.4	472	56.9
		Herbert C. Hoover	Republican	15,758,901	39.7	59	
		Norman Thomas	Socialist	881,951	2.2		
1936	48	**FRANKLIN D. ROOSEVELT**	Democratic	27,752,869	60.8	523	61.0
		Alfred M. Landon	Republican	16,674,665	36.5	8	
		William Lemke	Union	882,479	1.9		
1940	48	**FRANKLIN D. ROOSEVELT**	Democratic	27,307,819	54.8	449	62.5
		Wendell L. Willkie	Republican	22,321,018	44.8	82	
1944	48	**FRANKLIN D. ROOSEVELT**	Democratic	25,606,585	53.5	432	55.9
		Thomas E. Dewey	Republican	22,014,745	46.0	99	

Year	Number of States	Candidates	Parties	Popular Vote	% of Popular Vote	Electoral Vote	% Voter Participation
1948	48	**HARRY S. TRUMAN**	Democratic	24,179,345	49.6	303	53.0
		Thomas E. Dewey	Republican	21,991,291	45.1	189	
		J. Strom Thurmond	States' Rights	1,176,125	2.4	39	
		Henry A. Wallace	Progressive	1,157,326	2.4		
1952	48	**DWIGHT D. EISENHOWER**	Republican	33,936,234	55.1	442	63.3
		Adlai E. Stevenson	Democratic	27,314,992	44.4	89	
1956	48	**DWIGHT D. EISENHOWER**	Republican	35,590,472	57.6	457	60.6
		Adlai E. Stevenson	Democratic	26,022,752	42.1	73	
1960	50	**JOHN F. KENNEDY**	Democratic	34,226,731	49.7	303	62.8
		Richard M. Nixon	Republican	34,108,157	49.5	219	
1964	50	**LYNDON B. JOHNSON**	Democratic	43,129,566	61.1	486	61.9
		Barry M. Goldwater	Republican	27,178,188	38.5	52	
1968	50	**RICHARD M. NIXON**	Republican	31,785,480	43.4	301	60.9
		Hubert H. Humphrey	Democratic	31,275,166	42.7	191	
		George C. Wallace	American Independent	9,906,473	13.5	46	
1972	50	**RICHARD M. NIXON**	Republican	47,169,911	60.7	520	55.2
		George S. McGovern	Democratic	29,170,383	37.5	17	
		John G. Schmitz	American	1,099,482	1.4		

Year	Number of States	Candidates	Parties	Popular Vote	% of Popular Vote	Electoral Vote	% of Voter Participation
1976	50	**JIMMY CARTER**	Democratic	40,830,763	50.1	297	53.5
		Gerald R. Ford	Republican	39,147,793	48.0	240	
1980	50	**RONALD REAGAN**	Republican	43,901,812	50.7	489	52.6
		Jimmy Carter	Democratic	35,483,820	41.0	49	
		John B. Anderson	Independent	5,719,437	6.6		
		Ed Clark	Libertarian	921,188	1.1		
1984	50	**RONALD REAGAN**	Republican	54,451,521	58.8	525	53.1
		Walter F. Mondale	Democratic	37,565,334	40.6	13	
1988	50	**GEORGE H. W. BUSH**	Republican	47,917,341	53.4	426	50.1
		Michael Dukakis	Democratic	41,013,030	45.6	111	
1992	50	**BILL CLINTON**	Democratic	44,908,254	43.0	370	55.0
		George H. W. Bush	Republican	39,102,343	37.4	168	
		H. Ross Perot	Independent	19,741,065	18.9		
1996	50	**BILL CLINTON**	Democratic	47,401,185	49.0	379	49.0
		Bob Dole	Republican	39,197,469	41.0	159	
		H. Ross Perot	Independent	8,085,295	8.0		
2000	50	**GEORGE W. BUSH**	Republican	50,455,156	47.9	271	50.4
		Al Gore	Democrat	50,997,335	48.4	266	
		Ralph Nader	Green	2,882,897	2.7		
2004	50	**GEORGE W. BUSH**	Republican	62,040,610	50.7	286	60.7
		John F. Kerry	Democrat	59,028,444	48.3	251	

Candidates receiving less than 1 percent of the popular vote have been omitted. Thus the percentage of popular vote given for any election year may not total 100 percent.

Before the passage of the Twelfth Amendment in 1804, the electoral college voted for two presidential candidates; the runner-up became vice-president.

ADMISSION OF STATES

Order of Admission	State	Date of Admission	Order of Admission	State	Date of Admission
1	Delaware	December 7, 1787	26	Michigan	January 26, 1837
2	Pennsylvania	December 12, 1787	27	Florida	March 3, 1845
3	New Jersey	December 18, 1787	28	Texas	December 29, 1845
4	Georgia	January 2, 1788	29	Iowa	December 28, 1846
5	Connecticut	January 9, 1788	30	Wisconsin	May 29, 1848
6	Massachusetts	February 7, 1788	31	California	September 9, 1850
7	Maryland	April 28, 1788	32	Minnesota	May 11, 1858
8	South Carolina	May 23, 1788	33	Oregon	February 14, 1859
9	New Hampshire	June 21, 1788	34	Kansas	January 29, 1861
10	Virginia	June 25, 1788	35	West Virginia	June 30, 1863
11	New York	July 26, 1788	36	Nevada	October 31, 1864
12	North Carolina	November 21, 1789	37	Nebraska	March 1, 1867
13	Rhode Island	May 29, 1790	38	Colorado	August 1, 1876
14	Vermont	March 4, 1791	39	North Dakota	November 2, 1889
15	Kentucky	June 1, 1792	40	South Dakota	November 2, 1889
16	Tennessee	June 1, 1796	41	Montana	November 8, 1889
17	Ohio	March 1, 1803	42	Washington	November 11, 1889
18	Louisiana	April 30, 1812	43	Idaho	July 3, 1890
19	Indiana	December 11, 1816	44	Wyoming	July 10, 1890
20	Mississippi	December 10, 1817	45	Utah	January 4, 1896
21	Illinois	December 3, 1818	46	Oklahoma	November 16, 1907
22	Alabama	December 14, 1819	47	New Mexico	January 6, 1912
23	Maine	March 15, 1820	48	Arizona	February 14, 1912
24	Missouri	August 10, 1821	49	Alaska	January 3, 1959
25	Arkansas	June 15, 1836	50	Hawaii	August 21, 1959

POPULATION OF THE UNITED STATES

Year	Number of States	Population	% Increase	Population per Square Mile
1790	13	3,929,214		4.5
1800	16	5,308,483	35.1	6.1
1810	17	7,239,881	36.4	4.3
1820	23	9,638,453	33.1	5.5
1830	24	12,866,020	33.5	7.4
1840	26	17,069,453	32.7	9.8
1850	31	23,191,876	35.9	7.9
1860	33	31,443,321	35.6	10.6
1870	37	39,818,449	26.6	13.4
1880	38	50,155,783	26.0	16.9
1890	44	62,947,714	25.5	21.1
1900	45	75,994,575	20.7	25.6
1910	46	91,972,266	21.0	31.0
1920	48	105,710,620	14.9	35.6
1930	48	122,775,046	16.1	41.2
1940	48	131,669,275	7.2	44.2
1950	48	150,697,361	14.5	50.7
1960	50	179,323,175	19.0	50.6
1970	50	203,235,298	13.3	57.5
1980	50	226,504,825	11.4	64.0
1985	50	237,839,000	5.0	67.2
1990	50	250,122,000	5.2	70.6
1995	50	263,411,707	5.3	74.4
2000	50	281,421,906	6.8	77.0

IMMIGRATION TO THE UNITED STATES, FISCAL YEARS 1820–2005

Year	Number	Year	Number	Year	Number	Year	Number
1820–1989	55,457,531	1871–80	2,812,191	1921–30	4,107,209	1971–80	4,493,314
1820	8,385	1871	321,350	1921	805,228	1971	370,478
1821–30	143,439	1872	404,806	1922	309,556	1972	384,685
1821	9,127	1873	459,803	1923	522,919	1973	400,063
1822	6,911	1874	313,339	1924	706,896	1974	394,861
1823	6,354	1875	227,498	1925	294,314	1975	386,914
1824	7,912	1876	169,986	1926	304,488	1976	398,613
1825	10,199	1877	141,857	1927	335,175	1976	103,676
1826	10,837	1878	138,469	1928	307,255	1977	462,315
1827	18,875	1879	177,826	1929	279,678	1978	601,442
1828	27,382	1880	457,257	1930	241,700	1979	460,348
1829	22,520	1881–90	5,246,613	1931–40	528,431	1980	530,639
1830	23,322	1881	669,431	1931	97,139	1981–90	7,338,062
1831–40	599,125	1882	788,992	1932	35,576	1981	596,600
1831	22,633	1883	603,322	1933	23,068	1982	594,131
1832	60,482	1884	518,592	1934	29,470	1983	559,763
1833	58,640	1885	395,346	1935	34,956	1984	543,903
1834	65,365	1886	334,203	1936	36,329	1985	570,009
1835	45,374	1887	490,109	1937	50,244	1986	601,708
1836	76,242	1888	546,889	1938	67,895	1987	601,516
1837	79,340	1889	444,427	1939	82,998	1988	643,025
1838	38,914	1890	455,302	1940	70,756	1989	1,090,924
1839	68,069	1891–1900	3,687,564	1941–50	1,035,039	1990	1,536,483
1840	84,066	1891	560,319	1941	51,776	1991–2000	9,090,857
1841–50	1,713,251	1892	579,663	1942	28,781	1991	1,827,167
1841	80,289	1893	439,730	1943	23,725	1992	973,977
1842	104,565	1894	285,631	1944	28,551	1993	904,292
		1895	258,536	1945	38,119	1994	804,416
		1896	343,267	1946	108,721		

Year	Number	Year	Number	Year	Number	Year	Number
1843	52,496	1897	230,832	1947	147,292	1995	720,461
1844	78,615	1898	229,299	1948	170,570	1996	915,900
1845	114,371	1899	311,715	1949	188,317	1997	798,378
1846	154,416	1900	448,572	1950	249,187	1998	660,477
1847	234,968					1999	644,787
1848	226,527	**1901–10**	**8,795,386**	**1951–60**	**2,515,479**	2000	841,002
1849	297,024	1901	487,918	1951	205,717	**2001–5**	**4,904,341**
1850	369,980	1902	648,743	1952	265,520	2001	1,058,902
1851–60	**2,598,214**	1903	857,046	1953	170,434	2002	1,059,356
1851	379,466	1904	812,870	1954	208,177	2003	705,827
1852	371,603	1905	1,026,499	1955	237,790	2004	957,883
1853	368,645	1906	1,100,735	1956	321,625	2005	1,122,373
1854	427,833	1907	1,285,349	1957	326,867		
1855	200,877	1908	782,870	1958	253,265		
1856	200,436	1909	751,786	1959	260,686		
1857	251,306	1910	1,041,570	1960	265,398		
1858	123,126	**1911–20**	**5,735,811**	**1961–70**	**3,321,677**		
1859	121,282	1911	878,587	1961	271,344		
1860	153,640	1912	838,172	1962	283,763		
1861–70	**2,314,824**	1913	1,197,892	1963	306,260		
1861	91,918	1914	1,218,480	1964	292,248		
1862	91,985	1915	326,700	1965	296,697		
1863	176,282	1916	298,826	1966	323,040		
1864	193,418	1917	295,403	1967	361,972		
1865	248,120	1918	110,618	1968	454,448		
1866	318,568	1919	141,132	1969	358,579		
1867	315,722	1920	430,001	1970	373,326		
1868	138,840						
1869	352,768						
1870	387,203						

Source: U.S. Immigration and Naturalization Service, 2006.

IMMIGRATION BY REGION AND SELECTED COUNTRY OF LAST RESIDENCE, FISCAL YEARS 1820–2004

Region and Country of Last Residence[1]	1820	1821–30	1831–40	1841–50	1851–60	1861–70	1871–80	1881–90
All countries	8,385	143,439	599,125	1,713,251	2,598,214	2,314,824	2,812,191	5,246,613
Europe	7,690	98,797	495,681	1,597,442	2,452,577	2,065,141	2,271,925	4,735,484
Austria-Hungary	—[2]	—[2]	—[2]	—[2]	—[2]	7,800	72,969	353,719
Austria	—[2]	—[2]	—[2]	—[2]	—[2]	484[3]	63,009	226,038
Hungary	—[2]	—[2]	—[2]	—[2]	—[2]	7,124[3]	9,960	127,681
Belgium	1	27	22	5,074	4,738	6,734	7,221	20,177
Czechoslovakia	—[4]	—[4]	—[4]	—[4]	—[4]	—[4]	—[4]	—[4]
Denmark	20	169	1,063	539	3,749	17,094	31,771	88,132
France	371	8,497	45,575	77,262	76,358	35,986	72,206	50,464
Germany	968	6,761	152,454	434,626	951,667	787,468	718,182	1,452,970
Greece	—	20	49	16	31	72	210	2,308
Ireland[5]	3,614	50,724	207,381	780,719	914,119	435,778	436,871	655,482
Italy	30	409	2,253	1,870	9,231	11,725	55,759	307,309
Netherlands	49	1,078	1,412	8,251	10,789	9,102	16,541	53,701
Norway-Sweden	3	91	1,201	13,903	20,931	109,298	211,245	568,362
Norway	—[6]	—[6]	—[6]	—[6]	—[6]	—[6]	95,323	176,586
Sweden	—[6]	—[6]	—[6]	—[6]	—[6]	—[6]	115,922	391,776
Poland	5	16	369	105	1,164	2,027	12,970	51,806
Portugal	35	145	829	550	1,055	2,658	14,082	16,978
Romania	—[7]	—[7]	—[7]	—[7]	—[7]	—[7]	11	6,348
Soviet Union	14	75	277	551	457	2,512	39,284	213,282
Spain	139	2,477	2,125	2,209	9,298	6,697	5,266	4,419
Switzerland	31	3,226	4,821	4,644	25,011	23,286	28,293	81,988
United Kingdom[5,8]	2,410	25,079	75,810	267,044	423,974	606,896	548,043	807,357
Yugoslavia	—[9]	—[9]	—[9]	—[9]	5	—[9]	—[9]	—[9]
Other Europe	—	3	40	79	5	8	1,001	682

Asia	6	30	55	141	41,538	64,759	124,160	69,942
China[10]	1	2	8	35	41,397	64,301	123,201	61,711
Hong Kong	—[11]	8	39	36	43	69	163	269
India	1	—[11]	—[11]	—[11]	—[12]	—[12]	—[12]	—[12]
Iran	—[12]	—[13]	—[13]	—[13]	—[13]	—[13]	—[13]	—[13]
Israel	—[13]	—[14]	—[14]	—[14]	—[14]	—[14]	—[14]	—[14]
Japan	—[14]	—[15]	—[15]	—[15]	—[15]	186	149	2,270
Korea	—[15]	—[16]	—[16]	—[16]	—[16]	—[16]	—[15]	—[15]
Philippines	—[16]	20	—[16]	—[16]	—[16]	—[16]	—[16]	—[16]
Turkey	1	—[11]	7	59	83	131	404	3,782
Vietnam	—[11]	—	—[11]	—[11]	—[11]	—[11]	—[11]	—[11]
Other Asia	3	11	1	11	15	72	243	1,910
America	387	11,564	33,424	62,469	74,720	166,607	404,044	426,967
Canada & Newfoundland[17,18]	209	2,277	13,624	41,723	59,309	153,878	383,640	393,304
Mexico[18]	1	4,817	6,599	3,271	3,078	2,191	5,162	191,319
Caribbean	164	3,834	12,301	13,528	10,660	9,046	13,957	29,042
Cuba	—[12]	—[12]	—[12]	—[12]	—[12]	—[12]	—[12]	—[12]
Dominican Republic	—[20]	—[20]	—[20]	—[20]	—[20]	—[20]	—[20]	—[20]
Haiti	—[20]	—[20]	—[20]	—[20]	—[20]	—[20]	—[20]	—[20]
Jamaica	—[21]	—[21]	—[21]	—[21]	—[21]	—[21]	—[21]	—[21]
Other Caribbean	164	3,834	12,301	13,528	10,660	9,046	13,957	29,042
Central America	2	105	44	368	449	95	157	404
El Salvador	—[20]	—[20]	—[20]	—[20]	—[20]	—[20]	—[20]	—[20]
Other Central America	2	105	44	368	449	95	157	404
South America	11	531	856	3,579	1,224	1,397	1,128	2,304
Argentina	—[20]	—[20]	—[20]	—[20]	—[20]	—[20]	—[20]	—[20]
Colombia	—[20]	—[20]	—[20]	—[20]	—[20]	—[20]	—[20]	—[20]
Ecuador	—[20]	—[20]	—[20]	—[20]	—[20]	—[20]	—[20]	—[20]
Other South America	11	531	856	3,579	1,224	1,397	1,128	2,304
Other America	—[22]	—[22]	—[22]	—[22]	—[22]	—[22]	—[22]	—[22]
Africa	1	16	54	55	210	312	358	857
Oceania	1	2	9	29	158	214	10,914	12,574
Not specified[22]	300	33,030	69,902	53,115	29,011	17,791	790	789

Region and Country of Last Residence[1]	1891–1900	1901–10	1911–20	1921–30	1931–40	1941–50	1951–60	1961–70
All countries	3,687,564	8,795,386	5,735,811	4,107,209	528,431	1,035,039	2,515,479	3,321,677
Europe	3,555,352	8,056,040	4,321,887	2,463,194	347,566	621,147	1,325,727	1,123,492
Austria-Hungary	592,707[23]	2,145,266[23]	896,342[23]	63,548	11,424	28,329	103,743	26,022
Austria	234,081[3]	668,209[3]	453,649	32,868	3,563[24]	24,860[24]	67,106	20,621
Hungary	181,288[3]	808,511[3]	442,693	30,680	7,861	3,469	36,637	5,401
Belgium	18,167	41,635	33,746	15,846	4,817	12,189	18,575	9,192
Czechoslovakia	—[4]	—[4]	3,426[4]	102,194	14,393	8,347	918	3,273
Denmark	50,231	65,285	41,983	32,430	2,559	5,393	10,984	9,201
France	30,770	73,379	61,897	49,610	12,623	38,809	51,121	45,237
Germany	505,152[23]	341,498[23]	143,945[23]	412,202	114,058[24]	226,578[24]	477,765	190,796
Greece	15,979	167,519	184,201	51,084	9,119	8,973	47,608	85,969
Ireland[5]	388,416	339,065	146,181	211,234	10,973	19,789	48,362	32,966
Italy	651,893	2,045,877	1,109,524	455,315	68,028	57,661	185,491	214,111
Netherlands	26,758	48,262	43,718	26,948	7,150	14,860	52,277	30,606
Norway-Sweden	321,281	440,039	161,469	165,780	8,700	20,765	44,632	32,600
Norway	95,015	190,505	66,395	68,531	4,740	10,100	22,935	15,484
Sweden	226,266	249,534	95,074	97,249	3,960	10,665	21,697	17,116
Poland	96,720[23]	—[23]	4,813[23]	227,734	17,026	7,571	9,985	53,539
Portugal	27,508	69,149	89,732	29,994	3,329	7,423	19,588	76,065
Romania	12,750	53,008	13,311	67,646	3,871	1,076	1,039	2,531
Soviet Union	505,290[23]	1,597,306[23]	921,201[23]	61,742	1,370	571	671	2,465
Spain	8,731	27,935	68,611	28,958	3,258	2,898	7,894	44,659
Switzerland	31,179	34,922	23,091	29,676	5,512	10,547	17,675	18,453
United Kingdom[5,8]	271,538	525,950	341,408	339,570	31,572	139,306	202,824	213,822
Yugoslavia	—[9]	—[9]	1,888[9]	49,064	5,835	1,576	8,225	20,381
Other Europe	282	39,945	31,400	42,619	11,949	8,486	16,350	11,604

	(1)	(2)	(3)	(4)	(5)	(6)	(7)	(8)
Asia	74,862	323,543	247,236	112,059	16,595	37,028	153,249	427,642
China[10]	14,799	20,605	21,278	29,907	4,928	16,709	9,657	34,764
Hong Kong	—[11]	—[11]	—[11]		—[11]	—[11]	15,541[11]	75,007
India	68	4,713	2,082	1,886	496	1,761	1,973	27,189
Iran	—[12]	—[12]	—[12]	241[12]	195	1,380	3,388	10,339
Israel	—[13]	—[13]	—[13]	—[13]	—[13]	476[13]	25,476	29,602
Japan	25,942	129,797	83,837	33,462	1,948	1,555	46,250	39,988
Korea	—[15]	—[15]	—[15]	—[15]	—[15]	107[15]	6,231	34,526
Philippines	—[16]	—[16]	—[16]	—[16]	528[16]	4,691	19,307	98,376
Turkey	30,425	157,369	134,066	33,824	1,065	798	3,519	10,142
Vietnam	—[11]	—[11]	—[11]	—[11]	—[11]	—[11]	335[11]	4,340
Other Asia	3,628	11,059	5,973	12,739	7,435	9,551	21,572	63,369
America	38,972	361,888	1,143,671	1,516,716	160,037	354,804	996,944	1,716,374
Canada & Newfoundland[17,18]	3,311	179,226	742,185	924,515	108,527	171,718	377,952	413,310
Mexico[18]	971[19]	49,642	219,004	459,287	22,319	60,589	299,811	453,937
Caribbean	33,066	107,548	123,424	74,899	15,502	49,725	123,091	470,213
Cuba	—[12]	—[12]	—[12]	15,901[12]	9,571	26,313	78,948	208,536
Dominican Republic	—[20]	—[20]	—[20]	—[20]	1,150[20]	5,627	9,897	93,292
Haiti	—[20]	—[20]	—[20]	—[20]	191[20]	911	4,442	34,499
Jamaica	—[21]	—[21]	—[21]	—[21]	—[21]	—[21]	8,869[21]	74,906
Other Caribbean	33,066	107,548	123,424	58,998	4,590	16,874	20,935[21]	58,980
Central America	549	8,192	17,159	15,769	5,861	21,665	44,751	101,330
El Salvador	—[20]	—[20]	—[20]	—[20]	673[20]	5,132	5,895	14,992
Other Central America	549	8,192	17,159	15,769	5,188	16,533	38,856	86,338
South America	1,075	17,280	41,899	42,215	7,803	21,831	91,628	257,954
Argentina	—[20]	—[20]	—[20]	—[20]	1,349[20]	3,338	19,486	49,721
Colombia	—[20]	—[20]	—[20]	—[20]	1,223[20]	3,858	18,048	72,028
Ecuador	—[20]	—[20]	—[20]	—[20]	337[20]	2,417	9,841	36,780
Other South America	1,075	17,280	41,899	42,215	4,894	12,218	44,253	99,425
Other America	—[22]	—[22]	—[22]	31[22]	25	29,276	59,711	19,630
Africa	350	7,368	8,443	6,286	1,750	7,367	14,092	28,954
Oceania	3,965	13,024	13,427	8,726	2,483	14,551	12,976	25,122
Not specified[22]	14,063	33,523[25]	1,147	228	—	142	12,491	93

Region and Country of Last Residence[1]	1971–80	1981–89	1990–99	1991–2000	2001	2002	2003	2004	Total 184 Years 1820–2004
All countries	4,493,314	5,801,579	9,781,496	9,095,417	1,064,318	1,063,732	705,827	946,142	69,869,450
Europe	800,368	637,524	1,291,299	1,359,737	177,833	177,652	102,843	130,151	39,049,276
Austria-Hungary	16,028	20,152	N/A	24,882	2,318	4,016	2,181	3,683	4,379,862
Austria	9,478	14,566	5,094	15,500	1,004	2,657	1,163	2,442	1,851,712
Hungary	6,550	5,586	11,003	9,382	1,314	1,359	1,018	1,241	1,682,074
Belgium	5,329	6,239	5,783	7,090	1,002	842	518	746	220,754
Czechoslovakia[27]	6,023	6,649	7,597	9,816	1,921	1,862	1,474	1,870	162,744
Czech Republic	N/A	N/A	723	N/A	N/A	N/A	N/A	N/A	N/A
Slovak Republic	N/A	N/A	3,010	N/A	N/A	N/A	N/A	N/A	N/A
Denmark	4,439	4,696	5,785	6,079	741	655	436	568	378,891
France	25,069	28,088	26,879	35,820	5,431	4,596	2,933	4,209	840,576
Germany	74,414	79,809	60,082	92,606	22,093	21,058	8,102	10,270	7,237,594
Germany, East	N/A	N/A	105	N/A	N/A	N/A	N/A	N/A	N/A
Germany, West	N/A	N/A	7,338	N/A	N/A	N/A	N/A	N/A	N/A
Greece	92,369	34,490	15,403	26,759	1,966	1,516	914	1,213	736,272
Ireland	11,490	22,229	67,975	56,950	1,550	1,419	1,010	1,518	4,787,580
Italy	129,368	51,008	23,365	62,722	3,377	2,837	1,904	2,495	5,446,443
Netherlands	10,492	10,723	12,334	13,308	1,895	2,305	1,329	1,713	394,782
Norway-Sweden	10,472	13,252	15,720	17,893	2,561	2,097	1,520	2,011	2,172,036
Norway	3,941	3,612	4,618	5,178	588	464	386	457	760,792
Sweden	6,531	9,640	11,102	12,715	1,973	1,633	1,134	1,554	1,265,817
Poland	37,234	64,888	180,035	163,747	12,355	13,304	11,016	13,972	820,730
Portugal	101,710	36,365	25,428	22,916	1,654	1,320	821	1,062	529,034
Romania	12,393	27,361	55,303	51,203	6,224	4,525	3,311	4,064	274,168
Russia	N/A	N/A	110,921	N/A					
Soviet Union[28]	38,961	42,898	126,115	462,874	55,099	55,464	33,563	36,646	4,087,352
Former Soviet Republics[29]	N/A	N/A	255,552						
Spain	39,141	17,689	14,310	17,157	1,889	1,603	1,107	1,453	308,357
Switzerland	8,235	7,561	8,840	11,841	1,796	1,503	867	1,193	376,639
United Kingdom	137,374	140,119	138,380	151,866	20,258	18,057	11,220	16,680	5,337,231
Yugoslavia[28]	30,540	15,984	25,923	66,557	21,937	28,100	8,296	13,211	274,372

Region/Country									
Former Yugoslavian States	N/A	N/A	61,389	N/A	N/A	N/A	N/A	N/A	283,859
Other Europe	9,287	7,324	822,161	57,651	11,766	10,573	10,321	11,574	
Asia	1,588,178	2,416,278	2,965,360	2,795,672	337,566	326,871	236,039	314,489	10,029,817
China, People's Republic	124,326	306,108	410,736	419,114	50,821	55,974	37,395	45,942	1,523,622
Hong Kong	113,467	83,848	78,016	109,779	10,307	7,952	5,020	5,421	440,709
India	164,134	221,977	371,925	363,060	65,916	66,864	47,157	65,472	1,064,185
Iran	45,136	101,267	129,055	68,556	8,063	7,730	4,709	5,898	271,807
Israel	37,713	38,367	33,814	39,397	4,925	4,938	3,719	5,206	195,725
Japan	49,775	40,654	60,112	67,942	10,464	9,150	6,724	8,652	565,176
Korea	267,638	302,782	187,794	164,166	19,933	20,114	12,177	19,441	878,079
Philippines	354,987	477,485	526,835	503,945	50,870	48,674	43,258	54,632	1,728,032
Taiwan	N/A	N/A	112,464	N/A	N/A	N/A	N/A	N/A	N/A
Turkey	13,399	20,028	26,178	38,212	3,477	3,934	3,332	4,489	465,771
Vietnam	172,820	266,027	443,173	286,145	34,648	32,425	21,270	30,064	862,829
Other Asia	244,783	557,735	769,425	735,356	78,142	69,116	51,278	69,272	2,033,882
Africa	80,779	144,096	374,149	354,939	50,209	56,135	45,640	62,510	903,578
Oceania	41,242	38,401	49,040	55,845	7,253	6,536	5,102	6,929	286,287
America	1,982,735	2,564,698	4,529,512	4,486,806	473,351	478,777	306,793	407,471	19,220,746
Canada	169,939	132,296	138,165	191,987	30,203	27,299	16,555	22,437	4,584,066
Mexico	640,294	975,657	2,756,513	2,249,421	204,844	217,318	114,984	173,664	6,848,960
Caribbean	741,126	759,416	1,023,237	978,787	96,958	94,240	67,660	81,893	4,022,715
Cuba	264,863	135,142	170,675	169,322	26,073	27,520	8,722	15,385	995,732
Dominican Republic	148,135	209,899	365,598	335,251	21,256	22,474	26,157	30,049	945,323
Haiti	56,335	118,510	179,725	179,644	22,535	19,189	11,942	13,502	481,569
Jamaica	137,577	184,481	182,552	169,227	15,099	14,567	13,082	13,565	655,040
Other Caribbean	134,216	111,384	124,687	125,343	11,995	10,490	7,757	9,392	945,051
Central America	134,640	321,845	611,597	526,915	73,063	66,520	53,435	60,299	1,599,860
El Salvador	34,436	133,938	274,989	215,798	31,054	30,539	27,915	29,285	609,258
Other Central America	100,204	187,907	336,608	311,117	42,009	35,981	25,520	31,014	990,602
South America	295,741	375,026	569,650	539,656	68,279	73,400	54,155	69,177	2,054,956
Argentina	29,897	21,374	27,431	26,644	3,459	3,811	3,217	4,672	172,921
Colombia	77,347	99,066	140,685	128,499	16,333	18,488	14,455	17,887	491,015
Ecuador	50,077	43,841	81,204	76,592	9,694	10,564	7,040	8,351	268,008
Other South America	138,420	210,745	320,330	307,921	38,751	40,537	29,443	38,267	1,123,012
Other America	995	458	595	40	4	3	4	1	110,189
Unknown or not reported	N/A	N/A	2,486	42,418	18,106	17,761	9,410	24,592	379,746

Source: U.S. Immigration and Naturalization Service, 2006.

[1]Data for years prior to 1906 relate to country whence alien came; data from 1906–79 and 1984–89 are for country of last permanent residence; and data for 1980–99 refer to country of birth. Because of changes in boundaries, changes in lists of countries, and lack of data for specified countries for various periods, data for certain countries, especially for the total period 1820–2004, are not comparable throughout. Data for specified countries are included with countries to which they belonged prior to World War I.

[2]Data for Austria and Hungary not reported until 1861.

[3]Data for Austria and Hungary not reported separately for all years during the period.

[4]No data available for Czechoslovakia until 1920.

[5]Prior to 1926, data for Northern Ireland included in Ireland.

[6]Data for Norway and Sweden not reported separately until 1871.

[7]No data available for Romania until 1880.

[8]Since 1925, data for United Kingdom refer to England, Scotland, Wales, and Northern Ireland.

[9]In 1920, a separate enumeration was made for the Kingdom of Serbs, Croats, and Slovenes. Since 1922, the Serb, Croat, and Slovene Kingdom recorded as Yugoslavia.

[10]Beginning in 1957, China includes Taiwan.

[11]Data not reported separately until 1952.

[12]Data not reported separately until 1925.

[13]Data not reported separately until 1949.

[14]No data available for Japan until 1861.

[15]Data not reported separately until 1948.

[16]Prior to 1934, Philippines recorded as insular travel.

[17]Prior to 1920, Canada and Newfoundland recorded as British North America. From 1820 to 1898, figures include all British North America possessions.

[18]Land arrivals not completely enumerated until 1908.

[19]No data available for Mexico from 1886 to 1893.

[20]Data not reported separately until 1932.

[21]Data for Jamaica not collected until 1953. In prior years, consolidated under British West Indies, which is included in "Other Caribbean."

[22]Included in countries "Not specified" until 1925.

[23]From 1899 to 1919, data for Poland included in Austria-Hungary, Germany, and the Soviet Union.

[24]From 1938 to 1945, data for Austria included in Germany.

[25]Includes 32,897 persons returning in 1906 to their homes in the United States.

[26]Data for fiscal year 1998 have been revised due to changes in the count for asylees and cancellation of removal. The previously reported total was 660,477.

[27]Prior to 1993, data include independent republics; beginning in 1993, data are for unknown republic only.

[28]Prior to 1992, data include independent republic; beginning in 1992, data are for Yugoslavia only.

[29]Prior to 1992, data include previously independent republics only; beginning in 1992, data are for all former republics except Russia.

— represents zero.

NOTE: From 1820 to 1867, figures represent alien passengers arrived at seaports; from 1868 to 1891 and 1895 to 1897, immigrant aliens arrived; from 1892 to 1894 and 1898 to 1989, immigrant aliens admitted for permanent residence. From 1892 to 1903, aliens entering by cabin class were not counted as immigrants. Land arrivals were not completely enumerated until 1908. For this table, fiscal year 1843 covers 9 months ending September 1843; fiscal years 1832 and 1850 cover 15 months ending December 31 of the respective years; and fiscal year 1868 covers 6 months ending June 30, 1868.

PRESIDENTS, VICE-PRESIDENTS, AND SECRETARIES OF STATE

President	*Vice-President*	*Secretary of State*
1. George Washington, Federalist 1789	John Adams, Federalist 1789	Thomas Jefferson 1789 Edmund Randolph 1794 Timothy Pickering 1795
2. John Adams, Federalist 1797	Thomas Jefferson, Dem.-Rep. 1797	Timothy Pickering 1797 John Marshall 1800
3. Thomas Jefferson, Dem.-Rep. 1801	Aaron Burr, Dem.-Rep. 1801 George Clinton, Dem.-Rep. 1805	James Madison 1801
4. James Madison, Dem.-Rep. 1809	George Clinton, Dem.-Rep. 1809 Elbridge Gerry, Dem.-Rep. 1813	Robert Smith 1809 James Monroe 1811
5. James Monroe, Dem.-Rep. 1817	Daniel D. Tompkins, Dem.-Rep. 1817	John Q. Adams 1817
6. John Quincy Adams, Dem.-Rep. 1825	John C. Calhoun, Dem.-Rep. 1825	Henry Clay 1825
7. Andrew Jackson, Democratic 1829	John C. Calhoun, Democratic 1829 Martin Van Buren, Democratic 1833	Martin Van Buren 1829 Edward Livingston 1831 Louis McLane 1833 John Forsyth 1834
8. Martin Van Buren, Democratic 1837	Richard M. Johnson, Democratic 1837	John Forsyth 1837
9. William H. Harrison, Whig 1841	John Tyler, Whig 1841	Daniel Webster 1841

	President	Vice-President	Secretary of State
10.	John Tyler, Whig and Democratic 1841	None	Daniel Webster 1841 Hugh S. Legaré 1843 Abel P. Upshur 1843 John C. Calhoun 1844
11.	James K. Polk, Democratic 1845	George M. Dallas, Democratic 1845	James Buchanan 1845
12.	Zachary Taylor, Whig 1849	Millard Fillmore, Whig 1848	John M. Clayton 1849
13.	Millard Fillmore, Whig 1850	None	Daniel Webster 1850 Edward Everett 1852
14.	Franklin Pierce, Democratic 1853	William R. King, Democratic 1853	William L. Marcy 1853
15.	James Buchanan, Democratic 1857	John C. Breckinridge, Democratic 1857	Lewis Cass 1857 Jeremiah S. Black 1860
16.	Abraham Lincoln, Republican 1861	Hannibal Hamlin, Republican 1861 Andrew Johnson, Unionist 1865	William H. Seward 1861
17.	Andrew Johnson, Unionist 1865	None	William H. Seward 1865
18.	Ulysses S. Grant, Republican 1869	Schuyler Colfax, Republican 1869 Henry Wilson, Republican 1873	Elihu B. Washburne 1869 Hamilton Fish 1869
19.	Rutherford B. Hayes, Republican 1877	William A. Wheeler, Republican 1877	William M. Evarts 1877

	President	Vice-President	Secretary of State
20.	James A. Garfield, Republican 1881	Chester A. Arthur, Republican 1881	James G. Blaine 1881
21.	Chester A. Arthur, Republican 1881	None	Frederick T. Frelinghuysen 1881
22.	Grover Cleveland, Democratic 1885	Thomas A. Hendricks, Democratic 1885	Thomas F. Bayard 1885
23.	Benjamin Harrison, Republican 1889	Levi P. Morton, Republican 1889	James G. Blaine 1889 John W. Foster 1892
24.	Grover Cleveland, Democratic 1893	Adlai E. Stevenson, Democratic 1893	Walter Q. Gresham 1893 Richard Olney 1895
25.	William McKinley, Republican 1897	Garret A. Hobart, Republican 1897 Theodore Roosevelt, Republican 1901	John Sherman 1897 William R. Day 1898 John Hay 1898
26.	Theodore Roosevelt, Republican 1901	Charles Fairbanks, Republican 1905	John Hay 1901 Elihu Root 1905 Robert Bacon 1909
27.	William H. Taft, Republican 1909	James S. Sherman, Republican 1909	Philander C. Knox 1909
28.	Woodrow Wilson, Democratic 1913	Thomas R. Marshall, Democratic 1913	William J. Bryan 1913 Robert Lansing 1915 Bainbridge Colby 1920
29.	Warren G. Harding, Republican 1921	Calvin Coolidge, Republican 1921	Charles E. Hughes 1921
30.	Calvin Coolidge, Republican 1923	Charles G. Dawes, Republican 1925	Charles E. Hughes 1923 Frank B. Kellogg 1925

	President	Vice-President	Secretary of State
31.	Herbert Hoover, Republican 1929	Charles Curtis, Republican 1929	Henry L. Stimson 1929
32.	Franklin D. Roosevelt, Democratic 1933	John Nance Garner, Democratic 1933 Henry A. Wallace, Democratic 1941 Harry S. Truman, Democratic 1945	Cordell Hull 1933 Edward R. Stettinius, Jr. 1944
33.	Harry S. Truman, Democratic 1945	Alben W. Barkley, Democratic 1949	Edward R. Stettinius, Jr. 1945 James F. Byrnes 1945 George C. Marshall 1947 Dean G. Acheson 1949
34.	Dwight D. Eisenhower, Republican 1953	Richard M. Nixon, Republican 1953	John F. Dulles 1953 Christian A. Herter 1959
35.	John F. Kennedy, Democratic 1961	Lyndon B. Johnson, Democratic 1961	Dean Rusk 1961
36.	Lyndon B. Johnson, Democratic 1963	Hubert H. Humphrey, Democratic 1965	Dean Rusk 1963
37.	Richard M. Nixon, Republican 1969	Spiro T. Agnew, Republican 1969 Gerald R. Ford, Republican 1973	William P. Rogers 1969 Henry Kissinger 1973
38.	Gerald R. Ford, Republican 1974	Nelson Rockefeller, Republican 1974	Henry Kissinger 1974
39.	Jimmy Carter, Democratic 1977	Walter Mondale, Democratic 1977	Cyrus Vance 1977 Edmund Muskie 1980

	President	Vice-President	Secretary of State
40.	Ronald Reagan, Republican 1981	George H. W. Bush, Republican 1981	Alexander Haig 1981 George Schultz 1982
41.	George H. W. Bush, Republican 1989	J. Danforth Quayle, Republican 1989	James A. Baker 1989 Lawrence Eagleburger 1992
42.	William J. Clinton, Democrat 1993	Albert Gore, Jr., Democrat 1993	Warren Christopher 1993 Madeleine Albright 1997
43.	George W. Bush, Republican 2001	Richard B. Cheney, Republican 2001	Colin L. Powell 2001 Condoleezza Rice 2005

CREDITS

Granger Collection; **p. 158,** Library of Congress; **p. 163,** Courtesy of the Maryland Historical Society; **p. 165,** The Granger Collection; **p. 166,** The Granger Collection.

CHAPTER 7: p. 170, Bettmann/Corbis; **p. 175,** The Library Company of Philadelphia; **p. 177,** The Historical Society of Pennsylvania; **p. 179,** Library of Congress; **p. 181,** Library of Congress; **p. 184,** Independence National Historical Park.

CHAPTER 8: p. 190, Art Resource, NY; **p. 191,** Library of Congress; **p. 194,** Independence National Historical Park; **p. 198,** The Historical Society of Pennsylvania; **p. 200,** The Granger Collection; **p. 205,** The Granger Collection; **p. 209,** The Granger Collection; **p. 211,** The Granger Collection; **p. 212,** The Granger Collection.

CHAPTER 9: p. 220, Giraudon/Art Resource, NY; **p. 223,** Miriam and Ira D. Wallach Division of Art, Prints and Photographs, New York Public Library, Astor, Lenox and Tilden Foundations; **p. 228,** Library of Congress; **p. 231,** Library of Congress; **p. 235,** Library of Congress; **p. 243,** Library of Congress.

PART 3: p. 245, Library of Congress; **p. 246,** Library of Congress and The Granger Collection; **p. 247,** The Granger Collection; **p. 248,** Library of Congress and Courtesy of the Bancroft Library; **p. 249,** Library of Congress and Library of Congress; **p. 251,** Library of Congress.

CHAPTER 10: p. 253, Bettmann/Corbis; **p. 256,** Courtesy of the Maryland Historical Society; **p. 264,** Bettmann/Corbis; **p. 268,** Henry Clay Memorial Foundation; **p. 270,** Bettmann/Corbis.

CHAPTER 11: p. 275, Library of Congress; **p. 277,** Saint Louis Art Museum, Gift of Bank of America; **p. 279,** Library of Congress; **p. 282,** National Portrait Gallery; **p. 284,** Library of Congress; **p. 291,** Collection of the New-York Historical Society; **p. 296,** Library of Congress.

CHAPTER 12: p. 302, The Granger Collection; **p. 309,** Minnesota Historical Society; **p. 316,** American Textile History Museum, Lowell, MA; **p. 317,** The Granger Collection; **p. 318,** Library of Congress; **p. 321,** © Board of Trustees, National Gallery of Art, Washington; **p. 322,** Library of Congress; **p. 323,** National Park Service, Ellis Island Collection; **p. 327,** Library of Congress; **p. 328,** Library of Congress.

CHAPTER 13: p. 335, Bettmann/Corbis; **p. 339,** Library of Congress; **p. 342,** Bettmann/Corbis; **p. 343,** Bettmann/Corbis; **p. 345,** © American Antiquarian Society and The Walters Art Museum, Baltimore; **p. 347,** The Metropolitan Museum of Art; **p. 352,** Warder Collection.

CHAPTER 14: p. 357, The Granger Collection; **p. 361,** Library of Congress; **p. 363,** Library of Congress; **p. 367,** Richard Collier, Wyoming Department of State Parks and Cultural Resources; **p. 372,** National Archives; **p. 375,** Library of Congress.

PART 4: p. 385, The Granger Collection; **p. 386,** The Granger Collection and the Library of Congress; **p. 387,** The Granger Collection and The Granger Collection; **p. 388,** Library of Congress and the Library of Congress; **p. 389,** Library of Congress; **p. 390,** Library of Congress.

CHAPTER 15: **p. 393,** Bettmann/Corbis; **p. 395,** Prints and Photographs Division, Schomburg Center for Research, The New York Public Library; **p. 397,** Bettmann/Corbis; **p. 400,** The Charleston Museum; **p. 405,** Library of Congress; **p. 409,** The Granger Collection; **p. 411,** (*left*) The Granger Collection and (*right*) Collection of the New-York Historical Society.

CHAPTER 16: **p. 416,** The Granger Collection; **p. 420,** The Granger Collection; **p. 423,** The Granger Collection; **p. 425,** The Granger Collection; **p. 427,** The Granger Collection; **p. 437,** The Granger Collection; **p. 439,** Library of Congress; **p. 441,** Library of Congress.

CHAPTER 17: **p. 447,** Library of Congress; **p. 452,** Bettmann/Corbis; **p. 454,** Bettmann/Corbis; **p. 465,** (*top*) Library of Congress and (*bottom*) Library of Congress; **p. 470,** Library of Congress; **p. 472,** National Archives; **p. 475,** Library of Congress; **p. 478,** Bettmann/Corbis; **p. 480,** Bettmann/Corbis; **p. 484,** Library of Congress.

CHAPTER 18: **p. 488,** Library of Congress; **p. 490,** Library of Congress; **p. 492,** Library of Congress; **p. 495,** Library of Congress; **p. 499,** Library of Congress; **p. 507,** Bettmann/Corbis; **p. 512,** Library of Congress; **p. 515,** Library of Congress.

INDEX

Page numbers in *italics* refer to illustrations.